The Legal Environment of Business

The Legal Environment of Business:
Text, Cases and Readings
Second Edition

by

Michael P. Litka, M.A., J.D.
Professor of Business Law

and

James E. Inman, M.B.A., J.D.
Associate Professor of Business Law

both of the
College of Business Administration
The University of Akron

Grid Publishing, Inc., Columbus, Ohio

Printed in the United States.

1 2 3 4 5 6 ⊠ 5 4 3 2 1 0

Library of Congress Cataloging in Publication Data

Litka, Michael P.
    The legal environment of business.

    (Grid series in law)
    Includes index.
        1. Commercial law—United States—Cases.
I. Inman, James E., joint author   II.   Title.
KF888.L58   1980   346'.73'07   79-16507
ISBN 0-88244-195-7

CONTENTS

TABLE OF CASES

Preface

The *raison d'etre* of *The Legal Environment of Business* is to provide a text that covers a wide field of legal topics that especially impact upon business persons and business institutions. The book covers those areas of the law with which the reader should have a conceptual knowledge to understand better the environment in which decisions are formulated that affect both his individual rights and his business transactions. The text is designed to provide the reader with a conceptual view of the law, rather than as a number of mutually exclusive subjects with a "rule" orientation. An additional purpose is to demonstrate that the different areas of law are interrelated and that the reader, to develop an understanding of any one of the areas, must necessarily acquire some knowledge about others. Presently, the legal environment is so expansive, the number of legal principles so endless, and the details on any one subject so complex, that it is impossible to present all the legal principles in detail. Therefore, a broad environmental approach is useful to introduce legal reasoning in those vast areas of law in which the principles approach is not feasible in such limited time. However, the authors believe that complete abandonment of traditional business law subjects in an environmental text is inadvisable because many business students are exposed only once to a law course. Consequently, basic understanding of public policy positions in the substantive areas of business law are covered in a conceptual fashion. As such, *The Legal Environment of Business* provides an alternative for those instructors who prefer coverage of traditional business law subjects in a conceptual approach.

The environmental approach of *The Legal Environment of Business* was prepared with three major pedagogical principles in mind. First, the text includes a sufficiently broad coverage of the substantive, administrative, and institutional aspects of law to equip students with basic knowledge of the legal environment in which business must operate.

Secondly, the student is not "spoon-fed" with "black-letter" rules. The extensive use of court opinions followed by questions which test the student's understanding requires student comprehension and analysis. Insights are thereby developed in legal reasoning. Student synthesis of a series of cases leads to identification of trends in the policy of the law. Student evaluation of public policy is also encouraged. These aspects of legal reasoning, trend identification, and policy evaluation are consistently utilized throughout the text.

Finally, it attempts to instill an appreciation for the dynamic qualities of law in the settlement of controversies in both the social and business community. Recent developments in legal theory and processes are particularily emphasized in relation to business practices and problems. Student appreciation of the dynamic quality of both the legal process and the government-business relationship is essential in the formulation of modern managerial philosophy. Executive leadership qualities are fostered through the analytical and conceptual study of legal processes and trends, especially when coupled with the development of a value preference for sane and deliberate resolution of public policy in a free atmosphere of public debate of the issues. Business managers of the future must increasingly participate in public debate which formulates public policy.

The text is divided into three parts. Part I emphasizes materials designed to fascilitate student understanding of the purposes of law and the legal process. Topics include legal philosophy, judicial and administrative processes, dynamic qualities of law, and constitutional protection for individuals. These topics cut across all areas of life and are woven into the treatment of Part II on business law and Part III on government regulation. The text tries to stress for the student the changing character of the law as influenced by technology, morality, and other social forces. The development of the law is illustrated by a series of chronological and "landmark" decisions which modify or overturn precedents. The discussions of individual rights and citizenry are timely and thought provoking materials which, in connection with the legal dynamic study, emphasize both the successful and frustrating portions of working "within the system." Some students need to appreciate this orderly process of change if they are to effectively employ it, and others need such illustrations as reassurance of their faith in the American legal system.

In Part II the various concepts of property and property rights are discussed and contrasted by other materials which illustrate the evolving laws which restrict the use of private property to the detriment of society. This material is timely and of immense importance to the students and businessmen in relation to a privately directed economic system. The materials relating the substantive areas of traditional business law subjects include contracts, sales, negotiable instruments, secured transactions, agency, and corporate law. While these materials are of great importance, the authors believe only basic concepts are needed. Detailed rules are quickly forgotten and detail is achieved only at the cost of omitting other equally critical areas of study within the legal environment of business.

Part III concerns government regulation of business. Government regulation has so expanded in recent decades that it now has an enormous impact on business decision making. However, businessmen and students alike are confused by the myriad of regulatory agencies and are perplexed to discover just what their individual and corporate relationships are to such administrative bodies. Accordingly, the text provides materials to afford the student the opportunity to gain a basic understanding of the substantive regulations and institutional characteristics of the more important agencies in the legal environment of business.

The Legal Environment of Business includes brief discussions of the historical development of relevant law. The historical perspective is important in understanding trends in governmental processes. The judicial decisions selected, besides relating understanding of laws, often illustrate analytical style. Care was taken to select decisions which are interesting and enjoyable to the reader. While the cases were edited to eliminate unnecessary confusion over legal procedures and procedural terminology, they nevertheless provide the reader with a "feel" for the law. The discipline of law has much intuitive appeal and pragmatic attractiveness. These characteristics are shown in the selected material and create student interest and invite additional learning. The students often request additional course work in law as a direct result of having had their intellectual appetites whetted through the use of this environmental approach. Such demands by students for additional legal studies may well operate to the advantage of business law instructors also.

This second edition of *The Legal Environment of Business* proceeds with confidence since the first edition experienced a continuously expanding market. This edition has been prepared so that the previous user will recognize the essential attributes of the first edition, but appreciate the improvements incorporated into this edition. We believe the considerable changes integrated into this edition will heighten the text's receptibility by instructors and students alike.

The authors intend to cover the entire text in a four-hour semester course at The University of Akron. It is recommended that the instructor select pertinent portions from each of the three parts of the text if a shorter course is necessary. The authors believe the student should be exposed to each part, even if certain chapters or sub-chapters must be omitted. The text and courses of instruction may be supplemented by an accompanying student workbook which contains questions to test the student's understanding of the text and expand applications of concepts and principles. The problems of the workbook have been carefully prepared and are closely keyed to chapter material. Together, the text and workbook provide unique materials that provide a wide flexibility to the instructor in selecting substantive coverage and in determination of subject depth in his course design.

It is hoped that *The Legal Environment of Business* will provide materials useful in those courses in law that follow the environmental approach. The emphasis is on the concepts of law and the content reflects those areas of law which are of fundamental importance for every individual in a modern legal society.

M. P. Litka
J. E. Inman

PART I
THE LEGAL ENVIRONMENT

Historically, each society has its own set of values reflected in the goals that its legal system promotes for the good of its citizens. The substance of the law is attained by recognizing certain interests and defining the legal limits in which they will be permitted to operate. These goals, priorities, and limitations must change as societies evolve and become more complex.

The role of law in American history has been unique. Its legal environment evolved over a period of approximately two centuries and has been fashioned by public policies of three basic eras. It began with English Common Law which was refined and adopted to meet the problems of a new nation. It was modified by the impact of the Industrial Revolution and its values on American society and faced radical adjustments in the modern era of social awareness and welfare consciousness.

Part I begins with a discussion of legal philosophies and the objectives of the U.S. legal system (Chapter 1). American ideals are explored in the context of the constitutional system of government.

Legal institutions are created to resolve conflicting priorities which will ultimately occur as individual citizens desire their interests promoted over that of other citizens. The availability of legal process ensures an orderly society in the resolution of disputes. Consequently, Part I includes discussions of both the judicial (Chapter 2) and administrative processes (Chapter 3) which provide arenas and procedures for resolving conflict.

The dynamic aspects of the legal process are illustrated in Chapter 4. The changing nature of tort law and the judicial powers of interpretation are examined.

Chapter 5 explores the rights of the individual in the U.S. legal system. The basic rights afforded under the Bill of Rights are discussed in the context of differing controversies.

In total, Part I builds an understanding of the foundations of the legal system in the United States. Its dynamic qualities are explored, and an appreciation for the difficult "balancing" between societal interests and those of the individual is hopefully developed.

LEGAL PHILOSOPHY

What is law? What are the origin and nature of law? Who creates or determines law? What are the objectives of a legal system? These might be called jurisprudential or philosophical questions of law. They pose appropriate initial inquiries for the study of the legal environment of a politically organized society. In addition, discussions of legal philosophy provide foundations for better understanding the contemporary legal environment.

The following readings suggest explanations of the sources, forms, objectives, and functions of law. Each reading represents a different time period, which implys that contemporary legal philosophy has evolved from numerous sources, societies, and scholars. The reader should achieve a broader understanding of the several philosophies of law that exist in U.S. society and comprehend the basic objectives and structure of this legal system.

PHILOSOPHIES OF LAW

While there are a variety of legal philosophies there are a particular few that are most often discussed and widely known. An understanding of these basic philosophies will help the reader formulate and evaluate his own philosophy of law. Also, the reader can learn to evaluate better the statements of others who express some legal theory.

LEGAL POSITIVISM: LAW AS THE EXPRESSION OF POLITICAL POWER

Legal positivists argue that law is the command of the highest political authority. To "posit" means to put, place, or impose something. Hence, legal positivists view law as that which is laid down or "posited" by the highest political authority. The nineteenth century English lawyer, John Austin, wrote, "the subject matter of jurisprudence is positive law: . . . law set by political superiors to political inferiors."[1] Furthermore, legal positivists believe that ethical principles have no relevance to the study of law. Their concern is with the law "as it is" and not with the law "as it should be." They believe that value judgments have no place in the study of law. Furthermore, they assert that law is derived from some "basic norm." For example, a judicial decision is lawful, and just if it has been rendered in conformity with the proper statute; the statute is lawful if it is in conformity with the Constitution; and so forth. Therefore, the legal positivists believe laws are the logical and consistent rules derived from the "basic norm." The philosophical writings of a positivist are either the logical analysis of a derived rule or the continuous searching for a "basic norm" upon which to base the derived legal rule. The "basic norm" can take a variety of forms: a constitution, an assembly, a sovereign (king), or a mere acknowledgement of existing authority in some particular code or idea such as the Magna Carta. Some writings expressive of the philosophy of legal positivists follow.

> If we ask why the constitution is valid, perhaps we come upon an older constitution. Ultimately we reach some constitution that is the first historically and that was laid down by an individual usurper or by some kind of assembly. The validity of this first constitution is the last presupposition, the final postulate, upon which the validity of all the norms of our legal order depends.
>
> Hans Kelsen, *General Theory of Law and State,* (1965), p. 115.

> Law is the totality (a) of the rules of conduct, expressing the will of the dominant class and established in legal order, and (b) of customs and rules of community life sanctioned by state authority—their application being guaranteed by the compulsive force of the state in order to guard, secure, and develop social relationships and social orders advantageous and agreeable to the dominant class.
>
> A. Y. Vyshinsky, *The Law of the Soviet State,* (1948), p. 50.

> A law is defined as a rule of action backed by that compulsory power which is an essential mark of sovereignty. Compulsion implies the power to impose virtually unlimited penalties if the rule be centralized. Rivalry in this matter spells anarchy, and whatever body exercises this supreme power is, by that very fact, the sovereign body.
>
> Johnsen, *Selected Articles on Law Enforcement,* (1930), p. 83.

NATURAL LAW: LAW AS "HIGHEST HUMAN REASON" OR AS "DIVINE JUSTICE"

Natural law theories have their origin in the political thought of the Greeks and its later incorporation into the Roman law. The Greeks conceptualized the "jus naturale" which meant "the sum of those principles which ought to control human conduct, because founded in the very nature of man as a rational and social being."[2] This was largely synonymous with the Roman concept of law which consisted of those principles which were regarded "as so simple and reasonable that . . . they must be recognized everywhere and by everyone."[3]

Medieval lawyers and theologians added the concept that the law of nature was an expression of the Divine Will. They viewed the ultimate origin and final justification of the law to be God, since the law of nature is that part of God discoverable by human reason. They believed that natural law is not only that which is natural, but also that which is known through connaturality (by being inborn). As such, natural law is dependent on divine reason and therefore "binds men in conscience, and is the prime foundation of human law . . ."[4] The great English lawyer Blackstone wrote, "the will of the Maker is called the Law of Nature . . . . This law, being . . . dictated by God Himself, is obligatory upon all. No human laws are of any validity if contrary to this, as they derive their force and authority from this original."[5] The following materials are additional writings from natural law philosophers.

> There is in fact a true law—namely, right reason—which is in accordance with nature, applies to all men, and is unchangeable and eternal. By its commands this law summons men to the performance of their duties; by its prohibitions it restrains them from doing wrong. Its commands and prohibitions always influence good men, but are without effect upon the bad. To invalidate this law by human legislation is never morally right, nor is it permissible ever to restrict its operation, and to annul it wholly is impossible. Neither the senate nor the people can absolve us from our obligation to obey this law, and it requires no . . . (great lawyer) to expound and interpret it. It will not lay down one rule at Rome and another at Athens, nor will it be one rule today and another tomorrow. But there will be one law, eternal and unchangeable, binding at all times upon all peoples; and there will be, as it were, one common master and ruler of men, namely God, who is the author of this

law, its interpreter, and its sponsor. The man who will not obey it will abandon his better self, and, in denying the true nature of a man, will thereby suffer the severest of penalties, though he has escaped all the other consequences which men call punishment.

> Cicero, *On the Commonwealth,* (Sabine and Smith trans., 1950), pp. 215-16.

...[L]aws may be unjust through being opposed to the Divine good: such are the laws of tyrants inducing to idolatry, or to anything else contrary to the Divine law: and laws of this kind must nowise be observed, because...we ought to obey God rather than men...

> Thomas Aquinas, *Summa Theologica,* (Question 96, Article 4).

The law is the organization of the natural right of lawful defense. It is the substitution of a common force for individual forces. And this common force is to do only what the individual forces have a natural and lawful right to do: to protect persons, liberties, and properties; to maintain the right of each, and to cause justice to reign over us all.

> Bastiat, *The Law,* (1950), p. 7.

When, in the course of human events, it becomes necessary for one people to dissolve the political bonds which have connected them with another, and to assume, among the powers of the earth, the separate and equal station to which the laws of nature and of nature's God entitle them, a decent respect to the opinions of mankind requires that they should declare the causes which impel them to the separation.

> Thomas Jefferson, *Declaration of Independence,* (1776).

Misconceptions and dangers lurk in the view that ultimate conceptions of wisdom, justice and morality are embodied in a written legal instrument. The ultimates, identified with transcendent values, must, by their very nature, lie outside of the Constitution, just as basic rights have their source outside the Constitution...

It is sometimes said that the Supreme Court is the conscience of the nation. This, too, is specious. The Court cannot impose its own notion of conscience without correspondence to the accepted moral values of the community. It can lead, but within limits. In the end, its decision on ultimate values must be sustained by some higher law rooted in the common consciousness and understanding.

> Paul G. Kauper, "The Higher Law and the Rights of Man in a Revolutionary Society" (talk delivered at Old North Church, Boston, (1973).

THE HISTORICAL SCHOOL: LAW AS CUSTOM AND TRADITION

German jurists were among the first to argue that law was not something that could be developed by a mind that would understand and know law independent of experience (as in Natural Law theory). Likewise, to them a rule could not be put forth arbitrarily by a political authority (as in Legal Positivism). Law was to be understood only in terms of history of a particular race. Such an approach was clearly a challenge to both the natural law theory and legal positivism. The historical school believed that law was formulated in different societies by following certain similar patterns while passing through certain stages. It was the function of the historical school to observe various factors which contribute to the movement or changes in the law from one stage of development to another. Observe the following writings that emphasize the importance of custom and traditions to the formulation of laws.

Because law is that body of customs which are enforced by the community, it is that which regulates man's conduct toward his fellow men, which controls his gross passions and restrains his rude impulses.

> Lee, *Historical Jurisprudence,* (1911), p. 5.

The object ... is to present a general view of the Common Law. To accomplish the task, other tools are needed besides logic. It is something to show that the consistency of a system requires a particular result, but it is not all. The life of the law has not been logic; it has been experience. The felt necessitites of the time, the prevalent moral and political theories, intuitions of public policy, avowed or unconscious, even the prejudices which judges share with their fellow men, have had a good deal more to do than the syllogism in determining the rules by which men should be governed. The law embodies the story of a nation's development through many centuries, and it cannot be dealt with as if it contained only the axioms and corollaries of a book of mathematics. In order to know what it is, we must know what it has been, and what it tends to become. We must alternately consult history and existing theories of legislation. But the most difficult labor will be to understand the combination of the two into new products at every stage. The substance of the law at any given time pretty nearly corresponds, so far as it goes, with what is then understood to be convenient; but its form and machinery, and the degree to which it is able to work out desired results, depend very much upon its past.

Holmes, *The Common Law*, (1881), pp. 1-2.

A legal historian, Grant Gilmore, has suggested that lessons to be learned from the experience of the past two hundred years include the fact that law has never been, and never will be, the salvation of any society. He declared that the function of law is more modest—to provide a mechanism for an orderly adjustment to change during periods when there is consensus on the principles on which society is based. Moreover, he writes:

Law reflects but in no sense determines the moral worth of a society. The values of a reasonably just society will reflect themselves in a reasonably just law. The better the society, the less law there will be. In Heaven there will be no law, and the lion will lie down the lamb. The values of an unjust society will reflect themselves in an unjust law. The worse the society, the more laws there will be. In Hell there will be nothing but law, and due process will be meticulously observed.

Grant Gilmore, *The Ages of American Law*, (1977).

INSTRUMENTALISM: LAW AS AN INSTRUMENT OF SOCIAL ORDER

The historical school of legal philosophy has resulted in many derivative philosophies. One such derived philosophy could be labeled "instrumentalism." A modern exponent of instrumentalism is Wolfgang Friedmann who wrote, "Law must ... respond to social change if it is to fulfill its function as a paramount instrument of social order." Besides being adaptable to new social conditions, instrumentalists maintain that law must be understandable to the public so that they will respect it and follow it. However, since much of today's law has become so complex and largely unknown to the public, it is the public's faith in the "ideals" of the law that causes them to continue to uphold and respect the law. If the "man in the street" keeps his faith that law is rational and philosophically sound, law will remain as an instrument of social order.

In addition, instrumentalists believe law is the pragmatic decision-making of the processes that make or enact the law. A pragmatist follows a trial and error methodology to develop an acceptable solution to a social problem. The legal pragmatist would likewise use a trial and error technique in the formulation of the most appropriate law. Moreover, the pragmatist views law as a social instrument for the direction and control of individual and group activities.

The following writings illustrate some of the concepts of instrumentalism:

The term law ... does not include laws of God, natural laws, laws of morality or any other so-called laws which are not regulations of society enforceable by governmental means and may be briefly defined as societal regulations enforceable by governmental action.

Rodenbeck, *The Anatomy of the Law*, (1925), p. 6.

The really fundamental *sine qua non* of law in any society is the legitimate use of physical coercion. The law has teeth, and teeth that can bite, although they need not be bared, for as Holmes put it, "The foundation of jurisdiction is physical power, although in civilized times it is not necessary to maintain that power throughout proceedings properly begun." We would merely add to that declaration that it was not necessary to limit the latency of power to civilized times; primitive men often found that it was not necessary to display the power behind the law when the defendant acceded to proceedings carried through properly.

Hoebel, *Man in the Primitive World*, (1958), p. 363.

The law at bottom can only be what the mass of people actually does and tends to some extent to make other people do by means of governmental agencies.

Bently, *The Process of Government,* (1935), p. 276.

Law is not a brooding omnipresence in the sky, but a flexible instrument of social order, dependent on the political values of the society which it purports to regulate ...

Friedmann, *Law in a Changing Society,* (1955), p. xlii.

This doing of something about disputes, this doing of it reasonably, is the business of law. And the people who have the doing in charge, whether they be judges or sheriffs or clerks or jailers or lawyers, are officials of the law. What these officials do about disputes is, to my mind, the law itself.

Llewellyn, *The Bramble Bush,* (1930), p. 3.

Questions

1. How do you define "law"? Does it depend on your legal philosophy? Consider how a legal positivist defines law and answer the following question. Would the organized mass murders of the Nazi regime qualify as law to the positivist? To the theorist of Natural Law?
2. If you were the leader of a revolution against a tyrantical government, which legal philosophy would you probably declare to your followers?
3. Can you differentiate between law and justice?
4. Do Natural Law philosophers think all laws come from "highest reason" or God? What about a traffic law to drive on the right side of the road?
5. Plato's notion that law is the "will of the stronger" is based on the concept that "might makes right." Plato's viewpoint is similar to what philosophy?
6. Roscoe Pound's notion that law is formulated by "balancing competing interests" and Karl Llewellyn's notion that law is created by "official's manipulation of rules" are expressions similar to which basic philosophy?

THE OBJECTIVES OF A LEGAL SYSTEM

An obvious objective of a legal system is justice. However, in many instances, individual concepts of justice differ. In legal positivism, the objectives (what the legal system *ought* to achieve) are accepted as given by the sovereign political authority or the "basic law." Positivists would not inquire whether the objectives were right or wrong because positivists don't accept the notion of ultimate or enduring values. Positivists would merely seek "consistency" of rules with the basic norm. Therefore, the objectives of our legal system are largely the concepts of Natural Law theorists and the historical experiences of English-speaking people, because of their respective emphasis on what ought to be and on evolutionary reform. The English concepts of "justice" have had considerable impact on the objectives and purposes of our legal system.

PRESERVATION OF ORDER

Sir Frederick Pollock
The King's Peace
(from *Oxford Lectures and Other Discourses,* 1890)

Against the peace of Our Lady the Queen, her crown and dignity." This formula was once the necessary conclusion, as it is still the accustomed one, of every indictment for a criminal offence preferred before the Queen's justices. Even to those who have nothing to do with assizes or quarter sessions the Queen's Peace is a familiar term. By the widely spread office of justice of the peace it is brought home to the remotest corners of England. And it seems to us a natural thing that throughout the realm peace should be kept—in other words that unlawful force should be prevented and punished—in the Queen's name and by officers armed with her authority. This does not look, on the face of it, like a fact requiring any special explanation. Our conception of an executive power, under whatever names and in whatever forms it is exercised, is that its first business is to preserve order. And that this power should be one and uniform in every part of a land ruled by the same laws appears to us so far from remarkable that anything contrary to it has the air of a puzzle and an anomaly. Such is our modern point of view, too obvious (one would think) to be worth stating. Yet it is so modern that there was demonstrably a time when it was an innovation. It belongs to the political theory of sovereignty which has superseded the feudal theory of autonomous personal allegiance. It assumes that the rights of private feud and war, rights exercised without contradiction far into the Middle Ages, are for us intolerable and impossible. It assumes, moreover, that a central authority has become strong enough to subdue local competition and jealousy. These conditions have been brought about in Western Christendom only by long processes of growth, strife, and decay. Perhaps examples might be assigned of lands and institutions where even yet they are not wholly fulfilled. The establishment of the king's peace is a portion, and in England no small one, of the historical transformation which has given us the modern in the place of the medieval State . . .

Questions

1. What is the "first business" of executive powers?
2. How far should the executive powers extend? What did the sovereign's power replace? What was necessary before this replacement occurred?
3. Can you identify any similar processes of replacement of local powers by stronger central powers in this country?

GENERALITY, EQUALITY AND CERTAINTY

Sir Frederick Pollock
from *A First Book of Jurisprudence*
(1929)

Let us pass on, then, to consider what are the normal and necessary marks, in a civilised commonwealth, of justice administered according to law. They seem capable of being reduced to Generality, Equality, and Certainty. First, as to generality, the rule of justice is a rule for citizens as such. It cannot be a rule merely for the individual; as the medieval glossators put it, there cannot be one law for Peter and another for John. Not that every rule must or can apply to all citizens; there are divers rules for divers conditions and classes of men. An unmarried man is not under the duties of a husband, nor a trader under those of a soldier. But every rule must at least have regard to a class of members of the State, and be binding upon or in respect of that class as determined by some definite position in the community. This will hold however small the class may be, and even if it consists for the time being of only one individual, as is the case with offices held by only one person at a time. Certain rules of law will be found, in almost every country, to apply only to the prince or titular ruler of the State, or to qualify the application of the general law to him. But these rules are not lacking in the quality of generality, for in every case they apply not to the individual person as such, but to the holder of the office for the time being. . .

Next, the rule of generality cannot be fulfilled unless it is aided by the principle of equality. Rules of law being once declared, the rule must have the like application to all persons and facts coming within it. Respect of persons is incompatible with justice. Law which is the same for Peter and for John must be administered to John and to Peter evenly. The judge is not free to show favour to Peter and disfavour to John. As the maxim has it, equality is equity. So much is obvious and needs no further exposition. But it may be proper to point out that the rule of equality does not exclude judicial discretion. Oftentimes laws are purposely framed so as to give a considerable range of choice to judicial or executive officers as to the times, places, and manner of their application. It is quite commonly left to the judge to assign, up to a prescribed limit, the punishment of proved offences: indeed, the cases in which the court is deprived of discretion are exceptional in all modern systems ... Still, a judicial discretion, however, wide, is to be exercised without favour and according to the best judgment which the person intrusted with the discretion can form on the merits of each case. Differences of personal character and local circumstances are often quite proper elements in the formation of such a judgment, but any introduction of mere personal favour is an abuse. We still aim at assigning equal results to equal conditions. Judicial discretion is not an exception to the principle of equality, but comes in aid of it where an inflexible rule, omitting to take account of conditions that cannot be defined beforehand, would really work inequality. This implies that only such conditions are counted as are material for the purposes of the rule to be applied. Of course no two persons or events can be fully alike. What rules of law have to do is to select those conditions which are to have consequences of certain kinds: which being done, it is the business of the courts to attend to all those conditions, and, saving judicial discretion where it exists, not to any others ... The law cannot make all men equal, but they are equal before the law in the sense that their rights are equally the subject of protection and their duties of enforcement.

Further, as the requirement of generality leads to that of equality, so does the requirement of equality lead to that of certainty ... We must administer a general rule, and administer it equally. There can be no law without generality; there can be no just operation of law without equality. But we cannot be sure of a rule being equally administered at different times and in the cases of different persons unless the rule is defined and recorded. Justice ought to be the same for all citizens, so far as the ... conditions are the same. Now, to carry out this idea the dispenser of justice ought to be adequately furnished with two kinds of information. He should know what is accustomed to be done in like cases, and whenever new conditions occur he should know, or have the means of forming a judgment, which of them are material with a view of legal justice, and which are not. Moreover, there must be some means of securing an approximate uniformity of judgment; otherwise judges and magistrates of all degrees will make every one a law of his own for himself, and the principle of equality will not be satisfied ... Hence law becomes an artificial system which is always gathering new material. The controverted points of one generation become the settled rules of the next, and fresh work is built up on them in turn. Thus the law is in a constant process of approximation to an ideal certainty which, by the nature of the case, can never be perfectly attained at any given moment. Everyone who has studied the law knows that the approximation is apt to be a rough one, and is exposed to many disturbing causes ... For the practical purposes of a State governed according to law, that degree of certainty suffices which will satisfy the citizens that the law works on the whole justly and without favour ...

Questions

1. Pollock's principle of generality is that there "cannot be a rule merely for the individual ... But every rule must ... have regard to a class of members ..." When Pollock says there cannot be one law for Peter and another for John, does he assume Peter and John are (alike) in the same class? In other words, may the law discriminate between (or classify) persons so that different laws might be applied to different classes? May there be a law for Peter and another law for John, if Peter and John are not alike? Is this answered in Pollock's "divers rules for divers conditions and classes of men"?
2. Distinguish between "generality" and "equality"?
3. To facilitate the concept of "equality" under the law, is there any need for judicial discretion?
4. To achieve "certainty" in the administration of law, how are subsequent judges to know what occurred in the past?

UNIFORMITY

The Institute of Justinian (529)

In the name of Our Lord Jesus Christ.

The Emperor Caesar Flavius Justinian, conqueror of the Alamanni, the Goths, the Franks, the Germans, the Antes, the Alani, the Vandals, the Africans, pious, prosperous, renowned, victorious, and triumphant, ever august.

To the youth desirous of studying the law:

The imperial majesty should be armed with laws as well as glorified with arms, that there may be good government in times both of war and of peace, and the ruler of Rome may not only be victorious over his enemies, but may show himself as scrupulously regardful of justice as triumphant over his conquered foes.

With deepest application and forethought, and by the blessing of God, we have attained both of these objects. The barbarian nations which we have subjugated know our valour. Africa and other provinces without number being once more, after so long an interval, reduced beneath the sway of Rome by Victories granted by Heaven, and themselves bearing witness to our dominion. All peoples too are ruled by laws which we have either enacted or arranged. Having removed every inconsistency from the sacred constitutions, hitherto inharmonious and confused, we extended our care to the immense volumes of the older jurisprudence; and, like sailors crossing the mid-ocean, by the favour of Heaven have now completed a work of which we once despaired. When this, with God's blessing, had been done, we...commissioned...a book of Institutes, whereby you may be enabled to learn your first lessons in law...

Questions

1. In writing the *Institute of Justinian,* were the Romans interested in uniformity in application of the law over time or uniformity of law over geographical areas? Or both?
2. When a subsequent and similar case comes before the same court, what techniques would achieve uniformity in the application of law and avoid the result whereby one judge decides two exact cases differently?

THE AMERICAN LEGAL SYSTEM

The fundamental principles underlying modern legal environment in the United States were derived largely from preceding societies. The language of law often reflects the influence of natural law in its discussion of basic human rights and individual freedoms. In the United States philosophical underpinnings have combined natural law with American pragmatism and the desire to be ruled by the governed. The American legal system is effective, not because of the power to levy penalties on those who interfere with the legal rights of others, but because Americans believe in American ideals and generally respect the legal system as an evolutionary process of reform. The legal system is assigned the task of resolving the conflicting philosophies and establishing priorities among and between individuals and various groups of people.

AMERICAN IDEALS

DECLARATION OF INDEPENDENCE (1776)

We hold these truths to be self-evident, that all men are created equal; that they are endowed by their Creator with certain unalienable rights, that among these, are life, liberty, and the pursuit of happiness. That, to secure these rights, governments are instituted among men, deriving their just powers from the consent of the governed; that, whenever any form of government becomes destructive of these ends, it is the right of the people to alter or to abolish it, and to institute a new government, laying its foundation on such principles, and organizing its powers in such form, as to them shall seem most likely to effect their safety and happiness. Prudence, indeed, will dictate that governments long established, should not be changed for light and transient causes; and, accordingly, all experience hath shown, that mankind are more disposed to suffer, while evils are sufferable, than to right themselves by abolishing the forms to which they are accustomed. But, when a long train of abuses and usurpations, pursuing invariably the same object, evinces a design to reduce them under absolute despotism, it is their right, it is their duty, to throw off such government, and to provide new guards for their future security...

FRIEDMANN, *LAW IN A CHANGING SOCIETY*, (1959)

A democratic ideal of justice must rest on the three foundations of equality, liberty and ultimate control of the government by the people. It is, however, far from easy to give these concepts a specific content.

. . . We can still not formulate the principle of equality in more specific terms than Aristotle who said that justice meant the equal treatment of those who are equal before the law. We can give to this apparent tautology a more concrete meaning by saying that a democratic ideal of justice demands that inequalities shall be inequalities of function and service but shall not be derived from distinctions based on race, religion, or other personal attributes . . .

The meaning of "liberty" is hardly more easy to define. In terms of a democratic ideal of justice, liberty means certain rights of personal freedom which must be secure from interference by government. They include legal protection from arbitrary arrest, freedom of opinion and association, of contract, labour and many others. Briefly, they may be subsumed under the two broad categories of the freedom of the person and the freedom of the mind . . .

Lastly, the principle of control by the people means that law must ultimately be the responsibility of the elected representatives of the people. This is, indeed, a vital principle but it can say little about the technique by which the modern legislator can discharge this function.

Questions

1. What are some of the basic American ideals expressed in these writings?
2. Is it an American ideal to "take up arms" against any governmental decree which violates one of the American beliefs?

FEDERALISM

THE CONSTITUTION OF THE UNITED STATES OF AMERICA (1787)

We the people of the United States, in Order to form a more perfect Union, establish Justice, insure domestic Tranquility, provide for the common defense, promote the general Welfare, and secure the Blessings of Liberty to ourselves and our Posterity, do ordain and establish this Constitution for the United States of America.

KENT'S COMMENTARIES (1826-1830)

The government of the United States was erected by the free voice and joint will of the people of America, for their common defence and general welfare. Its powers apply to those great interests which relate to this country in its national capacity, and which depend for their stability and protection on the consolidation of the Union. It is clothed with the principal attributes of political sovereignty, and it is justly deemed the guardian of our best rights, the source of our highest civil and political duties, and the sure means of national greatness ... That the union of this country was essential to its safety, its prosperity and its greatness, had been generally known, and frequently avowed, long before the ... revolution ...

The Constitution of the United States has ... made a general delegation of ... specific powers for national purposes, and erected (the federal government) in the midst of numerous state governments retaining the exclusive control of their local concerns . . .

Questions

1. The powers of government are derived "from the consent of the governed." Did the people of the southern states have the "legal" philosophical right to secede from the union?
2. Is to "insure domestic tranquility" an extension of the concept of the "Queen's peace"? Does this notion partly explain the establishment of the federal government?
3. Why was a central government (national government) deemed necessary by the forefathers?
4. Contrast the American establishment of a Union for uniform laws with the Roman or Napoleonic quest for uniformity.

SEPARATION OF POWERS

KENT'S COMMENTARIES (1826-1830)

The power of making laws is the supreme power in a state, and the department in which it resides will naturally . . . act with such mighty force upon the public mind, that the line of separation between that and the other branches of the government ought to be marked very distinctly, and with the most careful precision.

The Constitution of the United States has effected this purpose . . . in a way well calculated to preserve the equal balance of the government and the harmony of its operations. It has not only made a general delegation of the legislative power to one branch of the government, of the executive to another, and of the judicial to the third, but it has specially defined the general powers and duties of each of those departments.

Questions

1. What is the "separation of powers" doctrine?
2. Is the separation of powers essential to effective government? Or, to protecting the people from despotism? Is the protection afforded by this doctrine a hinderance to effective government?

WRITTEN CONSTITUTIONS

MARBURY V. MADISON
5 U.S. (1 Cranch) 137 (1803)
Supreme Court of the United States

[*William Marbury was named a Justice of the Peace for the District of Columbia at the close of the administration of President John Adams. The new Jefferson administration through Secretary of State, James Madison, decided against delivering the commission which was not delivered at the end of Adam's term. Marbury filed suit in the Supreme Court of the United States to compel Madison to deliver his commission. Marbury's right to sue in the Supreme Court was authorized by the Judiciary Act of 1789. The Court's decision determined whether this congressional legislation could confer additional judicial power on the Supreme Court which had not been granted by the written Constitution.*]

■ ■ ■

MARSHALL, Chief Justice.

The question, whether an act, repugnant to the constitution, can become the law of the land, is a question deeply interesting to the United States . . . It seems only necessary to recognize certain principles, supposed to have been long and well established, to decide it.

. . . [T]he people have an original right to establish . . . their . . . government . . . This original and supreme will organizes the government, and assigns to different departments their respective powers. It may either stop here, or establish certain limits not to be transcended by those departments.

The government of the United States is of the latter description. The powers of the legislature are defined and limited; and that those limits may not be mistaken, or forgotten, the constitution is written. To what purpose are powers limited, and to what purpose is that limitation committed to writing, if these limits may, at any time, be passed by those intended to be restrained? The distinction between a government with limited and unlimited powers is abolished, if those limits do not confine the persons on whom they are imposed . . .

The constitution is either a superior paramount law, unchangeable by ordinary means, or it is on a level with ordinary legislative acts, and, like other acts, is alterable when the legislature shall please to alter it.

If the former part of the alternative be true, then a legislative act, contrary to the constitution, is not law: if the latter part be true, then written constitutions are absurd attempts on the part of the people, to limit a power, in its own nature, illimitable.

Certainly, all those who have framed written constitutions contemplate them as forming the fundamental and paramount law of the nation, and consequently, the theory of every such government must be that an act of the legislature, repugnant to the constitution, is void.

This theory is essentially attached to a written constitution, and is, consequently, to be considered, by this court, as one of the fundamental principles of our society . . .

It is, emphatically, the province and duty of the judicial department to say what the law is. Those who apply the rule to particular cases, must of necessity expound and interpret that rule. If two laws conflict with each other, the courts must decide on the operation of each.

So, if a law be in opposition to the constitution; if both the law and the constitution apply to a particular case, so that the court must either decide that case conformable to the law, disregarding the constitution; or conformable to the constitution, disregarding the law; the court must determine which of these conflicting rules governs the case. This is the very essence of judicial duty.

If then, the courts are to regard the constitution, and the constitution is superior to any ordinary act of the legislature, the constitution, and not such ordinary act, must govern the case to which they both apply . . .

It is also not entirely unworthy of observation, that in declaring what shall be the *supreme* law of the land, and *constitution* itself is first mentioned; and not the laws of the United States generally, but those only which shall be made in *pursuance* of the constitution, have that rank.

Thus, the particular phraseology of the constitution of the United States confirms and strengthens the principle, supposed to be essential to all written constitutions, that a law repugnant to the constitution is void; and that *courts*, as well as other departments, are bound by that instrument . . .

[*The Court concluded that the Judiciary Act was unconstitutional and not to be enforced by the courts. By so ruling, the Court acknowledged itself as the sole and final interrupter of the U.S. Constitution.*]

■ ■ ■

Questions

1. Oliver Wendell Holmes in the *Common Law* reminds us of errors often made by students; "that of supposing, because an idea seems very familiar and natural to us, that it has always been so. Many things which we take for granted

have had to be laboriously fought out or thought out in past times." Has the judiciary always had the power to declare acts of Congress unconstitutional? Do any precedents exist in England? The English Supreme Court is the House of Lords. Can the House of Lords declare acts of the House of Commons unconstitutional and null and void?

2. Does England have a written constitution? According to Marshall, why was the U.S. Constitution written?

UNITED STATES v. NIXON
418 U.S. 683 (1974)
Supreme Court of the United States

■ ■ ■

BURGER, Mr. Chief Justice.

On March 1, 1974, a grand jury of the United States District Court for the District of Columbia returned an indictment charging seven named individuals with various offenses, including conspiracy to defraud the Unites States and to obstruct justice. Although he was not designated as such in the indictment, the grand jury named the President, among others, as an unindicted coconspirator. On April 18, 1974, upon motion of the Special Prosecutor, a subpoena *duces tecum* was issued . . . to the President by the United States District Court . . . This subpoena required the production, in advance of the . . . trial date, of certain tapes, memoranda, papers, transcripts or other writings relating to certain precisely identified meetings between the President and others. The Special Prosecutor was able to fix the time, place, and persons present at these discussions because the White House daily logs and appointment records had been delivered to him . . . [T]he President's counsel, filed a "special appearance" and a motion to quash the subpoena . . . This motion was accompanied by a formal claim of privilege . . .

In the performance of assigned constitutional duties each branch of the Government must initially interpret the Constitution, and the interpretation of its powers by any branch is due great respect from the others. The President's counsel . . . reads the Constitution as providing an absolute privilege of confidentiality for all Presidential communications. Many decisions of this Court, however, have unequivocally reaffirmed the holding of Marbury v. Madison, that "[i]t is emphatically the province and duty of the judicial department to say what the law is.". . .

In support of his claim of absolute privilege, the President's counsel urges two grounds, one of which is common to all governments and one of whch is peculiar to our system of separation of powers. The first ground is the valid need for protection of communications between high Government officials and those who advise and assist them in the performance of their manifold duties; the importance of this confidentiality is too plain to require further discussion . . . .

The second ground asserted . . . in support of the claim of absolute privilege rests on · the doctrine of separation of powers. Here it is argued that the independence of the Executive Branch within its own sphere, insulates a President from a judicial subpoena in an ongoing criminal prosecution, and thereby protects confidential Presidential communications.

However, neither the doctrine of separation of powers, nor the need for confidentiality of high-level communications, without more, can sustain an absolute, unqualified Presidential privilege of immunity from judicial process under all circumstances . . . Absent a claim of need to protect military, diplomatic, or sensitive national security secrets, we find it difficult to accept the argument that even the very important interest in confidentiality of Presidential communications is significantly diminished by production of such material for *in camera* inspection with all the protection that a district court will be obliged to provide.

The impediment that an absolute, unqualified privilege would place in the way of the primary constitutional duty of the Judicial Branch to do justice in criminal prosecutions would plainly conflict with the function of the courts under Art. III. In designing the structure of our Government and dividing and allocating the sovereign power among three co-equal branches, the Framers of the Constitution sought to provide a comprehensive system, but the separate powers were not intended to operate with absolute independence . . . To read the Art. II powers of the President as providing an absolute privilege as against a subpoena essential to enforcement of criminal statutes on no more than a generalized claim of the public interest in confidentiality of nonmilitary and nondiplomatic discussions would upset the constitutional balance of "a workable government" and gravely impair the role of the courts under Art. III.

Since we conclude that the legitimate needs of the judicial process may outweigh Presidential privilege, it is necessary to resolve those competing interests in a manner that preserves the essential functions of each branch... A President and those who assist him must be free to explore alternatives in the process of shaping policies and making decisions and to do so in a way many would be unwilling to express except privately. These are the considerations justifying a presumptive privilege for Presidential communications. The privilege is fundamental to the operation of Government and inextricably rooted in the separation of powers under the Constitution. In Nixon v. Sirica, (1973), the Court of Appeals held that such Presidential communications are "presumptively privileged," and this position is accepted by both parties in the present litigation . . . But this presumptive privilege must be considered in light of our historic commitment to the rule of law . . . The very integrity of the judicial system and public confidence in the system depend on full disclosure of all the facts, within the framework of the rules of evidence. To ensure that justice is done, it is imperative to the function of courts that compulsory process be available for the production of evidence needed either by the prosecution or by the defense . . . .

In this case we must weigh the importance of the general privilege of confidentiality of Presidential communications in performance of the President's responsibilities against the inroads of such a privilege on the fair administration of criminal justice. The interest in preserving confidentiality is weighty indeed and entitled to great respect . . .

On the other hand, the allowance of the privilege to withhold evidence that is demonstrably relevant in a criminal trial would cut deeply into the guarantee of due process of law and gravely impair the basic function of the courts... Without access to specific facts a criminal prosecution may be totally frustrated. The President's broad interest in confidentiality of communications will not be vitiated by disclosure of a limited number of conversations preliminarily shown to have some bearing on the pending criminal cases.

We conclude that when the ground for asserting privilege as to subpoenaed materials sought for use in a criminal trial is based only on the generalized interest in confidentiality, it cannot prevail over the fundamental demands of due process of law in the fair administration of criminal justice. The generalized assertion of privilege must yield to the demonstrated, specific need for evidence in a pending criminal trial.

■ ■ ■

Questions

1. What is an *in camera* inspection?
2. On what basis did the Court conclude that presidential communications are presumptively privileged?
3. What conflicting constitutional interests did the Court weigh against the presidential privilege of confidentiality?
4. What coercive power does the Supreme Court possess to enforce its order against the president?

ENDNOTES

1. John Austin, *Lectures on Jurisprudence or the Philosophy of Positive Law,* rev. and ed. by Robert Campbell (2 vols., 5th ed., London: John Murray, 1929), Vol. I, p. 86.
2. J L. Brierly, *The Law of Nations,* (London: Oxford University Press, 1928), p. 10.
3. *Ibid*
4. Jacques Maritain, *The Range of Reason,* (New York: Charles Scribner's Sons, 1952), p. 28.
5. Sir William Blackstone, *Commentaries on the Laws of England,* ed. Wm. Hardcastle Browne (New York: L. K. Strouse and Co., 1892), pp. 7-8.

THE JUDICIAL PROCESS

The judicial process is a system of regularized and institutionalized procedures for resolving public and private disputes. The basic elements of this process are the courts, the jury, the judge, the procedures, and the adversary system. The courthouse may be described as the arena provided by an organized society for resolving controversy. Each participant acts out his part in this arena. The function of the jurors is to determine the facts from which the controversy arose. Collectively, the jury must decide which of the opposing versions alleged and testified to is correct. Thus, the jury is the "finder" of the facts.

The judge is normally not allowed to interfere with the jury's fact-finding process. The judge is, however, the sole authority on the law which is to be applied to the facts as the jury found them. In addition, the judge directs the pace of the litigation and administers the rules of procedures. Procedural rules provide the guidelines for the orderly operation of the courts.

The adversary system activates the judicial process. The parties to the controversy, through their lawyers, have the obligation for investigating, initiating, and maintaining the litigation. The court has no other means of obtaining the necessary information to resolve the controversy. The lawyers for each side must select the evidence essential to their cause. They attempt to present evidence which will convince the jury that their version of the facts is correct. The lawyers plan the sequence of the presentation of their witnesses, the questions that will be raised, and the evidence that will be needed to substantiate their claim. The theory of the adversary system is that the best decision will be rendered by the judge or jury if the parties presenting their views are real adversaries. If the parties have a real stake in the outcome of the case, they will present their case in a manner most favorable to their claim. Accordingly, the judge and jury can reach a better decision after having heard the best arguments on each side of the controversy.

The following materials emphasize the basic elements of the judicial process. These readings should assist the student in understanding the process of solving a legal controversy.

COURT SYSTEMS

A general familiarity with the court systems is necessary to understand the adjudicatory process. Initially, one should recognize that there is a distinction between a trial court and an appellate court. Trial courts, or courts of original jurisdiction, are courts where the cases are first heard and decided. It is in this arena that the opposing parties present their evidence and the jury determines its verdict. Ordinarily, a single judge presides over this hearing.

While most cases go no further than the trial court, a party dissatisfied with the outcome of the trial may usually request an appellate court to review the process and decisions of the trial court. The appellate court ordinarily consists of a number of judges who read the record or transcript of the proceedings in the trial court and review the legal briefs filed by counsel outlining the supposed error that occurred in the trial court. The appeallate court justices make their decisions from these written records and legal briefs. There are no new trials before the appellate courts. Rather, the appellate court will determine whether the lower court misinterpreted the law or committed some procedural error which necessitates a new trial in the lower court.

Each of the fifty states of the United States has its own court system. There are many differences in functions and labels given to the trial courts in the various states. Each state also has at least one appellate court. Some states provide intermediate appellate courts to relieve the highest appellate court of an excessive workload of appeal requests.

Figure 2-1

STATE COURT SYSTEMS

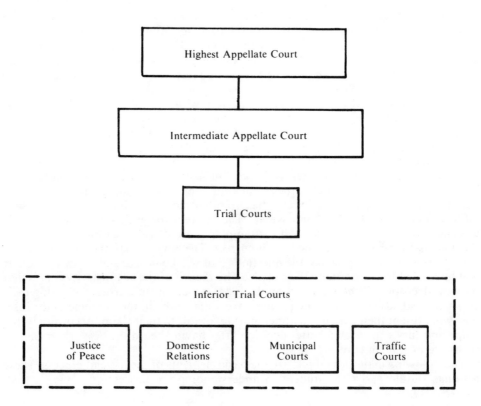

The federal court system is comparatively simple. The basic trial court at the federal level is the United States District Court. Appeals from these district courts are taken to the United States Court of Appeals which is divided into eleven circuits. Each circuit court hears appeals from decisions of district courts in its circuit. The highest appellate court in the federal system is the Supreme Court of the United States. Some cases can be appealed to the Supreme Court as a *right* granted in legislation. The Supreme court may also select cases that it regards of particular public importance for its determination by granting special permission through the *writ of certiorari*. Since legislative rights to appeal are infrequent, litigants cannot normally force the Supreme Court to hear their appeal.

Figure 2-2

FEDERAL COURT SYSTEM

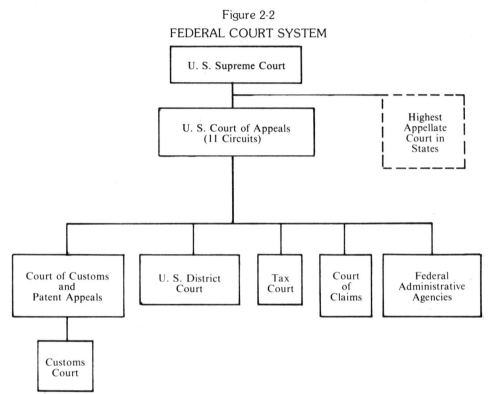

PROCEDURAL DUE PROCESS

The states maintain courts in which individuals may seek appropriate legal remedies when their lawful rights have been violated. Each court is governed by procedural rules which seek to ensure that any party that properly comes before the court will be granted "his day in court." The rules of the court provide for a systematic resolution of legal controversaries. The rules may vary from one court system to another, but they must comply with U.S. Constitutional requirements. However, mandatory compliance with the U.S. Constitution has not always been required. Historically, the Bill of Rights and its protections for the individual were added to the U.S. Constitution to limit the power of the *federal* government from becoming an oppressive central government similar to the crown's exercise of power over its subjects in the colonies. Each of the states already had its own constitution, which afforded similar protections to state citizens from oppressive state action. Consequently, the Bill of Rights was not applicable as a limitation on powers of *state* government.

After the Civil War, however, the Fourteenth Amendment was added to the U.S. Constitution as a limitation on the power of *state* governments and as a source of power to the federal government to protect individuals in certain instances from state governments. This amendment's basic purpose was to provide federal protection to the freed slaves of the South from oppressive state government. One protection afforded to individuals in the Fourteenth Amendment is that no state shall deprive an individual of his life, liberty, or property without following the requirements of "due process of law." This means, among other things, that the procedural rules used by state courts must conform to the requirements of "due process of law" as defined by the federal courts. Inevitably, this raises questions as to the proper definition of "due process." Some suggested that the Fourteenth Amendment "due process" clause was the equivalent of all the protections granted in the U.S. Bill of Rights and that, therefore, the protections for individuals afforded in the Bill of Rights were binding on the states as well as on the federal authorities. The following exerpt from a Supreme Court case provides the Court's answer to that question. (A copy of the Bill of Rights is provided in Chapter 5.)

DEFINING "DUE PROCESS"

MALINSKI v. PEOPLE OF STATE OF NEW YORK
324 U.S. 401 (1945)
Supreme Court of the United States.

■ ■ ■

DOUGLAS, Mr. Justice.

Apart from permitting Congress to use criminal sanctions as means for carrying into execution powers granted to it, the Constitution left the domain of criminal justice to the States. The Constitution, including the Bill of Rights, placed no restriction upon the power of the States to consult solely their own notions of policy in formulating penal codes and in administering them, excepting only that they were forbidden to pass any "Bill of Attainder" or "ex post facto Law", Constitution of the United States, Art. I, §10. This freedom of action remained with the States until 1868. The Fourteenth Amendment severely modified the situation. It did so not by changing the distribution of power as between the States and the central government. Criminal justice was not withdrawn from the States and made the business of federal law-making. The Fourteenth Amendment merely restricted the freedom theretofore possessed by the States in the making and the enforcement of their criminal laws.

Unlike the limitations of the Bill of Rights upon the use of criminal penalities by federal authority, the Fourteenth Amendment placed no specific restriction upon the administration of their criminal law by the States. Congress in proposing the Fourteenth Amendment and the States in ratifying it left to the States the freedom of action they had before that Amendment excepting only that after 1868 no State could . . . "deprive any person of life, liberty, or property, without due process of law", nor deny to any person the "equal protection of the laws." These are all phrases of large generalities . . . But they are generalities circumscribed by history and appropriate to the largeness of the problems of government with which they were concerned . . . The safeguards of "due process of law" and "the equal protection of the laws" summarize the history of freedom of English-speaking peoples running back to Magna Carta and reflected in the constitutional development of our people. The history of American freedom is, in no small measure, the history of procedure.

Here we are concerned with the requirement of "due process of law" in the enforcement of a state's criminal law. Experience has confirmed the wisdom of our predecessors in refusing to give a rigid scope to this phrase. It expresses a demand for civilized standards of law. It is thus not a stagnant formulation of what has been achieved in the past but a standard for judgment in the progressive evolution of the institutions of a free society. The suggestion that "due process of law," as guaranteed by the Fourteenth Amendment, is a compendious expression of the original federal Bill of Rights (Amendments I to VIII) has been rejected by this Court again and again .

The Due Process Clause of the Fourteenth Amendment thus has potency different from and independent of the specific provisions contained in the Bill of Rights . . .

A construction which gives due process no independent function but makes of it a summary of the specific provisions of the Bill of Rights would tear up by the roots much of the fabric of law in the several States. Thus, it would require all the States to prosecute serious crimes through the grand jury system long ago abandoned by many of them . . . to try such crimes by a jury of twelve which some of the States have seen fit to modify or abandon . . . and to have jury trials "In suits at common law, where the value in controversy shall exceed twenty dollars", a requirement which this Court has held over and over again for more than a hundred years does not apply to proceedings in state courts . . . .

And so, when a conviction, in a state court is properly here for review, under a claim that a right protected by the Fourteenth Amendment has been denied, the question is not whether the record can be found to disclose an infraction of one of the specific provisions of the first eight amendments . . .

The exact question is whether the criminal proceedings which resulted in his conviction deprived him of the due process of law by which he was constitutionally entitled to have his guilt determined. Judicial review of that guaranty of the Fourteenth Amendment inescapably imposes upon this Court an exercise of judgment upon the whole course of the proceedings in order to ascertain whether they offend those canons of decency and fairness which express the notions of justice of English-speaking peoples even toward those charged with the most heinous offenses. These standards of justice are not authoritatively formulated anywhere as though they were prescriptions in a pharmacopoeia. But neither does the application of the Due Process Clause imply that judges are wholly at large. The judicial judgment in applying the Due Process Clause must move within the limits of accepted notions of justice and is not to be based upon the idiosyncrasies of a merely personal judgment. The fact that judges among themselves may differ whether in a particular case a trial offends accepted notions of justice is not disproof that general rather than idiosyncratic standards are applied . . .

■ ■ ■

Notes and Questions

1. Why did the Court feel the Fourteenth Amendment's "due process" clause should not adopt all the Bill of Rights?
2. What alternate definition or standard is adopted by the Court for "due process"?
3. ". . . the due process clause of the 14th Amendment does not necessitate that the proceedings of a state court should be by a particular mode, but only that there shall be a regular course of proceedings in which notice is given of the claim asserted, and an opportunity afforded to defend against it." *Simon v. Croft,* 182 U.S. 427, 436 (1900).
4. According to the *Malinski* case, what test or standard would the Court use to determine if the defendant received a "regular course of proceedings"? A "notice of the claim asserted" against him? An "opportunity to defend" against it?
5. Technically, "procedural" due process refers to the regularity of the proceeding; that is, were the court rules of procedure properly and uniformly followed by the court? "Substantive" due process refers to the fairness of the rules of procedure so employed by the court; that is, assuming the rule is regularly and uniformly followed, is the rule so employed an appropriate rule according to the test laid down in the *Malinski* case? With these distinctions in mind, what kind of a violation of due process would it be to jail an unpopular political person without a trial? What if the jailing occurs after a regular and uniform

trial by following the state court rule that defendants do not have the right to cross-examine the accusors?

6. In the *Malinski* case, the Court rejected the notion that the Fourteenth's "due process" clause was the equivalent of the Bill of Rights. However, in the *Malinski* case, the Court continued a selective approach in defining the substance of the Fourteenth's "due process." This approach is called the "incorporation" or "absorption" theory which means that the Fourteenth's "due process" clause incorporates or absorbs in whole or in part various of the amendments in the Bill of Rights. In this manner, the incorporated amendment or portion thereof becomes applicable to the states also. Consider the following language from *Malaski* in which certain rights from the Bill of Rights are implied or incorporated into the Fourteenth's "due process."

> In the Bill of Rights, Eighteenth-century statesmen formulated safeguards against the recurrence of well-defined historic grievances. Some of these safeguards, such as the right of trial by a jury of twelve and immunity from prosecution unless initiated by a grand jury, were built on experience of relative and limited validity. "Few would be so narrow or provincial as to maintain that a fair and enlightened system of justice would be impossible without them" . . . (However), the freedom of the press or the free exercise of religion or freedom from condemnation without a fair trial, (are) express rights the denial of which is repugnant to the conscience of a free people. They express those "fundamental principles of liberty and justice which lie at the base of all our civil and political institutions" . . . and are implied in the comprehensive concept of "due process of law."

This incorporation process began rather slowly in the field of civil rights but became more popular during the fifties and sixties. Additional cases illustrating the incorporation theory will be explored in subsequent chapters. But, at this point, it should be noted that through the incorporation theory, the proponents of the position that due process equals the Bill of Rights have largely achieved their purpose. They lost the battle in *Malinski*, but through the process of time and the incorporation theory, they have largely won the war.

JURISDICTION

Jurisdiction refers to the power of a court to hear and decide a particular controversy. A court has power to decide cases when it has jurisdiction over the subject matter of the case and jurisdiction over the parties to the case. A court's jurisdiction over the dispute or subject matter is usually determined by the constitution or by some legislation. Either of these will specify the types of controversies that the particular court can resolve. State courts of general jurisdiction are normally empowered to hear all types of cases that are not specifically assigned to courts of limited or inferior jurisdiction. Inferior state courts (such as justice of the peace courts, mayor's courts or municipal courts), hear cases involving limited periods of punishments and fines. However, even if the court possesses subject matter jurisdiction, it still may not resolve the controversy if it is unable to achieve jurisdiction over the parties.

Jurisdiction over the parties to the controversy must be obtained before the court has the power to render a judgment. Jurisdiction over the person of the plaintiff is easily obtained. The plaintiff's filing of the suit is a voluntary submission to the power of the court. However, jurisdiction over the person of the defendant may be obtained by a variety of means in which a summons is delivered to the defendant. The summons contains a copy of the complaint against the defendant. The "service of process" may be delivered by a private person, a deputy sheriff, or the defendant may voluntarily pick up the "service" at the courthouse. "Service" is more often accomplished by delivery of the summons through registered mail.

Historically, the U.S. Supreme Court ruled that service of process by state courts could not be delivered beyond the borders of the state. However, in the 1940s this concept of territorial restrictions on the issuance of the summons was modified. Many states enacted what has been called "long-arm" statutes which provide for service of process beyond the state boundaries.

Out-of-state service was challenged in the U.S. Supreme Court as a denial of due process of law under the Fourteenth amendment in the case of *International Shoe Company vs. Washington* 326 U.S. 310 (1945). International Shoe contended that the company itself was not present in the State of Washington and that the notice sent by registered mail to the company was not a personal service that would have any force and effect outside the borders of the State of Washington. The Supreme Court denied the company's contention and said, "due process requires only that in order to subject the defendant to a judgment *in personam*, if he is not present within the territory of the form, he have certain minimum contacts with it such that the maintenance of the suit does not offend traditional notions of fair play and substantial justice ..." Subsequent to the *International Shoe* decision, many states adopted statutes giving extra territorial effect to their service of process. The following case illustrates the utilization of an Illinois long-arm statute in an attempt to compel an Ohio corporation to defend itself in an Illinois court.

GRAY v. AMERICAN RADIATOR & STANDARD SANITARY CORP.
176 N. E. 2d 761 (1961)
Supreme Court of Illinois

■ ■ ■

The suit was brought against the Titan Valve Manufacturing Company and others, on the ground that a certain water heater had exploded and injured the plaintiff. The complaint charges, ... that the Titan company, a foreign corporation, had negligently constructed the safety valve; and that the injuries were suffered as a proximate result thereof. Summons issued and was duly served on Titan's registered agent in Cleveland, Ohio. The corporation appeared specially, filing a motion to quash on the ground that it had not committed a tortious act in Illinois. Its affidavit stated that it does no business here; that it has no agent physically present in Illinois . . . [but] it is not disputed, for the purpose of this appeal, that a tortious act was committed. The issue depends on whether it was committed in Illinois, so as to warrant the assertion of personal jurisdiction by service of summons in Ohio.

The wrong in the case at bar did not originate in the conduct of a servant physically present here, but arose instead from acts performed at the place of manufacture. Only the consequences occurred in Illinois. It is well established, however, that in law the place of a wrong is where the last event takes place which is necessary to render the actor liable . . .

We think it is clear that the alleged negligence in manufacturing the valve cannot be separated from the resulting injury; and that for present purposes, like those of liability and limitations, the tort was committed in Illinois.

Under modern doctrine the power of a State court to enter a binding judgment against one not served with process within the State depends upon. . . whether he has certain minimum contacts with the State . . .

Where the business done by a foreign corporation in the State of the forum is of a sufficiently substantial nature, it has been held permissible for the State to entertain a suit against it even though the cause of action arose from activities entirely distinct from its conduct within the State . . . but where such business or other activity is not substantial, the particular act or transaction having no connection with the State of the forum, the requirement of "contact" is not satisfied.

In the case at bar the defendant's only contact with this State is found in the fact that a product manufactured in Ohio was incorporated in Pennsylvania, into a hot water heater which in the course of commerce was sold to an Illinois consumer . . .

Whether the type of activity conducted within the State is adequate to satisfy the requirement depends upon the facts in the particular case . . . The question cannot be answered by applying a mechanical formula or rule of thumb but by ascertaining what is fair and reasonable in the circumstances. In the application of this flexible test, the relevant inquiry is whether defendant engaged in some act or conduct by which he may be said to have invoked the benefits and protections of the law of the forum . . .

In the case at bar defendant does not claim that the present use of its product in Illinois is an isolated instance. While the record does not disclose the volume of Titan's business or the territory in which appliances incorporating its valves are marketed, it is a reasonable inference that its commercial transactions, like those of other manufacturers, result in substantial use and consumption in this State. To the extent that its business may be directly affected by transactions occurring here it enjoys benefits from the laws of this State, and it has undoubtedly benefited, to a degree, from the protections which our law has given to the marketing of hot water heaters containing its valve. Where the alleged liability arises, as in this case, from the manufacture of products presumably sold in contemplation of use here, it should not matter that the purchase was made from an independent middleman or that someone other than the defendant shipped the product into this State.

With the increasing specialization of commercial activity and the growing interdependence of business enterprises it is seldom that a manufacturer deals directly with consumers in other States. The fact that the benefit he derives from its laws is an indirect one, however, does not make it any the less essential to the conduct of his business; and it is not unreasonable, where a cause of action arises from alleged defects in his product, to say that the use of such products in the ordinary course of commerce is sufficient contact with this State to justify a requirement that he defend here.

As a general proposition, if a corporation elects to sell its products for ultimate use in another State, it is not unjust to hold it answerable there for any damage caused by defects in those products. Advanced means of distribution and other commercial activity have made possible these modern methods of doing business, and have largely effaced the economic significance of State Lines. By the same token, today's facilities for transportation and communication have removed much of the difficulty and inconvenience formerly encountered in defending lawsuits brought in other States.

Unless they are applied in recognition of the changes brought about by technological and economic progress, jurisdictional concepts which may have been reasonable enough in a simpler economy lose their relation to reality, and injustice rather than justice is promoted . . .

The principles of due process relevant to the issue in this case support jurisdiction in the court where both parties can most conveniently settle their dispute. The facts show that the plaintiff, an Illinois resident, was injured in Illinois. The law of Illinois will govern the substantive questions, and witnesses on the issues of injury, damages and other elements relating to the occurrance are most likely to be found here. Under such circumstances the courts of the place of injury usually provide the most convenient forum for trial . . . .

■ ■ ■

Notes and Questions

1. What reason did the court give for extending the state's jurisdictional powers over nonresident defendants in the *Gray* case?
2. Another type of jurisdiction is called jurisdiction *in rem*. In the case of *Pennington v. Fourth National Bank*, 243 U.S. 269 (1917), the Supreme Court said:

   "The 14th Amendment did not, in guaranteeing due process of law, abridge the jurisdiction which a state possessed over property within its borders, regardless of the residence or presence of the owner. That jurisdiction extends alike to tangible and to intangible property . . . The thing belonging to the absent defendant is seized and applied to the satisfaction of his obligation. The Federal Constitution presents no obstacle to the full exercise of this power."

3. The importance of possessing "jurisdiction" is that without it, the state court's judgment is void; and with it, the judgment is entitled to "full faith and credit" (that is, enforcement) throughout the fifty states. A state court's judgment which possessed both subject matter and person jurisdiction is enforceable in all states because the U.S. Constitution requires all states to give "full faith and credit" to the court judgments of the other states in the union. Does the "full faith and credit" clause suggest a reason for the out-of-state defendant to return and defend himself in a state court from which he has received a summons?

4. Subject matter jurisdiction for federal courts falls into one of two categories: (1) cases involving "federal questions"—questions concerning a provision of the federal constitution, a federal statute, or an international treaty, (2) cases involving "diversity of citizenship"—the respective parties are citizens of different states. All cases in the latter category could be tried in state courts. However, the apprehension of possible state court bias against the out-of-state party inspired the framers of the Constitution to allow such cases to be brought in federal courts. In addition to diversity of citizenship, the amount in controversy must exceed $10,000.

THEORY OF PLEADINGS

The pleadings, or documents in the case, serve to set the limits within which the litigation will operate and to give notice of the plaintiff's claim to the defendant to gain personal jurisdiction over the defendant. In the written complaint filed with the clerk of the court, the plaintiff's attorney will present his client's version of what transpired and relate the particular relief the plaintiff is seeking from the defendant. In contesting the plaintiff's case, the defendant's attorney will file an answer with the court denying all or some of the plaintiff's allegations about what occurred. These documents isolate the issues of fact—that is, where the parties' version of the facts differ. This divergence of alleged events must be resolved by a trial. Prior to a discussion of the aspects of a trial, the following materials are offered to provide a greater understanding of the pleading process.

A "COMPLAINT"

A COMPLAINT

IN THE COURT OF COMMON PLEAS
SUMMIT COUNTY, OHIO

Ernest Student)
221 North Street)
Akron, Ohio 44304
        and) No. _____
Dolly Student
221 North Street)
Akron, Ohio 44304
)
)
        Plaintiffs
    vs.) COMPLAINT

Herbert A. Worker   )
2631 East Market Street
Kent, Ohio 43204   )
     and
Worldwide Flush, Inc.
343 Industry Street
Kent, Ohio 43204   )

          Defendants   )

COUNT ONE

1. On May 6, 1970, plaintiff, Ernest Student, was driving an auto-
   mobile, owned jointly by Ernest Student and his wife, plaintiff
   Dolly Student, southwardly in the left traffic lane of Exchange
   Street, a multi-lane public highway in Akron, Ohio.

2. At the same time defendant, Herbert Worker, was driving an
   automobile, leased by defendant Worldwide Flush, Inc., southwardly in the right traffic lane of Exchange Street.

3. Negligently and without warning, defendant, Herbert Worker
   shifted from the right traffic lane to the left traffic lane of Exchange
   Street immediately in front of plaintiff Ernest Student, thus causing
   plaintiff, Ernest Student, to strike the left rear of defendant, Herbert
   Worker's automobile.

4. At the time of the impact defendant, Herbert Worker, was the
   agent of defendant, Worldwide Flush, Inc., and was acting within the
   scope of his agency and authority.

5. As a direct result of the impact plaintiff, Ernest Student, has
   suffered a rib fracture, a contusion over the sternum, and a rupture of
   an intervertebral disc at L-5, S-1. To date, he has expended $767.58 in
   medical expenses and has lost intermittently a total of 23 days of
   work. He has suffered great pain of body and mind and in the future
   will continue to do so and in the future will be compelled to expend
   additional sums for medical treatment and hospitalization and will
   suffer intermittently loss of wages. In addition, the automobile
   owned by plaintiffs, Ernest Student and Dolly Student, was damaged
   in the amount of $411.00. Being deprived of the use of the automobile
   for three weeks, plaintiff, Ernest Student, was required to expend
   $60.00 for public transportation.

     WHEREFORE, plaintiffs demand judgment against defendant,
Herbert Worker, or against Worldwide Flush, Inc., or against both of
them as follows:

   (a) In behalf of plaintiffs, Ernest Student and Dolly Student, for
       damage to their automobile in the sum of $411.00.
   (b) In behalf of the plaintiff, Ernest Student in the sum of $15,000.00,
       together with the costs of this action.

COUNT TWO

1. For a second claim plaintiff, Dolly Student, restates all that is alleged
   in paragraphs 1 through 4 of Count One.

2. Plaintiff, Dolly Student, further states that she is the wife of Ernest Student and that as a direct result of the injuries suffered by Ernest Student as set forth in paragraph 5 of Count One, plaintiff, Dolly Student, has been and will be deprived of the consortium of her husband, Ernest Student.

WHEREFORE, plaintiff, Dolly Student, demands judgment against defendant, Herbert Worker, or against defendant, Worldwide Flush, Inc., or against both of them in the sum of $5,000.00 together with the costs of this action.

> Chester Goodfellow, Attorney for Plaintiffs
> Goodfellow, Nice & Easy, Attorneys at Law
> 221 West Market Street
> Akron, Ohio 44304

AN ANSWER

AN ANSWER
IN THE COURT OF COMMON PLEAS
SUMMIT COUNTY, OHIO

Ernest Student 221 North Street Akron, Ohio 44304 and Dolly Student 221 North Street Akron, Ohio 44304	(((No. _____ ((

Plaintiffs
    vs.
Herbert A. Worker
2631 East Market Street
Kent, Ohio 43204
    and
Worldwide Flush, Inc.
343 Industry Street
Kent, Ohio 43204
	(ANSWER
	(
	
	(
	
	(

Defendant Herbert A. Worker:

1. Admits the allegations contained in paragraphs 1 and 2 of Count One of the complaint, and admits these same paragraphs as incorporated by reference in Count Two of the complaint.
2. Denies the allegations contained in paragraph 3 of Count One of the complaint, and denies the same paragraph as incorporated by reference in Count Two of the complaint.
3. Alleges that he is without knowledge or information sufficient to form a belief as to the truth of the allegations contained in paragraph

4 and 5 of Count One of the complaint, and alleges that he is without knowledge or information sufficient to form a belief as to the truth of the allegations contained in paragraph 4 as incorporated by reference in paragraph 1 of Count Two of the complaint, and further alleges that he is without knowledge or information sufficient to form a belief as to the truth of the allegations contained in paragraph 2 of Count Two of the complaint.

William Williams, Attorney for Defendant, Herbert Worker
Williams, Jones & Smith, Attorneys at Law
225 North High Street
Akron, Ohio 44304

Questions and Notes

1. What is the controversy in *Student v. Worker*? What facts are admitted? Which "facts" are in issue?

2. Historically, the rules of pleading were burdened with intricacies and technicalities. The emphasis was on pleading "facts." However, reformed efforts brought about "notice" pleading, with an emphasis upon giving notice of the complaint to the opposing parties. The "complaint" and "answer" in *Student v. Worker* illustrate the simplicity of "notice" pleading. Any further refinements or elaboration in the facts are to be "discovered" by other techniques separate from the pleading process. These privileges of "discovery" allow the parties to learn what sort of evidence the other party has that relates to the suit. Certain matters are not subject to discovery but, for the most part, any relevant matter may be ascertained. The techniques of discovery usually are written interrogatories, inspection of documents, physical examination of persons, and depositions. Such procedures allow for proper preparation for trials and aid pre-trial settlements. It also eliminates most "surprises" at the trial which might allow suits to be won or lost by tricks, rather than on the merits of the case. The broadest discovery processes are available in civil suits. Many states allow a limited aspect of discovery in criminal suits also.

SUMMARY JUDGMENT

DI SABATO v. SOFFES
193 N.Y.S. 2d 184 (1959)
Supreme Court, Appellate Division, N.Y.

■ ■ ■

One of the recognized purposes of summary judgment is to expedite the disposition of civil cases where no issue of material fact is presented to justify a trial. While the courts are cautioned to exercise the power to summarily direct judgment with full recognition that a party with a just claim or a valid defense is entitled to his day in court, timidity in exercising the power in favor of a legitimate claim and against an unmerited one, not alone defeats the ends of justice in a specific case, but contributes to calendar congestion which, in turn, denies to other suitors their rights to prompt determination of their litigation.

On a motion (for summary judgment...the Court is called upon to determine whether a bona fide issue exists. If the plaintiff's pleadings and other papers disclose no real defense and if the defendant fails to controvert such proof and establish by affidavits or other evidence the existence of a genuine defense, the Court may find that no triable issue exists and grant summary judgment (*General Investment Co. v. Interborough Rapid Transit Co.,* 139 N.E. 216, 219-220).

In the first case to reach this Court after the adoption of the Rule (*Dwan v. Massarene,* 880, 192 N.Y.S. 577, 582), it was said, "The defendant must show that he has a *bona fide* defense to the action, one which he may be able to establish. It must be a plausible ground of defense, something fairly arguable and of a substantial character. This he must show by affidavits or other proof. He cannot shelter himself behind general or specific denials * * * . He must show that his denial or his defense is not false and sham, but interposed in good faith and not for delay."

. . . With these principles in mind, we turn to the case at hand. The defendants have failed to submit a single affidavit, by anyone having knowledge of the facts, to controvert the prima facie showing of negligence which flows from the occurrence together with the examination before trial. A defendant is not privileged on a motion for summary judgment to ignore the rule that he must submit proof of a defense . . .

It is incumbent upon a defendant who opposes a motion for summary judgment to assemble, lay bare and reveal his proofs, in order to show that the matters set up in his answer are real and are capable of being established upon a trial.

■ ■ ■

Questions

1. What is a summary judgment? What are its purposes?
2. When is a summary judgment appropriately rendered?
3. What must a defendant do to avoid a summary judgment?
4. Why would a court grant a summary judgment against a plaintiff?
5. What must a plaintiff do to avoid a summary judgment?

CONDUCT OF THE TRIAL

The primary purpose of the trial is to resolve all controversy over questions of fact, that is, what events actually transpired. The pleadings serve to notify each party of the questions that each must be prepared to meet with the best evidence available to them. As the party that initiated the action, it is the obligation of the plaintiff to proceed first in presenting his case. Following the plaintiff's presentation of evidence, the defendant will attempt with his contra evidence to create doubt in the minds of the jurors concerning the plaintiff's version of the controversy. At the conclusion of the presentation of the evidence, the jury will return a verdict (finding of facts) in resolution of that portion of the legal controversy. In civil (non-criminal) cases, the plaintiff must present proofs to convince the jury by the preponderance of the evidence. This is a burden of proof that is much lower than the prosecutor's burden in a criminal case to convince the jury "beyond a reasonable doubt."

JURY SELECTION PROCESS

Prospective jurors are selected from a list of residents in the judicial district of the court. They are summoned to the courthouse and assigned to various trials. Prospective jurors are questioned concerning any possible connection with any of the participants in the trial or the possibility of some bias on the questions before the court. The opposing counsel may demand the exclusion of any prospective juror who demonstrates a specific cause for rejection. Moreover, opposing counsel have a limited number of "pre-emptory challenges" which allow prospective jurors to be dismissed without giving any reason. This privilege enables opposing counsel to exclude jurors who they feel may be hostile to their client's cause. Once the jury is empaneled, the lawyers present their opening statement. Then, the evidence is presented before the jury.

Since the jurors are not expert factfinders, they may have considerable difficulty in determining the truth from the evidence. Because the jurors are laypersons, the rules of evidence have been shaped over time to protect the jury from irrelevent, misleading, and unreliable evidence. Repetitious evidence and evidence that may be in violation of certain confidential relationships are also excluded. These rules of evidence have been developed over the years and are too numerous and complex for full discussion here. Indeed, even judges themselves often commit error by introducing inappropriate evidence or failing to admit evidence that should have been presented to the jury. Some of the excerpts from the cases that follow illustrate the difficulties involved in selecting the proper evidence to be presented to the jury.

IMMATERIAL

FUENTES v. TUCKER
187 P. 2d 752 (1947)
Supreme Court of California

■ ■ ■

It is a doctrine too long established to be open to dispute that the proof must be confined to the issues in the case and that the time of the court should not be wasted, and the jury should not be confused, by the introduction of evidence which is not relevant or material to the matters to be adjudicated. This is merely one aspect of the larger problem of delay in the conduct of litigation. Every court has a responsibility to the public to see that justice is administered efficiently and expeditiously and that the facilities of the court are made available at the first possible moment to those whose cases are awaiting trial. It would be an unwarranted waste of public funds, and a manifest injustice to the many litigants seeking an early trial date, to allow counsel in a particular case to occupy substantial periods of time in the useless presentation of evidence on matters not in controversy; and we know of no well considered opinion which asserts such a right.

One of the functions of pleadings is to limit the issues and narrow the proofs. If facts alleged in the complaint are not controverted by the answer, they are not in issue, and no evidence need be offered to prove their existence . . .

Evidence which is not pertinent to the issues raised by the pleadings is immaterial and it is error to allow the introduction of such evidence . . .

It follows, therefore, if an issue has been removed from a case by an admission in the answer, that it is error to receive evidence which is material solely to the excluded matter. This, of course, does not mean that an admission of liability precludes a plaintiff from showing how an accident happened if such evidence is material to the issue of damages. In an action for personal injuries, where liability is admitted and the only issue to be tried is the amount of damage, the force of the impact and the surrounding circumstances may be relevant and material to indicate the extent of plaintiff's injuries.

. . . Such evidence is admissible because it is relevant and material to an issue remaining in the case.

The defendant here by an unqualified statement in his answer admitted liability for the deaths of the children, and the sole remaining question in issue was the amount of damages suffered by the parents. In an action for wrongful death of a minor child the damages consist of the pecuniary loss to the parents in being deprived of the services, earnings, society, comfort and protection of the child . . .

The manner in which the accident occurred, the force of the impact, or defendant's intoxication could have no bearing on these elements of damage. The evidence, therefore, was not material to any issue before the jury, and its admission was error.

■ ■ ■

Questions

1. What is immaterial evidence? Why should it be excluded?
2. Why was the manner of the accident in *Fuentes* immaterial?

BEST EVIDENCE RULE

HERZIG v. SWIFT & CO.
146 F. 2d 444 (1945)
United States Court of Appeals, 2nd Cir.

■ ■ ■

This is an action under Florida law for the wrongful death of the decedent. The suit was commenced by the plaintiff, the decedent's administratrix, in the State court, but was removed to the district court because of diversity of citizenship.

In regard to proof of damages, the plaintiff's witnesses testified that the deceased was forty-three years old at the time of his death, that he was a partner in a firm which contracted for hoisting and rigging in building construction work, that his work included the physical labor involved in operating the machines, that he was, in the opinion of the witness, in good physical condition. The plaintiff offered testimony by one of the partners in the firm as to the amount of the partnership earnings, but this testimony was rejected on the ground that it was not the best evidence, that the books of the firm should have been produced to prove the firm's earnings.

At the conclusion of the plaintiff's case, the court dismissed the complaint on the ground that the failure to prove the earnings and savings of the decedent was a fatal defect as to proof of damages.

. . . "In its modern application, the best evidence rule amounts to little more than the requirement that the contents of a writing must be proved by the introduction of the writing itself, unless its absence can be satisfactorily accounted for." Here there was no attempt to prove the contents of a writing; the issue was the earnings of the partnership, which for convenience were recorded in books of account after the relevant facts occurred. Generally, this differentiation has been adopted by the courts. On the precise question of admitting oral testimony to prove matters that are contained in books of account, the courts have divided, some holding the oral testimony admissible, others excluding it. The federal courts have generally adopted the rationale limiting the "best evidence rule" to cases where the contents of the writing are to be proved. We hold, therefore, that the district judge erred in excluding the oral testimony as to the earnings of the partnership.

■ ■ ■

Questions

1. On what grounds was this case removed from the state court to the federal court?
2. Can you explain "the best evidence" rule and its correct application to this case?

PRIVILEGED COMMUNICATIONS

HURLBURT ET. AL. v. HURLBURT
28 N.E. 651 (1891)
Court of Appeals of New York

■ ■ ■

The plaintiffs objected to his evidence on the ground that he was an attorney, consulted professionally, and that the communications to him were privileged. The court overruled the objection, and received the evidence.

We think that in receiving this evidence there was no violation of the Code, which provides that "an attorney or counselor at law shall not be allowed to disclose a communication made by his client to him, or his advice given thereon, in the course of his professional employment." This section is a mere re-enactment of the common-law rule, and it cannot be supposed from the general language used that it was intended to change or enlarge that rule as it had been expounded by the courts. It has frequently been said that the object of the rule embodied in the section is to enable and encourage persons needing professional advice to disclose freely the facts in reference to which they seek advice, without fear that such facts will be made public to their disgrace or detriment by their attorney. Such a case as this is plainly not within the rule. Here Theron and his father were both interested in the advice which they sought, and they were both present at the same time, and engaged in the same conversation. Each heard what the other said, so that the disclosures made were not, as between them, confidential, and there can be no reason for treating such disclosures as privileged. It has frequently been held that the privilege secured by this rule of law does not apply to a case where two or more persons consult an attorney for their mutual benefit; that it cannot be invoked in any litigation which may thereafter arise between such persons, but can be in a litigation between them and strangers . . .

■ ■ ■

Questions

1. Why are confidential communications with an attorney privileged?
2. Why was this conversation with an attorney not privileged?
3. Can you think of any other confidential communications that are privileged? Why?

HEARSAY RULE

Hearsay evidence is testimony by someone who did not observe the event but who was told about the event by someone who did observe the event. The hearsay rule would preclude the testimony of the secondhand witness in favor of the "eye-witness" himself. The firsthand witness is the best evidence available. This witness could be put under oath and subjected to cross-examination as to his perception of the event. However, a great deal of valuable evidence would be lost to the courts if it excluded all hearsay. Consequently, numerous exceptions to the hearsay rule have been made to allow certain hearsay evidence to be admitted if it is likely to be trustworthy. The court attempts to assure itself that the original speaker or eye-witness is not available and that the original declarant possessed accurate perception, recall, and truthfulness. If these elements are established to the satisfaction of the court, the secondhand witness may testify as to what he heard the original declarant say.

GOODALE v. MURRAY ET AL.
227 Iowa 843 (1940)
Iowa Court of Appeals

■ ■ ■

The situation at the time of the execution of Dieckman's will meets every requirement justifying an exception to the rule. Dieckman and Scholz are dead and, of course,
not available for cross-examination. The only source of testimony was the witness
Bartels. Unless his testimony be accepted there is none available. The essential of
necessity is fully met. The same is true of the circumstantial guarantee of trustworthiness. What good reason can there be to suspect the sincerity or the truth or reliability
of what either the testator or Scholz did or said on the occasion? Scholz was his banker
and business adviser. They had previously discussed the making of the will. Scholz,
knowing the circumstances of this elderly bachelor, had advised him to make a will,
and had no doubt stressed the reasons why it was particularly advisable in his case.
Having concluded to make a will, he naturally, frankly and honestly told Scholz of his
testamentary wishes, and asked him to draw the will. Is there any reason why Scholz
would not prepare the instrument exactly as Dieckman wished it, or that he would
have read it to him falsely or incorrectly? He would have been both a knave and a fool
to have done otherwise, and would have exposed himself to early and certain detection. Had Scholz read the will other than Dieckman had instructed him to draw it,
Dieckman would have detected it when it was read, and had he violated his instructions in drawing the will, he would have been exposed as soon as Dieckman later at his
leisure read it. The situation itself was a guaranty of the verity of the declarations
testified to by Bartels. Three defects of hearsay testimony often mentioned by courts
and commentators are: 1. Inaccurate perception on the part of the declarant. 2. Faulty
memory on his part. 3. Untruthfulness on his part. In this case there was no basis or
occasion for either inaccurate perception or faulty memory, for neither memory nor
perception were called into action. Scholz merely read what he had just written. And
as already stated there was no reason for untruthfulness.

■ ■ ■

SCOPE OF CROSS-EXAMINATION

AH DOON v. SMITH
34 P. 1093 (1893)
Supreme Court of Oregon

■ ■ ■

. . . Under [the] statue, and the rule there provided, a party has no right to
cross-examine a witness except as to facts and circumstances stated on his direct
examination or connected therewith. But within this limitation great latitude should
be allowed in conducting the examination. It should not be limited to the exact facts
stated on the direct examination, but may extend to other matters which tend to limit,
explain, or qualify them, or to rebut or modify any inference resulting therefrom,
provided they are directly connected with the matter stated in the direct examination.
It is true the party against whom a witness is called cannot, on cross-examination,
go into an independent or affirmative case on his part, but must confine his examination to such facts connected with the direct examination as go to counteract so much of
the case of his adversary as the direct examination tends to prove; but the fact that
evidence called forth by a legitimate cross-examination also tends to sustain some
defense affords no reason why it should be excluded. A party will not be permitted to
glean out certain facts from his witness, which, without explanation, would give a false
coloring to the matter about which he testifies, and then save his witness from the
sifting process of a cross-examination, by which the real transaction could be shown.

When a witness is called and examined concerning any particular matter, the law imposes the obligation upon him to state the whole truth concerning such matter within his knowledge, and a direct examination, if perfectly fair, would generally disclose all the witness knows concerning the matter about which he is testifying; but, because the party calling him may so skillfully and adroitly conduct the examination in chief as to disclose only those facts which are in his favor, and conceal those which are against him, the law has given to the adverse party the right to cross-examination, for the purpose of bringing out the facts thus concealed.

Now, in this case, when the plaintiff was called and examined in chief concerning the alleged loan, the law imposed upon him the obligation to state the whole truth, and, if he had done so, he would have disclosed the fact that it was not a legitimate loan, but that he and the defendant were, at the time, engaged in an unlawful game; that he furnished defendant money to enable him to engage in it; that defendant lost the money so furnished, and plaintiff redelivered it to him, and this continued until the aggregate amount of such pretended loan reached the sum of $740; and that the remaining $145 sued for was money thus loaned and lost, and which defendant took from the gambling table. He would have thus disclosed and set forth facts upon which no court of justice would grant him relief . . .

■ ■ ■

Questions

1. What types of questions on cross-examination should be denied by the court?
2. Should court rules on the rights of cross-examination allow great latitude or confine the inquisitor? Consider the Supreme Court's attitude when it said; "In the Constitutional sense, trial by jury . . . necessarily implies at the very least that the evidence developed against a defendant shall come from the witness stand in a public courtroom where there is full judicial protection of the defendant's right of confrontation, of cross-examination, and of counsel." *Turner v. Louisiana,* 379 U.S. 466 (1965).

POST TRIAL

After the jury renders its verdict, one of the parties is likely to be dissatisfied with the outcome. There are a number of alternatives available to test the correctness of the jury's verdict or the court's judgment. The judgment is the final decision of the court (judge) determined by applying the proper law to the facts as found by the jury. The losing party may ask the judge to rule against the jury's verdict because it is clearly contrary to the evidence (judgment n.o.v.). In addition, the losing party may seek a new trial if there was some irregularity in the trial proceedings. Also, the losing party may appeal to determine whether the law that was applied in the case was properly applied or whether the law itself is a proper law for contemporary conditions. After the case has been argued before the appeals court and it renders a judgment, the legal controversy is usually terminated. If no appeal is advanced, it is terminated at the conclusion of the proceedings in the trial court.

Appeals beyond the first apellate court are normally not available as a matter of "right." Rather, the highest courts usually determine at their own discretion which of the lower court decisions they wish to hear. This procedure usually involves the filing of a petition by the party desiring an appeal with the highest court. The petition asks the high court to issue a "writ of certiorari" to the lower court. The "writ of certiorari" is an order by the high court to the lower court to certify a record of its proceedings for review by the high court. Of course, if the high court grants certiorari, this is not a determination of how the court will finally rule on the merits of the lower court decision. The decision on the merits will be decided only after a full hearing before the high court.

APPEAL FOR NEW TRIAL

DEAN v. TREMBLEY
137 A. 2d 880 (1958)
Superior Court of Pennsylvania

■ ■ ■

Counsel should make every effort to conduct themselves during the trial of a case as gentlemen, consistent with their affiliation with a respected and revered profession. It is to be expected that during the heat of a trial they might momentarily forget themselves and be guilty of breach of the decorum expected of them. This is excusable in the eyes of the jurors and of the Court, and is usually attributed to the zealousness of counsel in behalf of their client and their cause.

Likewise the conduct of a witness is within the control of the trial judge and it cannot be said that the actions of this witness in question were such as to prejudice the plaintiff or his case. The witness in question was called by the defendant, and any prejudice from his conduct or words would naturally inure to the benefit of the plaintiff and against the defendant. There was no occasion for the trial judge to do anything at the time of the alleged incident and therefore furnishes no cause to grant a new trial on account thereof.

The plaintiff also complains of the alleged error on the part of the trial judge in instructing the jury to disregard the evidence about the alleged failure of the defendant to furnish his name and address to the plaintiff following the accident and to offer the plaintiff aid and assitance. The jury was told that in connection with this evidence, they had a right to consider this fact in their deliberations as to whether or not the defendant was negligent, but were "not to be prejudiced or influenced by any alleged failure on his part to give his name and address or to render assistance." We are of the opinion that this portion of the charge was proper and consistent with our laws and constitute no basis for awarding a new trial. If the conduct of the defendant did constitute a violation of the law, it could not be the efficient or proximate cause of the accident.

A motion for a new trial will not be granted on the ground that the verdict is against the weight of the evidence where there is conflicting evidence on material questions, for this would be usurping the functions of the jury . . . An assignment that a jury's verdict is against the evidence is applicable only when it is not based on a conflict of testimony . . .

On a consideration of whether a verdict is against the evidence, all the evidence must be read in the light most favorable to the party in whose favor the verdict is rendered . . .

Our Courts have many times said, as Chief Justice Stern said in *Carrol v. Pittsburgh,* 368 Pa. 436, 84 A. 2d 505, 509:

> A new trial should not be granted because of a mere conflict in testimony or because the trial judge on the same facts would have arrived at a different conclusion . . . Neither should it ordinarily be granted on the ground that the verdict was against the weight of the evidence where the evidence is conflicting and the jury might have found for either party.

This guiding principle has been repeatedly reiterated by our Courts . . .

■ ■ ■

Questions

1. How was the conduct of the witness or of the attorneys relevant to the determination of whether to grant a new trial?
2. Why did the judge instruct the jury not to be prejudiced by the defendant's failure to give his name and address? Or to render assistance?

3. Do appellate courts "second guess" the jury? If the evidence is conflicting, should the appeals court pick the version of facts it prefers or leave the selection to the jury? Why?

4. What about the conduct of an unruly defendant? What can the judge do about him? The Supreme Court has provided some guidance in *Illinois v. Allen*, 397 U.S. 337 (1970).

> It is essential to the proper administration of criminal justice that dignity, order, and decorum be the hallmarks of all court proceedings in our country. The flagrant disregard in the courtroom of elementary standards of proper conduct should not and cannot be tolerated. We believe trial judges confronted with disruptive, contumacious, stubbornly defiant defendants must be given sufficient discretion to meet the circumstances of each case. No one formula for maintaining the appropriate courtroom atmosphere will be best in all situations. We think there are at least three constitutionally permissible ways for a trial judge to handle an obstreperous defendant like Allen: (1) bind and gag him, thereby keeping him present; (2) cite him for contempt; (3) take him out of the courtroom until he promises to conduct himself properly.

APPEAL FOR REVERSAL

STATE v. LISKA
32 Ohio App. 2d 317 (1971)
Court of Appeals of Ohio

■ ■ ■

This action comes here from the Berea Municipal Court on appeal from the appellant's convinction and fine of One Hundred Dollars ($100) for an alleged violation of R. C. 2921.05, the so-called "flag desecration" statute. For the reasons stated below, the judgment of the trial court is reversed as being contrary to law.

The appellant, Liska, a student at Baldwin-Wallace College, was arrested and charged with unlawfully and willfully exposing a contemptuous representation of the American flag on the rear window of his automobile. The alleged contemptuous representation consisted of a decal composed of thirteen red and white stripes with a peace symbol appearing on a blue field.

There is nothing in the record to indicate that the appellant was in violation of any traffic laws, nor that he was behaving in a disorderly manner when arrested. The appellant described himself at trial as a conscientious objector to the Viet Nam War and a pacifist, and testified that his purpose in displaying the decal in question was to make a political statement of peace. The state's evidence consisted only of the testimony of the arresting officer and a photograph of the offending decal as it appeared on appellant's car.

Appellant assigned the following as error:

(1) The court erred in concluding that appeallant's conduct was contemptuous as required by Section 2921.05 of the Revised Code of Ohio . . .

Allowing the state's evidence its most favorable stance, it is apparent that the most this appellant has done is to display a decal composed of thirteen red and white stripes and a blue square upon which is superimposed a peace symbol. On the evidence in this case that configuration indicates only the appellant's aspiration for peace for his country. We hold that the symbolic indication indicated by the facts of this case, without more, was, as a matter of law, not a contemptuous act within the meaning of R.C. 2921.05.

The conviction is reversed and the appellant discharged.

■ ■ ■

Questions

1. Did the appellant challenge the facts? Does this explain why he asked for a reversal and not a new trial?
2. In seeking a reversal, what is the appellant asserting as error by the trial court?

WRIT OF CERTIORARI

ROGERS v. MISSOURI PACIFIC RAILROAD CO.
352 U.S. 518 (1957)
Supreme Court of the United States

■ ■ ■

FRANKFURTER, Mr. Justice, Dissenting.

... It is sometimes said that the "integrity of the certiorari process" as expressed in the "rule of four" (that is, this Court's practice of granting certiorari on the vote of four Justices) requires all the Justices to vote on the merits of a case when four Justices have voted to grant certiorari ...

... [T]here is a ... basic reason why the "integrity of the certiorari process" does not require me to vote on the merits of these cases. The right of a Justice to dissent from an action of the Court is historic. Of course self-restraint should guide the expression of dissent. But dissent is essential to an effective judiciary in a democratic society, and especially for a tribunal exercising the powers of this Court. Not four, not eight, Justices can require another to decide a case that [one] regards as not properly before the Court. The failure of a Justice to persuade [the other Justices] does not require him to yield to their views, if [that Justice] has a deep conviction that the issue is sufficiently important. Moreover, the Court operates ultimately by majority. Even though a minority may bring a case here for oral argument, that does not mean that the majority has given up its right to vote on the ultimate disposition of the case as conscience directs. This is not a novel doctrine. As a matter of practice, members of the Court have at various times exercised this right of refusing to pass on the merits of cases that in their view should not have been granted review.

This does not make the "rule of four" a hollow rule. I would not change the practice. No Justice is likely to vote to dismiss a writ of certiorari as improvidently granted after argument has been heard, even though he has not been convinced that the case is within the rules of the Court governing the granting of certiorari.

In the usual instance, a doubting Justice respects the judgment of [fellow] brethren that the case does concern issues important enough for the Court's consideration and adjudication. But a different situation is presented when a class of cases is systematically taken for review. Then a Justice who believes that such cases raise insignificant and unimportant questions—insignificant and unimportant from the point of view of the Court's duties—and that an increasing amount of the Court's time is unduly drained by adjudication of these cases, cannot forego [a] duty to voice his dissent to the Court's action.

The "rule of four" is not a command of Congress. It is a working rule devised by the Court as a practical mode of determining that a case is deserving of review, the theory being that if four Justices find that a legal question of general importance is raised, that is ample proof that the question has such importance. This is a fair enough rule of thumb.

■ ■ ■

Questions

1. Why did Justice Frankfurter refuse to vote on the merits of this case?
2. Does Justice Frankfurter feel the "rule of four" should be abolished? What is the purpose of this rule?

RES JUDICATA

COMMISSIONER OF INTERNAL REVENUE v. SUNNEN
333 U.S. 591 (1948)
Supreme Court of United States

■ ■ ■

MURPHY, Mr. Justice.

It is first necessary to understand something of the recognized meaning and scope of *res judicata*, a doctrine judicial in origin. The general rule of *res judicata* applies to repetitious suits involving the same cause of action. It rests upon considerations of economy of judicial time and public policy favoring the establishment of certainty in legal relations. The rule provides that when a court of competent jurisdiction has entered a final judgment on the merits of a cause of action, the parties to the suit and their privies are thereafter bound "not only as to every matter which was offered and received to sustain or defeat the claim or demand, but as to any other admissible matter which might have been offered for that purpose." *Cromwell v. County of Sac.* 94 U.S. 351, 352. The judgment puts an end to the cause of action, which cannot again be brought into litigation between the parties upon any ground whatever, absent fraud or some other factor invalidating the judgment . . .

■ ■ ■

Questions

1. What is "res judicata"? Does it apply to the same parties or to different parties?
2. Does "res judicata" prohibit an appeal?

3

THE ADMINISTRATIVE PROCESS

Administrative law concerns the powers and procedures of administrative agencies, including the judicial review of administrative actions. An administrative agency is any governmental authority, other than courts and legislative bodies. Such an agency may be called a commission, bureau, authority, board, office, department, administration, division, or agency. Even executive officers, such as the president, governors, or mayors may exercise powers of an administrative authority.

The administrative process is the combination of methods and procedures used by administrative agencies in carrying out their tasks. Administrative law attempts to control governmental machinery and programs. Administrative law does not include the substantive law produced by the administrative agencies, such as tax law, labor law, securities law, and so forth.

The average person is much more directly and more often affected by the administrative process than by the judicial process. A large proportion of our population goes through life without ever becoming a party to a lawsuit. However, the administrative process affects nearly everyone in many different ways almost every day. Administrative agencies protect people from numerous problems: air and water pollution; excessive prices for utility services or transportation rates; unwholesome meats; unfair labor practices by employers and unions; false advertising; and physically unsafe airplanes, bridges, and elevators. The list incudes a wide range of items with which we have become so accustomed that we take them for granted.

Administrative agencies are so prevasive today that the volume of legislative rulemaking of federal agencies greatly exceeds the output of Congress. In addition, the number of informal decisions made by federal agencies is incalculable, and rules of state administrative bodies are yet to be added!

Administrative law and administrative agencies are as old as the Congress itself. The first Congress conferred power on the President to establish an agency which provided military pensions for "invalids ... wounded and disabled during the late war." Such payments were to be made "under such regulations as the President of the United States may direct."[1] Administrative law has been growing ever since. However, the growth of administrative agencies began to mushroom near the turn of the twentieth century. Such familiar acronyms as the ICC, the FTC, the FPC, the SEC, and the NLRB became part of America's vocabulary as the government increasingly sought to handle social and economic problems through the administrative process.

The rapid development and complexity of the American economy gave rise to a public concern for regulation of industry and trade to prevent abuses that might be detrimental to society. Initially, Congress attempted to legislate rules of proper conduct and have the attorney general's office enforce the laws. It soon became apparent, however, that this form of regulation was neither adequate nor effective, and in some instances, was impossible. The constant supervision and inspection necessary to insure compliance with the rules of regulation could not be fulfilled by either the legislature, the executive, or the judicial branches of government. Thus, there was a recognized need for a government body that was equipped for continuous supervision and that had the particular expertise required to cope with the technicalities of a dynamic economy. The complexity of the business environment, therefore, dictated the choice of the device of the administrative agency as a necessary instrument for the effective supervision and regulation of business activities.

Predictably, the growth of agencies and the administrative process has had a significant impact on the business community and, therefore, has resulted in both criticism and praise. More surprisingly, these conflicting positions are alternatively taken by first the political right criticizing while the political left praises, and then the left criticizes and the right praises. Such widespread confusion has led to the mistaken assumption that the administrative process, while the opposite of *laissez faire*, is likewise always antibusiness. But the fact is that businessmen have, at times, requested regulation or alternatively been successful at gaining a significant control over the agencies designed to regulate as "independent" bodies. Nevertheless, discussion of the proper role of the various administrative agencies is certain to raise diverse opinions from businessmen, regulators, and members of society.

DELEGATON DOCTRINE

The administrative agency is normally embodied with functions usually carried out by three separate branches of government. An administrative agency may exercise the legislative function by formulating rules to govern a particular trade or a specific business practice. The agency exercises an executive function when it investigates business activities and enforces its rules of proper conduct. Finally, the agency is empowered with the judicial function to hold a hearing and to determine if a particular defendant has violated any of the agency's rules.

Authorizing an agency to exercise legislative, judicial, and executive powers has violated the theory of separation of powers. And authorizing an agency to act legislatively violates the nondelegation doctrine as enunciated by the Supreme Court: "that legislative power of Congress cannot be delegated, is, of course, clear." *US v. Shreveport Grain and Elevator Co.,* 287 US 77, 85, (1932). Nevertheless, the combining of governmental powers in regulating through administrative agencies began from the practical standpoint that the task of government could be better performed through an agency. Consequently, the nondelegation doctrine did not doubt that the necessities of government required delegation of law making authority. Rather, the doctrine was concerned with whether there were sufficient limits and boundaries placed on the powers and actions of the administrative agencies.

LEGISLATIVE STANDARDS

SOUTH TERMINAL CORP. v. ENVIRONMENTAL PROTECTION AGCY.
501 F. 2d 646 (1974)
U.S. Court of Appeals (1st Cir.)

■ ■ ■

We are asked to review the Metropolitan Boston Air Quality Transportation Control Plan.

The plan is aimed at keeping two types of air-borne pollutants, photochemical oxidants and carbon monoxide, from exceeding within Greater Boston the national primary and secondary ambient air quality standards prescribed by the Environmental Protection Agency (EPA) under authority of the Clean Air Act. In the Act, Congress has directed EPA, using latest scientific knowledge, to establish nationwide air-quality standards for each pollutant having an adverse affect upon the public health or welfare. It has further directed each state to have a plan to "implement" those standards—that is, to see that within the state the level of each such pollutant does not exceed limits prescribed in the national standards ....

Several petitioners have argued that the powers of EPA, as construed by us, constitute an unconstitutional delegation to an agency of legislative powers. We do not find the argument persuasive. The last time that a delegation of power to an administrative agency was upset occurred in A.L.A. Schechter Poultry Corp. v. United States, 295 U.S. 495, (1935), and the unique conditions of that case are not repeated here.

In *Schechter* Congress had delegated to the President the power to approve industry "codes" drawn up by local businessmen. Congress had not prescribed a purpose to be served by the codes, nor had it set boundaries on the provisions the codes could contain. The Court consequently characterized the delegation as utterly without standards and impermissible. Justice Cardozo, concurring, wrote that the legislation was unconstitutional because the power granted was "not canalized within banks that keep it from overflowing. It is unconfined and vagrant ... Here in effect is a roving commission to inquire into evils and upon discovery correct them."

The power granted to EPA is not "unconfined and vagrant". The Agency has been given a well defined task by Congress—to reduce pollution levels "requisite to protect the public health", in the case of primary standards. The Clean Air Act outlines the approach to be followed by the Agency and describes in detail many of its powers. Perhaps because the task is both unprecedented and of great complexity, and because appropriate controls cannot all be anticipated pending the Agency's collection of technical data in different regions, the Act leaves considerable flexibility to EPA in the choice of means. Yet there are many benchmarks to guide the Agency and the courts in determining whether or not EPA is exceeding its powers, not the least of which is that the rationality of the means can be tested against goals capable of fairly precise definition in the language of science.

Administrative agencies are created by Congress because it is impossible for the Legislature to acquire sufficient information to manage each detail in the long process of extirpating the abuses identified by the legislation; the Agency must have flexibility to implement the congressional mandate. Therefore, although the delegation to EPA was a broad one, including the power to make essentially "local" rules and regulations when necessary to achieve the national goals, we have little difficulty concluding that the delegation was not excessive ...

■ ■ ■

Questions

1. Since 1935 the Supreme Court has not invalidated a single legislative delegation to an administrative agency. Does this suggest that this matter is no longer of concern to the Court? According to the Supreme Court, what must the Congress do in order to make delegation of legislative power constitutional? Does this provide a means for Congress to avoid a judicial veto of its delegations?
2. Does the standard in the EPA—"to protect the public health"—set boundaries on the agency and prevent "a roving commission to inquire into evils and upon discovery correct them"?
3. The famous legal philosopher, Blackstone, has stated the basic principle of separation of powers as: "In all tyrannical governments, the supreme magis-

tracy, or the right both of making and enforcing the laws is vested in one and the same man, or one and the same body of men; and wherever these two powers are united together, there can be no public liberty."[2] Is the separation of powers doctrine designed to create an effective and efficient government or a nontyrannical government?

CONGRESSIONAL CONTROLS

Other means of legislative control of administration agencies have developed besides congressional design of the primary standard and boundaries.

Appropriations

The power of the purse has become a traditional method of legislative check upon agency administration. In spite of the substantive declarations of Congress in many enactments, their enforcement and observance can be substantially weakened by refusal to appropriate funds for an adequate staff. Secondly, amendments to the original statutes creating agency powers can be added onto appropriation acts and thereby restrict future agency activities. Likewise, conditions attached to the spending of appropriated funds can modify the range of practical policy choices available to the agency.

Standing Committees

First, there exists the "subject matter" committees, one from each branch of Congress. These are charged with supervision of the content and substance of the relevant agency's assigned duties. The committee may act as a "watchdog" over the agency to determine whether additional legislation might be necessary to either expand or contract agency authority and influence. Secondly, a committee on Government Operations exists in both the House and Senate and is charged with the responsibility to ensure that the agencies operate with "economy and efficiency." When these committees are added to the appropriations committee, the result is that all agencies are answerable in certain contexts to at least six committees and maybe more.

Constituents Casework

Former Senator Paul H. Douglas has written: "Out of a deep instinctive wisdom, the American people have never been willing to confide their individual or collective destinies to civil servants over whom they have little control. They distrust and dislike a self-perpetuating bureaucracy, because they believe that ultimately it will not reflect the best interest of the people. They therefore turn to their elected representatives to protect their legitimate interests in their relationship with the public administrators."[3] The people feel this is part of a legislator's duties, as indeed it is, and if a legislator washes his or her hands of any such responsibility and refuses so to represent constituents, the legislator may expect very soon to be retired to private life. Attention to such matters, therefore, becomes a practical matter for political survival.

This legislator intervention is both praised and denounced. Whereas, the agency is charged to follow the law and its own rules and regulations, legislators sometimes demand a decision in favor of their constituents regardless of whether such decision is legitimate in terms of the law. On the other hand, the intervention of legislators can correct injustices and act as a check against administrator overzealousness or personal aggrandizement. The solution to these contradictory positions is easily stated: congressional intervention is to be limited to the "merits" of the case. However, individual judgments as to the "merits" differ and some legislators' insistence on winning rather than fairness for their constituents, create a real problem for administrators in terms of time involved and interference with decisionmaking.

Collectively, these alternate and continuous techniques of Congress provide better control by Congress over administrative agencies than the Congressional privilege of initially spelling out a precisely delegated administrative standard.

EXECUTIVE CONTROLS

What is the extent of power of the executive, the President, to direct and supervise administrative action? The power to appoint the agency chief is the President's most effective weapon of control. While this power is shared with the Senate, the President's nominees are most often accepted. Therefore, the President can be successful at changing the tempo and emphasis of the regulatory programs by the appointment process. Congress has often sought to diminish this presidential influence by providing certain statutory terms of office which require particular "cause" for removal from office. The question then arose: could the President ignore these constraints on his leadership role?

MYERS v. UNITED STATES
272 U.S. 52 (1926)
Supreme Court of the United States

[*Congress had enacted that postmasters were only to be removed with the Senate's consent. President Wilson removed Myers from his postmastership without asking for the Senate's approval. Myers sued for the salary he would have earned except for the "illegal" removal from office.*

The Supreme Court relied on Article II of the Constitution which says "The executive power shall be vested in a President," and that the President "shall take care that the laws be faithfully executed."]

■ ■ ■

TAFT, Chief Justice.

(The President) may properly supervise and guide their construction of the statutes under which they act in order to secure that unitary and uniform execution of the laws which Article II of the Constitution evidently contemplated in vesting general executive power in the President alone ... Of course, there may be duties so peculiarly and specifically committed to the discretion of a particular officer as to raise a question whether the President may overrule or revise the officer's interpretation of his statutory duty in a particular instance. Then, there may be duties of a quasi-judicial character imposed on executive officers and members of executive tribunals whose decisions after hearing affect interests of individuals, the discharge of which the President cannot in a particular case properly influence or control. But, even in such a case, he may consider the decision after its rendition as a reason for removing the officer, on the ground that the discretion regularly entrusted to the officer by statute has not been on the whole intelligently or wisely executed. Otherwise, he does not discharge his own constitutional duty of seeing that the laws are faithfully executed.

(Therefore, the provision of the statute which restricted the President's power of removal was in violation of the Constitution and invalid.)

■ ■ ■

HUMPHREY'S EXECUTOR v. UNITED STATES
295 U.S. 602 (1935)
Supreme Court of the United States

[*Humphrey, a Federal Trade Commissioner and a Republican, was removed from office by President Franklin D. Roosevelt who desired to staff the Commission with personnel of his own selection. Humphrey began suit for his salary, and after his death it was continued by his executor.*]

■ ■ ■

SUTHERLAND, Justice.

(The holding of the *Myers* case) goes far enough to include all purely executive officers, (but it does not) include an officer who occupies no place in the executive department and who exercises no part of the executive power vested by the Constitution in the President ... The Federal Trade Commission is an administrative body created by Congress to carry into effect legislative policies embodied in the statute in accordance with the legislative standard therein prescribed, and to perform other specified duties as a legislative or as a judicial aid. Such a body cannot in any proper sense by characterized as an arm or an eye of the executive. Its duties are performed without executive leave and, in the contemplation of the statute, must be free from executive control. In administering the provisions of the statute in respect of "unfair methods of competition"—that is to say in filling in and administering the details embodied by that general standard—the commission acts in part quasi-legislatively and in part quasi-judicially ...

We think it plain under the Constitution that illimitable power of removal is not possessed by the President in respect of officers of the character of those just named. The authority of Congress, in creating quasi-legislative or quasi-judicial agencies, to require them to act in discharge of their duties independently of executive control cannot well be doubted; and that authority includes, as an appropriate incident, power to fix the period during which they shall continue in office, and to forbid their removal except for cause in the meantime. For it is quite evident that one who holds his office only during the pleasure of another, cannot be depended upon to maintain an attitude of independence against the latter's will.

■ ■ ■

Questions

1. Weiner, a War Claims Commissioner nominated by President Truman, was removed by President Eisenhower who desired personnel of his own selection. Wiener sued for his salary and the Supreme Court said, "Judging ... the claim that the President could remove a member of an adjudicatory body like the War Claims Commission merely because he wanted his own appointees on such a Commission, we are compelled to conclude that no such power is given to the President directly by the Constitution, and none is impliedly conferred upon him by statute simply because Congress said nothing about it. The philosophy of *Humphrey's Executor*, in its explicit language as well, as its implications, precludes such a claim." *Wiener v. U.S.* 357 U.S. 349 (1958). How is the fact that this was "an adjudicatory body" relevant and helpful in making the decision?
2. When are agencies "independent" of presidential control? Why could Meyers be replaced in spite of Congressional restraint on his removal and Humphrey could not?
3. What is a "quasi-legislative" body? A "quasi-judicial" body?

The tasks of modern government are so large and difficult that Congress is delegating more and more legislative power. The problems are so complex that regulatory agencies are increasingly created and granted legislative power without meaningful standards to bridle agency actions. Regulatory agencies are forced to decide major questions that Congress could not anticipate nor, even if anticipated, effectively draft into meaningful standards. Consequently, protections from abuses of administrative action today lie less in "primary standards" and more in executive, legislative, or judicial checks on those broad powers delegated.

ADMINISTRATIVE INVESTIGATIONS

The stages of administrative agency procedures are depicted in Figure 3-1. Since the executive powers of administrative agencies normally include the power to investigate, the preliminary procedural steps often begin with some pressure being exerted on the agency to investigate some problem. Individual members of the public or Congressional representatives may complain or suggest to the administrative agency that they investigate a particular activity. Moreover, the administrative agency on its own initiative may begin an investigation.

Figure 3-1

STAGES OF ADMINISTRATIVE AGENCY PROCEDURES

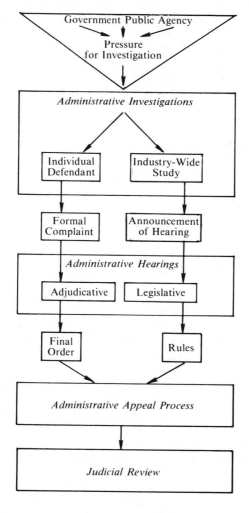

The agency in exercising its executive powers may follow either of two approaches in investigating an alleged problem. It may proceed against an individual defendant when it feels that the activity involved is peculiar to that defendant or it may proceed with an investigation of the entire industry if it believes the questionable practice is widespread. The Supreme Court affirmed this practice in *Moog Industries v. Federal Trade Commission* 355 U.S. 414, (1958) when it said:

   ...(A)lthough an allegedly illegal practice may appear to be operative throughout an industry, whether such appearances reflect fact and whether all firms in the industry should be dealt with in a single proceeding or should receive individualized treatment are questions that call for discretionary determination by the administrative agency ... Furthermore, the Commission alone is empowered to develop that enforcement policy best calculated to achieve the ends contemplated by Congress and to allocate its available funds and personnel in such a way as to execute its policy efficiently and economically.

Agencies normally possess a staff of attorneys, accountants, economists, or other appropriate specialists to aid in gathering the necessary information. Often the information gathered by the staff is published by the agency as a staff report. In such circumstances the determination or recommendations provided in such staff reports are not official positions of the agency. Nevertheless, the staff reports, made available to the public, aid the agency in making decisions about future actions.

The clash between administrative fact gathering and the interest of privacy is subject to emotional debate. For regulatory agencies to accomplish their purposes Congress conferred broad powers of investigation. However, the constitutional protections of privacy historically remained firm against bureaucratic snooping. Gradually, and particularly during the decade of the 1940s, constitutional protections weakened and grumbled. A new set of judicially determined constitutional principles developed based on the idea that administrative power of investigation is a necessity for modern administrative government. This clash between constitutional protections and the broad investigative powers are illustrated in the following cases.

INVESTIGATIVE PROCEDURES

HANNAH v. LARCHE
363 U.S. 420 (1960)
Supreme Court of the United States

■ ■ ■

WARREN, Mr. Chief Justice.

These cases involve the validity of certain Rules of Procedure adopted by the Commission on Civil Rights, which was established by Congress in 1957. They arise out of the Commission's investigation of alleged Negro voting deprivations in the State of Louisiana ... It was alleged, among other things, that the Commission's Rules of Procedure governing the conduct of its investigations were unconstitutional...

The specific question which we must decide (is) ... whether those procedures violate the Due Process Clause of the Fifth Amendment ....

Since the requirements of due process frequently vary with the type of proceeding involved, we think it is necessary at the outset to ascertain both the nature and function of this Commission. Section 104 of the Civil Rights Act of 1957 specifies the duties to be performed by the Commission. Those duties consist of (1) investigating written, sworn allegations that anyone has been discriminatorily deprived of his right to vote; (2) studying and collecting information "concerning legal developments constituting a denial of equal protection of the laws under the Constitution"; and (3) reporting to the President and Congress on its activities, findings, and recommendations. As is apparent from this brief sketch of the statutory duties imposed upon the Commission, its function is purely investigative and fact-finding. It does not adjudicate. It does not hold trials or determine anyone's civil or criminal liability. It does not issue orders. Nor does it indict, punish, or impose any legal sanctions. It does not make determinations depriving anyone of his life, liberty, or property. In short, the Commission does not and cannot take any affirmative action which will affect an individual's legal rights. The only purpose of its existence is to find facts which may subsequently be used as the basis for legislative or executive action.

The specific constitutional question, therefore, is whether persons whose conduct is under investigation by a governmental agency of this nature are entitled, by virtue of the Due Process Clause, to know the specific charges that are being investigated, as well as the identity of the complainants, and to have the right to cross-examine those complainants and other witnesses . . .

"Due Process" is an elusive concept. Its exact boundaries are undefinable, and its content varies according to specific factual contexts. Thus, when governmental agencies adjudicate or make binding determinations which directly affect the legal rights of individuals, it is imperative that those agencies use the procedures which have traditionally been associated with the judicial process. On the other hand, when governmental action does not partake of an adjudication, as for example, when a general fact-facting investigation is being conducted, it is not necessary that the full panoply of judicial procedures be used. Therefore, as a generalization, it can be said that due process embodies the differing rules of fair play, which through the years, have become associated with differing types of proceedings. Whether the Constitution requires that a particular right obtain in a specific proceeding depends upon a complexity of factors. The nature of the alleged right involved, the nature of the proceeding, and the possible burden on that proceeding, are all considerations which must be taken into account. . .

It is probably sufficient merely to indicate that the rights claimed by respondents are normally associated only with adjudicatory proceedings, and that since the commission does not adjudicate it need not be bound by adjudicatory procedures. Yet, the respondents contend and the court below implied, that such procedures are required since the Commission's proceedings might irreparably harm those being investigated by subjecting them to public opprobrium and scorn, the distinct likelihood of losing their jobs, and the possibility of criminal prosecutions. That any of these consequences will result is purely conjectural. There is nothing in the record to indicate that such will be the case or that past commission hearings have had any harmful effects upon witnesses appearing before the Commission. However, even if such collateral consequences were to flow from the Commission's investigations, they would not be the result of any affirmative determinations made by the Commission, and they would not affect the legitimacy of the Commission's investigative function.

On the other hand, the investigative process could be completely disrupted if investigative hearings were transformed into trial-like proceedings, and if persons who might be indirectly affected by an investigation were given an absolute right to cross-examine every witness called to testify. Fact-finding agencies without any power to adjudicate would be diverted from their legitimate duties and would be plagued by the injection of collateral issues that would make the investigation interminable. Even a person not called as a witness could demand the right to appear at the hearing, cross-examine any witness whose testimony or sworn affidavit allegedly defamed or incriminated him, and call an unlimited number of witnesses of his own selection. This type of proceeding would make a shambles of the investigation and stifle the agency in its gathering of facts.

In addition to these persuasive considerations, we think it is highly significant that the Commission's procedures are not historically foreign to other forms of investigation under our system. Far from being unique, the Rules of Procedure adopted by the Commission are similar to those which . . . have traditionally governed the proceedings of the vast majority of governmental investigating agencies.

. . . The best example is provided by the administrative regulatory agencies. Although these agencies normally make determinations of a quasi-judicial nature, they also frequently conduct purely fact-finding investigations. When doing the former, they are governed by the Administrative Procedure Act and the parties to the adjudication are accorded the traditional safeguards of a trial. However, when these agencies are conducting nonadjudicative, fact-finding investigations, rights such as apprisal, confrontation, and cross-examination generally do not obtain.

A typical agency is the Federal Trade Commission. Its rules draw a clear distinction between adjudicative proceedings and investigative proceedings. Although the latter are frequently initiated by complaints from undisclosed informants, and although the Commission may use the information obtained during investigations to initiate adjudicative proceedings, nevertheless, persons summoned to appear before investigative proceedings are entitled only to a general notice of "the purpose and scope of the investigation," and while they may have the advice of counsel, "counsel may not, as a matter of right, otherwise participate in the investigation." The reason for these rules is obvious. The Federal Trade Commission could not conduct an efficient investigation if persons being investigated were permitted to convert the investigation into a trial. ...[A]ny person investigated by the Federal Trade Commission will be accorded all the traditional judicial safeguards at a subsequent adjudicative proceeding, just as any person investigated by the Civil Rights Commission will have all of these safeguards, should some type of adjudicative proceeding subsequently be instituted....

We think it is fairly clear from this survey of various phases of governmental investigation that witnesses appearing before investigating agencies ... have generally not been accorded the rights of apprisal, confrontation, or cross-examination ...

Thus, the purely investigative nature of the Commission's proceedings, the burden that the claimed rights would place upon those proceedings, and the traditional procedure of investigating agencies in general, leads us to conclude that the Commission's Rules of Procedure comport with the requirements of due process. ...

■ ■ ■

Questions

1. What was the function or purpose of the hearing by the Commission on Civil Rights?
2. What rules of procedure did the witnesses desire? What reasons does the Court give to justify a reversal of the District Court's decision?
3. Is the reader familiar with any legislative investigative hearings? Did they seem fair?
4. What injuries did the potential witnesses in *Hannah* assert? Does this explain why Congress authorized the Civil Rights Commission in certain particular instances to proceed in a "closed doors" session?
5. Can you distinguish between the two basic types of hearings that the court discussed in *Hannah*?

SUBPOENA POWER

Administrative requests for information are enforced by the administrative agency applying to the courts for judicial enforcement if the defendant is uncooperative. Federal agencies apply to the appropriate federal District Court for a judicial order, which, if ignored, subjects the defendant to charges of "contempt of court." When the administrative agency is seeking judicial enforcement of its subpoena, the federal court may consider appropriate questions to determine whether the subpoena should be enforced. The courts generally determine whether the subpoena is overly broad or excessive in its request for relevant and material information. Of course, the material sought also must be subjects that Congress has authorized the agency to investigate. Historically, the courts took pains to avoid broad "fishing expeditions" by the administrative agencies. But, consider the new attitude of the Court expressed in the following case.

OKLA. PRESS PUB. CO. v. WALLING
327 U.S. 186 (1946)
Supreme Court of the United States

■ ■ ■

RUTLEDGE, Mr. Justice.

Petitioners ... insist that the question of coverage must be adjudicated before the subpoenas may be enforced. . . .

It is claimed that enforcement would permit the Administrator to conduct general fishing expeditions into petitioners' books, records and papers, in order to secure evidence that they have violated the Act, without a prior charge or complaint and simply to secure information upon which to base one, all allegedly in violation of the [4th] Amendment's search and seizure provision. . . .

Historically private corporations have been subject to broad visitorial power, both in England and in this country. And it long has been established that Congress may exercise wide investigative power over them, analogous to the visitorial power of the incorporating state, when their activities take place within or affect interstate commerce . . .

Without attempt to summarize or accurately distinguish all of the cases, the fair distillation, in so far as they apply merely to the production of corporate records and papers in response to a subpoena or order authorized by law and safeguarded by judicial sanction, seems to be that ... the Fourth ... guards against abuse only by way of too much indefiniteness or breadth in the things required to be "particularly described," ... [and] also the inquiry ... [must be] one the demanding agency is authorized by law to make and the materials specified are relevant. The gist of the protection is in the requirement, expressed in terms, that the disclosure sought shall not be unreasonable.

As this has taken form in the decisions, the following specific results have been worked out. It is not necessary, as in the case of a warrant, that a specific charge or complaint of violation of law be pending or that the order be made pursuant to one. It is enough that the investigation be for a lawfully authorized purpose, within the power of Congress to command. This has been ruled most often perhaps in relation to grand jury investigations, but also frequently in respect to general or statistical investigations authorized by Congress. The requirement of "probable cause, supported by oath or affirmation," literally applicable in the case of a warrant, is satisfied in that of an order for production by the court's determination that the investigation is authorized by Congress, is for a purpose Congress can order, and the documents sought are relevant to the inquiry. Beyond this the requirement of reasonableness, including particularity in "describing the place to be searched, and the persons or things to be seized," also literally applicable to warrants, comes down to specification of the documents to be produced adequate, but not excessive, for the purposes of the relevant inquiry. Necessarily, as has been said, this cannot be reduced to formula; for relevancy and adequacy or excess in the breadth of the subpoena are matters variable in relation to the nature, purpose and scope of the inquiry.

When these principles are applied to the facts of the present cases, it is impossible to conceive how a violation of petitioners' rights could have been involved ... All the records sought were relevant to the authorized inquiry, the purpose of which was to determine two issues, whether petitioners were subject to the Act and, if so, whether they were violating it. . . .

Petitioners stress that enforcement will subject them to inconvenience, expense and harrassment . . . There is no harrassment when the subpoena is issued and enforced according to law. The Administrator is authorized to enter and inspect, but the Act makes his right to do so subject in all cases to judicial supervision. Persons from whom he seeks relevant information are not required to submit to his demand, if in any respect it is unreasonable or overreaches the authority Congress has given. To it they may make "appropriate defence" surrounded by every safeguard of judicial restraint. . . .

■ ■ ■

Questions

1. On what grounds can the defendants object to a subpoena? Are these grounds to avoid the investigation or to narrow the investigation?
2. May a subpoena be avoided on the grounds that it will subject the defendant to inconvenience and expense?
3. Moreover, in *United States v. Morton Salt Co.*, 338 U.S. 632 (1950) an agency sought court enforcement of an order requiring a "complete statement (of) prices, terms and conditions of sale" during a certain period of time. The defendants maintained that the agency was on a fishing expedition. The Court responded by saying: "We will assume for the argument that this is so . . . We must not disguise the fact that sometimes, especially early in the history of the federal administrative tribunal, the courts were persuaded to engraft judicial limitations upon the administrative process. The courts could not go fishing, and so it followed neither could anyone else. . . . Even if one were to regard the request for information in this case as caused by nothing more than official curiosity, nevertheless law enforcing agencies have a legitimate right to satisfy themselves that corporate behavior is consistent with the law and the public interest." Considering this language, what protection remains of the 4th Amendment?
4. In 1967 the Supreme Court held in *Camara v. Municipal Court*, 387 U.S. 523. that fire and sanitation officers who inspect buildings may not make unconsented inspections without search warrants. However, the Court made the test for issuing a warrant for an unconsented inspection to be something less than the "probable cause" required for a search warrant seeking evidence of a felony. The Court recognizes the necessity of code enforcement inspections and "if reasonable legislative or administrative standards for conducting an area inspection are satisfied . . .", inspection warrants are likely to be issued as a matter of course. Hence, the Supreme Court's protection against unconsented searches is likely to be only temporary.
5. In 1978 the Supreme Court held that employers have a constitutional right to bar federal-job safety inspectors from their work places if the inspectors do not possess search warrants. While the Court ruled that the Occupatinal Safety and Health Administration did not have the right to make a warrantless inspection, the Court also made the process to get warrants relativly easy. OSHA can retain the surprise element in its inspection program by getting a warrant in advance without notifying the employer. The inspector will have to show the Court that the specific business has been chosen for a spot check on the basis of a general enforcement plan and that it is not being singled out for arbitrary reasons. The Court also made clear that its ruling did not necessarily mean that warrantless-search provisions in other regulatory laws were also unconstitutional. "The reasonableness of the warrantless search will depend upon the specific enforcement needs and privacy guarantees of each statute." *Marshall v. Barlow's Inc.* 98 S. Ct. 1816 (1978).

NONPERSONAL RECORDS

The Fifth Amendment prohibits compelling any person "in any criminal case to be a witness against himself." This protection is afforded the individual person in any proceeding of any kind, including administrative investigations. However, there are four ways for the administrative agency to get around the privilege against self-incrimination. Because these techniques are quite pervasive, the agencies have not found the Fifth Amendment to be a substantial obstacle to their investigations. The first limitation on the Fifth Amendment is illustrated in the following case.

UNITED STATES v. WHITE
322 U.S. 694 (1944)
Supreme Court of the United States

■ ■ ■

MURPHY, Mr. Justice.

Our attention is directed solely to the right of an officer of a union to claim the privilege against self-incrimination under the circumstances here presented.

Respondent contends that an officer of an unincorporated labor union possesses a constitutional right to refuse to produce, in compliance with a subpoena *duces tecum*, records of the union which are in his custody and which might tend to incriminate him. He relies upon the "unreasonable search and seizure" clause of the Fourth Amendment and the explicit guarantee of the Fifth Amendment that no person shall be compelled in any criminal case to be a witness against himself. We hold, however, that neither the Fourth nor the Fifth Amendment, both of which are directed primarily to the protection of individual and personal rights, requires the recognition of a privilege against self-incrimination under the circumstances of this case.

The constitutional privilege against self-incrimination is essentially a personal one, applying only to natural individuals. It grows out of the high sentiment and regard of our jurisprudence for conducting criminal trials and investigatory proceedings upon a plane of dignity, humanity and impartiality. It is designed to prevent the use of legal process to force from the lips of the accused individual the evidence necessary to convict him or to force him to produce and authenticate any personal documents or effects that might incriminate him . . .

Since the privilege against self-incrimination is a purely personal one, it cannot be utilized by or on behalf of any organization, such as corporation . . . Moreover, the papers and effects which the privilege protects must be the private property of the person claiming the privilege, or at least in his possession in a purely personal capacity. But individuals, when acting as representatives of a collective group, cannot be said to be exercising their personal rights and duties nor to be entitled to their purely personal privileges. Rather they assume the rights, duties and privileges of the artificial entity or association of which they are agents or officers and they are bound by its obligations. In their official capacity, therefore, they have no privilege against self-incrimination. And the official records and documents of the organization that are held by them in a representative rather than in a personal capacity cannot be the subject of the personal privilege against self-incrimination, even though production of the papers might tend to incriminate them personally . . .

Such records and papers are not the private records of the individual members or officers of the organization. Usually, if not always, they are open to inspection by the members and this right may be enforced on appropriate occasions by available legal procedures. They therefore embody no element of personal privacy and carry with them no claim of personal privilege.

The reason underlying the restriction of this constitutional privilege to natural individuals acting in their own private capacity is clear. The scope and nature of the economic activities of incorporated and unincorporated organizations and their representatives demand that the constitutional power of the federal and state governments to regulate those activities be correspondingly effective. The greater portion of evidence of wrongdoing by an organization or its representatives is usually to be found in the official records and documents of that organization. Were the cloak of the privilege to be thrown around these impersonal records and documents, effective enforcement of many federal and state laws would be impossible . . . The framers of the constitutional guarantee against compulsory self-disclosure, who were interested primarily in protecting individual civil liberties, cannot be said to have intended the privilege to be available to protect economic or other interests of such organizations so as to nullify appropriate governmental regulations.

Basically, the power to compel the production of the records of any organization, whether it be incorporated or not, arises out of the inherent and necessary power of the federal and state governments to enforce their laws, with the privilege against self-incrimination being limited to its historic function of protecting only the natural individual from compulsory incrimination through his own testimony or personal records.

It follows that labor unions, as well as their officers and agents acting in their official capacity, cannot invoke this personal privilege. This conclusion is not reached by any mechanical comparison of unions with corporations or with other entities nor by any determination of whether unions technically may be regarded as legal personalities for any or all purposes. The test, rather, is whether one can fairly say under all the circumstances that a particular type of organization has a character so impersonal in the scope of its membership and activities that it cannot be said to embody or represent the purely private or personal interests of its constituents, but rather to embody their common or group interests only. If so, the privilege cannot be invoked on behalf of the organization or its representatives in their official capacity. Labor unions—national or local, incorporated or unincorporated—clearly meet that test ...

These various considerations compel the conclusion that respondent could not claim the personal privilege against self-incrimination under these circumstances. The subpoena *duces tecum* was directed to the union and demanded the production only of its official documents and records. Respondent could not claim the privilege on behalf of the union because the union did not itself possess such a privilege. Moreover, the privilege is personal to the individual called as a witness, making it impossible for him to set up the privilege of a third person as an excuse for a refusal to answer or to produce documents. Hence respondent could not rely upon any possible privilege that the union might have ... Nor could respondent claim the privilege on behalf of himself as an officer of the union or as an individual. The documents he sought to place under the protective shield of the privilege were official union documents held by him in his capacity as a representative of the union. No valid claim was made that any part of them constituted his own private papers. He thus could not object that the union's books and records might incriminate him as an officer or as an individual.

The union and its officers acting in their official capacity lack the privilege at all times of insulating the union's books and records against reasonable demands of governmental authorities.

■ ■ ■

Questions

1. The court indicated that the Fifth and Fourth Amendment protections are personal protections. What does the Court mean by an essentially *personal* privilege against self-incrimination?
2. What basic reason did the Court use for restricting the constitutional protection of the Fifth Amendment?
3. Are the records of all "collective groups" subject to administrative investigative powers? May an administrative agency gain information from a corporation? From a nonincorporated eneity? From a religious organization? From a communist organization? From the National Association of Colored People?

PAPERS OUT-OF-CUSTODY

In 1973 the second of the four ways around the privilege against self-incrimination was clarified. In brief, it may be stated that the privilege may be denied to one whose records are in the custody of someone else.

COUCH v. UNITED STATES
409 U.S. 322 (1973)
Supreme Court of the United States

■ ■ ■

POWELL, Mr. Justice.

The question is whether the taxpayer may invoke her Fifth Amendment privilege against compulsory self-incrimination to prevent the production of her business and tax records in the possession of her accountant ...

It is important to reiterate that the Fifth Amendment privilege is a *personal* privilege: it adheres basically to the person, not to information that may incriminate him ... It is extortion of information from the accused himself that offends our sense of justice.

In the case before us the ingredient of personal compulsion against an accused is lacking. The summons and the order of the District Court enforcing it are directed against the accountant. He, not the taxpayer, is the only one compelled to do anything. And the accountant makes no claim that he may tend to be incriminated by the production. Inquisitorial pressure or coercion against a potentially accused person, compelling her, against her will, to utter self-condemning words or produce incriminating documents is absent. In the present case, no "shadow of testimonial compulsion upon or enforced communication by the accused" is involved ....

Petitioner's reliance on Boyd v. United States, 116 U.S. 616, (1886), is misplaced ...

Petitioner would, in effect, have us read *Boyd* to mark ownership, not possession, as the bounds of the privilege, despite the fact that possession bears the closest relationship to the personal compulsion forbidden by the Fifth Amendment. To tie the privilege against self-incrimination to a concept of ownership would be to draw a meaningless line. It would hold here that the business records which petitioner actually owned would be protected in the hands of her accountant, while business information communicated to her accountant by letter and conversations in which the accountant took notes, in addition to the accountant's own workpapers and photocopies of petitioner's records, would not be subject to a claim of privilege since title rested in the accountant. Such a holding would thus place unnecessary emphasis on the form of communication to an accountant and the accountant's own working methods, while diverting the inquiry from the basic purposes of the Fifth Amendment's protections. ...

Petitioner argues, nevertheless, that grave prejudice will result from a denial of her claim to equate ownership and the scope of the privilege. She alleges that "[i]f the IRS is able to reach her records the instant those records leave her hands and are deposited in the hands of her retainer whom she has hired for a special purpose then the meaning of the privilege is lost." That is not, however, the import of today's decision. We do indeed believe that actual possession of documents bears the most significant relationship to Fifth Amendment protections against governmental compulsions upon the individual accused of crime. Yet situations may well arise where constructive possession is so temporary and insignificant as to leave the personal compulsions upon the accused substantially intact. But this is not the case before us. Here there was no mere fleeting divestment of possession: the records had been given to this accountant regularly since 1955 and remained in his continuous possession until the summer of 1969 when the summons was issued. Moreover, the accountant himself worked neither in petitioner's office nor as her employee. The length of his possession of petitioner's records and his independent status confirm the belief that petitioner's divestment of possession was of such a character as to disqualify her entirely as an object of any impermissible Fifth Amendment compulsion.

Petitioner further argues that the confidential nature of the accountant-client relationship and her resulting expectation of privacy in delivering the records protect her, under the Fourth and Fifth Amendments, from their production. Although not in itself controlling, we note that no confidential accountant-client privilege exists under federal law, and no state-created privilege has been recognized in federal cases. Nor is there justification for such a privilege where records relevant to income tax returns are involved in a criminal investigation or prosecution. . .[T]here can be little expectation of privacy where records are handed to an accountant, knowing that mandatory disclosure of much of the information therein is required in an income tax return. What information is not disclosed is largely in the accountant's discretion, not petitioner's. Indeed, the accountant himself risks criminal prosecution if he willfully assists in the preparation of a false return. His own need for self-protection would often require the right to disclose the information given him. Petitioner seeks extensions of constitutional protections against self-incrimination in the very situation where obligations of disclosure exist and under a system largely dependent upon honest self-reporting even to survive. Accordingly, petitioner here cannot reasonably claim, either for Fourth or Fifth Amendment purposes, an expectation of protected privacy or confidentiality.

The criterion for Fifth Amendment immunity remains not the ownership of property but the " 'physical or moral compulsion' exerted." We hold today that no Fourth or Fifth Amendment claim can prevail where, as in this case, there exists no legitimate expectation of privacy and no semblance of governmental compulsion against the person of the accused. It is important in applying constitutional principles, to interpret them in light of the fundamental interests of personal liberty they were meant to serve. Respect for these principles is eroded when they leap their proper bounds to interfere with the legitimate interest of society in enforcement of its laws and collection of the revenues.

■ ■ ■

Questions

1. While not completely, the Supreme Court tied the privilege against self-incrimination to the concept of possession of papers. To what concept did the petitioner urge the privilege against self-incrimination be tied?
2. Did the Court say that some dispossessions of private papers would not destroy the personal privilege against self-incrimination in those papers?
3. Why does the Court reject the petitioner's contention of an accountant-client relationship of confidentiality which preserves the petitioner's privilege against self-incrimination?
4. Justice Douglas in his dissent wrote:

   One's privacy embraces what the person has in his home, his desk, his files, and his safe as well as what he carries on his person. It also has a very meaningful relationship to what he tells any confidant—his wife, his minister, his lawyer, or his tax accountant. The Constitutional fences of law are being broken down by an ever-increasingly powerful government that seeks to reduce every person to a digit.

   Does Douglas's concept of privacy extend too far? Why didn't the majority of justices, who also believe in privacy, agree with Douglas's extention of the privilege of self-incrimination?
5. What if Couch had taken his records to an attorney? Would the attorney-client privilege protect his records? The Supreme Court said:

   The fact that Schoeberlein is an accountant as well as a lawyer does not, of course, foreclose him for invoking the attorney-client privilege on appropriate occasions. Like any other attorney, however, Schoeberlein can refuse to disclose client communications only in accordance with the (law). . . The check stubs for 1965, 1966 and 1967 had been turned over by taxpayers to Schoeberlein for use in preparing the income tax returns for those years; the information contained thereon, insofar as it was relevant to taxpayers' income tax liability, was intended to be disclosed on the tax returns and to revenue agents who might audit the returns, and is, therefore, discoverable. Schoeberlein's work papers, developed for and used in connection with the preparation of the income tax returns, are not privileged, because (1) they were not prepared by the client and (2) were the basis for the information submitted to the government on the tax returns. . . which taxpayers had filed. They are not privileged. *U.S. v. Schoeberlein* 335 F. Supp. 1048 (1971).

A third way of preventing the privilege against self-incrimination from interferring with administrative investigations is Congressional enactment of "immunity" statutes. These statutes compel testimony and production of records even when the privilege of the Fifth Amendment applies. However, the statute confers immunity from prosecution for any offenses disclosed in such testimony and records. The Compulsory Testimony Act of 1893 provides:

> No person shall be excused from... testifying or from producing ... papers... before the... (administrative agency), or in obedience to the subpoena of the... (agency)... on the ground... that the... evidence... may tend to incriminate him.. but no person shall be prosecuted or subject to any penalty or forfeiture for or on account of any transaction, matter or thing, concerning which he may testify, or produce evidence, documentary or otherwise, before said... (agency), or in obedience to its subpoena... 27 Stat. 443 (1893), 49 U.S. C.A. 46.

In 1970 a amendment was added to this statute which requires that anyone who refuses to testify or to produce records may be fined or imprisoned. All major regulatory agencies have a similar provision to aid in the enforcement of their regulatory powers. The Supreme Court has ruled that such statutes are constitutional because prosecution for crimes revealed by such testimony may not be maintained. Other penalties, such as, loss of job, expulsion from organizations, requirement of state registration, or passport ineligibility do not effect the constitutionality of the statute.

The fourth way around the privilege against self-incrimination is the holding that the privilege does not apply to records require to be kept by statute or some valid regulation. In *Shapiro v. United States* 335 U.S. 1 (1948) the Supreme Court held that all business records, if required to be kept, are "public" and therefore subject to agency investigation and utilization in criminal prosecutions. The Court declared: "The Privilege which exists as to private papers cannot be maintained in relation to 'records required by law to be kept in order that there may be suitable information of transactions which are the appropriate subjects of governmental regulation and the enforcement of restrictions validly established.' " Moreover, in *California v. Byers,* 402 U.S. 424 (1971) the Court ruled that the privilege against self-incrimination cannot be evoked to prevent compelled disclosures unless the disclosures involve "substantial hazards of self-incrimination." since the defendant had been charged with failure to stop and identify himself at the scene of an auto accident as required by law, the Court had to determine whether such disclosures with respect to automobile accidents entailed a substantial risk of self-incrimination. The Court answered in the negative and emphasized that the statutory purpose was noncriminal and that self-reporting was indispensible to the fulfillment of the statute. The Court said: "A name, linked with a motor vehicle, is no more incriminating than the tax return, linked with the disclosure of income. It identifies but does not by itself implicate anyone in criminal conduct."

ADMINISTRATIVE HEARINGS

The Administrative Procedure Act (APA) contains provisions that pertain to the procedural aspects of activities by regulatory agencies. The APA prescribes procedures to be followed by administrative agencies in making rules and in adjudicatory proceedings. The cases in this section contrast the differences between rulemaking and adjudicatory hearings.

After preliminary investigations, an agency may begin an adjudicatory hearing by issuing a formal complaint against a particular defendant or defendants. The agency issues a complaint when it has "reason to believe" that the law has been violated in some manner. The defendants have a number of days in which to answer the complaint. Often the defendant may be interested in having the issue settled by the entry of a "consent order." The defendant is given an opportunity to negotiate an agreement with the agency which, if accepted, may become a consent order. In such consent orders, it is understood that the agreement is for purposes of settlement of the controversy and does not constitute an admission by the defendant of having violated the law. However, when a consent order is issued by the agency, it carries the force of law with respect to future behavior by the defendant. Any violations of such order by the defendant may result in civil penalties, such as a fine, for each violation. If the parties are not able to negotiate an agreement, an adjudicatory hearing is held to determine if a violation of the law as alleged in the complaint has, in fact, occurred.

Often administrative officials act against a person without affording the individual a hearing. Such instances are increasingly challenged as a denial of due process of law.

ADJUDICATIVE HEARING

DIXON v. ALABAMA STATE BOARD OF EDUCATION
294 F. 2d 150 (1961)
United States Court of Appeals, (5th Cir.)

■ ■ ■

The question (in this case)...is whether due process requires notice and some opportunity for hearing before students at a tax-supported college are expelled for misconduct....

The district court found the general nature of the proceedings before the State Board of Education, the action of the Board, and the official notice of explusion given to the students as follows:

"Investigations into this conduct were made by Dr. Trenholm, as president of the Alabama State College, the Director of Public Safety for the State of Alabama under directions of the Governor, and by the investigative staff of the Attorney General for the State of Alabama.

"On or about March 2, 1960, the State Board of Education met and received reports from the Governor of the State of Alabama, which reports embodied the investigations that had been made and which reports identified these six plaintiffs, together with several others, as the 'ring leaders' for the group of students that had been participating in... (demonstration) activities. During this meeting, Dr. Trenholm, in his capacity as president of the college reported to the assembled members of the State Board of Education that the action of these students in demonstrating on the college campus and in certain downtown areas was having a disruptive influence on the work of the other students at the college and upon the orderly operation of the college in general. Dr. Trenholm further reported to the Board that, in his opinion, he as president of the college could not control future disruptions and demonstrations. There were twenty-nine of the Negro students identified as the core of the organization that was responsible for these demonstrations. This group of twenty-nine included these six plaintiffs. After hearing these reports and recommendations and upon the recommendation of the Governor as chairman of the Board, the Board voted unanimously, expelling nine students, including these six plaintiffs, and placing twenty students on probation. This action was taken by Dr. Trenholm as president of the college, acting pursuant to the instructions of the State Board of Education. Each of these plaintiffs, together with the other students expelled, was officially notified of his expulsion on March 4th or 5th, 1960. No formal charges were placed against these students and no hearing was granted any of them prior to their explusion."....

Whenever a governmental body acts so as to injure an individual, the Constitution requires that the act be consonant with due process of law. The minimum procedural requirements necessary to satisfy due process depend upon the circumstances and the interests of the parties involved.

The precise nature of the private interest involved in this case is the right to remain at a public institution of higher learning in which the plaintiffs were students in good standing. It requires no argument to demonstrate that education is vital and, indeed, basic to civilized society. Without sufficient education the plaintiffs would not be able to earn an adequate livelihood, to enjoy life to the fullest, or to fulfill as completely as possible the duties and responsibilities of good citizens.

There was no offer to prove that other colleges are open to the plaintiffs. If so, the plaintiffs would nonetheless be injured by the interruption of their course of studies in mid-term. It is most unlikely that a public college would accept a student expelled from another public college of the same state. Indeed, expulsion may well prejudice the student in completing his education at any other institution. Surely no one can question that the right to remain at the college in which the plaintiffs were students in good standing is an interest of extremely great value.

Turning then to the nature of the governmental power to expel the plaintiffs, it must be conceded...that that power is not unlimited and cannot be arbitrarily exercised. Admittedly, there must be some reasonable and constitutional ground for expulsion or the courts would have a duty to require reinstatement. The possibility of arbitrary action is not excluded by the existence of reasonable regulations. There may be arbitrary application of the rule to the facts of a particular case. Indeed, that result is well nigh inevitable when the Board hears only one side of the issue. In the disciplining of college students there are no considerations of immediate danger to the public, or of peril to the national security, which should prevent the Board from exercising at least the fundamental principles of fairness by giving the accused students notice of the charges and an opportunity to be heard in their own defense. Indeed, the example set by the Board in failing so to do, if not corrected by the courts, can well break the spirits of the expelled students and of others familiar with the injustice, and do inestimable harm to their education....

For the guidance of the parties in the event of further proceedings, we state our views on the nature of the notice and hearing required by due process prior to expulsion from a state college or university. They should, we think, comply with the following standards. The notice should contain a statement of the specific charges and grounds which, if proven, would justify expulsion under the regulations of the Board of Education. The nature of the hearing should vary depending upon the circumstances of the particular case. The case before us requires something more than an informal interview with an administrative authority of the college. By its nature, a charge of misconduct, as opposed to a failure to meet the scholastic standards of the college, depends upon a collection of the facts concerning the charged misconduct, easily colored by the point of view of the witnesses. In such circumstances, a hearing which gives the Board or the administrative authorities of the college an opportunity to hear both sides in considerable detail is best suited to protect the rights of all involved. This is not to imply that a full-dress judicial hearing, with the right to cross-examine witnesses, is required. Such a hearing, with the attending publicity and disturbance of college activities, might be detrimental to the college's educational atmosphere and impractical to carry out. Nevertheless, the rudiments of an adversary proceeding may be preserved without encroaching upon the interests of the college. In the instant case, the student should be given the names of the witnesses against him and an oral or written report on the facts to which each witness testifies. He should also be given the opportunity to present to the Board, or at least to an administrative official of the college, his own defense against the charges and to produce either oral testimony or written affidavits of witnesses in his behalf. If the hearing is not before the Board directly, the results and findings of the hearing should be presented in a report open to the student's inspection. If these rudimentary elements of fair play are followed in a case of misconduct of this particular type, we feel that the requirements of due process of law will have been fulfilled.

Questions

1. What "interest" is advanced by the petitioners to entitle them to a hearing prior to administrative action? What interest is advanced by the administration that no hearing is required prior to their decision? According to the scales of justice in *Dixon*, the balance of these two interests was in whose favor? Why?

2. Is a student dismissed for poor academic performance entitled to a hearing prior to dismissal? The Supreme Court said:

> ...[R]espondent has been awarded at least as much due process as the Fourteenth Amendment requires. The School fully informed respondent of the faculty's dissatisfaction with her progress and the danger that this posed to timely graudation and continued enrollment. The ultimate decision to dismiss respondent was careful and deliberate. These prcedures were sufficient under the Due Process Clause of the Fourteeth Amendment...

> There is a...significant difference between the failure of a student to meet academic standards and the violation by a student of valid rules of conduct. This difference calls for far less stringent procedural requirements in the case of an academic dismissal. . . .

> Academic evaluations of a student, in contrast to disciplinary determinations, bear little resemblance to the judicial and administrative factfinding proceedings to which we have traditionally attached a full hearing requirement.

> The decision to dismiss respondent...rested on the academic judgment of school officials that she did not have the necessary...ability to perform adequately... and was making insufficient progress toward that goal. Such a judgment is by its nature more subjective and evaluative than the typical factual questions presented in the average disciplinary decision. Like the decision of an individual professor as to the proper grade for a student in his course, the determination whether to dismiss a student for academic reasons requires an expert evaluation of cumulative information and is not readily adapted to the procedural tools of judicial or administrative decision-making.

> Under such circumstances, we decline to ignore the historic judgment of educators and thereby formalize the academic dismissal process by requiring a hearing. The educational process is not by nature adversarial; instead it centers around a continuing relationship between faculty and students... We decline to further enlarge the judicial presence in the academic community and thereby risk deterioration of many beneficial aspects of the faculty-student relationship...
>
> *University of Missouri v. Horowitz*, 98 S. Ct. 948 (1978).

3. The Constitutional issue to be decided in *Goldberg v. Kelly*, 397 U.S. 254 (1970), was the narrow question of whether the due process clause requires that a recipient of state welfare benefits be afforded an evidentiary hearing *before* the termination of benefits. Decide this case using the balancing of interest approach of *Dixon*.

4. The Supreme Court has acknowledged that in "extraordinary situations" it is necessary for administrative officials to seize property without an opportunity for prior hearing. Immediate administrative action is needed "to collect the internal revenue of the United States, to meet the needs of a national war effort, to protect against economic disaster of a bank failure, and to protect the public from misbranded drugs and contaminated foods." *Fuentes v. Shevin*, 407 U.S. 67 (1972). Using the "balancing of interests" test, can you explain why the Court decided in favor of these "summary actions" by administrative officials?

Sometimes the "balancing of interests" between the litigants to determine if a *prior* hearing is required is not easily resolved or decided to everyone's satisfaction. Before reading the following case, how would you decide this question: Is a recipient of state disability payments entitled to an evidentiary hearing *prior* to an administrative decision to terminate those benefits? What are the "interests" of each side? In whose favor would you "balance" these interests?

MATHEWS v. ELDRIDGE
424 U.S. 333 (1976)
Supreme Court of the United States

■ ■ ■

POWELL, Justice.

Procedural due process imposes constraints on governmental decisions which deprive individuals of "liberty" or "property" interests within the meaning of the Due Process Clause of the Fifth or Fourteenth Amendment. The Secretary...recognizes ...that the interest of an individual in continued receipt of these benefits is a statutorily created "property" interest protected by the Fifth Amendment. (However), the Secretary contends that the existing administrative procedures...provide all the process that is constitutionally due before a recipient can be deprived of that interest...

Since a recipient whose benefits are terminated is awarded full retroactive relief if he ultimately prevails, his sole interest is in the uninterrupted receipt of this source of income pending final administrative decision on his claim. His potential injury is thus similar in nature to that of the welfare recipient in *Goldberg*...

Only in *Goldberg* has the Court held that due process requires an evidentiary hearing prior to a temporary deprivation. It was emphasized there that welfare assistance is given to persons on the very margin of subsistence.... As *Goldberg* illustrates, the degree of potential deprivation that may be created by a particular decision is a factor to be considered in assessing the validity of any administrative decisionmaking process... Still, the disabled worker's need is likely to be less than that of a welfare recipient. In addition to the possibility of access to private resources, other forms of government assistance will become available where the termination of disability benefits places a worker or his family below the subsistence level. In view of these potential sources of temporary income, there is less reason here than in *Goldberg* to depart from the ordinary principle, established by our decisions, that something less than an evidentiary hearing is sufficient prior to adverse administrative action.

An additional factor to be considered here is the fairness and reliability of the existing pretermination procedures, and the probable value, if any, of additional procedural safeguards. Central to the evaluation of any administrative process is the nature of the relevant inquiry. In order to remain eligible for benefits the disabled worker must demonstrate by means of "medically acceptable clinical and laboratory diagnostic techniques," that he is unable "to engage in any substantial gainful activity by reason of any *medically determinable* physical or mental impairment...." § 423(d)(1)(A) (emphasis supplied). In short, a medical assessment of the worker's physical or mental condition is required. This is a more sharply focused and easily documented decision than the typical determination of welfare entitlement. In the latter case, a wide variety of information may be deemed relevant, and issues of witness credibility and veracity often are critical to the decisionmaking process...

By contrast, the decision whether to discontinue disability benefits will turn, in most cases, upon "routine, standard, and unbiased medical reports by physician specialists," concerning a subject whom they have personally examined...The potential value of an evidentiary hearing, or even oral presentation to the decisionmaker, is substantially less in this context than in *Goldberg*...

A further safeguard against mistake is the policy of allowing the disability recipient's representative full access to all information relied upon by the state agency. In addition, prior to the cutoff of benefits the agency informs the recipient of its tentative assessment, the reasons therefor, and provides a summary of the evidence that it considers most relevant. Opportunity is then afforded the recipient to submit additional evidence or arguments, enabling him to challenge directly the accuracy of information in his file as well as the correctness of the agency's tentative conclusions. These procedures, again as contrasted with those before the Court in *Goldberg*, enable the recipient to "mold" his argument to respond to the precise issues which the decisionmaker regards as crucial....

In striking the appropriate due process balance the final factor to be assessed is the public interest. This includes the administrative burden and other societal costs that would be associated with requiring, as a matter of constitutional right, an evidentiary hearing upon demand in all cases prior to the termination of disability benefits... But more is implicated in cases of this type than ad hoc weighing of fiscal and administrative burdens against the interests of a particular category of claimants. The ultimate balance involves a determination as to when, under our constitutional system, judicial-type procedures must be imposed upon administrative action to assure fairness.... The judicial model of an evidentiary hearing is neither a required, nor even the most effective, method of decisionmaking in all circumstances. The essence of due process is the requirement that "a person in jeopardy of serious loss [be given] notice of the case against him and opportunity to meet it." All that is necessary is that the procedures be tailored, in light of the decision to be made, to "the capacities and circumstances of those who are to be heard," to insure that they are given a meaningful opportunity to present their case. In assessing what process is due in this case, substantial weight must be given to the good-faith judgments of the individuals charged by Congress with the administration of social welfare programs that the procedures they have provided assure fair consideration of the entitlement claims of individuals. This is especially so where, as here, the prescribed procedures not only provide the claimant with an effective process for asserting his claim prior to any administrative action, but also assure a right to an evidentiary hearing, as well as to subsequent judicial review, before the denial of his claim becomes final.

We conclude that an evidentiary hearing is not required prior to the termination of disability benefits and that the present administrative procedures fully comport with due process.

■ ■ ■

Questions

1. In *Goldberg*, the Court held that due process requires an evidentiary hearing prior to an administrative decision to terminate welfare assistance. How did the Court distinguish the petitioner's interests in disability payments from Goldberg's interest in welfare assistance?
2. What pretermination procedures were utilized by the administrative agency that were considered sufficiently fair to deny any evidentiary hearing prior to termination of benefits?

LEGISLATIVE HEARINGS

PHARMACEUTICAL MANUFACTURERS ASSOCIATION v. FINCH
307 F. Supp. 858 (1970)
U.S. District Court (Del.)

■ ■ ■

In this action for declaratory and injunctive relief, the Pharmaceutical Manufacturers Association ("PMA"), on behalf of its members, seeks a preliminary injunction restraining the Secretary of Health, Education and Welfare and the Commissioner of Food and Drugs from taking any action in reliance upon the regulations contained in the Commissioner's Order of September 19, 1969. The September regulations promulgated new standards of evidence necessary to demonstrate the effectiveness of drug products and applied those standards retroactively so as to place in jeopardy the continued marketing of thousands of drug products introduced before 1962 with Food and Drug Administration ("FDA") approval and the effectiveness of which FDA has not yet challenged....

...PMA contends that the regulations are invalid because they were issued without notice and opportunity for comment in violation of the Administrative Procedure Act....

[T]he Administrative Procedure Act requires that rule-making by an agency be preceded by "general notice of proposed rule-making" in the Federal Register at least thirty days before the effective date of the proposed rule, and further requires that the agency afford interested persons "an opportunity to participate in the rule making through submission of written data, views or arguments with or without opportunity for oral presentation." That procedure was not followed in this case. The September regulations were made effective by the Commissioner upon their publication in the Federal Register without prior notice or an opportunity for submission of comments by interested parties.

Exempt from the general requirements of notice and opportunity for comment are "interpretative rules, general statements of policy, or rules of agency organization, procedure, or practice." The Commissioner has characterized the September regulations as "procedural and interpretative" and thus contends that they fall within the exception to the notice and comment requirement. But the label placed on the September rules by the Commissioner does not determine whether the notice and comment provisions are applicable. As the Supreme Court has emphasized, in holding that a regulation of the Federal Communications Commission constituted an order subject to judicial review, "[T]he particular label placed upon it by the Commission is not necessarily conclusive, for it is the substance of what the Commission has purported to do and has done which is decisive."

...Rather that determination must be made in the light of the basic purpose of those statutory requirements. The basic policy of Section 4 at least requires that when a proposed regulation of general applicability has a substantial impact on the regulated industry, or an important class of the members or the products of that industry, notice and opportunity for comment should first be provided....

The all pervasive and substantial impact which the September regulations have upon the drug industry and in turn upon prescribing physicians and their patients, makes it imperative that the Commissioner comply with the notice and comment provisions of Section 4 before such regulations become effective....

■ ■ ■

Questions

1. The Administrative Procedure Act requires an agency to give notice and an opportunity to participate to those individuals affected by the creation of a new rule. However, the Administrative Procedure Act contains some exemptions. What exemptions did the Secretary of HEW rely upon to negate the necessity of notice and opportunity to participate? Why did the District Court not agree with the Secretary's determination on the status of this exemption?
2. The Supreme Court had previously decided a similar case that provided some guidance to the District Court. The Supreme Court ruled:

> The rule-making provisions of that Act, which the Board would avoid, were designed to assume fairness and mature consideration of rules of general application. They may not be avoided by the process of making rules in the course of adjudicatory proceedings. There is no warrant in law for the Board to replace the statutory scheme with a rule-making procedure of its own invention. Apart from the fact that the device fashioned by the Board does not comply with statutory command, it obviously falls short of the substance of the requirements of the Administrative Procedure Act. The "rule" created in *Excelsior* was not published in the Federal Register which is the statutory and accepted menas of giving notice of a rule as adopted; only selected organizations were given notice of the "hearing, " whereas notice in the Federal Register would have been general in character; under the Administrative Procedure Act, the terms of substance of the rule would have to be stated in the notice of hearing, and all interested parties would have an opportunity to participate in the rule making...

Adjudicated cases may and do, of course, serve as vehicles for the formulation of agency policies, which are applied and announced therein. They generally provide a guide to action that the agency may be expected to take in future cases. Subject to the qualified role of *stare decisis* in the administrative process, they may serve as precedents. But this is far from saying... that commands, decisions, or policies announced in adjudication are "rules" in the sense that they must, without more, be obeyed by the affected public.

NLRB v. Wyman-Gordon Co. 394 U.S. 759 (1969).

May adjudicated cases serve as precedent in future adjudicatory cases even if they cannot formulate "rules?"

RATE-MAKING HEARINGS

Many administrative agencies deal with a variety of rate-making problems. For example, there are rate structure problems which involve rate relationships. Rate structure refers to the relationship of the rate for one type of service to the rate charged for another service type. For instance, airlines charge one fare for coach and another fare for first class. The Civil Aeronautics Board has jurisdiction to determine and settle questions concerning this type of rate structure problem. When administrative agencies deal with problems of rate structure, they usually consider questions concerning cost of the service, value of the service, and its relationship with other rates. It obviously is a complex area.

In addition, administrative agencies face the problem of the level of rates; that is, whether all the rates of service provide a sufficient rate of return for the regulatees. Historically, the Supreme Court required administrative agencies to allow a level of rates for companies that provided a "fair return" on their investments. If the administrative agencies set the level of rates in such a fashion as to deny a "fair return," the Supreme Court ruled that such regulatory action would amounT to a "taking" of priVate property for public use without just compensation in violation of Fifth Amendment. Because of such judicial protection, the agencies would have to increase the rates. This "fair return" concept caused considerable problems because agencies had to make a determination of the company's rate base or investment in resources. The agencies had to determine which cost figures would be used in determining the rate base. Should original cost or replacement cost be used? Considerable litigation has been involved in these determinations.

However, in 1944 the Supreme Court set upon a new course. In *Federal Power Commission v. Hope Natural Gas Company*, 320 U.S. 591 (1944), the Court upheld the FPC's determination of rate levels without inquiring into the notion of a "fair return" on the company's rate base. Instead, the Court was concerned with setting of rate levels to sustain the financial and credit integrity of the enterprise to maintain its ability to attract capital. Consequently, the attention of federal regulatory bodies was shifted from the problem of rate base (cost of investment) to that of rate of return or ability to pay sufficient returns to investors and creditors to continue to attract capital. The effect of the *Hope* case has been to permit federal agencies to experiment with rate levels without being bound to some precise formula for the rate base. While federal agencies have been free to develop special experience and competence unencumbered by the past, many state authorities are still involved with the quagmire of determining the appropriate rate base and its consequential debates over original or replacement cost data.

Beside the difficulties involved in setting the appropriate rate levels, administrative agencies are increasingly faced with the demand for a wider participation (consumer groups) in the hearings which determine such rates.

HAHN v. GOTTLIEB
430 F.2d 1243 (1970)
United States Court of Appeals (1st Cir.)

■ ■ ■

In this appeal, we are asked to decide whether tenants in housing subsidized under the National Housing Act (NHA) have the right to an administrative hearing...

Plaintiffs are members of a tenants' association at the Castle Square project in Boston (the project), a development of low- and middle-income housing financed under NHA. Defendants Gottlieb and Druker (the landlord) are the current owners of the project. Prior to the expiration of the plaintiffs' leases in July 1969, the landlord filed a proposed monthly rent increase of $28 per apartment with the Federal Housing Administration (FHA). Plaintiffs sought an opportunity to be heard on the proposed increase; and, when the FHA failed to satisfy their request, they brought suit in the federal distict court...

...[T]he statute confers broad discretion on the Secretary of HUD. The Secretary is authorized to approve mortgagors and to supervise their operations "under a regulatory agreement or otherwise, as to rents, charges, and methods of operation, in such form and in such manner as in the opinion of the Secretary will effectuate the purposes of this section."

Implementing these broad grants of authority, the Secretary has promulgated regulations concerning priorities and income limits for occupancy in FHA projects. The Secretary also regulates the landlord's return on his investment by strictly supervising accounting practices, and, in the case of limited distribution mortgagors like defendants Gottlieb and Druker, by setting a six per cent ceiling on return. Applicaitons for rent increases must be submitted to the FHA, which takes into acount the rental income necessary to maintain a project's economic soundness and "to provide a reasonalbe return on the investment consistent with providing reasonable rentals to the tenants." FHA's agreement with the landlord in this case further provides that rental increases will be approved if necessary to compensate for increases in expense "over which the owners have no effective control."

The regulations illustrate that the success of a FHA project requires a flexible exercise of administrative discretion. The ultimate goal of the program is housing for low- and middle-class families, but this goal is to be achieved by expanding the range of housing needs which can be met by private enterprise. To provide low-income housing maintaining a sound investment requires considerable adaptability. We think Congress recognized this need for adaptability when it authorized the Secretary to regulate mortgagors by individual agreement as well as by general rule. Of course, the need for administrative flexibility does not of itself preclude an agency hearing or judicial review, but we must take care lest we kill the goose in our solicitude for the eggs.

Plaintiffs' initial claim is that they are entitled to a formal hearing before the FHA prior to the approval of any rent increase. This contention finds no support in the text of the National Housing Act. Plaintiffs claim, however, that both the right to a hearing and its procedural characteristics can be derived from the Due Process Clause of the Fifth Amendment...

The proceeding in which plaintiffs seek to assert their interest is basically an informal rate-making process. The landlord who seeks a rent increase submits documentation to the FHA showing his expenses, return on investment, and the like. The FHA staff then examines his proposal in the light of the terms of the regulatory agreement, the broad criteria of the regulations, and current economic conditions. Plaintiffs seek to encumber these negotiations with a formal hearing, the right to cross-examine adverse witnesses, and an impartial decision-maker, who must state the reasons for his decision and the evidence on which he relies. These procedural safeguards are characteristic of adjudicatory proceedings, where the outcome turns on accurate resolution of specific factual disputes. Such safeguards are not, however, essential in "legislative" proceedings, such as rate-making, where decision depends on broad familiarity with economic conditions...

The distinction between "legislative" and "adjudicative" facts is particularly apt in this case, where it is the tenants rather than the landlord who seek a hearing. The tenants are unlikely to have special familiarity with their landlord's financial conditions, the intricacies of project management, or the state of the economy in the surrounding area. Hopefully, the FHA can check the accuracy of the landlord's documentation without their assistance. They may be aware of construction defects in their own living areas, but if, contrary to (law), a building has been approved which does not conform to applicable standards, there would seem to be limited utility in rehearsing old mistakes each time a rental increase is sought. Of course, tenant's complaints about maintenance and living conditions ought to be heard, but such grievances can be dealt with without requiring a trial-type hearing with each rent increase. Indeed, an effective grievance system should be operable at all times, not merely when the landlord seeks to raise his rents. Thus, the elaborate procedural safeguards which plaintiffs demand are unlikely to elicit essential information in the general run of cases.

These procedures would, however, place a significant burden on the relationship between the landlord and the FHA. At present, applications for rent increases are merely one aspect of an on-going relationship between insured and insurer. Plaintiffs would turn these applications into occasions for full-scale review of the relationship, as their conduct in the hearing they have already received illustrates. Such reconsideration may delay economically necessary rent increases and discourage private investors from entering the FHA program at all. Equally important the project in question contains some 500 tenants, each of whom has the same interest in low-rent housing.

Applying the constitutionally relevant test, therefore, it seems to us that the government interest in a summary procedure for approving rent increases outweights the tenants' interest in greater procedural safeguards. The procedures demanded by plaintiffs would place substantial additional burdens on the insurer-insured relationship without necessarily improving the fundamental fairness of the proceedings. We, therefore, hold that tenants in housing financed under the National Housing Act are not constitutionally entitled to an administrative hearing on their landlord's proposals for increased rents...

■ ■ ■

Questions

1. What statutory authority does the FHA have over the owners of tenaments in which the FHA has supplied funds? What factors does the FHA consider in determining the appropriate rental rates for FHA housing?

2. Why did the Court rule that the tenants were not entitled to a hearing when FHA is considering rental increases? Do you agree with the reasoning?

3. In *Hahn* the Court was faced with a hearing which was to establish "legislative" facts for the purpose of determining appropriate rental rates. While it may be appropriate to deny tenants a hearing in regards to rate making, would the Court feel differently if the dispute concerned "adjudicative" facts? Consider *Escalera v. New York City Housing Authority,* 425 F. 2d 853 (2d Cir.), (1970) in which the housing authority terminated tenancies on the ground of nondesirability of the tenants. The procedural system to terminate included: conversations between the project manager and the tenant, tenant hearings before the Tenant Review Board which allowed the tenant to summarize his position but not present any witness, a Review Board decision based on items in the tenant's file which may be unknown to the tenant, and no findings or reasons for the termination were released to the tenant. Would the Court consider this procedural system to be sufficient for the establishment of "adjudicative" facts with which to make a fair determination of the tenant's rights.?

ADMINISTRATIVE APPEALS

In larger administrative agencies adjudicatory hearings are often held before "independent " administrative law judges. These individuals are civil servants performing judicial duties on assignment to various agencies. The decision of the administrative law judge articulates his "findings of fact" and "interpretations of law," which are later reviewed by the top officials of the agency. This review by the agency commissioners or board members is an internal appeal process to correct or affirm the decisions of the hearing judge. Consequently, a final decision or order by the agency is not rendered until the entire process has been completed. Upon completion, the decision of the agency is subject to review by the courts which usually involves an apellate court because the agency served as the "trial court." To allow the agency to correct its own internal errors and avoid unnecessary court congestion, the courts generally review only the "final orders" of the agencies. Sometimes a party may attempt an earlier review by the courts as the following case illustrates.

MYERS v. BETHLEHEM CORP.
303 U.S. 41 (1938)
Supreme Court of the United States

■ ■ ■

BRANDEIS, Mr. Justice.

The Industrial Union of Marine and Shipbuilding Workers of America, Local No. 5, made to the Board a charge that the Bethlehem Shipbuilding Corporation, Ltd., was engaging in unfair labor practices at its plant in Quincy, Massachusetts...

The Board duly notified the Corporation that a hearing on the complaint would be held on April 27, 1936, at Boston, Massachusetts, in accordance with Rules and Regulations of the Board, a copy of which was annexed to the notice; and that the Corporation "will have the right to appear, in person or otherwise, and give testimony."

On that day the Corporation filed, in the federal court for Massachusetts, the bill of equity...against A. Howard Myers, Acting Regional Director for...National Labor Relations Board, ...to enjoin them from holding "a hearing..."

...[T]he District Court issued a restraining order and... (it was) affirmed by the Circuit Court of Appeals... We are of opinion that the District Court was without power to enjoin the board from holding the hearings...

...The Act establishes standards to which the Board must conform. There must be complaint, notice and hearing. The Board must receive evidence and make findings. The findings as to the facts are to be conclusive, but only if supported by evidence. The order of the Board is subject to review by the designated court, and only when sustained by the court may the order be enforced. Upon that review all questions of the jursidiction of the Board and the regularity of its proceedings, all questions of constitutional right or statutory authority, are open to examination by the court. We construe the procedural provisions as affording adequate opportunity to secure judicial protection against arbitrary action in accordance with the well-settled rules applicable to administrative agencies set up by Congress to aid in the enforcement of valid legislation.

It is true that the Board has jurisdiction only if the complaint concerns interstate or foreign commerce. Unless the board finds that it does, the complaint must be dismissed. And if it finds that interstate or foreign commerce is involved, but the Circuit Court of Appeals concludes that such finding was without adequate evidence to support it, or otherwise contrary to law, the Board's petition to enforce it will be dismissed, or the employer's petition to have it set aside will be granted. Since the procedures before the Board is appropriate and the judicial review so provided is adequate, Congress had power to vest exclusive jurisdiction in the Board and the Circuit Court of Appeals.

The Corporation contends that, since it denies that interstate or foreign commerce is involved and claims that a hearing would subject it to irreparable damage, rights guaranteed by the Federal Constitution will be denied unless it be held that the District

Court has jurisdiction to enjoin the holding of a hearing by the Board. So to hold would, as the Government insists, in effect substitute the District Court for the Board as the tribunal to hear and determine what Congress declared the Board exclusively should hear and determine in the first instance. The contention is at war with the long settled rule of judicial administration that no one is entitled to judicial relief for a supposed or threatened injury until the prescribed administrative remedy has been exhausted. That rule has been repeatedly acted on in cases where, as here, the contention is made that the administrative body lacked power over the subject matter.

Obviously, the rule requiring exhaustion of the administrative remedy cannot be circumvented by asserting that the charge on which the complaint rests is groundless and that the mere holding of the prescribed administrative hearing would result in irreparable damage. Lawsuits also often prove to have been groundless; but no way has been discovered of relieving a defendent from the necessity of a trial to establish the fact.

■ ■ ■

JUDICIAL REVIEW

Judicial review is employed as a form of control over agency actions after administrative proceedings have concluded. However, the function of judicial review is restricted. The statute, for example, may provide that the agency's determination shall be "final" and not subject to review. Congress has delegated its power for agency exercise of discretion delegated to it.

Also, there are practical limits on judicial review. Court review is expensive, it involves delay and there is perhaps a fear of adverse publicity. Moreover, even if the court reverses the agency decision and remands the case, the agency can reach essentially the same decision again and merely correct its court declared error.

Nevertheless, judicial review is an important tool in controlling against administrative excesses. Even the fear of judicial review can act as a deterrent against overzealous officials who learn to think twice before they act.

STANDARDS FOR REVIEW

CITIZENS TO PRESERVE OVERTON PARK, INC. v. VOLPE
401 U.S. 412 (1971)
Supreme Court of the United States

■ ■ ■

MARSHALL, Justice.

A threshold question—whether petitioners are entitled to any judicial review—is easily answered. Section 701 of the Administrative Procedure Act, provides that the action of "each authority of the Government of the United States," which includes the Department of Transportation, is subject to judicial review except where there is a statutory prohibition on review or where "agency action is committed to agency discretion by law." In this case, there is no indication that Congress sought to prohibit judicial review and there is most certainly no "showing of 'clear and convincing evidence' of a * * * legislative intent" to restrict access to judicial review.

Similarly, the Secretary's decision here does not fall within the exception for action "committed to agency discretion." This is a very narrow exception. The legislative history of the Administrative Procedure Act indicates that it is applicable in those rare instances where "statutes are drawn in such broad terms that in a given case there is no law to apply."

Section 4(f) of the Department of Transportation Act and § 138 of the Federal-Aid Highway Act are clear and specific directives. Both the Department of Transportation

Act and the Federal-Aid to Highway Act provide that the Secretary "shall not approve any program or project" that requires the use of any public parkland "unless (1) there is no feasible and prudent alternative to the use of such land, and (2) such program includes all possible planning to minimize harm to such park * * *." This language is a plain and explicit bar to the use of federal funds for construction of highways through parks—only the most unusual situations are exempted. . .

Plainly, there is "law to apply" and thus the exemption for action "committed to agency discretion" is inapplicable. But the existence of judicial review is the only start: the standard for review must also be determined. For that we must look to § 706 of the Administrative Procedure Act, which provides that a "reviewing court shall * * * hold unlawful and set aside agency action, findings, and conclusions found" not to meet six separate standards. In all cases agency action must be set aside if the action was "arbitrary, capricious, an abuse of discretion, or otherwise not in accordance with law" or if the action failed to meet statutory, procedural, or constitutional requirements. . .

The court is first required to decide whether the Secretary acted within the scope of his authority. This determination naturally begins with a delineation of the scope of the Secretary's authority and discretion.

As has been shown, Congress has specified only a small range of choices that the Secretary can make. Also involved in this initial inquiry is a determination of whether on the facts the Secretary's decision can reasonably be said to be within that range. The reviewing court must consider whether the Secretary properly construed his authority to approve the use of parkland as limited to situations where there are no feasible alternative routes or where feasible alternative routes involve uniquely difficult problems. And the reviewing court must be able to find that the Secretary could have reasonably believed that in this case there are no feasible alternatives or that alternatives do involve unique problems.

Scrutiny of the facts does not end, however, with the determination that the Secretary has acted within the scope of his statutory authority. Section 706 (2) (A) requires a finding that the actual choice made was not "arbitrary, capricious, an abuse of discretion, or otherwise not in accordance with law." To make this finding the court must consider whether the decision was based on a consideration of the relevant factors and whether there has been a clear error of judgement.

Although this inquiry into the facts is to be searching and careful, the ultimate standard of review is a narrow one. The court is not empowered to substitute its judgment for that of the agency.

The final inquiry is whether the Secretary's action followed the necessary procedural requirements. Here the only procedural error alleged is the failure of the Secretary to make formal findings and state his reason for allowing the highway to be built through the park.

Undoubtedly, review of the Secretary's action is hampered by his failure to make such findings, but the absence of formal findings does not necessarily require that the case be remanded to the Secretary. Neither the Department of Transportation Act nor the Federal-Aid Highway Act requires such formal findings. Moreover, the Administrative Procedure Act requirements that there be formal findings in certain rule-making and adjudicatory proceedings do not apply to the Secretary's action here. And, although formal findings may be required in some cases in the absence of statutory directives when the nature of the agency action is ambiguous, those situations are rare. Plainly, there is no ambiguity here; the Secretary has approved the construction of I-40 through Overton Park and has approved a specific design for the project.

Thus it is necessary to remand this case to the District Court for plenary review of the Secretary's decision. That review is to be based on the full administrative record that was before the Secretary at the time he made his decision. But since the bare record may not disclose the factors that were considered or the Secretary's construction of the evidence it may be necessary for the District Court to require some exnation in order to determine if the Secretary acted within the scope of his authority and if the Secretary's action was justifiable under the applicable standard. The court may require the administrative officials who participated in the decision to give testimony explaining their action. Of course, such inquiry into the mental processes of administrative decisionmakers is usually to be avoided. But...it may be that the only way there can be effective judicial review is by examining the decisionmakers themselves.

The District Court is not, however, required to make such an inquiry. It may be that the Secretary can prepare formal findings that will provide an adequate explanation for his action. Such an explanation will, to some extent, be a *"post hoc* rationalization" and thus must be viewed critically. If the District Court decides that additional explanation is necessary, that court should consider which method will prove the most expeditious so that full review may be had as soon as possible.

■ ■ ■

Questions

1. The Administrative Procedure Act provides for judicial review except in two instances. What are those two exceptions to judicial review? Why did the Court think neither exception applied in this instance?
2. Having decided that the decision was subject to judicial review, the Court had to determine the appropriate standard for review. What standards are set in the Administrative Procedure Act?
3. What should the Court consider in deciding whether the Secretary acted within the scope of his authority?
4. Assuming that the Secretary did act within the scope of his statutory authority, the Court must determine whether the actual decision made by the Secretary was not "arbitrary, capricious, an abuse of discretion, or otherwise not in accordance with law." How is the Court to determine whether the decision made by the Secretary was arbitrary?
5. The Court on review can also determine whether the Secretary followed any necessary procedural requirements. What procedural error was alleged to have been violated by the Secretary? Did the Court conclude that this procedural requirement existed?

FEDERAL POWER COM'N V. FLORIDA POWER & LIGHT CO.
404 U.S. 453 (1972)
Supreme Court of the United States

■ ■ ■

WHITE, Mr. Justice.

We are asked to determine whether the Federal Power Commission exceeded its statutory authorization when it asserted jurisdiction over the Florida Power & Light Co....

In the case now before us the FPC hearing examiner and the Commission itself, utilizing two scientific tests, determined that the Florida Power & Light Co. (FP&L) generates energy that is transmitted in interstate commerce. They therefore held the company subject to the Commission's jurisdiction. Respondent RP&L argues that an alternative model better represents the flow of its electricity; by use of this model it purports to demonstrate that its power has not flowed in interstate commerce. The Court of Appeals for the Fifth Circuit rejected the FPC's tests as "not sufficient to prove the actual transmission of energy interstate." It did not approve FP&L's test. ("Both [the FPC and the FP&L tests] suffer from the same vice,"), but because the FPC must shoulder the burden of proof, its finding of jurisdiction was set aside....

A court must be reluctant to reverse results supported by such a weight of considered and carefully articulated expert opinion. Particularly when we consider a purely factual question within the area of competence of an administrative agency created by Congress, and when resolution of that question depends on "engineering and scientific" considerations, we recognize the relevant agency's technical expertise and experience, and defer to its analysis unless it is without substantial basis in fact. An appreciation of such different institutional capacities is reflected in the congressional directive defining the terms of judicial review of FPC action: "The finding of the Commission as to the facts, if supported by substantial evidence, shall be conclusive."

The Court of Appeals appears to have rejected the Commission's conclusions... (because) it apparently regarded these conclusions as supported by mere speculation rather than evidence. In its view, expert opinion about the nature of reality, however logically compelling, is not fact. Second, even if the Commission's views might be said to be supported by substantial evidence, the Court of Appeals apparently thought it important that the Commission acknowledged that its conclusions rest upon representations of a reality imperfectly understood. From this the Court of Appeals concluded that it was dealing with a "simplified characterization" that, despite the frequent use of that same characterization by other courts of appeals, was too uncertain in its application to any particular situation to be used as the basis for establishing jurisdiction.

We reverse and reinstate the FPC's order because we do not think these points are well taken...[W]e hold that well-reasoned expert testimony—based on what is known and uncontradicted by empirical evidence—may in and of itself be "substantial evidence" when first-hand evidence on the question (in this case how electricity moves...) is unavailable. This proposition has been so long accepted, and indeed has been so often applied specifically to challenges to the FPC's determination of technical matters, that we do not consider it fairly in dispute....

The elusive nature of electrons renders experimental evidence that might draw the fine distinctions required by this case practically unobtainable. That does not mean that expert testimony is insubstantial and that FP&L is beyond federal regulation...

The decision of the Court of Appeals is reversed and the case is remanded for reinstatement of the order of the Federal Power Commission.

■ ■ ■

Questions

1. Congress directed the Courts, when reviewing FPC Action, to uphold the findings of fact by the Commission, "if supported by substantial evidence." Why did the Court of Appeals feel the Commission's finding of fact was not supported by substantial evidence?
2. What evidence was found by the Supreme Court to be substantial enough to support the findings of the Federal Power Commission?

DISCLOSING INFORMATION

Administrative agencies in their regulatory functions accumulate a great deal of information concerning individuals in business enterprises. The chief administrative agent, the President, has from the beginning of our nation asserted a constitutional right to withhold information. Presidents have withheld information from Congress and others under the doctrine of executive privilege. Issues concerning the extent of executive privilege are complex and continuing. While no court has considered the doctrine in the context of executive withholding of information from Congress, executive privilege unquestionably exists and the courts have jurisdiction to consider problems concerning the privilege and in determining its scope. In 1974 part of the doctrine was determined to be constitutionally based under separation of powers in *United States v. Nixon* 418 U.S. 683, (Chapter I).

The Freedom of Information Act is a 1966 amendment of the Administrative Procedure Act. it requires disclosure of governmental records to anyone unless the governmental records are specifically exempted by the statute. District Courts are given jurisdiction to enforce its provisions. The Act requires that each agency shall make available to the public information in the following manner:

1. Substantive rules and general policies of general applicability adopted by the agency must be published in the Federal Register.
2. An agency must make available to the public its opinions, orders, statements of policy, interpretations, staff manuals, and instructions.
3. Each agency on request shall make the records concerning facts compiled by the agency in the course of investigation or facts filed with the agency promptly available to any person.

These disclosures must be made regardless of motive, interest or intent of the individual making the request. The request might include the right to inspect, copy or suggest corrections in the records. The federal District Court shall determine whether the record shall be disclosed or amended, with the burden of proof on the agency to justify its refusal to disclose or amend. Failure to obey District Court orders would result in contempt of court citations for non-compliance against the administrative officials.

Strangely, the Act did not mention executive privilege. Instead, the Act made the following exemptions from disclosure for matters

"(1) specifically required by Executive order to be kept secret in the interest of the national defense or foreign policy;
(2) related solely to the internal personnel rules and practices of an agency;
(3) specifically exempted from disclosure by statute;
(4) trade secrets and commercial or financial information obtained from a person and privileged or confidential;
(5) inter-agency or intra-agency memorandums or letters which would not be available by law to a party other than an agency in litigation with the agency;
(6) personnel and medical files and similar files the disclosure of which would constitute a clearly unwarranted invasion of personal privacy;
(7) investigtory files compiled for law enforcement purposes except to the extent available by law to a party other than an agency;
(8) contained in or related to examination, operating, or condition reports prepared by, on behalf of, or for the use of an agency responsible for the regulation or supervision of financial institutions; or
(9) geological and geophysical information and data, including maps, concerning wells."

ENVIRONMENTAL PROTECTION AGENCY v. MINK
410 U.S. 73 (1973)
Supreme Court of the United States

■ ■ ■

WHITE, Mr. Justice.

The Freedom of Information Act of 1966 provides that Government agencies shall make available to the public a broad spectrum of information, but exempts from its mandate certain specified categories of information...

(Petitioners') lawsuit began with an article that appeared in a Washington, D.C., newspaper in late July 1971. The article indicated that the President had received conflicting recommendations on the advisability of the underground nuclear test scheduled for that coming fall and, in particular, noted that the "latest recommendations" were the product of "a departmental under-secretary committee named to investigate the controversy." Two days later, Congresswoman Patsy Mink sent a telegram to the President urgently requesting the "immediate release of recommenda-tions and reports by inter-departmental committee. . . . " When the request was denied, an action under the Freedom of Information Act was commenced by Congresswoman Mink and 32 of her colleagues in the House.

. . .[T]he District Court granted summary judgment in (defendants) favor on the ground that each of the nine documents sought was exempted from compelled disclosure by §§ (b)(1) and (b)(5) of the Act. The Court of Appeals reversed, conclud-ing that subseciton (b)(1) of the Act permits the withholding of only the secret portions of those documents. . .

In addition, the Court of Appeals concluded that all nine contested documents fell within subsection (b)(5) of the Act, but construed that exemption as shielding only the "decisional processes" reflected in internal Government memoranda not "factual information" unless that information is "inextricably intertwined with policymaking processes.". . .

Subsection (b)(1) of the Act (hereafter Exemption) exempts from forced disclosure matters "specifically required by Executive order to kept secret in the interest of the national defense or foreign policy.". . .

. . . Manifestly, Exemption 1 was intended to dispel uncertainty with respect to public access to material affecting "national defense or foreign policy." Rather than some vague standard, the test was to be simply whether the President has determined by Executive Order that particular documents are to be kept secret. The language of the Act itself is sufficiently clear in this respect, but the legislative history disposes of any possible argument that Congress intended the Freedom of Information Act to subject executive security classifications to judicial review at the insistence of anyone who might seek to question them. . . .(It is). . .wholly untenable. . .that the Act in-tended to subject the soundness of executive security classifications to judicial review at the insistence of any objecting citizen. . . .

Disclosure of the three documents conceded to be "unclassified" is resisted solely on the basis of subsection (b)(5) of the Act (hereafter Exemption 5). . .By its terms. . . Exemption 5 creates an exemption for such documents only insofar as they "would not be available by law to a party. . .in litigation with the agency." This language clearly contemplates that the public is entitled to all such memoranda or letters that a private party could discover in litigation with the agency. Drawing such a line between what may be withheld and what must be disclosed is not without difficulties. . .Still, the legislative history of Exemption 5 demonstrates that Congress intended to incorporate generally the recognized rule that "confidential intra-agency advisory opinions. . .are privileged from inspection.". . .But the privilege that has been held to attach to intragovernmental memoranda clearly has finite limits, even in civil litigation. In each case, the question was whether production of the contested document would be "in-jurious to the consultative functions of government that the privilege of nondisclosure protects." Thus, in the absence of a claim that disclosure would jeopardize state secrets, memoranda consisting only of compiled factual material or purely factual material contained in deliberative memoranda and severable from its context would generally be available for discovery by private parties in litigation with the Govern-ment. Moreover, in applying the privilege, courts often were required to examine the disputed documents in order to determine which should be turned over or withheld. . . Virtually all of the courts that have thus far applied Exemption 5 have recognized that it requires different treatment for materials reflecting deliberative or policy-making processes on the one hand, and purely factual investigative matters on the other. . . .

. . .In the present case, the (defendant) proceeded on the theory that all of the nine documents were exempt from disclosure in their entirety under Exemption 5 by virtue of their use in the decisionmaking process. On remand, (defendants) are entitled to attempt to demonstrate the propriety of withholding any documents, or portions thereof. . .(on confidential-consultative grounds).

■ ■ ■

Questions

1. The Court of Appeals felt that Section (b)(1) permitted governmental withholding of only secret portions of the documents. Any portion of the document not "secret" should be available to the public. Why did the Supreme Court not agree with the interpretation of the court of Appeals?

2. The Court of Appeals concluded that Section (b)(5) shielded only "decisional processes" and not "factual information" unless such information was "inextricably intertwinned with policymaking process." Did the Supreme Court agree with the approach? How was the District Court to determine if such documents were merely factual?

The *Mink* case discussed the Freedom of Information Act and interpretation of the exemptions from disclosure. The nine exemptions of the act are not the only law that protects against "required" disclosure. Administrative officers may be governed by other statutory law, by the common law, by executive privilege, by executive orders, and agency-made law in the form of regulations, orders, or instructions. Often legislation confers discretionary powers on agency officers to disclose or not disclose specified information. Consequently, the courts often have to balance the Information Act with other statutes that may apply to the situation. These confusing rules and contradictory enactments have caused many commentators to assert that Congress created a rather shabby product in the Information Act. They maintain that many deficiencies in the act result from congressional inattention and indifference. Perhaps, this is because Congress prepared this legislation rather than following the lead of the executive branch of government. When the Executive has originated and promoted the legislation through Congress, it appears more coherent and internally consistent. In any case, the principle of open government with citizenery access to governmental information is vital to a free system of government. It is unfortunate that Congress was not able to achieve these goals in a more satisfactory fashion. However, the first steps in any new frontier are usually small.

ENDNOTES

1. K. C. Davis, *Administrative Law and Government*(St. Paul, Minn.: West Publishing Co., 1960), p. 25.
2. 1 Blackstone.
3. Paul H. Douglas, *Ethics in Government* (1952), pp. 85–88.

4

THE DYNAMICS
OF CHANGE

Today's laws have evolved on the basis of past experience and legal precedents set by expanding scientific knowledge and changing society. The U.S. legal system contains a dynamic process by which laws are constantly being created, altered, and adapted to contemporary society. Indeed, for the legal system to be effective in a free society, laws must be kept relevant to the "felt necessities" of society's members. The usual method of changing laws is legislation. However, another method of change and adaptation in the legal system is judicial modification of rules. Judges "make law" when they interpret a statute or a constitutional provision. They also make law when they create a new rule because no previous legislative rule or case precedent is directly applicable. Judge-made law is traditionally referred to as "common law"—a name first given to the rules fashioned by royal judges who rode throughout England fashioning rules to be common for all Englanders.

Judicial laws are largely formulated in appellate courts. Appellate courts attempt to obtain uniformity in law by resolving conflicting lower court opinions which differ on the interpretation of law. This process necessitates a written opinion by the court to explain exactly what legal questions the court is resolving, on what facts, and what reasons are given for the decision. The result of these appellate decisions is to clarify the court's conception of the current state of the law or to delcare new law as modern social conditions warrant.

At various times the appellate courts will be faced with fact situations that are presented for the "first" time. In such a case, new law will have to be established. It will be necessary for the court in reaching its decision to develop a judicial standard to guide lower courts in deciding future cases. In addition, members of society rely on appellate decisions as guides for their future actions. However, before appellate decisions are subsequently employed as "precedent" to determine the outcome of similar future cases, subsequent courts must feel that the rule has continuing usefulness as proper public policy in contemporary circumstances. Once a legal standard is accepted and cited as precedent, it is continually tested and refined by later courts in light of any changes that may have occurred in technology, social conditions, economic policy, or concepts of morality.

In dealing with the variety of cases cited and argued to the court as "precedent," the court will distinguish between the cases, accepting similar cases and pointing out the differences in others. The application of precedent to a present controversy is commonly referred to as *stare decisis et non quieta movere* (to adhere to precedent and not unsettle things that are settled). This process of *stare decisis* makes judicial decisions have a prospective effect as law for subsequent similar cases.

In the following materials, this dynamic character of the judicial process is explored. First, the field of tort law and its evolutionary qualities are presented. Then, a series of cases illustrate the enlargement of a legal standard because technological change affected its application. Additional cases show how the courts modify or change legal standards to fit current social conditions. Finally, some of the forces of resistance to change in legal standards by the courts and court attitudes on adhering to precedent in spite of changing conditions are explored.

DEVELOPING A RULE OF LAW

A body of law commonly called "torts" is primarily judge-made law and is concerned with compensating victims who are injured because of the "fault" of someone else. The latin word "tortus" means twisted, implying that someone's conduct is twisted away from society's norm of acceptable behavior. This "unreasonable" conduct causes the individual to be labelled at "fault" and as such, he must pay compensatory money damages to any victim injured as a result of his wrongful behavior.

A tort is not the same as a crime, though the same action by a person may constitute both a tort and a crime. The crime is an offense against the public at large which is prosecuted by the state. The purpose of such proceedings is to protect and vindicate the interest of the public by punishing the violator, by eliminating him from society, by reforming his behavior, or by deterring others from imitating his actions. The only role of the victim of criminal behavior is to serve as an accuser and witness in the criminal prosecution. In contrast, the victim of a tort brings a civil action against the tort-feasor to gain compensation for his sufferings caused by the tort. The court will aid the successful litigant in the collection of any monies awarded for his sufferings.

Liability for tortuous behavior has been imposed by judges on the following three fundamental grounds or legal theories:

1. *Intent* of the defendant to interfere with legally protected interests of the plaintiff.
2. *Negligence* of the defendant that causes harm to the plaintiff.
3. *Strict Liability* (without "fault") which is the imposition of liability for policy reasons, despite the absence of wrongful intent or negligence.

Under the common law, almost all torts have been categorized under some legal theory and given a name. However, some torts may not have a name and, of course, initially all of today's torts were without names. Observe the following language employed by a judge in an 1896 case:

> While no precedent is cited for such action, it does not follow that there is no remedy for the wrong, because every form of action, when brought for the first time, must have been without a precedent to support it. Courts sometimes of necessity abandon their search for precedents, and yet sustain a recovery upon legal principles clearly applicable to the new state of facts, although there was no direct precedent for it, because there had never been an occasion to make one... For instance, the action for enticing away a man's wife, now well established, was a first earnestly resisted upon the grond that no such action had ever been brought.... As we recently said by this court in an action then without precedent, "If the most that can be said is that the case is novel, and is not brought plainly within the limits of some adjudged case, we think such fact not enough to call for a reversal of the judgment." The question therefore is not whether there is any precedent for the action, but whether the defendant inflicted such a wrong upon the plaintiff as resulted in lawful damages. (Kujek v. Goldman et al., 150 N.Y. 176).

INTENTIONAL TORTS

Tortuous intent is the desire to bring about physical results or consequences which are disapproved by law. By voluntarily (intentionally) contracting muscles in his body, the actor "intents" a result. If the desire of the muscular contraction is to bring about an invasion of the legally protected interest of another, the actor's intent is tortuous whether the actual consequences were intended or not. For example, pulling a chair out from under a person about to be seated is intentionally desiring the consequence of physical impact of the person with the ground. As such, the defendant's assertions of intending no more than a practical joke or not intending to injure the plaintiff would not be acceptable as defenses because they describe the defendant's "motive" (inspiration for the act), rather than the "intent." The voluntary act (pulling away the chair) and the desire of particular results which invades another's personal interest (defendant's hitting the ground is the relevant "intent" in determination of intentional torts.

Litigation involving the interests of persons to have their physical self and property free of intentional invasion by others has created a number of specifically named torts. Some intentional torts are described as follows:

Battery

The intentional and offensive contact with another person without consent is a battery. While it is clear that persons are to be protected from indecent and hostile contact, other relatively trivial contacts made without consent can be a battery also. An unappreciated kiss, joke, or physical assistance can be a battery. Since a certain amount of personal contact is inevitable in a crowded world, consent to ordinary contacts is asumed. Time, place, and circumstances of the touching will affect its characterization as being reasonable or unpermitted.

Assault

The intentional act to arouse apprehension of immediate harmful or offensive contact in the mind of another is an assault. No actual contact is necessary, rather the individual is to be compensated for purely mental disturbance caused by the defendant's actions. It is an assault on another to raise a fist to strike, to aim a weapon, or to corner with a display a force. Because menacing actions are necessary to create the fear of "immediate" contact, mere words or threats are usually not assaults because no reasonable apprehension of immediate contact results.

Mental Distress

The law has been slow to accept the notion that peace of mind is entitled to legal protection. However, in recent years the intentional infliction of mental distress by extreme or outrageous conduct has been recognized as a tort. The actions necessary to establish this tort must be especially calculated to cause serious mental distress. Spreading false rumors that the plaintiff's son had hung himself, or wrapping up a gory dead rat in place of a loaf of bread for the plaintiff to open are examples of the kind of outrageous conduct that forms this kind of action. Moreover, prolonged and extreme measures to collect debts, evict tenants, or adjust insurance claims can result in this tortuous conduct.

False Imprisonment

A false imprisonment, or false arrest, is an intentional restraint on the free movement of another. "Imprisonment" doesn't mean iron bars and the like, but rather any restraint on freedom of movement may suffice. Free movement could be constrained by locking the plaintiff in a room; out of a room; by refusing him or her the right to exist an automobile or a store; or by compelling the plaintiff to accompany the defendant. The imprisonment need not last more than an appreciable amount of time. It is essential that the restraint be imposed against the plaintiff's will, though he need not resist to the point of physical violence. Under the common law, a storekeeper's detention of a suspected shoplifter who was ultimately found innocent can amount to a false arrest and subject the storekeeper to liability. However, most states have enacted legislation that protect the storekeeper from liability if his detention is reasonable and in good faith.

Trespass

Intentional trespass to land may be committed by entry upon the land, by casting objects upon it, or by remaining on the land after a right to entry has terminated. A similar trespass to personal properties may be committed also.

Conversion

A major interference with the personal property of another may be so serious as to justify the court, at the plaintiff's request, to order the intruder to buy the property from the plaintiff. The extent of interference is determined by many relevant factors; namely, the extent and duration of the interference, the defendant's intent, the harm done to the property, the degree of interference to the plaintiff, and the expense and inconvenience caused the plaintiff. The conversion occurs when the defendant intends to exercise control over another's personal property which is inconsistent with the owner's property rights and such exercise of control is determined to be a substantial interference.

Defamation

Defamation is the intentional publication to a third person of defamatory information which causes injury to the plaintiff's reputation. Defamatory information is any communication which tends to diminish esteem, respect, and goodwill in which the plaintiff is held. Language which causes contempt, derogatory, or unpleasant feelings against the plaintiff is likewise defamatory. It is generally true that if the defendant can establish the truthfulness of his remarks, no liability attaches to his words. In addition, certain defamatory communications are qualifiedly privileged and immune from prosecution—such as publications fairly made by a person in the discharge of some public or private duty, as an employee remark to a superior to protect the employer from the believed criminal behavior of another employee.

Privacy

Interferences with the right of the plaintiff "to be let alone" can amount to the tort of privacy. This tort is a creation of this century. Four kinds of invasions of plaintiff's right to privacy are embodied in this tort. The four invasions are: (1) intrusion upon the plaintiff's physical and mental solitude or seclusion (such as secret recording devices in plaintiff's bedroom); (2) public disclosure of private facts (such as public exhibition of films of a caesarean operation); (3) publicity which places the plaintiff in a false light in the public eye (such as using the face of an honest cab driver as an ornament in a story about cheating propensities of taxi drivers); (4) appropriation, for the defendant's advantage, of the plaintiff's name or likeliness (such as using plaintiff's name or picture without consent in an advertisement).

NEGLIGENCE

An unavoidable accident is an event which was not intended, and which, under all the circumstances, could not have been foreseen or prevented by exercise of reasonable precautions. There is no liability in such a case because there is no wrongful intent or failure to exercise proper care. However, if the event could have been prevented by the exercise of reasonable care, then the defendant's failure to be careful causes him to be liable under the tort of negligence.

Negligence, as a cause of action, is established by the plaintiff when four elements are proven:

1. A duty of care was owed by the defendant to those foreseeable individuals who would be exposed to unreasonable risk if the defendant didn't exercise due care in whatever he or she was doing. When the risk of injury to others is greater than the burden to take adequate precautions, the defendant is under the lawful duty to take those precautions.
2. The failure of the defendant to exercise reasonable care as a reasonable person under similar circumstances would have done.
3. A reasonably close causal connection between defendant's failure to exercise due care and the plaintiff's injury. This is commonly known as "proximate cause".
4. Actual injury or damage to the plaintiff. Such injury to the plaintiff may include property damage, medical bills, loss wages, and pain and suffering.

While many courts prefer not to attempt to define different degrees of negligence, various statutes often require such definitions. The distinctions usually made are as follows: slight negligence is the failure to exercise great care that persons of extraordinary prudence and foresight are accustomed to use, and gross negligence is the failure to exercise even scant care. Courts have difficulty in drawing a distinction between gross negligence and "reckless" conduct which is willful conduct in disregard of a known and probably risk.

Two usual defenses to a charge of negligence are contributory negligence and assumption of risk. Contributory negligence is negligence by the plaintiff that contributed to his or her own injuries. In the eyes of the law, both plaintiff and defendant are at "fault," and consequently, the plaintiff is unable to recover from the defendant. A few states by statute require the courts to compare the negligence of each party, and if the defendant's negligence outweighs the plaintiff's, the plaintiff is allowed to recover losses minus an amount attributed to his or her own negligence. This process of comparative negligence, in effect, apportions the loss between the unequally negligent parties.

The assumption of risk defense means the plaintiff, with knowledge of the risk, voluntarily entered some activity or relation agreeing to take his or her own chances. The legal result is that the defendant is not under a duty to the plaintiff as to those known and assumed risks.

STRICT LIABILITY

The last hundred years have witnessed the overthrow of the doctrine of "no liability without fault." As one writer put it, there is "a strong and growing tendency, where there is blame on neither side, to ask, in view of the exigencies of social justice, who can best bear the loss and hence to shift the loss by creating liability where there has been no fault." The courts are weighing various factors in our complex and dangerous civilization to determine, as a matter of social policy, which party is best able to shoulder the loss. The defendant is held liable on the court's conclusion that the responsibility *should* be the defendant's, as a matter of social adjustment of losses. This approach by the courts is a far cry from the common law determination of individual "fault" on the basis of intent or failure to exercise proper care. Rather, the normal basis of liability under strict liability is the creation of undue risk of harm to other members of the community while personally exercising ordinary care and intending no harm. For example, keeping a pet bear creates undue risk of harm to others if he escapes. While intending no harm and taking care to avoid escape, the owner would, nevertheless, be held strictly liable for any damages resulting from the bear's escape. It is usually said that legal liability for "ultra-hazardous activities" by the defendant which necessarily involve a risk of serious harm cannot be eliminated by the exercise of utmost care. The liability normally extends to the limits of the risk on society imposed by that dangerous activity. However, the plaintiff's assumption of risk will normally relieve the defendant of strict liability.

Strict liability theory has been extended into many fields of law. Sellers of goods have found increasing court propensities to find them strictly liable for defective good which cause harm to the purchasers. Carriers and inn-keepers are strictly liable for goods entrusted to their care unless statutes have modified such responsibility. However, strict liability theory is employed more often in legislation. Workmen's compensation, pure foods acts, child labor statutes, and numerous other enactments utilize strict liability theory. Likewise, no-fault auto insurance schemes ignore the determination of whose "fault" caused the accident.

EXPANDING ROLE OF PUBLIC POLICY

As the primary arena for the fair adjustment of conflicting claims by litigating parties, the law of torts is a continuous battleground of social theory with increasing realization that the interests of society are necessary ingredients in the resolution of private disputes. The notion of public policy in private cases is not new to tort law but certainly a more important variable in today's cases. Consequently, the courts are making more conscientious efforts to direct the law along lines which will achieve desirable social results. While the tort process may be a slow, confusing and often painful progress toward the best rule for society, ultimately the rules formulated must coincide with public opinion or the continuing processes of evolution in legal theory will be pushed at a faster pace.

Numerous cases in this chapter and other chapters contain illustrations of how public policy is granted an expanding influence in the determination of the court's decision.

EXTENDING A RULE OF LAW

In this section a series of tort cases from the courts of New York is presented to illustrate the flexibility of the common law and its evolving content over time.

The tort of defamation was previously defined as the injury to one's reputation caused by the tortfeasor's intentional publication to a third person of defamatory information. The injured person may recover damages for the injury to his reputation caused by the defamatory material. If the defamatory information is spoken orally to a third person, the tort is subcategorized as slander. If the defamatory information is written, it is called libel. Because the writing is permanent and, therefore, capable of more injury to the victim, the courts allow recovery for libel whether the victim can prove actual monetary damages to his reputation. In slander, since the words once said are then forever gone and potential injury thereby diminished, the victim must prove special monetary damages to be able to recover. There is one exception to this rule of special damages and that involves statements considered "slanderous per se." Statements considered "slanderous per se" include accusations of having committed serious crimes, of having contracted loathsome diseases, of lack of chastity and of incompetence in professional or occupational capacity. Each of these were considered so evil in themselves that special damages need not be proven, even though the statements were orally declared.

The cases that follow deal with the tort of defamation and the rule that special damages must be proven if the information published was merely accomplished by oral slander. The reader should note the extention of the definition of libel and how the judges reacted to the changing technological developments which expanded people's ability to harm one another through defamatory remarks.

DICTATION TO STENOGRAPHER— LIBEL?

OSTROWE v. LEE
175 N.E. 505 (1931)
Court of Appeals of New York

■ ■ ■

The complaint...charges that the defendant composed a letter accusing the plaintiff of the crime of larceny; that he dictated this letter to his stenographer; that the stenographer, in obedience to his orders, read the notes and transcribed them; and that the letter so transcribed was received by the plaintiff through the mails...The question is whether [this]...states the publication of a libel...

...A defamatory writing is not published if it is read by no one but the one defamed. Published, it is, however, as soon as read by any one else...The legal consequence is not altered where the symbols reproduced or interpreted are the notes of a stenographer. Publication there still is as result of the dictation, at least where the notes have been examined or transcribed.

Enough that a writing defamatory in content has been read and understood at the behest of the defamer.

The argument is made that the wrong in such a case is slander and not libel.

Very often a stenographer does not grasp the meaning of dictated words till the dictation is over and the symbols have been read. This is particularly likely to be the case where a defamatory charge is made equivocally or with evasive innuendoes. The author who directs his copyist to read, has displayed the writing to the reader as truly and effectively as if he had copied it himself.

To hold otherwise is to lose sight of history and origins. The schism in the law of defamation between the older wrong of slander and the newer one of libel is not the product of mere accident...It has its genesis in evils which the years have not erased. Many things that are defamatory may be said with impunity through the medium of speech. Not so, however, when speech is caught upon the wing and transmuted into print. What gives the sting to the writing is its permanence of form. The spoken word dissolves, but the written one abides and "perpetuates the scandal." When one speaks of a writing in this connection, one does not limit oneself to writings in manuscripts or books. Any symbol suffices—pictures, hieroglyphics, shorthand notes—if only what is written is intelligible to him who reads...There is publication of a libel if a stenographer reads the notes that have been taken by another. Neither the evil nor the result is different when the notes that he reads have been taken by himself.

■ ■ ■

Questions

1. When one *orally* dictates his message to a stenographer, why aren't his defamatory remarks labelled slander?
2. Would it be a libel if the stenographer understood the defamation as dictated, but never transcribed the notes?

MOTION PICTURE—LIBEL?

BROWN v. PARAMOUNT PUBLIX CORPORATIONS
270 N.Y.S. 545 (1934)
Supreme Court, Third Dept., New York

■ ■ ■

The defendant...produced for sale or distribution to and exhibition by moving picture houses throughout the country, a talking motion picture production under the title of "An American Tragedy," in which it has caused to be portrayed, by actors, scenes, characteristics, and otherwise what purports to be a reproduction of the lives of Chester Gillette. Grace Brown, and their families by the similarity of the characters, locations, scenes and incidents so closely associated with the actual incidents of the life oı said Chester Gillette and Grace Brown as to induce the public to believe that the same portrayed the conditions surrounding the lives of said characters. The defendant caused these films to be sent generally throughout the state of New York and especially in the locality where the plaintiff resides. After setting forth the plaintiff's good character as well as that of her husband, their respectability, and the proper rearing and education of their daughter, the complaint then alleges: "But that disregarding the character, appearance, reputation and good name of the plaintiff, the defendant willfully, wrongfully and maliciously, through the manufacture, use, lease and exhibition of said films and pictures, purporting of and concerning the plaintiff, the following false, untrue, slanderous, libelous and defamatory matter, to wit: that the plaintiff was an illiterate, unkempt, slovenly, neglectful and low-grade person; that she was the wife of a mean, illiterate, unkempt, lazy, low-type or degenerate person; that she had neglected her daughter, the said Grace Brown, both educationally and morally, or had compelled her, through lack of care, to seek her own livelihood as a mere child; that she had permitted her said daughter, Grace Brown, to carry on clandestine relations with Chester Gillette, or others, and so depicted the plaintiff, by the manner of said pictures and films, as to render the plaintiff an object of contempt and ridicule among her friends, neighbors, and those who knew her or knew of her; and that the references and allusions to the plaintiff were understood by her acquaintances and friends, and by the public generally, to apply to her; that by such allusions, innuendo and intimation, plaintiff was made therein to appear as poor-white-trash, and a disreputable, untidy product of the hills, without decent care for her daughter and as contributing to the condition in which her daughter found herself;...

...We are met here, however, with a novel and different situation. This is a comparatively new form of libel. It is not accomplished by the printed word, but by the somewhat recent invention of the talking motion picture. The exhibition is made to the public by means of projecting from a film onto a screen a series of a large number of still pictures so rapidly that the objects there displayed present the illusion of moving and acting as in everyday life. Accompanying these projected pictures are sounds mechanically reproduced and so synchronized that they appear to emanate from the objects on the screen. We are told that many of the scenes which upon the screen appear to be real are produced artificially and by illusion. Such a production may be libelous...In the hands of a wrongdoer these devices have untold possibilities toward producing an effective libel...We must base our decision on the allegations of the complaint alone. The production is defamatory of the plaintiff.

■ ■ ■

RADIO—LIBEL?

HARTMANN v. WINCHELL
73 N.E. 2d 30 (1947)
Court of Appeals of New York

■ ■ ■

Does the utterance of defamatory remarks, read from a script into a radio microphone and broadcast, constitute publication of libel?...

In *Snyder v. Andrews*, 1849, it was held that reading a defamatory letter in the presence of a stranger was a sufficient publication to sustain an action for libel...

We accept *Snyder v. Andrews*, as a correct statement of the rule which still prevails in this State but it is said that this rule can have no application to radio broadcasting because the persons who hear the broadcast do not know that the spoken words are being read from a writing.

Unless in the case of broadcasting we are prepared to do what Mansfield, C.J., in 1812 declared he could not do in *Thorley v. Kerry*, namely abolish the distinction between oral and written defamation, we must hold to the reason for the distinction so well expressed in a single phrase in *Ostrowe v. Lee*, 256, N.Y. 36, 39,. . . "What gives the sting to the writing is its permanence of form." This is true whether or not the writing is seen. Visibility of the writing is without significance and we hold that the defendant's defamatory utterance was libel, not slander. We do not reach the question, which has been much discussed, whether broadcasting defamatory matter which has not been reduced to writing should be held to be libellous because of the potentially harmful and widespread effects of such defamation. . .

■ ■ ■

Questions

1. Why are defamations through a motion picture held to be libel?
2. Why did the court say the defamation *spoken* through the radio was libel?
3. What question did the court in *Winchell* avoid answering?

Judge Fuld wrote a concurring opinion to the *Winchell* Case. As such, he voted with the majority justices that the defendant's broadcase was libel, but for a different reason. Since his reasons are not those of the majority, they cannot be cited as precedent. However, his views may be persuasive to future justices considering this type of case.

■ ■ ■

FULD, Judge (concurring).

Though I concur in the conclusion reached—that defendant's utterance over the radio is actionable per se, without allegation or proof of special damage—I cannot agree with the court's rationale. It impresses me as unreal to have liability turn upon the circumstances that defendant read from a script when,—so far as appears from the complaint before us, none of his listeners saw that script or, indeed, was even aware of its existence. As I see it, liability cannot be determined here without first facing and deciding the basic question whether defamation by radio, either with or without a script, should be held actionable per se because of the likelihood of aggravated injury inherent in such broadcasting.

Traditionally, the distinguished characteristics of a libel has been its expression in "some *permanent and visible* form, such as writing, printing, pictures, or effigies," whereas a slanderous statement "is made in spoken words. . . "

Where, as here, the contents of a defamatory writing reach a third person only in the form of spoken words, of "speech * * * upon the wing" (*Ostrowe v. Lee*, 256 N.Y. 36, 39), and with no hint of the existence of a writing, there is a publication of words, not of writing, which, *considered apart from the distinctive features of radio broadcasting*, would, by traditional standards, constitute slander rather than libel.

Our attention is directed to the decision of the English Court of Appeal in *Forrester v. Tyrrell* (1893), and to American cases in accord, that the reading aloud of a libelous document in the hearing and presence of a third person amounts to the publication of a libel. . .

There might, perhaps, be some basis for urging that where such a third person actually *witnesses* the reading of a written defamation, the extent of the consequent damage to reputation in the hearer's estimation is the same as if he had himself read the document. But, certainly, where he does not know, and is not made aware of the existence of a writing, and the scandalous matter reaches him only in the form of spoken words, the resultant injury is essentially the same as if the defamatory words had been uttered without any writing. . . The writing in such circumstances can have no "sting." See *Ostrowe v. Lee*.

If the base of liability for defamation is to be broadened in the case of radio broadcasting, justification should be sought not in the fiction that reading from a paper ipso facto constitutes a publication by writing, but in a frank recognition that sound policy requires such a result...

Abolition of the line between libel and slander would, I agree, be too extreme a break with the past to be achieved without legislation.... It is, however, the function of the courts, when called upon to determine which of two competing standards of liability shall be applied in a novel situation, to re-examine and reapply the old rules and to give them new content in the light of underlying vital principles.

The common-law action on the case for slander, in its sixteenth-century origin, embraced written as well as oral defamation, and the same rules were applicable to both... All other defamation was actionable only upon allegation and proof of special damage. The newer tort of libel—adapted by the common-law judges in the latter part of the seventeenth century...made the writing itself presumptive proof of damage.

This emphasis on the form of publication was apparently designed to cope with the new conditions created by the development of the printing press.

Another development, another invention—here the radio—invites a similar reappraisal of the old rules...

The primary reason assigned by the courts from time to time to justify the imposition of broader liability for libel than for slander has been the greater capacity for harm that a writing is assumed to have because of the wide range of dissemination consequent upon its permanence in form... When account is taken of the vast and far-flung audience reached by radio today—often far greater in number than the readers of the largest metropolitan newspaper...it is evident that the broadest of scandalous utterances is in general as potentially harmful to the defamed person's reputation as a publication by writing. That defamation by radio, in the absence of a script or transcription, lacks the measure of durability possessed by written libel, in nowise lessens its capacity for harm. Since the element of damage is, historically, the basis of the common-law action for defamation...and since it is as reasonable to presume damage from the nature of the medium employed when a slander is broadcast by radio as when published by writing, both logic and policy point the conclusion that defamation by radio should be actionable per se.

■ ■ ■

Questions

1. Was Judge Fuld concerned about the presence or absence of the script?
2. To Judge Fuld, what reasons justified the extension of the definition of libel?
3. How would Judge Fuld label a defamation uttered through a megaphone? Through an amplifier attached to a moving sound truck?

TELEVISION—LIBEL?

SHOR v. BILLINGSLEY
158 N.Y.S. 2d 476 (1956)
Supreme Court, N.Y. County, New York

■ ■ ■

Defendants move to dismiss each of the [three] causes of action for insufficiency. The complaint is based upon a telecast of "The Stork Club Show" over a nationwide network of stations and facilities... Defendant Stork operates "The Stork Club," defendant Mayfair prepared and produced "The Stork Club Show," defendant American Broadcasting telecast the show, and defendant Billingsley acted as a performer and master of ceremonies on the show.

Plaintiff earns his livelihood as the operator and manager of "The Toots Shor Restaurant," with which The Stork Club competes.

During the show, the following conversation was telecast between Billingsley and one Brisson, a guest on the program, and plaintiff's picture was telecast in connection therewith:

"Mr. Billingsley: I see, I would like to show you a few pictures taken here lately. The first—now, how did this picture get in here?

"Mr. Brisson: That is Toots Shor and a man I don't know.

"Mr. Billingsley: You want to know something?

"Mr. Brisson: Want to know something? I saw Toots Shor, he's a good-looking fellow, isn't he?

"Mr. Billingsley: Yes, he is. Want to know something? I wish I had as much money as he owes.

"Mr. Brisson: Owes you or somebody else?

"Mr. Billingsley: Everybody—oh, a lot of people.

"Mr. Brisson: He doesn't owe me anything, but he is a good-looking fellow just the same. A little (indicating)—you know.

"Mr. Billingsley: I wish I could agree with you."

Three causes of action for defamation are pleaded. All allege that the statements so telecast and the innuendoes necessarily implicit therein were false, which defendants knew or should have known, that they were uttered with malice and for the express purpose of injuring plaintiff in his business. The second cause of action adds the allegation that the statements were read by Billingsley from a prepared script or notes. The third adds the allegation that a permanent sound and motion picture film recording was made of the telecast, which recording was exhibited at various times to various individuals.

Defendants content that there is nothing defamatory in the portion of the dialogue complained of. Their argument runs: "Such a statement can hardly be considered defamatory or even inconsistent with our economic society which is fundamentally based upon credit. There is hardly an individual today who does not temporarily owe money and usually, the more solvent an individual, the greater is his or her capacity for credit. It would be no idle remark to wish that one had as much money as some of our 20th century financial wizards would owe on any given date."

Defendants may be able to convince a jury that their language should be given such an innocuous connotation. But I will not hold as a matter of law that the jury must reach such conclusion. Accordingly, the motion is denied as to the second cause of action, *Hartmann v. Winchell*, 296 N.Y. 296, and as to the third cause of action, *Brown v. Paramount-Publix Corp.*, 270 N.Y.S. 544. That leaves for consideration the real problem in the case—whether the first cause of action based upon a telecast not read from a prepared script sounds in libel or in slander.

This precise question has not been passed upon by our appellate courts, nor apparently in any other jurisdiction. *Hartmann v. Winchell*, held that the "utterance of defamatory remarks, *read from a script* into a radio microphone and broadcast, constitute(s) publication of libel," (italics supplied). It expressly did not reach the question "whether broadcasting defamatory matter which has not been reduced to writing should be held to be libellous because of the potentially harmful and widespread effects of such defamation." Fuld, J., concurring, held that it should "because of the likelihood of aggravated injury inherent in such broadcasting."

"Permanence of form" was the factor which justified such an extension; it is not necessarily a prerequisite to a libel. "That defamation by radio * * * lacks the measure of durability possessed by written libel, in nowise lessens its capacity for harm"(Fuld, J., concurring in *Hartmann v. Winchell*).

Cardozo himself was the first to recognize the duty of the courts to extend an established principle of law to a new technological development to which the logic of the principle applied, even though it was not covered by the literal language of the previous decisions. "Precedents drawn from the days of travel by stagecoach do not fit the conditions of travel today. The principle that the danger must be imminent does not change, but the things subject to the principle do change. They are whatever the needs of life in a developing civilization require them to be." Defendants argue that the application of the law of libel to broadcasting or telecasting without a script must be made (if at all) by the legislature rather than the courts. Such legislation has been enacted in England... However, I do not agree that such a change must await legislative action.

Our own courts experience no difficulty in applying the law of libel to the new instrumentality of the motion picture because "in the hands of wrongdoer these devices have untold possibilities toward producing an effective libel." *Brown v. Paramount-Publix Corp.*, 270 N.Y.S. 544, sustained a complaint for libel...

Accordingly, the motion to dismiss is denied as to the first three causes of action.

■ ■ ■

Questions

1. On what authority or theory of recovery did the court accept the second and third causes of action?
2. What reasons are advanced for accepting the first cause of action?
3. Why were the plaintiffs interested in extending the definition of libel from writings to motion pictures, radio or television?
4. What new standard for determination of libel is emerging from these cases?

While the states, like New York, were expanding the coverage of the laws of libel, the Supreme Court began another trend of decisions restricting the power of states to protect individual reputations through libel laws. In so doing, the Court has abolished several of the old common law rules of libel on the grounds that the danger posed to free speech outweighs the states' need for such rules to protect reputation of their citizens. For example, the Court has abolished the common law rule that if a publication is found by the court to be defamatory per se, the plaintiff need not prove that he had been damaged. The Court has held that damages must always be prove. *Gertz v. Robert Welch, Inc.* 418 U.S. 323, (1974). The Court has also abolished the rule that truth is a defense only when published with good motives and to a justifiable end. Truth is now an absolute defense to a libel suit, even when published for malicious purposes. *Time, Inc. v. Hill* 385 U.S. 374 (1967). Finally, the plaintiff must show that the publisher was at least negligent in failing to discover that the publication was false.

The result of these decisions by the Court has been to greatly curtail, if not altogether eliminate, the use of libel laws to protect reputation. Instead, the new tort of privacy is growing as a substitute means of individual protection.

PRIVACY - MODERN SUBSTITUTE FOR LIBEL?

SPAHN v. JULIAN MESSNER, INC.
274 N.Y.S. 2d 877 (1966)
Court of Appeals of New York

■ ■ ■

To the knowing and the novice alike, the name Warren Spahn brings to mind one of professional baseball's great left-handed pitchers. . . .

The size of the audience attracted to each game, whether in person or by transmission, is the profession's bread and butter. The individual player's income will frequently be a direct reflection of his popularity and ability to attract an audience. Professional privacy is thus the very antithesis of the player's need and goal.

With this background, the plaintiff, Warren Spahn, seeks an injunction and damages for the defendants' unauthorized publication of a fictitious biography of his life.

The action is predicated on section 51 of the Civil Rights Law, which authorizes the double remedy where a person's "name, portrait or picture is used within this state for advertising or for the purposes of trade" without that person's written consent. Its enactment may be traced directly to this court's opinion in Roberson v. Rochester Folding Box Co., 171 N.Y. 538, wherein we denied the existence of a legal right to privacy in New York but said that "The legislative body could very well interfere and arbitrarily provide that no one should be permitted for his own selfish purpose to use the picture or the name of another for advertising purposes without his consent.". . .

Over the years since the statute's enactment in 1903, its social desirability and remedial nature have led to its being given a liberal construction consonant with its over-all purpose. But at the same time, ever mindful that the written word or picture is involved, courts have engrafted exceptions and restrictions onto the statute to avoid any conflict with the free dissemination of thoughts, ideas, newsworthy events, and matters of public interest.

One of the clearest exceptions to the statutory prohibition is the rule that a public figure, whether he be such by choice or involuntarily, is subject to the often searching beam of publicity and that, in balance with the legitimate public interest, the law affords his privacy little protection.

But it is erroneous to confuse privacy with "personality" or to assume that privacy, though lost for a certain time or in a certain context, goes forever unprotected. Thus it may be appropriate to say that the plaintiff here, Warren Spahn, is a public personality and that, insofar as his professional career is involved, he is substantially without a right to privacy. That is not to say, however, that his "personality" may be fictionalized and that, as fictionalized, it may be exploited for the defendants' commercial benefit through the medium of an unauthorized biography.

The factual reporting of newsworthy persons and events is in the public interest and is protected. The fictitious is not. This is the heart of the cases in point.

The plaintiff's status as a public figure makes him newsworthy and thus places his biography outside the protection afforded by the statute. But the plaintiff does not seek an injunction and damages for the unauthorized publication of his biography. He seeks only to restrain the publication of that which purports to be his biography.

In the present case, the findings of fact go far beyond the establishment of minor errors in an otherwise accurate biography. They establish "dramatization, imagined dialogue, manipulated chronologies, and fictionalization of events". In the language of Justice Markowitz, who presided at the trial, "the record unequivocally establishes that the book publicizes areas of Warren Spahn's personal and private life, albeit inaccurate and distorted, and consists of a host, a preponderant percentage, of factual errors, distortions and fanciful passages". A sufficient number of specific instances of falsification are set forth in that opinion to make repetition here unnecessary.

It is urged upon us that application of the statute to the publication of a substantially fictitious biography will run afoul of the freedoms of speech and the press guaranteed by the First and Fourteenth Amendments to the Federal Constitution. . .

. . . The free speech which is encouraged and essential to the operation of a healthy government is something quite different from an individual's attempt to enjoin the publication of a fictitious biography of him. No public interest is served by protecting the dissemination of the latter. We perceive no constitutional infirmities in this respect.

We thus conclude that the defendants' publication of a fictitious biography of the plaintiff constitutes an unauthorized exploitation of his personality for purposes of trade and that it is proscribed by section 51 of the Civil Rights Law.

■ ■ ■

Questions

1. How was the law of privacy created in New York?
2. What is a "public figure"? Could a public figure prohibit the publication of an unauthorized factual biography? A fictitious biography?

CHANGING A RULE OF LAW

Cases tell us a great deal about the customs, habits, traditions, and moral standards of people at the time of their decision. The facts of each case and the attitude of the courts in explaining their result reflect the changing environment. Thus, as social, political, economic, and technological changes take place in our society, legal standards are modified and changed. The following cases dramatize situations in which the law has been kept contemporary by the courts. The courts make new laws by interpreting either the common law, the enactments of the legislatures, or the constitutions of the states and of the United States.

In the last half of the twentieth century with its advances in medical sciences, the debate concerning the rights of unborn children has increased. These debates have flourished in legislative halls and in executive and administrative processes. The following cases indicate that the courts have not been spared of these controversies either. The courts have been utilized as an instrument to settle controversies over the rights of the unborn in certain instances. One's philosophy, religious training, and moral standards influence one's conclusions concerning these difficult issues. Decisions by the courts on questions containing moral issues do not bring universal public agreement.

WRONGFUL INJURY

WOODS v. LANCET
303 N.Y. 349 (1951)
Supreme Court, Appellate Div., New York

■ ■ ■

The complaint served on behalf of this infant plaintiff alleges that, while the infant was in his mother's womb during the ninth month of her pregnancy, he sustained, through the negligence of defendant, such serious injuries that he came into this world permanently maimed and disabled. Defendant moved to dismiss the complaint as not stating a cause of action, thus taking the position that its allegations, though true, gave the infant no right to recover damages in the courts of New York. The Special Term granted the motion and dismissed the suit, citing *Drobner v. Peters,* 232 N.Y. 220...

...The precise question for us on this appeal is: shall we follow *Drobner v. Peters,* or shall we bring the common law of this State, on this question, into accord with justice? I think, as New York State's court of last resort, we should make the law conform to right.

...*Drobner v. Peters* must be examined against a background of history and of the legal thought of its time and of the thirty years that have passed since it was handed down. Early British and American common law gives no definite answer to our questions, so it is not profitable to go back farther than *Dietrich Inhabitants v. Northampton,* 138 Mass. 14, decided in 1884, with an opinion by Justice Holmes, and, apparently the first American case...

The principal ground asserted by the Massachusetts Supreme Court, for a denial of recovery was that "the unborn child was a part of the mother at the time of the injury" and that "any damage to it which was not too remote to be recovered for at all was recoverable by her" (the mother)...

There were, in the early years of this century, rejections of such suits by other courts, with various fact situations involving before-birth traumas... and quite recently, Massachusetts has reaffirmed the Dietrich rule... Thus, when *Drobner v. Peters* came to this court in 1921, there had been no decisions upholding such suits,...

In *Drobner v. Peters*, this court, finding no precedent for maintaining the suit, adopted the general theory of *Dietrich v. Inhabitants of Northampton*, taking into account, besides the lack of authority to support the suit, the practical difficulties of proof in such cases, and the theoretical lack of separate human existence of an infant *in utero*. It is not unfair to say that the basic reason for *Drobner v. Peters* was absence of precedent. However, since 1921, numerous and impressive affirmative precedents have been developed...

What, then, stands in the way of a reversal here? Surely, as an original proposition, we would, today, be hard put to it to find a sound reason for the old rule. Following *Drobner v. Peters*, would call for an affirmance but the chief basis for that holding (lack of precedent) no longer exists. And it is not a very strong reason, anyhow, in a case like this... Negligence law is common law, and the common law had been molded and changed and brought up-to-date in many another case. Our court said, long ago, that it had not only the right, but the duty to re-examine a question where justice demands it,... That opinion notes that Chancellor Kent, more than a century ago, had stated... that decisions which seem contrary to reason "ought to be examined without fear, and revised without reluctance, rather than to have the character of our law impaired, and the beauty and harmony of the system destroyed, by the perpetuity of error."... We act in the finest common-law tradition when we adapt and alter decisional law to produce common-sense justice.

The other objection to recovery here is the purely theoretical one that a foetus *in utero* has no existence of its own separate from that of its mother, that is, that it is not "a being *in esse*"...

To hold, as matter of law, that no viable foetus has any separate existence which the law will recognize is for the law to deny a simple and easily demonstrable fact. This child, when injured, was in fact, alive and capable of being delivered and of remaining alive, separate from its mother. We agree with the dissenting Justice below that "To deny the infant relief in this case is not only a harsh result, but its effect is to do reverence to an outmoded, timeworn fiction not founded on fact and within common knowledge untrue and unjustified."

The judgments should be reversed...

LEWIS, Judge (dissenting).

I agree with the view of a majority of the court that prenatal injury to a child should not go unrequited by the one at fault. If, however, an unborn child is to be endowed with the right to enforce such requital by an action at law, I think that right should not be created by a judicial decision on the facts in a single case. Better, I believe, that the right should be the product of legislative action taken after hearings at which the Legislature can be advised, by the aid of medical science and research, not only as to the stage of gestation at which a foetus is considered viable, but also as to appropriate means—by time limitation for suit and otherwise—for avoiding abuses which might result from the difficulty of tracing causation from prenatal injury to postnatal deformity. When, in England, the right—unknown to the common law—was created which permitted suit to recover damages for negligently causing the death of a human being, it was accomplished by legislative action. In our own jurisdiction a similar right of action—carefully limited as to time and by other measures to prevent abuse—has long been the subject of statute law adopted by the process incident to statutory enactment. That same process, in my opinion, is peculiarly appropriate for the solution of the problem now before us where unknown factors abound.

Accordingly, I dissent and vote for affirmance.

■ ■ ■

Questions

1. What technological change required a modification of the law in *Woods*? What "difficulties of proof" exist in a case like *Woods*? Do these "difficulties" suggest reasons for the old rule denying recovery to the infant?
2. Should the lack of precedent preclude the formation of the new law? Should a previous legal fiction (infant has no existence separate from its mother) preclude a new ruling enlightened by medical science?
3. Why did the dissending judge want to follow the precedent of *Drobner v. Peters*?

WRONGFUL PREGNANCY

TROPPI v. SCARF
187 N.W. 2d 511 (1971)
Court of Appeals of Michigan

■ ■ ■

In August 1964, plaintiffs were the parents of seven children, ranging in age from six to sixteen years of age. John Troppi was 43 years old, his wife 37.

While pregnant with an eighth child, Mrs. Troppi suffered a miscarriage. She and her husband consulted with their physician and decided to limit the size of their family. The physician prescribed an oral contraceptive, Norinyl, as the most desirable means of insuring that Mrs. Troppi would bear no more children. He telephoned the prescription to defendant, Frank H. Scarf, a licensed pharmacist. Instead of filling the prescription, Scarf negligently supplied Mrs. Troppi with a drug called Nardil, a mild transquilizer.

Believing that the pills she had purchased were contraceptives, Mrs. Troppi took them on a daily basis. In December 1964, Mrs. Troppi became pregnant. She delivered a well-born son on August 12, 1965.

Plaintiff's complaint alleges four separate items of damage: (1) Mrs. Troppi's lost wages; (2) medical and hospital expenses; (3) the pain and anxiety of pregnancy and childbirth, and (4) the economic cost of rearing the eighth child....

We begin by noting that the fundamental conditions of tort liability are present here. The defendant's conduct constituted a clear breach of duty. A pharmacist is held to a very high standard of care in filling prescriptions. When he negligently supplied a drug other than the drug requested, he is liable for resulting harm to the purchaser.

We assume, for the purpose of appraising the correctness of the ruling dismissing the complaint, that the defendant's negligence was a cause in fact of Mrs. Troppi's pregnancy. The possibility that she might become pregnant was certainly a foreseeable consequence of the defendant's failure to fill a prescription for birth control pills; we therefore, could not say that it was not a proximate cause of the birth of the child.

Setting aside, for the moment, the subtleties of the damage question, it is at least clear that the plaintiffs have expended significant sums of money as a direct and proximate result of the defendant's negligence. The medical and hospital expenses of Mrs. Troppi's confinement and her loss of wages arose from the defendant's failure to fill the prescription properly. Pain and suffering, like that accompanying childbirth, have long been recognized as compensable injuries.

This review of the elements of tort liability points up the extraordinary nature of the trial court's holding that the plaintiffs were entitled to no recovery as a matter of law.

We have here a negligent, wrongful act by the defendant, which act directly and proximately caused injury to the plaintiffs. . . .

In *Shaheen v. Knight* (Pa. 1957), a Pennsylvania court ruled that a physician who violated his promise to perform an elective sterilization operation was not liable for the consequences of his breach of contract. . . .

Underlying the *Shaheen* opinion are two principal ideas. The first is that the birth of a healthy child confers such an undoubted benefit upon the plaintiff as to outweigh, as a matter of law, the expenses of delivering and rearing the child. The second is that if the child is really unwanted, plaintiff has a duty to place him for adoption, in effect to mitigate damages. . .

Our review has been conducted to determine whether the defendant in this case should be exempted from the consequences of his negligence. We conclude that there is no valid reason why the trier of the fact should not be free to assess damages as it would in any other negligence case. . . .

Overriding Benefit. It is arguable that the birth of a healthy child confers so substantial a benefit as to outweigh the expenses of his birth and support. In the great majority of cases, this is no doubt true, else, presumably, people would not choose to multiply so freely. But can we say, as a matter of law, that a healthy child always confers such an overriding benefit?

Thus, if the defendant's tortious conduct conferred a benefit to the same interest which was harmed by his conduct, the dollar value of the benefit is to be subtracted from the dollar value of the injury in arriving at the amount of damages properly awardable.

Since pregnancy and its attendant anxiety, incapacity, pain and suffering are inextricably related to child bearing, we do not think it would be sound to attempt to separate those segments of damage from the economic costs of an unplanned child in applying the "same interest" rule. Accordingly, the benefits of the unplanned child may be weighed against all the elements of claimed damage.

The trial court evidently believes, as did the court in *Shaheen v. Knight*, that application of the benefits rule prevents any recovery for the expenses of rearing an unwanted child. This is unsound. Such a rule would be equivalent to declaring that in every case, as a matter of law, the services and companionship of a child have a dollar equivalent greater than the economic costs of his support, to say nothing of the inhibitions, the restrictions, and the pain and suffering caused by pregnancy and the obligation to rear the child.

There is a growing recognition that the financial "services" which parents can expect from their offspring are largely illusory. As to companionship, cases decided when "loss of companionship" was a compensable item of damage for the wrongful death of a child reveal no tendency on the part of juries to value companionship so highly as to outweigh expenses in every foreseeable case. . . .

What must be appreciated is the diversity of purposes and circumstances of the women who use oral contraceptives. Unmarried women who seek the pleasures of sexual intercourse without the perils of unwed motherhood, married women who wish to delay slightly the start of a family in order to retain the career flexibility which many young couples treasure, married women for whom the birth of another child would pose a threat to their own health or the financial security of their families, all are likely users of oral contraceptives. Yet it is clear that in each case the consequences arising from negligent interference with their use will vary widely. A rational legal system must award damages that correspond with these differing injuries. The benefits rule will serve to accomplish this objective.

Consider, for example, the case of the unwed college student who becomes pregnant due to a pharmacist's failure to fill properly her prescription for oral contraceptives. Is it not likely that she has suffered far greater damage than the young newlywed who, although her pregnancy arose from the same sort of negligence, had planned the use of contraceptives only temporarily, say, while she and her husband took an extended honeymoon trip? Without the benefits rule, both plaintiffs would be entitled to recover substantially the same damages.

Application of the benefits rule permits a trier of fact to find that the birth of a child has materially benefitted the newly wed couple, notwithstanding the inconvenience of an interrupted honeymoon, and to reduce the net damage award accordingly. Presumably a trier of fact would find that the "family interests" of the unmarried coed has been enhanced very little.

The essential point, of course, is that the trier must have the power to evlauate the benefit according to all the circumstances of the case presented. Family size, family income, age of the parents, and marital status are some, but not all, the factors which the trier must consider in determining the extent to which the birth of a particular child represents a benefit to his parents. That the benefits so conferred and calculated will vary widely from case to case is inevitable.

Mitigating Damages. It has been suggested that parents who seek to recover for the birth of an unwanted child are under a duty to mitigate damages by placing the child for adoption. If the child is "unwanted", why should they object to placing him for adoption, thereby reducing the financial burden on defendant for his maintenance?

However, to impose such a duty upon the injured plaintiff is to ignore the very real difference which our law recognizes between the avoidance of conception and the disposition of the human organism after conception. . . At the moment of conception, an entirely different set of legal obligations is imposed upon the parents. A living child almost universally gives rise to emotional and spiritual bonds which few parents can bring themselves to break.

Once a child is born he obviously should be treated with love regardless of whether he was wanted when he was conceived. Many, perhaps most, persons living today are conceptional accidents in the sense that their parents did not desire that a child result from the particular intercourse in which the person was conceived. Nevertheless, when the child is born, most parents accept him with love. That the plaintiffs accepted their eighth child does not change the fact that the birth of another child, seven years younger than the youngest of their previously born children, unbalanced their life style and was not desired by them.

The doctrine which requires a plaintiff to take measures to minimize the financial consequencs of a defendant's negligence requires only that reasonable measures be taken. . . .

In determining reasonableness, the best interests of the child must be considered. The law has long recognized the desirability of permitting a child to be reared by his natural parents. The plaintiffs may have believed that the hazards of adoption would damage the child.

A child will not be taken from his mother without her consent. . . The mother's right to keep the child is not dependent on whether she desired the conception of the child.

As a matter of personal conscience and choice parents may wish to keep an unwanted child. Indeed, parents have been known to keep children that many think should be institutionalized, e.g., mentally retarded children, not because of any anticipated joy or happiness that the child will bring to them but out of a sense of obligation. So, too, the parents of an unplanned, healthy child may feel, and properly so, that whether they wanted the child or not is beside the point once the child is born and that they have an obligation to rear the child as best they can rather than subject him to rearing by unknown persons.

Further, even though the parents may not want to rear the child they may conclude that the psychological impact on them of rejecting the child and placing him for adoption, never seeing him again, would be such that, making the best of a bad situation, it is better to rear the child than to place him for adoption.

Many women confronted with an unwanted pregnancy will abort the fetus, legally or illegally. Some will bear the child and place him for adoption. Many will bear the child, keep and rear him. The defendant does not have the right to insist that the victim of his negligence have the emotional and mental makeup of a woman who is willing to abort or place a child for adoption. If the negligence of a tortfeasor results in conception of a child by a woman whose emotional and mental makeup is inconsistent with aborting or placing the child for adoption, then, under the principle that the tortfeasor takes the injured party as he finds him, the tortfeasor cannot complain that the damages that will be assessed against him are greater than those that would be determined if he had negligently caused the conception of a child by a woman who was willing to abort or place the child for adoption.

While the reasonableness of a plaintiff's efforts to mitigate is ordinarily to be decided by the trier of fact, we are persuaded to rule, as a matter of law, that no mother, wed or unwed, can reasonably be required to abort (even if legal) or place her child for adoption. The plaintiffs are entitled to have the jurors instructed that if they find that negligence of the defendant was a cause in fact of the plaintiff's injury, they may not, in computing the amount, if any, of the plaintiff's damages, take into consideration the fact that the plaintiffs might have aborted the child or placed the child into adoption.

Uncertainty of Damages. Of the four items of damage claimed by plaintiffs, each is capable of reasonable ascertainment. The medical and hospital expenses and Mrs. Troppi's lost wages may be computed with some exactitude. Plaintiffs' claimed pain and anxiety, if not capable of precise determination, is a component of damage which triers of fact traditionally have been entrusted to ascertain. As to the costs of rearing the child until his majority, this is a computation which is routinely performed in countless cases.

It should be clear that ascertainment of *gross* damages is a routine task. Whatever uncertainty attends the final award arises from application of the benefits rule, which requires that the trier of fact compute the dollar value of the companionship and services of an unwanted child. Placing a dollar value on these segments may well be more difficult than assessing damages for, say, Mrs. Troppi's lost wages. But difficulty in determining the amount to be subtracted from the gross damages does not justify throwing up our hands and denying recovery altogether.

The assessment of damages in this case is properly within the competence of the trier of fact. The element of uncertainty in the net recovery does not render the damages unduly speculative.

Reversed and remanded for trial.

■ ■ ■

Questions

1. Did the analogous area of a physician's liability for failure of a nontherapeutic sterilization operation resulting in the birth of an unwanted child provide relevant precedent?

2. What actual loss or injury resulted in *Troppi?*

3. In *Shaheen v. Knight*, (1957) the court concluded that "we are of the opinion that to allow damages for the normal birth of a normal child is foreign to the universal public sentiment of the people." Do sentiments change?

4. Mitigation of damages involves the responsibility of the injured party to take reasonable steps to avoid or minimize further loss. In order to mitigate their damages, must the plaintiff place their unwanted newborn child for adoption?

5. The court concluded that although the benefits of having the child are to be deducted from the gross damages, such benefits do not as a matter of law override the damages suffered. Can you give any examples?

6. Would the awarding of damages to the parents for "wrongful conception" cause the child to feel unwanted and emotionally like a "bastard?"

   The first case to expressly reject (this)...argument and to hold that the parents of an unplanned normal child could recover all damages proximately caused by a negligently performed sterilization operation was *Custodio v. Bauer*, 251 Cal. App.2d 303, (1967).

   Rejecting the argument that an award of damages could reduce the child to an emotional bastard, the court found that the possibility of psychological harm was

no greater than in any other case where a child learns that his existence is the
result of his parents' ineptitude at birth control. Most persuasively, the court
observed that modern attitudes with respect to family establishment and the use
of contraceptives had changed, and further insinuated that the birth of an unplanned child may now be viewed by some as something less than a "blessed
event.".

Sherlock v. Stillwater Clinic, 260 N.W. 2d 169 (Minn. 1977).

When the courts are called upon to interpret a statute enacted by the legislature,
their task is one of interpreting the words according to the "legislative intent."
However, it is not always easy to determine the intent of the legislature. Consequently,
courts use differing techniques and give differing weights to those techniques in
reaching their decisions. In the following case the court must determine the proper
interpretation of a statute. Each of the parties to the case argue differing interpretations and advance various techniques of statutory interpretation to support their
cause. The reader should note not only the decision of the case in relation to the rights
conferred by the legislature on the unborn child, but also the various techniques of
legislative interpretation utilized by the court in reaching its decision.

WRONGFUL DISCRIMINATION

BURNS v. ALCALA
420 U.S. 575 (1975)
Supreme Court of the United States

■ ■ ■

POWELL, Mr. Justice.

Respondents, residents of Iowa, were pregnant at the time they filed this action.
Their circumstances were such that their children would be eligible for Aid to Families
with Dependent Children (AFDC) benefits upon birth. They applied for welfare
assistance but were refused on the ground that they had no "dependent children"
eligible for the AFDC program. Respondents then filed this action against petitioners,
Iowa welfare officials. On behalf of themselves and other women similarly situated,
respondents contended that the Iowa policy of denying benefits to unborn children
conflicted with the federal standard of eligibility under § 406(a) of the Social Security
Act... The District Court...held that unborn children are "dependent children"
within the meaning of § 406(a)... The Court has held that under... the Social
Security Act, federal participation in state AFDC programs is conditioned on the
State's offering benefits to all persons who are eligible under federal standards. The
State must provide benefits to all individuals who meet the federal definition of
"dependent child" and who are "needy" under state standards, unless they are
excluded or aid is made optional by another provision of the Act... The definition of
"dependent child" appears in § 406(a) of the Act... The section makes no mention of
pregnant women or unborn children as such.

Respondents contend, citing dictionary definitions, that the word "child" can be
used to include unborn children. This is enough, they say, to make the statute
ambiguous and to justify construing the term "dependent child" in light of legislative
purposes and administrative interpretation....

Our analysis of the Social Security Act does not support a conclusion that the
legislative definition of "dependent child" includes unborn children. Following the
axiom that words used in a statute are to be given their ordinary meaning in the
absence of persuasive reasons to the contrary, and reading the definition of "dependent child" in its statutory context, we conclude that Congress used the word "child" to
refer to an individual already born, with an existence separate from its mother.

As originally enacted in 1935, the Social Security Act made no provision for the
needs of the adult taking care of a "dependent child." It authorized aid only for the

child and offered none to support the mother... The failure to provide explicitly for the special circumstances of pregnant women strongly suggests that Congress had no thought of providing AFDC benefits to "dependent children" before birth.

The purposes of the Act also are persuasive. The AFDC program was originally conceived to substitute for the practice of removing needy children from their homes and placing them in institutions, and to free widowed and divorced mothers from the necessity of working, so that they could remain home to supervise their children...

Congress did not ignore the needs of pregnant women or the desirability of adequate prenatal care. In Title V of the Social Security Act, Congress provided federal funding for prenatal and postnatal health services to mothers and infants, explicitly designed to reduce infant and maternal mortality. In selecting this form of aid for pregnant women, Congress had before it proposals to follow the lead of some European countries that provided "maternity benefits" to support expectant mothers for a specified period before and after childbirth. If Congress had intended to include a similar program in the Social Security Act, it very likely would have done so explicitly rather than by relying on the term "dependent child," at best a highly ambiguous way to refer to unborn children.

Respondents have also relied on HEW's regulation allowing payment of AFDC benefits on behalf of unborn children. They ask us to defer to the agency's long-standing interpretation of the statute it administers. Respondents have provided the Court with copies of letters and interoffice memoranda that preceded adoption of this policy in 1941... These papers suggest that the agency initially may have taken the position that the statutory phrase "dependent children" included unborn children.

A brief filed by the Solicitor General on behalf of HEW in this case disavows respondents' interpretaiton of the ACT. HEW contends that unborn children are not included in the federal eligibility standard and that the regulation authorizing federal participation in AFDC payments to pregnant women is based on the agency's general authority to make rules for efficient administraiton of the Act. The regulation is consistent with this explanation. It appears in a subseciton with other rules authorizing temporary aid, at the option of the States, to individuals in the process of gaining or losing eligibility for the AFDC program. For example, one of the accompanying rules authorizes States to pay AFDC benefits to a relative 30 days before the eligible child comes to live in his home. HEW's current explanation of the regulation deprives respondents' argument of any significant support...

Nor can respondents make a convincing claim of congressional acquiescence in HEW's prior policy. In 1972, in the context of major Social Security legislation, both Houses of Congress passed bills to revise the AFDC system. One seciton of the bill passed in the Senate would have amended the definition of "dependent child" expressly to exclude unborn children. The House bill would have substituted an entirely new definition of eligibility... The accompanying committee report specified that under the new definition unborn children would not be eligible for aid. Both bills passed the respective Houses of Congress, but none of the AFDC amendments appeared in the final legislation, because the House and Senate conferees were unable to agree on the underlying principle of welfare reform. All efforts to amend AFDC were postponed for another session of Congress. Under the circumstances, failure to enact the relatively minor provision relating to unborn children cannot be regarded as approval of HEW's practice of allowing optional benefits. To the extent this legislative history sheds any light on congressional intent, it tends to rebut the claim that Congress by silence has acquiesced in the former HEW view that unborn children eligible for AFDC payments...

MARSHALL, Mr. Justice, dissenting.

As the majority implicitly acknowledges, the evidence available to help resolve the issue of statutory construction presented by this case does not point decisively in either direciton. When it passed the Social Security Act in 1935 Congress gave no indication that it meant to include or exclude unborn children from the definition of "dependent child." Nor has it shed any further light on the question other than to consider, and fail to pass, legislation that would indisputably have excluded unborn children from coverage.

The majority has parsed the language and touched on the legislative history of the Act in an effort to muster support for the view that unborn children were not meant to benefit from the Act. Even given its best face, however, this evidence provides only modest support for the majority's position. The lengthy course of administrative practice cuts quite the other way. Although the question is a close one, I agree with the conclusion reached by five of the six courts of appeals that have considered this issue, and would accordingly affirm the judgment below.

■ ■ ■

Questions

1. Some courts utilize a techinque of statutory interpretation called the "plain meaning rule." With this rule the words used by the legislature are to be given their usual and ordinary meaning in the context in which they are used. Did the court in *Burns* use this rule?
2. The second technique of legislative interpretation is "purpose" interpretation. The words are to be interpreted in light of the purpose of Congress in passing the law. The purpose may indicate a certain interpretation that is not consistent with the plain meaning of the words actually used by the legislature. Did the court in *Burns* follow this procedure of interpretation?
3. Often in deciding the proper interpretation of a statute, the court defers great weight to the judgment or interpretation of the administrative agency empowered to enforce the statute. Was any such deference shown in *Burns?*
4. The dissenting justice relies on what sources of statutory interpretation? Does he place differing weights on the techniques of statutory interpretation?

WRONGFUL DEATH

ROE v. WADE
410 U.S. 113 (1973)
Supreme Court of the United States

■ ■ ■

BLACKMUN, Mr. Justice.

The Texas statutes under attack here are typical of those that have been in effect in many States for approximately a century... These make it a crime to "procure an abortion," as therein defined, or to attempt one, except with respect to "an abortion procured or attempted by medical advice for the purpose of saving the life of the mother." Similar statutes are in existence in a majority of the States.

It perhaps is not generally appreciated that the restrictive criminal abortion laws in effect in a majority of states today are of relatively recent vintage. Those laws, generally proscribing abortion or its attempt at any time during pregnancy except when necessary to preserve the pregnant woman's life, are not of ancient or even of common law origin. Instead, they derive from statutory changes effected, for the most part, in the latter half of the 19th century...

The common Law. It is undisputed that at the common law, abortion performed *before* "quickening"—the first recongizable movement of the fetus *in utero,* appearing usually from the 16th to the 18th week of pregnancy—was not an indictable offense...

It is thus apparent that at common law, at the time of the adoption of our Constitution, and throughout the major portion of the 19th century, abortion was viewed with less disfavor than under most American statutes currently in effect. Phrasing it another way, a woman enjoyed a substantially broader right to terminate a pregnancy than she does in most States today. At least with respect to the early stage of pregnancy, and very possibly without such a limitation the opportunity to make this choice was present in this country well into the 19th century. Even later, the law continued for some time to treat less punitively an abortion procured in early pregnancy...

Three reasons have been advanced to explain historically the enactment of criminal abortion laws in the 19th century and to justify their continued existence.

It has been argued occasionally that these laws were the product of a Victorian social concern to discourage illicit sexual conduct. Texas, however, does not advance this justification in the present case, and it appears that no court or commentator has taken the argument seriously...

A second reason is concerned with abortion as a medical procedure. When most criminal abortion laws were first enacted, the procedure was a hazardous one for the woman... Thus it has been argued that a State's real concern in enacting a criminal abortion law was to protect the pregnant woman, that is, to restrain her from submitting to a precedure that placed her life in serious jeopardy.

Modern medical techniques have altered this situation. Appellants... refer to medical data indicating that abortion in early pregnancy, that is, prior to the end of the first trimester, although not without its risk, is now relatively safe. Mortality rates for women undergoing early abortions, where the procedure is legal, appear to be as low or lower than the rates for normal childbirth. Consequently, any interest of the State in protecting,the woman from an inherently hazardous procedure, except when it would be equally dangerous for her to forgo it, has largely disappeared. Of course, important State interests in the area of health and medical standards do remain. The State has a legitimate interest in seeing to it that abortion, like any other medical procedure, is performed under circumstances that insure maximum safety for the patient. This interest obviously extends at least to the performing physician and his staff, to the facilities involved, to the availability of after-care, and to adequate provision for any complication or emergency that might arise. The prevalence of high mortality rates at illegal "abortion mills" strengthens, rather than weakens, the State's interest in regulating the conditions under which abortions are performed. Moreover, the risk to the woman increases as her pregnancy continues. Thus the State retains a definite interest in protecting the woman's own health and safety when an abortion is proposed at a late stage of pregnancy.

The third reason is the State's interest—some phrase it in terms of duty—in protecting prenatal life. Some of the argument for this justification rests on the theory that a new human life is present from the moment of conception. the State's interest and general obligation to protect life then extends, it is argued, to prenatal life. Only when the life of the pregnant mother herself is at stake, balanced against the life she carries within her, should the interest of the embryo of fetus not prevail. Logically, of course, a legitimate state interest in this area need not stand or fall on acceptance of the belief that the life begins at conception or at some other point prior to live birth. In assessing the State's interest, recognition may be given to the less rigid claim that as long as at least *potential* life is involved, the State may assert interests beyond the protection of the pregnant woman alone...

It is with these interests, and the weight to be attached to them, that this case is concerned.

The Constitution does not explicitly mention any right of privacy. In a line of decisions, however... the court has recognized that a right of personal privacy, or a guarantee of certain areas or zones of privacy, does exist under the constitution... They also make it clear that the right has some extension to activities relating to marriage, procreation, contraception, and child rearing and education...

This right of privacy, whether it be founded in the Fourteenth Amendment's concept of personal liberty and restrictions upon state action, as we feel it is, or, as the District court determined, in the Ninth Amendment's reservation of rights to the people, is broad enough to encompass a woman's decision whether or not to terminate her pregnancy. The detriment that the State would impose upon the pregnant woman by denying this choice altogether is apparent. Specific and direct harm medically diagnosable even in early pregnancy may be involved. Maternity, or additional offspring, may force upon the woman a distressful life and future. Psychcological harm may be imminent. Mental and physical health may be taxed by child care. There is also the distress, for all concerned, associated with the unwanted child, and there is the problem of bringing a child into a family already unable, psychologically and otherwise, to care for it. In other cases, as in this one, the additional difficulties and continuing stigma of unwed motherhood may be involved. All these are factors the woman and her responsible physician necessarily will consider in consultation.

On the basis of elements such as these, appellants... argue that the woman's right is absolute and that she is entitled to terminate her pregnancy at whatever time, in whatever way, and for whatever reason she alone chooses. With this we do not agree. Appellant's arguments that Texas either has no valid interest at all in regulating the abortion decision, or no interest strong enough to support any limitation upon the woman's sole determination, is unpersuasive. The Court's decisions recognizing a right of privacy also acknowledge that some state regulation in areas protected by that right is appropriate. As noted above, a state may properly assert important interests in safeguarding health, in maintaining medical standards, and in protecting potential life. At some point in pregnancy, these respective interests become sufficiently compelling to sustain regulation of the factors that govern the abortion decision. The privacy right involved, therefore, cannot be said to be absolute. In fact, it is not clear to us that the claim asserted... that one has an unlimited right to do with one's body as one pleases bears a close relationship to the right of privacy previously articulated in the Court's decisions. The Court has refused to recognize an unlimited right of this kind in the past.

We therefore conclude that the right of personal privacy includes the abortion decision, but that this right is not unqualified and must be considered against important state interests in regulation...

Where certain "fundamental rights" are involved, the Court has held that regulation limiting these rights may be justified only by a "compelling state interest," and that legislative enactments must be narrowly drawn to express only the legitimate state interests at stake...

Texas urges that, apart from the Fourteenth Amendment, life begins at conception and is present throughout pregnancy, and that, therefore, the State has a compelling interest in protecting that life from and after conception. We need not resolve the difficult question of when life begins. When those trained in the respective disciplines of medicine, philosphy, and theology are unable to arrive at any consensus, the judiciary, at this point in the development of man's knowledge, is not in a position to speculate as to the answer...

In view of all this, we do not agree that, by adopting one theory of life, Texas may override the rights of the pregnant woman that are at stake. We repeat, however, that the State does have an important and legitimate interest in preserving an protecting the health of the pregnant woman, whether she be a resident of the State or a non-resident who seeks medical consultation and treatment there, and that it has still *another* important and legitimate interest in protecting the potentiality of human life. These interests are separate and distinct. Each grows in substantiality as the woman approaches term and, at a point during pregnancy, each becomes "compelling."

With respect to the State's important and legitimate interest in the health of the mother, the "compelling" point, in the light of present medical knowledge, is at approximately the end of the first trimester. This is so because of the now established medical fact... that until the end of the first trimester mortality in abortion is less than mortality in normal childbirth. It follows that, from and after this point, a State may regulate the abortion procedure to the extent that the regulation reasonably relates to the preservation and protection of maternal health. Examples of permissible state regulation in this area are requirements as to the qualifications of the person who is to perform the abortion; as to the licensure of that person; as to the facility in which the procedure is to be performed, that is, whether it must be a hospital or may be a clinic or some other place of less-than-hospital status; as to the licensing of the facility; and the like.

This means, on the other hand, that, for the period of pregnancy prior to this "compelling" point, the attending physician, in consultation with his patient, is free to determine, without regulation by the State, that in his medical judgment the patient's pregnancy should be terminated. If that decision is reached, the judgment may be effectuated by an abortion free of interference by the States.

With respect to the State's important and legitimate interest in potential life, the "compelling" point is at viability. This is so because the fetus then presumably has the capability of meaningful life outside the mother's womb. State regulation protective of fetal life after viability thus has both logical and biological justifications. If the State is interested in protecting fetal life after viability, it may go so far as to proscribe abortion during that period except when it is necessary to preserve the life or health of the mother.

Measured against these standards, the Texas Penal Code, in restricting legal abortions to those "procured or attempted by medical advice for the purpose of saving the life of the mother," sweeps too broadly. The statute makes no distinction between abortions performed early in pregnancy and those performed later, and it limits to a single reason, "saving" the mother's life, the legal justification for the procedure. The statute, therefore, cannot survive the constitutional attack made upon it here...

This holding we feel, is consistent with the relative weights of the respective interests involved, with the lessons and example of medical and legal history, with the lenity of the common law and with the demands of the profound problems of the present day. The decision leaves the State free to place increasing restrictions on abortion as the period of pregnancy lengthens, so long as those restrictions are tailored to the recognized state interests. The decision vindicates the right of the physician to administer medical treatment according to his professional judgment up to the points where important state interests provide compelling justifications for intervention. Up to those points the abortion decision in all its aspects is inherently, and primarily, a medical decision, and basic responsibility for it must rest with the physician. If an individual practitioner abuses the privilege of exercising proper medical judgment, the usual remedies, judicial and intra-professional, are available.

■ ■ ■

Questions

1. What "law" was the Court "interpreting" in *Roe*?
2. For the stage of pregnancy prior to the end of first trimester, the abortion decision and its effectuation must be left to whom?
3. What may the state do during the second trimester?
4. After the fetus has reached "viability," may the state proscribe abortion?
5. May the state proscribe an abortion which is necessary for the preservation of the life or health of the mother?

ADHERING TO PRECEDENT

In our legal system, the mandate of the courts has been to apply and interpret settled law as well as modify law to new social conditions. Often when adhering to legal precedent and refusing to alter existing law, the courts have decided to leave any change in the law to the decision processes of the legislature. This deference to the legislative process is illustrated in the following cases.

DEFERENCE TO LEGISLATURE

The Constitution of the United States made the central government one of limited powers. Article I, Section 8, of the U.S. Constitution details the legislative power of the U.S. Congress. Any attempt by the Congress to legislate in an area not specifically delegated by the Constitution is unconstitutional and of no legal effect. One of the powers granted to Congress is to regulate "interstate commerce." Historically, the court interpreted this to mean that Congress could not regulate business activities that were not "interstate commerce" but rather involved *intra* state commerce only. The following 1921 case dealt with whether baseball was interstate or intrastate commerce. If intrastate, the federal legislation, the Sherman Act, was inapplicable to baseball.

FEDERAL BASEBALL CLUB OF BALTIMORE v. NATIONAL LEAGUE
259 U.S. 200 (1921)
Supreme Court of the United States

■ ■ ■

HOLMES, Mr. Justice.

This is a suit for threefold damages brought by the plaintiff under the Anti-Trust Acts of... 1890 (Sherman Act)... The defendants are the National League of Professional Baseball Clubs and the American League of Professional Baseball Clubs, unincorporated associations, composed respectively of groups of eight incorporated baseball clubs, joined as defendants:... and three other persons having powers in the Federal League of Professional Baseball Clubs... It is alleged that these defendants conspired to monopolize the baseball business...

The plaintiff is a baseball club incorporated in Maryland, and with seven other corporations was a member of the Federal League of Professional Baseball Players, a corporation under the laws of Indiana, that attempted to compete with the combined defendants. It alleges that the defendants destroyed the Federal League by buying up some of the constituent clubs and in one way or another inducing all those clubs except the plaintiff to leave their League, and that the three persons connected with the Federal league and named as defendants, one of them being the President of the League, took part in the conspiracy. Great damage to the plaintiff is alleged. The plaintiff obtained a verdict for $80,000 in the (trial) Court and a judgment for treble the amount was entered, but the Court of Appeals, after an elaborate discussion, held that the defendants were not within the Sherman Act...

...The clubs composing the Leagues are in different cities and for the most part in different States. The end of the elaborate organizations and sub-organizations that are described in the pleadings and evidence is that these clubs shall play against one another in public exhibitions for money, one or the other club crossing a state line in order to make the meeting possible... Of course the scheme requires constantly repeated travelling on the part of the clubs, which is provided for, controlled and disciplined by the organizations, and this it is said means commerce among the States. But we are of opinion that the Court of Appeals was right. The business is giving exhibitions of baseball, which are purely state affairs. It is true that in order to attain for these exhibitions the great popularity that they have achieved, competitions must be arranged between clubs from different cities and States. But the fact that in order to give the exhibitions the Leagues must induce free persons to cross state lines and must arrange and pay for their doing so is not enough to change the character of the business. According to the distinction insisted upon in *Hooper v. California*, 155 U.S. 648, 655, the transport is a mere indicent, not the essential thing. That to which it is incident, the exhibition, although made for money would not be called trade or commerce in the commonly accepted use of those words. As it is put by the defendant, personal effort, not related to production, is not a subject of commerce. That which in its consummation is not commerce does not become commerce among the States because the transportation that we have mentioned takes place. To repeat the illustrations given by the Court below, a firm of lawyers sending out a member to argue a case, or the Chautauqua lecture bureau sending out lecturers, does not engage in such commerce because the lawyer or lecturer goes to another State.

If we are right, the plaintiff's business is to be described in the same way and the restrictions by contract that prevented the plaintiff from getting players to break their bargains and the other conduct charged against the defendants were not an interference with commerce among the States.

■ ■ ■

Questions

1. What reasons did the Court cite for baseball not being in interstate commerce?
2. Did the Court also conclude that a lawyer's services, though he may cross state lines, are not interstate commerce?

TOOLSON v. NEW YORK YANKEES
346 U.S. 356 (1953)
Supreme Court of the United States

■ ■ ■

Per CURIAM.

In *Federal Baseball Club of Baltimore v. National League*, this Court held that the business of providing public baseball games for profit between clubs of professional baseball players was not within the scope of the federal antitrust laws. Congress has had the ruling under consideration but has not seen fit to bring such business under these laws by legislation having prospective effect. The business has thus been left for thirty years to develop, on the understanding that it was not subject to existing antitrust legislation. The present cases ask us to overrule the prior decision and, with retrospective effect, hold the legislation applicable. We think that if there are evils in this field which now warrant application to it of the antitrust laws it should be by legislation. Without re-examination of the underlying issues, the judgments below are affirmed on the authority of *Federal Baseball Club of Baltimore v. National League* so far as that decision determines that Congress had no intention of including the business of baseball within the scope of the federal antitrust laws.

BURTON, Mr. Justice (dissenting).

Whatever may have been the situation when the *Federal Baseball Club* case was decided in 1922, I am not able to join today's decision which, in effect, announces that organized baseball, in 1953, still is not engaged in interstate trade or commerce. In the light of organized baseball's well-known and widely distributed capital investments used in conducting competitions between teams constantly traveling between states, its receipts and expenditures of large sums transmitted between states, its numerous purchases of materials in interstate commerce, the attendance at its local exhibitions of large audiences often traveling across state lines, its radio and television activities which expand its audiences beyond state lines, its sponsorship of interstate advertising, and its highly organized "farm system" of minor league baseball clubs, coupled with restrictive contracts and understandings between individuals and among clubs or leagues playing for profit throughout the United States, and even in Canada, Mexico and Cuba, it is a contradiction in terms to say that the defendants in the cases before us are not now engaged in interstate trade or commerce as those terms are used in the Constitution of the United States and in the Sherman Act....

■ ■ ■

Notes and Questions

1. Does the Court's statement, "Without re-examination of the underlying issues..." suggest the Court doesn't want to consider those issues because they recognize the growth of the baseball business undermines the previous reasons for the rule?
2. What reason did the court give for not exercising its power of reversal when, as in this case, the reason for the original rule had disappeared?
3. Consider the following excerpt from *Flood v. Kuhn*, 407 U.S. 258 (1972):

> We continue to be loath, 50 years after *Federal Baseball* and almost two decades after *Toolson*, to overturn those cases judicially when Congress, by its positive inaction has allowed those decisions to stand for so long and, far beyond mere inference and implication, has clearly evinced a desire not to disapprove them legislatively.

> Accordingly, we adhere once again to *Federal Baseball* and *Toolson* and to their application to professional baseball. We adhere also to *International Boxing* and *Radovich* and to their respective applications (of the antitrust laws) to professional boxing and professional football. If there is any inconsistency or illogic in all this, it is an inconsistency and illogic of long standing that is to be remedied by the Congress and not by this Court. If we were to act otherwise, we would be withdrawing from the conclusion as to congressional intent made in *Toolson* and from the concerns as to retrospectivity therein expressed. Under these circumstances, there is merit in consistency even though some might claim that beneath that consistency is a layer of inconsistency.

Why allow antitrust laws in boxing and football, but not baseball? What consistency is the Court talking about?

INADEQUATE KNOWLEDGE

POWELL v. TEXAS
392 U.S. 514 (1967)
Supreme Court of the United States

■ ■ ■

MARSHALL, Mr. Justice.

In late December 1966, appellant was arrested and charged with being found in a state of intoxication in a public place, in violation of Texas Penal Code... His counsel urged that appellant was "afflicted with the disease of chronic alcoholism", "that his appearance in public (while drunk was)... not of his own volition", and therefore that to punish him criminally for that conduct would be cruel and unusual, in violation of the Eighth and Fourteenth Amendments to the United States Constitution.

The principal testimony was that of Dr. Davis Wade, a Fellow of the American Medical Association, duly certificated in psychiatry... Dr. Wade sketched the outlines of the "disease" concept of alcoholism; noted that there is no generally accepted definition of "alcoholism"; alluded to the ongoing debate within the medical profession over whether alcohol is actually physically "addicting" or merely psychologically "habituating"; and concluded that in either case a "chronic alcoholic" is an "involuntary drinker," who is "powerless not to drink," and who "loses his self-control over his drinking." He testified that he had examined appellant, and that appellant is a "chronic alcoholic," who "by the time he has reached (the state of intoxication)... is not able to control his behavior, and (who)... has reached this point because he has an uncontrollable compulsion to drink." Dr. Wade also responded in the negative to the question whether appellant has "the willpower to resist the constant excessive consumption of alcohol." He added that in his opinion jailing appellant without medical attention would operate neither to rehabilitate him or to lessen his desire for alcohol....

Appellant testified concerning the history of his drinking problem. He reviewed his many arrests for drunkenness; testified that he was unable to stop drinking; stated that when he was intoxicated he had no control over his actions and could not remember them later, but that he did not become violent; and admitted that he did not remember his arrest on the occasion for which he was being tried. On cross-examination, appellant admitted that he had had one drink on the morning of the trial and had been able to discontinue drinking... The State made no effort to obtain expert psychiatric testimony of its own, or even to explore with appellant's witness the question of appellant's power to control the frequency, timing, and location of his drinking bouts, or the substantial disagreement within the medical profession concerning the nature of the disease, the efficacy of treatment and the prerequisites for effective treatment... Instead, the State contented itself with a brief argument that appellant had no defense to the charge because he "is legally sane and knows the difference between right and wrong."

Following this abbreviated exposition of the problem before it, the trial court indicated its intention to disallow appellant's claimed defense of "chronic alcoholism."...

In the first place, the record in this case is utterly inadequate to permit the sort of informed and responsible adjudication which alone can support the announcement of an important and wideranging new constitutional principle. We know very little about the circumstances surrounding the drinking bout which resulted in this conviction, or about Leroy Powell's drinking problem, or indeed about alcoholism itself....

...Debate rages within the medical profession as to whether "alcoholism" is a separate "disease" in any meaningful biochemical, physiological or psychological sense, or whether it represents one peculiar manifestation in some individuals of underlying psychiatric disorders...

It is one thing to say that if a man is deprived of alcohol his hands will begin to shake, he will suffer agonizing pains and ultimately he will have hallucinations; it is quite another to say that a man has a "compulsion" to take a drink, but that he also retains a certain amount of "free will" with which to resist. It is simply impossible, in the present state of our knowledge, to ascribe a useful meaning to the latter statement. This definitional confusion reflects, of course, not merely the undeveloped state of the psychiatric art but also the conceptual difficulties inevitably attendant upon the importation of scientific and medical models into a legal system generally predicated upon a different set of assumptions.

Despite the comparatively primitive state of our knowledge on the subject, it cannot be denied that the destructive use of alcoholic beverages is one of our principal social and public health problems...

There is as yet no known generally effective method for treating the vast number of alcoholics in our society... Most psychiatrists are apparently of the opinion that alcoholism is far more difficult to treat than other forms of behavioral disorders, and some believe it is impossible to cure by means of psychotherapy; indeed, the medical profession as a whole, and psychiatrists in particular, have been severely criticised for the prevailing reluctance to undertake the treatment of drinking problems. Thus it is entirely possible that, even were the manpower and facilities available for a full-scale attack upon chronic alcoholism we would find ourselves unable to help the vast bulk of our "visible"—let alone our "invisible"—alcoholic population.

However, facilities for the attempted treatment of indigent alcoholics are woefully lacking throughout the country. It would be tragic to return large numbers of helpless, sometimes dangerous and frequently unsanitary inebriates to the streets of our cities without even the opportunity to sober up adequately which a brief jail term provides... Yet the medical profession cannot, and does not, tell us with any assurance that, even if the buildings, equipment and trained personnel were made available, it could provide anything more than slightly higher-class jails for our indigent habitual inebriates. Thus we run the grave risk that nothing will be accomplished beyond the hanging of a new sign—reading "hospital"—over one wing of the jailhouse....

Faced with this unpleasant reality, we are unable to assert that the use of the criminal process as a means of dealing with the public aspects of problem drinking can never be defended as rational. The picture of the penniless drunk propelled aimlessly and endlessly through the law's "revolving door" of arrest, incarceration, release and rearrest is not a pretty one. But before we condemm the present practice across the board, perhaps we ought to be able to point to some clear promise of a better world for these unfortunate people. Unfortunately, no such promise has yet been forthcoming. If, in addition to the absence of a coherent approach to the problem of treatment, we consider that almost complete absence of facilities and manpower for the implementation of a rehabilitation program, it is difficult to say in the present context that the criminal process is utterly lacking in social value. This court has never held that anything in the Constitution requires that penal sanctions be designed solely to achieve therapeutic or rehabilitative effects, and it can hardly be said with assurance that incarceration serves such purposes any better for the general run of criminals than it does for public drunks.

Ignorance likewise impedes our assessment of the deterrent effect of criminal sanctions for public drunkenness. The fact that a high percentage of American alcoholics conceal their drinking problems, not merely by avoiding public displays of intoxication, but also by shunning all forms of treatment, is indicative that some powerful deterrent operates to inhibit the public revelation of the existence of alcoholism. Quite probably this deterrent effect can be largely attributed to the harsh moral attitude which our society has traditionally taken toward intoxication and the shame which we have associated with alcoholism. Criminal conviction represents the degrading public revelation of what AngloAmerican society has long condemned as a moral defect, and the existence of criminal sanctions may serve to reinforce this cultural taboo, just as we presume they serve to reinforce other, stronger feelings against murder, rape, theft, and other forms of antisocial conduct...

It is not difficult to imagine a case involving psychiatric testimony to the effect that an individual suffers from some aggressive neurosis which he is able to control when sober; that very little alcohol suffices to remove the inhibitions which normally contain these aggressions, with the result that the individual engages in assaultive behavior without becoming actually intoxicated; and that the individual suffers from a very strong desire to drink, which is an "exceedingly strong influence" but "not completely overpowering." Without being untrue to the rationale of this case, should the principles advanced in dissent be accepted here, the Court could not avoid holding such an individual constitutionally unaccountable for his assaultive behavior.

Traditional commonlaw concepts of personal accountability and essential considerations of federalism lead us to disagree with appellant. We are unable to conclude, on the state of this record or on the current state of medical knowledge, that chronic alcoholics in general, and Leroy Powell in particular, suffer from such an irresistible compulsion to drink and to get drunk in public that they are utterly unable to control their performance of either or both of these acts and thus cannot be deterred at all from public intoxication...

It is simply not yet the time to write into the Constitution formulas cast in terms whose meaning, let alone relevance, are not yet clear either to doctors or to lawyers.

■ ■ ■

Questions

1. In *Robinson v. California,* 370 U.S. 660, (1962), the state made it a crime to "be addicted to the use of narcotics." The court held that "a state statute which imprisons the person thus inflicted (with narcotics addiction) as a criminal, even though he has never touched any narcotic drug within the state or been guilty of any irregular behavior there, inflicts a cruel and unusual punishment..." In effect, California was making a particular status (narcotic addiction on a crime. The court ruled that California could not make such status a

crime any more than it could make the status of being mentally ill or a leper a crime. Would this case form an argument for Leroy Powell?

2. Was Powell convicted of being a chronic alcoholic (status) or for being in public while drunk (behavior)? Could California make it a crime to *use* an unprescribed narcotic?

3. Why was the court not willing to allow chronic alcoholism as a defense like mental illness is a defense to other crimes? Could a defendant like Powell resist intoxication and prevent himself from appearing in public places?

RIGHTS OF THE INDIVIDUAL

Law, as an instrument of social control, prescribes the environment in which society functions and suggests guidelines for individuals in carrying out their daily activities. Law similiarly defines the rights and liberties of individuals within society, and the rights of society in regard to its members. In its present form, law is a result of many years of change and a concerted effort to keep social controversy within limits.

Under the scheme of social order in the United States, which emphasizes "freedoms," society must protect the security of the individual. However, due to the many races and creeds that make up society, it has been necessary to shield many types of life, traditions, opinions, and beliefs. This fact alone implies that there are many guarantees for the individual under U.S. laws. It further suggests the existence of an organized society maintaining those protections and public order. Therefore, on those occasions when a collective social need is recognized as necessary in the public interest, it must be given priority over an individual need that, in some other circumstances, might justify priority.

It is virtually impossible to classify the many interests for which individuals might claim the right to be protected by the government or from the government. Nevertheless, whatever the situation, legal institutions have been established to protect individual interests and to arbitrate conflicting interests.

Included in the following materials is a copy of the Bill of Rights and several Supreme Court cases involving "fundamental personal rights" and those rights labeled "a fundamental right, esential to a fair trial."

BILL OF RIGHTS

■ ■ ■

AMENDMENT. I

Congress shall make no law respecting an establishment of religion, or prohibiting the free exercise thereof; or abridging the freedom of speech. or of the press; or the right of the people peaceably to assemble, and to petition the Government for a redress of grievances.

AMENDMENT. II.

A well regulated Militia, being necessary to the security of a free State, the right of the people to keep and bear Arms, shall not be infringed.

AMENDMENT. III.

No Soldier shall, in time of peace be quartered in any house without the consent of the owner, nor in time of war, but in a manner to be prescribed by law.

AMENDMENT. IV.

The right of the people to be secure in their persons, houses, papers, and effects, against unreasonable searches and seizures, shall not be violated, and no Warrants shall issue, but upon probable cause, supported by Oath or affirmation, and particularly describing the place to be searched, and the persons or things to be seized.

AMENDMENT. V.

No person shall be held to answer to a capital or otherwise infamous crime, unless on a presentment of indictment of a Grand Jury, except in cases arising in the land or naval forces, or in the Militia, when in actual service in time of War or public danger; nor shall any person be subject for the same offense to be twice put in jeopardy of life or limb; nor shall be compelled in any criminal case to be a witness against himself, nor be deprived of life, liberty, or property, without due process of law; nor shall private property be taken for public use, without just compensation.

AMENDMENT. VI.

In all criminal prosecutions, the accused shall enjoy the right to a speedy and public trial, by an impartial jury of the State and district wherein the crime shall have been committed, which district shall have been previously ascertained by law, and to be informed of the nature and cause of the accusation; to be contronted with the witnesses against him; to have compuslory process for obtaining witnesses in his favor, and to have the Assistance of Counsel for his defense.

AMENDMENT. VII.

In suits at common law, where the value in controversy shall exceed twenty dollars, the right of trial by jury shall be preserved, and no fact tried by a jury, shall be otherwise reexamined in any Court of the United States, than according to the rules of the common law.

AMENDMENT. VIII.

Excessive bail shall not be required, nor excessive fines imposed, nor cruel and unusual punishment inflicted.

AMENDMENT. IX.

The enumeration in the constitution, of certain rights, shall not be construed to deny or disparage others retained by the people.

AMENDMENT. X.

The Powers not delegated to the United States by the Constitution nor prohibited by it to the States, are reserved to the States respectively, or to the people.

***AND

AMENDMENT. XIV.

Section 1. All persons born or naturalized in the United States, and subject to the jurisdiction thereof, are citizens of the United States and of the State wherein they reside. No State shall... deprive any person of life, liberty, or property, without due process of law; nor deny to any person within its jurisdiction the equal protection of the laws....

■ ■ ■

"FUNDAMENTAL PERSONAL RIGHTS"

Often, the courts are faced with difficult decisions involving constitutionally protected rights, such as freedom of speech, press, religion or privacy. These problems are too varied and multifaceted to be solved by any simple formula. Moreover, the courts feel a special responsibility to safeguard these rights. Therefore, the resolution of conflict between society's desire to regulate and the individual person's right to freedom involve many controversial decisions. The court must define the rights and determine to what extent the state may regulate these rights to preserve order, quiet, and peace. Just when does a speaker become a danger to society? Does a hostile audience justify restricting the speaker? Besides these questions concerning free speech, the reader can well imagine the additional problems dealing with school prayers, with free press, and with decisions concerning abortion. The following cases have been selected to give the reader an appreciation of the problems facing the courts in protecting individual rights. The court must resolve the controversies themselves and at the same time develop protection for basic rights by defining the prospective scope of individual and state responsibilities.

FREE SPEECH

COLLIN v. SMITH
447 F. Supp. 676 (1978)
U.S. District Court (N.D. Ill.)

■ ■ ■

Plaintiffs, the National Socialist Party of America and its leader, Frank Collin, bring this action challenging three ordinances of the Village of Skokie, Illinois, on the grounds that the ordinances deprive them of their rights to freedom of speech and assembly in violation of the First and Fourteenth Amendments to the United States Constitution...

Skokie is a municipal corporation north of Chicago, which is generally regarded in the Chicago area as a predominantly Jewish community...

Plaintiff Collin testified that the National Socialist Party is "a Nazi organization" and that in public appearances its members wear uniforms reminiscent of those worn by members of the German Nazi Party during the rule of the Third Reich. Specifically, plaintiffs employ the swastika as a party symbol. Among their more controversial political views, plaintiffs believe that black persons are "biologically inferior" to whites and should be "repatriated" to Africa, and that American Jews have excessive influence in government and close ties to international Communism. Collin stated that this Jewish influence should be "exposed and documented and presented to the American public", but denied that plaintiffs endorse the Third Reich's "final solution" to the problem of Jewish influence—genocide.

In late 1976, plaintiffs planned a series of demonstrations in Jewish communities, including Skokie... News of the planned demonstration caused considerable consternation in Skokie... As a result of this sentiment, the Village decided to attempt to prevent the demonstration. It enacted the three ordinances at issue in this action.

Ordinance #994 is a comprehensive permit system for all parades or public assemblies of more than 50 persons anywhere within Skokie. It requires all permit applicants to obtain $300,000 in liability insurance and $50,000 in property damage insurance. Ordinances #995 and #996 are both criminal measures: #995 prohibits the dissemination of material which incites racial or religious hatred, with intent to incite such hatred; #996 prohibits public demonstrations by members of political parties while wearing military-style uniforms...

On June 22, 1977, Collin applied for a permit under #994... The application was denied by defendant John Matzer, the Village Manager, on the grounds that plaintiffs planned to wear military-style uniforms in violation of #996. Plaintiffs responded by bringing this action...

The question, then, is not whether there are some ideas that are completely unacceptable in a civilized society. Rather the question is which danger is greater: the danger that allowing the government to punish "unacceptable" ideas will lead to suppression of ideas that are merely uncomfortable to those in power; or the danger that permitting free debate on such unacceptable ideas will encourage their acceptance rather than discouraging them by revealing their pernicious quality. This question is one of the fundamental dilemmas of free speech, and it is certainly open to public debate, but for the purposes of this case, the question has been definitively settled by the Supreme Court.

From the beginning the court has held that speech may be punished only when it actually causes some social harm which the government can legitimately prevent. For many years, however, the Court held that certain doctrines, such as the violent overthrow of the government, we so inherently harmful to society that their mere advocacy in any form could be prohibited. Justices Holmes and Brandeis consistently dissented from these opinions on the grounds that allowing the prohibition of mere advocacy would inevitably lead to untrammeled censorship. They took the position that advocacy even of violence or lawlessness could be punished only when it occurred in a situation in which the advocacy posed a "clear and present danger" of actually inciting the lawless actions advocated.

The Holmes-Brandeis approach gained ascendancy through the 1940's and 1950's as the Court retreated from the position that all advocacy of Communism could be prohibited...

Since the court has thus squarely rejected the theory that some ideas are too dangerous to permit their advocacy, it follows that plaintiffs have the right to advocate their political views within Skokie...

Thus, the ordinances may not prohibit advocacy which falls short of incitement of imminent lawless action. However it has long been established that certain kinds of language are of so little utility in the conveyance of ideas that they can be prohibited on the basis of harms less serious than the threat of imminent lawlessness. Such speech is generally referred to as "unprotected" and it includes "the lewd and obscene, the profane, the libelous and the insulting or 'fighting' words—those which by their very utterance inflict injury or incite an immediate breach of peace." *Chaplinsky v. New Hampshire,* 315 U.S. 568, 572 (1942). Defendants' position is that language which intentionally incites racial hatred is unprotected speech...

The doctrine of unprotected speech was first developed in cases involving abusive epithets and insults. In *Cantwell v. Connecticut,* 310 U.S. 296, (1940), and *Chaplinsky v. New Hampshire,* 315 U.S. 568, (1942), members of the Jehovah's Witnesses sect were convicted of inciting breaches of the peace on the basis of their use of language which the Court characterized as highly offensive...

This analysis would seem to suggest that the government may generally prohibit speech which is not a communication of ideas or opinion. The Court, however, avoided such a broad approach to the restriction of unprotected speech in favor of an inquiry into the conduct of the speaker, the circumstances in which the speech was employed, and the actual likelihood that it would provoke a breach of peace. Cantwell's speech had consisted of a phonograph record which he played on a public street. He had asked permission to play the record, had stopped when asked to do so, and had at no time been belligerent, offensive or truculent. His conviction was reversed. Chaplinsky, on the other hand, had called another a "damned racketeer" and "damned Facist" to his face in a belligerent manner; his conviction was affirmed.

This narrow approach to unprotected speech was emphasized by *Terminiello v. City of Chicago,* 337 U.S. 1, (1949). Terminiello was convicted for disorderly conduct on the basis of an inflammatory speech filled with offensive epithets... The Illinois Supreme Court affirmed, finding no constitutional problem since Terminiello's speech had been so offensive and insulting that it was unprotected under *Cantwell* and *Chaplinsky.* The Supreme Court reversed without even considering whether the speech was unprotected. Inviting dispute, creating unrest and stirring anger are among the "high purposes" of free debate, the Court said, and therefore no speech could be punished merely because it accomplished those purposes.

Thus, *Cantwell, Chaplinsky* and *Terminiello* established a two-part test for the restriction of the "fighting words" class of unprotected speech. The speech must, considered objectively, be abusive and insulting rather than a comunication of ideas, and it must actually be used in an abusive manner in a situation which presents an actual danger that it will cause a breach of peace. The Court has several times emphasized that care must be taken to insure that what is restricted is insulting and offensive *language*, not the communication of offensive *ideas*."It is firmly settled that under our Constitution the public expression of ideas may not be prohibited merely because the ideas themselves are offensive to some of their hearers." Even where the audience is so offended by the ideas being expressed that it becomes disorderly and attempts to silence the speaker, it is the duty of the police to attempt to protect the speaker, not to silence his speech if it does not consist of unprotected epithets.

In *Cohen v. California,* 403 U.S. 15, (1971), the Court discussed in detail the rule that even unproteced speech may only be suppressed when it threatens a harm...Although the government need not prove an actual threat of an imminent breach of the peace in order to restrict unprotected speech, the Court said in *Cohen* the state's position amounted to an asertion that it could ban certain offensive epithets even without showing a possible breach, either because such epithets are inherently likely to cause violent reactions or inorder to maintain a "suitable level of discourse within the body politic." Neither rationale, the Court said, was strong enough to justify establishing the "inherently boundless' precedent that the government could ban certain forms of language solely because of their offensiveness. To permit such bans would place unacceptable restrictions on free and uninhibited debate...

In light of these princiles, it is apparent that the line between protected and unprotected speech in matters relating to race and religion is an extraordinarily difficult one to draw. On the one hand, slurs and insults which rely upon the victim's racial and religious heritage are among the most vicious and abusive epithets known...

On the other hand, it is equally clear that discussion of race and religion will often involve the exposition of ideas and positions that are inherently offensive to many, but which are nevertheless protected by the First Amendment...

The question remains whether the language of Ordinance # 995 is sufficiently precise to focus exclusively on the personally abusive use of epithets in situations where the possibility of breaches of the peace justifies the epithets' suppression and still permit the intemperate and emotional debate which may accompany any discussion of race and religion. Our courts have employed the doctrines of vagueness and of overbreadth to make this determination.

A law is unconstitutionally vague when it fails to give reasonable notice of the conduct which is prohibited and gives law enforcement personnel the opportunity to enforce it according to their personal prejudices. In First Amendment cases the doctrine has an added dimension, since a vague statute which covers speech-related activities may be enforced only against those who express unpopular opinions and thus be used as a device for censorship.

Statutes which punish speech solely on the basis of the emotion it arouses in other persons are vulnerable to findings of vagueness, particularly where the emotion involved is subjective and difficult to define with precision...

The Skokie ordinance punishes language which intentionally incites hatred. This standard is... subjective and impossible to clearly define... *Terminiello* and its progeny establish that there is a constitutional right to incite unrest, dissatisfaction, and even anger with social conditions. The distinction between inciting anger with a social condition and hatred of the person or group perceived to be responsible for that condition is impossible to draw with the requisite clairty, and depends to a great extent upon the frame of mind of the listener... A society which values "uninhibited, robuts and wide-open" debate cannot permit criminal sanctions to turn upon so fine a distinction. Ordinance # 995 is unconstitutionally vague.

Even assuming that the distinction can be defined with sufficient clarity, however, the court also finds that the Ordinance is overbroad. A law is overbroad for First Amendment purposes when, even though it is directed at unprotected speech, it can also be applied to protected speech. Such a law is considered completely unconstitutional on its face even though it is capable of application in a constitutional manner, on the theory that the very existence of laws which can be applied to protected speech exercises an unacceptable inhibiting effect on free debate...

The Skokie ordinance punishes the mere "dissemination" of material which incites hatred, with dissemination broadly defined to include such relatively passive activities as distributing leaflets and wearing "symbolic" clothing. It is clearly not aimed solely at personally abusive, insulting behavior... The court cannot agree that the requirement that the language intentionally incite hatred is an adequate substitute for this limitation.

It may very well be true that hatred tends to spawn violence and that, unlike the unrest and dissatisfaction referred to in *Terminiello,* hatred serves no useful social function in itself. Nevertheless, the incitement of hatred is often a byproduct of vigorous debate on highly emotional subjects, and the basic message of *Cohen* is that a great deal of useless, offensive and even potentially harmful language must be tolerated as part of the "verbal cacophony" that accompanies uninhibited debate, not for its own sake, but because any attempt to excise it from the public discourse with the blunt instrument of criminal sanctions must inevitably have a dampening effect on the vigor of that discourse...

The requirement that speech pose an imminent danger of violence before it may be suppressed is relaxed to a great extent when the speech serves no useful social purpose, but Ordinance # 995 seeks to dispense with the requirement entirely, and this it may not do. The ordinance in unconstitutionally overbroad...

In resolving this case in favor of the plaintiffs, the court is acutely aware of the very grave dangers posed by public dissemination of doctrines of racial and religious hatred.

In this case, a small group of zealots, openly professing to be followers of Nazism, have succeeded in exacerbating the emotions of a large segment of the citizens of the Village of Skokie who are bitterly opposed to their views and revolted by the prospect of their public appearance.

When feelings and tensions are at their highest peak, it is a temptation to reach for the exception to the rule announced by Mr. Justice Holmes, "if there is any principle of the Constitution that more imperatively calls for attachment than any other it is the principle of free thought—not free thought for those who agree with us but freedom for the thought that we hate."

Freedom of thought carries with it the freedom to speak freely and to publicly assemble to express one's thoughts.

The long list of cases reviewed in this opinion agrees that when a choice must be made, it is better to allow those who preach racial hate to expend their venom in rhetoric rather than to be panicked into embarking on the dangerous course of permitting the government to decide what its citizens may say and hear. As Mr. Justice Harlan reminded us in *Cohen,* where a similar choice was made, "That the air may at times seem filled with verbal cacophony is not a sign of weakness but of strength." The ability of American society to tolerate the advocacy even of the hateful doctrines espoused by the plaintiffs without abandoning its commitment to freedom of speech and assembly is perhaps the best protection we have against the establishment of any Nazi-type regime in this country.

■ ■ ■

Questions

1. May the State (through the Village of Skokie) prevent individuals from stating their political philosophy if it is noxious and reprehensible? May the State prohibit advocacy of force and violence against the State?
2. What is the theory of the "marketplace of ideas"? Has this theory been accepted or rejected by the Supreme Court?
3. What is "unprotected" speech? Can you identify examples? What are "fighting words"? Are racial slurs fighting words and capable of government suppression?
4. When is a law (ordinance) unconstitutionally vague? Why were the ordinances of Skokie considered unconstitutionally vague?
5. When is an ordinance unconstitutionally overbroad? Why were the ordinances of Skokie unconstitutionally overbroad?

6. Were the Skokie Park District ordinances which required $350,000 in liability in property damage insurance before permission could be obtained to demonstrate in the Skokie Park constitutional? The court concluded that this drastic restriction on the right of freedom of speech and assembly was unconstitutional and said:

> The government may impose financial burdens on the exercise of the First Amendment rights, such as permit fees, only when the amount involved is reasonable and directly related to the accomplishment of the legitimate governmental purposes. In this case, defendants have presented no evidence whatsoever of the Village's need for such a burdensome insurance requirement... (Moreover), the ordinance is objectionable because some organizations may be exempted from its requirements and there are no principled standards for determining which organizations are exempt... It is well established that permits systems which were so devoid of standards that they allow government officials to engage in covert censorship in their administration are particularly vulnerable to First Amendment challenge.

7. In October of 1978 the Supreme Court refused certiorari in the *Collin* Case. Justices Harry Blackman and Byron White argued for review saying the case offered a chance to decide if "there is no limit whatsoever to the exercise of free speech."

SYMBOLIC SPEECH

TINKER v. DES MOINES INDEPENDENT COM. SCH. DIST.
393 U.S. 503 (1969)
Supreme Court of the United States

■ ■ ■

FORTAS, Mr. Justice.

Petitioner John F. Tinker, 15 years old, and petitioner Christopher Eckhardt, 16 years old, attended high schools in Des Moines, Iowa. Petitioner Mary Beth Tinker, John's sister, was a 13 year old student in junior high school.

In December 1965, a group of adults and students in Des Moines held a meeting at the Eckhardt home. The group determined to publicize their objections to the hostilities in Vietnam and their support for a truce by wearing black armbands during the holiday season and by fasting on December 16 and New Year's Eve. Petitioners and their parents had previously engaged in similar activities, and they decided to participate in the program.

The principals of the Des Moines schools became aware of the plan to wear armbands. On December 14, 1965, they met and adopted a policy that any student wearing an armband to school would be asked to remove it, and if he refused he would be suspended until he returned without the armband. Petitioners were aware of the regulation that the school authorities adopted.

On December 16, Mary Beth and Christoper wore black armbands to their schools: John Tinker wore his armband the next day. They were all sent home and suspended from school until they would come back without their armbands. They did not return to school until after the planned period for wearing armbands had expired—that is, until after New Year's Day.

This complaint was filed in the United States District Court by petitioners, through their fathers...

After an evidentiary hearing the District Court dismissed the complaint. It upheld the constitutionality of the school authorities' action on the ground that it was reasonable in order to prevent disturbance of school discipline. 258 F. Supp. 971 (1966)...

The District Court recognized that the wearing of an armband for the purpose of expressing certain views is the type of symbolic act that is within the Free Speech Clause of the First Amendment...

First Amendment rights, applied in light of the special characteristics of the school environment, are available to teachers and students. It can hardly be argued that either students or teachers shed their constitutional rights to freedom of speech or expression at the schoolhouse gate... On the other hand, the Court has repeatedly emphasized the need for affirming the comprehensive authority of the States and of school officials, consistent with fundamental constitutional safeguards, to prescribe and control conduct in the schools. Our problem lies in the area where students in the exercise of First Amendment rights collide with the rules of the school authorities.

The problem posed by the present case does not relate to regulation of the length of skirts or the type of clothing, to hair style, or deportment. It does not concern aggressive, disruptive action or even group demonstrations. Our problem involves direct, primary First Amendment rights akin to "pure speech."

The school officials banned and sought to punish petitioners for a silent, passive expression of opinion, unaccompanied by any disorder or disturbance on the part of petitioners. There is here no evidence whatever of petitioners' interference, actual or nascent, with the schools' work or of collision with the rights of other students to be secure and to be let alone... There is no indication that the work of the schools or any class was disrupted. Outside the classrooms, a few students made hostile remarks to the children wearing armbands, but there were no threats or acts of violence on school premises.

...In our system, undifferentiated fear or apprehension of disturbance is not enough to overcome the right to freedom of expression. Any departure from absolute regimentation may cause trouble. Any variation from the majority's opinion may inspire fear. Any word spoken, in class, in the lunchroom, or on the campus, that deviates from the views of another person may start an argument or cause a disturbance. But our Constitution says we must take this risk, *Terminiello v. Chicago,* 337 U.S. 1, (1949); and our history says that it is this sort of hazardous freedom—this kind of openness—that is the basis of our national strength and of the independence and vigor of Americans who grow up and live in this relatively permissive, often disputatious , society.

In order for the State in the person of school officials to justify prohibition of a particular expression of opinion, it must be able to show that its action was caused by something more than a mere desire to avoid the discomfort and unpleasantness that always accompany an unpopular viewpoint. Certainly where there is no finding and no showing that engaging in the forbidden conduct would "materially and substantially interfere with the requirements of appropriate discipline in the operation of the school," the prohibition cannot be sustained.

It is also relevant that the school authorities did not purport to prohibit the wearing of symbols of political or controversial significance. The record shows that students in some of the schools wore buttons relating to national political campaigns, and some even wore the Iron Cross, traditionally a symbol of Nazism. The order prohibiting the wearing of armbands did not extend to these. Instead, a particular symbol—black armbands worn to exhibit opposition to this Nation's involvement in Vietnam—was singled out for prohibition. Clearly, the prohibition of expression of one particular opinion, at least without evidence that it is necessary to avoid material and substantial interference with schoolwork or discipline, is not constitutionally permissible.

In our system, state-operated schools may not be enclaves of totalitarianism. School officials do not possess absolute authority over their students. Students in school as well as out of school are "persons" under our Constitution. They are possessed of fundamental rights which the State must respect, just as they themselves must respect their obligations to the State. In our system, students may not be regarded as closed-circuit recipients of only that which the State chooses to communicate. They may not be confined to the expression of those sentiments that are officially approved. In the absence of a specific showing of constitutionally valid reasons to regulate their speech, students are entitled to freedom of expression of their views.

■ ■ ■

Questions

1. What is "symbolic speech?"
2. Does the *Tinker* decision justify the wearing of skirts at any length or see-through clothing as an expression of symbolic free speech?
3. At what point can school officials prohibit student conduct which the student asserts is symbolic speech?

FREE PRESS

MILLS v. ALABAMA
384 U.S. 214 (1966)
Supreme Court of the United States

■ ■ ■

BLACK, Mr. Justice.

The question here is whether it abridges freedom of the press for a State to punish a newspaper editor for doing no more than publishing an editorial on election day urging people to vote a particular way in the election...

Whatever differences may exist about interpretations of the First Amendment, there is practically universal agreement that a major purpose of that amendment was to protect the free discussion of governmental affairs. This of course includes discussions of candidates, structures and forms of government, the manner in which government is operated or should be operated, and all such matters relating to political processes. The Constitution specifically selected the press, which includes not only newspapers, books, and magazines, but also humble leaflets and circulars to play an important role in the discussion of public affairs. Thus the press serves and was designed to serve as a powerful antidote to any abuses of power by governmental officials and as a constitutionally chosen means for keeping officials elected by the people responsible to all the people whom they were selected to serve. Suppression of the right of the press to praise or criticize governmental agents and to clamor and contend for or against change, which is all that this editorial did, muzzles one of the very agencies the Framers of our Constitution thoughtfully and deliberately selected to improve our society and keep it free. The Alabama Corrupt Practices Act by providing criminal penalties for publishing editorials such as the one here silences the press at a time when it can be most effective. It is difficult to conceive of a more obvious and flagrant abridgment of the constitutionally guaranteed freedom of the press.

Admitting that the state law restricted a newspaper editor's freedom to publish editorials on election day, the Alabama Supreme Court nevertheless sustained the constitutionality of the law on the ground that the restrictions on the press were only "reasonable restrictions". The court reached this conclusion because it thought the law imposed only a minor limitation on the press—restricting it only on election days—and because the court thought the law served a good purpose. It said:

> "It is a salutary legislative enactment that protects the public from confusive last-minute charges and countercharges and the distribution of propaganda in an effort to influence voters on an election day; when as a practical matter, because of lack of time, such matters cannot be answered or their truth determined until after the election is over."

This argument, even if it were relevant to the constitutionality of the law, has a fatal flaw. The state statute leaves people free to hurl their campaign charges up to the last minute of the day before election. The law held valid by the Alabama Supreme Court then goes on to make it a crime to answer those "last-minute" charges on election day, the only time they can be effectively answered. Because the law prevents any adequate reply to these charges, it is wholly ineffective in protecting the electorate "from confusive last-minute charges and countercharges." We hold that no test of reasonableness can save a state law from invalidation as a violation of the First Amendment when that law makes it a crime for a newspaper editor to do no more than urge people to vote one way or another in a publicly held election.

■ ■ ■

Questions

1. Upon what basis did the Alabama Supreme Court uphold the statute prohibiting the election day editorial?
2. The Supreme Court felt the "reasonableness" argument was not relevant to the determination of the statute's constitutionality. Why not?
3. According to the Supreme Court, what "fatal flaw" in logic did the Alabama Court make?

OBSCENITY

In 1957 the U.S. Supreme Court held that obscenity, like libel and "fighting words," is not within the area of constitutionally protected speech or press. However, the Court said that sex and obscenity are not synonymous. The Court observed:

Obscene material is material which deals with sex in a manner appealing to prurient interest. The portrayal of sex, e.g., in art, literature and scientific works, is not itself sufficient reason to deny material the constitutional protection of freedom of speech and press... It is therefore vital that the standards for judging obscenity safeguard the protection of freedom of speech and press for material which does not treat sex in a manner appealing to prurient interest." *Roth v. United States* 354 U.S. 476 (1957).

The Court clarified further the definition of obscenity in the following case. The reader should note the elements that must be proven to establish the obscene nature of the materials before the government may suppress it.

MEMOIRS v. MASSACHUSETTS
383 U.S. 413 (1966)
Supreme Court of the United States

■ ■ ■

BRENNAN, Justice.

This is an obscenity case in which *Memoirs of a Woman of Pleasure* (commonly known as *Fanny Hill*), written by John Cleland in about 1750, was adjudged obscene in a proceeding that put on trial the book itself, and not its publisher or distributor...

As authorized by § 28D, G. P. Putnam's Sons intervened in the proceedings in behalf of the book, but it did not claim the right provided by that section to have the issue of obscenity tried by a jury. At the hearing before a justice of the Superior Court...the court received the book in evidence and...heard the testimony of experts and accepted other evidence, such as book reviews, in order to assess the literary, cultural, or educational character of the book... The trial justice entered a final decree, which adjudged *Memoirs* obscene and delcared that the book "is not entitled to the protection of the First and Fourteenth amendments to the Constitution of the United States against action by the Attorney General..." The Massachusetts Supreme Judicial Court affirmed the decree....

The term "obscene" appearing in the Massachusetts statute has been interpreted by the Supreme Court to be as expansive as the Constitution permits... Thus the sole question before the state courts was whether *Memoirs* satisfies the test of obscenity established in *Roth v. United States*, 354 U.S. 476 (1957).

We defined obscenity in *Roth* in the following terms: "Whether to the average persons, applying contemporary community standards, the dominant theme of the material taken as a whole appeals to prurient interest." Under this definition, as elaborated in subsequent cases, three elements must coalesce: it must be established that a dominant theme of the material taken as a whole appeals to a prurient interest in sex; (b) the material is patently offensive because it affronts contemporary community standards relating to the description or representation of sexual matters; and (c) the material is utterly without redeeming social value.

The Supreme Judicial Court purported to apply the *Roth* definition of obscenity and held all three criteria satisfied. We need not consider the claim that the court erred in concluding that *Memoirs* satisfied the prurient appeal and patent offensiveness criteria: for reversal is required because the court misinterpreted the social value criterion. The court applied the criterion in this passage:

> "It remains to consider whether the book can be said to be 'utterly without social importance.' We are mindful that there was expert testimony, much of which was strained, to the effect that *Memoirs* is a structural novel with literary merit; that the book displays a skill in characterization and a gift for comedy; that it plays a part in the history of the development of the English novel; and that it contains a moral, namely, that sex with love is superior to sex in a brothel. But the fact that the testimony may indicate this book has some minimal literary value does not mean it is of any social importance. We do not interpret the 'social importance' test as requiring that a book which appeals to prurient interest and is patently offensive must be unqualifiedly worthless before it can be deemed obscene."...

The Supreme Judicial Court erred in holding that a book need not be "unqualifiedly worthless before it can be deemed obscene." A book can not be proscribed unless it is found to be utterly without redeeming social value. This is so even though the book is found to possess the requisite prurient appeal and to be patently offensive. Each of the three federal constitutional criteria is to be applied independently; the social value of the book can neither be weighed against nor cancelled by its prurient appeal or patent offensiveness. Hence, even on the view of the court below that *Memoirs* possessed only a modicum of social value, its judgment must be reversed as being founded on an erroenous interpretation of a federal constitutional standard...

■ ■ ■

Questions

1. What elements must be proven to establish the obscene nature of a publication?
2. Is the definition of obscenity so difficult to prove that state governments find it difficult to prohibit it?
3. Are "contemporary community standards" national or local in scope? In *Miller v. California*, 413 U.S. 15 (1973) the Court stated that community standards need not be national; that standards of one state may differ from those of another state or community; and that the same publication may affort the standards of one community but not those of another. Moreover, in *Hamling v. U.S.* 418 U.S. 87 (1974), the Court stated:

   > A juror is entitled to draw on his knowledge of the view of the average person in the community from which he comes for making the required determination...
   > (of affronting community standards).

4. May the States restrict what minors see and read when it could not restrict adults from seeing and reading such material? The Court answered affirmatively in *Ginsberg v. New York* 390 U.S. 629 (1968) because the "well-being of its children is...a subject within the State's constitutional power to regulate..." The State legislature might conclude that exposure to such materials

constitutes an "abuse" from which children should be safeguarded. *Ginsberg* upheld the conviction of a salesman who sold "girlie" magazines to minors.

FREEDOM FROM GOVERNMENT ESTABLISHMENT OF RELIGION

ENGEL v. VITALE
370 U.S. 421 (1962)
Supreme Court of the United States

■ ■ ■

BLACK, Mr. Justice.

The Board of Education of Union Free School District No. 9, New Hyde Park, New York, acting in its official capacity under state law, directed the School District's principal to cause the following prayer to be said aloud by each class in the presence of a teacher at the beginning of each school day:

"Almighty God, we acknowledge our dependence upon Thee, and we beg Thy blessings upon us, our parents, our teachers and our Country."

This daily procedure was adopted on the recommendation of the State Board of Regents. These state officials composed the prayer which they recommended and published as part of their "Statement on Moral and Spiritual Training in the Schools," saying: "We believe that this Statement will be subscribed to by all men and women of good will, and we call upon all of them to aid in giving life to our program."

It is a matter of history that this very practice of establishing governmentally composed prayers for religious services was one of the reasons which caused many of our early colonists to leave England and seek religious freedom in America. The Book of Common Prayer, which was created under governmental direction and which was approved by Acts of Parliament in 1548 and 1549, set out in minute detail the accepted form and content of prayer and other religious ceremonies to be used in the established, tax-supported Church of England. The controversies over the Book and what should be its content repeatedly threatened to disrupt the peace of that country as the accepted forms of prayer in the established church changed with the views of the particular ruler that happened to be in control at the time...

It is an unfortunate fact of history that when some of the very groups which had most strenuously opposed the established Church of England found themselves sufficiently in control of colonial governments in this country to write their own prayers into law, they passed laws making their own religion the official religion of their respective colonies. Indeed, as late as the time of the Revolutionary War, there were established churches in at least eight of the thirteen former colonies and established religions in at least four of the other five. But the successful Revolution against English political domination was shortly followed by intense opposition to the practice of establishing religion by law. This opposition crystallized rapidly into an effective political force in Virginia where the minority religious groups such as Presbyterians, Lutherans, Quakers and Baptists had gained such strength that the adherents to the established Episcopal Church were actually a minority themselves. In 1785–1786, those opposed to the established Church, led by James Madison and Thomas Jefferson, who, though themselves not members of any of these dissenting religious groups, opposed all religious establishments by law on grounds of principle, obtained the enactment of the famous "Virginia Bill for Religious Liberty" by which all religious groups were placed on an equal footing so far as the State was concerned. Similar though less far-reaching legislation was being considered and passed in other States.

By the time of the adoption of the Constitution, our history shows that there was a widespread awareness among many American of the dangers of a union of Church and State. These people knew, some of them from bitter personal experience, that one of the greatest dangers to the freedom of the individual to worship in his own way lay in the Government's placing its official stamp of approval upon one particular kind of prayer or one particular form of religious services...

The First Amendment was added to the constitution to stand as a guarantee that neither the power nor the prestige of the Federal Government would be used to control, support or influence the kinds of prayer the American people can say—that the people's religions must not be subjected to the pressures of government for change each time a new political administration is elected to office. Under that Amendment's prohibition against governmental establishment of religion, as reinforced by the provisions of the Fourteenth Amendment, government in this country, be it state or federal, is without power to prescribe by law any particular form of prayer which is to be used as an official prayer in carrying on any program of governmentally sponsored religious activity.

There can be no doubt that New York's state prayer program officially establishes the religious beliefs embodied in the Regents' prayer... Neither the fact that the prayer may be denominationally neutral nor the fact that its observance on the part of the students is voluntary can serve to free it from the limitations of the Establishment Clause... The Establishment Clause... is violated by the enactment of laws which establish an official religion whether those laws operate directly to coerce nonobserving individuals or not. This is not to say, of course, that laws officially prescribing a particular form of religious worship do not involve coercion of such individuals. When the power, prestige and financial support of government is placed behind a particular religious belief, the indirect coercive pressure upon religious minorities to conform to the prevailing officially approved religion is plain. But the purposes underlying the Establishment Clause go much further than that. Its first and most immediate purpose rested on the belief that a union of government and religion tends to destroy government and to degrade religion... The Establishment Clause thus stands as an expression of principle on the part of the Founders of our Constitution that religion is too personal, too sacred, too holy, to permit its "unhallowed perversion" by a civil magistrate. Another purpose of the Establishment Clause rested upon an awareness of the historical fact that governmentally established religions and religious persecutions go hand in hand... It was in large part to get completely away from this sort of systematic religious persecution that the Founders brought into being our Nation, our Constitution, and our Bill of rights with its prohibition against any governmental establishment of religion. The New York Laws officially prescribing the Regents' prayer are inconsistent both with the purposes of the Establishment Clause and with the Establishment Clause itself.

It has been argued that to apply the constitution in such a way as to prohibit state laws respecting an establishment of religious services in public schools is to indicate a hostility towards religion or toward prayer. Nothing, of course, could be more wrong. The history of man is inseparable from the history of religion. And perhaps it is not too much to say that since the beginning of that history many people have devoutly believed that "More things are wrought by prayer than this world dreams of"... And there were men of this same faith in the power of prayer who led the fight for adoption of our Constitution and also for our Bill of Rights with the very guarantees of religious freedom that forbid the sort of governmental activity which New York has attempted here. These men knew that the First Amendment, which tried to put an end to governmental control of religion and of prayer, was not written to destroy either. They knew rather that it was written to quiet well-justified fears which nearly all of them felt arising out of an awareness that governments of the past had shackled men's tongues to make them speak only the religious thoughts that government wanted them to speak and to pray only to the God that government wanted them to pray to. It is neither sacrilegious to say that each separate government in this country should stay out of the business of writing or sanctioning official prayers and leave that purely religious function to the people themselves and to those the people choose to look to for religious guidance.

Questions

1. How was the Establishment Clause violated if the prayer was to be voluntary?
2. Would you conclude from *Engel* that the court is anti-God?
3. James Madison, the Author of the First Amendment wrote:

> (I)t is proper to take alarm at the first experiment on our liberties. * * *
> Who does not see that the same authority which can establish Christianity,
> in exclusion of all other Religions, may establish with the same ease any
> particular sect of Christians, in exclusion of all other Sects? That the
> authority which can force a citizen to contribute three pence only of his
> property for the support of any one establishment, may force him to
> conform to any other establishment in all cases whatsoever? II Writings
> of Madison 183, at 185-186.

Does Madison's warning against the "first experiment on our liberties" apply
to the financing of private religious education by the federal government?

FREE EXERCISE OF RELIGION

IN RE BROOKS' ESTATE
205 N.E. 2d 435 (1965)
Supreme Court of Illinois

■ ■ ■

On and sometime before May 7, 1964, Bernice Brooks was in the McNeal General
Hospital, Chicago, suffering from a peptic ulcer. She was being attended by Dr.
Gilbert Demange, and had informed him repeatedly during a two-year period prior
thereto that her religious and medical convictions precluded her from receiving blood
transfusions. Mrs. Brooks, her husband and two adult children are all members of the
religious sect commonly known as Jehovah's Witnesses. Among the religious beliefs
adhered to by members of this group is the principle that blood transfusions are a
violation of the law of God, and that transgressors will be punished by God...
Premised upon the belief that "The blood is the soul" (Deuteronomy 12:33) and that
"We cannot drain from our body part of that blood, which represents our life, and still
love god with our whole soul, because we have taken away part of 'our soul—our
blood—' and given it to someone else" (Blood, Medicine and the Law of God, p. 8),
members of Jehovah's witnesses regard themselves commanded by God to neither give
nor receive transfusions of blood.

Mrs. Brooks and her husband had signed a document releasing Dr. Demange and
the hospital from all civil liability that might result from the failure to administer
blood transfusions to Mrs. Brooks. The patient was assured that there would thereafter be no further effort to persuade her to accept blood.

Notwithstanding these assurances, however, Dr. Demange, together with several
assistant State's attorneys, and the attorney for the public guardian of Cook County,
Illinois, appeared before the probate division of the circuit court with a petition by the
public guardian requesting appointment of that officer as conservator of the person of
Bernice Brooks and further reguesting an order authorizing such conservator to
consent to the administration of whole blood to the patient. No notice of this
proceeding was given any member of the Brooks family. Thereafter, the conservator of
the person was appointed, consented to the administration of a blood transfusion, it
was accomplished and ... successfully so...

Appellees argue that society has an overriding interest in protecting the lives of its
citizens which justifies the action here taken. As supporting this conclusion they rely
upon the compulsory vaccination cases; the polygamous marriage proscriptions;
those cases sustaining statutes prohibiting the handling of snakes during religious

rituals; and Wallace v. Labrenz 411 Ill. 618, upholding the appointment of a guardian who consented to a blood transfusion administered to the minor child of members of Jehovah's Witnesses...

These cases are not determinative of the instant issue, and some are, in fact, supportive of a conclusion contrary to that urged by appellees. We believe the compulsory vaccination cases inapposite since society clearly can protect itself from the dangers of loathsome and contagious disease, a question with which we are not concerned; the polygamous marriage bans were upheld because the practice consisted of overt acts determined to be deleterious to public morals and welfare (no overt immoral activity appears here); the... "snake handling" prohibitions also involved affirmative action deemed detrimental to the public welfare; and Labrenz involved blood transfusions to a minor child...

It seems to be clearly established that the First Amendment of the United States Constitution as extended to the individual States by the Fourteenth Amendment to that constitution, protects the absolute right of every individual to freedom in his religious belief and the exercise thereof, subject only to the qualification that the exercise thereof may properly be limited by governmental action where such exercise endangers, clearly and presently, the public health, welfare or morals...

Applying the constitutional guarantees and the interpretations thereof... to the facts before us we find a competent adult who has steadfastly maintained her belief that acceptance of a blood transfusion is a violation of the law of God. Knowing full well the hazards involved, she has firmly opposed acceptance of such transfusions, notifying the doctor and hospital of her convictions and desires, and executing documents releasing both the doctor and the hospital from any civil liability which might be thought to result from a failure on the part of either to administer such transfusions. No minor children are involved. No overt or affirmative act of appellants offers any clear and present danger to society—we have only a governmental agency compelling conduct offensive to appellant's religious principles. Even though we may consider appellant's beliefs unwise, foolish or ridiculous, in the absence of an overriding danger to society we may not permit interference therewith in the form of a conservatorship established in the waning hours of her life for the sole purpose of compelling her to accept medical treatment forbidden by her religious principles, and previously refused by her with full knowledge of the probable consequences. In the final analysis, what has happened here involves a judicial attempt to decide what course of action is best for a particular individual, notwithstanding that individual's contrary views based upon religious convictions. Such action cannot be constitutionally countenanced...

■ ■ ■

Questions

1. "Whilst legislation for the establishment of a religion is forbidden, and its free-exercise permitted, it does not follow that everything which may be so-called (must) be tolerated." *Davis v. Veson* 133 U.S. 333 (1889). When can the state prohibit religious practices?
2. What religious activities are listed by the court in *Brooks* as properly prohibited by the state proscriptions?
3. How did the court differentiate this case allowing Mrs. Brook's religious practice from the case outlawing the religious practice of polygamous marriages? Do you agree that there is a difference?
4. Can the state require a religious oath for a public official?

EQUAL EDUCATION

The Equal Protection Clause of the Fourteenth Amendment pledges to the state citizenry the protection of equal laws. However, laws may classify, which will result in treating people differently or unequally. The Court must deal with this paradox of requiring equal treatment without denying legislative bodies the right to classify. It has taken a middle course of requiring "reasonable" classifications. The Constitution does not require that different things be treated in law as though they are the same. It merely requires equality in the sense that those similarly situated are to be similarly treated. Hence, the Court's task is to determine whether the legislative classification is a reasonable classification and rationally related to the purpose of the legislature.

The prohibition of the Equal Protection Clause goes no further than to prohibit invidious discrimination. As such, the Clause in a historical context supported only minimal judicial intervention. On the other hand, the Warren Court during the late sixties began to utilize the Equal Protection Clause as a favorite tool for judicial protection of "fundamental" rights that are not specifically specified in the Constitution. Under this transformation, the Equal Protection Clause becomes more important. The Court has held that when the statutory classification is based upon certain "suspect" criteria or affects "fundamental rights," such as classifications will be held to deny equal protection of the law unless they are justified by a "compelling" governmental interest. Two "suspect" categories that can be upheld only upon proof of a compelling governmental interest are racial classifications and classifications affecting "fundamental rights," such as a citizen's right to vote. The following two cases illustrate the Court's utilization of the "new" Equal Protection Clause to protect against "suspect" racial discrimination and State manipulation of the "fundamental right" to vote. To uphold the State laws in these "suspect" areas, the States must prove a "compelling governmental interest" requires the classification.

BROWN v. BOARD OF EDUCATION OF TOPEKA
347 U.S. 483 (1954)
Supreme Court of the United States

■ ■ ■

WARREN, Mr. Chief Justice.

...[M]inors of the Negro race, through their legal representatives, seek the aid of the courts in obtaining admission to the public schools of their community on a nonsegregated basis. In each instance, they have been denied admission to schools attended by white childre under laws requiring or permitting segregation according to race. This segregation was alleged to deprive the plaintiffs of the equal protection of the laws under the Fourteenth Amendment. In each of the cases...a three-judge federal district court denied relief to the plaintiffs on the so-called "separate but equal" doctrine announced by this Court in *Plessy vs. Ferguson,* 163 U.S. 537, ... Under that doctrine, equality of treatment is accorded when the races are provided substantially equal facilities, even though these facilities be separate...

The plaintiffs contend that segregated public schools are not "equal" and cannot be made "equal," and that hence they are deprived of the equal protection of the laws...

...[One] reason for the inconclusive nature of the Amendment's history, with respect to segregated schools, is the status of public education at that time. In the South, the movement toward free common schools, supported by general taxation, had not yet taken hold. Education of white children was largely in the hands of private groups. Education of Negroes was almost nonexistent, and practically all of the race were illiterate. In fact, any education of Negroes was forbidden by law in some states. Today, in contrast, many Negroes have achieved outstanding success in the arts and sciences as well as in the business and professional world. It is true that public school education at the time of the Amendment had advanced further in the North, but the effect of the Amendment on Northern States was generally ignored in the congressional debates. Even in the North, the conditions of public education did not approximate those existing today. The curriculum was usually rudimentary: ungraded schools were common in rural areas; the school term was but three months a year in many states; and compulsory school attendance was virtually unknown. As a consequence, it is not suprising that there should be so little in the history of the Fourteenth Amendment relating to its intended effect on public education.

In approaching this problem, we cannot turn the clock back to 1868 when the Amendment was adopted, or even to 1896 when *Plessy v. Ferguson* was written. We must consider public education in the light of its full development and its present place in American life throughout the Nation. Only in this way can it be determined if segregation in public schools deprives these plaintiffs of the equal protection of the laws.

Today, education is perhaps the most important function of state and local governments. Compulsory school attendance laws and the great expenditures for education both demonstrate our recognition of the importance of education to our democratic society. It is required in the performance of our most basic public responsibilites, even service in the armed forces. It is the very foundation of good citizenship. Today it is a principal instrument in awakening the child to cultural values, in preparing him for later professional training, and in helping him to adjust normally to his environment. In these days, it is doubtful that any child may reasonably be expected to succeed in life if he is denied the opportunity of an education. Such an opportunity, where the state has undertaken to provide it, is a right which must be made available to all on equal terms.

We come then to the question presented: Does segregation of children in public schools solely on the basis of race, even though the physical facilities and other "tangible" factors may be equal, deprive the children of the minority group of equal educational opportunities? We believe that it does.

In *Sweatt v. Painter,* (339 U.S. 629), in finding that a segregated law school for Negroes could not provide them equal educational opportunities, this Court relied in large part on "those qualities which are incapable of objective measurement but which make for greatness in a law school." In *McLaurin v. Oklahoma State Regents,* (339 U.S. 637), the Court, in requiring that a Negro admitted to a white graduate school be treated like all other students, again resorted to intangible considerations: "* * * his ability to study, to engage in discussions and exchange views with added force to children in grade and high schools. To separate them from others of similar age and qualifications solely because of their race generates a feeling of inferiority as to their status in the community that may affect their hearts and minds in a way unlikely ever to be undone. The effect of this separation on their hearts and minds in a way unlikely ever to be undone. The effect of this separation of their educational opportunities was well stated by a finding in the Kansas case by a court which nevertheless felt compelled to rule against the Negro plaintiffs:

> "Segregation of white and colored children in public schools has a detrimental effect upon the colored children. The impact is greater when it has the sanction of the law; for the policy of separating the races is usually interpreted as denoting the inferiority of the Negro group. A sense of inferiority affects the motivation of a child to learn. Segregation with the sanction of law, therefore, has a tendency to (retard) the educational and mental development of Negro children and to deprive them of some of the benefits they would receive in a racial-(ly) integrated school system."

Whatever may have been the extent of psychological knowledge at the time of *Plessy v. Ferguson,* this finding is amply supported by modern authority. Any language in *Plessy v. Ferguson* contrary to this finding is rejected.

We concule that in the field of public education the doctrine of "separate but equal" has no place. Separate educational facilities are inherently unequal. Therefore, we hold that the plaintiffs and others similarly situated for whom the actions have been brought are, by reason of the segregation complained of, deprived of the equal protection of the laws guaranteed by the Fourteenth Amendment.

■ ■ ■

Questions

1. Why was the Fourteenth Amendment not used against racially separate schools when it was first added to the Constitution?
2. What "intangible effect" causes racially separate educational facilities to be unequal? Did we always know of the "effect?"
3. Legally compelled segregation in other public facilites has been declared unconstitutional, such as public beaches, buses, golf courses, parks, court-rooms, and prison facilities. What would be the reasoning of these decisions?
4. The *Brown* decision outlawed *de jure* segregation, that is segregation of races by law. In effect, the decision outlawed the State mandated legal separation by race of children in educational facilities. However, President Nixon reminded us that, "There is a fundamental distinction between so-called *'de jure'* and *'de facto'* segregation: *de jure* segregation arises by law or by the deliberate act of school officials and it's unconstitutional; *de facto* segregation results from residential housing patterns and does not violate the Constitution." *New York Times.* (March 25, 1970). Hence, attacks against racially segregated schools must prove that the separation was from deliberate State (School Board) action to be found illegal.

EQUAL REPRESENTATION

In *Colegrove v. Greene* 328 U.S. 549 (1946) the Supreme Court considered a federal court action to enjoin Illinois officials from proceeding with an election of Congress-men on the grounds that the Illinois Law apportioning Congressional districts was unconstitutional. The districts were not of approximate equality in population. The Supreme Court dismissed the complaint and said:

> ...(E)ffective working of our government revealed this issue to be of a peculiar political nature... It is hostile to a democratic system to involve the judiciary in the politics of people... Authority for dealing with such problems resides elsewhere... The short of it is that the Constitution has conferred upon Congress exclusive authority to secure fair representation by the States in the popular House and left to that House determination whether States have fulfilled their responsibilities... Whether congress faithfully dis-charged its duty or not, the subject has been committed to the exclusive control of Congress... Courts ought not to enter this political thicket.....

The Supreme Court held that nonjusticiability of political questions was primarily a function of the separation of powers doctrine. The Court felt that under the U.S. system of government these questions were more appropriately handled by other political departments and that the Court lacked satisfactory criteria to make a judicial determination of the issue. In 1962 in the case of *Baker v. Carr* 369 U.S. 186 the Supreme Court expressed a change of attitude. The Court concluded that the issue had not been committed to the exclusive enforcement of other departments of government and was not lacking judicially discoverable and manageable standards for determina-tion of the issue. The holding that this question was justiciable opened a whole new area of controversial decisions by the Supreme Court.

REYNOLDS v. SIMS
377 U.S. 533 (1964)
Supreme Court of the United States

■ ■ ■

WARREN, Mr. Chief Justice.

In *Baker v. Carr*, 369 U.S. 186, we held that a claim asserted under the Equal Protection Clause challenging the constitutionality of a State's apportionment of seats in its legislature, on the ground that the right to vote of certain citizens was effectively impaired since debased and diluted, in effect presented a justiciable controversy subject to adjudication by federal courts. The spate of similar cases filed and decided by lower courts since our decision in *Baker* amply shows that the problem of state legislative malapportionment is one that is perceived to exist in a large number of the States. In *Baker*, a suit involving an attack on the apportionment of seats in the Tennessee Legislature, we remanded to the District Court, which had dismissed the action, for consideration on the merits. We intimated no view as to the proper constitutional standards for evaluating the validity of a state legislative apportionment scheme. Nor did we give any consideration to the question of appropriate remedies....

In *Gray v. Sanders*, 372 U.S. 368, we held that the Georgia county unit system, applicable in statewide primary elections, was unconstitutional since it resulted in a dilution of the weight of the votes of certain Georgia voters merely because of where they resided. After indicating that the Fifteenth and Nineteenth Amendments prohibit a State from overweighting or diluting votes on the basis of race or sex, we stated:

How then can one person be given twice or ten times the voting power of another person in a statewide election merely because he lives in a rural area or because he lives in the smallest rural county? Once the geographical unit for which a representative is to be chosen is designated, all who participate in the election are to have an equal vote—whatever their race, whatever their sex, whatever their occupation, whatever their income, and wherever their home may be in that geographical unit. This is required by the Equal Protection Clause of the Fourteenth Amendment. The concept of "we the people" under the Constitution visualizes no preferred class of voters but equality among those who meet the basic qualifications. The idea that every voter is equal to every other voter in his State, when he casts his ballot in favor of one of several competing candidates, underlies many of our decisions.

Continuing, we stated that "there is no indication in the Constitution that homesite or occupation affords a permissible basis for distinguishing between qualified voters within the State." And, finally, we concluded: "The conception of political equality from the Declaration of Independence, to Lincoln's Gettysburg Address, to the Fifteenth, Seventeenth, and Nineteenth Amendments can mean only one thing—one person, one vote."...

In *Wesberry v. Sanders*, 376 U.S. 1, decided earlier this Term, we held that attacks on the constitutionality of congressional districting plans enacted by state legislatures do not present nonjusticiable questions and should not be dismissed generally for "want of equity." We determined that the constitutional test for the validity of congressional districting schemes was one of substantial equality of population among the various districts established by a state legislature for the election of members of the Federal House of Representatives....

Logically, in a society ostensibly grounded on representative government, it would seem reasonable that a majority of the people of a State could elect a majority of that State's legislators. To conclude differently, and to sanction minority control of state legislative bodies, would appear to deny majority rights in a way that far surpasses any possible denial of minority rights that might otherwise be thought to result. Since legislatures are responsible for enacting laws by which all citizens are to be governed, they should be bodies which are collectively responsive to the popular will. And the concept of equal protection has been traditionally viewed as requiring the uniform treatment of persons standing in the same relation to the governmental action questioned or challenged. With respect to the allocation of legislative representation, all voters, as citizens of a State, stand in the same relation regardless of where they live...

Since the achieving of fair and effective representation for all citizens is concededly the basic aim of legislative apportionment, we conclude that the Equal Protection Clause guarantees the opportunity for equal participation by all voters in the election of state legislators. Diluting the weight of votes because of place of residence impairs basic constitutional rights under the Fourteenth Amendment just as much as invidious discriminations based upon factors such as race, or economic status. Our constitutional system amply provides for the protection of minorities by means other than giving them majority control of state legislatures. And the democratic ideals of equality and majority rule, which have served this Nation so well in the past, are hardly of any less significance for the present and the future. . . .

We hold that, as a basic constitutional standard, the Equal Protection Clause requires that the seats in both houses of a bicameral state legislature must be apportioned on a population basis. Simply stated, an individual's right to vote for state legislators is unconstitutionally impaired when its weight is in a substantial fasion diluted when compared with votes of citizens living in other parts of the State. . .

■ ■ ■

Questions and Note

1. *Gray v. Sanders* outlawed unequal representation in which kind of election? What kind in *Wesberry v. Sanders*? What kind in *Reynolds v. Sims*?

2. . . . The actions of local government are the actions of the State. A city, town, or county may no more deny the equal protection of the laws than it may abridge freedom of speech, establish an official religion, arrest without probable cause, or deny due process of the law.

   When the State apportions its legislature, it must have due regard for the Equal Protection Clause. Similarly, when the State delegates lawmaking power to local government and provides for the election of local officials from districts specified by statute, ordinance, or local charter, it must insure that those qualified to vote have the right to an equally effective voice in the election process. . . *Avery v. Midland County* 390 U.S. 474 (1968).

3. Can you think of a reason why the Supreme Court refused certiorari to dismissed suits challenging the constitutionality of the respective powers of the President and Congress in making foreign policy and in committing armed forces abroad?

MARIHUANA RIGHTS

Having opened the door of the "new" Equal Protection Clause in protection of "fundamental rights," the Court has been flooded with requests to recognize additional fundamental rights. Consider the short exerpts from the following cases.

COMMONWEALTH v. LEIS
243 N.E. 2d 898 (1969)
Supreme Court of Massachusetts

■ ■ ■

The defendants insist that the right to smoke marihuana is guaranteed by the Constitutions of the Commonwealth and of the United States and must be balanced against the interests of the State in prohibiting its use. No such right exists. It is not specifically preserved by either Constitution. The right to smoke marihuana is not "fundamental to the American scheme of justice necessary to an Anglo-American regime of ordered liberty." It is not within a "zone of privacy" formed by "penumbras" of the First, Third, Fourth and Fifth Amendments and the Ninth Amendment of the Constitution of the United States. The defendants have no right, fundamental or otherwise, to become intoxicated by means of the smoking of marihuana.

The defendants maintain that the Narcotic Drugs Law "has singled out for prohibition and punishment possessors of and possessors of with intent to sell, marihuana, while the laws permit the regulated use, sale and possession of substances far more harmful than marihuana, punish less harshly possession and sale of substances far more harmful than marihuana, and punish equally harshly substances far more harmful than marihuana." Therefore, they say that it violates art. I of the Declaration of Rights of the Constitution of the Commonwealth and the Equal Protection Clause of the Fourteenth Amendment of the Constitution of the United States....

They concede that the Legislature may select the kinds of behavior that it wishes to proscribe. They claim, however, that this "does not mean that a Legislature may actually proscribe behavior of one class of people (e.g., those who choose to obtain a mild state of intoxication with marihuana) and allow another class of people to freely indulge in behavior of an exactly similar nature (e.g., those who choose to obtain a mild state of intoxication with alcohol)."

We do not think that a statute which proscribes generally certain conduct can be said to be discriminatory simply because a certain group of persons tend to engage more often in that conduct than others. Such "de facto" discrimination does not violate the Equal Protection Clause. There are at least two distintions between alcohol and the "mind-altering" intoxicants that are defined by the law to be narcotic drugs. First, alcohol is susceptible to a less restrictive alternative means of control. There are recognized, accurate means of determining its use and its abuse. Second, the effects of alcohol upon the user are known. We think that the Legislature is warranted in treating this known intoxicant differently from marihuana, LSD or heroin, the effects of which are largely still unknown and subject to extensive dispute. The Legislature is free to recognize degrees of harm and may confine its restrictions to instances where it determines the need for them is clearest....

■ ■ ■

Questions

1. How did the Court determine that smoking of marihuana was not a "fundamental" right?
2. Why did the Court feel the classification of marihuana smoking as a crime was not an "unequal" law?

A FUNDAMENTAL RIGHT, ESSENTIAL TO A FAIR TRIAL

One primary concern of our legal system is the security of the individual. Our political problems as a colony and the abuse of the legal system by the Crown against unpopular political persons gave rise to various efforts to protect individuals from arbitrary government actions. Accordingly, the Constitution contains numerous prohibitions against unreasonable action by government officials. The principles under which the acused is to be held accountable for the alleged crime and the appropriate conduct of the enforcement officials emphasize the protection of individual liberties. The constitutional framework in these civil libertarian areas has been defined and clarified by the U.S. Supreme Court in a case-by-case application of the Constitution to conflicts between the alleged suspect and law enforcement officials. The following cases illustrate the case approach used by the Supreme Court in resolving the controversy before it and in maintaining the delicate balance between law enforcement and civil liberties.

RIGHT AGAINST UNLAWFUL SEARCH AND SEIZURE

MAPP v. OHIO
367 U.S. 643 (1961)
Supreme Court of the United States

■ ■ ■

CLARK, Mr. Justice.

On May 23, 1957, three Cleveland police officers arrived at appellant's residence in that city pursuant to information that "a person (was) hiding out in the home, who was wanted for questioning in connection with a recent bombing, and that there was a large amount of policy paraphernalia being hidden in the home." Miss Mapp and her daughter by a former marriage lived on the top floor of the two-family dwelling. Upon their arrival at that house, the officers knocked on the door and demanded entrance but appellant, after telephoning her attorney, refused to admit them without a search warrant. They advised their headquarters of the situation and undertook a surveillance of the house.

The officers again sought entrance some three hours later when four or more additional officers arrived on the scene. When Miss Mapp did not come to the door immediately, at least one of the several doors to the house was forcibly opened and the policemen gained admittance. Meanwhile Miss Mapp's attorney arrived, but the officers, having secured their own entry, and continuing in their defiance of the law, would permit him neither to see Miss Mapp nor to enter the house. It appears that Miss Mapp was halfway down the stairs from the upper floor to the front door when the officers, in this highhanded manner, broke into the hall. She demanded to see the search warrant. A paper, claimed to be a warrant, was held up by one of the officers. She grabbed the "warrant" and placed it in her bosom. A struggle ensued in which the officers recovered the piece of paper and as a result of which they handcuffed appellant because she had been "belligerent"... in resisting their official rescue of the "warrant" from her person. Running roughshod over appellant, a policeman "grabbed" her, "twisted (her) hand," and she "yelled (and) pleaded with him" because "it was hurting." Appellant, in handcuffs, was then forcibly taken upstairs to her bedroom where the officers searched a dresser, a chest of drawers, a closet and some suitcases. They also looked into a photo album and through personal papers belonging to the appellant. The search spread to the rest of the second floor including the child's bedroom the living room, the kitchen and a dinette. The basement of the building and a trunk found therein were also searched. The obscene materials for possession of which she was ultimately convicted were discovered in the course of that widespread search... "There is, in the record, considerable doubt as to whether there ever was any warrant for the search of defendant's home."

The State says that even if the search were made without authority, or otherwise unreasonably, it is not prevented from using the unconstitutinally seized evidence at trial, citing *Wolf v. People of State of Colorado,* (1949), in which this Court did indeed hold "that in a prosecution in a State court for a State crime the Fourteenth Amendment does not forbid the admission of evidence obtained by a unreasonable search and seizure."....

Today we once again examine *Wolf*...and, after its dozen years on our books, are led by it to close the only courtroom door remaining open to evidence secured by official lawlessness in flagrant abuse of that basic right, reserved to all persons as a specific guarantee against that very same unlawful conduct. We hold that all evidence obtained by searches and seizures in violation of the Constitution is, by that same authority, inadmissible in a state court....

...Therefore, in extending the substantive protections of due process to all constitutionally unreasonable searches—state or federal—it was logically and constitutionally necessary that the exclusion doctrine—an essential part of the right to privacy—be also insisted upon as an essential ingredient of the right... In short, the admission of the new constitutional right...(of privacy) could not consistently tolerate denial of its most important constitutional privilege, namely, the exclusion of the evidence which an accused had been forced to give by reason of the unlawful seizure. To hold otherwise is to grant the right but in reality to withhold its privilege and enjoyment... This court has not hesitated to enforce as strictly against the States as it does against the Federal Government the rights of free speech and of a free press, the rights to notice and to a fair, public trial, including, as it does, the right not to be convicted by use of a coerced confession... Why should not the same rule apply to what is tantamount to coerced testimony by way of unconstitutional seizure of goods, papers, effects, documents, etc.? We find that, as to the Federal Government, the Fourth and Fifth Amendments and, as to the States, the freedom from unconscionable invasions of privacy and the freedom from convictions based upon coerced confessions...together...assure in either sphere...that no man is to be convicted on unconstitutional evidence.

Moreover, our holding that the exclusionary rule is an essential part of both the Fourth and Fourteenth Amendments is not only the logical dictate of prior cases, but it also makes very good sense. There is no war between the Constitution and common sense. Presently, a federal prosecutor may make no use of evidence illegally seized, but a State's attorney across the street may, although he supposedly is operating under the enforceable prohibitions of the same Amendment. Thus the State, by admitting evidence unlawfully seized, serves to encourage disobedience to the Federal Constitution which it is bound to uphold... In non-exclusionary States, federal officers, being human, were by it invited to and did, as our cases indicate, step across the street to the State's attorney with their unconstitutionally seized evidence. prosecution on the basis of that evidence was then has in a state court in utter disregard of the enforceable Fourth Amendment. If the fruits of an unconstitutional search had been inadmissible in both state and federal courts, this inducement to evasion would have been sooner eliminated...

Federal-state cooperation in the solution of crime under constitutional standards will be promoted, if only by recognition of their now mutual obligation to respect the same fundamental criteria in their approaches.

...There are those who say, as did Justice (then Judge) Cardozo, that under our constitutional exclusionary doctrine " (t)he criminal is to go free because the constable has blundered." In some cases this will undoubtedly be the result. But, as was said in *Elkins*, "there is another consideration—the imperative of judicial integrity." The criminal goes free, if he must, but it is the law that sets him free. Nothing can destroy a government more quickly than its failure to observe its own laws, or worse, its disregard of the charter of its own existence... Nor can it lightly be assumed that, as a practical matter, adoption of the exclusionary rule fetters law enforcement. Only last year this Court expressly considered that contention and found that "pragmatic evidence of a sort" to the contrary was not wanting...

The ignoble shortcut to conviction left open to the State tends to destroy the entire system of constitutional restraints on which the liberties of the people rest. Having once recognized that the right to privacy embodied in the Fourth Amendment is enforceable against the States, and that the right to be secure against rude invasions of privacy by state officers is, therefore, constitutional in origin, we can no longer permit that right to remain an empty promise. Because it is enforceable in the same manner and to like effect as other basic rights secured by the Due Process Clause, we can no longer permit it to be revocable at the whim of any police officer who, in the name of law enforcement itself, chooses to suspend its enjoyment. Our decision, founded on reason and truth, gives to the individual no more than that which the Constitution guarantees him, to the police officer no less than that to which honest law enforcement is entitled, and, to the courts, that judicial integrity so necessary in the true administration of justice.

■ ■ ■

Comment and Questions

1. Previously, the highest court of California felt compelled to adopt the exclusionary rule in California because other remedies have failed to secure complete compliance with the constitutional provision in the Fourth Amendment. Are there no other ways to discipline police against unlawful searches besides refusing to use his illegally gathered evidence? Must the criminal go free because the constable has blundered?

2. Is judicial integrity blemished if courts use evidence seized in violation of the Fourth Amendment?

3. The Supreme Court concluded that the exclusionary rule of *Mapp* should not apply to "state court convictions which had become final before rendition" of the *Mapp* decision. Why not?

4. In 1969 the Supreme Court ruled: "We hold the First and Fourteenth Amend-

ments prohibit making mere private possession of obscene material a crime...
As we have said, the States retain broad power to regulate obscenity; that
power simply does not extend to mere possession by the individual in the
privacy of his own home..."

The Court's argument included: "Whatever may be the justifications for
other statutes regulating obscenity, we do not think they reach into the privacy
of one's own home. If the First Amendment means anything, it means that a
state has no business telling a man, sitting alone in his own house, what books
he may read or what films he may watch. Our whole Constitutional heritage
rebels at the thought of giving government the power to control men's
minds..." *Stanley v. Georgia* 394 U.S. 557 (1969).

Under the more recent decision of *Stanley*, would the Court conclude that
Miss Mapp's *First* Amendment rights also were violated by the State of Ohio?

RIGHT TO COUNSEL

GIDEON v. WAINWRIGHT
372 U.S. 335 (1963)
Supreme Court of the United States

■ ■ ■

BLACK, Mr. Justice.

Petitioner was charged in a Florida state court with having broken and entered a
poolroom with intent to commit a misdemeanor. This offense is a felony under Florida
law. Appearing in court without funds and without a lawyer, petitioner asked the
court to appoint counsel for him, whereupon the following colloquy took place:

"THE COURT: Mr Gideon, I am sorry, but I cannot appoint Counsel to represent you in
this case. Under the laws of the State of Florida, the only time the Court can appoint
Counsel to represent a Defendant is when that person is charged with a capital offense. I
am sorry, but I will have to deny your request to appoint Counsel to defend you in this
case.

"THE DEFENDANT: The United States Supreme Court says I am entitled to be
represented by Counsel."

Put to trial before a jury, Gideon conducted his defense about as well as could be
expected from a layman. He made an opening statement to the jury, cross-examined
the State's witnesses, presented witnesses in his own defense, declined to testify
himself, and made a short argument "emphasizing his innocence to the charge contained in the Information filed in this case." The jury returned a verdict of guilty, and
petitioner was sentenced to serve five years in the state prison. Later, petitioner filed in
the Florida Supreme Court this *habeas corpus* petition attacking his conviction and
sentence on the ground that the trial court's refusal to appoint counsel for him denied
him rights "guaranteed by the Constitution and the Bill of Rights by the United States
Government." Treating the petition for *habeas corpus* as properly before it, the State
Supreme Court, "upon consideration thereof" but without an opinion, denied all
relief. Since 1942, when *Betts v. Brady*, 316 U.S. 455, was decided by a divided Court,
the problem of a defendant's federal constitutional right to counsel in a state court has
been a continuing source of controversy and litigation in both state and federal courts.
To give this problem another review here, we granted *certiorari*.

The facts upon which Betts claimed that he had been unconstitutionally denied the
right to have counsel appointed to assist him are strikingly like the facts upon which
Gideon here bases his federal constitutional claim... Like Gideon, Betts sought

release by *habeas corpus*, alleging that he had been denied the right to assistance of counsel in violation of the Fourteenth Amendment. Betts was denied any relief, and on review this Court affirmed. It was held that a refusal to appoint counsel for an indigent defendant charged with a felony did not necessarily violate the Due Process Clause of the Fourteenth Amendment... The Court said:

> "Asserted denial (of due process) is to be tested by an appraisal of the totality of facts in a given case. that which may, in one setting, constitute a denial of fundamental fairness, shocking to the universal sense of justice, may, in other circumstances, and in the light of other considerations, fall short of such denial." 316 U.S., at 462...

We accept *Betts v. Brady's* assumption, based as it was on our prior cases, that a provision of the Bill of Rights which is "fundamental and essential to a fair trial" is made obligatory upon the States by the Fourteenth Amendment. We think the Court in *Betts* was wrong, however, in concluding that the Sixth Amendment's guarantee of counsel is not one of these fundamental rights. Ten years before *Betts v. Brady,* this Court, after full consideration of all the historical data examined in *Betts,* had unequivocally declared that "the right to the aid of counsel is of this fundamental character." *Powell v. Alabama.* While the Court at the close of its *Powell* opinion did by its language, as this Court frequently does, limit its holding to the particular facts and circumstances of that case, its conclusions about the fundamental nature of the right to counsel are unmistakable... In returning to these old precedents, sounder we believe than the new, we but restore constitutional principles established to achieve a fair system of justice. Not only these precedents but also reason and reflection require us to recognize that in our adversary system of criminal justice, any person haled into court, who is too poor to hire a lawyer, cannot be assured a fair trial unless counsel is provided for him. This seems to us to be an obvious truth. Governments, both state and federal, quite properly spend vast sums of money to establish machinery to try defendants accused of crime. Lawyers to prosecute are everywhere deemed essential to protect the public's interest in an orderly society. Similarly, there are few defendants charged with crime, few indeed, who fail to hire the best lawyers they can get to prepare and present their defenses. That government hires lawyers to presecute and defendants who have the money hire lawyers to defend are the strongest indications of the wide-spread belief that lawyers in criminal courts are necessitites, not luxuries. The right of one charged with crime to counsel may not be deemed fundamental and essential to fair trials in some countries, but it is in ours. From the very beginning, our state and national constitutions and laws have laid great emphasis on procedural and substantive safeguards designed to assure fair trials before impartial tribunals in which every defendant stands equal before the law. This noble ideal cannot be realized if the poor man charged with crime has to face his accusers without a lawyer to assist him... Twenty-two States, as friends of the Court, argue that *Betts* was an "anachronism when handed down" and that it should not be overruled. We agree.

■ ■ ■

Questions

1. Why is the trial "unfair" if the indigent defendant is denied counsel?
2. Does "effective" assistance of counsel mean something other than successful assistance?

RIGHT AGAINST SELF-INCRIMINATION

The Fifth Amendment right against compulsory self-incrimination has received considerable attention in the opinions of the Supreme Court. The Court's decisions have referred to this right as "the mainstay of our adversary system of criminal justice," *Johnson v. New Jersey*, 384 U.S. 719 (1966) and as "one of the great landmarks of man's struggle to make himself civilized." *Ullman v. U.S.* 350 U.S. 422 (1956).

The privilege against compulsory self-incrimination was developed by painful opposition to the ecclesiastical inquisitions and Star Chamber proceedings of centuries ago. Accounts of those ancient investigations reveal a premium was placed upon compelling subjects of the investigation to admit guilt from their own lips. The Framers of the Constitution desired to protect citizens against such compulsion.

Cases in United States which involve the Self-incrimination Clause obviously, by definition involve an element of coercion. The Clause provided that a person may not be *compelled* to give evidence against himself. Cases involving self-incriminating statements often depict servere pressures on the accused to admit guilt. Factual situations have ranged from the classical third degree torture, to prolonged isolation from family or friends in a hostile setting, and to a simple desire on part of the physically or mentally exhausted suspect to have the seemingly endless interrogation end. As a consequence of recurring cases such as these, the Supreme Court attempted to develop a rule to avoid these techniques of compulsion.

MIRANDA v. STATE OF ARIZONA
384 U.S. 436 (1966)
Supreme Court of the United States

■ ■ ■

WARREN, Mr. Chief Justice.

The cases before us raise questions which go to the roots of our concepts of American criminal jurisprudence: the restraints society must observe consistent with the Federal Constitution in prosecuting individuals for crime. More specifically, we deal with the admissibility of statements obtained from an individual who is subjected to custodial police interrogation and the necessity for procedures which assure that the individual is accorded his privilege under the Fifth Amendment to the Constitution not to be compelled to incriminate himself.

We dealt with certain phases of this problem recently in *Escobedo v. State of Illinois,* (1964). There, as in the four cases before us, law enforcement officials took the defendant into custody and interrogated him in a police station for the purpose of obtaining a confession. The police did not effectively advise him of his right to remain silent or of his right to consult with an attorney. Rather, they confronted him with an alleged accomplice who accused him of having perpetrated a murder. When the defendant denied the accusation and said "I didn't shoot Manuel, you did it," they handcuffed him and took him to an interrogation room. There, while handcuffed and standing, he was questioned for four hours until he confessed. During this interrogation, the police denied his request to speak to his attorney, and they prevented his retained attorney, who had come to the police station, from consulting with him. At his trial, the State, over his objections, introduced the confession against him. We held that the statements thus made were constitutionally inadmissible.

We start here, as we did in *Escobedo,* with the premise that our holding is not an innovation in jurisprudence, but is an application of principles long recognized and applied in other settings. We have undertaken a thorough re-examination of the *Escobedo* decision and the principle it announced, and we reaffirm it. That case was but an explication of basic rights that are enshrined in our Constitution—that "No person * * * shall be compelled in any criminal case to be a witness against himself," and that "the accused shall * * * have the Assistance of Counsel"—rights which were put in jeopardy in that case through official overbearing. These precious rights were fixed in our Constitution only after centuries of persecution and struggle...

Our holding will be spelled out with some specificity in the page which follow but briefly stated it is this: the prosecution may not use statements, whether exculpatory or inculpatory, stemming from custodial interrogation of the defendant unless it demonstrates the use of procedural safeguards effective to secure the privilege against self-incrimination. By custodial interrogation, we mean questioning initiated by law enforcement officers after a person has been taken into custody or otherwise deprived of his freedom of action in any significant way. As for the procedural safeguards to be employed, unless other fully effective means are devised to inform accused persons of their right of silence and to assure a continuous opportunity to exercise it, the following measures are required. Prior to any questioning, the person must be warned that he has a right to remain silent, that any statement he does make may be used as evidence against him, and that he has a right to the presence of an attorney, either retained or appointed. The defendant may waive effectuation of these rights, provided the waiver is made voluntarily, knowlingly and intelligently. If, however, he indicates in any manner and at any stage of the process that he wishes to consult with an attorney before speaking there can be no questioning. Likewise, if the individual is alone and indicates in any manner that he does not wish to be interrogated, the police may not question him. The mere fact that he may have answered some questions or volunteered some statements on his own does not deprive him of the right to refrain from answering any further inquiries until he has consulted with an attorney and thereafter consents to be questioned.

The constitutional issue we decide in each of these cases is the admissibility of statements obtained from a defendant questioned while in custody or otherwise deprived of his freedom of action in any significant way. In each, the defendant was questioned by police officers, detectives, or a prosecuting attorney in a room in which he was cut off from the outside world. In none of these cases was the defendant given a full and effective warning of his rights at the outset of the interrogation process. In all the cases, the questioning elicited oral admissions, and in three of them, signed statements as well which were admitted at their trials. They all thus share salient features—incommunicado interrogation of individuals in a police-dominated atmosphere, resulting in self-incriminating statements without full warnings of constitutional rights.

An understanding of the nature and setting of this in-custody interrogation is essential to our decisions today. The difficulty in depicting what transpires at such interrogations stems from the fact that in this country they have largely taken place incommunicado. From extensive factual studies undertaken in the early 1930's, including the famous Wickersham Report to Congress by a Presidential Commission, it is clear that police violence and the "third degree" flourished at that time.

. . . Interrogation still takes place in privacy. Privacy results in secrecy and this in turn results in a gap in our knowledge as to what in fact goes on in the interrogation rooms. A valuable source of information about present police practices, however, may be found in various police manuals and texts which document procedures employed with success in the past, and which recommend various other effective tactics. These texts are used by law enforcement agencies themselves as guides. It should be noted that these texts professedly present the most enlightened and effective means presently used to obtain statements through custodial interrogation. . . In essence, it is this: To be alone with the subject is essential to prevent distraction and to deprive him of any outside support. The aura of confidence in his guilt undermines his will to resist. He merely confirms the preconceived story the police seek to have him describe. Patience and persistence, at times relentless questioning, are employed. To obtain a confession, the interrogator must "patiently maneuver himself or his quarry into a position from which the desired object may be obtained." When normal procedures fail to produce the needed result, the police may resort to deceptive strategems such as giving false legal advice. It is important to keep the subject off balance, for example, by trading on his insecurity about himself or his surroundings. The police then persuade, trick or cajole him out of exercising his constitutional rights. . .

Today, then, there can be no doubt that the Fifth Amendment privilege is available outside of criminal court proceedings and serves to protect persons in all settings in which their freedom of action is curtailed in any significant way from being compelled to incriminate themselves. We have concluded that without proper safeguards the process of in-custody interrogation of persons suspected or accused of crime contains inherently compelling pressures which work to undermine the individual's will to resist and to compel him to speak where he would not otherwise do so freely. In order to combat these pressures and to permit a full opportunity to exercise the privilege against self-incrimination, the accused mut be adequately and effectively apprised of his rights and the exercise of those rights must be fully honored. . .

Our decision is not intended to hamper the traditional function of police officers in investigating crime.

. . . When an individual is in custody on probable cause the police may, of course, seek out evidence in the field to be used at trial against him. Such investigation may include inquiry of persons not under restraint. General on-the-scene questioning as to facts surrounding a crime or other general questioning of citizens in the fact-finding process is not afected by our holding. It is an act of responsible citizenship for individuals to give whatever information they may have to aid in law enforcement. In such situations the compelling atmosphere inherent in the process of in-custody interrogation is not necessarily present.

In dealing with statements obtained through interrogation we do not purport to find all confessions inadmissible. Confessions remain a proper element in law enforcement. Any statement given freely and voluntarily without compelling influences is, of course, admissible in evidence. The fundamental import of the privilege while an individual is in custody is not whether he is allowed to talk to the police without the benefit of warnings and counsel, but whether he can be interrogated. There is no requirement that police stop a person who enters a police station and states that he wishes to confess to a crime, or a person who calls the police to offer a confession or any other statement he desires to make. Volunteered statements of any kind are not barred by the Fifth Amendment and their admissibility is not affected by our holding today. . . .

■ ■ ■

Questions

1. What four warnings or information must the police give to one under police custody prior to questioning?
2. Does the *Miranda* decision effectively destroy any ability to secure confession to crimes?
3. What is a waiver of rights that is voluntarily, knowingly, and intelligently given? What is custodial interrogation? At what point is a person within custody?
4. ". . .[R]etroactive application of. . . *Miranda* would seriously disrupt the administration of our criminal laws. It would require the retrial or release of numerous prisoners found guilty by trustworthy evidence in conformity with previously announced constitutional standards. . . [W]e conclude that. . . *Miranda*, like *Mapp v. Ohio*. . . should not be applied retroactively. . . [T]hese decisions should apply only to trials begun after the decisions were announced. . ." *Johnson v. New Jersey* 384 U.S. 719 (1966). Why?

SCHMERBER V. CALIFORNIA
384 U.S. 757 (1966)
Supreme court of the United States

■ ■ ■

BRENNAN, Mr. Justice.

We hold that the privilege protects an accused only from being compelled to testify against himself, or otherwise provide the State with evidence of a testimonial or communicative nature, and that the withdrawal of blood and use of the analysis in question in this case did not involve compulsion to these ends. . .

It is clear that the protection of the privilege reaches an accused's communications, whatever from they might take, and the compulsion of responses which are also communications, for example, compliance with a subpoena to produce one's papers. . . On the other hand, both federal and state courts have usually held that it offers no protection against compulsion to submit to fingerprinting, photographing, or measurements, to write or speak for identification, to appear in court, to stand, to assume a stance, to walk, or to make a particular gesture. The distinction which has emerged, often expressed in different ways, is that the privilege is a bar against compelling "communications" or "testimony," but that compulsion which makes a suspect or accused the source of "real or physical evidence" does not violate it. ...(However), there will be many cases in which such a distinction is not readily drawn Some tests seemingly directed to obtain "physical evidence," for example, lie detector tests measuring changes in body function during interrogation, may actually be directed to eliciting responses which are essentially testimonial. To compel a person to submit to testing in which an effort will be made to determine his guilt or innocence on the basis of physiological responses, whether willed or not is to evoke the spirit and history of the Fifth Amendment...

In the present case, however, no such problem of application is presented. Not even a shadow of testimonial compulsion upon or enforced comunication by the accused was involved either in the extraction or in the chemical analysis. Petitioner's testimonial capacitites were in no way implicated: indeed, his participation, except as a donor, was irrelevant to the results of the test, which depend on chemical analysis and on that alone. Since the blood test evidence, although an incriminating product of compulsion, was neither petitioner's testimony nor evidence relating to some communicative act or writing by the petitioner, it was not inadmissible on privilege grounds...

The question is also squarely presented... whether the chemical analysis introduced is evidence in this case should have been excluded as the product of an unconstitutional search and seizure.

The overriding function of the Fourth Amendment is to protect personal privacy and dignity against unwarranted intrusion by the State...

...[T]he Fourth Amendment's proper function is to constrain, not against all intrusions as such, but against intrusions which are not justified in the circumstances, or which are made in an improper manner. We must decide whether the police were justified in requiring petitioner to submit to the blood test, and whether the means and procedures employed in taking his blood respected relevant Fourth Amendment standards of reasonableness.

...Here, there was plainly probable cause for the officer to arrest petitioner and charge him with driving an automobile while under the influence of intoxicating liquor...

Similarly, we are satisfied that the test chosen to measure petitioner's blood-alcohol level was a reasonable one...

Finally, the record shows that the test was performed in a reasonable manner. Petitioner's blood was taken by a physician in a hospital environment according to accepted medical practices...

We thus conclude that the present record shows no violation of petitioner's right under the Fourth and Fourteenth Amendments to be free of unreasonable searches and seizures...

■ ■ ■

Questions

1. How did the court distinguish between involuntary confessions and involuntary "taking of blood"?
2. What elements of "reasonableness" did the Court consider in determining if the research was reasonable under the Fourth Amendment?

HARRIS v. NEW YORK
401 U.S. 222 (1971)
Supreme Court of the United States

■ ■ ■

BURGER, Mr. Chief Justice.

The State of New York charged petitioner with twice selling herion to an undercover police officer...

Petitioner took the stand in his own defense. He admitted knowing the undercover police officer but denied a sale on January 4, 1966. He admitted making a sale of contents of a glassine bag to the officer on January 6 but claimed it was baking powder and part of a scheme to defraud the purchaser.

On cross-examination petitioner was asked whether he had made specified statements to the police immediately following his arrest—statements that partially contradicted petitioner's direct testimony at trial. In response to the cross-examination, petitioner testified that he could not remember virtually any of the questions or answers recited by the prosecutor...

The trial judge instructed the jury that the statements attributed to petitioner by the prosecution could be considered only in passing on petitioner's credibility and not as evidence of guilt...

At trial the prosecution made no effort in its case in chief to use the statements allegedly made by petitioner, conceding that they were inadmissible under *Miranda v. Arizona*. The transcript of the interrogation used in the impeachment, but not given to the jury, shows that no warning of a right to appointed counsel was given before questions were put to petitioner when he was taken into custody. Petitioner makes no claim that the statements made to the police were coerced or involuntary.

... *Miranda* barred the prosecution from making its case with statements of an accused made while in custody prior to having or effectively waiving counsel. It does not follow from *Miranda* that evidence inadmissible against an accused in the prosecution's case in chief is barred for all purposes, provided of course that the trustworthiness of the evidence satisfies legal standards.

In Walder v. United States, 347 U.S. 62, (1954), the Court permitted physical evidence, inadmissible in the case in chief, to be used for impeachment purposes.

> "It is one thing to say that the Government cannot make an affirmative use of evidence unlawfully obtained. It is quite another to say that the defendant can turn the illegal method by which evidence in the Government's possession was obtained to his own advantage, and provide himself with a shield against contradiction of his untruths"...

... Petitioner's testimony in his own behalf concerning the events contrasted sharply with what he told the police shortly after his arrest. The impeachment process here undoubtedly provided valuable aid to the jury in assessing petitioner's credibility, and the benefits of this process should not be lost, in our view, because of the speculative possibility that impermissible police conduct will be encouraged thereby. Assuming that the exclusionary rule has a deterrent effect on proscribed police conduct, sufficient deterrence flows when the evidence in question is made unavailable to the prosecution in its case in chief.

Every criminal defendant is privileged to testify in his own defense, or to refuse to do so. But that privilege cannot be construed to include the right to commit perjury. Having voluntarily taken the stand, petitioner was under an obligation to speak truthfully and accurately, and the prosecution here did no more than utilize the traditional truth-testing devices of the adversary process...

The sheild provided by *Miranda* cannot be perverted into a license to use perjury by way of a defense, free from the risk of confrontation with prior inconsistent utterances. We hold, therefore, that petitioner's credibility was appropriately impeached by use of his earlier conflicting statements.

BRENNAN, Mr. Justice, dissents.

... We settled this proposition in *Miranda* where we said:

"The privilege against self-incrimination protects the individual from being compelled to incriminate himself in *any* manner * * *. [S]tatements merely intended to be exculpatory by the defendant are often *used to impeach his testimony at trial * * *. These statements are incriminating in any meaningful sense of the word and may not be used without the full warnings and effective waiver required for any other statement."* 384 U.S., at 476-477, (emphasis added).

This language completely disposes of any distinction between statements used on direct as opposed to cross-examination. "An incriminating statement is as incriminating when used to impeach credibility as it is when used as direct proof of guilt ana no constitutional distinction can legitimately be drawn."

The objective of deterring improper police conduct is only part of the larger objective of safeguarding the integrity of our adversary system. The constitutional foundation underlying the privilege is the respect a government * * * must accord to the dignity and integrity of its citizens." These values are plainly jeopardized if an exception against admission of tainted statements is made for those used for impeachment purposes. Moreover, it is monstrous that courts should aid or abet the law-breaking police officer. The Court today tells the police that they may freely interrogate an accused incommunicado and without counsel and know that although any statement they obtain in violation of *Miranda* cannot be used on the State's direct case, it may be introduced if the defendant has the temerity to testify, in his own defense. This goes far toward undoing much of the progress made in conforming police methods to the Constitution.

■ ■ ■

Questions and Comment

1. How did the Court determine that failure to give the *Miranda* warnings did not preclude use of the defendant's statement to impeach his testimony?
2. Why does the disenting Justice feel the use of the defendant's statement for impeachment purposes is improper.
3. During the course of a consented search of a car that had been stopped by officers for traffic violations, evidence was discovered that was used to convict defendant of unlawfully possessing a check. The Court of Appeals, in reversing the District Court, held that the prosecution had failed to prove that consent to the search had been made with the understanding that it could freely be withheld. The Supreme Court reversed the Court of Appeals and held that when the subject of a search is not in custody and the State would justify a search on the basis of his consent, the fourth and fourteenth amendments require that it demonstrate that the consent was in fact voluntary; voluntariness is to be determined from the totality of the surrounding circumstances. While knowlege of a right to refuse consent is a factor to be taken into account, the State need not prove that the one giving permission to search knew that he had a right to withhold his consent. In effect, no police warning of the right to refuse a search was needed. The Court said:

    "(A search by consent may) occur on the highway, or in a person's home or office, and under informal and unstructed conditions. The circumstances that prompt the initial request to search may develop quickly or be a logical extension of investigative police questioning. The police may seek to investigate further suspicious circumstances or to follow up leads developed in questioning persons at the scene of a crime. These situations are a far cry from the structured atmosphere of a trial...and...are...far removed from 'custodial interrogation' as in *Miranda v. Arizona...*" *Schneckloth v. Bustamonte* 412 U.S. 218 (1973). Comment.

4. Can *Harris* and *Schneckloth* decisions be partly explained as an effort by the conservative Burger court to relax the decisions which were rendered by the liberal Warren Court?

PUBLIC TRIAL

SHEPPARD v.MAXWELL
384 U.S. 333 (1966)
Supreme Court of the United States

■ ■ ■

CLARK, Mr. Justice.

Marilyn Sheppard, petitioner's pregnant wife, was bludgeoned to death in the upstairs bedroom of their lakeshore home in Bay Village, Ohio, a suburb of Cleveland...

From the outset officials focused suspicion on Sheppard...

The principle that justice cannot survive behind walls of silence has long been reflected in the "Anglo-American distrust for secret trials."

A responsible press has always been regarded as the handmaiden of effective judicial administration, especially in the criminal field. its function in this regard is documented by an impressive record of service over several centuries. The press does not simply publish information about trials but guards against the miscarriage of justice by subjecting the police, prosecutors, and judicial processes to extensive public scrutiny and criticism. This Court has, therefore, been unwilling to place any direct limitations on the freedom traditionally exercised by the news media for "[w]hat transpires in the court room is public property."

...And where there was "no threat or menace to the integrity of the trial," we have consistently required that the press have a free hand, even though we sometimes deplored its sensationalism.

But the Court has also pointed out that "[l]egal trials are not like elections, to be won throught the use of the meeting-hall, the radio, and the newspaper." And the Court has insisted that no one be punished for a crime without "a charge fairly made and fairly tried in a public tribunal free of prejudice, passion, excitement, and tyrannical power."

Freedom of discussion should be given the widest range compatible with the essential requirement of the fair and orderly administration of justice." But it must not be allowed to divert the trial from the "very purpose of a court system * * * to adjudicate controversies, both criminal and civil, in the calmness and solemnity of the courtroom according to legal procedures." Among these "legal procedures" is the requirement that the jury's verdict be based on evidence received in open court, not from outside sources. Thus, in *Marshall v. United States*, we set aside a federal conviction where the jurors were exposed "through news accounts" to information that was not admitted at trial. We held that the prejudice from such material "may indeed be greater" than when it is part of the prosecution's evidence "for it is then not tempered by protective procedures"...

While we cannot say that Sheppard was denied due process by the judge's refusal to take precautions against the influence of pretrial publicity alone, the court's rulings must be considered against the setting in which the trials was held. In light of this background, we believe that the arrangements made by the judge with the news media caused Sheppard to be deprived of that "judicial serenity and calm to which [he] was entitled." The fact is that bedlam reigned at the courthouse during the trial and newsmen took over practically the entire courtroom, hounding most of the participants in the trial, especially Sheppard. At a temporary table within a few feet of the jury box and counsel table sat some 20 reporters staring at Sheppard and taking notes. The erection of a press table for reporters inside the bar is unprecedented. The bar of the court is reserved for counsel, providing them a safe place in which to keep papers and exhibits, and to confer privately with client and co-counsel. It is designed to protect the witness and the jury from any distractions, intrusions or influences, and to permit bench discussions of the judge's rulings away from the hearing of the public and the jury... Indeed, every court that has considered this case, save the court that tried it, has deplored the manner in which the news media inflamed and prejudiced the public... Nor is there doubt that this deluge of publicity reached at least some of the jury. On the only occasion that the jury was queried, two jurors admitted in open court to hearing the highly inflamatory charge that a prison inmate claimed Sheppard as the father of her illegitimate child...

The court's fundamental error is compounded by the holding that it lacked power to control publicity about the trial. From the very inception of the proceedings the judge announced that neither he nor anyone else could restrict prejudicial news accounts. And he reiteratd this view on numerous occasions. Since he viewed the news media as his target, the judge never considered other means that are often utilized to reduce the appearance of prejudicial material and to protect the jury from outside influence. We conclude that these procedures would have been sufficient to guarantee Sheppard fair trial and so do not consider what sanctions might be available against a recalcitrant press...

The carnival atmosphere at trial could easily have been avoided since the courtroom and courthouse premises are subject to the control of the court. As we stressed in *Estes*, the presence of the press at judicial proceedings must be limited when it is apparent that the accused might otherwise be prejudiced or disadvantaged. Bearing in mind the massive pretrial publicity, the judge should have adopted stricter rules governing the use of the courtroom by newsmen, as Sheppard's counsel requested. The number of reporters in the courtroom itself could have been limited at the first sign that their presence would disrupt the trial. They certainly should not have been placed inside the bar. Furthermore, the judge should have more closely regulated the conduct of newsmen in the courtroom...

Secondly, the court should have insulated the witnesses. All of the newspapers and radio stations apparently interviewed prospective witnesses at will, and in many instances disclosed their testimony... Although the witnesses were barred from the courtroom during the trail the full verbatim testimony was available to them in the press. This completely nullified the judge's imposition of the rule.

Thirdly, the court should have made some effort to control the release of leads, information, and gossip to the press by police officers, witnesses, and the counsel for both sides. Much of the information thus disclosed was inaccurate, leading to groundless rumors and confusion... Effective control of these sources—concededly within the court's power—might well have prevented the divulgence of inaccurate information, rumors, and accusations that made up much of the inflammatory publicity, at least after Sheppard's indictment.

More specifically, the trial court might well have proscribed extrajudicial statements by any lawyer, party, witness, or court official which divulged prejudicial matters, such as the refusal of Sheppard to submit to interrogation or take any lie detector test; any statement made by Sheppard to officials; the identity of prospective witnesses or their probable testimony; any belief in guilt or innocence; or like statements concerning the merits of the case. Had the judge, the other officers of the court, and the police placed the interest of justice first, the news media would have soon learned to be content with the task of reporting the case as it unfolded in the courtroom—not pieced together from extrajudicial statements.

...Due process requires that the accused receive a trial by an impartial jury free from outside influences. Given the pervasiveness of modern communications and the difficulty of effacing prejudicial publicity from the minds of the jurors, the trial courts must take strong measures to ensure that the balance is never weighed against the accused. And appellate tribunals have the duty to make an independent evaluation of the circumstances. Of course, there is nothing that proscribes the press from reporting events that transpire in the courtroom. But where there is a reasonable likelihood that prejudicial news prior to trial will prevent a fair trial, the judge should continue the case until the threat abates, or transfer it to another county not so permeated with publicity. In addition, sequestration of the jury was something the judge should have raised... with counsel...

The courts must take steps by rule and regulation that will protects their processes from prejudicial outside interferences. Neither prosecutors, counsel for defense, the accused, witnesses, court staff nor enforcement officers coming under the jurisdiction of the court should be permitted to frustrate its function. Collaboration between counsel and the press as to information affecting the fairness of a criminal trial is not only subject to regulation but is highly censurable and worthy of disciplinary measures.

Since the state trial judge did not fulfill his duty to protect Sheppard from the inherently prejudicial publicity which saturated the community and to control disruptive influences in the courtroom, we must reverse the denial of the habeas petition. The case is remanded to the District Court with instructions to issue the writ and order that Sheppard be released from custody unless the State puts him to its charges again within a reasonable time.

■ ■ ■

Questions

1. What must the Court do to protect the jury from prejudicial news? Why not have "secret trials."?

2. What could the judge do to avoid the "carnival atmosphere" at the trial? What public policy is served by judicial "gags" on court participants?

3. As a result of *Baldwin v. New York*, 399 U.S. 66 (1970), the defendant has a constitutional right to trial by jury in all cases where the possible penalty is more than six months. However, in *Johnson v. Louisiana*, 406 U.S. 356 (1972), and *Apodaca v. Oregon*, 406 U.S. 404 (1972), the Supreme Court held that there is no federal constitutional right to a unanimous jury verdict. Moreover, the Supreme Court held in *Williams v. Florida*, 400 U.S. 1010 (1970), that the Fourteenth Amendment did not require a jury of twelve and implied that the states may provide for a different number of jurors for different classes of crime. However in *Ballew v. Georgia*, 435 U.S. 223 (1978), the Court held that a conviction by a five-man jury violated the Sixth Amendment. In 1979 the Court decided that the same rule applies to a conviction by a six-man jury that is split five to one. *Burch v. Louisiana* No. 78-90. Why is a "jury of twelve members with unanimous verdict" not considered a fundamental right?

4. Does the defendant have a constitutional right to appeal his conviction? The Supreme Court has said:

> The right to an appeal from a conviction for crime is today so established that this leads to the easy assumption that it is fundamental to the protection of life and liberty and therefore a necessary ingredient of due process of law. "Due Process" is, perhaps, the least frozen concept of our law — the least confined to history and the most absorptive of powerful social standards of a progressive society...(Yet), it is significant that no appeals from convictions in the federal courts were afforded... for nearly a hundred years; and, despite the civilized standards of criminal justice in modern England, there was no appeal from convictions... until 1907. Thus, it is now settled that due process of law does not require a State to afford review of criminal judgments. Nor does the equal protection of the laws deny a State the right to make classifications in law when such classifications are rooted in reason. Since capital offenses are *sui generis,* a State may take account of the irrevocability of death by allowing appeals in capital cases and not in others. The States have exercised this discriminating power. The different States

and the same State from time to time have conditioned criminal appeals by fixing the time within which an appeal may be taken, by delimiting the scope of review, by shaping the mechanism by which alleged errors may be brought before the appellate tribunal, and so forth. *Griffin v. Illinois* 351 U.S. 12 (1952).

PART II
CONCEPTS OF
BUSINESS LAW

Organized society in an industrial democracy is the source of all sanctions in the field of business operations. Private business management receives its sanction through the right of private property. This is basically the right to hold, control, and use property in the personal interests of individuals or groups with due regard for the public interests. Private property is the basis for decentralization of political and economic power and a secure foundation for individual freedoms. The "free enterprise" system is founded on the right of private property and the decentralization of control over national economic resources.

Society has delegated to individuals the right to own and use physical property for the production and distribution of goods and services to the public. The owners of this property, to maintain a "free" system, are obliged to provide goods and services in the quality and quantity needed by society. The right to profit—that is, to increase one's holdings of private property—is dependent upon the ability of business organizations to discharge their service responsibilities to the public. To the extent that business is able to comply with this responsibility, it is not necessary for organized society to modify the rights and privileges of private property and of private management of economic resources.

Some modification of the rights of private property becomes necessary as industrial economies become more complex. Increased modification of private property rights are necessary when the liberties granted by society are abused. When individuals or business leaders misuse their authority to the detriment of the public interest, it seems necessary to increase the regulation of business activity. Each governmental regulation is a modification of the right of private property and contributes to a further breakdown of the "free enterprise" system.

Basic business law is formulated as an expression of the public policy at a given period of time. Initially, public policy favored the rights of private property and free contractual relations. Governmental policy was restricted to enforcing contractual rights and otherwise protecting the rights of private property. However, public policy is dynamic and its directions vary with the current needs of society. Consequently, a business contract found valid in one age may be unacceptable in another. Unbridled use of land in frontier times cannot be tolerated in today's crowded cities. The historical public preference for sole proprietorships gave way to the corporate device as an instrument of capitalistic expansion and organizational efficiency. The evolving content of public policy and its impact on the basic tenants of private property, contracts, financial transactions, and business organizations are presented in Part II.

Chapter 6 includes a study of property concepts and their application in business affairs. The materials in Chapter 7 present an overview of contracts and "sales," which are the basic business transactions. Chapter 8 contains a discussion of the financial aspects of business transactions, and Chapter 9 deals with the organization of business, including concepts of agency, partnerships, and corporations.

6

PROPERTY

One of the fundamental foundations of society in the United States is that of private property. Inherent in private property is the right of the owner to obtain governmental assistance in maintaining exclusive use and enjoyment of the property. This was not always the situation, however. Prior to the formation of an organized society to grant and protect the rights of private property, the concept of property was not known. Every person could take possession of as much land or movable obects as was unappropriated and as necessities dictated. Use of these possessions was dependent on the ability to maintain exclusive occupancy and control.

As nomadic tribes of hunters and fishermen began to group themselves into societies for defense, it became apparent that rules and group enforcement of those rules would be needed to protect an individual's possessions. In some instances, the inhabitants of these primitive societies attempted to solve their problem by drawing lines upon the ground throughout the settlement and mutually agreeing among themselves that within these "landmarks," the respective landholders alone had a possessory right during their period of occupancy. Later, as societies became more permanent, this possessory theory evolved into a "lawful" claim of ownership protected by society. The legal theory of "ownership" affords protection to property holders whether or not the owners have actual possession. Hence, the legal process is esential to the concept of ownership. One author wrote, "Property and law are born together, and die together. Before laws were made there was no property; take away laws, and property ceases." [1]

After the fall of the Roman Empire and its protection of property rights, alliances between communitites again became a necessity to provide common protection and defense. These alliances evolved into kingdoms with ownership of the unappropriated lands passing to the sovereign. As one early English lawyer, Blackstone, once wrote, "the King is esteemed in the eyes of the law as the original propietor of all the lands in the kingdom." Others acquired ownership rights, at first, as the king allowed and, subsequently, as the people demanded. As society evolved, so the legal concepts of property changed.

In America, with the propspect of developing the vast natural rsources available and with enterprising individuals eager for the task, substantial changes were needed in the restrictive English property laws. English landholding involved the obligations of rent or service to the crown. In contrast, America created a "free" system of landholding. Land was free to be bought and sold like other properties without any obligation owed to the government. In fact, the self-sufficiency afforded to citizens though private property rights formed the basis on which the U.S. economic and political systems were organized. American land-law was conceived as the means to secure and to protect both personal liberties and property rights. As John Adams exclaimed, "Property must be secure, or liberty cannot exist." Another author has argued:

> What maintains liberty... more than any other thing is the great mass of people who are independent because they have, as Aristotle said, "a moderate and sufficient property." They resist the absolute state. An official, a teacher, a scholar, a minister, a journalist, all those whose business it is to make articulate and to lead opinion, will act the part of free men if they can resign or be discharged without subjecting their wives, their children, and themselves to misery and squalor.[2]

In the early nineteenth century, American concern for expansion and economic development of the continent dictated the use of property rights as the tool for expansion. Homestead laws and land grants fostered the development of farming, railroads, and educational institutions in the west. However, by the end of the nineteenth century and with the rise of financial and industrial "empires," large concentrations of power and wealth developed. As a result, America became increasingly concerned for the personal rights of poor individuals whose "rights" were unsecured by property holdings. Government, therefore, assumed a positive duty to promote the welfare of society, even at the expense of the rights of private property.

In the twentieth century, land-law has evolved toward increasing limitations on the freedom of land use. Wasteful use of property was restrained by laws providing for proper utilization of soil and the conservation of natural resources. The doctrine of reasonable use of land has been eroded by zoning and city planning. More recently, society has further restricted property rights in its concern for a good quality natural environment.

Presently, it would seem that a *societal* theory of land use prevails over that of individual determination of property use. The traditional absolute freedom of private decision in regard to property use, which initially was thought incapable of restriction without subverting the very foundations of all liberties, is now within the purview of governmental control.

PROPERTY RIGHTS AND LIMITATIONS

In its most technical legal sense, property is an intangible concept signifying the rights, privileges, and powers that the law recognizes as vested in an individual in relation to others as to certain things tangible or intangible. It includes every interest anyone may have in anything that may be the subject of ownership, including the right to freely possess, use, enjoy, and dispose of the same. The sum of these proprietary rights is designated as "title" to property.

Property rights are classified in law according to the nature of the object concerning which rights are claimed. Immovable property—land and those things permanently attached to it—is considered real property, whereas movable items, or chattels, are designated as personal property. Land can be possessed and controlled: however, personal property is not only possessed and controlled, it may also be handled, manually transferred, altered, and destroyed with relative ease.

Proprietary rights are exclusive rights of the individual owner and are protected against infringement by others. In the final analysis, these rights represent a relationship between the owner and other individuals with respect to objects that can be owned. Part of those rights include the relationship between owners of private property and the government's power to regulate or take that property interest. The following materials emphasize the changing relationship between the power of the state and individual property rights.

EMINENT DOMAIN

IN RE FORSSTROM
38 P. 2d 878 (1934)
Supreme Court of Arizona

[The City of Tulsa believed a railroad-street crossing to be a hazard to public travel. Consequently, the City determined to construct an underpass below the tracks. In agreement with the State of Arizona the City by eminent domain condemned the property required for construction of the underpass and paid "just compensation" to acquire it. The underpass also deprived the plaintiff, an adjacent property holder, of entry and exit onto the street. He maintains that such deprivation was a "taking" of an "appurtenant" to his property which is entitled to compensation.]

■ ■ ■

Eminent domain is the right and power of a sovereign state to appropriate private property to particular uses, and it embraces all cases whereby under the authority of the state the property of the individual is appropriated permanently without his consent, for the purpose of being devoted to some particular use for the pubic good. This right is an inherent one which pertains to sovereignty as a necessary, constant, and unextinguishable attribute, and constitutional provisions in regard to it do not create or grant the power, but are limitations thereon. But the right has always carried with it, even in the absence of constitutional limitations, the principle that in some manner and to some extent compensation must be made for its exercise.

In order that we may understand the better what is meant by a "taking" of property. we should have a clear knowledge of what property really is. The word is used at different times to express many varying ideas. Sometimes it is taken in common parlance to denote a physical object, as where one says an automobile or a horse is his property. On carful consideration, however, it is plain that "property" in the true and legal sense does not mean a physical object itself, but certain rights over the object. A piece of land in an unexplored and uninhabited region which belongs to no one does not necessarily undergo any physical change merely by reason of its later becoming the property of any person. A wild animal may be exactly the same physically before and after it is captured, but, when it is running free in the forest, no one would speak of it as property. We must therefore look beyond the physical object itself for the true definition of property. Many courts and writers have attempted to define it, using different words, but meaning in essence the same thing. One of the great writers on jurisprudence says:

> "Property is entirely the creature of the law.* * *There is no form, or color, or visible trace, by which it is possible to express the relation which constitutes property. It belongs not to physics, but to metaphysics; it is altogether a creature of the mind." *Bentham Works* (Ed. 1843) vol. 1, p. 308.

We think that "property" may well be defined as the right to the possession, use, and disposition of things in such manner as is not inconsistent with law.

When real property is considered, a man has not only rights of use, of possession and disposition in a particular area of land, but he has at times other rights over contiguous and surrounding areas affecting the use of the particular area, and these are as much his property as the right to the use of the area he possesses. Such, for instance, are the right to the support of soil, to light and air, to access, the right to be undisturbed by nuisances on the adjoining property, and similar matters. Of course, these rights vary greatly in accordance with circumstances, but, whenever they do exist, and to the extent to which they are secured by law, they are truly property as much as the right to use the land to which they appertain. It would follow from these definitions and explanations of the meaning of the term "property" that since it consists, not in tangible things themselves, but in certain rights in and appurtenant to them, it would logically follow that, when a person is deprived of any of these rights, he is to that extent deprived of his property, and that it is taken in the true sense, although his title and possession of the physical object remains undisturbed. Any substantial interference, therefore, with rights over a physical object which destroys or lessens its value, or by which the use and enjoyment thereof by its owner is in any substantial degree abridged or destroyed, is both in law and in fact a "taking" of property...

We are satisfied that the word "taking," when used in constitutions or statutes in regard to property, and particularly realty, includes the permanent taking or diminishing of any of the rights which one has by reason of and appurtenant to his ownership of the realty in question, as well as a deprivation of the title to the physical object...The very purpose of establishing streets in a city is to afford access, light, and air to the property through which they pass, and it is therefore generally held that all lots abutting upon a street have these easements appurtenant thereto. This right of access extends to the use of the street as an outlet from the abutting property by any mode of travel or conveyance appropriate to the highway in such manner as is customary or reasonable...[I]t certainly could not be abolished or narrowed by the ...(government) without compensation therefor.

Questions

1. What is eminent domain? What is its source?
2. What is property? What are the "rights" of property?
3. Besides the appurtenant of entry and exit, what other appurtenant rights exist for real property?
4. The court mentioned "the right to be undisturbed by nuisances." How would you define a "nuisance?" Would it depend on the circumstances? Can you think of any example? Just as one has the right to be free of nuisances, so does one's neighbor. Consequently, the rights of private property are restricted in the sense that property use may not be a nuisance to the neightbors.

POLICE POWER

FRED F. FRENCH INV. CO., INC. v. CITY OF NEW YORK
350 N.E. 2d 381 (1976)
Court of Appeals of New York

■ ■ ■

The issue is whether the rezoning of buildable private parks exclusively as parks open to the public, thereby prohibiting all reasonable income productive or other private use of property, constitutes a deprivation of property rights without due process of law in violation of constitutional limitations...

The power of the State over private property extends from the regulation of its use under the police power to the actual taking of an easement or all or part of the fee under the eminent domain power. The distinction, although definable, between a compensable taking and a noncompensable regulation is not always susceptible of precise demarcation. Generally, as the court stated in *Lutheran Church in Amer. v. City of New York*, 316 N.E.2d 305, 310: "[G]overnment interference [with the use of private property] is based on one of two concepts—either the government is acting in its enterprise capacity, where it takes unto itself private resources in use for the common good, or in its arbitral capacity, where it intervenes to straighten out situations in which the citizenry is in conflict over land use or where one person's use of his land is injurious to others. Where government acts in its enterprise capacity, as where it takes land to widen a road, there is a compensable taking. Where government acts in its arbitral capacity, as where it legislates zoning or provides·the machinery to enjoin noxious use there is simply noncompensable regulation."...

In the present case, while there was a significant diminution in the value of the property, there was no actual appropriation or taking of the parks by title or governmental occupation... There was no physical invasion of the owner's property; nor was there an assumption by the city of the control or management of the parks. Indeed, the parks served the same function as before the amendment, except that they were now also open to the public. Absent factors of governmental displacement of private ownership, occupation or management, there was no "taking" within the meaning of constitutional limitations. There was, therefore, no right to compensation as for a taking in eminent domain.

Since there was no taking within the meaning of constitutional limitations, it is necessary to determine whether the zoning amendment was a valid exercise of the police power under the due process clauses of the State and Federal Constitutions.

The broad police power of the State to regulate the use of private property is not unlimited. Every enactment under the police power must be reasonable. An exercise of the police power to regulate private property by zoning which is unreasonable constitutes a deprivation of property without due process of law.

What is an "unreasonable" exercise of the police power depends upon the relevant converging factors. Hence, the facts of each case must be evaluated in order to determine the private and social balance of convenience before the exercise of the power may be condemned as unreasonable. A zoning ordinance is unreasonable, under traditional police power and due process analysis, if it encroaches on the exercise of private property rights without substantial relation to a legitimate governmental purpose. A legitimate governmental purpose is, of course, one which furthers the public health, safety, morals or genral welfare. Moreover, a zoning ordinance, on similar police power analysis, is unreasonable if it is arbitrary, that is, if there is no reasonable relation between the end sought to be achieved by the regulation and the means used to achieve that end.

Finally, and it is at this point that the confusion between the police power and the exercise of eminent domain most often occurs, a zoning ordinance is unreasonable if it frustrates the owner in the use of his property, that is, if it renders the property unsuitable for any reasonable income productive or other private use for which it is adapted and thus destroys its economic value, or all but a bare residue of its value.

The ultimate evil of a deprivation of property, or better, a frustration of property rights, under the guise of an exercise of the police power is that it forces the owner to assume the cost or providing a benefit to the public without recoupment. There is no attempt to share the cost of the benefit among those benefited, that is, society at large. Instead, the accident of ownership determines who shall bear the cost initially. Of course, as further consequence, the ultimate economic cost of providing the benefit is hidden from those who in a democratic society are given the power of deciding whether or not they wish to obtain the benefit despite the ultimate economic cost, however initially distributed. In other words, the removal from productive use of private property has an ultimate social cost more easily concealed by imposing the cost on the owner alone. When successfully concealed, the public is not likely to have any objection to the "cost-free" benefit.

In this case, the zoning amendment is unreasonable and, therefore, unconstitutional because, without due process of law, it deprives the owner of all his property rights, except the bare title and a dubious future reversion of full use. The amendment renders the park property unsuitable for any reasonable income productive or other private use for which it is adapted and thus destroys its economic value...

It is recognized that the "value" of property is not a concrete or tangible attribute but an abstraction derived from the economic uses to which the property may be put. Thus, the development rights are an essential component of the value of the underlying property because they constitute some of the economic uses to which the property may be put. As such, they are a potentially valuable and even a transferable commodity and may not be disregarded in determining whether the ordinance has destroyed the economic value of the underlying property.

Solutions must be reached for the problems of modern zoning, urban and rural conservation, and last but not least landmark preservations, whether by particular buildings or historical districts. Unfortunately, the land planners are now only at the beginning of the path to solution. In the process of traversing that path further, new ideas and new standards of constitutional tolerance must and will evolve. It is enough to say that the loose-ended transferable development rights in this case fall short of achieving a fair allocation of economic burden...

The legislative and administrative efforts to solve the zoning and landmark problem in modern society demonstrate the presence of ingenuity. That ingenuity further pursued will in all likelihood achieve the goals without placing an impossible or unsuitable burden on the individual property owner, the public fisc, or the general taxpayer. These efforts are entitled to and will undoubtedly receive every encouragement. The task is difficult but not beyond management. The end is essential but the means must nevertheless conform to constitutional standards.

■ ■ ■

Questions

1. Why did the court conclude in *French Inv. Co.* that there was no "taking" of plaintiff's property?
2. How did the court determine if the exercise of police power was reasonable?
3. What is the "evil" of frustrating private property rights under the guise of an exercise of the police power?
4. What is the extent of the police power? Consider the words of the U.S. Supreme Court:

> ...We deal, in other words, with what traditionally has been known as the police power. An attempt to define its reach or trace its outer limits is fruitless, for each case must turn on its own facts. The definition is essentially the product of legislative determinations addressed to the purpose of government, purposes neither abstractly nor historically capable of complete definition. Subject to specific constitutional limitations, when the legislature has spoken, the public interest has been declared in terms well-nigh conclusive. In such cases the legislature, not the judiciary, is the main guardian of the public needs to be served by social legislation...

> Public safety, public health, morality, peace and quiet, law and order--these are some of the more conspicuous examples of the traditional application of the police power to municipal affairs. Yet they merely illustrate the scope of the power and do not delimit it... The concept of the public welfare is broad and exclusive. The values it represents are spiritual as well as physical, aesthetic as well as monetary. It is within the power of the legislature to determine that the community should be beautiful as well as healthy, spacious as well as clean, well-balanced as well as carefully patrolled...

> If those who govern the (City)... decide that (it)... should be beautiful as well as sanitary, there is nothing in the Fifth Amendment that stands in the way. *Berman v. Parker* 348 U.S. 26 (1954).

FARRELL v. DREW
227 N.E.2d 824 (1967)
Court of Appeals of New York

■ ■ ■

The sole issue... is the constitutionality of section 143-b of the Social Welfare Law, known as the Spiegel Law, providing rent abatement for welfare tenants who live in buildings that contain a "violation of law * * * which is dangerous, hazardous or detrimental to life or health."...

The legislation, designed to operate as an effective weapon in the fight against slum housing in general was adopted only after it became apparent that existing sanctions, including criminal sanctions, were inadequate to cope with the problems of building law enforcement...

In the cases before us, the landlord does not challenge the Legislature's power to require that building law violations be corrected. Her attack is directed solely against the sanction chosen by the legislature to attain its objective of safe housing. Specifically, her contention is that the rent abatement provided by section 143-b works a denial of equal protection of the laws, a deprivation of property without due process...

(The landlord)... urges that it denies equal protection of the laws on the ground that it is aimed only at *landlords* of welfare recipients. However, it is settled that such legislation is not unconstitutional as long as a "reasonable basis" exists for differentiating among the members of the same...

In the situation presented by the cases before us, it is the landlords of welfare recipients who, the Legislature found, "conspicuously offend". To be sure, they are not the only landlords who fail to make repairs in slum dwellings. But welfare recipients have even less freedom than other tenants of deteriorated buildings in selecting a place to live and the landlords of welfare recipients, secure in their receipt of rent directly from public funds, have even less incentive than other landlords to make repairs. Under circumstances such as these, if the Legislature chooses to select one class of landlords and impose a special sanction against them, the equal protection clause does not forbid it.

It is likewise clear that the State may, in the exercise of its police power, provide for the curtailment of rent payments to landlords as a means of inducing them to eliminate dangerous housing conditons.

We have, in the past, upheld and applied statutes or regulations, not too unlike the one before us, which provide for (1) rent reduction, (2) partial rent abatement and (3) rent receivership...

It is clear, too, that section 143-b does not effect any unconstitutional impairment of the landlord's...rights... It is 'fundamental' * * * that the state may establish regulations reasonably necessary to secure the general welfare of the community by the exercise of its police power, although the rights of private property are [thereby] * * * curtailed...

The remedial legislation challenged in the case before us is reasonably aimed at correcting the evil of substandard housing and may not be stricken as unconstitutional even though the means devised to accomplish that result may, to some extent, impair... the landlord's... (property rights).

■ ■ ■

Questions

1. Why was the discrimination against landlords of welfare recipients not a denial of equal protection of the law?
2. How has the police power been utilized to regulate the property use in this and other cases? Are such regulations a denial of due process?

REITMAN v. MULKEY
387 U.S. 369 (1967)
Supreme Court of the United States

■ ■ ■

WHITE, Mr Justice.

The question here is whether Art. I, §26, of the California Constitution denies "to any person *** the equal protection of the laws" within the meaning of the Fourteenth Amendment of the Constitution of the United States. Section 26 of Art. I, an initiated measure submitted to the people as Proposition 14 in a statewide ballot in 1964, provides in part as follows:

Neither the State nor any subdivision or agency thereof shall deny, limit or abridge, directly, the right of any person, who is willing or desires to sell, lease or rent any part or all of his real property, to decline to sell, lease or rent such property to such person or persons as he, in his absolute discretion, chooses."

The real property covered by § 26 is limited to residential property and contains an exception for state-owned real estate...

First, the court considered whether § 26 was concerned at all with private discriminations in residential housing. This involved a review of past efforts by the California Legislature to regulate such discriminations. The Unruh Act, on which respondents based their cases, was passed in 1959. The Hawkins Act, formerly Health & Safety Code, followed and prohibited discriminations in publicly assisted housing. In 1961, the legislature enacted proscriptions against restrictive covenants. Finally, in 1963, came the Rumford Fair Housing Act, superseding the Hawkins Act and prohibiting racial discriminations in the sale or rental of any private dwelling containing more than four units. That act was enforceable by the State Fair Employment Practice Commission.

It was against this background that Proposition 14 was enacted. Its immediate design and intent, the California court said, were "to overturn state laws that bore on the right of private sellers and lessors to discriminate," the Unruh and Rumford Acts, and "to forestall future state action that might circumscribe this right." This aim was successfully achieved: the adoption of Proposition 14 "generally nullifies both the Rumford and Unruh Acts as they apply to the housing market," and establishes "a purported constitutional right to *privately* discriminate on grounds which admittedly would be unavailable under the Fourteenth Amendment *should state action* be involved."...

The California court could very reasonably conclude that § 26 would and did have wider impact than a mere repeal of existing statutes. Section 26 mentioned neither the Unruh nor Rumford Act in so many words. Instead, it announced the constitutional right of any person to decline to sell or lease his real property to anyone to whom he did not desire to sell or lease. Unruh and Rumford were thereby *pro tanto* repealed. But the section struck more deeply and more widely. Private discriminations in housing were now not only free from Rumford and Unruh but they also enjoyed a far different status than was true before the passage of those statutes. The right to discriminate, including the right to discriminate on racial grounds, was now embodied in the State's basic charter, immune from legislative, executive, or judicial regulation at any level of the state government. Those practicing racial discriminations need no longer rely solely on their personal choice. they could now invoke express constitutional authority, free from censure or interference of any kind from official sources. All individuals, partnerships, corporations and other legal entities, as well as their agents and representatives, could now discriminate with respect to their residential real property, which is defined as any interest in real property of any kind or quality, "irrespective of how obtained or financed," and seemingly irrespective of the relationship of the State to such interests in real property. Only the State is excluded with respect to property owned by it.

This Court has never attempted the "impossible task" of formulating an infallible test for determining whether the State "in any of its manifestations" has become significantly involved in private discriminations. "Only by sifting facts and weighing circumstances" on a case-by-case basis can a "nonobvious involvement of the State in private conduct be attributed its true significance." Here the California court, armed as it was with the knowledge of the facts and circumstances concerning the passage and potential impact of § 26, and familiar with the milieu in which that provision would operate, has determined that the provision would involve the State in private racial discriminations to an unconstitutional degree. We accept this holding of the California court.

■ ■ ■

Questions

1. May the state prohibit racial discrimination in the sale or rental of private dwellings?
2. Why was the Proposition 14 in *Teitman* considered "state action" which violates the 14th Amendment?

OWNERSHIP AND POSSESSION

The terms "ownership" and "possession" are not synonymous. They refer to two separate rights to property--rights that need not be held by the same person. The owner has title to the things he owns: he has a series of rights in the property which are protected by law. Possession, on the other hand, is simply the right to control a physical object. It may be had by right of ownership or may be had temporarily by one who is not the owner. For example, if A rents his house to B, A retains ownership but B takes possession.

Possession may be actual or constructive. Actual possession indicates physical control over an object. Constructive possession indicates that while the posessor's legal rights to the article still exist, the article is not under his or her physical control. For example, a man has actual possession of anything he carries on his person, such as a watch or a wallet; he would have only constructive possession of these same items had he left them at home.

Property in land is traditionally dealt with in terms of estates. The extent to which an owner may enjoy ownership of real property is describe as his or her estate. The quality, nature, and extent of an interest in real property will depend on the type of estate held. From this arises the interchangeable use of the terms "real property" and "real estate." Although, technically, the former refers to the land itself and the latter to an interest in the land, the distinction is seldom observed. Some estates include the right of possession while others do not.

ESTATES

The most substantial estate is the fee simple absolute. This estate has a potentially infinite duration in that the owner's rights, if not conveyed away during the owner's lifetime or by will at death, are statutorily inherited by his or her heirs. One wishing to convey a fee simple absolute to, say, John Doe, traditionally uses the language "to John Doe and his heirs." This does not mean that any interest is thereby conveyed to Doe's heirs. They inherit nothing if John conveys his fee simple absolute to another by deed or will. The words referring to heirs describe Doe's estate rather than designating the heirs of John Doe as owners also.

The special works, "and his heirs," are used to denote the intention of the grantor to pass full rights, a fee simple absolute, in the real property. The word "heirs" signifies the grantor's intention to pass full ownership because he also intended the land to be inheritable by the grantee's heirs. The use of the word "heirs" is indispensible to the effective expression of an intention to create a fee simple estate in the grantee. Omission of the word necessarily reduces the estate granted to one for life. The requirement of "words of inheritance" for the creation of a fee simple by deed is firmly embedded in the law. Although courts acknowledge that this rule is intent-defeating and seems to be supported by no modern policy, the courts often repeat that: "This is the rule of the common law from which the courts cannot escape.... (I)t has been so long established... that the courts cannot now overrule the cases laying it down, without imperiling vested rights." *Grainger v. Hamilton* 90 S.E. 2d at 211 (1955).

In the following case, the bank as grantor used the word, "heirs," but in the wrong place. It did not use the word "heirs" in relation to Nathan and Alice Palmer, the grantees. Rather, the bank used "heirs" in relation to the survivor of Nathan and Alice. Does this imply that Nathan and Alice had an interest in their land only during their life (life estate) and that the survivor held the (remainder) full ownership (fee)? That is what the defendant argued. And if the defendant was right, when Alice later deeded her "interest" to Nathan, only her life estate was passed. Consequently, Nathan possessed both life estates (that is, he and his heirs could live on the property as long as Nathan or Alice lived), but the remaining full ownership (fee) was to go to the survivor of Nathan or Alice. Alice still held her contingent remainder. Since Nathan died first, Alice claims to own the (remainder) property, the entire fee, as the survivor.

The opponent of Alice, a grantee from Nathan, claims the missing word "heirs" is of no consequence and that the bank's deed created a joint ownershi of the absolute fee by Nathan and Alice. If so, then when Alice deeded her "interest"(joint tenancy in the fee absolute) to Nathan, she lost all interest in the property.

Because the word "heirs" was misplaced, the court was forced to decide which of these two interpretations of the deed was correct.

PALMER v. FLINT
161 A 2d 837 (1960)
Supreme Court of Maine.

■ ■ ■

This is a petition for a declaratory judgment to determine the right or status of the parties hereto in certain real estate... [T]he Federal Land Bank of Springfield... conveyed this real estate to Nathan H. Palmer and his wife, Alice E. Palmer (now Alice E. Flint), the... defendant. The granting and habendum clauses in this deed... both read as follows: "Unto the said Nathan H. Palmer and Alice E. Palmer as joint tenants, and not as tenants in common, to them and their assigns and to the survivor, and the heirs and assigns of the survivor forever." Alice E. Palmer obtained a decree of divorce from Nathan H. Palmer... and by quitclaim deed without covenant... she conveyed the premises to Nathan H. Palmer. Nathan H. Palmer conveyed the property to Frank L. Palmer, who reconveyed to Nathan and his sister, Roxa B. Palmer, the plaintiff herein, "as joint tenants and not as tenants in common, to them and their heirs and assigns, and to the survivor of them, and to the heirs and assigns of such survivor forever." Nathan H. Palmer died.

The real controversy in this case is between the plaintiff Roxa B. Palmer and the defendant Alice E. Flint...

The plaintiff contends:
(1) That the deed from the Federal Land Bank of Springfield created in the grantees an estate in joint tenancy in fee simple...

The defendant contends:
(1) That the conveyance from the Federal Land Bank of Springfield conveyed a joint life estate to the grantees with a contingent remainder in fee to the survivor.
(2) That the quitclaim deed of Alice E. Palmer to her former husband was inoperative to convey to him her contingent remainder.

There is no doubt that the entire fee in the property was conveyed by the Land Bank of Springfield. The necessary words of inheritance for that purpose were used. The problem before us is the determination of the respective estates of the grantees in the fee conveyed...

In some jurisdictions a conveyance to two persons and the survivor of them, in the absence of words of inheritance applying to both grantees, or other circumstances indicating an intention to create a fee simple in each, has been construed to create a cotenancy in the grantees for their lives, with a contingent remainder in the survivor...

Does the use of the word "heirs" in the phrase "and the heirs of the survivor forever," and in no other part of the granting or habendum clauses of the deed, preclude a severance of the property and thus create a life estate in the grantees with a contingent fee in the survivor, as claimed by the defendant? We believe not. The intention to create a joint tenancy, so clearly expressed in this deed, carries with it the intent to endow such tenancy with all of the well-recognized incidents of a joint tenancy at common law. If the intention of the parties to create a joint tenancy, clearly expressed as in this deed, is in conflict with technical rules of the common law in the construction of deeds, then that intent takes precedence over and overrides those technical rules which are attempted to be used to justify the creation of such an unusual estate as that claimed by the defendant. If the parties had desired to create the estate claimed by the defendant, they could have indicated such intent by apt language. They did not do so. The deed contained no reference to a life estate, nor did it refer to any estate in remainder.   We hold that . . . the deed conveyed the entire estate disposed of by the grantor, a fee, to the grantees as joint tenants . . . If our ruling in this respect be considered a departure from the technical rules of the common law, let it be said that it is made in the interest of the security of property titles and in accordance with the intention of the parties clearly expressed in the instrument of conveyance.

■ ■ ■

Questions

1. Considering the language of the deed, "unto the said Nathan H. Palmer and Alice E. Palmer as joint tenants, and not as tenants in common, to them and their assigns and to the survivor, and the heirs and assigns of the survivor," where would you insert the word "heirs" to avoid this litigation? Was "heirs" properly inserted in the deed from Frank Palmer to Nathan and his sister, Roxa?

2. What is a life estate? What is a "contingent remainder?" Under the common law, a contingent remainder could not be transferred because the owner of a contingent remainder did not know whether the contingency would occur and vest his interests in the property. Consequently, if Alice had a life estate and a contingent remainder, then Alice's quit claim deed transferred her life estate only, because her contingent remainder could not be passed to Nathan. Considering these technical rules of the common law, do you agree with Holmes when he said, "It is revolting to have no better reason for a rule of law than that so it was laid down in the time of Henry IV. It is still more revolting if the grounds upon which it was laid down have vanished long since, and the rule simply persists from blind imitation of the past." Holmes, *Collected Legal Papers* (1920) 187.

3. Must the words "and his heirs" be used to convey a fee simple absolute? Would the phrase "to A in fee simple absolute" suffice? In the overwhelming majority of states, any form of expression of intention to convey a fee simple absolute is given effect. Usually this result is based upon a statute.

DEFEASIBLE FEES

OLDFIELD v. STOECO HOMES, INC.
139 A.2d 291 (1958)
Supreme Court of New Jersey

■ ■ ■

Suit was instituted by plaintiffs, residents and taxpayers of the City of Ocean City, with the object of having several resolutions of the City of Ocean City extending the time for performance of certain conditions in a deed declared invalid, (and) for the further relief of having lands owned by the defendants forfeited and returned to the city. The defendants are Stoeco Homes, Inc., the purchaser from Ocean City . . . and the City of Ocean City . . .

In 1951 Ocean City held title to a large number of lots of undeveloped land in a low-lying area of the city... Ocean City, recognizing that an extensive redevelopment of these swampy areas would benefit the community, indicated its willingness to sell the lots...

While the deed from Ocean City to Stoeco contained various conditions and restrictions, the core provisions around which this dispute centers are:...

> (b) Within one (1) year following the date of this Deed, Stoeco...shall fill all of the lots of land...
>
> (d) All such lands shall be filled to at least the now established and existing grades of the City of Ocean City, New Jersey...
>
> The City of Ocean City reserves the right to change or modify any restriction, condition or other requirements hereby imposed in a manner agreeable to or as permitted by law.
>
> A failure to comply with the covenants and conditions of paragraphs (b) and (d) hereof will automatically cause title to all lands to revert to the City of Ocean City; and a failure of any other restrictions and convenants may cause title to revert to the City as to any particular land, lot or lots involved in any violation.

...(U)nfavorable dredging conditions, not originally contemplated, created serious engineering and financial problems for Stoeco.

By June 29, 1952, one year after obtaining the deed, Stoeco had still not completed the substantial portion of filling and grading, nor had it done so by February of 1953. Ocean City, more interested in redevelopment than declaring a default, passed a resolution on February 20, 1953 to change and modify the terms and conditions of the sale of the land... The general import of the resolution was that Stoeco was to be given until December 31, 1954 to complete the filling and grading of all lots purchased...

First, we consider the issue relating to the nature of the estate created. It is said that a fee simple determinable differs from a fee simple subject to a condition subsequent in that, in the former, upon the happening of the stated event the estate "ipso facto" or "automatically" reverts to the grantor or his heirs, while in the latter the grantor must take some affirmative action to divest the grantee of this estate. The interest remaining in the grantor in a fee simple determinable has been denominated a possibility of reverter, while the interest remaining in the grantor of a fee simple subject to a condition subsequent, i.e., the right to re-enter upon the happening of the prescribed contingency, has been denominated a power of termination.

It is further alleged that a fee simple determinable estate is more onerous than an estate in fee simple subject to condition subsequent in that the defenses of waiver and estoppel which are applicable to the latter are unavailing in the former...

Plaintiffs assert that the language of automatic reverter in the deed indicates beyond cavil that the estate created was a fee simple determinable and that therefore the municipality's effort to waive the breach of performance was uneffectual.

While language is the primary guide for the ascertainment of whether a given deed attempts to condition or limit an estate, still it is the instrument as a whole and not a particular phrase aborted from the context which provides the basis for the attainment of our ultimate task, which is to effectuate the intention of the parties. The particular words, upon which are predicated the right, or lack of it, to a forfeiture are often emphasized. Thus, it has been said that such words as "so long as," "until" or "during," followed by words of reverter, are appropriate to create a fee simple determinable, whereas such words as "upon condition that" or "provided that" are usual indicators of an estate upon condition subsequent. But that particular forms of expression, standing alone and without resort to the purpose of the instrument in question, are not determinative is at once apparent to a discerning surveyor of the case authorities...

The ancient land law imputed a thaumaturgic quality to language... If the judicial eye in scanning the instrument chanced upon a pet phrase the inquiry was ended without resorting to the arduous effort of reconciling evident inconsistencies therein. The universal touchstone today is the intention of the parties to the instrument creating the interest in land.

If the four corners of the deed provide a coherent expression of the parties' intent, we need search no further, but if an ambiguity or a reasonable doubt appears from a perusal of the particular symbols of expression our horizons must be broadened to encompass the circumstances surrounding the transaction... To the foregoing must be added certain constructional biases developed in a hierarchical fashion and predicated upon the proposition that the law abhors a forfeiture. Thus, if... the choice is between an estate in fee simple determinable and an estate on condition subsequent, the latter is preferred.

To focus attention solely on the words "automatically cause title to revert" is to ignore and refuse effect to the following provisions: "This conveyance is also subject to the following *conditions*, requirements, reservations, covenants and restrictions:" (Court's Emphasis) and "A failure to comply with the *convenants* and *conditions of paragraphs (a), (b) and (d) hereoff...*" (Court's Emphasis). Moreover, the deed contained the following clause: "The City of Ocean City reserves the right to change or modify any restriction, condition or other requirements hereby imposed in a manner agreeable to or as permitted by law."

The repeated use of the word "condition" and the provision reserving the right to alter the arrangement in the clauses are sufficient to cast a reasonable doubt upon what is intended. Accordingly, we shall consider the surrounding circumstances in order to ascertain the intention of the parties in creating the estate.

With this in mind, we proceed to a determination of whether the limitation as to time was a condition subsequent which could be waived by the city in its discretion or limitation (fee simple determinable).

To hold that the condition as to time was so essential to the scheme of the parties that to violate it by a day would result in an immediate and automatic forfeiture of the estate is to distort beyond recognition what the parties intended. There is no indication that time was of the essence of the agreement... No immediacy or sense of urgency in relation to the time within which this development was to take place is apparent. It may be fairly inferred that the one-year limitation was originally put in because Stoeco conceived that the fill from the drained lagoons on the west side would be of sufficient quantity and quality that the task could easily be completed within one year. But, as is often the case, difficulties were encountered with the plan, and at last it had to be discarded in favor of alternative and more expensive methods of grading and filling than those originally contemplated. In light of this impediment, the parties renegotiated for the time in which performance was to be made. To say that the parties intended a forfeiture irrespective of future contingencies impeding the original scheme is to ignore and refuse legal efficacy to the following language previously referred to in the resolutions and deed: "The City of Ocean City reserves the right to change or modify any restriction, condition or other requirements hereby imposed in a manner agreeable to or as permitted by law."...

It is our conclusion that the parties contemplated that the estate created was not to expire automatically at the end of a year and that therefore it is one subject to a condition subsequent...

■ ■ ■

Questions

1. The word "estate" suggests a relationship between a person and others concerning some particular property. Hence, estate means the interest which a person has in property. The description of that estate details the rights and privileges of the estate holder in relation to others. Several types of estates have been discussed. Can you describe the particular attributes of the following estates?
   Fee Simple Absolute
   Fee Simple Determinable
   Fee Simple Subject to a condition subsequent

Life Estate
Contingent Remainder
Possibility of Reverter
Power of Termination
Remainder

2. What main or controlling rule of interpretation is used by the court to interpret deeds?

CONCURRENT OWNERSHIP

Several persons may have simultaneous interest of a *different* nature in the same thing (that is, one has a fee simple determinable and another the possibility of reverter), but they may also have simultaneous interests of an *identical* nature in the same property (that is, they both own the same type of estate). Simultaneous or concurrent ownership comprehends the situation in which two or more persons share ownership in the same subject. In law, concurrent ownership is synonymous with "co-tenancy" which means the two or more owners simultaneously share equal rights in possession and use of the property subject. Cotenancy can exist in basically two types—joint tenancy and tenancy in common. Tenancy in common is easily defined as the type of co-ownership that exists if the co-ownership is not a joint tenancy. Joint tenancy requires special attention to be created.

Four unities are said to be necessary to create a joint tenancy; unities of interest, title, time, and possession. Unity of interest means the parties must equally share identical estates (both share a fee simple absolute or both share a life estate). Unity of title and time means the parties must claim their interest through the same instrument or deed which granted them their rights at the same time. Unity of possession means each party has the right to share possession of the property subject. Consequently, any deed that grants two or more persons equal interests in the same estate and grants equal rights to possession has created the four unities prerequisite for a joint tenancy. However, the additional language of "suvivorship" or the word "jointly" is necessary to form a joint tenancy. Under the "right of survivorship," the surviving co-tenant becomes the sole owner of the property on the demise of the other co-tenant. The heirs of the deceased co-tenant get no interest in the property. In contrast, the fractional interest of a tenant-in-common passes to his heirs. Finally, it should be noted that a transfer of the fractional interest by a joint tenant causes a severance of the unities and thereby terminates the joint tenancy. The new tenant receiving the transfer of ownership becomes a tenant-in-common with the remaining tenant (the former joint tenant).

■ ■ ■

Questions

1. What kind of tenancy exists if the deed reads: "To A and B and their heirs..."?
2. What kind of tenancy exists if the deed reads: "To A and B, as joint tenants, with rights of survivorship and not as tenants in common..."?
3. What kind of tenancy was intended in the deed in *Palmer v. Flint?*

MORTGAGE LAW

The history of mortgage law is the history of a long struggle between lender and borrower over their respective rights in a mortgage default situation. Mortgage law is derived from England and began with a fourteenth century mortgage which transferred the ownership from borrower to lender. The lender received *title* to the property, but his fee simple was subject to a condition subsequent (debt payment). In effect, the lender's title was subject to defeasance if the debt was timely paid. This mortgage theory has been carried forward today but has been modified in several states so that the lender acquires only a lien, rather than title, on the mortgaged property.

In lien-theory states, the mortgagee (lender) obtains the right to foreclose (capture the property or its value) with the aid of the court. In a title-theory state, the lender brings an action to terminate the borrower's power (of termination) to defease the property away from the lender. The lien theory is the more modern view and prevails in most states.

PEOPLE v. NOGARR
330 P.2d 858 (1958)
Court of Appeal of California

■ ■ ■

Is a mortgage upon real property executed by one of two joint tenants enforceable after the death of that joint tenant?

The facts are not in dispute. The appellant, Elaine R. Wilson, hereinafter called "Elaine," and Calvert S. Wilson, hereinafter called "Calvert," were husband and wife. On April 10, 1950, they acquired the real property in question as joint tenants... In July 1954 Elaine and Calvert separated. On October 11, 1954 Calvert executed his promissory note to his parents, the respondents, Frank II. and Alice B. Wilson, hereinafter called "respondents." This note was in the sum of $6,440. At the same time he executed and delivered to respondents a mortgage upon the real property in question. Elaine did not have knowledge of or give her consent to the execution of this mortgage. On June 23, 1955, Calvert died...

It is appellant's contention that execution of the mortgage by Calvert did not operate to terminate the joint tenancy and sever his interest from that of Elaine, but that the mortgage was a charge or lien upon his interest as a joint tenant only and that therefore upon his death, his interest having ceased to exist, the lien of the mortgage terminated and that Elaine was... (sole owner).

We have reached the conclusion that appellant's contention must be sustained. In order that a joint tenancy may exist four unities are required: unity of interest, unity of title, unity of time and unity of possession. So long as these unities exist the right of survivorship is an incident of the tenancy, and upon the death of one joint tenant the survivor becomes the sole owner in fee by right of survivorship and no interest in the property passes to the heirs, devisees or personal representatives of the joint tenant first to die.

It is undisputed in the present case that a joint tenancy in fee simple existed between Elaine and Calvert at the time of the execution of the mortgage, that at that time there existed all of the four unities, that consequently Elaine upon the death of Calvert became the sole owner of the property in question... unless the execution by Calvert of the mortgage destroyed one of the unities and thus severed the joint tenancy and destroyed the right of survivorship.

Under the law of this state a mortgage is but a hypothecation of the property mortgaged. It creates but a charge or lien upon the property hypothecated, without the necessity of a change of possession and without any right of possession in the mortgagee, and does not operate to pass the legal title to the mortgagee.

Inasmuch as the mortgage was but a lien or charge upon Calvert' interest, and as it did not operate to transfer the legal title or any title to the mortgagees or entitle the mortgages to possession, it did not destroy any of the unities, and therefore the estate in joint tenancy was not severed and Elaine and Calvert did not become tenants in common. It necessarily follows that, as the mortgage lien attached only to such interest as Calvert had in the real property, when his interest ceased to exist the lien of the property expired with it.

Respondents have directed our attention to decisions of other jurisdictions which they assert support their contention that a joint tenant has a right to mortgage his interest and that this operates to sever the joint tenancy. Examination of each of the cases relied upon by respondents discloses that all... of them were rendered in jurisdictions where a mortgage operated not merely as a lien or chage upon the mortgagor's interest but as a transfer or conveyance of his interest, the conveyance being subject to defeasance upon the payment of the mortgage debt. It is evident that in those jurisdictions where a mortgage operates to convey title to the mortgagee the unity of title is destroyed...and...there is a severance of the joint tenancy.

■ ■ ■

Questions

1. Why did the court conclude that the mortgage by Calvert was not a severance of the joint tenancy?
2. Would the result have been different in *Nogarr* if California had a title theory of mortgage?
3. Should a creditor take a mortgage with only one signature on property owned by joint tenants?

DEEDS

A deed is a written instrument in which the grantor expresses an intention to pass an interest in real property to the grantee. Deeds differ in the kind of interest they convey: (1) a *quit claim* deed conveys the interest of the grantor, if any, without specifying the interest, and makes no warranties; (2) a *general warranty* deed transfers a specified interest and obligates the grantor on certain warranties.

A *general warranty* deed ordinarily contains the following warranties: (1) a covenant of seisen (2) a covenant of the right to convey (3) a covenant against encumbrances (4) a covenant for quiet enjoyment and (5) a covenant for further assurances.

A *covenant of seisen* is a guaranty that the grantor owns the exact estate that he intends to convey to the grantee. It is a covenant to the effect that the grantor has and conveys the title described in the conveyance. In a quit claim deed, the grantor purports to convey his interest, if any, to the grantee; and in the absence of fraud, if the grantor had nothing, the grantee gets nothing.

A *covenant of right to convey* is a guaranty that the grantor has the right to make the conveyance.

A *convenant against encumbrances* is an undertaking by the grantor that no lien or burden not describe in the conveyance is outstanding against the property. In other words, he warrants that the property is free from any encumbrances such as mortgages, tax liens, mechanic's liens, or judgment liens, except those, if any, detailed in the deed.

A *covenant for quiet enjoyment* is a general warranty that the grantee will not be disturbed by possessory or title claims not already disclosed, and, if such are established and are settled by the grantee, that the grantor will reinburse him for the sums expended. Actually, the grantor agrees to defend the title to the property against all who claim to have a superior title.

A *covenant for further assurance* is a promise by the grantor that he will execute any additional document that may be required to perfect the title of the grantee.

BOEHRINGER v MONTALTO
254 N.Y.S. 276 (1931)
Supreme Court, Westchester County, New York

■ ■ ■

(Plaintiff) sues... for breach of covenant against incumbrances.

The (defendant) conveyed the property to the (plaintiff) by (a general warranty)... deed... and... the property conveyed was warranted free from incumbrances.

In now develops that the Bronx Valley sewer commission had procured... the right to construct and maintain the Bronx Valley sewer through the premises, and that the sewer has been constructed across the porperty at a depth of 150 feet... (and) provided no right of access from the surface of the property.

At a time when nobody foresaw the use to which the air above the land might be put, a maxim appears in the law to the effect that he who owns the soil owns everything above and below, from heaven to hell...

In *Smith v. New England Aircraft Co.*, 270 Mass. 511, the Supreme Judicial Court of Massachusetts stated that it would assume that private ownership extends to all reasonable heights above the underlying land; that the experience of mankind, although not necessarily a limitation upon rights, is the basis upon which air space must be regarded.

The Massachusetts court held in that case that the statutory regulation of 500 feet as the minimum altitude flight by aircraft was a permissible exercise of the police power, although the experience of mankind indicates many structures exceeding 500 feet in height.

It therefore appears that the old theory that the title of an owner of real property extends indefinitely upward and downward is no longer an accepted principle of law in its entirety. Title above the surface of the ground is now limited to the extent to which the owner of the soil may reasonably make use thereof.

By analogy, the title of an owner of the soil will not be extended to a depth below ground which the owner may not reasonably make use thereof.

It is concluded that the depth at which the Bronx Valley sewer exists is beyond the point to which the owner can conceivably make use of the property, and is therefore not an incumbrance...

■ ■ ■

Notes

1. The warranties in a deed give some protection to the buyer that his purchase is clear and fee of claims by other persons against the property. However, the seller may die or become financially insolvent in which case the claim of the buyer against the seller will be barren. Accordingly, other measures of protection of the buyer's investment should be taken. While the methods differ in the various states, every state makes some provision for the recording of deeds and other documents that effect title to real property. Every purchaser should search the public records for determination that the seller possesses a "clear title." Public records give priority to those documents first recorded over rival claimants to the same property. An attorney skilled in the task of searching the public records should be employed for such tasks.

2. A careful investigation of the public record may disclose many monetary claims against the property. All unpaid taxes, mortgages, or other restrictions against the property can be noted through a search of the public records. However, the buyer is subject to possible errors in indexing, errors in the examination process, and to claims of those whose rights would not be revealed in the public records. The records would not reveal forged deeds or wills, invalid or undisclosed wills, undisclosed errors, or deeds by persons supposedly single but secretly married. A host of other possible hidden defects in the title may exist. Detection against these risks can be obtained only by purchasing title insurance. Title insurance is a contract to indemnify the buyer against losses through defects in title to real property. The insurance company guarantees the buyer against loss due to any defects in title and to pay all expenses in defense of any lawsuits attacking the title.

CLASSES OF PERSONAL PROPERTY

Personal property is classified as "chattels real" and "chattels personal." Chattels real are temporary interests in land; a prime example is a lease for a specified period of time. All other personal property is chattels personal.

Personal property may be further subdivided into tangible or intangible property. Tangible personal property includes all movable property, even large items such as animals, cars, and standing trees that have been sold and are to be removed from the land. Intangible property includes things to which one does not have a right of possession but to which legal rights in the subject matter are granted. For example, A may purchase a copy of a book copyrighted by B; A owns and enjoys the exclusive possesion of the tangible book, but B owns the intangible property right to republish additional copies of the book. This intangible property right of B will receive court protection. Additional examples of intangible property are evidenced in pieces of paper; such as negotiable instruments, bank accounts, insurance policies, and stock certificates. The following cases are illustrative of intangible property and the variety of rules associated with the various forms of personal property.

INTANGIBLE PERSONAL PROPERTY

PITTSBURGH ATHLETIC CO. v. KQV BROADCASTING CO.
24 F. Supp. 490 (1938)
District Court of Pennsylvania

■ ■ ■

This is an action in which the plaintiffs ask for a preliminary injunction to restrain defendant from broadcasting play-by-play reports and descriptions of baseball games played by the "Pirates," a professional baseball team owned by Pittsburgh Athletic Company, both at its home baseball park in Pittsburgh, known as "Forbes Field," and at baseball parks in other cities.

The plaintiff, Pittsburgh Athletic Company, owns a professional baseball team known as the "pirates," and is a member of an association known as the "National League." With the several teams of the members of the League, the "Pirates" play baseball both at its home field and at the home fields of the other members of the League in various cities. The home games are played at a baseball park known as "Forbes Field" which is enclosed by high fences and structures so that the public are admitted only to the park to witness the games at Forbes Field by the payment of an admission ticket, which provides that the holder of the admission ticket agrees not to give out any news of the game while it is in progress.

The Pittsburgh Athletic Company has granted by written contract, for a valuable consideration, to General Mills, Inc., the exclusive right to broadcast, play-by-play, descriptions or accounts of the games played by the "Pirates" at this and other fields. The National Broadcasting Company, also for a valuable consideration, has contracted with General Mills, Inc., to broadcast by radio over stations KDKA and WWSW, play-by-play decriptions of these games. The Socony-Vacuum Oil Company has purchased for a valuable consideration a half interest in the contract of the General Mills, Inc.

The defendant operates at Pittsburgh a radio broadcasting station known as KQV, from which it has in the past broadcast by radio play-by-play descriptions of the games played by the "Pirates" at Pittsburgh, and asserts its intention to continue in so doing. The defendant secures the information which it broadcasts from its own paid observers whom it stations at vantage points outside Forbes Field on premises leased by defendant. These vantage points are so located that the defendant's observers can see over the enclosures the games as they are played in Forbes Field.

On this state of facts, we are of the opinion that the plaintiffs have presented a case which entitles them under the law to a preliminary injunction.

It is perfectly clear that the exclusive right to broadcast play-by-play descriptions of the games played by the "Pirates" at their home field rests in the plaintiffs, General Mills, Inc., and the Socony-Vacuum Oil Company under the contract with the Pittsburgh Athletic Company. That is a property right of the plaintiffs with which defendant is interfering when it broadcasts the play-by-play description of the ball games obtained by the observers on the outside of the enclosure.

The plaintiffs and the defendant are using baseball news as material for profit. The Athletic Company has, at great expense, acquired and maintains a baseball park, pays the players who participate in the game, and have, as we view it, a legitimate right to capitalize on the news value of their games by selling exclusive broadcasting rights to companies which value them as affording advertising mediums for their merchandise. This right the defendant interferes with when it uses its broadcasting facilites for giving out the identical news obtained by its paid observers stationed at points outside Forbes Field for the purpose of securing information which if cannot otherwise acquire. This, in our judgment... is a violation of the property rights of the plaintiffs. For it is our opinion that the Pittsburgh Athletic Company, by reason of its creation the game, its control of the park, and its restriction of the dissemination of news therefrom, has a property right in such news, and the right to control the use thereof for a reasonable time following the games.

The communication of news of the ball games by the Pittsburgh Athletic Company, or by its licensed news agencies, is not a general publication and does not destroy that right...

Defendant seeks to justify its action on the ground that the informationit receives from its observers stationed on its own property without trespassing on plaintiff's property, may be lawfuly broadcast by it. We cannot follow defendant's counsel in this contention for the reasons above stated. The cases cited by them we have carefully studied and are unable to accept as authority...

■ ■ ■

Questions

1. Describe the property that was protected in the *Pittsburgh Athletic Co.* case.
2. Does the *Pittsburgh Athletic Co.* case explain why the National Football League, on all broadcasts of football games, reserves to themselves any further rights to rebroadcast?

BAILMENTS

WEINBERG v. WAYCO PETROLEUM COMPANY
402 S.W. 2d 597 (1966)
St. Louis Court of Appeals

■ ■ ■

There is only one issue presented in this appeal and that is to determine whether the relationship between the parties was, as plaintiff contends, that of bailee and bailor.

With respect to cases involving automobiles and the contents thereof when loss occurs after the automobile is left in a parking lot, the relationship between the parties is usually one of bailment or license, and whether it is one or the other depends upon the circumstances of the particular case and especially upon the manner in which the parking lot in question is being operated and with whom control of the allegedly bailed article or articles is vested. The obligations of the parties flow from the relationship (bailment or license) once it is established.

A "bailment" in its ordinary legal sense imports the delivery of personal property by the bailor to the bailee who keeps the property in trust for a specific purpose, with a contract, express or implied, that the trust shall be faithfully executed, and the property returned or duly accounted for when the special purpose is accomplished or that the property shall be kept until the bailor reclaims it. This court has said that "* * * the term 'bailment' * * * signifies a contract resulting from the delivery of goods by bailor to bailee on condition that they be restored to the bailor, according to his directions, so soon as the purposes for which they were bailed are answered." We need not examine all the elements of bailment to determine whether or not the relationship exists in the instant case. In Suits v. Electric Park Amusement Co., it was held "* * * there must be a delivery to the bailee, either actual or constructive. * * * It has been held that such a full delivery of the property must be made to the bailee as will entitle him to exclude for the period of the bailment the possession thereof, even of the owner. * * *"

In National Fire Ins. Co. v. Commodore Hotel (1961), 107 N.W. 2d 708, the plaintiff was a guest at a luncheon held at the defendant's hotel. She hung her mink jacket in an unattended cloakroom on the main floor across from the lobby desk. After the luncheon the plaintiff went to the cloakroom to retrieve her jacket and discovered it was gone. The court held that no negligence had been established against the defendant and stated:

"* * *...[W]e do not feel that it is incumbent upon a hotel or restauraunt owner to keep an attendant in charge of a free cloakroom for luncheon or dinner guests or otherwise face liability for loss of articles placed therein. The maintenance of such rooms without attendants is a common practice, and where the proprietor has not accepted control and custody of articles placed therein, no duty rests upon him to exercise any special degree of care with respect thereto.
"Likewise, failure to post a warning disclaiming responsibility would not seem to constitute negligence when, as here, a guest is aware that a cloakroom is unattended, adjacent to the loby, and accessible to anyone; and has used it under similar circumstances on many prior occasions. The absence of such warning signs does not appear to have been material in a number of decisions absolving proprietors from liability although when posted they appear to be regarded as an added factor in establishing such nonliability."

It is obvious from the facts in the instant case that there was no delivery to Wayco sufficient to create the relationship of bailee and bailor between the parties here involved. Cases of the nature here involved are to be distinguished from those where the parking operation is such that the attendants collect a fee and assume authority or control of the automobile by parking it and/or retaining the keys so that the car can be moved about to permit the entrance or exit of other automobiles and where the tickets that are given to the owner of the automobile are issued for the purpose of identifying the automobile for redelivery. In such instances a bailment relationship is almost invariably held to exist.

In the instant case Wayco never secured control or authority over the plaintiff's automobile. No agent or employee of Wayco parked it or kept the keys to it or issued any ticket whereby the automobild could be identified by comparison of a portion of the ticket left with the automobile when it was parked. The plaintiff parked his own automobile, locked it, and took the keys with him. Certainly Wayco, the alleged bailee, did not have the right under these circumstances to exclude the purposes of the owner or even of anyone else who might have had the keys. In the instant case the plaintiff never made a delivery, actual or constructive, of the automobile to Wayco under circumstances leading to the creation of a bailee-bailor relationship between them. Other jurisdictions where the factual situation present have been similar to the instant case have ruled that no bailment was created.

Of course, if Wayco was not a bailee of the plaintiff's automobile, it was not a bailee of the contents...

■ ■ ■

Questions

1. What is a bailment? Why did the court rule in *Weinberg* that no bailment existed?
2. What is the duty of the bailor to the bailee in relation to the bailed property? What is the duty of a lessor of parking space to the lessee's auto?

3. May a bailor by contract relieve himself of his duty of care over the bailed property? Might this practice be unfair to the bailee in certain circumstances? Should the court protect against such efforts of the bailor to avoid responsibility?

TANGIBLE PERSONAL PROPERTY

SCHLEY v. COUCH
284 S.W. 2d 333 (1955)
Supreme Court of Texas

■ ■ ■

Petitioner was the owner of a tract of land near Hamilton, Texas, upon which was situated a dwelling house with an attached garage and storeroom. At the time petitioner moved upon the premises there was a concrete floor covering only the front half of the garage, and the remaining half was a dirt floor. . . . [P]etitioner employed a Mr. Tomlinson and his crew of workmen—among whom was respondent—to put a concrete floor in the rear half of the garage . . .

. . . While digging in this soil, respondent's pick struck a hard object and respondent found the $1,000 sued for buried in the ground. The money was in currency. The owner of the money is unknown.

. . . Respondent sued petitioner for the money . . . The trial court submitted the case to the jury upon two special issues. One inquired if the money were "lost" property, and the other inquired if the money were "mislaid" property. The jury answered the money was "mislaid" property, and upon that verdict the trial court rendered judgment in favor of the defendant as bailee for the true owner. Upon appeal the Court of Civil Appeals reversed the trial court's judgment and rendered judgment for the respondent against the defendant for the money. The Court of Civil Appeals held that the money constituted neither "lost" nor "mislaid" property, but fell into yet a third category known in some jurisdictions as "treasure trove." It accordingly held the right of possession to be in the finder.

Neither party claims to be the true owner of the money, but each claims the right to have possession of the money for the benefit of the true owner, should he ever appear and establish his claim. Title to the money is not involved, but only the right of possession thereof.

This is a case of first impression in Texas. If the money constitutes treasure trove the decision of the Court of Civil Appeals is correct and in accordance with the decided cases from other jurisdictions. However, we have decided not to recognize the "treasure trove" doctrine as the law in Texas, but that this case should be governed by the rules of law applicable to lost and mislaid property. There is no statutory law in Texas regarding the disposition of such property, or provisions defining the respective rights of various claimants. The rule of treasure trove is of ancient origin and arose by virtue of the concealment in the ground and other hiding places of coin, bullion, and plate of the Roman conquerors when they were driven from the British Isles. These Romans expected to return at a later date and reclaim their buried and hidden treasures. For a time laws were in effect which gave all this treasure trove which might be discovered to the sovereign, but it was later held to belong to the finder, and this regardless of whether he was in ownership or possession of the land where the treasure was found. The doctrine only applied to "money or coin, gold, silver, plate, or bullion found hidden in the earth or other private places, the owner thereof being unknown." Black, Law Dictionary. Such doctrine has never been officially recognized in Texas, although it has been recognized and applied under the common law in many states of the American Union. We can see no good reason at the present time and under present conditions in our nation, to adopt such a doctrine. Therefore, we treat the money involved herein as no different from other personal property and will adjudicate the possession thereof in accordance with the rules governing personal property generally . . .

Lost property may be retained by the finder as against the owner or possessor of the premises where it is found.

On the other hand, "mislaid property is to be distinguished from lost property in that the former is property which the owner intentionally places where he can again resort to it, and then forgets. Mislaid property is presumed to be left in the custody of the owner or occupier of the premises upon which it is found, and it is generally held that the right of possession to mislaid property as against all except the owner is in the owner or occupant of such premises."

The facts of this case show that the bills were carefully placed in the jar and then buried in the ground and further show that the owner did not part with them inadvertently, involuntarily, carelessly or through neglect. Rather it shows a deliberate, conscious and voluntary act of the owner desiring to hide his money in a place where he thought it was safe and secure, and with the intention of returning to claim it at some future date. All the evidence indicates that the money must have been buried in the garage after the garage had been built. That was only a scant four years prior to the finding of the money...

The facts in this case show, as a matter of law, that the property is not to be classed in the category of lost property. Conceivably, there may be cases in which the issue as to whether the property is lost or mislaid property would be for determination by a jury under appropriate instructions by the court. The trial judge submitted the matter to a jury in the present case. There were no objections raised by either party to the definitions of "lost" and "mislaid" property as contained in the charge. The jury upon consideration of all the facts found that the property was mislaid rather than lost property.

Property which is found embedded in the soil under circumstances repelling the idea that it has been lost is held to have the characteristics of mislaid property. The finder acquires no rights thereto, for the presumption is that possession of the article found is in the owner and, accordingly it is held that the right to possession of such property is in the landowner....

Respondent relies strongly upon the case of *Danielson v. Roberts* to sustain his right to recover the money from petitioner. In that case the money was found in an old rusty half-gallon tin can containing a number of musty and partially deteriorated tobacco sacks. This demonstrated the money had been buried for some considerable period of time, and the court said: "The circumstances under which it was discovered, the condition of the vessel in which it was contained, and the place of deposit (in an old hen house) * * * all tend * * * to indicate that it had been buried for some considerable time, and that the owner was probably dead or unknown." In all the other cases relied upon by respondent the property was held to be either lost property or treasure trove, and belonged to the finder. That is recognized as the correct rule of law in such cases, but we have held, under the facts of this case, the property herein not to be lost property, but to be mislaid property, and the well recognized rules of law award the possession to the owner of the premises upon which the property is found. This being mislaid property, the right to possession thereof is in the owner of the premises where it was found.

The judgment of the Court of Civil Appeals is reversed and the judgment of the trial court is affirmed.

CALVERT, Justice (concurring).

I can agree to the judgment rendered herein but there is much in the majority opinion to which I cannot agree. I suggest that in an effort to simplify the law of found property, as applied in other common law jurisdictions, by declining to approve and adopt the law of "treasure trove" in this state, the majority opinion has only succeeded in confusing it.

The majority opinion declares, as a matter of law, that the property involved in this case is not to be classed as "lost" property because the facts show conclusively it was not "involuntarily parted with through neglect, carelessness or inadvertence." It then declares the property to be "mislaid property."

In none of the cases analyzed did the courts treat the property involved as mislaid property. In no case cited to this court or found by us has it been held that property found imbedded in the soil fell in the category of mislaid property, or had the characteristics of mislaid property.

The majority opinion fails to recognize a fourth category of found property... that is, the category of personal property found imbedded in the soil. The majority opinion has adopted the rule applicable to this category of property but has defined it as mislaid property. There is no need for this departure from the common-law rules. The rule as stated in American Jurisprudence is as follows: "Where property, not treasure trove, is found imbedded in the soil under circumstances repelling the idea that it has been lost, the finder acquires no title thereto... All we need do in order to achieve our objective of rejecting the law of treasure trove is to eliminate from the foregoing rule the words "not treasure trove", thus adopting the rule that all personal property or chattels found imbedded in the soil under circumstances repelling the idea that has been lost will be held to be rightfully in the possession of the owner of the soil as against all the world except the true owner.

If we are to disavow the doctrine of treasure trove—and I doubt the wisdom of doing so—I would not undertake to narrow the classifications of found property to "lost" and "mislaid" property. I certainly would not hold that the classification of property found imbedded in the soil was a jury question, and I would not hold that the length of the period for which it had been buried had any effect in determining whether it was lost or mislaid property. I would simply hold that all property found imbedded in the soil, including that known as treasure trove in England and other jurisdictions, was, as a matter of law, to be held in the possession of the landowner as bailee or trustee for the true owner.

■ ■ ■

Questions

1. In *Schley v. Couch,* the court cited the case of *Danielson v. Roberts* in which some boys found money buried in the soil beneath a henhouse. The court awarded the money to the boys. How did the majority opinion in *Schley* rationalize the *Danielson* case with the rule they accepted as law in *Schley?*
2. The concurring opinion in *Schley* suggests three types of property that can be found and, therefore, three rules as to who gets possession of the found property. What are the three types of property? Three rules?
3. In *Erickson v. Sinykin,* 223 Minn. 232, the court approved the trial court's finding that money discovered under a hotel room carpet had been abandoned, though the only evidence of abandonment was the likelihood, in view of its age, that the money had been undisturbed for over fifteen years. Why label "abandoned?" Who would get the money under the regular rules of misplaced or lost?

ENDNOTES

1. Betham, *Theory of Legislation Principles of the Civil Code,* Part I, 113, (Dumont ed., Hildreth Trans., 1864).
2. Lippman, *The Method of Freedom,* (The MacMillan Co., 1934), p. 102.

7

BUSINESS TRANSACTIONS

When the feudal practice of self-sufficiency began to decline and society proceeded to develop the rudimentary economic concepts of division of labor, specialization, and exchange of surpluses, there developed also the need to safeguard the exchange process. As the new capitalistic system developed, so the common law traditions transformed the "contract" from elementary judicial concepts into a practical tool of merchants for protecting their bargains. In effect, the contract brought rationality and order to the exchange process by court enforcement of merchants' promises. The contract concept requires that the reasonable expectations arising from promises receive protection of law. With such knowledge, most merchants will carry out their bargains as promised, and those who breach promises are ordered by the courts to compensate the aggrieved party.

It is no accident that the contract concept is especially adaptable to the free enterprise system. The contract is the inevitable counterpart of free enterprise. The legal system, responsive to society's needs, modified the contract to accommodate the business community. Since the courts could not anticipate every type of business transaction required by merchants, the courts, by delegation of authority to individuals, permitted the parties to draw up their own set of rules and embody them into their agreements. Merchants, therefore, are free to contract as the business situation dictates and this freedom of contract, as accorded by the courts, is an integral part of the *free enterprise* system. Indeed, much of the legal history of contracts reflects the concepts of free enterprise. Rugged individualism is mirrored in the rule that the party must protect himself in the bargain he strikes. It is not the court's duty to protect him from his foolish bargains. Moreover, the business community coupled with court enforcement of contracts was theorized as being efficiently regulated by competition without necessity of further governmental involvement. Therefore, *laissez-faire* flourished as the concept explaining the role of government in the free enterprise system. Indeed, free enterprise, as we know it, it inseparable from the contract concept.

Early American contract law reflected society's concern for individual freedom of decision. The fundamental natural rights expounded by our forefathers included the right to freely and voluntarily enter into contracts. The Constitution included a contract clause which prohibited state governments from impairing the obligations of contracts. They sought to prevent local governments from interfering with the individual in the exercise of his free will. However, since natural justice meant living up to the bargain, it became the positive duty of courts to maintain and enforce contracts.

Together with the rights of private property, the freedom to contract has formed the basis of the free enterprise system, which developed the natural resources of the American continent.

Contract law expanded during the Industrial Revolution. To facilitate commercial dealings, judges fashioned new relationships and new rules. The freedoms of contract law and the evolutionary qualities of the legal system provided the business community with the legal instruments needed to foster the expansion of the industrial society.

However, with the coming of the twentieth century and the concentration of wealth and power in large economic units, contracts with freely negotiated terms were often replaced by the contract that offered a take-it-or-leave-it bargain. Consequently, the attitudes of the courts began to change. Judges sometimes refused to enforce contracts which they considered unequal or unfair bargains. The social unrest and change in this century resulted in the belief that society should provide fairer standards of work and living for its citizens. The more recent aspects of "social justice" has caused contracts to be "regulated" on the basis of reasonableness and judged on the basis of equality of bargaining power. In short, government regulation of contractual terms has flourished in this modern era, obviously reducing the freedoms of contract law.

CONTRACT ESSENTIALS

Today, to accommodate the business community, the ceremony necessary to create a contract must be reduced to the absolute minimum. As such, the bargains can be made quickly and performed with efficiency. The legal requirements to form a contract are:

1. A genuine agreement (normally, an offer and acceptance);
2. Consideration (mutuality of legal inducement);
3. Legal capacity or competency of the parties;
4. Lawful purpose, (i.e., not declared illegal by statute or judicial decision).

OBJECTIVE INTENT

LUCY v. ZEHMER
84 S.E. 2d 516 (1954)
Supreme Court of Appeals of Virginia

■ ■ ■

This suit was instituted by W.O. Lucy and J.C. Lucy, against A.H. Zehmer and Ida S. Zehmer, his wife, defendants, to have specific performance of a contract by which it was alleged the Zehmers had sold to W.O. Lucy a tract of land known as the Ferguson farm, for $50,000...

The instrument sought to be enforced was written by A.H. Zehmer on December 20, 1952, in these words: "We hereby agree to sell to W.O. Lucy the Ferguson Farm complete for $50,000, title satisfactory to buyer," and signed by the defendants, A.H. Zehmer and Ida S. Zehmer.

A.H. Zehmer admitted that at the time mentioned W.O. Lucy offered him $50,000 cash for the farm, but that he, Zehmer, considered that the offer was made in jest; that so thinking... he wrote out "the memorandum" quoted above and induced his wife to sign it; that he did not deliver the memorandum to Lucy, but that Lucy picked it up, read it, put it in his pocket, attempted to offer Zehmer $5 to bind the bargain, which Zehmer refused to accept, and realizing for the first time that Lucy was serious, Zehmer assured him that he had no intention of selling the farm and that the whole matter was a joke. Lucy left the premises insisting that he had purchased the farm...

The defendants insist that the evidence was ample to support their contention that the writing sought to be enforced was prepared as a bluff or dare to force Lucy to admit that he did not have $50,000; that the whole matter was a joke; that the writing was not delivered to Lucy and no binding contract was ever made between the parties.

It is an unusual, if not bizarre, defense. When made to the writing admittedly prepared by one of the defendants and signed by both, clear evidence is required to sustain it...

If it be assumed, contrary to what we think the evidence shows, that Zehmer was jesting about selling his farm to Lucy and that the transaction was intended by him to be a joke, nevertheless the evidence shows that Lucy did not so understand it but considered it to be a serious business transaction and the contract to be binding on the Zehmers as well as on himself. The very next day he arranged with his brother to put up half the money and take a half interest in the land. The day after that he employed an attorney to examine the title. The next night, Tuesday, he was back at Zehmer's place and there Zehmer told him for the first time, Lucy said, that he wasn't going to sell and he told Zehmer, "You know you sold that place fair and square." After receiving the report from his attorney that the title was good he wrote to Zehmer that he was ready to close the deal.

Not only did Lucy actually believe, but the evidence shows he was warranted in believing, that the contract represented a serious business transaction and a good faith sale and purchase of the farm.

In the field of contracts, as generally elsewhere, "We must look to the outward expression of a person as manifesting his intention rather than to his secret and unexpressed intention. 'The law imputes to a person an intention corresponding to the reasonable meaning of his words and acts. ' "

At no time prior to the execution of the contract had Zehmer indicated to Lucy by word or act that he was not in earnest about selling the farm. They had argued about it and discussed its terms, as Zehmer admitted, for a long time. Lucy testified that if there was any jesting it was about paying $50,000 that night. The contract and the evidence show that he was not expected to pay the money that night. Zehmer said that after the writing was signed he laid it down on the counter in front of Lucy. Lucy said Zehmer handed it to him. In any event there had been what appeared to be a good faith offer and a good faith acceptance, followed by the execution and apparent delivery of a written contract. Both said that Lucy put the writing in his pocket and then offered Zehmer $5 to seal the bargain. Not until then, even under the defendants' evidence, was anything said or done to indicate that the matter was a joke. Both of the Zehmers testified that when Zehmer asked his wife to sign he whispered that it was a joke so Lucy wouldn't hear and that it was not intended that he should hear.

The mental assent of the parties is not requisite for the formation of a contract. If the words or other acts of one of the parties have but one reasonable meaning, his undisclosed intention is immaterial except when an unreasonable meaning which he attaches to his manifestations is known to the other party...

An agreement or mutual assent is of course essential to a valid contract but the law imutes to a person an intention corresponding to the reasonable meaning of his words, and acts. If his words and acts, judged by a reasonable standard, manifest an intention to agree, it is immaterial what may be the real but unexpressed state of his mind.

So a person cannot set up that he was merely jesting when his conduct and words could warrant a reasonable person in believing that he intended a real agreement.

Whether the writing signed by the defendants and now sought to be enforced by the complainants was the result of a serious offer by Lucy and a serious acceptance by the defendants, or was a serious offer by Lucy and an acceptance in secret jest by the defendants, in either event it constituted a binding contract of sale between the parties.

The (plaintiffs) are entitled to have specific performance of the contract...

■ ■ ■

Questions

1. What is meant by "objective intent" to form a contract? Can you contrast it with "subjective intent?" Which intent is relevant for determination of serious intent to contract?
2. The usual remedy for breach of contract is a money payment to compensate for

any damages caused by the breach. However, if the remedy of money payment is inadequate to accomplish justice, the courts will decree "specific performance" (that is, order the party who breached to specifically perform as he promised). Historically, the money-payment (or "damages")remedy has been generally held inadequate when there is failure to deliver a "unique" performance. Thus, if a seller refused to deliver his antique 1918 Ford that he had contracted to sell, the court would order its delivery since a money-payment remedy would be inadequate to compensate the injured buyer. Had the Ford been a modern and a more readily available model, the specific performance remedy would be denied and the buyer's remedy would have to be "damages" (the *extra* amount of money over the contract price necessary to buy the modern Ford elsewhere). In *Lucy* why was the court willing to grant the remedy of specific performance?

3. A contract is formed and based upon a "meeting of minds" or agreement by the parties. Sometimes there are disputes as to whether an "offer" had been extended or whether the communications was merely an *invitation* to another to enter into negotiations.

> The commonest example of offers meant to open negotiations and to call forth offers in the technical sense are advertisements, circulars and trade letters sent out by business houses. While it is possible that the offers made by such means may be in such form as to become contracts, they are often merely expressions of a willingness to negotiate.
>
> Business advertisements published in newspapers and circulars sent out by mail or distributed by hand stating that the advertiser has a certain quantity or quality of goods which he wants to dispose of at certain prices, are not offers which may become contracts as soon as any person to whose notice they may come signifies his acceptance by notifying the other that he will take a certain quantity of them. They are merely invitations to all persons who may read them that the advertiser is ready to receive offers for the goods at the price stated. *Craft v. Elder & Johnson Co.* 38 N.E. 2d 416 (1941).

Can you think of any reason why an advertisment should not be held to be an "offer?" What if you advertise your auto in the newspaper and four people arrive and accept your advertised "offer." Are you now in breach of three contracts?

MUTUAL MISTAKE

OSWALD v. ALLEN
417 F. 2d 43 (1969)
United States Court of Appeals, 2nd Cir.

■ ■ ■

Dr. Oswald, a coin collector from Switzerland, was interested in Mrs. Allen's collection of Swiss coins. In April of 1964 Dr. Oswald was in the United States and arranged to see Mrs. Allen's coins. The parties drove to the Newburgh Savings Bank of Newburgh, New York, where two of her collections referred to as the Swiss Coin Collection and the Rarity Coin Collection were located in separate vault boxes. After examining and taking notes on the coins in the Swiss Coin Collection, Dr. Oswald was shown several valuable Swiss coins from the Rarity Coin Collection. He also took notes on these coins and later testified that he did not know that they were in a separate "collection." The evidence showed that each collection had a different key number and was housed in labeled cigar boxes.

On the return to New York City, Dr. Oswald sat in the front seat of the car while Mrs. Allen sat in the back with Dr. Oswald's brother, Mr. Victor Oswald, and Mr. Cantarella of the Chase Manhattan Bank's Money Museum, who had helped arrange the meeting and served as Dr. Oswald's agent. Dr. Oswald could speak practically no English and so depended on his brother to conduct the transaction. After some negotiation a price of $50,000 was agreed upon. Apparently the parties never realized that the references to "Swiss coins" and the "Swiss Coin Collection" were ambiguous. The trial judge found that Dr. Oswald thought the offer he had authorized his brother to make was for all of the Swiss coins, while Mrs. Allen thought she was selling only the Swiss Coin Collection and not the Swiss coins in the Rarity Coin Collection...

Appellant attacks the conclusion of the Court below that a contract did not exist since the minds of the parties had not met. The opinion below states:

"* * * plaintiff believed that he had offered to buy all Swiss coins owned by the defendant while defendant reasonably understood the offer which she accepted to relate to those of her Swiss coins as had been segregated in the particular collection denominated by her as the 'Swiss Coin Collection'."

The trial judge based his decision upon his evaluation of the credibility of the witnesses, the records of the defendant, the values of the coins involved, the circumstances of the transaction and the reasonable probabilities. Such findings of fact are not to be set aside unless "clearly erroneous." There was ample evidence upon which the trial judge could rely in reaching this decision.

In such a factual situation the law is settled that no contract exists. The Restatement of Contracts in section 71(a) adopts the rule of *Raffles v. Wichelhaus*, 159 Eng. Rep. 375 (Ex. 1864). Professor Young states that rule as follows:

"when any of the terms used to express an agreement is ambivalent, and the parties understand it in different ways, there cannot be a contract unless one of them should have been aware of the other's understanding." Young, "Equivocation in Agreements," 64 *Colum. L. Rev.* 619, 621 (1964).

Even though the mental assent of the parties is not requisite for the formation of a contract, the facts found by the trial judge clearly place this case within the small group of exceptional cases in which there is "no sensible basis for choosing between conflicting understandings." The rule of *Raffles v. Wichelhaus* is applicable here.

■ ■ ■

Questions

1. Generally, for a contract to be rescindable for a mistake, the mutual mistake of the parties must go "to the whole substance of the agreement." What determines whether a mistake goes to the "substance" of the contract? There are generally two types of mutual mistakes which involve "the whole substance of the agreement." First, as in *Oswald*, each party was thinking, and reasonably so, of different subject matters (the Swiss coin collection, versus *all* Swiss coins). This kind of mutual mistake involves the identification of differing subject matters by each party and goes to the entire "substance of the agreement." The second kind of mutual mistake is illustrated by the case of the "barren cow." The buyer and the seller had made a contract for the sale of a barren cow, both thinking she was incapable of breeding. Later, the seller refused to deliver the cow for the $80 purchase price because she was with calf. The court ruled:

...the mistake or misapprehension of the parties went to the whole substance of the agreement. If the cow was a breeder, she was worth at least $750; if barren, she was worth not over $80. The parties would not have made the contract of sale except upon the understanding and belief that she was incapable of breeding, and of no use as a cow. It is true she is now the identical animal that they thought her to be when the contract was made; there is no mistake as to the identity of the creature. Yet the mistake was not of the mere quality of the animal, but went to the very nature of the thing. A barren cow is substantially a different creature than a breeding one... If the mutual mistake had simply related to the fact whether she was with calf or not for one season, then it might have been a good sale, but the mistake affected the character of the animal for all time, and for its present and ultimate use. She was not in fact the animal, or the kind of animal, the defendants intended to sell or the plaintiff to buy. She was not a barren cow, and, if this fact had been known, there would have been no contract. The mistake affected the substance of the whole consideration, and it must be considered that there was no contract to sell... the cow as she actually was. The thing sold and bought had in fact no existence... *Sherwood v. Walker* 66 Mich. 568 (1887).

This kind of mutual mistake is usually referred to as a mistake as to the existence of the subject matter.

2. The cases make a distinction between a statement of fact and a statement of opinion. A misstatement of fact may be grounds for rescission of the contract, whereas an honest statement of opinion may not. If A expresses an opinion in order to induce B to enter into a bargain and B relies on that statement of opinion in deciding to enter into the contract, why should B not be allowed to rescind if he proves that A was mistaken in his opinion?

.3. It is important to note that the duty of the court is to enforce the contract or bargain of the parties and not to rewrite the contract. The concept of freedom to contract, in effect, includes the right to make foolish as well as sharp bargains. The court's duty is not to protect every fool. If actual fraud is perpetrated upon one of the parties, the court will afford a remedy just as in the case of mutual mistakes. But, otherwise, the court enforces contracts as drawn by the parties.

CONSIDERATION

Contract law is commonly supposed to exist for the enforcement of promises. But not all promises are to receive legal enforcement. Friends who fail to show up for a promised engagement are not subject to legal suits for damages. Nor is a promise to make a gift enforceable. The question naturally arises, how do you determine which promises are legally enforceable? The courts have drawn certain lines and limitations that are largely the product of English and American history. Other countries have other methods to determine which promises are enforceable. But in the United States, the test of legally enforceable promises is the doctrine of "consideration." The idea of consideration is the idea of a bargain. The promise given is conditioned upon the receiving of an agreed exchange. The promisor is to receive a benefit in exchange for his promise or the prmisee is to experience some detriment at the promisor's request. Having received what he bargained for, the promisor is now held to his promise. But failure to receive consideration means the promisor need not keep his promise. Nevertheless, the application of the doctrine of consideration in particular situations is not always easy as the following cases illustrate.

HAMER v. SIDWAY
27 N.E. 256 (1891)
Court of Appeals of New York

■ ■ ■

The question which provoked the most discussion by counsel on this appeal, and which lies at the foundation of plaintiff's asserted right of recovery, is whether by virtue of a contract defendant's testator, William E. Story, became indebted to his newphew, William E. Story, 2d. on his twenty-first birthday in the sum of $5,000. The trial court found as a fact that "on the 20th day of March, 1869, * * * William E. Story agreed to and with William E. Story, 2d. that if he would refrain from drinking liquor, using tobacco, swearing, and playing cards or billiards for money until he should become twenty-one years of age, then he, the said William E. Story, would at that time pay him, the said William E. Story, 2d. the sum of $5,000 for such refraining, to which the said William E. Story, 2d. agreed," and that he "in all things fully performed his part of said agreement." The defendant contends that the contract was without consideration to support it, and therefore invalid. He asserts that the promisee, by refraining from the use of liquor and tobacco, was not harmed, but benefited; that that which he did was best for him to do, independently of his uncle's promise—and insists that it follows that,, unless the promisor was benefited, the contract was without consideration...

Such a rule could not be tolerated, and is without foundation in the law. The exchequer chamber in 1875 defined "consideration" as follows: "A valuable consideration, in the sense of the law, may consist either in some right, interest, profit, or benefit accruing to the one party, or some forbearance, detriment, loss, or responsibility given, suffered, or undertaken by the other." Courts "will not ask whether the thing which forms the consideration does in fact benefit the promisee or a third party, or is of any substantial value to any one. It is enough that something is promised, done, forborne, or suffered by the party to whom the promise is made as consideration for the promise made to him." Anson, Cont. 63. "In general a waiver of any legal right at the request of another party is a sufficient consideration for a promise." Pars. Cont. *444. "Any damage, or suspension, or forbearance of a right will be sufficient to sustain a promise." 2 *Kent. Comm.* (12th Ed.) *465. Pollock in his work on Contracts, (page 166,) after citing the definition given by the exchequer chamber, already quoted, says: "The second branch of this judicial description is really the most important one. 'Consideration' means not so much that one party is profiting as that the other abandons some legal right in the present, or limits his legal freedom of action in the future, as an inducement for the promise of the first." Now, applying this rule to the facts before us, the promisee used tabacco occasionally, drank liquor, and he had a legal right to do so. That right he abandoned for a period of years upon the strength of the promise of the testator that for such forbearance he would give him $5,000. We need not speculate on the effort which may have been required to give up the use of those stimulants. It is sufficient that he restricted his lawful freedom of action within certain prescribed limits upon the faith of his uncle's agreement, and now, having fully performed the conditions imposed, it is of no moment whether such performance actually proved a benefit to the promisor, and the court will not inquire into it; but, were it a proper subject of inquiry, we see nothing in this record that would permit a determination that the uncle was not benefited in a legal sense. Few cases have been found which may be said to be precisely in point, but such as have been, support the position we have taken.

■ ■ ■

Questions

1. Would the result in *Hamer* have been different if the uncle had merely promised to pay his nephew $5,000 on his 21st birthday? How is this promise different from the promise in *Hamer*?
2. To be consistent with the concept of freedom to contract, should the court determine if the value of the two considerations are approximately equal (that

is, a fair bargain)? Or should the court not inquire whether the consideration is adequate as long as the court finds some consideration from each side?

SCHUMM v. BERG
231 P. 2d 39 (1951)
Supreme Court of California

■ ₅ ■

Plaintiff, Johan Richard Wallace Schumm, is a minor born on February 7, 1948. Defendants are the executors of the estate of Wallace Beery, decreased. According to the complaint, the following facts appear: Plaintiff is the son of Beery and Gloria Schumm, neither of whom was married. He was conceived as the result of an act of sexual intercourse between Beery and Gloria on May 18, 1947. In August, 1947, Gloria's request of Beery that he marry her to legitimatize the expected child being refused, she demanded that he acknowledge his paternity of the expected child or she would institute proceedings to have him declared the father and for support of the child. Beery believed, and it was a likely result, that such a suit would be damaging to his social and professional standing as a prominent motion picture star. Under these circumstances, in August, 1947, while Gloria was pregnant with the child...and for his express benefit, [she] entered into an oral agreement with Beery as follows:...

"(a) The said Gloria Schumm during the remainder of the period of her said pregnancy until the birth of said child shall institute no action or proceeding in any Court to establish judicially the fact that said Wallace Beery is or will be the father of said child.

"(b) Upon the marriage of said Gloria Schumm and Hans Schumm, said expected child if born alive shall be surnamed 'Schumm' and its name if a male shall include said Berry's Christian name 'Wallace,' or if a female, shall include said Beery's nickname 'Wally.'

"(c) Wallace Beery, if said child be born alive, recognizes and acknowledges the claim of Gloria Schumm in behalf of said expected child that he is morally and legally responsible for the support and education of said child in a manner suitable to said Wallace Beery's circumstances, station in life and standard of living from the date of birth of said child until said child shall become 21 years of age, or until the death of said child, whichever shall occur sooner...

Pursuant thereto Gloria married Hans Schumm on August 21, 1947, and on the birth of plaintiff, gave him the name above mentioned including "Wallace" and the surname "Schumm"; no proceeding was instituted until after the birth. Beery refused to comply with any of the provisions of the contract, except he paid nine weekly installments of $25, beginning July 6, 1948. Damages of $104,135 are claimed. Beery died and a claim against his estate was rejected....

Defendants contend that for various reasons there was no consideration for the contract...

Defendants assert that Gloria's promise not to institute suit and to name plaintiff after Beery is not consideration. We cannot agree with either assertion.

On the first proposition, the argument runs to the effect that it is the illegitimate *child's* right to enforce the obligation of the father to support it; that the mother has no right except to bring the action in a representative capacity on the child's behalf; that, therefore, in agreeing not to sue she had suffered no detriment, for having no right, she gave up nothing; that a forbearance to sue on a void claim is not good consideration...

The mother does have a definite interest in maintaining the action, for the obligation to support is imposed upon both the mother and father. If the mother does not bring an action against the father and he refuses to give support, she will have to bear it. To the extent that she obtains relief against the father in such an action she is relieved of that burden. In agreeing to refrain from suing she is thereby suffering a detriment.

Gloria had the legal right to bring an action after conception and before birth...

Gloria's promise to name plaintiff after Beery (given name Wallace) was adequate consideration to support the contract. It was a detriment to Gloria and a benefit to Beery...

Reason supports the rule, for having a child bear its father's name is commonly considered a privilege and honor, and Beery assumed it was, for he obtained such a promise running to him... The validity of consideration does not depend on its value. Defendants refer to recitations in the contract that Beery was prominent and did not want the possible adverse publicity resulting from the instigation of a paternity suit. But that was only for the period prior to birth, and as seen, the promise to name the child after him was in his favor and presumably he considered it valuable...

■ ■ ■

Notes and Questions

1. "The (husband) had assualted his wife, who took refuge in (a neighbor's) house. The next day the husband gained access to the house and began another assault upon his wife. The wife knocked (the husband) down with an axe, and was on the point of cutting his head open or decapitating him while he was (lying) on the floor, and the plaintiff (neighbor) intervened, caught the axe as it was descending, and the blow intended for (the husband) fell upon (the neighbor's) hand, mutilating it badly, but saving (the husband's) life.

    Subsequently, (the husband) orally promised to pay the plaintiff (neighbor) her damages; but...failed to pay anything...

    The question presented is whether there was a consideration recognized by our law as sufficient to support the promise. The Court is of the opinion that, however much the (husband) should be impelled by common gratitude to alleviate the plaintiff's misfortune, a humanitarian act of this kind, voluntarily performed, is not such consideration as would entitle her to recover at law." *Harrington v. Taylor* 35 SE 2d 227, (N. Carolina, 1945).

    Why, under the doctrine of consideration, is there no recovery in these circumstances? Was the consideration (hand in front of the axe) given in response to a bargain?

2. Because the doctrine of consideration has not been completely satisfactory in all situations, another rule has been developed as a substitute for consideration and yet binding the promisor to his promise. The rule is called "promissory estoppel" and is stated in the Restatement, Contracts 390 (1932) as:

    > A promise which the promisor should reasonably expect to induce action or forebearance of a definite and substantial character on the part of the promisee and which does induce such action or forebearance is binding if injustice can be avoided only by enforcement of the promise.

    In one case, the court in discussing this doctrine stated,

    > We think the promissory estopped doctrine... extends to commercial transactions... "To hold a defendant liable under this doctrine there must be a promise which reasonably leads the promisee to rely on it to his detriment, with injustice otherwise not being avoidable. If the (statement made)... for any reason is not a promise affirmatively to do something, then the plaintiff cannot recover. Likewise if there is no reasonably foreseeable likelihood of reliance by the person receiving the offer or promise, the doctrine does not permit recovery. And the reliance must be justifiable... Finally, there must be some substantial detriment due to the reliance"... *N. Litterio & Co. v. Glassman Construction Co.* 319 F 2d 736 (D.C. Cir, 1963)

Can you think of any instances in which promissory estopped would require the enforcement of a promise unsupported by consideration?

PAROL EVIDENCE RULE

KELEHER v. LA SALLE COLLEGE
147 A. 2d 835 (1959)
Supreme Court of Pennsylvania

■ ■ ■

On March 2, 1953 Brother E. Stanislaus... defendant's President, wrote plaintiff to the effect that defendant could not offer him a new contract upon the expiration of the 1952-1953 contract, assigning as the reason therefor the necessity that defendant curtail its expenditures because of rising costs and diminishing enrollment. On March 7, 1953 the plaintiff wrote Brother Stanislaus questioning his authority to revoke "academic tenure" which plaintiff stated had been given him in June 1951 by Brother Paul (the defendant's former President)...

On September 18, 1953 plaintiff instituted an...action against defendant for an alleged breach of an *oral* contract of employment. In this action plaintiff alleged that in June of 1951, Brother Paul, defendant's President, entered into an *oral* contract with plaintiff increasing his salary to $4,160,... giving him "tenure of academic employment," and that the revocation without cause, of his tenure and employment by defendant, violated and breached this oral contract. Defendant's answer denied the existence of any oral contract and averred that plaintiff's employment arose soley under the two written contracts of June 15, 1951 and June 15, 1952.

When the matter came for trial... defendant's counsel offered in evidence the written contract of June 15, 1952 and, in response to a question addressed to him by defendant's counsel, plaintiff acknowledged that the signature on this written contract was his signature. After plaintiff's counsel had placed in evidence the March and April 1953 correspondence between plaintiff and Brother Stanislaus, the trial court granted "a motion for a nonsuit...

...(T)he fundamental issue is whether, in view of the written undertaking of June 15, 1952 between the parties, the plaintiff should be permitted to prove by parol evidence the terms of the alleged oral contract of June 1951

Walker v. Saricks, 63 A. 2d 9, 10, well states the Pennsylvania Parol Evidence Rule: "Where parties, without any fraud or mistake, have deliberately put their engagements in writing, the law declares the writing to be not only the best, but the only, evidence of their agreement.

All preliminary negotiations, conservations and verbal agreements are merged in and superseded by the subsequent written contract * * * and unless fraud, accident, or mistake be averred, the writing constitutes the agreement between the parties, and its terms cannot be added to nor subtracted from by parol evidence..."

The written contract of June 15, 1952 is clear and free of any ambiguity. It purports to encompass all the terms and conditions of the relationship between plaintiff and defendant concerning the former's employments as a teacher during the academic year 1952-1953. Plaintiff now seeks to prove an oral agreement which would clearly alter and vary the terms of this written contract in a most material instance, to wit, the length of plaintiff's employment. The written contract distinctly and unambiguously sets forth that plaintiff is employed for the academic year 1952-1953. What plaintiff wants to prove is that, as the result of an oral contract, he acquired "academic tenure" by which we understand permanent tenure. That plaintiff's oral contract would vary and alter the written contract is clear beyond any peradventure of doubt.

Plaintiff neither alleges nor does he seek to prove any fraud, accident or mistake, but simply contends that the parol evidence rule is inapplicable because the written contract did not constitute an integration of the alleged oral contract and that both the oral and the written contract are co-existent. A comparison of the subject-matter of the written contract with that of the alleged oral contract clearly indicates an integration of the latter by the former. To allow plaintiff to prove an oral contract under these circumstances would violate the parol evidence rule, a rule to which this Court requires rigid adherence. Both the spirit and the letter of the parol evidence rule... and a host of... decisions, compel the rejection of evidence as to any alleged oral contract in June 1951 between all parties.

For the reasons stated, judgment is directed to be entered for the defendant.

■ ■ ■

Notes and Questions

1. What type of exceptions to the parol evidence rule were alluded to in *La Salle*?
2. People usually put their contracts in writing, not necessarily because the law requires it, but because the writing serves as evidence of the existence of the contract. Does the parol evidence rule suggest another reason for putting contracts in writing?
3. When the language used in an agreement might be interpreted two or more ways, extrinsic (outside the writing) evidence may be considered, not to vary or modify the terms of the written agreement but to aid the court in ascertaining the true intent of the parties. Suppose the written contract called for the delivery of "300 chickens." Could one of the parties introduce extrinsic evidence of the "trade" meaning of the word "chicken?"
4. The parol evidence rule is not a bar to admission of testimony if the parties do not intend the writing to be the repository of all of the terms of their agreement. The terms not incorporated in the writing are still a part of the binding contract even though they are provable only by parol testimony. What the intention of the parties was is a question of fact. Did the parties in *La Sale* intend the writing to be the full "repository of all terms of their agreement?"

CAPACITY TO CONTRACT

KIEFER v. FRED HOWE MOTORS, INC.
158 NW 2d 288 (1968)
Supreme Court of Wisconsin

■ ■ ■

The law governing agreements made during infancy reaches back over many centuries. The general rule is that "* * * the contract of a minor, other than for necessaries, is either void or voidable at his option."...

The underpinnings of the general rule allowing the minor to disaffirm his contracts were undoubtedly the protection of the minor. It was thought that the minor was immature in both mind and experience and that, therefore, he should be protected from his own bad judgments as well as from adults who would take advantage of him. The doctrine of the voidability of minors' contracts often seems commendable and just. If the beans that the young naive Jack purchased from the crafty old man in the fairy tale "Jack and the Bean Stalk" had been worthless rather than magical, it would have been only fair to allow Jack to disaffirm the bargain and reclaim his cow. However, in today's modern and sophisticated society the "infancy doctrine" seems to lose some of its gloss.

Paradoxically, we declare the infant mature enough to... be responsible for his torts and crimes, but not mature enough to assume the burden of his own contractual indiscretions. In Wisconsin, the infant is deemed mature enough to use a dangerous instrumentality—a motor vehicle—at sixteen, but not mature enough to purchase it without protection until he is twenty-one.

No one really questions that a line as to age must be drawn somewhere below which a legally defined minor must be able to disaffirm his contract for nonnecessities. The law over the centuries has considered this age to be twenty-one...

Undoubtedly, the infancy doctrine is an obstacle when a major purchase is involved. However, we believe that the reasons for allowing that obstacle to remain viable at this point outweigh those for casting it aside. Minors require some protection from the pitfalls of the market place. Reasonable minds will always differ on the extent of the protection that should be afforded...

Disaffirmance.

The (dealer) questions whether there has been an effective disaffirmance of the contract in this case.

Williston, while discussing how a minor may disaffirm a contract, states:

> "Any act which clearly shows an intent to disaffirm a contract or sale is sufficient for the purpose. Thus a notice by the infant of his purpose to disaffirm * * * a tender or even an offer to return the consideration or its proceeds to the vendor, * * * is sufficient."

The testimony of Steven Kiefer and the letter from his attorney to the dealer clearly establish that there was an effective disaffirmance of the contract.

Misrepresentation.

(The dealer's) last argument is that the (minor) should be held liable in tort for damages because he misrepresented his age. Dealer would use these damages as a set-off against the contract price sought to be reclaimed by (the minor).

The 19th-century view was that a minor's lying about his age was inconsequential because a fraudulent representation of capacity was not the equivalent of actual capacity. This rule has been altered by time. There appear to be two possible methods that now can be employed to bind the defrauding minor: he may be estopped from denying his alleged majority, in which case the contract will be enforced or contract damages will be allowed; or he may be allowed to disaffirm his contract but be liable in tort for damages. Wisconsin follows the latter approach.

In *Wisconsin Loan & Finance Corp. v. Goodnough*, Mr. Chief Justice Rosenberry said:

> "...In this case, if there is an estoppel which operates to prevent the defendant from repudiating the contract and he is liable upon it, the damages will be the full amount of the note plus interest and a reasonable attorney's fee. If he is held liable, on the other hand, in deceit, he will be liable only for the damages which the plaintiff sustained in this case, the amount of money the plaintiff parted with, which was $352 less the $25 repaid. There seems to be sound reason in the position of the English courts that to hold the contract enforceable by way of estoppel is to go contrary to the clearly declared policy of the law... The contract (should not be)...enforced, he is held liable (instead) for deceit as he is for other torts such as slander...and trespass..."

Having established that there is a remedy against the defrauding minor, the question becomes whether the requisites for a tort action in misrepresentation are present in this case.

The trial produced conflicting testimony regarding whether Steven Kiefer had been asked his age or had replied that he was "twenty-one." Steven and his wife, Jacqueline, said "No," and Frank McHalsky, (the dealer's) salesman, said "Yes." Confronted with this conflict, the question of credibility was for the trial court to decide, which it did by holding that Steven did not orally represent that he was "twenty-one." This finding is not contrary to the great weight and clear preponderance of the evidence and must be affirmed.

Even accepting the trial court's conclusion that Steven Kiefer had not orally represented his age to be over twenty-one, the (dealer) argues that there was still a misrepresentation. The "motor vehicle purchase contract" signed by Steven Kiefer contained the following language just above the purchaser's signature:

> "I represent that I am 21 years of age or over and recognize that the dealer sells the above vehicle upon this representation."

Whether the inclusion of this sentence constitutes a misrepresentation depends on whether elements of the tort have been satisfied. They were not. In *First Nat. Bank in Oshkosh v. Scieszinski* it is said:

> "To be actionable the false representation must consist, first of a statement of fact which is untrue; second, that it was made with the intent to defraud and for the purpose of inducing the other party to act upon it; third, that he did in fact rely on it and was induced thereby to act, to his injury or damage."

No evidence was adduced to show that the plaintiff had an intent to defraud the dealer. To the contrary, it is at least arguable that the majority of minors are, as the plaintiff here might well have been, unaware of the legal consequences of their acts.

Without the elements of scienter being satisfied, the plaintiff is not susceptible to an action in misrepresentation. Furthermore, the reliance...must be..."justifiable reliance." We fail to see how the dealer could be justified in the mere reliance on the fact that the plaintiff signed a contract containing a sentence that said he was twenty-one or over. The trial court observed that the plaintiff was sufficiently immature looking to arouse suspicion. The (dealer) never took any affirmative steps to determine whether the plaintffif was in fact over twenty-one. It never asked to see a draft card, identification card, or the most locical indicium of age under the circumstances, a driver's license. Therefore, because there was no intent to deceive, and no justifiable reliance, the (dealer's) action for misrepresentation must fall.

HALLOWS, Chief Justice (dissenting).

My...ground...(for) dissent is that an automobile to this plaintiff was a necessity and therefore the contract could not be disaffirmed. Here, we have a minor, aged 20 years and 7 months, the father of a child, and working. While the record shows there is some public transportation to his present place of work, it also shows he borrowed his mother's car to go to and from work. Automobiles for parents under 21 years of age to go to and from work in our current society may well be a necessity and I think in this case the record shows it is. An automobile as a means of transportation to earn a living should not be considered a non-necessity because the owner is 5 months too young. I would reverse.

■ ■ ■

Questions

1. Why protect minors by giving them an escape from the contract?
2. What must a minor do to disaffirm?
3. In Wisconsin, a minor may be held liable for the tort of fraud or misrepresentation. What elements must be proven to establish the tort of fraud? Which elements were not proven in *Kiefer*?
4. Minors are held liable for contractual consumption of "necessaries" and the dissenting justice in *Kiefer* felt the auto was a necessity. Why do you think the majority of the court didn't think an auto was a necessity?
5. How drunk does one have to be to lose the legal capacity to contract?

> "Mere drunkenness is not sufficient to release a party from his contracts. To render a transaction voidable on account of the drunkenness of a party to it, the drunkenness must have been such as to have drowned reason, memory, and

judgment, and to have impaired the mental facilities to such an extent as to render the party non compos mentis (not of sound mind) for the time being... Though the mind of a person may be to some extent impaired by age or disease, still if he has the capacity to comprehend and act rationally in the transaction in which he is engaged—if he can understand the nature of his business and the effect of what he is doing, and can exercise his will with reference thereto—his acts will be valid. *Martin v. Harsh et. al.* 83 N.E. 164 (1907).

CONDITIONS

LACH v. CAHILL
85 A. 2d 481 (1951)
Supreme Court of Errors of Connecticut

■ ■ ■

The plaintiff sues to recover a deposit he made with one of the defendants upon a written agreement to purchase a house belonging to the other. The trial court concluded that the agreement never came into existence because it was subject to a condition which had not been fulfilled. It rendered judgment for the plaintiff for the return of the deposit and the defendants appealed.

The finding,... discloses the following facts: On November 10, 1949, the plaintiff signed an agreement with the defendant Cahill, acting through his agent, the defendant Rabbett, to purchase Cahill's house in Windsor Locks for $18,000 and paid a deposit of $1,000. A few days later Cahill also signed the agreement and accepted the deposit. The contract contained the following provision: "This agreement is contingent upon buyer being able to obtain mortgage in the sum of $12,000 on the premises, and have immediate occupancy of the premises." The conveyance was to be made by warranty deed within thiry days after acceptance of the agreement by the seller.

The plaintiff had been a practicing attorney for a little more than one year, was married and the father of three small children. Rabbett knew the financial position of the plaintiff and that he contemplated a bank mortgage payable in installments over a reasonable period of time. On November 14, the plaintiff applied to the First National Bank of Windsor Locks for a $12,000 mortgage, which was denied. Thereafter, in the period up to November 21, he unsuccessfully applied for a mortgage loan at five different banks and loaning institutions. He was informed that the banks in Hartford were not interested in placing loans on outlying property. He conferred with the federal housing administration examiners, who advised him that although he was a veteran his income did not meet the requirements for an F.H.A. guaranteed loan. Rabbett informed the plaintiff not later than November 18 that Cahill was definitely not interested in a purchase mortgage. On December 1, the plaintiff wrote to Cahill that he was unable to secure a mortgage in the amount of $12,000 and requested the return of the deposit...

The decisive issues in the case are whether the ability of the plaintiff to secure a $12,000 mortgage was a condition precedent to his duty to perform his promise to purchase and whether he made a reasonable effort to secure the mortgage. Unless both questions are answered in the affirmative the plaintiff cannot recover. A condition precedent is a fact or event which the parties intend must exist or take place before there is a right to performance... A condition is distinguished from a promise in that it creates no right or duty in and of itself but is merely a limiting or modifying factor... If the condition is not fulfilled, the right to enforce the contract does not come into existence... Whether a provision in a contract is a condition the nonfulfillment of which excuses performance depends upon the intent of the parties, to be ascertained from a fair and reasonable construction of the language used in the light of all the surrounding circumstances when they executed the contract.

The plaintiff was a young man of limited means, just starting in his profession and under the necessity of finding a home for his wife and their three small children. He required a mortgage payment in reasonable instalments over a period of time if he was to complete the prospective purchase of Cahill's house. The court properly concluded that the language used, read in the light of the situation of the parties, expressed an intention that the plaintiff should not be held to an agreement to purchase unless he could secure a mortgage for $12,000 on reasonable terms as to the amount and time of instalment payments.

The condition in the contract implied a promise by the plaintiff that he would make reasonable efforts to secure a suitable mortgage...The performance or nonperformance of this implied promise was a matter for the determination of the trial court. The conclusion reached upon the facts was proper...

■ ■ ■

Notes and Questions

1. Generally, the problems arising under contract law involve either (1) a dispute concerning whether the contract exists, or (2) a dispute where the parties admit the contract but disagree concerning their rights under the contract. Which type of dispute existed in *Lach?*

2. As in *Lach*, the condition is said to be "precedent" when some event must occur before the party becomes bound to complete his performance or duty. Failure of that event to occur obviously relieves the party from any duty under the contract.
   On the other hand, when the party has already become bound to complete his performance but will be relieved from such responsibilty by the happening of some event, the condition is "subsequent." A condition subsequent can be illustrated by conditions commonly contained in insurance policies. After an auto accident, (condition precedent) the insurance company is bound by the contract to pay the insured for his loss. But if the insured fails to notify the insurance company within a stipulated time period as stated in the policy (the condition subsequent), the insurance company is relieved from its duty ot indemnify the insured.

3. There are also what are called "conditions concurrent" though this term is more of a misnomer. Its real meaning is that when the performance of the parties are to occur concurrently, then it is a condition precedent to a suit by either party that such a party do something to put the other in default. The something that must be done will vary according to the circumstances, but it is generally called making a "tender" of his performance (that is, offering his half of the bargain and if the second party refuses or can't concurrently perform, then he is in default). In effect, the "concurrent conditions" concept requires tender of performance as a condition that must occur before the other party is bound to perform which, if he fails, puts him in breach.

CERTAINITY OF DAMAGES

EVERGREEN AMUSEMENT CORPORATION v. MILSTEAD
112 A. 2d 901 (1955)
Court of Appeals of Maryland

■ ■ ■

The appellant, by counterclaim, sought recovery of lost profits for the period of delay. The court held the amount claimed to have been so lost to be too uncertain and speculative, and refused evidence proffered to support appellant's theory...

The real reliance of the Evergreen Amusement Corporation is on the slowness of the contractor in completing the work. It says that the resulting delay in the opening of the theater from June first to the middle of August cost it twelve thousand five hundred dollars in profits. It proffered a witness to testify that he had built and operated a majority of the drive-in theaters in the area, that he is in the theater equipment business and familiar with the profits that drive-in theaters make in the area, that a market survey was made in the area before the site of the theater was selected, and that it had shown the need for such a theater in the neighborhood. It was said he would testify as to the reasonably anticipated profits during the months in question by comparing the months in its second year of operation with those in which it could not operate the year before, and would say that the profits would have been the same. His further testimony would be, it was claimed, that weather conditions, the population, and competition were all approximately the same in the year the theater opened and the following year...

We think the court did not err in refusing the proffered evidence. Under the great weight of authority, the general rule clearly is that loss of profit is a definite element of damages in an action for breach of contract or in an action for harming an established business which has been operating for a sufficient length of time to afford a basis of estimation with some degree of certainty as to the probable loss of profits, but that, on the other hand, loss of profits from a business which as not gone into operation may not be recovered because they are merely speculative and incapable of being ascertained with the requisite degree of certainty. Restatement, Contracts, Sec. 331, states the law to be that damages are recoverable for profits prevented by breach of contract "only to the extent that the evidence affords a sufficient basis for estimating their amount of money with reasonable certainty", and that where the evidence does not afford a sufficient basis, "damages may be measured by the rental value of the property." Comment "d" says this: "If the defendant's breach has prevented the plaintiff from carrying on *a well-established business,* the amount of profits thereby prevented is often capable of proof with reasonably certainty. On the basis of its past history, a reasonable prediction can be made as to its future." That damages for profits anticipated from a business which has not started may not be recovered, is laid down in 25 C.J.S., Damages, §42.

See also "The Requirement of Certainty for Proof of Lost Profits," 64 Harvard Law 317. The article discusses the difficulties of proving with sufficient certainty the profits which were lost, and then says: "These difficulties have given rise to a rule in some states that no new business can recover for its lost profits." While this Court has not laid down a flat rule (and does not hereby do so), nevertheless, no case has permitted recovery of lost profits under comparable circumstances...

It would seem that a new theater would not for some time be well enough known to attract the same number of patrons it would draw after a period of operation. We think the court was right in basing the damages for delay in the completion of the site on fair rental value...

■ ■ ■

LIQUIDATED DAMAGES

As in *Evergreen Amusement Corporation* it is often difficult to estimate with any degree of certainty the amount of actual damage that will result from a breach of contract. Often contracts provide that if the party has not completed his or her performance by a specified time, he or she must pay a certain amount of money per day until performance is completed. These "damages" are referred to as liquidated damages, and the injured party has a right to claim the amount specified as the measure of damages. For liquated damages to be recovered, the amount stipulated must be reasonable and bear some relationship to the probable damages incurred by the injured party. Furthermore, the amount of damages stipulated must be intended as compensation for possible breach and not as a penalty to force performance. Liquidated damages will be interpreted as a penalty when the amount stipulated is out of proportion to the possible loss. However, once the court decides that the amount is reasonable, that amount will be awarded without inquiry to the actual damages sustained by the injured party. While a liquated damage provision is involved in the following case, the central issue involves the determination of whether "consequential damages" may be recovered.

CONSEQUENTIAL DAMAGES

KRAUSS v. GREENBARG
137 F. 2d 569 (1943)
United States Court of Appeals, 3rd. Cir.

■ ■ ■

On July 30, 1940, the defendants who used the business name of King Kard Overall Company, received an award and contract from the War Department of the United States to supply 698,084 pairs of leggings. The contract called for deliveries of certain quantities of leggings at stated intervals and provided for a sum as liquidated damages for each day of delay. By a memorandum of the same date the defendants (Greenbarg) placed an order with the plaintiff (Krauss), whose business was carried on under the name of American Cord and Webbing Company, for the webbing to be used in making the leggings. The order provided for certain quantities of webbing to be delivered at given dates.   On March 11, 1941, the webbing company (Krauss) started suit in the Eastern District of Pennsylvania to recover $15,326.13 for the webbing sold and delivered to the overall company (Greenbarg) pursuant to the latter's order. The buyers (Greenbarg) admitted nonpayment but filed a counterclaim for $22,740.99. The jury returned a vedict in favor of the overall company for the counterclaim and judgment was entered for the difference... The webbing company filed this appeal.

The issues raised on this appeal concern the counterclaim. The theory of the counterclaim is that the webbing company did not maintain the scheduled deliveries of the webbing and as a result thereof the overall company could not meet its schedule with the Government. Because of this it incurred the per diem penalty provided for in the government contract for each day's delay in deliveries which amounted to $22,740.99. These special damages it seeks to charge to the webbing company. The latter admits that it failed to deliver the webbing as per schedule. It denies, however, liability on its part for the special damages sought...

The rule governing special damages in contract cases applied in the Pennsylvania decisions has been laid down in the leading English case of *Hadley v. Baxendale*, 9 EX. 341 (1854). It is that special damages for breach of contract are not recoverable unless they can fairly and reasonably be considered as arising naturally from the breach or as being within the contemplation of the parties, at the time the contract was made, as the probable result of the breach.

Where the consequential damages claimed were within the contemplation of the parties at the time of the contracting as the probable result of the breach, their recovery has been allowed. The question stressed as ultimately determinative in all these cases is whether at the time of making the contract the party who broke his promise knew that his breach would probably result in the kind of special damages claimed and thus could be said to have foreseen them. If he did, then he was liable for the consequential damages.

On the question in the case at bar we have a special finding by the jury. At the trial of the case the court submitted three questions to the jury. One asked whether Krauss (the webbing company) knew, at the time he made his contract with Greenbarg (the overall company), that the latter's contract with the Government provided that delay in delivery would subject it to penalty. The jury answered yes. This finding, which is unassailed, establishes definitely that the webbing, which it undertook to furnish, was not delivered as scheduled in the contract and as a result the leggings could not be delivered on time, the overall company would incur the special damages it now claims.

■ ■ ■

Questions

1. In *Krauss*, who must have foreseen the loss for the court to allow recovery for consequential damages? When must the loss have been foreseen? Why?
2. What type of reactions (specifically) might a businessman have to the greater risk associated with a breach of the contract when he is told of a potential consequential damage?
3. While contract law seeks to compensate the aggrieved contracting party, do *Evergreen* and *Krauss* suggest some realistic protection for the breacher also? From what type of risks?

ILLEGALITY

Historically, the common law courts have refused to enforce illegal bargains. An agreement is considered illegal if its formation or performance is a crime or tort, or otherwise opposed to public policy. The parties to such agreement are not entitled to the aid of the courts. Agreements for bribery, fraud, wagers, usery, and agreements obstructing legal process (such as the suppression of evidence) are clearly obnoxious to society. Besides these relatively few judicially declared illegal agreements, the law of contracts was oriented to private agreements between private individuals as they freely determine their bargain. Freedome to contract was overwhelming public policy. However, the Supreme Court made it clear in 1911 that the freedom to contract was not an absolute right. In the opinion of the court,

> ...freedom of contract is a qualified and not an absolute right. There is no absolute freedom to do as one wills or to contract as one chooses. The guaranty of liberty does not withdraw from legislative supervision that wide department of activity which consists of the making of contracts, deny to government the power to provide restrictive safequards. Liberty implies the absence of arbitrary restraint, not immunity from reasonable regulations and prohibitions imposed in the interests of the community. *Chicago B & Q.R. v. Maguire,* 219 U.S. 549 (1911)

Nevertheless, in the early twentieth century the Supreme Court held numerous governmental intrusions into the freedom of contract as unconstitutional. They ruled against the initial congressional efforts in the field of minimum wage and child labor laws, finding such legislation to be an unconstitutional interference with the liberty of contract. In the 1930s, however, the Supreme Court changed its point of view and upheld congressional intrusion into the freedom of contract because the consequences of sub-standard wages and of child labor abuses were too harmful to the welfare of individuals and society. Consequently, in the modern era numerous legislative attempts to define contractual terms have been upheld and represent a general move to make modern law more "just."

Courts have recognized that contracts presented before the court are no longer a single instrument drafted for those particular parties. Instead, contracts of insurance, contracts of purchase of goods, or contracts for a bank loan are all prepared in a uniform fashion with an industry-wide pattern. Such contracts often require that the consumers conform to the industry terms, or do without that industry's goods. The appreciation that such contractual terms result from unequal bargaining power has resulted in judicial and congressional modification and regulation of contract. The Supreme Court has said that

> when a widely diffused public interest has become enmeshed in a network of multitudinous private arrangements, the authority of the state "to safeguard the vital interests of its people"...is not to be gain said by abstracting one such arrangement from its public context and treating it as though it were an isolated private contract constitutionally immune from impaiment. *East New York Savings Bank v. Hahn,* 326 U.S. 230, 232, (1945).

As a result, local, state, and national laws have been created which statutorally regulate contractual terms. For example, the terms of insurance policies are regulated by statutes, credit terms and consumer loans are often dictated by statutes, and contracts in the marketing of goods may run afowl of statutes or court decisions which condemn certain practices as unfair methods of competition.

These statutory and judicial restrictions on the freedom of contract have had an important impact upon commerical activities. It reduces the freedom to contract from the theoretical absolute privilege of selecting contractual terms to a governmentally modified privilege. Such modifications have gone so far as in certain instances, to even regulate with whom one contracts (sex, race, and so forth). Becoming familiar with these numerous substantive governmental "regulations" in the formulation of contracts is of fundamental importance in understanding the concept of illegality and in recognizing such intrusion as a continuing technique of government to rectify perceived inequities in bargaining power and to achieve social justice.

SALES

The word "sales" has a particular legal meaning. In general, a "sale" is a contract or a transfer of legal title of *tangible personal property* from seller to buyer for a monetary consideration. Personal property is all property that is not "real" property, (land and things permanently attached thereto). Examples of tangible personal property would be desks, shoes, candy, or other tangible items not attached to real estate. Intangible personal property is evidenced in stocks, bonds, copyrights, or patent rights. Thus, "sales" is the body of law covering and applicable only to transfers of tangible personal property for a price; it does not apply to intangible property or to contracts for services.

Historically, merchants have sought distinctive treatment for their business transactions. In early medieval times, disputes among merchants were settled in their own courts by elder merchants who primarily resolved the controversy by applying rules developed through business customs. The courts of the "Law Merchant" were swift in operation for the benefit of traveling merchants and, in applying business customs as rules, the merchants could come to know the law and develop the law to fit their particular needs.

Later, many of the rules of the Law Merchant were incorporated into the common law courts of England and eventually brought to the courts of the colonies. However, the law developed by the various states of the union followed different paths and this diversity of rules was not conducive to the business community with its mass production and expanding markets. Therefore, efforts were begun to make the law of "sales" uniform among the several states. The result was the Uniform Sales Act which was enacted by most states. Much of the Uniform Sales Act was later made part of the Uniform Commercial Code (UCC) which covers not only "sales" law but other laws of the mercantile environment as well. The UCC has been adopted in some manner by all the states of the union.

Article 2 of the UCC embodies the law of "sales." Article 2 employs several new and unique concepts in the effort to reform sales law to better conform to the customs and practices of merchants.

BATTLE OF THE FORMS

Perhaps the most drastic of all things that can go wrong for merchants is to assume that they have a binding contract only to discover that they do not. Under contract principles, the acceptance of a contract offer must be unequivocal, that is, accept the exact terms of the offer without alteration or addition of different terms. This is sometimes called the "mirror-image" rule because the terms of the acceptance must be the mirror-image of the terms of the offer. Prior to the UCC, the parties, each using their respective forms provided by their individual attorneys and drawn with terms to their own individual advantage, would correspond with one another and believe they had formed a contract. However, if a dispute occurred, the parties would find the law saying that they had not formed a contract because the terms on the buyer's offer (order form) and the terms on the seller's acceptance (acknowledgment) did not conform. Since there was no mirror-image acceptance, there was no binding contract. In effect, one party was winning the suit for the wrong reason which, in terms of respect for the law, is as bad as the wrong party winning—which, of course, might also occur since the court was not really reaching the merits of the dispute.

The UCC attempted to deal with this problem which has been called the "battle of the forms." The code attempts to solve the "battle of the forms" controversy through Section 2-207 which allows the formation of the contract even though the writings of the parties do not agree. The seller's acknowledgment form can contain new terms (not the mirror-image) and yet, still form a contract. The policy of 2-207 is to form the contract as the parties intended and then determine the terms of their bargain. Merchants often form their agreements without establishing all the terms to the contract. The Code recognizes this reality and molds the law to fit the practice of merchants. Another section of the Code [2-204(3)] provides that "Even though one or more terms are left open a contract for sale does not fail for indefiniteness if the parties have intended to make a contract and there is a reasonably certain basis for giving an appropriate remedy." The court can normally fashion an appropriate remedy because the Code has what might be called "filler" provisions which normally establish "reasonable" terms whenever the merchants fail to establish their own exact terms. In this way, the contract is found to exist, and the court can get to the merits of the controversy and in more probability determine justice between the parties.

C. ITOH & CO., INC. v. JORDAN INTERNATIONAL
552 F. 2d 1228 (7th Cir., 1977)
United States Court of Appeals

■ ■ ■

The pertinent facts may be briefly restated. Itoh sent its purchase order for steel coils to Jordan which contained no provision for arbitration. Subsequently, Jordan sent Itoh its acknowledgment form which included...a broad arbitration term on the reverse side of the form. On the front of Jordan's form, the following statement also appears:

> Seller's acceptance is...expressly conditioned on Buyer's assent to the additional or different terms and conditions set forth below and printed on the reverse side. If these terms and conditions are not acceptable, Buyer should notify Seller at once.

After the exchange of documents, Jordan delivered and Itoh paid for the steel coils. Itoh never expressly assented or objected to the additional arbitration term in Jordan's form...

The instant case, therefore, involves the classic "battle of the forms," and Section 2—207 furnishes the rules for resolving such a controversy. Hence, it is to Section 2—207 that we must look to determine whether a contract has been formed by the exchange of forms between Jordan and Itoh and, if so, whether the additional arbitration term in Jordan's form is to be included in that contract...

Under Section 2—207 it is necessary to first determine whether a contract has been formed under Section 2—207 (1) as a result of the *exchange of forms* between Jordan and Itoh.

At common law, "an acceptance . . . which contained terms additional to . . . those of the offer . . . constituted a rejection of the offer . . . and thus became a counter-offer." Thus, the mere presence of the additional arbitration term in Jordan's acknowledgement form would, at common law, have prevented the exchange of documents between Jordan and Itoh form creating a contract, and Jordan's form would have automatically become a counter-offer.

Section 2—207 (1) was intended to alter this inflexible common law approach to offer and acceptance:

> This section of the Code recognizes that in current commercial transactions, the terms of the offer and those of the acceptance will seldom be identical. Rather, under the current "battle of the forms," each party typically has a printed form drafted by his attorney and containing as many terms as could be envisioned to favor that party in his sales transactions. Whereas under common law the disparity between the fine-print terms in the parties' forms would have prevented the consummation of a contract when these forms are exchanged, Section 2—207 recognizes that in many, but not all, cases the parties do not impart such significance to the terms on the printed forms. . . . Thus, under Subsection (1), a contract . . . [may be] recognized notwithstanding the fact that an acceptance . . . contains terms additional to . . . those of the offer...

And it is now well-settled that the *mere presence* of an additional term, such as a provision for arbitration, in one of the parties' forms will not prevent the formation of a contract under Section 2—207 (1).

However, while Section 2—207 (1) constitues a sharp departure from the common law "mirror image" rule, there remain situations where the inclusion of an additional term in one of the forms exchanged by the parties will prevent the consummation of a contract *under that section.* Section 2—207 (1) contains a proviso which operates to prevent an exchange of forms from creating a contract where "acceptance is expressly made conditional on assent to the additional. . . terms." In the instant case, Jordan's acknowledgement form contained the following statement:

> Seller's acceptance is . . . *expressly conditional* on Buyer's *assent* to the additional or different terms and conditions set forth below and printed on the reverse side. If these terms and conditions are not acceptable, Buyer should notify Seller at once.

The arbitration provision at issue on this appeal is printed on the reverse side of Jordan's acknowledgment, and there is no dispute that Itoh never expressly assented to the challenged arbitration term.

The Court of Appeals for the Sixth Circuit has held that the proviso must be construed narrowly...

. . .[H]owever, it is clear that the statement contained in Jordan's acknowledgement form comes within the Section 2—207(1) proviso.

Hence, the exchange of forms between Jordan and Itoh did not result in the formation of a contract under Section 2—207(1), and Jordan's form became a counteroffer. "[T]he consequence of a clause conditioning acceptance on assent to the additional or different terms is that *as of the exchanged writings, there is no contract.* Either party may at this point in their dealings walk away from the transaction." However, neither Jordan nor Itoh elected to follow that course; instead, both parties proceeded to performance—Jordan by delivering and Itoh by paying for the steel coils.

At common law, the "terms of the counter-offer were said to have been accepted by the original offeror when he proceeded to perform under the contract without objecting to the counter-offer." Thus, under pre-Code law, Itoh's performance (*i. e.,* payment for the steel coils) probably constituted acceptance of the Jordan counter-offer, including its provision for arbitration. However, a different approach is required under the Code.

Section 2—207(3) of the Code first provides that "[c]onduct by both parties which recognizes the existence of a contract is sufficient to establish a contract for sale although the writings of the parties do not otherwise establish a contract." As the court noted in *Dorton,* at 1166:

> [W]hen no contract is recognized under Subsection 2—207(1) . . . the entire transaction aborts at this point. If, however, the subsequent conduct of the parties—particularly, performance by both parties under what they apparently believe to be a contract—recognizes the existence of a contract, under Subsection 2—207(3) such conduct by both parties is sufficient to establish a contract, not withstanding the fact that no contract would have been recognized on the basis of their writings alone.

Thus, "[s]ince . . . [Itoh's] purchase order and . . . [Jordan's] counter-offer did not in themselves create a contract, Section 2—207(3) would operate to create one because the subsequent performance by both parties constituted 'conduct by both parties which recognizes the existence of a contract.' "

What are the terms of a contract created by conduct under Section 2—207(3) rather than by an exchange of forms under Section 2—207(1)? As noted above, at common law the terms of the contract between Jordan and Itoh would be the terms of the Jordan counter-offer. However, the Code has effectuated a radical departure from the common law rule. The second sentence of Section 2—207(3) provides that where, as here, a contract has been consummated by the conduct of the parties, "the terms of the particular contract consist of those terms on which the writings of the parties agree, together with any supplementary terms incorporated under any other provisions of this Act." Since it is clear that the Jordan and Itoh forms do not "agree" on arbitration, the only question which remains *under the Code* is whether arbitration may be considered a supplementary term incorporated under some other provision of the Code. . .

Since provision for arbitration is not a necessary or missing term which would be supplied by one of the Code's "gap-filler" provisions unless agreed upon by the contracting parties, there is no arbitration term in the Section 2—207(3) contract which was created by the conduct of Jordan and Itoh in proceeding to perform even though no contract had been established by their exchange of writings.

We are convinced that this conclusion does not result in any unfair prejudice to a seller who elects to insert in his standard sales acknowledgement form the statement that acceptance is expressly conditional on buyer's assent to additional terms contained therein. Such a seller obtains a substantial benefit *under Section 2—207(1)* through the inclusion of an "expressly conditional" clause. If he decides after the exchange of forms that the particular transaction is not in his best interest, Subsection (1) permits him to walk away from the transaction without incurring any liability so long as the buyer has not in the interim expressly assented to the additional terms. Moreover, whether or not a seller will be disadvantaged *under Subsection (3)* as a consequence of inserting an "expressly conditional" clause in his standard form is within his control. If the seller in fact does not intend to close a particular deal unless the additional terms are assented to, he can protect himself by not delivering the goods until such assent is forthcoming. If the seller does intend to close a deal irrespective of whether or not the buyer assents to the additonal terms, he can hardly complain when the contract formed under Subsection (3) as a result of the parties' conduct is held not to include those terms. Although a seller who employs such an "expressly conditional" clause in his acknowledgement form would undoubtedly appreciate the dual advantage of not being bound to a contract under Subsection (1) if he elects not to perform and of having his additional terms imposed on the buyer under Subsection (3) in the event that performance is in his best interest, we do not believe such a result is contemplated by Section 2—207. Rather, while a seller may take advantage of an "expressly conditional" clause under Subsection (1) when he elects not to perform, he must accept the potential risk under Subsection (3) of not getting his additional terms when he elects to proceed with performance without first obtaining buyer's assent to those terms. Since the seller injected ambiguity into the transaction by inserting the "expressly conditional" clause in his form, he, and not the buyer, should bear the consequence of that ambiguity under Subsection (3).

■ ■ ■

Questions

1. What is meant by the "battle of the forms"? What is the "mirror image" rule?
2. Under 2—207(1), how does one differentiate between an acceptance and a counter offer?
3. Did the parties form a contract by their writings?
4. Under the common law, Itoh's performance (that is, payment for the steel coils) probably constituted acceptance of the Jordan counter offer, including its provision for arbitration. How does Section 2—207(3) of the Code change this result?

STATUTE OF FRAUDS

Certain types of contracts, although they fulfill the requirements of a valid contract, are not enforceful unless they are reduced to writing. The written contract has been a requisite for legal enforceability for certain types of agreements since the passage by the English Parliament in 1677 of the Statute of Frauds. Its theory involved the requirement that contracts be in writing to prevent the perpetration of frauds. Consequently, even if the plaintiff can prove with reasonable certainty the terms of the oral contract, the court will not enforce the contract when the defendant claims the protection of the statute. In essence, when a contract is the type that is required to be written by the statute, oral evidence is not allowed. The success of the Statute of Frauds in prevention of frauds has been minimal, but its viability as law has endured.

The Statute of Frauds applies only to the enforcement of executory contracts. If both parties have fully performed their obligations under an agreement, the courts treat the bargain as binding and allow it to stand. Although the law may vary somewhat from state to state, the more important kinds of agreements generally required by the statute to be put in writing are as follows:

1. Contracts to guarantee the debts or obligations of another,
2. Contracts that can not be completed within one year from the date in which the agreement is made,
3. Contracts for the transfer of an interest in real property, and
4. Contracts for the sale of tangible personal property valued at $500 or more.

The courts have not always been hospitable to the Statute of Frauds. Consequently, many judicial exceptions to the statute have been created. For example, A's promise to work for B for ten years must be in writing to be enforceable because it is not capable of being performed in less than a year. However, if A's promise is to work for his entire life for B, the courts do not require a writing because such promise is capable of being completely performed in less than a year.

When a written contract is required, the writing, or connected writings, must contain all the essential terms of the contract. The written memoranda should contain the following information:

1. Essential terms of the contract,
2. Names and identities of the parties to the contract, and
3. Signature of the party to be charged.

The written evidence of an agreement is enforceable only against the party or parties who have signed it. The party's signature denies him the right to assert the protection of the statute. However, Article 2 of the UCC has made an important change in this theory concerning signatures as the following case illustrates.

COOK GRAINS, INC. v. FALLIS
395 S.W. 2d 555 (1965)
Supreme Court of Arkansas

■ ■ ■

Plaintiff, Cook Grains, Inc., filed this suit alleging that it entered into a valid contract with defendant, Paul Fallis, whereby Fallis sold and agreed to deliver to

Cook 5,000 bushels of soybeans at $2.54 per bushel. It is alleged that Fallis breached the alleged contract by failing to deliver the beans, and that as a result thereof Cook has been damaged in the sum of $1,287.50. There was a judgement for Fallis. The grain company has appealed.

Plaintiff introduced evidence to the effect that its agent, Lester Horton, entered into a verbal agreement with defendant whereby defendant sold and agreed to deliver to plaintiff grain company 5,000 bushels of beans; that delivery was to be made in September, October, and November, 1963. Fallis denied entering into such a contract. He contends that although a sale was discussed, no agreement was reached. He also contends that (the written confirmation of the oral understanding sent by Cook Grains to Fallis as) the alleged contract is barred (from court enforcement) by the statute of frauds.

The plaintiff grain company concedes that ordinarily the alleged cause of action would be barred by the statute of frauds, but contends that here the alleged sale is taken out of the statute of frauds by the Uniform Commercial Code. It is as follows:

§ 2-201 "Formal requirements—Statute of frauds.—(1) Except as otherwise provided in this section a contract for the sale of goods for the price of $500 or more is not enforceable by way of action or defense unless there is some writing sufficient to indicate that a contract for sale has been made between the parties and signed by the party against whom enforcement is sought or by his authorized agent or broker.

"(2) Between merchants if within a reasonable time a writing in confirmation of the contract and sufficient against the sender is received and the party receiving it has reason to know its contents, it satisfies the requirements of subsection (1) against such party unless written notice of objection to its contents is given within ten (10) days after it is received.* * * "

Thus, it will be seen that under the statute, if defendant is a merchant he would be liable on the alleged contract because he did not, within ten days, give written notice that he rejected it.

The solution of the case turns on the point of whether the defendant Fallis is a "merchant" within the meaning of the statute. § 852104 provides:

" 'Merchant' means a person who deals in goods of the kind or otherwise by his occupation holds himself out as having knowledge or skill peculiar to the practices or goods involved in the transaction or to whom such knowledge or skill may be attributed by his employment of an agent or broker or other intermediary who by his occupation holds himself out as having such knowledge or skill. * * * "

There is not a scintilla of evidence in the record, or proffered as evidence, that defendant is a dealer in goods of the kind or by his occupation holds himself out as having knowledge or skill peculiar to the practices of dealers in goods involved in the transaction, and no such knowledge or skill can be attributed to him.

The evidence in this case is that defendant is a farmer and nothing else. He farms about 550 acres and there is no showing that he has any other occupation. Our attention has been called to no case, and we have found none holding that the word farmer may be construed to mean merchant.

...There is nothing whatever in the statute indicating that the word "merchant" should apply to a farmer when he is acting in the capacity of a farmer, and he comes within that category when he is merely trying to sell the commodities he has raised.

Notes 1 and 2 under § 2—104 (Uniform Commercial Code) defining merchant indicate that this provision of the statute is meant to apply to professional traders. In Note 1 it is stated: "This section lays the foundation of this policy defining those who are to be regarded as professionals or 'merchants,' * * *" It is said in Note 2: "The term 'merchant' as defined here roots in the 'law merchant' concept of a professional in business. * * *"

In construing a statute its words must be given their plain and ordinary meaning.

■ ■ ■

Questions

1. What is the "written confirmation" exception to the Statute of Frauds?
2. Why was the "written confirmation" exception not applied to *Fallis?*

Notes

1. Compare *Cook Grains* with this language in *Ohio Grain Co. v. Swisshelm* 40 Ohio App. 2d 203 (1973).

> A buyer who agrees to purchase farm products at a stated price in cash may send to the seller a timely written confirmation specifying the terms, and the quality and standards required, and may hold a seller who has the knowledge or skill of merchants, to the terms and conditions specified, unless the seller gives timely notice of his objection.
>
> An experienced farmer, who previously sold soybeans, keeps abreast of the soybean market, and sells livestock and other farm products from time to time, is "chargeable with the knowledge or skill of merchants... in selling his current crop of soybeans."

2. The signature of each party to the agreement should be the one he ordinarily uses in business transactions, although the law does not make this requirement. It may be printed. It may be an initial, a mark, or any other symbol, as long as the party intends to authenticate the document. The signature need not appear at the end of the memorandum, but it must appear somewhere.

UNCONSCIONABLE

In additional to the traditional limition on contractual freedom imposed by the concept of illegality, the law is evolving toward the requirement that contracts be fair and be formed in good faith. The law is becoming increasingly concerned with the use of superior bargaining power to obtain favorable terms from those that are unable to protect themselves.

In the case of sales under Article 2 of the UCC, the seller must act in good faith, which for a merchant-seller is defined as "honesty in fact and the observance of reasonable commercial standards of fair dealing in the trade." UCC Section 2—103 (1) (b). Other statutes, such as the Federal Automotive Dealer's Day in Court Act likewise are imposing duties of good faith bargaining. Such terms in the law empower the judges with greater latitude of interpretation to achieve "social justice." A more obvious example of expanding judicial power to modify contracts is the power afforded to the court to modify contractual terms if they are too harsh or oppresive to one of the two parties. Traditionally, the courts have refused to enforce a "too harsh" liquidated damage clause and in a more modern context, the UCC provides that:

> If the court... finds the contract or any clause of the contract to have been unconscionable at the time it was made, the court may refuse to enforce the contract, or it may enforce the remainder of the contract without the unconscionable clause, or it may so limit the application of any unconscionable clause as to avoid any unconscionable result. UCC Section 2—302 (1).

To exercise the unconscionability provision, the court need not receive proof of fraud. Whenever there is grossly disproportinate bargaining power between the parties, so that the weaker party "just signs on the dotted line," the court can modify the grossly unfair terms to avoid results which are contrary to public policy.

CAMPBELL SOUP CO. v. WENTZ
172 F.2d 80 (1948)
U.S. Court of Appeals (3rd. Cir.)

■ ■ ■

On June 21, 1947, Campbell Soup Company (Campbell), a New Jersey corporation, entered into a written contract with George B. Wentz and Harry T. Wentz, who are Pennsylvania farmers, for delivery by the Wentzes to Campbell of all the Chantenay red cored carrots to be grown on fifteen acres of the Wentz farm during the 1947 season. The contract provides. . . for delivery of the carrots at the Campbell plant in Camden, New Jersey. The prices specified in the contract ranged from $23 to $30 a ton.

The Wentzes harvested approximately 100 tons of carrots from the fifteen acres covered by the contract. Early in January, 1948, they told a Campbell representative that they would not deliver their carrots at the contract price. The market price at the time was at least $90 per ton, and the Chantenay red cored carrots were virtually unobtainable. . .

On January 9, 1948, Campbell (sued). . . the Wentz brothers. . . to compel specific performance of the contract.

We think that on the question of adequacy of the legal remedy the case is one appropriate for specific performance. It was expressly found that at the time of the trial it was "virtually impossible to obtain Chantenay carrots in the open market."

. . . We see no reason why a court should be reluctant to grant specific relief when it can be given without supervision of the court or other time-consuming processes against one who has deliberately broken his agreement. Here the goods of the special type contracted for were unavailable on the open market, the plaintiff had contracted for them long ahead in anticipation of its needs, and had built up a general reputation for its products as part of which reputation uniform appearance was important. We think if this were all that was involved in the case specific performance should have been granted.

The reason that we shall affirm instead of reversing with an order for specific performance is found in the contract itself. We think it is too hard a bargain and too one-sided an agreement to entitle the plaintiff to relief in a court of conscience. For each individual grower the agreement is made by filling in names and quantity and price on a printed form furnished by the buyer. This form has quite obviously been drawn by skillful draftsmen with the buyer's interests in mind.

Paragraph 2 provides for the manner of delivery. Carrots are to have their stalks cut off and be in clean sanitary bags or other containers approved by Campbell. This paragraph concludes with a statement that Campbell's determination of conformance with specifications shall be conclusive.

The defendants attack this provision as unconscionable. We do not think that it is, standing by itself. We think that the provision is comparable to the promise to perform to the satisfaction of another and that Campbell would be held liable if it refused carrots which did not conform to the specifications.

The next paragraph allows Campbell to refuse carrots in excess of twelve tons to the acre. The next contains a covenant by the grower that he will not sell carrots to anyone else except the carrots rejected by Campbell nor will he permit anyone else to grow carrots on his land. Paragraph 10 provides liquidation damages to the extent of $50 per acre for any breach by the grower. There is no provision for liquidated or any other damages for breach of contract by Campbell.

The provision of the contract which we think is the hardest is paragraph 9. . . . It will be noted that Campbell is excused from accepting carrots under certain circumstances. But even under such circumstances the grower, while he cannot say Campbell is liable for failure to take the carrots, is not permitted to sell them elsewhere unless Campbell agrees. This is the kind of provision which the late Francis H. Bohlen would call "carrying a good joke too far." What the grower may do with his product under the circumstances set out is not clear. He has covenanted not to store it anywhere except on his own farm and also not to sell to anybody else.

We are not suggesting that the contract is illegal. Nor are we suggesting any excuse for the grower in this case who has deliberately broken an agreement entered into with Campbell. We do think, however, that a party who has offered and succeeded in getting an agreement as tough as this one is, should not come to a chancellor and ask court help in the enforcement of is terms. That equity does not enforce unconscionable bargains is too well established to require elaborate citation.

. . . As already said, we do not suggest that this contract is illegal. All we say is that the sum total of its provisions drives too hard a bargain for a court of conscience to assist.

■ ■ ■

Questions

1. Why did the court think "damages" was an inadequate remedy and that specific perfomrmance was appropriate in this instance?
2. The court identified several provisions of the contract which it considered carefully drawn to protect the buyer's interest. Which of those provisions did the court find particularly "hardest" on the seller?
3. Did the court find the contract to be illegal? Did the court find any of the provisions in the contract unconscionable? Just what did the court rule?

SHELL OIL CO. v. MARINELLO.
307 A 2d 598 (1973)
Supreme Court of New Jersey

■ ■ ■

This case involves the interpretation of a lease and a dealer agreement entered into between Shell Oil Company (Shell) and Frank Marinello (Marinello), one of its service station operators, and a determination of the extent of Shell's right to terminate such lease and agreement. . .

In 1959 (Shell) leased the station to Marinello, and at the same time entered into a written dealer agreement with the lessee. The original lease was for a one-year term and was regularly renewed in writing for fixed terms. The last lease between Shell and Marinello is dated April 28, 1969 and runs for a three-year term ending May 31, 1972, and from year-to-year thereafter, but is subject to termination by Marinello at any time by giving at least 90 days notice and by Shell at the end of the primary period or of any such subsequent year by giving at least 30 days notice. . .

. . . The last dealer agreement is also dated April 28, 1969, and is for a three-year term ending May 31, 1972 and from year-to-year thereafter, but is subject to termination at any time by giving at least 10 days notice.

By letter dated April 14, 1972, Shell notified Marinello that it was terminating the aforesaid lease and the dealer agreement effective May 31, 1972. Marinello immediately filed suit in the Superior Court, Chancery Division, seeking to have Shell enjoined from taking its proposed action, and asking for reformation of the "agreement" between the parties. . .

These instruments, and the business relationship created thereby, cannot be viewed in the abstract. Shell is a major oil company. It not only controls the supply, but, in this case, the business site. The record shows that while the product itself and the location are prime factors in the profitability of a service station, the personality and efforts of the operator and the good will and clientele generated thereby are of major importance. The amount of fuel, lubricants and TBA (files, batteries and accessories) a station will sell is directly related to courtesy, service, cleanliness and hours of operation, all dependent on the particular operator.

Marinello testified that when the station was offered to him in 1959 he was told by Shell representative that the station was run down, but that a good operator could make money and that if he built up the business his future would be in the station. . .

Viewing the combined lease and franchise against the foregoing background, it becomes apparent that Shell is the dominant party and that the relationship lacks equality in the respective bargaining positions of the parties. For all practical purposes Shell can dictate its own terms. The dealer, particularly if he has been operating the station for a period of years and built up its business clientele, when the time for renewal of the lease and dealer agreement comes around, cannot afford to risk confrontation with the oil company. He just signs on the dotted line.

Where there is grossly disproportionate bargaining power, the principle of freedom to contract is non-existent and unilateral terms result. In such a situation courts will not hesitate to declare void as against public policy grossly unfair contractual provisions which clearly tend to the injury of the public in some way.

Applying the foregoing to the case before us, it is clear that the provisions of the lease and dealer agreement giving Shell the right to terminate its business relationship with Marinello, almost at will, are the result of Shell's disproportionate bargaining position and are grossly unfair. That the public is affected in a direct way is beyond question. We live in a motor vehicle age. Supply and distribution of motor vehicle fuels are vital to our economy. In fact, the Legislature has specifically concluded that the distribution and sale of motor fuels within this State is affected with a public interest.

It is a fallacy to state that the right of termination is bilateral. The oil company can always get another person to operate the station. It is the incumbent dealer who has everything to lose since, even if he had another location to go to, the going business and trade he built up would remain with the old station.

The relationship between Shell and Marinello is basically that of franchise. The lease is an integral part of that same relationship. Our Legislature in enacting the Franchise Practices Act, has declared that distribution and sales through franchise arrangements in New Jersey vitally affect the general economy of the State, the public interest and the public welfare. The Act prohibits a franchisor from terminating, cancelling or failing renew a franchise without good cause which is defined as the failure by the franchisee to substantially comply with the requirements imposed on him by the franchise.

The Act does not directly control the franchise relationship herein since Marinello's last renewal antedates the effective date of the statute. However, the Act reflects the legislative concern over long-standing abuses in the franchise relationship, particularly provisions giving the franchisor the right to terminate, cancel or fail to renew the franchise. To that extent the provisions of the Act merely put into statutory form the extant public policy of this State. . .

We hold that the provision giving Shell the absolute right to terminate on 10 days notices is void as against the public policy of this State, and that said public policy requires that there be read into the existing lease and dealer agreement, and all future lease and dealer agreements which may be negotiated in good faith between the parties, the restriction that Shell not have the unilateral right to terminate, cancel or fail to renew the franchise, including the lease, in absence of a showing that Marinello has failed to substantially perform his obligations under the lease and dealer agreement, *i. e.,* for good cause. . .

■ ■ ■

Questions

1. What particular provision of the contract is declared void as against public policy?
2. What reasons are advanced by the court for finding a portion of the contract against public policy?
3. Does New Jersey's Franchise Practices Act interefere with the liberty of contract? What reasoning of the legislature prompted passage of the Act?

PRODUCT LIABILITY

Product liability refers to those cases involving the liability of the seller, manufacturer, processor, or supplier for injuries caused to the person or property of the buyer or user because of a defect in the product sold. This area of the law has had rapid change with pronounced effects upon sellers of products. The reslut has been to substantially increase the liability of the seller, manufacturer, processor, and supplier of goods and to increase the classes of injured parties who may seek recovery in such cases.

Initially, products liability was restricted in application to the sale of foodstuffs for human consumption. It has since been expanded to include almost any product that causes injuries with the person or property of the buyer. This liability of the seller has been predicated on either negligence, breach of implied warranty, or strict liability.

Negligence — Some jurisdictions adhere to the use of negligence as the theory of recovery in products liability cases. This theory requires that the plaintiff trace the defective condition of the product to a fault (negligence) in manufacturing. A manufacturer must exercise due care to make his product safe for the purpose for which it is intended. This requires the exercise of care in the design of the product, in the selection of materials, in selection of component parts, in the inspection and testing, and in giving adequate warnings of any dangers in the use of the product which an ordinary person might not be able to detect. The Restatement of the Law of Torts, Second, Section 395 provides:

A manufacturer who fails to exercise reasonable care in the manufacture of a chattel, which, unless carefully made, he should recognize as involving an unreasonable risk of causing substantial bodily harm to those who lawfully use it for a purpose for which it is manufactured and those whom the supplier should expect to be in the vicinity of its probable use, is subject to liability for bodily harm caused to them by its lawful use in a manner and for a purpose for which it is manufactured.

The liability for negligence of a seller other than the manufacturer (retailers and wholesalers) is set forth in Section 401. It provides:

A seller of a chattel manufactured by a third person who knows or has reason to know that the chattel is, or is likely to be, dangerous when used by a person to whom it is delivered or for whose use it is supplied, or to others whom the seller should expect to share in or be endangered by its use, is subject to liability for bodily harm caused thereby to them if he fails to exercise reasonable care to inform them of the danger or otherwise to protect them against it.

This liability is imposed upon the seller (retailer or wholesaler) based upon his "reason to know" the dangerous character of the product. The retailers' duty is to exercise reasonable care to inform the purchaser or user of this danger in order to protect the consumer from it. Section 402 excuses from liability the seller of goods manufactured by a third person if the seller does not know or have reason to know of the dangerous character of the goods. Moreover, Section 402 indicates that the retailer or wholesaler will not be liable for failure to inspect or test the goods before selling them. This Section, therefore, protects the retailer who sells goods that are prepackaged or placed in sealed containers by a manufacturer. The seller-retailer would not be liable for negligence based upon the theory of failure to inspect. However, in those states utilizing an alternate theory of liability, the retailer may be liable even if he is not negligent.

NEGLIENT DESIGN

LARUE v. NATIONAL U. ELEC. CORP.
571 F.2d 51 (1978)
U.S. Court of Appeals (5th Cir.)

■ ■ ■

Conrad Larue brought this diversity action in January 1973, on behalf of his minor son Michael, for injuries suffered by Michael. The complaint charged National Union Electric Corp. with negligent design and manufacture of a vacuum cleaner. National Union denied all liability and alleged contributory negligence on the part of Michael. After a trial in March, 1977...the jury...(found) for Michael on the negligence count. The jury determined that $125,000 would fully compensate Michael but that his own comparative negligence required reduction of the award to $93,750. National Union and Larue both appeal, the former...attacking the verdict as contrary to law..., and the later arguing the issue of comparative negligence should not have been submitted to the jury.

On January 25, 1971, Michael Larue, then 11 years old, was playing with his parents' canister-type vacuum cleaner, a Eureka Model 842A. He and his sister were home because they had missed the bus for school; his father was at work and his mother in school. The previous evening his mother had taken out the two filters that rested above the fan housing and motor in order to clean them. The morning of the accident the vacuum cleaner was left out in a hallway, plugged in, with the filters not yet replaced and the hood that covered its top half left open...

According to Michael's testimony, he was sitting on the yellow plastic filter support, which in turn rested on the metal casing that covered the fan and engine, riding the vacuum cleaner as if it were a toy car. He was dressed in pajamas. His older sister was in another room watching television. At some point in his play the motor was turned on. Michael continued to ride the vacuum cleaner until his penis slipped through openings in the filter support and casing into the fan. He immediately suffered an amputation of the head of his penis and part of the shaft. He rushed outside to seek help, was taken to the hospital, and underwent the first of a number of complicated operations to repair the damage to his penis...

The principal issue at trial was the adequacy of safety features in the Eureka vacuum cleaner in light of foreseeable risks of injury resulting from household use. The Larues contended National Union had failed to take sufficient precautions both by not installing a shield over the opening in the engine and fan casing to prevent insertion of stray parts of the human body and by not using an "interlock" switch that would prevent the motor from turning on while the hood was up. The strongest evidence in support of these contentions was the testimony of plaintiff's expert, Dr. Paul, a design engineer on the MIT faculty. Dr. Paul...explained that the rotation of the fan at 15,000 rpm left it invisible. Someone fiddling around with the interior of the machine, and especially a child, would have no warning of the danger created by the sharp, quickly moving fan blades. Some amount of exposure to the risk was inherent in the design, as the filters that covered the fan casing periodically had to be removed. Dr. Paul testified that suction created by the fan was sufficient to pull in stray items through the overlarge openings. He asserted that the safety devices that could eliminate this risk—a shield or an interlock switch—were feasible and, at least with regard to the switch, inexpensive.

To demonstrate the reasonableness of installing a protective shield over the fan housing, plaintiff produced a Eureka 4001 vacuum cleaner, manufactured during the same period as the 842A model and marketed overseas. The 4001 was in all material respects identical to the 842A, except that it was wired to take the higher voltages used in Europe and contained a shield over the fan housing such as would have prevented Michael's accident. The shield was required by Swedish safety regulations....

National Union...argues that regardless of the nature of the hazard presented by the vacuum cleaner, this accident resulted from unforeseeable misuse of the product for which the manufacturer cannot be charged with liability. That question was submitted to the jury as part of the issue of negligence. National Union...agrues that as a matter of law this use and the ensuing accident were simply not foreseeable...

In the analogous situation of a storeowner's duty of care to child invitees on the premises, the Supreme Judicial Court of Maine has ruled that the critical factor is "the *resonableness,* or the *unreasonableness,* of the risks of harm engendered by the premises, facilities, instrumentalities, or combinations thereof, in the light of the *totality of the circumstances,* as the ordinarily prudent storekeeper would apprehend the circumstances and foresee the dangers of harm generated by them,—including the reasonably recognizable dangers resulting from the reasonably foreseeable *misuse* of the premises by children in the light of their known, or reasonably recognizable, propensities."

Orr v. First National Stores, Inc., 280 A.2d 785, 792 (Me. 1971) [Emphasis in original.] In determining what kind of reasonable foreseeable misuse might arise from the play of children, the court recognized

"that children as old as thirteen years of age are likely to act dangerously to themselves even though, upon reflection, they know better."

Id. at 790. It also observed:

"It should be emphasized that it is unessential that the *precise* manner in which injuries might have occurred, or were sustained, be foreseeable, or foreseen. It is sufficient that there is a reasonable generalized gamut of greater than ordinary dangers of injury and that the sustaining of injury was within this range..."

Id. at 794.

It was undisputed that National Union realized that the Eureka 842A vacuum cleaner would be used in households where children would be present and appreciated the risks of children playing with the insides of the machine. Based on all the evidence presented at trial, there was a sufficient basis for holding that the vacuum cleaner presented an unreasonable risk of harm to children who might reasonably be foreseen to explore and fiddle with the device. The inadvertent intrusion of Michael's penis into the fan, perhaps the product of the machine's suction, fell within this class of dangers, even though the precise circumstances of the accident might have been improbable. Under the principles expressed in *Orr,* the district court had a sufficient basis for refusing to rule that as a matter of law the injury to Michael was so unforeseeable as to be outside the scope of National Union's duty to consumers of its product.

By the same token, we reject plaintiff's argument that the evidence concerning the hidden danger presented by the vacuum cleaner was so unequivocal as to bar the district court from letting the issue of Michael's own negligence go to the jury. Plaintiff exaggerates the strength of his own case. Evidence was presented suggesting that the vacuum cleaner motor was switched on as long as two minutes before the accident; during that time Michael continued to ride the machine. Perhaps, as plaintiff's expert contended, the fan blades rotated at too great a speed to be visible, but the jury well might have believed that the sould of the motor alone should have been enough to warn Michael that some danger existed. There was evidence that Michael was familiar with the operation of machinery in general and engines in particular. The district court properly submitted the issue of comparative negligence to the jury.

■ ■ ■

Questions

1. Was the use of the machine as a toy car by a child "reasonably foreseeable" by the manufacturer?
2. What is "comparative negligence"? Was it properly applied in *LaRue?*

BREACH OF WARRANTY

A second type of theory of recovery against the seller of a defective product is called breach of warranty. A warranty under the law of sales (UCC Article 2) is an obligation imposed by law upon the seller with respect to the goods. Such warranties can arise from (1) the mere fact of the transaction of sale (a warranty of title) or (2) by affirmations of fact or promise by the seller to the buyer (warranties of quality). The latter warranties are referred to as express warranties, which are explicit undertakings by the seller with respect to quality, description, or performability of the goods. These expressed warranties constitute a portion of the bargain between the parties. Accordingly, if the seller chooses not to give any expressed warranties, he is free to avoid this potential liability by refusing to affirm the quality or nature of his goods. Of course, the buyer is thereby put on notice and perhaps less likely to make the purchase.

In addition, the merchant-seller who deals in goods of a certain kind impliedly warrants the "merchantability" of those goods. This warranty is implied by law into the bargain without any express bargaining on the matter by the parties. To be merchantable, the goods must be of such quality as to pass in the market without objection and to be honestly resalable by the buyer in the normal course of business. The implied warranty of merchantability is an obligation on the merchant-seller that the goods are reasonably fit for the general purpose for which they are manufactured and sold and, also, that they are of fair, average, and merchantable quality. When goods are sold to a consumer, merchantability generally means reasonably fit for consumption.

The second implied warranty is the warranty of "fitness for *particular* purpose" which arises when a seller has reason to know the particular purpose of the buyer and the buyer is relying on the seller's skill and judgment in selecting goods to fit that particular purpose. Fitness for the buyer's particular purpose may be the same as merchantability. A restauranteur impliedly warrants that the meals are fit for the *particular* purpose and *ordinary* purpose for which goods are sold—human consumption.

The implied warranties are imposed on the seller by law, not by the bargaining of the parties. However, the UCC makes clear that the seller may modify or exlude these implied warranties with the buyer's consent. However, the disclaimers must be positive, explicit, unequivocal, and conspicuous, so that the buyer's acknowledgment of the change in implied warranties is clear. In additon, since the Code requires that notice of any breach of warranty be given to the seller in a reasonable time after the defect has occurred, the buyer's failure to notify the seller may result in being barred from any remedy.

Many states require that since the warranty extends with the contract of sale of the goods, the absence of a contractual relationship (privity) with the seller would preclude recovery by a victim that was not the buyer of the goods from the defendant-seller. However, many courts have abolished the requirement of "privity." The Code itself has relaxed the requirement of privity of contract. It permits recovery for breach of warranty that causes injury to members of the family or the household of the buyer or guests to his home even though such persons are without privity of contract.

The contributory negligence of the buyer is no defense to an action for a breach of warranty. However, the buyer's discovery of a defect would preclude his recovery against the seller for injuries caused by the known defect (voluntary assumption of risk).

Warranties are limited to sales of goods. No warranty attaches to the performance of a service. If the service is performed negligently, the cause of action accruing is for that negligence. In contrast, the case of a sale of goods gives rise to a breach of warranty action without proof of fault by the seller. Consequently, victims prefer a breach of warranty action over an action for negligence. Therefore, problems often arise over the determination of whether the transaction was a service or a sale. In one case, it was held that injuries to scalp and hair from the application of a product in a beauty treatment was not a "sale" and, consequently, no breach of warranty action could be maintained. The victim was left with only a negligence action in which she must prove that the beauty operator failed to exercise reasonable care. Contrast this result with the following case.

NEWMARK v. GIMBEL'S INCORPORATED
246 A. 2d 11 (1968)
Supreme Court, Appellate Division of New Jersey

■ ■ ■

Mrs. Newmark sued for injury to her skin and loss of hair following a permanent wave treatment at defendant's beauty parlor...She was waited on by one Valente, a beauty technician, who told her that her fine hair was not right for the special permanent and that she needed a "good" permanent wave. She agreed to this...

Valente admitted that the permanent wave procedure followed was at his suggestion. It is conceded that the permanent wave solution he used was "Candle Glow," a product of Helene Curtis. Valente testified that the processing products he used were applied as they were taken from the original packages or containers, and that it was common for a customer to feel a burning or tingling sensation when the waving lotion was applied. He stated that persons were affected "in varying degrees" by the treatment. When he began the treatment there was "nothing wrong" with her hair or scalp...

The core question here presented is whether warranty principles permit a recovery against a beauty parlor operator for injuries sustained by a customer as a result of use on the customer of a product which was selected and furnished by the beauty parlor operator...

...In ruling that warranty did not apply here the trial judge reasoned that the transaction between the parties amounted to the rendition of services rather than the sale of a product, hence defendant could be held liable only for negligence in the performance of such services. Our consideration of the question convinces us that his ruling was a mistaken one.

It would appear clear that the instances in which implied warranties may be imposed are not limited to "sales" that come strictly within the meaning of Article 2 of the Uniform Commercial Code...

In *Cintrone v. Hertz Truck Leasing,* 45 N.J. 434, 446 (1965), the court said:

> "There is no good reason for restricting such warranties to sales. Warranties of fitness are regarded by law as an incident of a transaction because one party to the relationship is in a better position than the other to know and control the condition of the chattel transferred and to distribute the losses which may occur because of a dangerous condition the chattel possesses. These factors make it likely that the party acquiring possession of the article will assume it is in a safe condition for use and therefore refrain from taking precautionary measures himself...

The policy reasons applicable in the case of sales would likewise justify the extension of liability for breach of warranty to any commercial transaction where one person supplies a product to another, whether or not the transaction be technically considered as a sale...The rational underlying the liability of a retailer for defects in a product obtained from a reputable supplier and sold to a customer, has been explained as follows:

> ...If reliance upon the seller is needed, it may be found in the customer's reliance on the retailer's skill and judgment in selecting his sources of supply. broader considerations are also urged. The retailer should bear this as one of the risks of his enterprise. He profits from the transaction and is in a fairly strategic position to promote safety through pressure on his supplier. Also, he is known to his customers and subject to their suits, while the maker is often unknown and may well be beyond the process of any court convenient to the customer. Moreover, the retailer is in a good position to pass the loss back to his supplier, either through negotiations or through legal proceedings."2 Harper and James, *Torts,* §28.30, p. 1600 (1956).

Weighing the foregoing policy considerations, we are satisfied and hold that, stripped of its nonessentials the transaction here in question, consisting of the supplying of a product for use in the administration of a permanent wave to plaintiff, carried with it an implied warranty that the product used was reasonably fit for the purpose for which it was to be used.

Mrs. Newmark was a regular customer of defendant and had a weekly appointment to have her hair washed and set. On the day in question she received something in addition—a permanent wave. In essence, it involved application of a permanent wave lotion or solution and thereafter a neutralizer. The lotion was selected by one of defendant's operators who was familiar with her scalp and hair from current examination and prior visits. The product was secured from sources known to defendant and only defendant knew of any special instructions concerning its use. The risk from use of the lotion was incident to the operation of defendant's business, a business which yielded it a profit and placed it in a position to promote safety through pressure on suppliers. It was in a position to protect itself by making inquiry or tests to determine the susceptibility of customers to the use of the product, or by using another lotion which did not present the possibility of an adverse effect. It could secure indemnity from its suppliers through legal proceedings or otherwise. The fact that there was no separate charge for the product did not preclude its being considered as having been supplied to the customer in a sense justifying the imposition of an implied warranty against injurious defects therein. . .

While the statement of facts presently before us leaves something to be desired, we are satisfied that the jury could have found from the evidence that the product was defective within the intent of the statute. In the first place the record does not show that plaintiff's dermatitis was the result of an allergic attack peculiar to her own sensitivities. Neither medical witness so testified. Second, the product was accompanied by an instruction in the form of a warning from which it could be inferred that its use, in the absence of certain precautions, could adversely affect an appreciable number of persons. Some support for such an inference is found in Valente's testimony that a burning or tingling sensation is fairly common (in such cases) and that each person was affected "in varying degrees." It is conceded that plaintiff testified that she had received permanent wave treatments prior to and for two years subsequent to the incident in question with no adverse effects to her hair or scalp.

It follows that the issue of defendant's liability for breach of implied warranties of fitness for purpose and merchantability should have been submitted to the jury.

■ ■ ■

Questions

1. Why did the trial judge decide there was no cause of action for breach of warranty?

2. What "policy reasons" justify the "extension of liability for breach of warranty to any commercial transaction where one person supplies a product to another, whether or not the transaction be technically considered as a sale. . ."?

3. Forty-four states have enacted statutes which expressly provide that a blood transfusion is a service and not a sale, or alternatively state that the hospital is not liable in blood transfusions except for negligence or willful misconduct. Such statutes protect the hospital in the sale of blood which may contain a hepatitis virus because such viruses cannot be detected and excluded from blood components. Is this reason sufficient to override the policy reasons for imposing liability for defective goods in a "sale"?

FIT FOR HUMAN CONSUMPTION?

HUNT v. FERGUSON-PAULUS ENTERPRISES
415 P. 2d 13 (1966)
Supreme Court of Oregon

The plaintiff bought a cherry pie from the defendant through a vending machine owned and maintained by the defendant. On biting into the pie one of plaintiff's teeth was broken when it encountered a cherry pit. He brought this action to recover damages for the injury, alleging breach of warranty of fitness of the pie for human consumption. In a trial to the court without a jury the court found for the defendant and plaintiff has appealed.

Under... (the law) if the cherry pie purchased by the plaintiff from the defendant was not reasonably fit for human consumption because of the presence of the cherry pit there was a breach of warranty and plaintiff was entitled to recover his damages thereby caused.

In the consideration of similar cases some of the courts have drawn a distinction between injury caused by spoiled, impure, or contaminated food or food containing a foreign substance, and injury caused by a substance natural to the product sold. In the latter class of cases, these courts hold there is no liability on the part of the dispenser of the food. Thus in the leading case of *Mix v. Ingersoll Candy Co.*, 59 P. 2d 144, the court held that a patron of a restaurant who ordered and paid for chicken pie, which contained a sharp sliver or fragment of chicken bond, and was injured as a result of swallowing the bone, had no cause of action against the restauranteur either for breach of warranty or negligence. Referring to cases in which recovery had been allowed the court said:

"All of the cases are instances in which the food was found not to be reasonably fit for human consumption, either by reason of the presence of a foreign substance, or an impure and noxious condition of the food itself, such as for example glass, stones, wires, or nails in the food served, or tainted, decayed, diseased, or infected meats of vegetables."

The court when on to say that:

"* * * despite the fact that a chicken bone may occasionally be encountered in a chicken pie, such chicken pie, in the absence of some further defect, is reasonably fit for human consumption. Bones which are natural to the type of meat served cannot legitimately be called a foreign substance, and a consumer who eats meat dishes ought to anticipate and be on his guard against the presence of such bones."

Further the court said:

"Certainly no liability would attach to a restaurant keeper for the serving of a T-bone steak, or a beef stew which contained a bone natural to the type of meat served, or if a fish dish should contain a fish bone, or if a cherry pie should contain a cherry stone—although it be admitted that an ideal cherry pie would be stoneless." 59 P.2d at 148.

The so-called "foreign-natural" test of the *Mix* case has been applied in the following cases: *Silva v. F. W. Woolworth Co.*, 83 P. 2d 76 (turkey bone in "special plate" of roast turkey); *Musso v. Picadilly Cafeterias*, 178 So. 2d 421 (cherry pit in a cherry pie); *Courter v. Dilbert Bros.*, 186 N.Y.S. 2d 334 (prune pit in prune butter); *Adams v. Great Atlantic & Pacific Tea Co.*, 112 S.E. 2d 92 (crystalized grain of corn in cornflakes); *Webster v. Blue Ship Tea Room Inc.*, 198 N.E. 2d 309 (fish bone in a fish chowder).

Other courts have rejected the so-called foreign-natural test in favor of what is known as the "reasonable expectation" test, among them the Supreme Court of Wisconsin, which, in *Betehia v. Cape Cod Corp.*, 103 N.W. 2d 64, held that a person who was injured by a chicken bone in a chicken sandwich served to him in a restaurant, could recover for his injury either for breach of an implied warranty or for negligence. "There is a distinction," the court said, "between what a consumer expects to find in a fish stick and in a baked or fried fish, or in a chicken sandwich made from sliced white meat and in roast chicken. The test should be what is reasonably expected by the consumer in the food as served, not what might be natural to the ingredients of that food prior to preparation. What is to be reasonably expected by the consumer is a jury question in most cases; at least, we cannot say as a matter of law that a patron of a restaurant must expect a bone in a chicken sandwich either because chicken bones are occasionally found there or are natural to chicken."

Among other decisions adopting the resonable expectation test are: *Bonenberger v. Pittsburgh Mercantile Co.*, 28 A. 2d 913, (oyster shell in canned oysters used in making oyster stew); *Bryer v. Rath Packing Co.*, 156 A. 2d 442, (chicken bone in chow mein); *Varone v. Calaro*, 199 N.Y.S. 2d 755 (struvite in canned tuna).

In view of the judgment for the defendant, we are not required in this case to make a choice between the two rules. Under the foreign-natural test the plaintiff would be barred from recovery as a matter of law. The reasonable expectation test calles for determination of a question of fact...

The court has found the fact in favor of the defendant and this court has no power to disturb the finding...

Questions

1. What is the foreign-natural test? How would it be applied in this instance to determine if a breach of the warranty of merchanability occurred?
2. What is the "reasonable expectation" test? According to this test, was there a breach of the warranty of merchantability?

STRICT LIABILITY

The most recent and far reaching development in the field of products liability is that of strict liability in tort. The theory of strict liability, for those states which are adopting this approach, is best expressed in Section 402A of the Restatement of Torts, Second, which provides:

(1) One who sells any product in a defective condition unreasonably dangerous to the user or consumer or to his property is subject to liability for physical harm thereby caused to the ultimate user or consumer, or to his property, if

(a) the seller is engaged in the business of selling such a product (no distinction between a manufacturer or retailer), and
(b) it is expected to and does reach the user or consumer without substantial change in the condition in which it is sold.

(2) The rule stated in Subsection (1) applies although

(a) the seller has exercised all possible care in the preparation and sale of his product, and
(b) the user or consumer has not bought the product from or entered into any contractual relation with the seller.

It is to be emphasized that the above (2) (a) makes clear that negligence is not the basis of this liability. The seller may still be liable in spite of the fact that he "has exercised all possible care in the preparation of the sale of his product." The elements of this action were summarized by the Supreme Court of Wisconsin in *Dippel v. Sciano*, 155 N.W. 2d 55 (1967), as follows:

From a reading of the plain language of the rule, the plaintiff must prove (1) that the product was in defective condition when it left the possession or control of the seller, (2) that it was unreasonably dangerous to the user or consumer, (3) that the defect was a cause (a substantial factor) of the plaintiff's injuries or damages, (4) that the seller engaged in the business of selling such product or, put negatively, that this is not an isolated or infrequent transaction not related to the principal business of the seller, and (5) that the product was one which the seller expected to and did reach the user or consumer without substantial change in the condition it was when he sold it.

This liability is imposed by law as a matter of public policy. It arises out of common law in tort and does not require any contract and, therefore, it is not subject to any disclaimer or modification by contractual agreement. The expanding scope of this liability is being developed by the courts in various states.

At common law, contributory negligence of the plaintiff is a bar to his recovery on any action based on negligence of the defendant. However, under strict liability (or negligence) in a products liability case, the plaintiff's failure to discover the defect or to guard against the probability of its existence (contributory negligence) is no defense for the seller of a defective product. Nevertheless, the maker or seller of a product is entitled to assume that the product he sells will be put to its normal use. The plaintiff's use of the product in some unintended, unusual, or unforseeable manner will prevent recovery from the defendant on the ground of assumption of risk. Moreover, the plaintiff who used a product with a known defect would be precluded from recovery of injury resulting from the defect.

EMBS v. PEPSI-COLA BOTTLING CO.
OF LEXINGTON, KENTUCKY, INC.
528 S.W. 2d 703 (1975)
Court of Appeals of Kentucky

■ ■ ■

On the afternoon of July 25, 1970 plaintiff entered the self-service retail store operated by the defendant, Stamper's Cash Market, Inc., for the purpose of "buying soft drinks for the kids." She went to an upright soft drink cooler, removed five bottles and placed them in a carton. Unnoticed by her, a carton of Seven-up was sitting on the floor at the edge of the produce counter about one foot from where she was standing. As she turned away from the cooler she heard an explosion that sounded "like a shotgun." When she looked down she saw a gash in her leg, pop on her leg, green pieces of bottle on the floor and the Seven-Up carton in the midst of the debris. She did not kick or otherwise come into contact with the carton of Seven-Up prior to the explosion. Her son, who was with her, recognized the green pieces of glass as part of a Seven-Up bottle.

She was immediately taken to the hospital by Mrs. Stamper, a managing agent of the store. Mrs. Stamper told her that a Seven-Up bottle had exploded and that several bottles had exploded that week. Apparently, all of the physical evidence went out with the trash. The location of the Seven-Up carton immediately before the explosion was not a place where such items were ordinarily kept.

The defendant, Arnold Lee Vice, was the distributor of Seven-Up in the Clark County area...

The defendant, Pepsi-Cola Bottling Co. of Lexington, Kentucky, Inc., was the bottler who produced and supplied Vice with his entire stock of Seven-Up...

In *Dealers Transport Co. v. Battery Distributing Co.*, 402 S.W. 2d 441 (1966) we adopted the view of strict liability in tort expressed in Section 402A of the American Law Institute's Restatement, Second, Torts...

Our expressed public policy will be furthered if we minimize the risk of injury and property damage by charging the costs of injuries against the manufacturer who can procure liability insurance and distribute its expense among the public as a cost of doing business; and since the risk of harm from defective products exists for mere bystanders and passersby as well as for the purchaser or user, there is no substantial reason for protecting one class of persons and not the other. The same policy requires us to maximize protection for the injured third party and promote the public interest in discouraging the marketing of products having defects that are a menace to the public by imposing strict liability upon retailers and wholesalers in the distributive chain responsible for marketing the defective product which injures the bystander. The imposition of strict liability places no unreasonable burden upon sellers because they can adjust the cost of insurance protection among themselves in the course of their continuing business relationship.

We must not shirk from extending the rule to the manufacturer for fear that the retailer or middleman will be impaled on the sword of liability without regard to fault. Their liability was already established under Section 402A of the Restatement of Torts 2d. As a matter of public policy the retailer or middleman as well as the manufacturer should be liable since the loss for injuries resulting from defective products should be placed on those members of the marketing chain best able to pay the loss, who can then distribute such risk among themselves by means of insurance and indemnity agreements. . .

The result which we reach does not give the bystander a "free ride." When products and consumers are considered in the aggregate, bystanders, as a class, purchase most of the same products to which they are exposed as bystanders. Thus, as a class, they indirectly subsidize the liability of the manufacturer, middleman and retailer and in this sense do pay for the insurance policy tied to the product.

Public policy is adequately served if parameters are placed upon the extension of the rule so that it is limited to bystanders whose injury from the defect is reasonably foreseeable.

For the sake of clarity we restate the extension of the rule. The protections of Section 402A of the Restatement, Second, Torts extend to bystanders whose injury from the defective product is reasonably foreseeable. . .

It matters not that the evidence be circumstantial for as Thoreau put it "Some circumstantial evidence is very strong, as when you find a trout in the milk." There are some accidents, as where a beverage bottle explodes in the course of normal handling, as to which there is common experience that they do not ordinarily occur without a defect; and this permits the inference of a defect. This is particularly true when there is evidence in the case of the antecedent explosion of other bottles of the same product.

In cases involving multiple defendants the better reasoned view places the onus of tracing the defect on the shoulders of the dealers and the manufacturer as a policy matter, seeking to compensate the plaintiff and to require the defendants to fight out the question of responsibility among themselves.

■ ■ ■

Questions

1. How is public policy best served by imposing strict liability upon sellers, distributors and manufacturers for defective products?
2. What is the limit of "strict liability"? Is the seller liable for all possible damages following from a defective product?

In many states, implied warranty of merchantability is more akin to the concept of strict liability in tort than it is to a warranty attached to a contract of sale. The court's desire to impose strict liability upon the seller is merely camouflaged in contractual terms of warranty. Confusion in legal terminology results, but the result in increasing liability on sellers is the same. In those states adopting a strict liability theory in products liability, whether under Section 402A of the Restatement of Torts or under a strict liability theory of implied warranty, the courts are increasingly inclined to expand the concept of liability beyond the mere sale of goods. The following case is illustrative of the expanding concepts of strict liability in areas outside of the sale of tangible personal property.

HUMBER v. MORTON
426 S.W. 2d 554 (1968)
Supreme Court of Texas

■ ■ ■

The widow Humber brought suit against Claude Morton, alleging that Morton was in the business of building and selling new houses; that she purchased a house from him which was not suitable for human habitation in that the fireplace and chimney were not properly constructed and because of such defect, the house caught fire and partially burned the first time a fire was lighted in the fireplace. Morton defended upon (the)... ground... that the doctrine of "caveat emptor" applied to all sales of real estate...

According to Morton, the only warranty contained in the deed was the warranty of title, i.e. "to warrant and forever defend... the said premises unto the said Ernestine Humber, her heirs and assigns, * * *," and that he made no other warranty written or oral, in connection with the sale. While it is unusual for one to sell a house without saying something good about it... we shall assume that such conversation as may have taken place did not involve anything more than mere sales talk or puffing, and that no express warranties, either oral or written, were involved. However, it is undisputed that Morton built the house and then sold it as a new house. Did he thereby impliedly warrant that such house was constructed in a good workmanlike manner and was suitable for human habitation? We hold that he did. Under such circumstances, the law raises an implied warranty...

It might further be pointed out that generally in Texas, the notion of implied warranty arising from sales is considered to be a tort rather than a contract concept...

We return to the crucial issue in the case—Does the doctrine of caveat emtor apply to the sale of a new house by a builder-vendor?

In 1964, the Colorado Supreme Court in Carpenter v. Donohoe, 388 P. 2d 399, extended the implied warranty rule... to cover sales of a new house by a builder-vendor. The court said:

> "We hold that the implied warranty doctrine is extended to include agreements between builder-vendors and purchasers for the sale of newly constructed buildings, completed at the time of contracting. There is an implied warranty that builders-vendors have complied with the building code of the area in which the structure is located. Where, as here, a home is the subject of sale, there are implied warranties that the home was built in workmanlike manner and is suitable for habitation."

While it is not necessary for us to pass upon a situation in which the vendor-purchaser relationship is absent, the case of *Schipper v. Levitt & Sons,* 207 A. 2d 314 (1965), is important as much of the reasoning set forth in the opinion is applicable here. The Supreme Court of New Jersey recognized "the need for imposing on builder-vendors an implied obligation of reasonable workmanship and habitability which survives delivery of the deed." This was a case in which a person other than a purchaser had been injured by a defective water heater which had been installed in a new house by Levitt, the builder-vendor. The opinion cited and quotes from *Carpenter v. Donohoe* but proceeded upon the theory of strict liability in tort. The court placed emphasis upon the close analogy between a defect in a new house and a manufactured chattel. The opinion states:

> "The law should be based on current concepts of what is right and just and the judiciary should be alert to the neverending need for keeping its common law principles abreast of the times. Ancient distinctions which make no sense in today's society and tend to descredit the law should be readily rejected...

> "When a vendee buys a development house from an advertised model... he clearly relies on the skill of the developer and on its implied representation that the house will be erected in reasonably workmanlike manner and will be reasonably fit for habitation. He has no architect or other professional adviser of his own, he has no real competency to inspect on his own, his actual examination is, in the nature of things, largely superficial, and his oppourtunity for obtaining meaningful protective changes in the conveyancing documents prepared by the builder vendor is neglibible. If there is improper construction such as a defective heating system or a defective ceiling, stairway and the like, the well-being of the vendee and others is seriously endangered and serious injury is foreseeable. The public interest dictates that if such injury does result from the defective construction, its cost should be borne by the responsible developer who created the danger and

who is in the better economic position to bear the loss rather than by the injured party who justifiably relied on the developer's skill and implied representation."

If at one time in Texas the rule of caveat emptor had application to the sale of a new house by a vendor-builder, that time is now past. . .

Obviously, the ordinary purchaser is not in a position to ascertain when there is a defect in a chimney flue, or vent of a heating apparatus, or whether the plumbing work covered by a concrete slab foundation is faulty. . .

The caveat emptor rule as applied to new houses is an anachronism patently out of harmony with modern home buying practices. It does a disservice not only to the ordinary prudent purchaser but to the industry itself by lending encouragement to the unscrupulous, fly-by-night operator and purveyor of shoddy work. . .

■ ■ ■

Questions

1. What policy reasons are advanced by the court to expand the doctrine of implied warranty to the sale of a newly constructed building?
2. Should the doctrine of implied warranty or strict liability be extended to the sale of used goods? A used house?

8

FINANCIAL
TRANSACTIONS

Most societies that have developed a considerable amount of trade have found it expediate to use some form of commercial paper (negotiable instruments) to settle accounts between merchants. It is the use of these documents that facilitates the distribution of goods and services, since it is often impractical to transfer large sums of money with speed and safety.

Although there is evidence of usage earlier, it was during the late sixteenth and early seventeenth centuries that the use of commercial paper necessitated the creation of a special body of law. The commercial transactions of this period were primarily created at a local fair, which was authorized by the crown which conferred the privilege of the fair upon a noblemen or bishop. This privilege included the right to conduct court hearings in resolution of disputes between the merchant. The merchants, before moving on, wanted to settle their accounts at the fair. The decisions at these courts became known as the *law merchant*, with the custom and usage of the traders becoming an important aspect of this law. Later, whenever the courts of the crown were required to make decisions involving commercial transactions, they incorporated the *law merchant* in formulation of their common law decisions.

Commercial law in early America adopted the English common law and developed on a case-by-case basis. However, with each state having a separate legal system, unnecessary complexity evolved in multistate business transactions due to the diversity of rules in the various states. Merchants were faced with a variety of rules with regard to settling accounts with other merchants. Consequently, efforts were begun to provide more uiformity of law concerning business transactions.

In 1896 the National Conference of Commissioners on Uniform State Laws proposed the Negotiable Instruments Law NIL as part of their business law with some variation. This variation, along with differing judicial interpretations because of the ambiguities in draftmanship, somewhat frustrated the quest for uniformity.

In 1952 the Commissioners approved the Uniform Commercial Code (UCC) for submission to the states. Its purpose was to clarify and modernize business law, including the area of negotiable instruments. The code has been adopted in its entirety in all states, except Louisiana which as adopted a portion of it. The code was further clarified with a 1972 amendment. Presently, the UCC provides the basic legal framework for most business transactions.

The concept of "finance" has many different and broad connotations. Generally, however, it can be reduced to either (1) lending of money, or (2) the sale of goods with an extension of time for the payment of purchase price. In lending funds, businessmen often employ the use of "negotiable instruments" whether the lending involves simple promissory notes or more complex corporate bonds.

The extension of time for payments in the sale of goods involves certain risks. One method often employed by merchants to reduce such risks is to assure the right to repossess the goods if the debtor-buyer defaults in payment. To accomplish such results, the merchant must comply with the body of law known as "secured transactions."

The following materials explore the basic conceptual aspects of the law of "negotiable instruments" and "secured transactions."

COMMERCIAL PAPER

Commercial paper or negotiable instruments are special types of contracts. They are written in a special form requiring the future payment of money by one of the parties, either directly or through a third person. One of the parties has the contract right to receive the payment of money and may transfer this right to other parties through what is called negotiations.

As commerical activity expanded in the sixteenth century, merchants found themselves short of cash. Buyers began to write short contracts that required their unconditional payment of money on the seller's demand (or at a stated time interval) as a substitute for an immediate cash payment. Since buyer-merchants appreciated this opportunity of delayed payment, they tended to pay the obligation on its due date. Later, as the practice expanded, the seller-merchants holding these contracts to receive future payment began to transfer them to their suppliers in payment for goods or debts. In effect, these payment-on-demand or future payment contracts began to pass as effective substitutes for money and serve as instruments for granting of credit. To preserve and encourage these practices, the law developed special rules for these contracts. These rules have endured and today are embodied in Articles 3 and 4 of the Uniform Commercial Code.

It is important for the reader to remember that these contracts are to pass freely among merchants—as substitutes for money. Therefore, to facilitate this free transferability, the instrument must be readily identifiable. The following materials outline the essentials for formation of a negotiable instrument.

TYPES OF PAPER

Commercial paper includes written promises (promissory notes) or orders (drafts) to pay money that are created to be transferred to others as substitute for money. Paying a debt by check involves the use of commercial paper in place of a cash transaction. Moreover, commercial paper is also used for the extension of credit. This is easily illustrated by the promissory note in which the debtor has sixty days or more before payment is due. Obviously, the creditor cannot collect this sum until the sixty days or more have passed.

According to the UCC a negotiable promissory note is an unconditional promise in writing made by one person (the maker) to another (the payee) whereby the signature of the maker is attached to a promise to pay on demand or on a definite time a sum certain in money to the payee or the order of the payee or to the bearer. A promissory note payable on demand immediately serves as a substitute for money and a promissory note payable on a future date serves as an extension of credit to the maker of the note.

A negotiable draft (bill of exchange) is an unconditional order in writing addressed and signed by one person (drawer) to another person (drawee) who is required to pay on demand or on a definite time a sum certain in money to a designated payee or his or her order, or to the bearer. In effect, a draft is an order or command by the drawer to the drawee to pay money to a third person, the payee. The drawee who is ordered to pay the money is not required to do so unless he or she "accepts" the order. On becoming the "acceptor" the drawee becomes primarily obligated to pay the instrument which is often thereafter called a "trade acceptance."

Figure 8-1
PROMISSORY NOTE

$450.00	Grand Rapids, Mich. *March 20* 19
Thirty days	AFTER DATE *I* PROMISE TO PAY TO
THE ORDER OF *Carolsue Furniture Company*	
Four hundred fifty and $^{no}/_{100}$ ——— DOLLARS	
PAYABLE AT *Second National Bank*	
VALUE RECEIVED WITH INTEREST AT 5 %	
No. 85 Due *April 19, 19*	*Fred E. Hart*

Figure 8-2
SIGHT DRAFT

$950.00	CLEVELAND, OHIO February 11, 19 ____
At sight —————————————————————————————	PAY TO THE
ORDER OF Fredna Pearce	
Nine hundred fifty and 50/100 - - - - - - - - - - - - - - - DOLLARS	
VALUE RECEIVED AND CHARGE TO ACCOUNT OF	
TO Mary Lynn Britton	SHARONANN APPLIANCES
No. 167 Gary, Indiana By	*Clara Bell*

A check is a draft in which the drawee is a bank and which is payable on demand. It is an order by the depositor (drawer) upon his or her bank (drawee) to pay a sum of money to the order of another person (payee). According to UCC's Section 3-104 the instrument to be negotiable must:

1. Be signed by the maker or drawer,
2. Contain an unconditional promise or order to pay a sum certain in money,
3. Be payable on demand or at a definite time, and
4. Be payable to order or to bearer.

Besides the signature of the maker or the drawer, the instrument must contain an *unconditional* promise or order to pay a sum certain in money. As such, the promisor or acceptor of the draft agrees to make payment with no conditions attached to that agreement. Because of the absence of any condition on payment, the instrument may be more readily passed to other parties prior to its maturity date as a substitute for cash payment. Subsequent parties are willing to take the negotiable instrument because no conditions are attached to the requirement to pay on the maturity date. In *D'Andrea v. Feinberg* 256 N.Y.S. 2d 504 (1965) the court was faced with the question of whether a note was nonnegotiable because it contained the notation "as per contract." The court said:

> "The note meets all the requirements of section 3-104 of the U.C.C. with the possible exception that it does not contain an unconditional promise because of the legend "as per contract." Section 3-105(1)(c) expressly states that an unconditional promise "is not made conditional by the fact that the instrument * * * (c) refers to or states that it arises out of a separate agreement or refers to a separate agreement for rights as to prepayment or acceleration."
>
> The official comment on the above quoted provision. . . is that it was "intended to resolve a conflict, and to reject cases in which a reference to a separate agreement was held to mean that payment of the instrument must be limited in accordance with the terms of the agreement, and hence was conditioned by it." The court is satisfied that the legend "as per contract" does not affect the negotiability of an instrument as would a statement that the instrument "is subject to or governed by any other agreement."
>
> The court determines that the note being sued upon is a negotiable instrument. . .

MATURITY DATE

FERRI v. SYLVIA
214 A. 2d 470 (1965)
Supreme Court of Rhode Island

■ ■ ■

The note, which is dated May 25, 1963, obligates defendants to pay to plaintiff or her order $3,000 "within ten (10) years after date." The trial justice determined that the maturity of the note was uncertain, admitted testimony of the parties as to both their intentions or prior agreements, and premised upon such extrinsic evidence found that plaintiff "could have the balance that may be due at any time she needed it and that she could call for and demand the full payment of any balance that may be due or owing her at the time of her demand."

The question is whether the note is payable at a fixed or determinable future time. If the phrase "within ten (10) years after date" lacks explicitness or is ambiguous then clearly parol evidence was admissible for the purpose of ascertaining the intention of the parties. . .

At the law merchant it was generally settled that a promissory note or a bill of exchange payable "on or before" a specified date fixed with certainty the time of payment. The same rule has been fixed by statute first under the negotiable instruments law, and now pursuant to the uniform commercial code. The code in §3-109(1) reads as follows: "An instrument is payable at a definite time if by its terms it is payable (a) on or before a stated date or at a fixed period after a stated date * * *."

The courts (have). . . said that the legal rights of the holder of an "on or before" instrument were clearly fixed and entitled him to payment upon an event that was certain to come, even though the maker might be privileged to pay sooner if he so elected. They held, therefore, that the due date of such an instrument was fixed with certainty and that its negotiability was unaffected by the privilege given the maker to accelerate payment. . .

On principle no valid distinction can be drawn between an instrument payable "on or before" a fixed date and one which calls for payment "within" a stipulated period. This was the holding in Leader v. Plante, 95 Me. 339, where the court said. . . "'Within' a certain period, 'on or before' a day named and 'at or before' a certain day, are equivalent terms and the rules of construction apply to each alike."

. . . We hold that the payment provision of a negotiable instrument payable "within" a stated period is certain as well as complete on its face and that such an instrument does not mature until the time fixed arrives.

For the foregoing reasons it is clear that the parties unequivocally agreed that the plaintiff could not demand payment of the note until the expiration of the ten-year period. It is likewise clear that any prior or contemporaneous oral agreements of the parties relevant to its due date were so merged and integrated with the writing as to prevent its being explained or supplemented by parol evidence.

■ ■ ■

Questions

1. Is "within ten years after date" a definite maturity date?
2. Since the maker has the privilege to accelerate payment prior to the maturity date when "within" or "on or before" language is used, does this imply that the maker does not have the right of early payment when such language is absent?

MAGIC WORDS

HAGGARD v. MUTUAL OIL & REFINING CO.
263 S.W. 745 (1924)
Court of Appeals of Kentucky

■ ■ ■

The single question presented by this appeal is whether or not the following check is a negotiable instrument:

"$2,500.00 Winchester, Ky., July 10, 1920
"The Winchester Bank, of Winchester, Ky.:
Pay to Arco Refinery Construction Company twenty-five hundred and no/100 dollars, for constructing refinery, switch, and loading racks, Win. Ky.

"Mutual Oil & Refining Co.
"By C. L. Bell, Pres."

"An instrument to be negotiable must conform to the following requirements: * * * (4) Must be payable to the order of a specified person or to bearer."

Since, as the check itself shows, and as is admittedly true, the maker, in issuing the check, drew a line through the printed words "or bearer," we need only to examine it to ascertain whether or not it was "payable to the order of a specified person," for unless so, it lacked one of the essentials prescribed for negotiability...

It will be noticed that the above check is not payable to the order of the payee, nor to the payee or its order, but is payable simply to the payee. It therefore seems to us too clear for dispute that this check is not payable to order, and is therefore, as the lower court held, not negotiable.

■ ■ ■

Questions

1. Must an instrument contain either the word "order" or "bearer" on the face of the instrument in order to be a "negotiable instrument?"
2. Assuming the instrument is payable to "bearer," does that mean the instrument is the same as cash or currency as far as the risk of loss is concerned? Suppose you lose an instrument payable to bearer. If it is presented to the maker-payer, how would he know the instrument is being presented by a finder? (or thief?) If the maker paid the funds to the finder (or thief), should he be required to pay again to the true owner who lost the instrument? Does this suggest an obvious

advantage of "order" instruments? Order instruments can only be transferred by the indorsement (or order) of the person whose name is designated as payee. Anyone taking or holding the order instrument without a valid indorsement does not have ownership over the instrument or a right to collect payment. The payer-maker could not pay the finder and discharge his duty to pay the person designated by the instrument or the indorsement.

NEGOTIATION

Often the purpose for creating a negotiable instrument is to create an instrument that is more readily transferable than ordinary contract rights. Consequently, the law is designed to enhance that transferability. The method of transferring or negotiating an instrument depends on the terms of the instrument or the indorsements. If the instrument is order paper, it can be negotiated only by indorsement and delivery. If it is bearer paper, it may be negotiated by delivery alone.

An instrument payable to order may be negotiated by indorsement only by the person to whom the instrument was made payable (payee). The indorsement must be placed on the instrument and is usually contained on the reversed side of the instrument. The indorsement is made by the payee merely signing his name or adding certain additional words as part of his indorsement. When the indorser signs only his name, the indorsement is called a *blank indorsement* because it does not indicate the person to whom the instrument is to be paid. Any person in possession of a paper with a blank indorsement may sue upon the instrument without proving ownership of the paper. The effect of a blank indorsement is to make the instrument a "bearer" paper.

A *special indorsement* consists of the signature of the indorser and words designating the person to whom the indorser makes the instrument payable, that is, the indorsee. In effect, a special indorsement preserves the "order" status of the paper or transforms "bearer" paper into "order" paper.

A *restrictive indorsement* specifies a particular purpose of the indorsement and specifies the use that is to be made of the paper. The usual kind of restrictive indorsement is an indorsement "for deposit only." This indorsement indicates that the intent of the indorsor is to have the instrument presented for payment and the proceeds deposited to his or her account. The depository bank must collect payment and apply the proceeds consistent with the indorsement.

Negotiations by blank, special, or restrictive indorsements (all unqualified indorsements) do two things: (1) pass ownership of the instrument, and (2) impose secondary liability upon the indorser for the amount of the instrument. If the primary parties (maker or drawee-acceptor) fail to pay the holder of the instrument after a proper presentment for payment, the holder may give notice of the dishonor by the primary party to the indorser within the specified time limit and thereby require the indorsor to "make good" the instrument by paying it himself. In effect, the indorsor's secondary liability is a *conditional* promise of payment if the primary party is unable or unwilling to pay. The conditions which the holder must perform are a proper presentment for payment (on the due date) and proper notice of dishonor (within three days).

Should the indorsor desire not to provide this conditional promise of payment to the indorsee, the indorsor would utilize a *qualified indorsement* which disclaims or destroys the secondary liability of the indorsor. The qualified indorsement is created by including the words "without recourse" in the body of the indorsement. A qualified indorsement does not affect the passage of title to the negotiable instrument.

A person who becomes a party to a negotiable instrument to add his or her credit to the paper is called an *accommodation party*. If he or she is a maker, he or she is called an accommodation maker; if an indorsor, an accommodation indorser. For example, when a bank is unwilling to lend money to A on the strength of A's credit rating, B may sign the note as a co-maker with A to bolser A's credit. In such instance, B is an accommodation maker. Moreover, if A was attempting to cash a check while in a strange city, B as a resident and depositor with a bank in that city could indorse A's check and thereby lend his or her credit to the check to induce the bank to cash the check. The accommodation party, whether a maker or indorsor, receives no owner-ship interest in the instrument, but merely lends credit to support another party. If the accommodation party is required to pay the instrument, he or she may recover the amount of payment from the person accommodated.

Figure 8-3
TYPES OF INDORSEMENT

Peter Payee

Blank Indorsement

Pay to John Doe
Peter Payee

Special Indorsement

For Deposit
Peter Payee

Restrictive Indorsement

Without Recourse
Peter Payee

Qualified Indorsement

INDORSER'S SECONDARY LIABILITY

HANE v. EXTEN
259 A. 2d 290 (1969)
Court of Appeals, Maryland

■ ■ ■

John B. Hane is the indorsee of the note (made by)...Theta Electronic Laborato-ries, Inc. (Theta) in the stated amount of $15,377.07, with interest at six per cent per annum. The note was dated 10 August 1964; stipulated that the first monthly payment of $320.47 would be due five months from date, or on 10 January 1965; and that "in the event of the failure to pay the interest or principal, as the same becomes due on this Note the entire debt represented hereby shall at the end of thirty (30) days become due and demandable * * *." The note was indorsed without recourse to Hane by George B. Thomson, the original payee, on 26 November 1965. A default having occurred in the making of the monthly payments, Hane...on 7 June 1967 sued Theta and Gerald M. Exten...who had (indorsed as an accommodation party on)...Theta's note...[T]he case came on for trial on the merits before the court without a jury. From a judgment for the Extens. . . ,Hane has appealed.

This case raises the familiar question: Must Hane show that the Extens were given notice of presentment and dishonor before he can hold them on their indorsement?

The court below, in finding for the Extens, relied on the provisions of Uniform Commercial Code. . .

"Unless the indorsement otherwise specifies (as by such words as 'without recourse') every indorser engages that upon dishonor and any necessary notice of dishonor and protest he will pay the instrument according to its tenor at the time of his indorsement to the holder or to any subsequent indorser who takes it up.". . .

§3-501(1) (b) provides that "Presentment for payment is necessary to charge any indorser" and §3-501(2) (a) that "Notice of any dishonor is necessary to charge any indorser," in each case subject, however, to the provisions of §3-511 which recite the circumstances under which notice of dishonor may be waived or excused, none of which is here present. §3-502(1) (a) makes it clear that unless presentment or notice of dishonor is waived or excused, unreasonable delay will discharge an indorser. . .

There was testimony from which the trier of facts could find as he did that presentment and notice of dishonor were unduly delayed.

It is clear that Hame held the note from November, 1965, until some time in April 1967, before he made demand for payment. U.C.C. §3-503(1)(d) provides that "Where an instrument is accelerated presentment for payment is due within a reasonable time after the acceleration." "Reasonable time" is not defined in §3-503, except that §3-503(2) provides, "A reasonable time for presentment is determined by the nature of the instrument, any usage of banking or trade and the facts of the particular case." But §1-204(2) characterizes it: "What is a reasonable time for taking any action depends on the nature, purpose and circumstances of such action."

Reasonableness is primarily a question for the fact finder. . .

We see no reason to disturb the lower court's finding that Hane's delay of almost 18 months in presenting the note "was unreasonable from any viewpoint."

As regards notice of dishonor, §3-508 (2) requires that notice be given by persons other than banks "before midnight of the third business day after dishonor or receipt of notice of dishonor." Exten, called as an adverse witness by Hane, testified that his first notice that the note had not been paid was. . . on 7 June 1967. Hane's brother testified that demand had been made about 15 April 1967. He was uncertain as to when he had given Exten notice of dishonor, but finally conceded that it was "within a week." The lower court found that the ambiguity of this testimony, coupled with Exten's denial that he had received *any* notice before 7 June fell short of meeting the three day notice requirement of the U.C.C. The date of giving notice of dishonor is a question of fact, solely for determination by the trier of facts.

In the absence of evidence that presentment and notice of dishonor were waived or excused, Hane's unreasonable delay discharged the Extens.

■ ■ ■

Questions

1. Did Hane unduly delay the presentment of the instrument for payment? When was the instrument to be presented for payment?
2. Did Hane give timely notice of the dishonor of the instrument? Within what time period was Hane required to give the notice of dishonor?
3. What is the legal result of Hane's failure to properly present the instrument for payment and failure to give notice of dishonor within the prescribed time period?
4. In *Hane* the time of presentment for payment was to be within a reasonable time after the instrument was accelerated, (that is, all future payments are accelerated to a current date and presently due). Acceleration protects the

creditor from having to sue for each monthly or yearly installment as it comes due. Rather, If a periodic payment is missed, the creditor can, if the note has an authorizing clause, accelerate and demand payment for all periodic payments (present & future) under the note. However, when a note is not accelerated, the holder of the note is to present it for payment, not within a reasonable time, but *on* the due date. Failure to make a timely presentment for payment will discharge the secondarily liable parties.

DRAWER'S SECONDARY LIABILITY

GILL v YOES
360 P.2d 506 (1961)
Supreme Court of Oklahoma

■ ■ ■

The plaintiff in this case, Deane Gill, was the owner of an airplane which he had for sale. A man by the name of C.J. Hobson desired to buy this plane from Gill. The price of the plane was $8,000. Hobson agreed to buy the plane. He got the defendant Jackie Yoes to draw a draft on the Phoenix Savings and Loan Company of Muskogee, Oklahoma, in favor of Gill and gave the draft to Gill in payment for the plane. The defendant Jackie Yoes had no money in the Savings and Loan Company but had made application to it for a loan on property she owned but none was made to her. The draft was turned down by the Savings and Loan Company. Title to the plane was taken in the name of the defendant and application for registration in defendant's name was made. After the delivery of the plane Hobson took and flew it away and it was later destroyed in an accident. Soon after the draft was drawn it was presented for payment which was refused. Plaintiff immediately got in touch with the defendant and demanded that she make the draft good. This she refused to do, so the plaintiff brought suit on the draft.

The defendant claimed that she had nothing to do with the purchase of the plane except that she did sign the draft for $8,000 to pay for it; that she knew nothing about the deaings between Hobson and plaintiff; that she had no need for a plane and that she did not buy it. She did testify that she did try to borrow money from the Phoenix Savings and Loan Company on her property in Stigler, Oklahoma, but the loan was never completed...

The case was tried to a jury and a verdict was rendered for the defendant. The plaintiff had moved for a directed verdict at the close of the defendant's case...

By giving a negotiable instrument,...(the) drawer of the instrument..."engages that on due presentment the instrument will be...paid...according to its tenor...

...There is no question in this case that the defendant executed the draft involved herein. It was on the strength of this draft that the airplane was turned over to Hobson. If this draft had not been delivered to plaintiff certainly he would not have executed the bill of sale and transferred the airplane. The defendant by her answer injected into this case the proposition that the draft given for the plane was for the benefit of a third party, one Hobson. It is really immaterial whether the draft was given for the purchase of the plane by either Hobson or the defendant just so long as it was given...

The judgement is reversed with directions to the trial court to render judgment for the plaintiff...

■ ■ ■

Questions

1. What is the drawer's obligation under a negotiable draft or check? Are any conditions attached to the obligation?
2. Is the drawer's responsibility on a draft similar to the responsibility of an indorsor?

3. While secondary parties (indorsors and drawers) may be relieved from responsibility on a negotiable instrument because of improper presentment or improper notice of dishonor, primary parties (makers of notes and acceptors of drafts) are not thereby relieved for failure of proper presentment or notice of dishonor. The primarily obligated parties are forever bound to pay the instrument according to its terms.

4. Why should a secondarily liable party (drawer or indorser) be relieved of liability on a delay of presentment or of notice of dishonor? Consider the following situation:

> Joe Worker received his paycheck from his employer, Goodandrich, which was drawn on the First National Bank of Pleasantville. Joe Worker stopped by the saloon on his way home that evening and cashed the check by indorsement with Bart Barkeeper. Barkeeper held on to the check for a month before tendering it for payment to The First National Bank. During that month, the employer, Goodandrich, became insolvent and applied to the Bankruptcy Court for dissolution. Consequently, the Bank, without any deposits by Goodandrich, refused to honor the check. Therefore, Barkeeper attempted to sue Joe Worker on his indorsement to make the check good. Would it be fair to Joe Worker to require that he pay the check when Barkeeper could have gotten full payment had he made a proper presentment of the check in the first part of the month? Barkeeper's delay forces someone to absorb the loss.

As between Barkeeper and Joe Worker, who should absorb the loss?

TRANSFEROR'S WARRANTIES

When one makes a sale of tangible personal property, certain warranties (title and merchantability) are implied by law in the transaction of sale. The seller is held liable for breach of any of those warranties. Likewise, when one sells a negotiable instrument (by negotiating it for value), warranties are also implied by law in this transfer. The transferor warrants:

1. He or she has good title to the instrument or is properly authorized to obtain payment;
2. All signatures are genuine or authorized;
3. The instrument has not been materially altered;
4. No defense of any party is good against him; and
5. He or she has no knowledge of any insolvency proceedings against the maker or acceptor, or the drawer of an unaccepted instrument.

While the transferee of a negotiable instrument normally relies on the indorsor's secondary liability as a protection against the insolvency of the primary party, the warranties may be important in certain instances; perhaps no indorsement was made, the indorsement was qualified (without recourse), or the transferee failed to make a proper presentment or to give proper notice of dishonor. In such cases, the transferee may sue the transferor if the transferor has breached any of the above warranties. However, it should be noted that the warranty of no defenses is changed when the transfer is made by a qualified endorsement. When the indorser signs "without recourse," the no-defense warranty (number 4 above) changes to a warranty of "no knowledge of a defense." In this warranty, the transferree must prove the transferor *knew* of the defense of the maker at the time the transfer of the instrument occurred. Failure to prove such "knowledge" would mean the transferee has failed to prove a breach of warranty.

Charging an individual with an interest rate higher than the state's legal rate is usury. Depending upon the state, various penalties can result from usury. In most states the penalty imposed is inability to collect the usurious interest. In the following case Fair Finance was not able to collect from the maker the usurious part of the interest on a note. Therefore, Fair Finance attempted to force Forco, who had sold the note to Fair Finance, to "make good" this part of the note. Forco had indorsed the instrument without recourse and the warranty of no defense was thereby changed to a warranty of no knowledge of a defense. Therefore, the question before the court was whether Forco had "knowledge" of the defense of usury at the time of transfer of the instrument?

FAIR FINANCE CO. v. FOURCO, INC.
237 N.E. 2d 406 (1968)
Court of Appeals of Ohio

■ ■ ■

In this appeal on questions of law, the plaintiff, Fair Finance Company (appellant here), says it purchased from the defendant, Fourco, Inc. (appellee here), a certain promissory note which was endorsed "without recourse" and delivered to the Fair Finance Company. When Fair Finance Company sought to collect on the note from the maker thereof, it was determined by the trial court in a hearing that, at the time of transfer from Fourco, Inc., to Fair Finance Company, the amount due on the note was $1,361.96 less than the amount represented to Fair Finance Company as the amount due on such note, and $1,361.96 less than Fair Finance Company paid Fourco, Inc., for such promissory note.

An action to recover the claimed overpayment was instituted by Fair Finance Company against Fourco, Inc.; the case was tried on written stipulations of fact and submitted in this manner to the trial court. That court... says:

"It is the finding of the court that the defendant at the time of endorsing the note without recourse had no notice of usury by the maker of this note; that the defendant having transferred without recourse is not liable to the plaintiff."

...Fair Finance Company admits that Fourco, Inc., had no knowledge of the defense of improper computation until after an attempt to obtain payment by court action against the maker was instituted. There is no claim of fraud in the sale and purchase of this promissory note. Counsel for the Fair Finance Company, in their statements to the trial court and to this court, said: "We do claim unintentional misrepresentation." This claim of misrepresentation arises from the fact that interest on the note was calculated by the vendor, Fourco, Inc., at the beginning of the interest period and taken in advance instead of at the end of the interest period.

Is the claim of "unintentional misrepresentation" such that it is exempt from the provisions of Section 1303.53 (B) (4) and (C), Revised Code? We find no reported cases in Ohio, or elsewhere, interpreting this section of the Uniform Commercial Code.

The vendor in the instant case, Fourco, Inc., used its own printed note to obtain the written promise of the maker. the terms of that note concerning the computation of interest were its handiwork. The computation of interest was not made by the maker but by the vendor of the note who now wishes, because of its own error and improper computation of interest, to be relieved of liability because of the endorsement "without recourse." Is this such a lack of knowledge of a defense as releases the vendor-endorser from liability? We think it is not, for we believe that where an endorsement of a promissory note "without recourse" is made by a vendor-payee, who computes the interest incorrectly in determining the face value of that note at the time of sale, and where the form of note and terms thereof are those of the vendor-payee, such vendor-payee has knowledge of that wrongful computation, and the defense arising therefrom within the terms of Code.

It is the conclusion of this court that the judgment must be reversed, and, as there is no dispute as to the facts, final judgment shall be ordered entered herein for the appellant, Fair Finance Company, for the amount admitted by the parties hereto as being the improper computation of interest by Fourco, Inc.

■ ■ ■

Questions

1. Did Fourco have "knowledge" of the defense of usury at the time of transfer of the instrument? How did the court conclude Fourco did have knowledge? Do you agree with the court's logic? With the result?
2. Wayne obtained a negotiable instrument by fraudulent means and negotiated it to Percival with the indorsement "without recourse on me pay to the order of J. J. Percival, J. C. Wayne." When the instrument was dishonored, Percival sought to hold Wayne, claiming breach of warranty. How should the court decide? Why?

HOLDER IN DUE COURSE

An important concept of negotiable instruments is the "holder in due course" doctrine. This doctrine is designed to increase the effectiveness of the instruments as substitues for money by encouraging their free tansferability and by making them more desirable for investment purposes. To allow the instrument to circulate as freely as money itself, this rule of law gives a subsequent holder of the instrument (if he qualifies) greater rights to collect payment from the maker than the original payee had. For example, if a maker of a promissory note gives the note to a payee in payment for a refrigerator which was never delivered, the maker would not have to pay the party (payee) who sold the refrigerator. However, if the payee who sold the refrigerator had transferred the note to a "holder in due course," such holder could collect payment from the maker in spite of the nondelivery of the refrigerator. In effect, the rights of the holder (transferee) to collect are greater than the rights of the payee. This role of greater rights in the transferee is unique to commercial paper in that, under contract law, a transfer of contract rights in a similiar situation results in the holder receiving only the rights of his or her transferor and no better. Under contract law, any defense of the maker would be effective to stop payment to the payee or the transferee. Therefore, contrary to contract law, the "holder in due course" doctrine gives the holder a superior position (that is, ability to collect payment regardless of the maker's defenses) and thereby encourages the potential purchaser of an instrument to take the paper. This doctrine allows negotiable instruments to circulate with greater freedom as substitutes for money. (See Figure 8-4).

ILLINOIS VALLEY ACCEPTANCE CORP. v. WOODARD
304 N.E. 2d 859 (1975)
Court of Appeals of Indiana

■ ■ ■

Woodard was a part time salesman for Moody Manufacturing Company (Moody), a manufacturer of grain bins and grain handling equipment. In May of 1966, Moody, as "borrower", had entered into a Finance Agreement with Acceptance listed as "the lender". This agreement made provision, among other things, for Moody to sell acceptable accounts to Acceptance for face value with 15% being reserved for deductions, expenses, accumulated interest, etc. On the 24th of December, 1968, Woodard

Figure 8-4 .

CHARTS CONTRASTING LAW OF ASSIGNMENT AND LAW OF NEGOTIATION

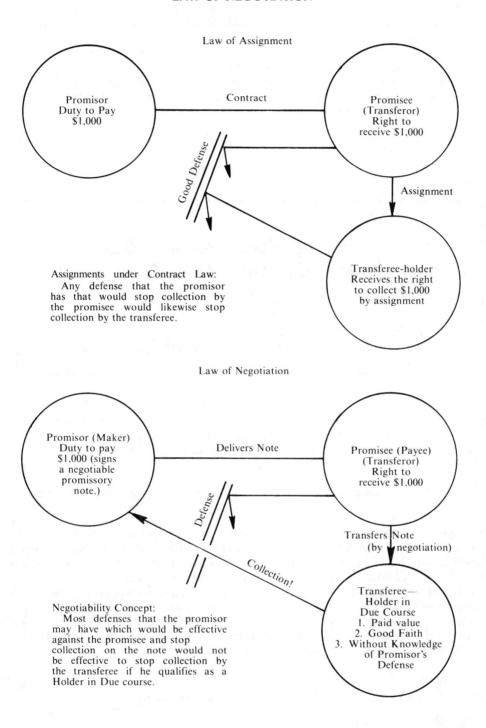

Law of Assignment

Promisor
Duty to Pay
$1,000

Contract

Promisee
(Transferor)
Right to
receive $1,000

Good Defense

Assignment

Transferee-holder
Receives the right
to collect $1,000
by assignment

Assignments under Contract Law:
Any defense that the promisor has that would stop collection by the promisee would likewise stop collection by the transferee.

Law of Negotiation

Promisor (Maker)
Duty to pay
$1,000 (signs
a negotiable
promissory
note.)

Delivers Note

Promisee (Payee)
(Transferor)
Right to
receive $1,000

Defense

Transfers Note
(by negotiation)

Collection!

Transferee—
Holder in
Due Course
1. Paid value
2. Good Faith
3. Without Knowledge
of Promisor's
Defense

Negotiability Concept:
Most defenses that the promisor may have which would be effective against the promisee and stop collection on the note would not be effective to stop collection by the transferee if he qualifies as a Holder in Due course.

signed, as acceptor, the trade acceptance which is the subject of this litigation. Moody was the drawer and payee. At that time it was in blank with the face value subsequently being filled in for the face amount of $8,815.62. In the four or five years prior to 1968, Woodard had signed several trade acceptances in blank for Moody for the purposes of covering the purchase of materials which he sold. The face amount was ultimately to be filled in when it was determined how much he had ordered. The December, 1968 trade acceptance was endorsed by Moody's secretary and given to Acceptance several days after Woodard had signed it. Between February and April, 1970, and several months past the due date, Moody went bankrupt. When Acceptance presented the instrument for payment it was refused by Woodard. Additionally, Woodard never received the materials presented by the trade acceptance, nor was he aware it had been negotiated by Moody to Acceptance...

Figure 8-5

TRADE ACCEPTANCE

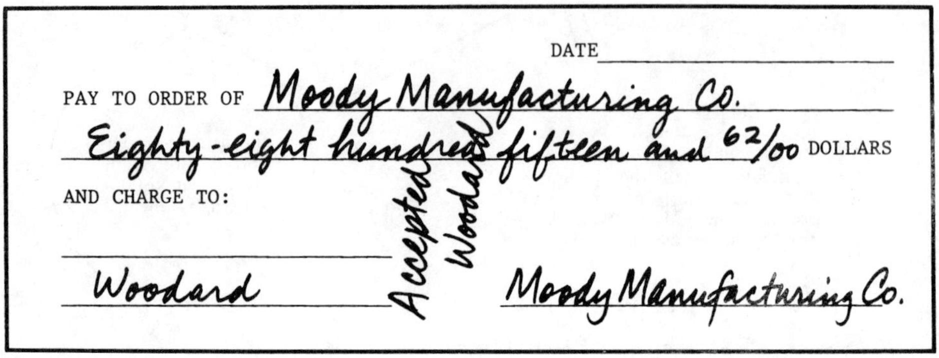

DATE ______

PAY TO ORDER OF Moody Manufacturing Co.

Eighty-eight hundred fifteen and 62/00 DOLLARS

AND CHARGE TO:

Accepted Woodard

Woodard

Moody Manufacturing Co.

This case is to be decided under the provisions of the Uniform Commercial Code... It provides that only a holder can recover on the instrument. The applicable section reads:

> "(2) When signatures are admitted or established, production of the instrument entitles the holder to recover on it unless the defendant establishes a defense."

Acceptance's acknowledged status as a holder was not sufficient for it to recover because Woodard raised the defenses of fraud and failure of consideration, each a valid defense. These defenses, however, may have been cut off if Acceptance was a holder in due course. The holder in due course takes the instrument "free from all defenses of any party to the instrument with whom the holder has not dealt," subject to several exceptions. To avail itself of this "super-plaintiff" status, Acceptance had the burden of establishing by a preponderance of the evidence that it was "in all respects a holder in due course." "In all respects" means that Acceptance had to establish the existence of each of the elements set forth in 3—302...

It provides:

"(1) A holder in due course is a holder who takes the instrument

(a) for value; and
(b) in good faith; and
(c) without notice that it is overdue or has been dishonored or of any defense against or claim to it on the part of any person."

The evidence, when examined with the foregoing requisites in mind, establishes Acceptances as a holder in due course. Briefly summarized that evidence shows the trade acceptance being endorsed over to Acceptance by Moody. Moody in turn received a draft for 85% of the face value of the trade acceptance. There was nothing irregular with the acceptance and the transaction was similar to other prior transactions between the parties. At that time Acceptance had no knowledge that the trade acceptance had been signed in blank and that the goods had not been delivered.

A portion of Woodard's aruguments appears to be directed to the questions of good faith and notice...

The Finance Agreement, introduced into evidence by Woodard, may have been an attempt to establish something akin to the doctrine of close connectedness, characterized by Woodard as the lack of an arms-length transaction, for the purpose of showing that Acceptance was so closely related to Moody commercially that it knew, or should have known, either Moody was in poor financial shape or that it had not delivered the goods represented by the trade acceptance. Acceptance's summary judgment affidavit as well as the testimony given at the trial belies such a relationship.

Woodard further argues that there was no value given for the trade acceptance and that the Finance Agreement between Moody and Acceptance was merely a borrowing agreement. The evidence shows that Acceptance paid Moody 85% of the face vlaue of trade acceptance and held the remainder in reserve. There can be little question that the value concept was satisfied...

Woodard's affirmative defense of want of consideration is not available against a holder in due course.

Turning next to the question of fraud, 3-305(2)(c), allows a defense against a holder in due course based upon "such misrepresentation as has induced the party to sign the instrument with neither knowledge nor reasonable opportunity to obtain knowledge of its character or its essential terms." The comments subsequent to this statute state that fraud in the essence or fraud in the factum is a valid defense against a holder in due course with the theory being that the "signature is ineffective because he did not intend to sign such an instrument at all." Woodard's past conduct in signing blank trade acceptances for Moody negates a defense based on the foregoing. Woodard testified he was familiar with the forms and knew they constituted a promise to pay...

It is our conclusion that the evidence conclusively demonstrated Acceptance to be a holder in due course.

Questions

1. Was Acceptance a holder in due course? Did it give value? In good faith? Without notice of any defense?
2. What were Woodard's defenses? Why were these defenses not good against the holder in due course?

BURCHETT v. ALLIED CONCORD FINANCIAL CORP.
396 P. 2d 186 (1965)
Supreme Court of New Mexico

[Kelly was an agent selling aluminum siding for a firm named Consolidated Products. He talked with the Burchetts and their neighbors, the Beevers, at their homes offering to install aluminum siding on their houses for a stipulated price in exchange for their permission to use their houses as "show houses." Kelly told them they would receive a credit of $100 for each aluminum siding contract sold within a 25 mile radius and that such credit would be applied to their contractual indebtedness for installation of the siding on their homes. The couples believed that by this method they would receive the improvements for nothing. Kelly handed each couple a form of a printed contract to read. While they were reading the contracts, Kelly was filling out blanks on other forms. They signed, without reading, these forms filled out by Kelly, assuming them to be the same as those which they had read. The contracts clearly stated on the same pages on which the signatures of the purchasers appeared; "No one is authorized on behalf of this company to represent this job to be 'a sample home for a free job.'" What the couples had signed were notes and mortgages on their property to cover the cost of the aluminum siding and the contracts contained no mention of credits for "promoting" other sales. The aluminum siding was installed, although the jobs were not completely satisfactory. Shortly afterwards, the Burchetts and the Beevers received letters from Allied Concord Financial Corp., informing them that it had purchased the notes and mortgages and that they were delinquent in their first payment. The Burchetts and the Beevers brought this action to have the notes and mortgages cancelled. The defendant, Consolidated Products, appeals from judgments avoiding the instruments.]

■ ■ ■

In both cases, the trial court found that the notes and mortgages, although signed by the plaintiffs were fraudulently procured. The court also found that the defendant paid a valuable consideration for the notes and mortgages, althought at a discount, and concluded as a matter of law that the defendant was a holder in due course. . . . The only real question in the case is whether, under these facts, plaintiffs, by substantial evidence, satisfied the provisions of the statute relating to their claimed defense as against a holder in due course.

In 1961, . . . our legislature adopted, with some variations, the Uniform Commercial Code. The provision of the code applicable to this case appears as. . . §3-305(2)(c). . . which, so far as material, is as follows:

"To the extent that a holder is a holder in due course he takes the instrument free from
  "(2) all defenses of any party to the instrument with whom the holder has not dealt except. . .
  "(c) such misrepresentation as has induced the party to sign the instrument with neither knowledge nor reasonable opportunity to obtain knowledge of its character or its essential terms;. . ."

Although fully realizing that the official comments appearing as part of the Uniform Commerical Code are not direct authority for the construction to be placed upon a section of the code, nevertheless they are persuasive and represent the opinion of the National Conference of Commissioners on Uniform State Laws and the American Law Institute. The purpose of the comments is to explain the provisions of the code itself, in an effort to promote uniformity of interpretation. We believe that the official comments following §3-305 (2) (c), Comment No. 7, provide an excellent guideline for the disposition of the case before us. We quote the same in full:

"7. Paragraph (c) of subsection (2) is new. It follows the great majority of the decisions under the original Act in recognizing the defense of 'real' or 'essential' fraud, sometimes called fraud in the essence or fraud in the factum, as effective against a holder in due course. The common illustration is that of the maker who is tricked into signing a note in the belief that it is merely a receipt or some other document. The theory of the defense is that his signature on the instrument is ineffective because he did not intend to sign such an instrument at all. Under this provision the defense extends to an instrument signed with knowledge that it is a negotiable instrument, but without knowledge of its essential terms.

"The test of the defense here stated is that of excusable ignorance of the writing signed. The party must not only have been in ignorance, but must also have had no reasonable opportunity to obtain knowledge. In determining what is a reasonable opportunity all relevant factors are to be taken into account, including the age and sex of the party, his intelligence, education and business experience; his ability to read or to understand English, the representations made to him and his reason to rely on them or to have confidence in the person making them; the presence or absence of any third person who might read or explain the instrument to him, or any other possibility of obtaining independent information; and the apparent necessity or lack of it, for acting without delay.

"Unless the misrepresentation meets this test, the defense is cut off by a holder in due course."

We observe that the inclusion of subsection (2) (c) in §3-305 of the Uniform Commercial Code was an attempt to codify or make definite the rulings of many jurisdictions on the question as to the liability to a holder in due course of a party who either had knowledge, or a reasonable opportunity to obtain the knowledge, of the essential terms of the instrument, before signing. Many courts were in the past called upon to determine this question under the Uniform Negotiable Instruments Law. Almost all of the courts that were called upon to rule on this question required a showing of freedom from negligence, in order to constitute a good defense against a bona fide holder of negotiable paper.

The reason for the rule, both as it was applied under the Negotiable Instruments Law and as is warranted under the Uniform Commercial Code, is that when one of two innocent persons must suffer by the act of a third, the loss must be borne by the one who enables the third person to occasion it.

We believe that the test set out in Comment No. 7 above quoted is a proper one and should be adhered to by us. . . Thus the only question is whether, under the facts of this case, the misrepresentations were such as to be a defense as against a holder in due course.

Applying the elements of the test to the case before us, Mrs. Burchett was 47 years old and had a ninth grade education, and Mr. Burchett was approximately the same age, but his education does not appear. Mr. Burchett was a foreman of the sanitation department of the city of Clovis and testified that he was familiar with some legal documents. Both the Burchetts understood English and there was no showing that they lacked ability to read. Both were able to understand the original form of contract which was submitted to them. As to the Beevers, Mrs. Beevers was 38 years old and had been through the ninth grade. Mr. Beevers had approximately the same education, but his age does not appear. However, he had been working for the same firm for about nine years and knew a little something about mortgages, at least to the extent of having one upon his property. Mrs. Beevers was employed in a supermarket, and it does not appear that either of the Beevers had any difficulty with the English language and they made no claim that they were unable to understand it. Neither the Beevers nor the Burchetts had ever had any prior association with Kelly and the papers were signed upon the very day that they first met him. There was no showing of any reason why they should rely upon Kelly or have confidence in him. The occurrences took place in the homes of the defendants, but other than what appears to be Kelly's "chicanery," no reason was given which would warrant a reasonable person in acting as hurriedly as was done in this case. None of the defendants attempted to obtain any independent information either with respect to Kelly or Consolidated Products, nor did they seek out any other person to read or explain the instruments to them. As a matter of fact, they apparently didn't believe this was necessary because, like most people, they wanted to take advantage of "getting something for nothing." There is no dispute but that the plaintiff did not have actual knowledge of the nature of the instruments which they signed, at the time they signed them. Defendant urges that plaintiffs had a reasonable opportunity to obtain such knowledge but failed to do so, were therefore negligent, and that their defense was precluded.

We recongize that the reasonable opportunity to obtain knowledge may be excused if the maker places reasonable reliance on the representations. The difficulty in the instant case is that the reliance upon the representations of a complete stranger (Kelly) was not reasonable, and all of the parties were of sufficient age, intelligence, education, and business experience to know better. . . See *First National Bank of Philadelphia v. Anderson*, which held that the mere failure to read a contract was not sufficient to allow the maker a defense under §3-305 of the Uniform Commercial Code. In our opinion, the plaintiffs here are barred for the reasons hereinabove stated.

Although we have sympathy with the plaintiffs, we cannot allow it to influence our decision. They were certainly victimized, but because of their failure to exercise ordinary care for their own protection, an innocent party cannot be made to suffer.

■ ■ ■

Questions and Notes

1. In *Burchett* the makers were asserting the defense of fraud. Since there are different kinds of fraud, the plaintiffs were attempting to assert the fraud that is a good defense against a holder in due course. This fraud is called fraud in the essence or fraud in the factum. How would you define this type of fraud? Why were the plaintiffs not able to establish fraud in the essence?

2. Allied Concord Financial Corp. was a holder in due course of the notes and mortgages. Suppose that subsequently, newspaper reports of the defenses of the makers were made known to the world. Thereafter, purchasers of the notes, with notices of the defenses, could not become holders in due course. Purchasers would be most hesitant to buy the instrument. This inability of the present holder to further negotiate the instrument would frustrate the purpose of negotiable instrument law. Therefore, to avoid this result the Shelter Doctrine allows buyers of the instrument, in spite of their knowledge of the defenses of the maker at the time they purchased the instrument, to acquire the "rights" of the transferor-holder in due course. The doctrine "shelters" purchasers of an instrument from a holder in due course by giving the purchasers the rights of the seller (his holder in due course status). Since Allied Concord Financial Corp. could easily recover as a holder in due course, allowing its transferee to take Allied's "rights" as a holder in due course would not change the legal liabilities of the maker of the instrument. Consequently, the Shelter Doctrine enhances the marketability of the instrument by providing a "market" in which a holder in due course can more readily sell the instrument. Therefore, a purchaser from Allied Concord Financial Corp. could acquire the "rights" of a holder in due course even if they knew of the fraudulent transaction with the Burchetts and Beevers.

3. Because of cases like the Burchetts and the Beevers, numerous commentators have argued that the holder-in-due-course concept is an unfair law when applied in consumer sales. They maintain that financial institutions should not be allowed to collect payment from the consumer when the consumer has not received a fair value from the merchant-seller. State legislative and judicial attempts to modify the holder-in-due-course concept in consumer sales have only been modestly successful. Consequently, after several years of extensive hearings and investigations, the Federal Trade Commission in 1975 adopted a Trade Regulation Rule which provides that:

> In connection with any sale or lease of goods or services to consumers, in or affecting commerce as "commerce" is defined in the Federal Trade Commission Act, it is an unfair or deceptive act or practice within the meaning of Section 5 of that Act for a seller, directly or indirectly to:
> (a) Take or receive a consumer credit contract which fails to contain the following provision in at least ten point, bold face, type:

NOTICE

AN HOLDER OF THIS CONSUMER CREDIT CONTRACT IS SUBJECT TO ALL CLAIMS AND DEFENSES WHICH THE DEBTOR COULD ASSERT AGAINST THE SELLER OF GOODS OR SERVICES OBTAINED PURSUANT HERETO OR WITH THE PROCEEDS HEREOF, RECOVERY HEREUNDER BY THE DEBTOR SHALL NOT EXCEED AMONTS PAID BY THE DEBTOR HEREUNDER.

or, (b) Accept, as full or partial payment for such sale or lease, the *proceeds* of any purchase money loan (as purchase money loan is defined herein), unless any consumer credit contract made in connection with such purchase money loan contains the following provision in at least ten point, bold face, type:

NOTICE
ANY HOLDER OF THIS CONSUMER CREDIT CONTRACT IS
SUBJECT TO ALL CLAIMS AND DEFENSES WHICH THE
DEBTOR COULD ASSERT AGAINST THE SELLER OF GOODS
OR SERVICES OBTAINED PURSUANT HERETO OR WITH
THE PROCEEDS HEREOF, RECOVERY HEREUNDER BY THE
DEBTOR SHALL NOT EXCEED AMOUNTS PAID BY THE
DEBTOR HEREUNDER.

The FTC Rule protects the rights of consumers who purchase on credit and incur obligations to financial institutions by preserving the consumers' claims and defenses. The consumers' claims and defenses could not be cut off by a purchaser of an instrument containing a "notice" like that above. Failure to include this notice provision subjects the merchant-seller to prosecution by the FTC for violating its rules. As a result, the holder in due course doctrine is no longer effective in retail installment sales to consumers. Results as occurred in *Burchett* will thereby be avoided.

UNAUTHORIZED INDORSEMENTS

A forged or unauthorized indorsement is wholly inoperative as the indorsement of the person whose name has been written. Acordingly, the possessor of "order" paper with a forge indorsement is not the owner of the instrument. If payment of a negotiable instrument is made to one who claims ownership through a forged indorsement, the payor has improperly paid the instrument and has not thereby extinguished his liability to the rightful owner of the paper. The payor must pay the instrument again to the rightful owner unless the true owner is barred by negligence from asserting any claim against the payor. Anyone receiving payment on an instrument received through a forged or unauthorized indorsement becomes a converter because the person has dealt with the instrument without having ownership therein, inconsistent with the true owner's property rights in the instrument. As such, the true owner may recover the value of the instrument from the converting party, unless the true owner is by some negligence precluded from recovery. The following two cases deal with unauthroized indorsements and how liability on the instrument may be shifted because of the negligence of one of the parties.

SALSMAN v. NATIONAL COMMUNITY BANK OF RUTHERFORD
246 A 2d 162 (1968)
Supreme Court of New Jersey

■ ■ ■

Plaintiffs, payee and special indorsee of a check, sue defendant collecting bank for applying the proceeds of the check to the account of an attorney, Harold Breslow, who improperly indorsed the check...

In May 1965 plaintiff Elizabeth A Odgers (now Elizabeth A. Salsman) retained an attorney, Harold Breslow, to handle matters arising out of the death of her husband Arthur J. Odgers...

Arthur J. Odgers had been an officer and stockholder in a company in which he had a one-third interest. He participated in the company's profit-sharing plan and had designated his wife as sole beneficiary. In payment of benefits under the plan, Mrs. Odgers received a cashier's check of the First National City Bank made out to her order in the amount of $159,770.02. The check is dated August 13, 1965. Breslow then informed Mrs. Odgers that the check was not hers but belonged to the estate, and that the proceeds must be held in a separate account for payment of taxes and other purposes. Mrs. Odgers was told by Breslow that the check "must be put in the estate account of Arthur Odgers"...

Breslow wrote on the back of the cashier's check, "Pay to the order of Estate of Arthur J. Odgers." He requested Mrs. Odgers to indorse the check in this fashion, and she did so. Under this special indorsement, when he was no longer in the presence of Mrs. Odgers, Breslow wrote, "Estate of Arthur J. Odgers—for deposit Harold Breslow, Trustee." Under this purported indorsement Breslow's secretary then wrote, "For deposit Harold Breslow Trustee." Mrs. Odgers had no knowledge of the subsequent indorsement. The check was then sent by mail to defendant National Community Bank of Rutherford for collection, and the proceeds were collected and deposited in Breslow's general trustee account. Defandant bank did not inquire into the authority of Breslow to indorse the checks for the estate. There was no estate account in defendant's bank, although Mrs. Odgers had qualified as administratix of the estate on July 9, 1965.

From August 1965 until March 1966 Mrs. Odgers inquired of Breslow on many occasions as to the status of the profit-sharing funds... As time passed Mrs. Odgers became more suspicious and began to investigate the disposition of the funds...

Mrs. Odgers then contacted another attorney and he assisted her in further investigation... An appointment was then made with Breslow for March 30. On that date, at his office, Breslow confessed to Mrs. Odgers and her present husband, Salsman, that he had appropriated the funds to his own use... Breslow has since pleaded guilty to the charge of embezzlement and misappropriation of funds and is presently serving a prison sentence. He also resigned from the New Jersey Bar. In April 1966 Mrs. Odgers started an action against Breslow and on June 3, 1966 obtained judgment in her favor. Some monies were recovered by execution on that judgment. The balance not yet recovered is $117,437.43...

In the absence of defenses such as negligence, estoppel or ratification, the payee is entitled to recover against a bank making collection from the drawee based upon a forged or unauthorized indorsement of a check... This has been the established law throughout the country...

The check in question was indorsed by the payee. Mrs. Odgers, to the order of the Estate of Arthur J. Odgers. There was no valid indorsement thereafter by the estate of Arthur J. Odgers. [The U.C.C.] provides that an instrument may be payable to the order of "an estate, trust or fund, in which case it is payable to the order to the representative of such estate, trust or fund ***." The check was not indorsed by the administratrix of the estate, the only person who had authority in law to indorse the check. Breslow was not a trustee of the estate, and the purported indorsement for the estate by "Harold Breslow, Trustee" was unauthorized and ineffective. Breslow testified that he never told plaintiff that he would act as her agent. His purported indorsement was not authorized as the agent for the administratrix nor as a representative of the estate...

The check in question could not be negotiated without an authorized indorsement of the special indorsee, the estate of Arthur J. Odgers. [The U.C.C.] provides that "Any unauthorized signature is wholly inoperative as that of the person whose name is signed unless he ratifies it or is precluded from denying it ***." There is no evidence in this case which shows a ratification by Mrs. Odgers of the conduct of Breslow; there has been nothing shown to preclude her from denying the indorsements in question, and there is no evidence of any negligence on her part which contributed to the misapplication of the funds.

Mrs. Odgers had relied upon an attorney who was then reputable. She followed his instructions and was not negligent in assuming that the check would be deposited into the estate account after she indorsed it to the order of the estate... Although she had not signed signature cards as administratrix in order to open such an account, Mrs. Odgers cannot be held negligent on the theory that she should have suspected that the check might not have been deposited in an estate account. Mrs. Odgers made repeated inquiries concerning the funds and was given various explanations by Breslow as to their disposition and as to her inability to deal with them at the stage in the administration of the estate. Her conduct was not unreasonable or imprudent.

Receiving the funds without a proper indorsement and crediting the funds to one not entitled thereto constitutes a conversion of the funds. A holder is one who receives an instrument which is indorsed to his order or in blank...

The bank cannot be a holder, or a holder in due course... without a valid indorsement of this check by the estate of Arthur J. Odgers. 3-419(1)(c) provides that an instrument is converted when it is paid on a forged indorsement. 1-201(43) provides that an unauthorized signature or indorsement is one made without authority (actual, implied or apparent) and includes a forgery...

3-419(3) clearly implies the liability of a depositary or collecting bank in conversion when it deals with an instrument or its proceeds on behalf of one who is not the true owner, where the bank does not act in accordance with "reasonable commercial standards." Defendant did not act in accordance with reasonable commercial standards... In the *Teas v. Third National Bank and Trust Co.*, the Court... held... that a depositary bank was derelict in its duty to the check's payee in failing to inquire as to an attorney's right to indorse the check and place the proceeds in his own account to his own credit. The court held that the form of the checks, payable to an executor and to an estate, put the bank on notice that the attorney had no power to do what he did, and that the bank's breach of its duty to make appropriate inquiry rendered it liable to the payee...

In the present case there are sufficient facts to justify the conclusion that defendant bank is liable regardless of how we view the conduct of Mrs. Odgers in giving the check to Breslow...[T]he indorsement purportedly made on behalf of the estate was a "for deposit" indorsement, a restrictive indorsement. This is another fact which should have alerted the bank to a misapplication of the funds...

Thus, even if the indorsement for the estate had been authorized, defendant bank would be liable for failing to deposit the proceeds to the credit of the estate as required by that indorsement...

■ ■ ■

Questions

1. What kind of indorsement did Mrs. Odgers make on the back of the cashier's check from the insurance company? Did Breslow have the authority to indorse for the estate of Arthur J. Odgers?
2. Did the National Community Bank of Rutherford have a valid indorsement (ownership) for collection of the proceeds of the check? What should the bank have done to protect itself from this type of error?
3. Was the National Community Bank of Rutherford negligent in another regard? What did the "for deposit only" indorsement indicate? What was the bank's duty in relation to this restrictive indorsement?

IMPOSTER RULE

The UCC contains a body of rules involving situations in which the payee's name on an negotiable instrument is forged, but the indorsement is ruled effective. The law makes the forgery effective only for the purpose of transferring the loss away from the bank which normally would absorb the loss because it dealt with an instrument with a forged indorsement. The loss is transferred to the drawer of the instrument because his or her behavior has been less than acceptable to society's standards in relation to negotiable instruments. The following case illustrates one of those instances. The reader should consider the question; "As between the drawer of the check and the bank who paid over a forged indorsement, who should bear the loss?"

PHILADELPHIA TITLE INSURANCE CO v. FIDELITY-PHILADELPHIA TRUST CO.
212 A. 2d 222 (1965)
Supreme Court of Pennsylvania

■ ■ ■

Edmund Jezemski and Paula Jezemski were husband and wife, estranged and living apart. Edmund Jezemski was administrator and sole heir of his deceased mother's estate, one of the assets of which was premises 1130 North Fortieth Street, Philadelphia. Mrs. Jezemski, without her husband's knowledge, arranged for a mortgage to be placed on this real estate. This mortgage was obtained for Mrs. Jezemski through John M. McAllister, a member of the Philadelphia Bar, and Anthony DiBenedetto, a real estate dealer, and was to be insured by Philadelphia Title Insurance Company, the plaintiff. Shortly before the date set for settlement at the office of the title company, Mrs. Jezemski represented to McAllister and DiBenedetto that her husband would be unable to attend the settlement. She came to McAllister's office in advance of the settlement date, accompanied by a man whom she introduced to McAllister and DiBenedetto as her husband. She and this man, in the presence of McAllister and DiBenedetto, executed a deed conveying the real estate from the estate toEdmund Jezemski and Paula Jezemski... and also executed the mortgage... which had been prepared. McAllister and DiBenedetto, accompanied by Mrs. Jezemski, met at the office of the title company on the date appointed for settlement, the signed deed and mortgage were produced, the mortgagee handed over the amount of the mortgage, and the title company delivered its check to Mrs. Jezemski for the net proceeds of $15,640.82, made payable... to Mr. and Mrs. Jezmski individually and Mr. Jezemski as administrator of his mother's estate...

Paula Jezemski, one of the payees... presented (the check), with purported endorsements of all the payees, at the Penns Grove National Bank and Trust Company in Penns Grove, New Jersey, for cash. Edmund Jezemski received none of the proceeds, either individually or as administrator of the estate of Sofia Jezemski; and it is conceded that the endorsements purporting to be his were forged. The Penns Grove bank negotiated the check through the Philadelphia National Bank, and it was eventually paid by Fidelity-Philadelphia Trust Company, which charged the amount of the check against the deposit account of plaintiff...

There is no question that the man whom Mrs. Jezemski introduced to McAllister and DiBenedetto was not Edmund Jezemski, her husband. It was sometime later that Edmund Jezemski, when he tried to convey the real estate, discovered the existence of the mortgage. When he did so he instituted an action in equity which resulted in the setting aside of the deed and mortgage and the repayment of the fund advanced by the mortgagee.

The parties do not dispute the proposition that as between the payor bank (Fidelity-Philadelphia) and its customer (Title Company), the former must bear the loss occasioned by the forgery of a payee's endorsement (Edmund Jezemski) upon a check drawn by its customer and payed by it...

However, the banks argue that this case falls within an exception to the above rule, making the forged indorsement of Edmund Jezemski's name effective so that Fidelity-Philadelphia was entitled to charge the account of its customer, the Title Company, who was the drawer of the check. The exception asserted by the banks is found in §3-405(1) (a) of the Uniform Commercial Code-Commercial Paper which provides:

"An indorsement by any person in the name of a named payee is effective if (a) an imposter by use of the mails or otherwise has induced the maker or drawer to issue the instrument to him or his confederate in the name of the payee; * * *."

The lower court found and the Title Company does not dispute that an imposter appeared before McAllister and DiBenedetto, impersonated Mr. Jezemski, and, in their presence, signed Mr. Jezemski's name to the deed, bond and mortgage; that Mrs. Jezemski was a confederate of the impostor; that the drawer, Title Company, issued the check to Mrs. Jezemski naming her and Mr. Jezemski as payees; and that some person other than Mrs. Jezemski indorsed his name on the check. In effect, the only agrument made by the Title Company to prevent the applicability of Section 3-405(1)

(a) is that the imposter, who admittedly played a part in the swindle, *did not "by the mails or otherwise" induce the Title Company* to issue the check within the meaning of Section 3-405(1) (a). The argument must fail.

Both the words of Section 3-405(1) (a) and the official Comment thereto leave no doubt that the imposter can induce the drawer to issue him or his confederate a check within the meaning of the section even though he does not carry out his impersonation before the very eyes of the drawer. Section 3-405 (1) (a) says the inducement might be by "the mails or otherwise.". . .

Moreover, the Legislature's use of the word "otherwise" and the Comment, which suggests that results should not turn upon "the type of fraud which the particular imposter committed," indicates that the Legislature did not intend to limit the applicability of the section to cases where the imposter deals directly with the drawer (face-to-face, mails, telephone, etc.). Naturally, the Legislature could not have predicted and expressly included all the ingenious schemes designed and carried out by imposters for the purpose of defrauding the makers or drawers of negotiable instruments. Something had to be left for the courts by way of statutory construction. For purposes of imposing the loss on one or two "innocent" parties, either the drawer who was defrauded or the drawee bank which payed out on a forged endorsement, we see no reason for distinguishing between the drawer who is duped by an impersonator communicating directly with him through the mails and a drawer who is duped by an impersonator communicating indirectly with him through third persons. Thus, both the language of the Code and common sense dictates that the drawer must suffer the loss in both instances. . . .

■ ■ ■

Questions

1. How could the Trust Co. protect itself from this type of loss? Who is in a better position to stop this type of injury — the bank or the drawer?
2. Suppose Widget Co. employs a bookkeeper, Smart, who prepares company paychecks. Smart prepares a paychcek for eight hours of overtime work to Joe Worker. However, Joe never worked the overtime and doesn't expect or receive the check. Smart indorses "Joe Worker" and then deposits the check to his own account. When the check clears, it is returned to Widget Co. who allows Smart to reconcile the bank statement. After several years of this practice, the Widget Co. sues the bank for paying on checks with forged indorsements. Should Widget Co. recover against the bank?

NEGLIGENT PREPARATION OF CHECKS

PARK STATE BANK v. ARENA AUTO AUCTION, INC.
207 N.E. 2d 158 (1965)
Appellate Court of Illinois

■ ■ ■

This case comes into Court by reason of certain mistakes made by employees of the involved parties following the normal routine of customary business details so characteristic of the rapidly changing society and world in which we live.

Defendant, Arena Auto Auction, Inc., created the problem brought to court by the issuance of its check dated December 17, 1963, and by the mailing of it to Plunkett Auto Sales, Rockford, Illinois. For clarity's sake, we will refer to the Rockford Plunkett and the Alabama Plunkett by the geographical designations rather than by their corporate names. . . Rockford Tom Plunket might well have felt, upon receiving said check, that he was the recipient of some give-away or promotional scheme, for it later appears that he had sold no merchandise, a fact of which he was well aware, to the

Defendant. We might visualize Rockford Tom Plunkett as a fast-thinking, old-time horse trader, now engaged in the business of buying and selling used automobiles. He, being well known to the Plaintiff Bank by reason of his borrowing and having cashed one previous check of the Defendant, after holding this check from December 17th or 18th until January 3rd, 1964, and after due reflection on his part, signed his name to the check and presented it for payment to Charlotte Parish, head teller, who, promptly and without question, turned over to him the check-designated sum of $1,435.00.

On January 9, 1964, the said check was returned to the Plaintiff Bank by reason of a stop-payment order by the maker, and came into the hands of the Assistant Vice-President, Mr. Marconi, whose duties are to assist in the operation of the financial institution, to know its customers, and, equally, to earn a profit for the Plaintiff. Vice-President Marconi promptly called his personal friend, Jack Clark of the Arena Auto Auction, Inc., who, to cover the shortcomings of his secretary, called at the Plaintiff Bank on January 10, 1964, to make the explanation. Now, Jack Clark, being in the business of operating a automobile auction and using the speed of their operation to explain the error, commented thus: "This guy here (meaning Rockford Tom Plunkett) wasn't supposed to get the check. It was another Plunket in Alabama. But Alabama Plunkett wasn't in our books, so that's why our gals sent the check to Rockford Plunkett, and that's why we stopped payment on our check."

But, to put the frosting on the cake, or as Counsel put it, to add insult to injury, Defendant, Arena Auto Auction, Inc., issued their second check in the same amount to the same payee, and again sent the check to Rockford Tom Plunkett. Again we can visualize quick-thinking Rockford Tom Plunkett's surprise, for this truly must come from the money tree. He loses no time in going to the same financial institution as before. Not so fortunate on this second occasion, poor Rockford Tom Plunkett, as he tendered the second check, is questioned as to why payment was stopped on the first one. In his effort to secure quick payment he stated, "This check is to replace the first. Cash this check, give me back the first one, and I will return it to the Arena Auto Auction."

Mindful of the first experience, the Vice-President was reluctant to follow this advice and informed poor Tom that he was in difficulty. Rockford Tom Plunkett, seeing that the Vice-President could be right, promptly left the State of Illinois and established his abode in a more sunny climate...

So now we find the Plaintiff Bank in the embarrassing position of having cashed a check and having had payment of that check stopped. Desirous of not losing money, they start suit to recover from the Arena Auto Auction...(The trial judge)...decided in favor of the Plaintiff and against the Arena Auto Auction, Inc., who appeals to this Court.

From a purely legal point of view, there are two questions raised. First, did Rockford Tom Plunkett commit a forgery by signing his own name to a check ostensibly issued to him. Without passing on the very technical question of whether or not these facts constitute a forgery, this is apparently admitted by all parties concerned, for they cite cases in the Trial Court and in this Court, holding that a forgery passes no title by which one can recover as a bar to the Plaintiff recovering. The Plaintiff Bank relies upon Chapter 26, Illinois Revised Statutes, 1963, Section 3—406; which, being a new section of our Commercial Code, is as follows:

> "Any person who by his negligence substantially contributes to a material alteration of the instrument or to the making of an unauthorized signature is precluded from asserting the alteration or lack of authority against a holder in due course or against a drawee or other payor who pays the instrument in good faith in accordance with the reasonable commercial standards of the drawee's or payor's business."

Without repeating the various errors previously recited, it appears to this Court presumptuous on the part of Arena Auto Auction, Inc., Defendant, to insist that they did nothing for which they should be held accountable. We point out the interval of lapsed time before they, in their fast-thinking, fast-operating business, decide first to stop payment.

Secondly, bearing in mind the erroneous sending of a second check to the same payee, and considering the custom of the trade as set forth by the testimony of the several gentlemen of the financial world as to the routine handling of checks in banking institutions, it is our considered conclusion that to require the recipient Bank to stop and question persons known to that Bank and presenting checks in routine business and issued by makers likewise known to the Bank, would be placing cogs in the wheels of business, which, in turn, would bring those wheels of the banking business to an astounding and abrupt halt. This, as we see it, was neither the intent nor the purpose of our legislators in passing the section in our Commercial Code to which reference was made.

We, therefore and accordingly, do conclude that the Trial Court was correct in holding that the Defendant, by their own negligence, substantially assisted in making it possible that an unauthorized person's signature passed title to the funds represented by said check.

■ ■ ■

Questions

1. Did Rockford Tom Plunkett committ forgery by signing his own name to a check which was meant to be issued to another?
2. The court determined that the Arena Auto Auction, Inc. was precluded from recovery because of its negligence. What did the court identify as negligent behavior?

SECURED TRANSACTIONS

Historically, numerous credit devices were utilized to provide a creditor with protection beyond his or her right to sue the debtor. Such devices afford the creditor the right to repossess certain properties in the hands of the debtor. These devices are known as "secured transactions" and are governed by the law in Article 9 of the UCC.

A secured credit sale is a sale in which possession of certain property passes to the buyer but the seller retains a "security interest" in the goods until the buyer has paid in full. The seller's security interest entitles him or her to repossess the goods when the buyer fails to make a required payment or in some other way commits a breach of the purchase contract. The right of repossession is in addition to the lender's right to sue for the contractual indebtedness.

The UCC is not designed solely to aid creditors. Article 9 has also increased the protection given to buyers over that which was available under former law. However, numerous commentators feel that Article 9 is unfairly balanced in favor of creditors and, consequently, special consumer protection statutes have been enacted in some jurisdictions to increase the protection available to debtor-buyers.

A security interest for the protection of the creditor arises when the debtor grants such security interest to the creditor by a written security agreement signed by the debtor and describes the property involved, called collateral. The description of the collateral need only reasonably identify such property and is sufficient when it would enable a third person aided by additional information to determine which goods were involved. The security interest of the creditor and the right of repossession can be effective not only against the debtor, but also against the creditors of the debtor and purchasers of the collateral from the debtor (if the creditor takes the appropriate legal steps). When the creditor's security interest becomes effective against third persons (in addition to the debtor), it is said to be "perfected." The usual way of perfecting a security interest is to file a "financing statement" in some public recorder's office. The filing of this document gives "notice" to other parties of the existence of the secured transaction between the debtor and creditor. As such, other parties may modify their transactions and dealings with the debtor in light of this knowledge concerning the secured creditor's priority over certain property (the collateral) in the hands of the debtor.

Article 9 defines different categories of property and provides different rules for each category. A *consumer good* is a good which is used or bought primarily for personal, family, or household purpose. It is the intended use, rather than the nature of the article, which determines its categorical definition. For example, any goods purchased for resale to consumers would not be a consumer good in the hands of such resaler. Instead, the merchant's purchase of goods with the intention of resale is categorized as *inventory*. Likewise, *equipment* used in business is not a consumer good, nor inventory. Depending upon the type of property involved, the filing requirements and other rules of law vary.

CREATION OF THE SECURITY INTEREST

MOSLEY v. DALLAS ENTERTAINMENT COMPANY, INC.
496 S.W. 2d 237 (1973)
Court of Civil Appeals of Texas

■ ■ ■

Dallas Entertainment Company, Inc. sued Bill Mosley for conversion of a cash register alleging that plaintiff was a secured party under a security agreement covering the cash register and that defendant, Mosley, had purchased the cash register from the plaintiff's debtor without its consent and had sold same to a third party. The trial court sitting without a jury, granted judgment against defendant, Bill Mosley, in the amount of $950.00, from which judgment defendant...appeals....

The evidence shows that in June, 1970, plaintiff, Dallas Entertainment Company, Inc., was the holding company for a private club located in Dallas and known as the Music Box. Plaintiff sold the entire club to Follies Buffet of Dallas, Inc. Among the various items of personal property allegedly sold with the club was a certain cash register. In connection with the sale of the club, a financing statement was prepared showing Dallas Entertainment Company as the secured party and Follies Buffet of Dallas, Inc., as debtor. The financing statement was filed in the office of the Texas Secretary of State on July 2, 1970...

Defendant, Bill Mosley, was in the business of buying and selling used cash registers and does not dispute the fact that he purchased the cash register from Follies Buffet in December, 1970, and that he subsequently sold the cash register to a customer in the course of his business. It is not contended that defendant had actual knowledge of plaintiff's alleged security interests in the cash register....

...Defendant attacks the judgment on the ground that there is no evidence or alternatively that the evidence is insufficient to show plaintiff was a secured party under a Security Agreement executed by the debtor because plaintiff failed to produce a written security agreement...

In reply plaintiff contends first that there is competent oral testimony to prove the existence of a security agreement and secondly that the financing statement itself amounts to a security agreement...

In paragraph 5 of the Uniform Commercial Code Comment following Section 9.203, we find this statement:

> "The formal requisites stated in this Section are not only conditions to the enforceability of a security interest against third parties. They are in the nature of a Statute of Frauds. Unless the secured party is in possession of the collateral, his security interest, absent a writing which satisfies subsection (1)(b), is not enforceable even against the debtor, and cannot be made so on any theory * * *"

In American Card Company, Inc. v. H. M. H. Co., 196 A.2d 150 (1966), the court specifically rejected the argument that the security agreement could be established by parol, stating that oral assertions were without probative force to supply the absence of a required security agreement in writing. . . .

Since the foregoing statute requires the secured party to show that the debtor has signed a security agreement containing a description of the collateral, we hold that the oral testimony of the secured party is without probative force to establish a security interest for the simple reason that it fails to satisfy the statutory requirement that the security agreement be in writing and signed by the debtor.

This brings us to the question of whether the judgment may be sustained on the theory that the financing statement amounts to a security agreement. The financing statement in this case appears to have been written on the Secretary of State's standard form. As noted above, it recites a general description of the collateral in which a security interest is claimed. It is signed by the creditor, plaintiff, and by a party alleged to be the agent of Follies. . . Nowhere in the instrument does it grant the creditor a security interest in the collateral nor does it identify the obligation owed to the creditor.

The code makes no provisions for a naked financing statement to be enforced as a security agreement. It merely gives notice of the existence of a security iterest but in itself does not create a security interest. A financing statement cannot serve as a security agreement where it does not grant the creditor an interest in the collateral and does not identify the obligation owed to the creditor. Since the financing statement offered by plaintiff fails to contain any language showing the alleged debtor granted the creditor (plaintiff) an interest in the collateral and since plaintiff was unable to produce a written security agreement signed by defendant, plaintiff failed to establish a cause of action. It therefore follows that the judgment must be reversed and rendered in favor of defendant.

■ ■ ■

Questions

1. Why did the court rule the pro-offered evidence could not be used to establish the existence of a security agreement?
2. Why was the financing statement not sufficient as a security agreement? Did the financing statement omit some "magic word"?
3. What are the basic elements of a security agreement? What are the basic elements of the financing statement?

PURCHASE MONEY SECURITY INTERESTS

Secured transactions often arise in either of two situations. First, a person desires to purchase goods but lacks the cash or the necessary credit rating to get the goods on open credit, so the seller retains a security interest in the goods sold. Secondly, the potential buyer secures financing from a third party who takes a security interest in the goods purchased to secure the repayment of the loan. Either type of arrangement is called a "purchase money security interest" because the security interest is taken or retained to secure the payment of the *purchase* price. Consequently, a purchase money security interest arises whenever the lender supplies the funds that purchase the collateral. Since the lender is supplying funds to purchase goods on credit and thereby aiding the selling of goods which help promote the health of the nation's economy, the purchase money security interest holder is often given a preferred status under the law. One instance of the preferred status is illustrated in the following case which involves a "floating lien." It will be noted that the rights of the purchase money security interest holder may take priority (if he takes the proper steps to protect himself) over the holder of the floating lein.

"FLOATING LIEN"

The "floating lien" concept was created with the enactment of Article 9 of the UCC. To create the security interest in goods called a "floating lien,"the Code requires a written security agreement with certain provisions. The security agreement must include a provision that the collateral, *whenever acquired*, secures the indebtedness under the agreement. This provision permits the goods, which may be broadly defined as all inventory or equipment, to vary. The items of inventory or equipment may be sold and replaced with sebsequent purchases which immediately become subject to the secured party's interests. It is not necessary to create a new security agreement each time that items are sold and replaced. The new items automatically become covered by the previous security agreement. It is as though there is "a floating lien," hovering above the collateral (inventory or equipment) at all times, despite sales or replacements in the broadly described collateral. The concept of a floating lien eliminates the burden of repetitive filing that was required under prior law. Once the floating lien holder has filed the financing statement in the recorder's office, no additional filing is needed as the inventory is sold or replaced. The financing statement is considered "notice" to all other would-be creditors of the debtor that the secured party has an interest in the goods in the hands of the debtor. Other creditors informed by the financing statement of the debtor-creditor relationship may modify their credit extension policies accordingly.

Often the floating lien language (whenever acquired) is followed by a provision covering *future advances* of funds. This provision means that new advances of funds can be made by the lender to the debtor and these funds are secured by the prior security interest which was created in the security agreement of the original loan. Therefore, the amount of the indebtedness may vary under this provision as payments of the debt are made and as the lender may choose to extend more loans to the debtor or additional inventory. A future advances provision makes unnecessary the execution of a new security agreement each time new funds are lent. When both the future advances provision and the after-acquired property clause are combined, the items of the collateral may change without defeating the secured party's interest in the collateral. New funds may be advanced to the debtor to secure new inventory on a continuous basis. The once executed security agreement and the once filed financing statement are sufficient for this continuing relationship between the debtor and creditor for an extended period of time (usually seven years). The floating lien concept and the future advances concept eliminated the repetitious creation of security agreements and financing statements required under the old law. As such, Article 9 greatly improves the processes of financing inventory and equipment.

The security interest holder of a floating lien is capable of being made secondary in priority by two parties. First, a purchaser from the merchant-debtor in an ordinary business transaction takes title to the goods free of the lender's security interest. This, of course, is what the lender expects, in that he or she anticipates repayment of the loan from the proceeds of such sale. The holder of the floating lien may not recover the good sold to the purchaser if the lien holder is unable to secure repayment of the debt from the debtor-merchant.

Secondly, the holder of a floating lien may become secondary in priority to a subsequent creditor who lends funds to the debtor on a purchase money basis. The sale of goods to the debtor-merchant on a purchase-money-security-interest basis creates a security interest in such seller that takes priority over the floating lien if the purchase money seller files his financing statement within ten days of giving possession of the sold item to the debtor-merchant and, in addition, notifies the floating lien holder of this sale on a purchase money basis. In this way, the debtor-merchant may expand his inventory lines or equipment needs and thereby secure new lines of credit from different sources in spite of the "floating lien" which hovers over all of his inventory or equipment. The new items are exempt from the floating lien and, instead, are pledged to the purchase-money-security-interest holder. However, should the seller on a purchase money basis not comply with necessary steps to gain priority over the floating lien, the goods would come under the floating lien of the original lender, who would gain priority to those goods on the debtor's default.

NATIONAL CASH REGISTER COMPANY v. FIRESTONE & CO.
191 N.E. 2d 471 (1963)
Supreme Court of Massachusetts

■ ■ ■

The underlying question is the relative standing of two security interests. On June 15, 1960, the plaintiff, a manufacturer of cash registers, and one Edmond Carroll, doing business in Canton as Kozy Kitchen, entered into a conditional sale contract for a cash register. On November 18, 1960, the defendant, which was in the financing business, made a loan to Carroll, who conveyed certain personal property to the defendant as collateral under a security agreement. The defendant filed a financing statement with the Town Clerk of Canton on November 22, 1960. Between November 19 and November 25 the plaintiff delivered a cash register to Carroll in Canton. On November 25, the contract of June 15 was canceled and superseded by a new contract for the same cash register but provided for different terms of payment. The plaintiff filed a financing statement with respect to this contract with the Town Clerk of Canton on December 20 and with the Secretary of State on December 21. Carroll subsequently became in default both on the contract with the plaintiff and on the security agreement with the defendant. In December the defendant took possession of the cash register, and although notified on January 17, 1961, of the plaintiff's asserted right sold it at auction on the following day.

The defendant's security agreement recites that Carroll in consideration of $1,911 paid by it does "hereby grant, sell, assign, transfer and deliver to Grantee the following goods, chattels, and automobiles, namely: The business located at and numbered 574 Washington Street, Canton, Mass. together with all its good-will, fixtures, equipment and merchandise. The fixtures specifically consist of the following: *All contents of luncheonette including equipment such as: booths and tables; stand and counter; tables; chairs; booths; steam tables; salad unit; potato peeler; U.S. Slicer; range; case; fryer; compressor; bobtail; milk dispenser; silex; 100 Class air conditioner; signs; pastry case; mixer; dishes; silverware; tables; hot fudge; Haven Ex.; 2 door station-wagon 1957 Ford A57R107215* together with all property and articles now, and which may hereafter be, used or mixed with, added or attached to, and/or substituted for, any of the foregoing described property."

In the defendant's financing statement the detailed description of the "types (or items) of property" is the same as the words in supplied italics in the security agreement. There is no specific reference to a cash register in either document, and no mention in the defendant's financing statement of property to be acquired thereafter.

Under the Uniform Commercial Code after-acquired property, such as this cash register, might become subject to the defendant's security agreement when delivered and likewise its delivery under a conditional sale agreement with retention of title in the plaintiff would not, in and of itself, affect the rights of the defendant. Although the plaintiff could have completely protected itself by perfecting its interest before or within ten days of the delivery of the cash register to Carroll, it did not try to do so until more than ten days after delivery. Thus the principal issue is whether the defendant's earlier security interest effectively covers the cash register...

Contrary to the plaintiff's contention, we are of opinion that the security agreement is broad enough to include the cash register, which concededly did not have to be specifically described. The agreement covers "All contents of luncheonette including equipment such as," which we think covers all those contents and does not mean "equipment, to wit." There is a reference to "all property and articles now, and which may hereafter be, used * * * with, (or) added * * * to* * * any of the foregoing described property." We infer that the cash register was used with some of the other equipment even though the case stated does not expressly state that the luncheonette was operated.

We now come to the question whether the defendant's financing statement should have metioned property to be acquired thereafter before a security interest in the cash register could attach. The code. . . reads in part: "A financing statement is sufficient if it is signed by the debtor and the secured party, gives an address of the secured party from which information concerning the security interest may be obtained, gives a mailing address of the debtor and contains a statement indicating the types, or describing the items, of collateral."

In this official comment to this section appears the following: "2. This Section adopts the system of 'notice filing' which has proved successful under the Uniform Trust Receipts Act. What is required to be filed is not, as under chattel mortgage and conditional sales acts, the security agreement itself, but only a simple notice which may be filed before the security interest attaches or thereafter. The notice itself indicates merely that the secured party who has filed may have a security interest in the collateral described. Further inquiry from the parties concerned will be necessary to disclose the complete state of affairs. Section 9-208 provides a statutory procedure under which the secured party, at the debtor's request, may be required to make disclosure. Notice filing has proved to be of great use in financing transactions involving inventory, accounts and chattel paper, since it obviates the necessity of refiling on each of a series of transactions in a continuing arrangement where the collateral changes from day to day. Where other types of collateral are involved, the alternative procedure of filing a signed copy of the security agreement may prove to be the simplest solution."

The framers of the Uniform Commercial Code, by adopting the "notice filing" system, had the purpose to recommend a method of protecting security interest which as the same time would give subsequent potential creditors and other interested persons information and proceedures adequate to enable the ascertainment of the facts they needed to know. In this respect the completed Code reflects a decision of policy reached after several year's study and discussion by experts. We conceive our duty to be the making of an interpretation which will carry out the intention of the framers of uniform legislation. . .

In view of the broad purposes of the act we do not give a restrictive construction to the provision which sets forth what constitutes a "suficient" financing statement. The defendant's financing statement is signed by the debtor and the secured party and gives both the address of the latter from which information is be be obtained and the mailing address of the debtor. It is argued, however, that the "statement indicating the types, or describing the items, of collateral" is inadequate because it fails to include a reference to the after-acquired clause of its security agreement, and so it not a resonable identification of the cash register. . .

The words, "All contents of luncheonette," including, as we have held, all equipment, were enough to put the plaintiff on notice to ascertain what those contents were. This is not a harsh result as to the plaintiff, to which, as we have indicated, [The U.C.C.] made available a simple and sure procedure for completely protecting its purchase money security interest.

■ ■ ■

Questions

1. In the *NCR* case, did the financing statement of Firestone contain an "after-acquired property" clause? Was it necessary to make the "after-acquired property" language of the security agreement effective?
2. Did Firestone's financing statement contain "notice" of the after-acquired property clause in the security agreement?
3. The court said that NCR could have protected itself from defendant's "floating lien." How?

PROTECTION FROM A BONA FIDE PURCHASER OF COLLATERAL

STERLING ACEPTANCE CO. v. GRIMES
168 A. 2d 600 (1961)
Supreme Court of Pennsylvania

■ ■ ■

Sterling Acceptance Company brought action. . . against Patrick Grimes, Jr. and George Homish to obtain possession of a 1958 Dodge automobile which Grimes had purchased new from Homish, a dealer. . .

Homish, who traded as Homish Sales & Service, was an automobile dealer in Aliquippa, Beaver County, for approximately 40 years. On May 29, 1958 he sold Grimes a new 1958 Dodge automobile for which Grimes paid him the sale price in full, including the sales tax and the fee for registration of the title. Grimes paid Homish $2,060 in cash and transferred to Homish title to a 1955 Dodge automobile for which he was given an allowance of $1,636.14. Possession of the new Dodge was given to Grimes. An application for title to the new car was signed by Grimes and given to Homish for mailing to the Bureau of Motor Vehicles in Harrisburg. The purchase of the automobile by Grimes was made from Homish's inventory in the ordinary course of Homish's business at his place of business in Aliquippa. When the certificate of title did not arrive, Grimes contacted Homish several times, and was told that the delay was caused by the authorities in Harrisburg. Finally, after frequent evasions, Homish told Grimes that he was in financial difficulties and that he had not mailed the application for the certificate of title.

Over two years prior to the sale of the Dodge to Grimes, a Blanket Security Agreement was filed by the acceptance company in the office of the Prothonotary of Beaver County. The agreement covered a security interest of the plaintiff in the sale of all new and used vehicles by Homish. This agreement was filed in compliance with §9-302 of the Uniform Commercial Code of April 6, 1953. . .

Article 9 of the Uniform Commercial Code, supra, deals with secured transactions, including liens on personal property intended to be sold in the ordinary course of business. Section 9-307 provided: "(1) In the case of inventory and in the case of other goods as to which the secured party files a financing statement in which he claims a security interest even though perfected and even though the buyer knows of the terms of the security agreement.". . .

According to the comment on §9-307 of the Uniform Commercial Code, "The theory is that when goods are inventory or when proceeds are claimed the secured party contemplates that his debtor will make sales, and so the debtor has effective power to do so, even though his buyers know the goods they buy were subject to the security interest."

Under the provision of the Uniform Commercial Code, the plaintiff must look to Homish for repayment of the loan it made to him, and not to the automobile in the possession of Grimes, who paid the full purchase price to Homish.

■ ■ ■

Notes and Questions

1. U.C.C. Section 2-403 provides: " * * * (2) Any entrusting of possession of goods to a merchant who deals in goods of that kind gives him power to transfer all rights of the entruster to a buyer in ordinary course of business. (3) 'Entrusting' includes any delivery and any acquiescence in retention of possession regardless of any condition expressed between the parties to the delivery or acquiescence and regardless of whether the procurement of the entrusting or the possessor's disposition of the goods have been such as to be larcenous under the criminal law."

    Can you think of specific situations of "entrusting"? What do you suspect is the policy reason for such a law?

2. U.C.C. Section 9-302 (2) provides that, "The filing provisions of this Article do not apply *** to a security interest ***(b) in property subject to a statute of this state which provides for central filing of, or which requires indication on a certificate of title of, such security interests in such property. Compliance with any such statute is equivalent to filing under this article."

Can you think of any such property in your state subject to central filing or a certificate of title on which security interests are noted?

3. In *Sterling Acceptance v. Grimes*, Section 9-307 (1) says the buyer takes free of a security interest in goods classified as "inventory." Does this cover goods pledged to a merchant-creditor in the hands of a consumer-debtor who chooses to sell the goods? The next case deals with this problem.

U.G.I. v. McFALLS
18 D & C 2nd 713 (1959)
United States Bankruptcy Court

■ ■ ■

The complaint avers as follows: "On September 13, 1957, the plaintiff and Robert Henry, of 23 Parkside Avenue, Lancaster, Pennsylvania, entered into a written security agreement lease by which plaintiff sold to the said Robert Henry one household laundry dryer described in the security agreement lease as CD-85 Whirlpool Dryer. The dryer as delivered by the plaintiff to Robert Henry on September 18, 1957. By the terms of said security agreement lease, title to the dryer did not pass to Robert Henry until payments totaling $204.97 had been made to the plaintiff and a bill of sale for the dryer given by the plaintiff to Robert Henry...

In the month of January, 1958, Robert Henry failed to pay an installment of $8.54 due at that time under the said security agreement lease and has not paid any amount whatsoever since that time. By the terms of said security agreement lease, upon default in the payment of any installment for a period of ten days, the plaintiff is entitled to possession of the dryer. On or about the early part of March,, 1958, Robert Henry sold and delivered the dryer to the defendant. The defendant is a dealer in used household appliances and purchased the dryer for purposes of resale. On July 8, 1958, the plaintiff demanded of the defendant the return of the dryer to it but the defendant refused to return the dryer, and refuses to return the dryer at the present time. The value of the dryer at the time of its conversion by the defendant was $180.00."

Defendant, William H. McFalls,... raises but one question, namely: Does plaintiff have a cause of action against defendant because of plaintiff's failure to file a financing statement in accordance with the Uniform Commercial Code?

The Uniform Commercial Code defines "consumer goods" as goods "used or bought for use primarily for personal, family or household purposes." There can be no question, therefore, that the description in the complaint of the article sold to Robert Henry as "one household laundry dryer" is within the above definition of "consumer goods." The question then is, does plaintiff bring itself within the exception of the Uniform Commercial Code which provides as follows: "A financing statement must be filed to perfect all security interests except those covered in subsection (2)... (d) a purchase money security interest in consumer goods; but filing is required if the goods are part of the realty or a motor vehicle required to be licensed."

...Under (the) Code... these transactions might qualify as purhase money security interests that would be effective without filing." This court is in accord with this statement and finds that plaintiff has brought itself within (the) exception of the Uniform Commercial Code.

This then leaves one remaining question, was defendant a buyer of goods, such as is contemplated in the code, which provides as follows: "In the case of consumer goods... a buyer takes free of a security interest even though perfected if he buys without knowledge of the security interest for value and for his own personal, family or household purposes or his own farming operations unless prior to the purchase the secured party has filed a financing statement covering such goods."

We have previously stated that the goods purchased by defendant were clearly "consumer goods" and were not purchased for defendant's own personal family or household purposes. Since. . . it is averred that defendant is a dealer in used household appliances and purchased the dryer for purposes of resale, plaintiff therefore did not have to file a financial statement covering such goods as provided by the Uniform Commerical Code. . . and defendant did not purchase the same from Robert Henry free of the security interest of plaintiff.

■ ■ ■

Questions

1. A purchase money security interest in consumer goods can be "perfected" without filing. What does this mean? Does the security interest holder have protection against other creditors of the debtor? Against *all* buyers from the debtor? Or only *some* buyers from the debtor?

REPOSSESSION PROCESS
FUENTES v. SHEVIN
407 U.S. 67 (1972)
Supreme Court of the United States

■ ■ ■

STEWART, Mr. Justice.

Margarita Fuentes is a resident of Florida. She purchased a gas stove and service policy from the Firestone Tire and Rubber Company (Firestone) under a conditional sales contract calling for monthly payments over a period of time. A few months later, she purchased a sterophonic phonograph from the same company under the same sort of contract. The total cost of the stove and stereo was about $500, plus an additional financing charge of over $100. Under the contracts, Firestone retained title to the merchandise, but Mrs. Fuentes was entitled to possession and until she should default on her installment payments.

For more than a year, Mrs. Fuentes made her installment payments. But then, with only about $200 remaining to be paid, a dispute developed between her and Firestone over the servicing of the stove. Firestone instituted an action in a small claims court for repossession of both the stove and stereo, claiming that Mrs. Fuentes had refused to make her remaining payments. Simultaneously with the filing of that action and before Mrs. Fuentes had even received a summons to answer its complaint, Firestone obtained a writ of replevin ordering a sheriff to seize the disputed goods at once.

In conformance with Florida procedure, Firestone had only to fill in the blanks on the appropriate form documents and submit them to the file clerk of the small claims court. The clerk signed and stamped the documents and issued a writ of replevin. Later the same day, a local deputy sheriff and an agent of Firestone went to Mrs. Fuentes' home and seized the stove and stereo

Shortly thereafter, Mrs. Fuentes instituted the present action in a federal district court, challenging the constitutionality of the Florida prejudgment replevin procedures under the Due Process Clause of the Fourteenth Amendment. . .

For more than a century the central meaning of precedural due process has been clear: "Parties whose rights are to be affected are entitled to be heard; and in order that they may enjoy that right they must be notified." It is equally fundamental that the right to notice and an opportunity to be heard "must be granted at a meaningful time and in a meaningful manner."

The primary question in the prsent case is whether (the) state statute (is) constitutionally defective in failing to provide for hearing "at a meaningful time." The florida replevin process guarantees an opportunity for a hearing after the seizure of goods,... But... the Florida... statute (does not) provide for notice or an opportunity to be heard *before* the seizure. The issue is whether procedural due process in the context of these cases requires an opportunity for a hearing *before* the State authorizes its agents to seize property in the possession of a person upon the application of another.

The constitutional right to be heard is a basic aspect of the duty of government to follow in a fair process of decision making when it acts to deprive a person of his possessions. The purpose of this requirement is not only to ensure abstract fair play to the individual. Its purpose, more particularly, is to protect his use and possession of property from arbitrary encroachment—to minimize substantively unfair or mistaken deprivations of property, a danger that is especially great when the State seizes goods simply upon the application of and for the benefit of a private party. So viewed, the prohibition against the deprivation of property without due process of law reflects the high value, embedded in our constitutional and political history, that we place on a person's right to enjoy what is his, free of governmental interference... It has long been recognized that "fairness can rarely be obtained by secret, one-sided determination of facts decisive of rights... (And no) better instrument has been devised for arriving at truth than to give a person in jeopardy of serious loss notice of the case against him and opportunity to meet it."

If the right to notice and a hearing is to serve its full purpose, then, it is clear that it must be granted at a time when the deprivation can still be prevented. At a later hearing, an individual's possessions can be returned to him if it was unfairly or mistakenly taken in the first place. Damages may even be awarded to him for the wrongful deprivation. But no later hearing and no damage award can undo the fact that the arbitrary taking that was subject to the right of precedural due process has already occurred. "This Court has not... embraced the general proposition that a wrong may be done if it can be undone."

This is no new principle of constitutional law. The right to a prior hearing has long been recognized by this Court under the Fourteenth and Fifth Amendments. Although the Court has held that due process tolerates variances in the *form* of a hearing "appropriate to the nature of the case," and depending upon the importance of the interests involved and the nature of the subsequent proceedings (if any), "the Court has traditionally insisted that, whatever its form, opportunity for that hearing must be provided before the deprivation at issue takes effect.

"That the hearing required by due process is subject to waiver, and is not fixed in form does not affect its root requirement that an individual be given an opportunity for a hearing *before* he is deprived of any significant property interest, except for extraordinary situation where some valid governmental interest is at stake that justifies postponing the hearing until after the event."...

The Florida prejudgment replevin statute serves no such important governmental or general public interest. It allows summary seizure of a person's possessions when no more than private gain is directly at stake...

The statute, moreover, abdicate[s] effective control over state power. Private parties, serving their own private advantage, may unilaterally invoke state power to replevy goods from another. No state official participates in the decision to seek a writ; no state official reviews the basis for the claim to repossession; and no state official evaluates the need for immediate seizure. There is not even a requirement that the plaintiff provide any information to the court on these matters. The State acts largely in the dark... We hold that the Florida... prejudgment replevin provisions work a deprivation of property without due process of law insofar as they deny the right to a prior opportunity to be heard before chattels are taken from their possessor. Our holding, however, is a narrow one. We do not question the power of a State to seize goods before a final judgment in order to protect the security interests of creditors so long as those creditors have tested their claim to the goods through the process of a fair prior hearing. The nature and form of such prior hearings, moreover, are legitimately open to many potential variations and are a subject, at this point, for legislation—not adjudication. Since the essential reason for the requirement of a prior hearing is to prevent unfair and mistaken deprivations of property, however, it is axiomatic that the hearing must provide a real test.

■ ■ ■

Questions

1. When the creditor proceeds by judicial process, *Fuentes* requires that notice to the debtor and a preliminary hearing prior to repossession be held. What additional risk does this process put upon the lender?

2. The Georgia Garnishment Statute was attacked in *North Georgia Finishing, Inc. v. Di-Chem.*419 U.S. 601 (1975). The writ of garnishment was issuable on the affidavit of the creditor or his attorney, and the latter need not have personal knowledge of the facts. The affidavit need contain only conclusory allegations. The writ was issuable by the court clerk, without participation by a judge.On service of the writ, the debtor was deprived of the use of the property in the hands of the garnishee (bank). A sizeable bank account was frozen, and the only method to dissolve the garnishment was to file a bond to protect the plaintiff-creditor. There was no provision for an early hearing at which the creditor would be required to demonstrate probable cause for the garnishment. Indeed, it appeared that without the filing of a bond the defendant-debtor's challenge to the garnishment would not be entertained, whatever the grounds may be. Was the Georgia Garnishment Statute constitutional?

3. *Fuentes* dealt with the application of due process protections to consumers who are victims of contracts of adhesion and who might be irreparably damaged by temporary deprivation of household necessities. Should the principles of *Fuentes* be applied in a commercial setting involving parties of equal bargaining power? The Supreme Court said: "It may be that consumers deprived of household applicances will more likely suffer irreparably than corporations deprived of bank accounts, but the probability of irreparable injury in the latter case is sufficiently great so that some procedures are necessary to guard against the risk of initial error."

PRIVATE REPOSSESSION

BENSCHOTER v. FIRST NATIONAL BANK OF LAWRENCE
542 P. 2d 1042 (1975)
Supreme Court of Kansas

■ ■ ■

This is an appeal from an order of the trial court granting a creditor judgment thereby affirming the creditor's "self-help" repossession of the plaintiff's property (pledged as security for a loan) pursuant to [UCC] 9-503. The provision...reads:

"Unless otherwise agreed a secured party has on default the right to take possession of the collateral. In taking possession a secured party may proceed without judicial process if this can be done without breach of the peace or may proceed by action...

The plaintiff first argues the due process requirements of the Fourteenth Amendment of the United States Constitution requires that he should have been given notice and a prior hearing... Under this clause, state action is necessary to invoke the Fourteenth Amendment. Acts of private individuals, however discriminatory or wrongful, are outside the scope of the Fourteenth Amendment.

The state action test is generally met when conduct formerly private becomes so entwined with governmental policies and so impregnated with governmental character as to become subject to the constitutional limitations placed upon state action. The courts have never attempted the imposible task of formulating an infallible test for determining whether the state in any of its manifestations has become significantly involved in private conduct. Only by sifting facts and weighing circumstances on a case-by-case basis can a non-obvious involvement of the state in private conduct be attributed its true significance.

The plaintiff's primary argument is that the state has passed a law which authorizes or encourages "self-help repossession" so state action must be present. But the Federal Circuit Courts have unanimously rejected this argument. The state courts have also unanimously rejected this contention...

One reason for the almost unanimous acceptance of self-help repossession is that 9-503, did not change the common law or the previously codified statutory law. The right to peaceful self-help repossession of property under circumstances such as are here involved, far from being a right created by 9-503, has roots deep in the common law... Therefore, 9-503 injects no new element upon which a finding of state action may be based.

Had 9-503, changed our law, a finding of state action would still not be required.

Statutes regulate many forms of private activities in some manner or another. Subjecting all behavior that conforms to some statute to complete due process guarantees would emasculate the state action concept and create chaos in our society.

Recent United States Supreme Court cases have held that conforming to some state regulation is not sufficient state action to trigger application of the Fourteenth Amendment. (*Moose Lodge No. 107 v. Irvis*, 407 U.S. 163, [conforming to liquor regulations]; and *Jackson v. Metropolitan Edison Co.*, 419 U.S. 345, [conforming to utility tariffs].) The same is true whan a creditor conforms to 9-503, no state action is present...

Plaintiff further relies on several of the more modern creditors' rights cases. *Sniadach v. Family Finance Corp.*, 395 U.S. 337, (prejudgment garnishment of wages); and *Fuentes v. Shevin*, 407 U.S. 67, (prejudgment replevin statute). These decisions of the United States Supreme Court reversed state laws which allowed state agents, the state court in *Sniadach* and the sheriff in *Fuentes*, to seize property without prior notice and prior hearings.

Here no state official, be he judge, clerk of the court or police officer, is involved in the prejudgment self-help repossession of the collateral. As such no state action is present...

The plaintiff suggests that the better course of action would be for the bank and other secured parties to institute legal proceedings pursuant 9-503, under which "the secured party" may "proceed by action." However, that is not necessary. The secured party may choose the remedy it wishes; either self-help repossession or judicial action in accordance with the due process guarantees of the Fourteenth Amendment.

Commentaries on the practical and economic aspects of self-help repossession make a strong argument that absent self-help repossession credit would be more restricted or would cost more or both...

Debtors are not without remedy. If the bank or secured party repossesses before default, or breaches the peace during repossession after default, it may be liable for damages.

A default having been established, the next question is whether the defendant took repossession of the securd propert by "stealth" and thereby committed a "breach of the peace" under the facts in this case. The plaintiff asserts that the defendant used "stealth" to effect the repossession because the repossession occurred without the plaintiff's knowledge and arguable, at a time when the defendant knew the plaintiff would not be at his place of residence. The deposition testimony of the parties submitted to the court for consideration upon the motion for summary judgment fails to bear out the plaintiff's contention that defendant knew the plainfiff would not be home. In fact, the plaintiff's deposition testimony tends to establish the contrary. To support the plaintiff's assertion that "stealth" is part of a breach of the peace the plaintiff argues it should be defined to cover, without more, a repossession that is effected without the debtor's knowledge...

Here plaintiff had knowledge that the property might be taken. He had received repeated warnings from the defendant and he *agreed to the taking of repossession upon his continued default*... Thus the defendant had permission to be on the property, both from the plaintiff and his seventeen-year-old son at the time of their entry. Had the seventeen-year-old son refused to let the defendant repossess (*Morris v. Bk. & TR Co.*, 21 Ohio St. 2d 25, 254 N.E. 2d 683 [1970]), or had he requested the defendant to wait until his father returned, a different case might be presented. (*Luthy v. Philip Werlein Co.*, 163 La. 752, 112 So. 709 [1927].)...

As a matter of law this court cannot say "stealth", as the term is used in the context of this case by the plaintiff, constitutes a "breach of the peace".

...[S]tealth, in the sense of the debtor's lack of knowledge of the creditor's repossession, does not make an otherwise lawful repossession an unlawful repossession.

White and Summers in their Handbook of the Law under the Uniform Commercial Code, discuss the essential requirement that repossession be peaceful and what constitutes a breach of the peace, as follows:

> ...To determine if a breach of the peace has occurred, courts inquire mainly into: (1) whether there was entry by the creditor upon the debtors premises; and (2) whether the debtor or one acting on his behalf consented to the entry and repossession."

Using this basis for any analysis the trial court correctly found there was no breach of the peace in this case.

■ ■ ■

Questions

1. In *Benschoter* why did the court reject the plaintiff's argument that "self-help repossession" authorized by statute amounts to "state action"?
2. How is *Benschoter* different from the cases of *Sniadach* and *Fuentes*?
3. Are there any good reasons for private repossessions? Why not force all creditors to proceed by judicial action?
4. Private repossession is permissible only if obtained without breach of the peace. Is it a "breach of the peace" for a creditor to repossess the property without giving the debtor any notice of the repossession? May the creditor repossess over the protests of the debtor? Or the debtor's family? Or may the creditor break and enter?

9

BUSINESS ORGANIZATIONS

Each society selects the methods of organization best suited for allocating resources and products in the design of its economic system. The United States has placed its primary emphasis in economic organization on private ownership of productive property and the freedom of contractual relations as the means to distribute products and incomes. In America's early development, the freedom of "private" enterprise was as sacred as political liberty and, indeed, it was of critical importance in preserving political liberties. This emphasis on a "free" economic system was partly a reaction to the English mercantilist system which favored some merchants over others. Americans believed that political restrictions on disfavored merchants discouraged their initiative to the detriment of society. The American economic system was to be open for all participants willing to entertain the risks of a free market.

During the American colonial period, most business enterprises were organized as sole proprietorships or partnerships. The corporate form of business organization was not popular in America, despite the fact that English mercantile trading companies and a minuscule of native business corporations were already carrying on business activities here. The "free market" writings of Adam Smith, who was against incorporated enterprises, were widely circulated in America. The English mercantile companies were politicaly protected monopolies. American wanted no part of these large, exclusive and monopolistic companies, nor were Americans interested in creating their own.

What few corporations were created had to be accomplished under a special enactment of the state legislature. No more than 250 corporate bodies were begun during the first decade after the Constitution. The impact of the Industrial Revolution and episodes of corruption and bribery of state legislators to create particular corporations initiated the need for reform in the processes of creating incorporated bodies. The industrialization process requires large amounts of capital and the corporte form of organization provides a most successful vehicle to raise capital funds. The increasing pressures for incorporation lead nearly all states to enact general incorporation statutes which allow persons to form corporations without special legislative favor.

As long as business corporations remained local, the states theoretically retained full control over corporate activities. However, when the Supreme Court held that a state could not exclude the interstate commercial activities of a foreign (chartered in another state) corporation, business organizations that intended to engage in interstate activity sought out those states for incorporation which provided a "liberal" corporate law favoring the interests of the incorporators. Initially, New Jersey became the most favored state of incorporation, and Delaware soon followed. Governor Woodrow Wilson, however, took New Jersey out of the "corporation home" competition with his tough reforms in 1913.

Corporations have steadily grown and have increasingly acquired power within society. With theoretical perpetual existence and minimal state regulation or oversight, corporations have become self-perpetuating and largely autonomous. As a result, it has often been argued that federal control over the formation of corporations that do business in interstate commerce should be instigated. However, federal intervention in corporate affairs has mainly taken the form of superimposed regulatory legislation and the rejection of any federal incorporation law. In the modern era state legislation has attempted to balance more fairly the interest of shareholders, management, employees, and the public interest in corporate affairs. Moreover, judicial decisions have attempted to enhance business morality in corporate affairs by increasingly recognizing fiduciary duties on the part of directors, officers, and controlling stockholders.

Any study of American business organizations must begin with the important laws of agency. Agency law governs the power of an agent or employee of a business organization in relation to outsiders. In adition, agency law articulates basic principles concerning the legal relationships within the businss firm itself.

AGENCY

Agency is a legal relationship based on consent of the parties that one party, the agent, will represent another, the prncipal, in contractual matters with third persons. Since a principal may appoint an agent to arrange most any transaction that he or she may legally conduct himself, an obvious purpose of an agency is to expand the principal's business interest by operating through agents. The agency relationship usually arises out of a contractual agreement between the parties, but it is possible to form an agency from mere consent without a contract. The crux of the agency status is that the agent acts for the benefit of the principal and is therefore subject to the principal's control.

By definition, an agent acts for the principal on contractual matters. In contrast, an employee acts for the employer (principal) on physical things and in service to the employer without power to make contracts for the employer. However, the employee is subject to the employer's direction and control.

An independent contractor is one who is not subject to direction or control by an employer (principal). Instead, the contractor is hired to acomplish the contractual result or end product through the exercise of skill and management. As such, an independent contractor is neither an agent nor an employee because he or she is not subject to the right of control by the principal.

RESPONDENT SUPERIOR

While agency is a voluntarily assumed status, the relationship is largely governed by a body of law that defines the resepctive rights and liabilities of the principal and agent to each other and to third persons. That body of law has been developed through the common law traditions in England and the United States through hundreds of years. One rule that has been settled for over 250 years is yet strange to many. That rule is *respondeat superior*; that is, let the master (principal) respond by paying compensatory damage awards to others who are torturously injured by the acts of the agent-employee. The master-principal must bear liability for the servant-agent's torts, if such torts were committed in the "course of the agent's employment." Mr. Justice Holmes wrote:

> I assume that common sense is opposed to making one man pay for another man's wrong, unless he actually has brought the wrong to pass according to the ordinary canons of legal responsibility. . . I therefore assume that common sense is opposed to the fundamental theory of agency.[1]

While the initial reaction of common sense may be opposed to *respondeat superior*, many writers have approved of the doctrine. Its long survival and present vigor indicate the rule must satisfy some instinct of public policy. Justifiactions advanced for the rule tend to be based on concepts of morality or economics.

In a moral sense, it is argued that since the principal has the power of control, the principal should take the responsibility for the agent's acts, or that since he or she gets the benefits of the agent's acts, he or she should bear the burden of the agent's misconduct. Moreover, while it is true that the principal is innocent, so is the person insured, and as between the two, the person (principal) who initiated the activity (set the agent into action) should bear the loss.

Economically, it is argued that making the principal liable will induce him or her to exercise greater care in employing and supervising agents. The public will thereby benefit from less agent misconduct. Also, since injuries should be compensated, the public is better served if the master, who is likely to have greater financial responsibility, is held liable. This latter theory is called the "deep-pocket principle." Finally, the entrepreneur theory argues that the compensation of victims should be treated like any other cost of doing business. Ultimately, such costs will be covered, like any business expense, through the fees paid by consumers for the business service. Imposing liability upon the principal thereby provides a means of fair and reasonable allocation of loss throughout society. Spreading the loss in this manner provides social justice for both the victims and the innocent principal.

No matter the justification chosen, *respondeat superior* is a viable and expanding legal principle as the following two cases illustrate.

TEXACO, INC. v. LAYTON
395 P. 2d 393 (1964)
Supreme Court of Oklahoma

■ ■ ■

This wrongful death action was brought by plaintiff Daniel Layton, Jr., as administrator of the estate of Jimmy Alexander, who, with two others, was burned to death in a fire in a filling station in Oklahoma City. Plaintiff did not sue the operator of the filling station, but elected to prosecute his action against Texaco, Inc., only.

There is no dispute as to the events surrounding the fire. The operator of the station was Bob Anderson, who leased it from Texaco, Inc., the defendant in the trial court. Anderson also had a "Gasoline Consignment Agreement" with Texaco. On the night of the fire, Anderson was not at the filling station but had left it in charge of Clarence Little, his employee. A truck driver and regular customer named Mauldin drove into the station for some gasoline, and told Little that he must first have some water cleaned out of his "saddle tank." He then drove the truck into the washroom for that purpose. Jimmy Alexander, plaintiff's decedent, had driven into the station with his father for some gasoline, and they entered the wash room to wait while the work on Mauldin's gas tank was being done. In the wash room were two gas appliances with pilot lights, a hot water heater and an overhead "space heater." Little opened the drain plug on the gas tank and drained the gas into two open containers which he set to one side. He "blew out the lines" with a compressed air hose and then applied the compressed air hose to the tank itself. At this time there was an explosion and fire which casued the deaths of Jimmy Alexander, his father, and Clarence Little.

Verdict and judgment were for plaintiff and against Texaco, and Texaco appeals.

The argument on appeal chiefly concerns the contractual relationship between Texaco and Anderson. In general, Texaco argues that the relationship was that of bailor and bailee, or principal and commission factor; and that the doctrine of respondeat superior does not arise from the existence of such relationships merely, but arises only where, in addition to the contractual relationship, it is shown that the superior (or principal, or bailor) had the right to control, or actually did control, the subordinate (or bailee, or commission factor) in the manner of the doing of the thing which resulted in the injury.

Plaintiff agrees generally with this statement of the law, but argues that the right to control is to be found in the contracts themselves, and that "The record in this case is replete with instances of actual control exercised by Texaco over the physical movements of Anderson and the other employees at this Texaco station"...

Winkelstein et al. v. Solitare, 129 N.J.L. 38, is particularly enlightening in this connection. The agreed facts in that case were that defendant Solitare went to the home of a friend to pick up his wife and take her home. He offered a ride to other guests who were present. He was in the driver's seat of the automobile; his wife got in beside him; and his sister-in-law, Ann Solitare, was to his wife's right. Defendant said "Ann, it is cold in here; close the door." The sister-in-law thereupon closed the door of the car upon the finger of the female plaintiff, who had grasped the door frame for support while entering the back seat of the car.

Defendant's motion for directed verdict upon the ground that "the negligence of Ann, the sister-in-law, was the act of an independent third party and not the act of the defendant's agent, servant or employee, so that if she were guilty of negligence, that negligence could not be imputed or attributed to the defendant as the master or principal" was sustained. The Supreme Court of New Jersey reversed the judgment and granted a new trial saying:

> "* * * The closing of the door was at defendant's express direction, and in his presence; and thus the wrongful act in the execution of the comand was his own. * * *

> "* * * The actor was the agent or servant of defendant so as to render him liable for her wrongful act in the performance of the service thus undertaken at his request.... [T]o constitute that relation as to third persons, it is not requisite that 'any actual contract should subsist between the parties, or that compensation should be expected by the servant. * * * 'The real test as to third persons... is whether the act is done by one for another, however trivial, with the knowledge of the person sought to be charge as master, or with his assent, express or implied...'"

The points illustrated by the New Jersey case are (1) it is not necessary, in respondeat superior cases, to show the existence of a master-servant, or "superior-subordinate," relationship "in its full sense"; and (2) it *is* necessary to show such a relationship in respect to the transaction out of which the injury arose.

It also illustrates the fact that the doctrine of respondeat superior is not limited to instances in which the superior has the *right* to control the transaction out of which the injury arose, but extends also to instances in which the superior *actually exercises control*, regardless of any inherent or contractual right to do so...

In summary, it may be said that the basic inquiry in any respondeat superior case in which the specific act of negligence by the subordinate is admitted (as it is in this case) is whether the superior had the right to control, or actually did control in some measure, the actions of the subordinate in respect to the transaction out of which the injury arose.

With that principle in mind, we now examine the record before us to see if the doctrine of respondeat superior is applicable in this case. We agree at the outset that plaintiff has pointed out many instances in which, under the two written contracts between Texaco and Anderson, Texaco retains the right to a substantial degree of control over Anderson. These "controls" concern such things as the retail price of gasoline to be collected by Anderson; the keeping and examination of records and taking of inventories; the prohibition of the sale of other brands under the Texaco trademark; the amount of Anderson's commission; the term of the lease and the related gasoline consignment agreement; and Anderson's credit policy. Without setting out in further detail the contents of the two instruments, it is sufficient to say that we do not find in either of them a "right" on the part of Texaco to control Anderson in the transaction out of which the injury arose. The remaining inquiry is whether, aside from the rights of Texaco under it contracts with Anderson, it actually did through Anderson control Little, in some measure, in the act which he admittedly performed negligently.

In this connection, there was evidence that Texaco inspectors visited the Anderson station about twice each month. Or these visits they filled out inspection report forms entitled "Texaco Dealer's Registered Rest Room-Sparkle Report" and "Service Station Inspection Report." Anderson testified that on some occasions the inspectors would give him a copy of the report and at other times they did not. The aparkle report is apparently prepared in triplicate for the information of the Zone Manager the State Manager, and the Division Office.

There was testimony from former employes that the station was inspected for cleanliness "and to see if it was run right" that the inspectors talked to Mr. Anderson and "told him how they wanted it run", that they would "tell us what we were doing wrong", that the inspectors were present when gasoline in open containers was being used in the washroom and grease room, and must have seen it; that on several occasions the inspectors spent some time in the role of filling station attendant, showing them "how to perform" their work; that they were never instructed not to drain gas tanks in the washroom. Most of former employees' testimony was denied by the inspectors.

Inspectors testified that their activities were for purely instructional and advisory purposes, and that their recommendations and suggestions were not binding upon Mr. Anderson; that he on occasion did not follow their suggestions; and that their purpose was merely to increase Anderson's volume of business, and his profits. They agreed that in increasing Anderson's profits, they also increased the profits to Texaco.

Anderson testified that the filling station attendants were his employee and not Texaco's; that he prescribed their working hours and wages, and that they took their instructions from him. He also testified that Texaco furnished him with no written set of rules and regulations to follow. . .

As heretofore noted there is testimony in this case to the effect that the inspections were made to "see if it (the station) was run right," and inspectors told Mr. Anderson "how they wanted it run", and would tell us "what we were doing wrong." In view of all the facts and circumstances appearing from the record, and the ease with which Texaco was authorized to cancel their consignment agreement upon five days notice, without cause if it so elected, we are unable to determine as a matter of law the extent of the control which Texaco exercised upon Anderson and his employees in the operation of the station. . .

As we have seen, insofar as the applicability of the doctrine of respondeat superior under the particular facts in this case is concerned, the written contracts between the parties did not justify a peremptory instruction by the court that Anderson was Texaco's agent for the purpose of the sale of gasoline only, since the contracts do not show on their face that Texaco retained the *right* to control Anderson or his employees in respect to the transaction out of which the injury arose.

Since the evidence with respect to whether Texaco *actually exercised control* in that respect is in conflict, it created at the most a question of fact for the jury, and not a question of law for the court, on this point. It is reversible error for the court, in its instructions, to invade the province of the jury, assume a controverted fact as proved or treat it as a question of law, and withhold the same from the determination of the jury.

■ ■ ■

Questions

1. Texaco could have been liable under the Doctrine of *Respondeat Superior* if Texaco had the "right to control" the service station manager's activities in regards to the transaction out of which the injury arose. What right of control was retained by Texaco in its contractual dealings with the service manager?
2. Texaco could be liable under the Doctrine of *Respondeat Superior* if it "actually exercised control" over the service station manager in relation to the activity in which the injury arose. Did Texaco "actually exercise control" over

the service station manager in relation to the transaction out of which the injury arose? How was that determined?

THE AGENT'S AUTHORITY

Agents possess authority (power to make contracts for the principal) when the principal consents to such authority. This authority may arise by the principal manifesting consent to the agent's authority either expressly in words or impliedly by the principal's conduct. The authority granted to conduct a transaction includes the authority to do acts that are incidental to such authority or are reasonably necessary to accomplish the purpose of the authority conferred. The agent has the authority to follow usual business customs of the trade in carrying out his or her authority. In emergency situations, the agent's authority extends to additional acts reasonably believed necessary to protect the principal. Therefore, whether expressed in words, implied from conduct, or incidental or necessary to accomplish the agency purpose, the principal's consent is given and the agent possesses *actual* authority. In such situations, third parties dealing through the agent may make binding contracts between themselves and the principal. The agent is not bound on the contract but is merely the instrumentality through which the principal has contracted. Simply stated, the principal is bound on all contracts negotiated by the agent if such contracts were within the actual authority of the agent as conferred by the principal.

Dealing with a person who claims to be an agent but who possesses no actual authority conferred by the principal will not bind the principal to the bargain made by the unauthorized agent. Consequently, it is advisable for a third party to take additional steps to determine the extent of the authority which has been conferred by the principal. While the principal may not be bound by any unauthorized agency, the agent who so respresents himself or herself may be liable to the third party for breach of implied warranty that he or she had authority as an agent.

Sometimes agents are placed in positions by a principal, but secret instructions limiting the agent's actual authority are given by the principal. May the principal escape liability to a third party on a contract made by such agent in which the agent violated the secret limitation and exceeded actual authority, but which to the third party appeared to be within the agent's authority as revealed by his or her position? The following case provides an answer.

LINDSTROM v. MINNESOTA LIQUID FERTILIZER COMPANY
119 N.W. 2d 855 (1963)
Supreme Court of Minnesota

■ ■ ■

Action for labor and materials furnished by plaintiff, Anund T. Lindstrom, to defendant, Minnesota Liquid Fertilizer Company, a Minnesota corporation.

The labor and material furnished by plaintiff were ordered by one Hurley Weaver, who represented to plaintiff that he was acting for defendant in the transactions. Defendant denies that he was its agent or employee and contends that the evidence compelled a finding that his status was merely that of a lessee of defendant's plant and equipment, without authority to bind defendant in any way...

Defendant is engaged in the sale and distribution of mixed liquid anhydrous ammonia fertilizer. Its home office at the time involved was in Minneapolis, and it has various branch plants throughout the state, one of which has been located at Farmington since 1954. The Farmington branch consists of an office building; a 30,000-pound steel storage tank adjacent to rail trackage; and smaller movable tanks and equipment. Defendant's name, "Minnesota Liquid Fertilizer Co.," is painted on a large sign above the office building and on the steel storage tank in letters of substantial size and prominence, and is also painted on the small storage tanks and equipment.

On July 30, 1955, one Hurley Weaver was placed in charge of the Farmington

Branch. Under agreements with defendant covering the period from August 1, 1955, to August 1, 1958, he was authorized to use the plant building and equipment there and required to maintain the same at his own expense...

Under the plan of operation between defendant and Weaver, liquid fertilizer was shipped to Farmington in rail tank cars cosigned to Weaver for resale to farmers in the area. Weaver distributed this to customers in field tanks, using defendant's equipment and applicators in applying it in the fields. In this work he was assisted by Richard Aronson, whom he had employed. In addition to defendant's equipment, Weaver also used a pick-up truck and two tractors of his own in performing the worked described. On this truck the name "Hurley Weaver" appeared above the name "Minnesota Liquid Fertilizer Co."

In dealing with customers, Weaver was authorized to fix the price of the fertilizer sold. Each month he was billed by defendant for the amount of fertilizer removed from the steel tank and sold to customers based upon a measurement scale on the tank. When he or Aronson collected from customers for fertilizer sold, they would deposit the amount collected in the First National Bank of Farmington in a checking account in defendant's name. Defendant withdrew from this account any money which was due it for the fertilizer or for any advances which it had made to Weaver during the month and then forwarded the remainder to Weaver so he could pay his accounts and withdraw any earnings due him therefrom.

Defendant's president visited the Farmington branch on various occasions while Weaver was operating it. During the summer months defendant's sales manager likewise visited it once every 2 weeks. Another official in charge of the sale of a "mixed liquid" fertilizer also visited it on one or two occasions. On such occasions they could observe defendant's name prominently displayed on the office building, the large storage tank, and the movable equipment, and could observe that nothing on such property or equipment referred to Weaver as a lessee or as an independent contractor. On brochures forwarded by defendant to prospective customers in the area, the location of the Farmington branch was set forth together with directions to "SEE YOUR AGROVITA LESSEE MANAGER." Defendant's name and Minneapolis address were likewise printed thereon.

Since February 1956 plaintiff has operated a small blacksmith and welding shop at Farmington. On May 8, 1956, Weaver first contracted him and requested that he perform certain welding services and supply parts and material for certain of the equipment used in connection with applying fertilizer. At Weaver's request, plaintiff then opened a charge account, on the first sales ticket to which Weaver printed in pencil the name "Minn. Liq. Fert. Co. Farmington, Minn," as the customer to be charged for items ordered by Weaver. Thereafter, until July 1958, he ordered various items of labor and material for the operation of the Farmington branch and for the maintenance of various equipment of defendant which had been entrusted to his care. All of these items were required for the conduct of defendant's business in the Farmington area, and were on Weaver's instructions charged to its account. By July 17, 1958, the total charges against defendant on this account were $2,438.90 less $100 paid by Weaver in July 1956.

Plaintiff testified that at various times when Weaver came to plaintiff's shop he had observed defendant's name on the pick-up truck which Weaver then drove; that he had also observed defendant's name on the plant building and equipment at Farmington; that he had looked up defendant's credit and financial standing in Dun and Bradstreet; and that at all times he assumed, in accordance with Weaver's statements, that defendant was the customer for which such services and materials were being furnished. He also testified that he had talked with Weaver about the account on numerous occasions during the years in which it was active and that at no time did Weaver indicate anything other than that defendant was responsible for and would pay the charges thereon; and that shortly after such conversations he (Weaver) would see to it that defendant paid it...

The agreement between defendant and Weaver, which included a lease of defendant's Farmington property and equipement to Weaver, would not foreclose a finding that the relationship of principal and agent existed as between them. . . It makes little difference whether the agreement between the parties is in form of an agency contract or a lease. . .

The evidence here adequately supports a finding that defendant, by its actions, had made Weaver its *actual* as well as its ostensible manager of the Farmington branch. In its advertising material distributed in the Farmington area prospective customers were requested to refer to the "local manager" and "Agro-Vita Lessee Manager" of defendant's Farmington branch. In its letter of August 22, 1958, it definitely revealed that Weaver was actually looked upon by defendant as the manager of the Farmington branch as well as lessee of certain of the physical assets thereof.

Further, at all times its corporate name was painted in large letters on the buildings, tanks, and equipment of this branch, with nothing thereon to indicate that Weaver was lessee of such business or operated it as an independent contractor. It is well settled that, in so far as third parties are concerned, the relationship of principal and agent may be evidenced by acts on the part of the alleged principal or appearances of authority he permits another to have which lead to the belief that an agency has been created. . .

It has been held that, where a party permits his name to be used on property or equipment which is placed under the control or direction of another and thus makes such other an ostensible agent, an agency by estoppel will result. . .

In *Restatement, Agency (2d)* §8 comments *a* and *b*, this principle is expressed and illustrated as follows:

> "(a) Apparent authority results from a manifestation by a person that another is his agent, the manifestation being made to a third person and not, as when authority is created, to the agent."

> "(b) The manifestation of the principal may be made directly to a third person, or may be made to the community, *by signs, by advertising,* by authorizing the agent to state that he is authorized, or by continuously employing the agent.". . .

The jury's finding that a principal and agent relationship existed between defendant and Weaver would render defendant liable for acts performed by Weaver within the scope of his apparent authority as plant manager. Any secret limitations placed thereon by defendant would not absolve it from liability to third persons such as plaintiff who dealt with Weaver as defendant's manager and who were unaware of any limitations upon his authority as such. . . The authority of an agent is generally held to be co-extensive with the property or business entrusted to his care.

In the case of a department or branch manager the authority ordinarily would extend to his purchases of material and employment of services for the preservation and upkeep of the property and the operation of the business.

Under the principles and authorities referred to the evidence above described was more than adequate to establish that Weaver's actions in ordering the described work and material from plaintiff for the maintenance of defendant's property and equipment and the operation of its business in the Farmington area were within the scope of his real or apparent authority as plant manager of the Farmington branch.

■ ■ ■

Questions

1. What is an agency by estoppel? What elements of proof are necessary to establish an agency by estoppel?
2. Would the decision be different if the lease contract had declared that Weaver was not an "agent" of Minnesota Liquid Fertilizer Company?

DUTIES BETWEEN AGENT AND PRINCIPAL

When the agent has completed his or her performance and the services were not intended gratuitous, the principal has the duty to compensate the agent. If not previously agreed on, the reasonable value of the agent's services is due the agent. Likewise, if the agent incurs expenses in carrying out the principal's task, the principal has the duty to reimburse the agent. Also, should the agent incur liability to a third person through no fault of the agent but for carrying out the instructions of the principal, the principal must indemnify the agent against the loss.

The agent has the duty to obey the principal's instructions. Failure to follow orders will make the agent liable to the principal for any resulting damage. The agent must exercise care and skill in carrying out the principal's affairs. Negligence or incompetence in professed skills will render the agent liable. Also, it is the duty of the agent to keep the principal's account and not to mingle his or her own property with that of the principal. The agent will lose his or her property if mingling results in inability to identify his or her portion. The agent also must inform the principal of any notices given to him or her for the principal.

While all of these duties are important, the highest duty of the agent is that of loyalty and good faith. The agent is a fiduciary (person in position of trust) to the principal and must not violate that trust by self-enrichment at the expense of the principal.

FIDUCIARY RESPONSIBILITIES

GENERAL AUTOMOTIVE MANUFACTURING CO. v. SINGER
120 N.W 2d 659 (1963)
Supreme Court of Wisconsin

■ ■ ■

Study of the record discloses that Singer was engaged as general manager of Automotive's operations. Among his duties was solicitation and procurement of machine shop work for Automotive. Because of Singer's high reputation in the trade he was highly successful in attracting orders....

As time went on a large volume of business attracted by Singer was offered to Automotive but which Singer decided could not be done by Automotive at all, for lack of suitable equipment, or which Automotive could not do at a competitive price. When Singer determined that such orders were unsuitable for Automotive he neither informed Automotive of these facts nor sent the orders back to the customer. Instead, he made the customer a price, then dealt with another machine shop to do the work at a less price, and retained the difference between the price quoted to the customer and the price for which the work was done. Singer was actually behaving as a broker for his own profit in a field where by contract he had engaged to work only for Automotive. We concur in the decision of the trial court that this was inconsistent with the obligations of a faithful agent or employee.

Singer finally set up a business of his own, calling himself a manufacturer's agent and consultant, in which he brokered orders for products of the sort manufactured by Automotive,—this while he was still Automotive's employee and without informing Automotive of it. Singer had broad powers of management and conducted the business activities of Automotive. In this capacity he was Automotive's agent and owed a fiduciary duty to it...Under his fiduciary duty to Automotive Singer was bound to the exercise of the utmost good faith and loyalty so that he did not act adversely to the interests of Automotive by serving or acquiring any private interest of his own...He was also bound to act for the furtherance and advancement of the interest of Automotive...

If Singer violated his duty to Automotive by engaging in certain business activities in which he received a secret profit he must account to Automotive for the amounts he illegally received...

The present controversy centers around the question whether the operation of Singer's side line business was a violation of his fiduciary duty to Automotive...

The trial court found that Singer's side line business, the profits of which were

$64,088.08, was in direct competition with Automotive. However, Singer argues that in this business he was a manufacturer's agent or consultant, whereas Automotive was a small manufacturer of automotive parts. The title of an activity does not determine the question whether it was competitive but an examination of the nature of the business must be made. In the present case the conflict of interest between Singer's business and his position with Automotive arises from the fact that Singer received orders, principally from a third party called Husco, for the manufacture of parts. As a manufacturer's consultant he had to see that these orders were filled as inexpensively as possible, but as Automotive's general manager he could not act adversely to the corporation and serve his own interests. On this issue Singer argues that when Automotive had the shop capacity to fill an order he would award Automotive the job, but he contends that it was in the exercise of his duty as general manager of Automotive to refuse orders which in his opinion Automotive could not or should not fill and in that case he was free to treat the order as his own property. However, this argument ignores, as the trial court said,"defendant's agency with plaintiff and the fiduciary duties of good faith and loyalty arising therefrom."

Rather than to resolve the conflict of interest between his side line business and Automotive's business in favor of serving and advancing his own personal interests, Singer had the duty to exercise good faith by disclosing to Automotive all the facts regarding this matter... Upon disclosure to Automotive it was in the latter's discretion to refuse to accept the orders from Husco or to fill them if possible or to sub-job them to other concerns with the consent of Husco if necessary, and the profit, if any, would belong to Automotive. Automotive would then be able also to decide whether to expand its operations, install suitable equipment, or to make further arrangements with Singer or Husco. By failing to disclose all the facts relating to the orders from Husco and by receiving secret profits from these orders, Singer violated his fiduciary duty to act solely for the benefit of Automotive. Therefore he is liable for the amount of the profits he earned in his side line business...

■ ■ ■

Questions

1. Why was Singer found liable to Automotive? What should Singer have done to avoid this liability?
2. What is a fiduciary

SOLE PROPRIETORSHIP AND PARTNERSHIP

The form of organization selected for a particular business firm is dependent on a number of factors. The type of business, capital requirements, tax considerations, degree of delegated responsibilities, governmental regulations, and the individual's desire to exercise control are all relevant factors in the final choice. The most appropriate form of business organization for any particular business can be selected only after a full appreciation of all the facts involved and a careful consideration of tax and other aspects. Sometimes different forms of organization recommend themselves at different stages of the business life.

The individual or sole proprietorship is the oldest, simplest, and most prevalent form of business organization. It can be organized in an informal fashion and is subject to minimal governmental regulation. The sole proprietor retains full control in management of the organization and is entitled to all profits or losses. The sole proprietorship ends on the proprietor's death or retirement, but the business normally is freely transferable to others. A sole proprietorship is taxed as an individual. Smaller enterprises and new entrants into the business environment often utilize a sole proprietorship form of organization.

Partnerships are also more numerous than business corporations. A partnership is an association of two or more persons to carry on as co-owners a business for profit. A partnership can be formed with little formality, although it is a sound practice to define the relationships among the partners in written detail. Sometimes statutes require the public filing of the partnership name. Most partnership law is governed by the Uniform Partnership Act (UPA). However, the partners in their written agreement often may vary from the statutory pattern imposed by the UPA.

The partnership requires no minimum capital contribution except as the partners agree. Partners may contribute cash, property, or personal services to the partnership. Partners may lend money or property to the partnership, and provision for interest on such contributions should be made in the written agreement. The written agreement should also deal with matters concerning the withdrawal of the capital contributed by each party.

Unless the partners agree otherwise in their written partnership agreement, each partner has an equal voice in the management and control of the partnership. Ordinarily matters will be determined by a majority vote; however, extraordinary matters, such as the sale of the business itself, require unanimous approval.

Because a partnership is a co-agency, the acts of either partner within the apparent scope of the partnership business bind the partnership for any liability arising therefrom. Each partner has authority to bind the partnership to contracts of both good and bad bargains. Likewise, all partners are subject to the further potential liability arising from the torts committed by a partner while acting within the scope of the partnership business. This liability of the partners is not limited to their capital contribution, but extends to their personal resources as well. Under the Doctrine of Marshalling of Assets, the partnership creditors must first proceed against partnership assets before proceeding against the partners individually. A creditor of an individual partner must first proceed against the latter's personal property before attempting to attach the partnership interest.

A retiring partner remains personally liable for partnership debts incurred while he or she was a partner. The retiring partner will also be liable for new debts to persons who had previously extended credit to the partnership and who have not received actual notice of the retirement. Hence, retirement requires notification to all creditors and "publication" of a notice to all other potential creditors so that they cannot claim any right against the retiring partner. The retiring partner cannot sell his or her interest in the partnership without the consent of all the other partners.

A dissolution of the partnership can occur at the end of the specified term of the partnership existence, on death of a partner, bankruptcy of the partnership, withdrawal of the partner, or expulsion of a general partner by virture of the contractual agreement or by court order. Unless the contractual agreement provides otherwise, dissolution is followed by winding up and termination of the partnership. In winding up, the assets of the general partnership are distributed in the following priority: (a) claims of creditors, (b) a debt obligation to a partner, (c) capital contributions of partners, and (d) partner's claims in respect to profits.

Unless there is an agreement to the contrary, profits are to be shared equally by the partners regardless of any differences in the amounts of their capital contributions. Losses are shared in the same proportion as profit. Any contractual provisions for the sharing of losses are effective among the partners, but do not affect the partners' liability to partnership creditors.

A limited partnership may not be created unless there is a statute authorizing limited partnerships. Four-fifths of the states have enacted the Uniform Limited Partnership Act. Most of the principles applicable to general partnerships apply in limited partnerships. However, a limited partnership can be created only in accordance with the formalities prescribed by the statute, which includes the filing and possible publication of a limited partnership certificate. Often the name of the limited partnership must include the word "limited" or its abbreviation, Ltd. Ordinarily, the name of the limited partners cannot be included in the name of the limited partnership. A limited partner can contribute cash or other property to the limited partnership but may not contribute services or otherwise take part in the control of the business. As such, the limited partner is immune from liability beyond his contribution. Limited partnerships are created for the purpose of attracting additional capital to the partnership venture.

CORPORATIONS

The corporation, in terms of business volume and capital assets, is the most important form of business enterprise. Inumerable variations are possible in setting up a corporation. Corporations range in size from a one-shareholder corporation to the more than two million sharesholders of American Telephone & Telegraph Company. The term "incorporate" literally means to form into a body. By definition, therefore, an incorporation is an entity and is so regarded for most legal purposes.

Each state has general incorporation statues that define the purposes for which corporations may be formed and detail the steps to be taken for incorporation. In applying for corporate recognition by the state, it is usually necessary to list:

1. The name and address of each incorporator
2. The purpose or purposes for which the corporation is being organized
3. The name of the corporation
4. The kind of stock it intends to issue, the number of shares authorized, and other relevant stock information
5. The period of corporate existence, which may be perpetual

The application, signed by all the incorporators and sometimes acknowledged by a notary public, is forwarded to a state official, usually the Secretary of State. The Secretary issues, a Charter which, together with the general incorporation statute, sets forth the powers, rights, and privileges of the corporation. Often, the Charter must be filed in the proper recording office in the County in which the principal office of the business is to be located. Normally, corporate life begins when the charter has been issued. Additional requirements of law call for the subscription and payment to the corporation of, at least, the minimum amount of capital stock, for stockholder approval of corporate by-laws which govern internal relations, and for stockholder election of directors who appoint corporate officers.

PROMOTER'S CONTRACTS

A promoter is one who does the preliminary work necessary to bring a corporation into existence. The promoter often conceives the business or negotiates its purchase and performs any task necessary for the proposed venture to begin operations. In this function, however, the prometer cannot act as an agent of the corporation since the corporation is not legally in existence. He or she cannot be an agent for a nonexisting principal. The corporation, once it comes into existence, cannot automatically be held liable on contracts made in its behalf by the promoter. However, once corporate life begins, the corporation is free to adopt or reject the contracts made by the promoter. For the corporation to adopt the promoter's contracts, the contracts must be valid and within the legal authority of the corporation. In addition, the corporation must adopt the contracts in their entirety. However, unless a provision of the contract specifically exempts them from personal liability, promoters themselves normally continue to be liable on pre-incorporation contracts and are not relieved from liability by the corporation's adoption of the contract. However, the courts have developed numerous rules in resolving promoter's liability on contracts negotiated for the benefit of a proposed corporation. Determine the rule of the law followed in *Robertson v. Levy* and contrast its approach with the view expressed in *Philipsborn and Co. v. Suson.*

ROBERTSON v. LEVY
197 A. 2d 443 (1964)
Court of Appeals, Dist. of Columbia

■ ■ ■

On December 22, 1961, Martin G. Robertson and Eugene M. Levy entered into an agreement whereby Levy was to form a corporation, Penn Ave. Record Shack, Inc., which was to purchase Robertson's business. Levy submitted articles of incorporation to the Superintendent of Corporations on December 27, 1961, but no certificate of corporation was issued at this time. Pursuant to the contract an assignment of lease was enter into on December 31, 1961, between Robertson and Levy, the latter acting as president of Penn Ave. Record Shack, Inc. On January 2, 1962, the articles of incorporation were rejected by the Superintendent of Corporations but on the same day Levy began to operate the business under the name Penn Ave. Record Shack, Inc. Robertson executed a bill of sale to Penn Ave. Record Shack, Inc. on January 8, 1962, disposing of the assets of his business to that "corporation" and receiving in return a note providing for installment payments signed "Penn Ave. Record Shack, Inc. by Eugene M. Levy, President." The certificate of incorporation was issued on January 17, 1962. One payment was made on the note. The exact date when the payment was made cannot be clearly determined from the record, but presumably it was made after the certificate of incorporation was issued. Penn Ave. Record Shack, Inc. ceased doing business in June 1962 and is presently without assets. Robertson sued Levy for the balance due on the note as well as for additional expenses incurred in settling the lease arrangement with the original lessor.

The case presents the following issues on appeal: Whether the president of an "association" which filed its articles of incorporation, which were first rejected but later accepted, can be held personally liable on an obligation entered into by the "association" before the certificate of incorporation has been issued, or whether the creditor is "estopped" from denying the existence of the "corporation" because, after the certificate of incorporation was issued, he accepted the first installment payment on the note.

The Business Corporation Act of the District of Columbia, Code 1961, Title 29, is patterned after the Model Business Corporation Act which is largely based on the Illinois Business Corporation Act of 1933. On this appeal, we are concerned with an interpretation of sections 29-921c and 29-950 of our act. Several states have substantially enacted the Model Act, but only a few have enacted both sections similar to those under consideration. . .

For a full understanding of the problems raised, some historical grounding is not only illuminative but necessary. In early common law times private corporations were looked upon with distrust and disfavor. This distrust of the corporate form for private enterprise was eventually overcome by the enactment of statutes which set forth certain prerequisites before the status of corporation was achieved, and by court decisions which eliminated other stumbling blocks. Problems soon arose, however, where there was substantial compliance with the prerequisites of the statute, but not complete formal compliance. Thus the concept of *de jure* corporations, *de facto* corporations, and of "corporations by estoppel" came into being.

Taking each of these in turn, a *de jure* corporation results when there has been conformity with the mandatory conditions precedent (as opposed to merely directive conditions) established by statute. A *de jure* corporation is not subject to direct or collateral attack either by the state in a *quo warranto* proceeding or by any other person.

A *de facto* corporation is one which has been defectively incorporated and thus is not *de jure*. The Supreme Court has stated that the requisites for a corporation *de facto* are: (1) A valid law under which such a corporation can be lawfully organized: (2) An attempt to organize thereunder; (3) Actual user of the corporate franchise. Good faith in claiming to be and in doing business as a corporation is often added as a further condition. A *de facto* corporation is recognized for all purposes except where there is a direct attack by the state in a *quo warranto* proceeding. The concept of *de facto* corporation has been roundly criticized.

Cases continued to arise, however, where the corporation was not *de jure*, where it was not *de facto* because of failure to comply with one of the four requirements above, but where the courts, lacking some clear standard or guideline, were willing to decide on the equities of the case. Thus another concept arose, the so-called "corporation by estoppel." This term was a complete misnomer. There was no corporation, the acts of the associates having failed even to colorably fulfill the statutory requirements; there was no estoppel in the pure sense of the word because generally there was no holding out followed by reliance on the part of the other party. Apparently estoppel can arise whether or not a *de facto* corporation has come into existence. Estoppel problems arose where the certificate of incorporation has been issued as well as where it had not been issued, and under the following general conditions: where the "association" sues a third party and the third party is estopped from denying that the plaintiff is a corporation; where a third party sues the "association" as a corporation and the "association" is precluded from denying that it was a corporation; where a third party sues the "association and the members of that asociation cannot deny its existence as a corporation where they participated in holding it out as a corporation; where a third party sues the individuals behind the "association" but is estopped from denying the existence of the "corporation"; where either a third party, or the "association is estopped from denying the corporate existence because of prior pleadings.

One of the reasons for enacting modern corporation statutes was to eliminate problems inherent in the *de jure, de facto* and estopped concepts. Thus sections 29-921c and 950 were enacted as follows:

> "§29-921c. Effect of issuance of incorporation.
> "Upon the issuance of the certificate of incorporation the corporate existence shall begin, and such certificate of incorporation shall be conclusive evidence that all conditions precedent required to be performed by the incorporators have been compiled with and that the corporation has been incorporated under this chapter, except as against the District of Columbia in a proceeding to cancel or revoke the certificate of incorporation."

> "§29-950. Unauthorized assumption of corporate powers.

> "All persons who assume to act as a corporation without authority so to do shall be jointly and severally liable for all debts and liabilities incurred or arising as a result thereof."

...No longer must the courts inquire into the equities of a case to determine whether there has been "colorable compliance" with the statute. The corporation comes into existence only when the certificate has been issued. Before the certificate issues, there is no corporation *de jure, de facto* or by estoppel. After the certificate is issued under section 921c, the *de jure* corporate existence commences. Only after such existence has begun can the corporation commence business through compliance with section 29-921d, by paying into the corporation the minimum capital, and with section 921a(f), which requires that the capitalization be no less than $1,000. These latter two sections are given further force and effect by section 29-918 (a)(2) which declares that directors of a corporation are jointly and severally liable for any assets distributed or any dividends paid to shareholders which renders the corporation insolvent or reduces its net assets below its stated capital...

The portion of § 29-291c which states that the certificate of incorporation will be "conclusive evidence" that all conditions precedent have been performed eliminates the problems of estoppel and *de facto* corporations once the certificate has been issued. The existence of the corporation is conclusive evidence against all who deal with it. Under § 29-950, if an individual or group of individuals assumes to act as a corporation before the certificate of incorporation has been issued, joint and several liability attaches. We hold, therefore, that the impact of these sections, when considered together, is to eliminate the concepts of estoppel and *de facto* corporateness under the Business Corporation Act of the District of Columbia. It is immaterial whether the third person believed he was dealing with a corporation or whether he intended to deal with a corporation. The certificate of incorporation provides the cut off point; before it is issued, the individuals, and not the corporation, are liable.

Turning to the facts of this case, Penn Ave. Record Shack, Inc. was not a corporation when the original agreement was entered into, when the lease was assigned, when Levy took over Robertson's business, when operations began under the Penn Ave. Record Shack, Inc. name, or when the bill of sale was executed. Only on January 17 did Penn Ave. Record Shack, Inc. become a corporation. Levy is subject to personal liability because, before this date, he assumed to act as a corporation without any authority so to do. Nor is Robertson estopped from denying the existence of the corporation because after the certificate was issued he accepted one payment on the note. An individual who incurs statutory liability on an obligation under section 29-950 because he has acted without authority, is not relieved of that liability where, at a later time, the corporation does come into existency by complying with section 29-921c. Subsequent partial payment by the corporation does not remove this liability.

The judgement appealed from is reversed with instructions to enter judgment against (Levy) on the note and for damages proved to have been incurred by (Robertson) for breach of the lease.

Questions

1. What is a corporation *de jure?* Corporation *de facto?* Corporation by estoppel? Why did these various conceptions become necessary? Who would win the case in *Roberton* if these common law rules were followed?
2. How did the Model Business Corporation Act attempt to solve and eliminate any issues of corporate existence?
3. Before a corporation begins to do business with the public, the Model Act requires that the minimum capital of the corporation be paid into the corporation. Which type of liability exists and on whom if this provision is not followed?

PHILIPSBORN & CO. v. SUSON
322 N.E. 2d 45 (1974)
Supreme Court of Illinois

■ ■ ■

It is plaintiff's theory "that in the absence of a knowing agreement to the contrary" Suson, as the promoter of Estates, "is personally liable on a pre-incorporation contract..." It argues that "The general rule concerning promoters' contracts is that the promoter will be personally liable on contracts signed on behalf of a nonexistent corporation unless the contract provides to the contrary."...

The parties to this appeal appear to be in agreement that, unless the parties to the transaction agree otherwise, an individual who conducts the ordinary affairs of a business in the name of a nonexistent corporation is personally liable, both at common law, and by statute, on contracts made in connection with the business. However, the authorities dealing with a promoter's personal liability on contracts made for the benefit of a proposed corporation present a wide array of factual situations and many so-called general rules...A number of the decisions...state that where a promoter had become liable on a pre-incorporation contract, he was not, in the absence of an agreement to that effect, discharged from liability merely because the corporation was later organized....

We find the ... reasoning more persuasive...(in those cases where) liability...depends upon the intent of the parties.

In our opinion...(a) contract is to be construed to give effect to the intent of the parties,...and effect must be given to the contract as written and any documents executed contemporaneously therewith....In this transaction, so far as this record reflects, plaintiff required no showing of Estates' assets nor did it make any inquiry concerning its solvency...Clearly, under these circumstances, plaintiff looked only to

Estates for (payment)...and the fact that Estates had not at that time been formed furnished no basis for the imposition of personal liability on Suson for the payment...On this record we hold that whether or not Estates existed as a corporate entity at the time the (contract) was executed, or whether plaintiff knew that it was not, was not controlling.

■ ■ ■

Questions

1. In *Philipsborn and Co.* the court imposed liability on the promoter based upon a retroactive speculation as to the intent of the parties. In *Robertson,* the court applied a mechanical rule that the promoter is liable if no corporation exists unless the contract provides otherwise. Which of these two rules do you prefer? Why?

2. Is there a difference between representing a "corporation" without disclosing its nonexistence and representing a "proposed corporation" in which its nonexistence is disclosed? Does this explain the court's unwillingness in *Philipsborn* to follow the mechanical rule of liability?

STOCK SUBSCRIPTIONS

LITTLE SWITZER, BREW, CO. v. LITTLE SWITZER, BREW, CO.
197 S.E. 2d 301 (1973)
Supreme Court of Appeals of West Virginia

■ ■ ■

Little Switzerland Brewing Company was incorporated and a charter was issued by the Secretary of State on January 28, 1968. The company had authorized capital stock of $200,000 consisting of 2,000,000 shares at the par value of ten cents a share. On February 18, 1968 Fred Ellison andd Charles E. Oxley were made directors of the company after they purchased 5,000 shares at $5 per share...

Little Switzerland contends that 275 citizens throughout the State of West Virginia subscribed for shares in the company prior to September 22, 1968. On September 25, 1968 Charles E. Oxley and Fred J. Ellison signed stock subscription agreements to purchase 5,000 shares of stock at $10 a share... The "Note" that accompanied the stock subscription agreement was titled "Noninterest Bearing-Nonobligatory Note" and merely stated that Oxley and Ellison would pay "at their discretion" $50,000 to Little Switzerland Brewing Company....

On March 24, 1970, eight of the ten directors of the company met and passed a resolution 7 to 1 to cancel the stock subscription agreements of Ellison...and Oxley...On March 26, 1970 an involuntary petition for bankruptcy was filed against Little Switzerland Brewing Company...

This action was instituted for the benefit of the creditors of the Little Switzerland Brewing Company pursuant to an order of the bankruptcy court in order to collect the defendant's money for their stock subscriptions. The authority for such action is contained in Code, 31-1-35, in the following language:

> Every stockholder of every corporation of this State shall be liable for the benefit of the creditors of such corporation for the amount of his subscription to the stock of such corporation, less the amount which he shall already have paid thereon, until he shall have paid such subscription in full, according to the terms thereof, * * * and, in the event of the insolvency of the corporation, all such liabilities of the stockholders shall be considered assets of the corporation and may be enforced by the receiver, trustee or other person winding up the affairs of the corporation, notwithstanding any release, agreement or arrangement, short of actual payment, which may have been made between the corporation and such stockholders....

It should be noted that the defendants in the instant case were not only stockholders but were also directors of the company and it is their contention that the stock subscription agreements were only options to buy stock. However, the agreements were used to assure the Commissioner of Securities that the public offering had been fully subscribed and to free the other stock of the Little Switzerland Brewing Company for over-the-counter trading. The contention of the defendants would appear to be that the subscription agreements in question were merely fictitious or colorable subscriptions; but if this were done to induce others to subscribe and there was an understanding that there was to be no liability on the part of the defendants, the subscriptions are nevertheless just as binding on the subscribers as if they were made in good faith. . .

It has been held that a corporation has no authority to accept subscriptions to its capital stock upon special terms, where the terms are such as to constitute a fraud upon other subscribers, or upon persons who become creditors of the corporation, and the invalidity of such terms or conditions will not release the subscriber from liability upon his subscription. . . .

The Supreme Court of the United States has consistently held since the case of Sawyer v. Hoag, that the capital stock of an insolvent corporation is a trust fund for the payment of its debts; that the law implies a promise by the subscribers of stock who did not pay for it to make such payment when demanded by the creditors of the corporation; and that any extrinsic agreement limiting the subscriber's liability therefor is void against creditors. . .

It has been repeatedly held by this Court that the officers and directors of an insolvent corporation are trustees for the creditors.

It is clear from the authorities that the defendants in the instant case are liable for their stock subscriptions.

The answer to the second question involved in the case presented here is that the directors of the corporation did not have the authority in any event to release the defendants from liability on their stock subscription agreements. In the first place the directors of a solvent corporation have no authority to release any stockholder from liability on stock subscription agreements unless authorized by the stockholders of the corporation. Then, too, where a corporation is insolvent such action by the corporation is prohibited by statute. This statute not only provides that the defendants, as stockholders of the Little Switzerland Brewing Company, shall be liable for the benefit of the creditors of Little Switzerland for the amount of their stock subscriptions, but also that in the event of insolvency of Little Switzerland all such liability of the stockholders shall be considered as assets of the corporation and may be enforced by the proper person notwithstanding any release agreement or arrangement which may have been made between the corporation and the stockholders.

■ ■ ■

Questions

1. The defendants contend the stock subscription and agreement was merely an option to buy stock. On what grounds did the court reject this contention?
2. Why were the directors powerless to release the defendants from liability on their stock subscription agreement?

ILLEGAL ISSUANCE OF STOCK

UNITED STEEL INDUSTRIES, INC. v. MANHART
405 S.W. 2d 231 (1966)
Court of Civil Appeals of Texas

■ ■ ■

Plaintiffs Manhart filed this suit individually and as major stockholders against defendants United Steel Industries, Inc., Hurt, and Griffitts, alleging the corporation had issued Hurt 5000 shares of its stock in consideration of Hurt agreeing to perform CPA and bookkeeping services for the corporation for one year in the future; and had issued Griffitts 4000 shares of its stock in consideration for the promised conveyance of a 5 acre tract of land to the Corporation, which land was never conveyed to the Corporation. Plaintiffs assert the 9000 shares of stock were issued in violation of Article 2.16 Business Corporation Act, and prayed that such stock be declared void and cancelled....

Article 12, Section 6, Texas Constitution...provides: "No corporation shall issue stock * * * except for money paid, labor done, or property actually received * * *." And Article 2.16 Texas Business Corporation Act provides:

"Payment for Shares.

"A. The consideration paid for the issuance of shares shall consist of money paid, labor done, or property actually received. Shares may not be ussued until the full amount of the consideration, fixed as provided by law, has been paid.* * *

"B. Neither promissory notes nor the promise of future services shall constitute payment or part payment for shares of a corporation.

"C. In the absence of fraud in the transaction, the judgement of the board of directors * * * as to the value of the consideration received for shares shall be conclusive."

The Fifth Circuit in Champion v. CIR, 303 F. 2d 887 construing the foregoing constitutional provision and Article 2.16 of the Business Corporation Act, held:

"Where it is provided that stock can be issued for labor done, as in Texas * *, the requirement is not met where the consideration for the stock is work or services to be performed in the future.**"

The 5000 shares were issued before the future services were rendered. Such stock was illegally issued and voil.

Griffitts was issued 10,000 shares partly in consideration for legal services to the Corporation and partly in exchange for the 5 acres of land. The stock was valued at $1 per share and the land had an agreed value of $4000. The trial court found (upon ample evidence) that the 4000 shares of stock issued to Griffitts was in consideration of his promise to convey the land to the Corporation; that Giffitts never conveyed the land; and the issuance of the stock was illegal and void.

The judgement of the board of directors "as to the value of consideration received for shares" is conclusive, but such does not authorize the board to issue shares contrary to the Constitution, for services to be performed in the future (as in the case of Hurt), or for property not received (as in the case of Griffitts).

■ ■ ■

Questions

1. The Texas Constitution provides for the issuance of stock upon three grounds. What are the three bases upon which stock may be issued?
2. Why was the stock issued to Hurt to be cancelled? What reasons were given for cancelling Griffitts' stock?

DISREGARDING THE CORPORATE ENTITY

BERGER v. COLUMBIA BROADCASTING SYSTEM, INC.
453 F. 2d 991 (5th Cir. 1972)
United States Court of Appeals

[Berger contracted with CBS Films, Inc. whereby Berger would produce an International Fashion Festival to be filmed by CBS Films, Inc. Subsequently, CBS, Inc., the parent corporation of CBS Films, Inc., contracted with another party to produce a fashion spectacular similar to the plaintiff's festival. Consequently, Berger instituted this action against CBS, Inc. alleging that the defendant breached the contract entered into between plaintiff and Films, which was asserted to be the alter ego of the defendant. The District Judge concluded that Films were merely an instrumentality of the defendant, and he proceeded to treat the two corporations as one.]

■ ■ ■

It is elemental jurisprudence that a corporation is a creature of the law, endowed with a personality separate and distinct from that of its owners, and that one of the principal purposes for legal sanctioning of a separate corporate personality is to accord stockholders an opportunity to limit their personal liability. There does exist, however, a large class of cases in which the separateness of a corporate entity has been disregarded and a parent corporation held liable for the acts of its subsidiary because the subsidiary's affairs had been so controlled as to render it merely an instrument or agent of its parent. But the dual personality of parent and subsidiary is not lightly disregarded, since application of the instrumentality rule operates to defeat one of the principal purposes for which the law has created the corporation. Therefore, to justify judicial derogation of the separateness of a corporate creature, an aggrieved party must prove something more than a parent's mere ownership of a majority or even all of the capital stock and the parent's use of its power as an incident of its stock ownership to elect officers and directors of the subsidiary.

In formulating a basis for predicating liability of a parent corporation for the acts of its subsidiary, courts have developed various legal theories and descriptive terms to explain the relationship between a subsidiary and its dominating parent. For example, under the "identity" theory the separate corporate entity of the dominated subsidiary is disregarded and the parent and subsidiary are treated as one corporation. Furthermore, a dominated subsidiary has been labeled an instrument, agent, adjunct, branch, dummy, department, or tool of the parent corporation. In Lowendahl v. Baltimore & O.R.R., 1936, 247 App. Div. 144, a New York court analyzed the various terms and legal theories and concluded that the instrumentality rule furnished the most practical theory for toppling a parent coporation's immunity. The court in *Lowendahl* then postulated the following three elements as the quantum of proof necessary to sustain application of the instrumentality rule:

"(1) Control, not mere majority or complete stock control, but complete domination, not only of finances, but of policy and business practice in respect to the transaction attacked so that the corporate entity as to this transaction had at the time no separate mind, will or existence of its own; and

"(2) Such control must have been used by the defendant to commit fraud or wrong, to perpetrate the violation of a statutory or other positive legal duty, or a dishonest and unjust act in contravention of plaintiff's legal rights; and

"(3) The aforesaid control and breach of duty must proximately cause the injury or unjust loss complained of."

. . . The district court held that at all relevant times Films was merely an instrumentality of the defendant based on the following findings: (1) the board of directors of Films consisted solely of employees of the defendant: (2) the organization chart of CBS, Inc. included Films; and (3) all lines of employee authority from Films passed through employees of the defendant and other subsidiaries to the chairman of the board of CBS, Inc. In addition, the trial judge was greatly influenced by the fact that several witnesses, including a comptroller of one of the defendant's subsidiaries, testified that Films ws a "division" of CBS, Inc. . . .

. . . In our opinion complete stock ownership, common officers and directors, and the use of organizational charts illustrating lines of authority are all business practices common to most parent-subsidiary relationships, and such proof of a parent's potential to dominate its subsidiary is precisely the kind of evidence that New York courts have consistently rejected as insufficient in proving a community of management between corporations. Furthermore, with respect to the testimony concerning Films' status as a division of the defendant, we think this evidence under New York law is equally unpersuasive. For purposes of application of the instrumentality rule, descriptive characterization is simply not an adequate alternative to a factual showing of the essential "act of operation."

"Our prequisition of the record in this case reveals that the evidence concerning the defendant's "act of operation" is totally insufficient to sustain any possible finding that, with respect to the transaction attached, Films possessed at the time no separate mind, will, or existence of its own...Faced with the total absence of any evidence showing the defendant's actual domination of its subsidiary Films during the period in which the plaintiff's contract was executed and allegedly breached, this court has no alternative but to reverse the decision of the district court on the simple basis that plaintiff has failed to prove, in accordance with New York law, that Films was the alter ego of the defendant. We reiterate that under the substantive law of the State of New York a parent's potential to dominate its subsidiary is insufficient to justify application of the instrumentality rule. New York law respects corporate identity, and its destruction by piercing or surrogation requires substantiation of facts, not just organizational charts and labels.

■ ■ ■

Questions

1. In *Berger* the court laid down three elements as the quantum of proof necessary to disregard a corporate entity. What were those three elements?
2. Why did the district court determine that CBS Films was the mere instrumentality of CBS, Inc.? On what grounds did the appellate court conclude that CBS Films was not the mere instrumentality of CBS, Inc.?

SHAREHOLDER'S RIGHTS

A share of stock represents an investment in a corporation. It represents an intangible personal property right, but does not confer the right to share in the operational management of the firm (although it does confer voting rights) nor a right to any specific asset. Basically, the share of stock is evidence of a profit-sharing contract between the shareholder and the corporation. However, in addition to the voting franchise, the shareholder obtains protection for the investment through the right to inspect the corporate books and records and the right to bring a derivative suit for certain types of injury suffered by the corporation as a result of mismanagement.

A shareholder is an individual whose name appears on the books of the corporation as the owner of shares of stock and who is entitled to participate in stockholder meetings of the corporation. The majority vote of the shareholders binds the cororation and all its members in any transaction or proceeding within the scope of corporate business as authorized by the corporate charter.

Action by the shareholders may be taken in a regular meeting or properly called special meeting. A regular meting is one prescribed by the charter or by-laws, whereas a special meeting is usually called by the directors. Oftern no notice is required for the annual meeting because information regarding it is set forth in the articles or by-laws. Where statutes, articles, or by-laws do not provide the time and place for this meeting, personal notice must be given to all shareholders. When giving special notice, the directors must include a statement detailing the matters to be acted upon. Any action taken at this special meeting other than those described in the notice would be illegal.

Shareholders have four basic means of remeding corporate weaknesses for mismanagement:

1. They may elect new directors if they feel that the existing management is not adequate.
2. They may bring an individual suit if their individual rights are impaired.
3. They may enjoin management from illegal or unauthorized activities.
4. They may bring a derivative suit to enforce a corporate cause of action.

A shareholder may sue the corporation in his or her individual capacity as a shareholder if the corporation has deprived him or her of any right that naturally accrued to him or her as a shareholder. For example, a shareholder may bring suit if voting rights are denied or if the corporation has failed to pay a dividend when all other shareholders have been paid.

The shareholders have the right to demand that the capital of the corporation not be subjected to risk not provided for in the charter. An individual shareholder may bring suit to enjoin the directors, officers, or agents of the corporation from engaging in conduct that would impair the corporate assets. However, because most charters today provide for a wide series of activities by the corporation, most activities of the corporation would not be considered outside the corporate purposes.

If the directors, officers, or agents are acting outside the scope of their authority, are guilty of negligent conduct, or are engaging, or about to engage, in fraudulent activities with other shareholders that would be injurious to the corporation, a shareholder may bring a "derivative" suit. Because the shareholder has no individual rights against these persons for neglect in mismanagement resulting in damages to the corporation, he or she must bring the suit as a corporate cause of action. The corporate officials, for differing reasons, may decide not to initiate this corporate action. In such case, the shareholder may derivately bring the action if he or she properly follows the requirements of the state laws. Mere dissatisfaction with corporate management, however, will not normally justify a "derivative" suit.

PREEMPTIVE RIGHTS

STOKES v. CONTINENTAL TRUST CO.
78 N.E. 1090 (1906)
Court of Appeals of New York

■ ■ ■

What is the nature of the right acquired by a stockholder through the ownership of shares of stock? What rights can he assert against the will of a majority of the stockholders and all the officers and directors? While he does not own and can not dispose of any specific property of the corporation, yet he and his associates own the corporation itself, its charter, franchises and all rights conferred thereby, including the right to increase the stock. He has an inherent right to his proportionate share of any dividend declared, or of any surplus arising upon dissolution, and he can prevent waste or misappropriation of the property of the corporation by those in control. Finally, he has the right to vote for directors and upon all propositions subject by law to the control of the stockholders and this is his supreme right and main protection. Stockholders have no direct voice in transacting the corporate business,but throught their right to vote they can select those to whom the law intrusts the power of management and control.

. . . The power to manage . . . (corporate) affairs resides in the directors, who are its agents, but the power to elect directors resides in the stockholders. This right to vote for directors and upon propositions to increase the stock . . . is about all the power the stockholder has. So long as the management is honest, within the corporate powers and involves no waste, the stockholders can not interfere, even if the administration is feeble and unsatisfactory, but must correct such evils through their power to elect other directors. Hence, the power of the individual stockholder to vote in proportion to the number of his shares, is vital and can not be cut off or curtailed by the action of all the other stockholders even with the cooperation of the directors and officers. . .

We are thus led to lay down the rule that a stockholder has an inherent right to a proportionate share of new stock issued for money only and not to purchase property for the purposes of the corporation or to effect a consolidation, and while he can waive that right, he can not be deprived of it without his consent except when the stock is issued at a fixed price not less than par and he is given the right to take at that price in proportion to his holding. . .

■ ■ ■

Questions

1. What are the stockholders' pre-emptive rights? At least three rights were mentioned in *Stokes.*
2. The conclusion in *Stokes* is that the stockholder has the pre-emptive right in the issuance of new stock. Does this suggest that the stockholder has no pre-emptive rights in the reissuance of treasury stock?
3. The court also ruled that pre-emptive rights exist for stock issued for "money only" and not stock issued "to purchase property" or issued "to effect a consolidation." Are these additional limitations on stockholders' pre-emptive rights?
4. Statutory enactments concerning pre-emptive rights are becoming increasingly frequent. The majority of jurisdictions expressly authorize the articles of incorporation to deny or limit pre-emptive rights and other jurisdictions would presumably follow the same result by implication. Are pre-emptive rights necessary in corporations of large size and with wide dispersal of their shares?

VOTING RIGHTS

GENERAL INV. CO. v. BETHLEHEM STEEL CORP.
100 A. 347 (1917)
Court of Chancery of New Jersey

■ ■ ■

This is an application for a temporary injunction to restrain Bethlehem Steel Corporation from increasing its capital stock... The stock is to have all the characteristics of common, except that it will have no vote...

The question is... whether a stockholder is entitled to require that any new stock issued should be vested with the privilege of voting...

Turning to the statute:

> Every corporation organized under this act shall have power to create two or more kinds of stock, of such classes, with such designations, preferences and voting powers or restrictions or qualifications thereof as shall be stated and expressed in the certificate of incorporation or any certificate of amendment thereof.

No broader language could have been used, and, unless the usual meaning of these words is to be restricted by reason of the existence of some public policy, it is inconceivable to me that a corporation may not issue this class of common stock, or call it what you will. I have failed to find the existence of any such public policy. The matter is one for the stockholders to determine by their contract. If the public does not want to buy it, it does not have to. The legal rights of the present stockholders are not affected; they contracted at the time they went in that they would have the advice, consultation with, and action by (or rather the opportunity of securing such adivce, consultation, and action) of the then existing stock (and this subject to its reduction in accordance with law): but there was no contract that the corporation would, if it created further stock, give that further stock the voting privilege, so that the present stockholders might have the opportunity of securing advice by and consultation with and action by the new stockholders.

The essential elements of common stock are that the holders have an opportunity to make profit if there is any and participate in the assets after all other claims are paid, and beat the loss if there be such...

That the purpose of the plan is to retain control in the present stockholders does not vitiate it. The question is one of good faith. There is no charge of bad faith in the present case.

There are many cases in other states not necessary to cite holding that it is within the power of stockholders to combine for the purpose of maintaining a management in control, and if done in good faith there s no legal objection to it. The mere fact that one of the results of the plan may be to perpetuate the control in the hands of its present stockholders does not vitiate the plan. The stockholders were entitled to vote as their selfish interest dictated.

Questions

1. Voting rights, depending upon the jurisdiction involved, may be (a) straight, (b) cumulative, (c) class, (d) contingent, (e) disporportionate, or (f) nonvoting. In straight voting, each share carries one vote for each matter to be voted on. Cumulative voting gives each share as many votes as there are directors to be elected, with the shareholder being permitted to cumulate all his or her votes for one director or distribute them as desired. Cumulative voting is designed to assure minority representation on the board of directors. Class voting involves separate voting by classes of stock for separate classes of directors or for certain other matters. Contingent voting rights are dependent on a named contingency, often the default of specified dividends and the return of the original status when the contingency is over. Disproportionate voting rights involve fractional or multiple votes per share of certain classes of stock. Nonvoting stock is self-explanatory. Of course, each of these differing types of voting rights are dependent on the statute enacted in each of the states. Which kind of voting rights were to be granted by Bethlehem Steel Corporation?

2. The New York Stock Exchange, since 1926, has barred the listing of nonvoting common stock. Since 1940 it has barred the listing of nonvoting preferred stock which does not have the right as a class to elect at least two directors when six quarterly dividends, consecutive or nonconsecutive, are in default. Is the desire to be listed on the New York Stock Exhange strong enough to force large companies to grant voting rights?

3. May shareholders form a contractual agreement to vote as required by the contract? The leading case answering this question was *Manson v. Curtis* 223 NY. 313, 119 N.E. 559 (1918), in which the court said:

   > An ordinary agreement, among a minority in number, but a majority in shares, for the purpose of obtaining control of the corporation by the election of particular persons as directors is not illegal. Shareholders have the right to combine their interests and voting powers to secure such control of the corporation in the adoption of and adhesion by it to a specific policy and course of business. Agreements upon a sufficient consideration between them, of such intendment and effect, are valid and binding, if they do not contravene any express charter or statutory provisions or contemplate any fraud, oppression or wrong against other stockholders or other illegal object.

4. May a stockholder sell his right? The rule as stated in Fletcher, *Cyclopedia Corporations*, (Rev. Ed., 1967) Section 2066:

   > ...[A]ny agreement by a stockholder to sell his vote or to vote in a certain way, or a consideration personal to himself is contrary to public policy and void.

5. Most states provide that the shareholders are entitled to vote by proxy. The proxy holder is the shareholder's agent for voting purposes at the meeting. In larger corporations, management's control of the proxy machinery tends to perpetuate management in office. Corporate funds may be used by management to solicit proxies and obtain a quorum at shareholder meetings. Often the Securities and Exchange Commission has the power to regulate proxies under the federal law. The SEC may utilize the courts to gain compliance of its rules and, in addition, private persons have been entitled to seek court enforcement of SEC proxy rules.

RIGHT TO INSPECT CORPORATE RECORDS

STATE EX REL. PILLSBURY v. HONEYWELL, INC.
191 N.W. 2d 406 (1971)
Supreme Court of Minnesota

■ ■ ■

Petitioner appeals from an order...denying...a petition for writs of mandamus to compel respondent, Honeywell, Inc., (Honeywell) to produce its original shareholder ledger, current shareholder ledger, and all corporate records dealing with weapons and munitions manufacture...

Petitioner attended a meeting on July 3, 1969, of a group involved in what was known as the "Honeywell Project." Participants in the project believed that American involvement in Vietnam was wrong, that a substantial portion of Honeywell's production consisted of munitions used in that war, and that Honeywell should stop this production of munitions...

On July 14, 1969, petitioner ordered his fiscal agent to purchse 100 shares of Honeywell. He admits that the sole purpose of the purchase was to give himself a voice in Honeywell's affairs so he could persuade Honeywell to cease producing munitions...

This court has had several occasions to rule on the propriety of shareholders' demands for inspection of corporate books and records...

While inspection will not be permitted for purposes of curiosity, speculation, or vexation, adverseness to management and a desire to gain control of the corporation for economic benefit does not indicate an improper purpose.

Several courts agree with petitioner's contention that a mere desire to communicate with other shareholders is, per se, a proper purpose. This would seem to confer an almost absolute right to inspection. We believe that a better rule would allow inspections only if the shareholder has a proper purpose for such communication...

The act of inspecting a corporation's shareholder ledger and business records must be viewed in its proper perspective. In terms of the corporate norm, inspection is merely the act of the concerned owner checking on what is in part his property. In the context of the large firm, inspection can be more akin to a weapon in corporate warfare. The effectiveness of the weapon is considerable:

> Considering the huge size of many modern corporations and the necessarily complicated nature of their bookkeeping, it is plain that to permit their thousands of stockholders to roam at will through their records would render impossible not only any attempt to keep their records efficiently, but the proper carrying on of their businesses." Cooke v. Outland, 265 N.C. 601, (1965).

Because the power to inspect may be the power to destroy, it is important that only those with a bona fide interest in the corporation enjoy that power.

That one must have proper standing to demand inspection has been recognized by statutes in several jurisdictions. Courts have also balked at compelling inspection by a shareholder holding an insignificant amount of stock in the corporation.

Petitioner's standing as a shareholder is quite tenuous. He only owns one share in his own name, bought for the purposes of this suit. He had previously ordered his agent to buy 100 shares, but there is no showing of investment intent. While his agent had a cash balance in the $400,000 portfolio, petitioner made no attempt to determine whether Honeywell was a good investment or whether more profitable shares would have to be sold to finance the Honeywell purchase...

Petitioner had utterly no interest in the affairs of Honeywell before he learned of Honeywell's production of fragmentation bombs. Immediately after obtaining this knowledge, he purchased stock in Honeywell for the sole purpose of asserting ownership privileges in an effort to force Honeywell to cease such production...

But for his opposition to Honeywell's policy, petitioner probably would not have bought Honeywell stock, would not be interested in Honeywell's profits and would not desire to communicate with Honeywell's shareholders. His avowed purpose in buying Honeywell stock was to place himself in a position to try to impress his opinions favoring a reordering of priorities upon Honeywell management and its other shareholders. Such a motivation can hardly be deemed a proper purpose germane to his economic interest as a shareholder...

We do not mean to imply that a shareholder with a bona fide investment interest could not bring this suit if motivated by concern with the long- or short-term economic effects on Honeywell resulting from the production of war munitions. Similarly, this suit might be appropriate when a shareholder has a bona fide concern about the adverse effects of abstention from profitable war contracts on his investment in Honeywell.

In the instant case, however, the trial court, in effect, has found from all the facts that petitioner was not interested in even the long-term well-being of Honeywell or the enhancement of the value of his shares. His sole purpose was to persuade the company to adopt his social and political concerns, irrespective of any economic benefit to himself or Honeywell. This purpose on the part of one buying into the corporation does not entitle the petitioner to inspect Honeywell's books and records.

Petitioner argues that he wishes to inspect the stockholder ledger in order that he may correspond with other shareholders with the hope of electing to the board one or more directors who represent his particular viewpoint... While a plan to elect one or more directors is specific and the election of directors normally would be a proper purpose, here the purpose was not germane to petitioner's or Honeywell's economic interest. Instead, the plan was designed to further petitioner's political and social beliefs. Since the requisite propriety of purpose germane to his or Honeywell's economic interest is not present, the allegation that petitioner seeks to elect a new board of directors is insufficient to compel insepction.

■ ■ ■

Questions

1. Why did the court rule that petitioner's "proper purpose" to inspect was absent?
2. Did the petitioner have "proper standing" to demand inspection?
3. Statutes of the various states often modify the shareholder's right of inspection for proper purpose. Under SEC Proxy rules corporate management has an additional option in dealing with a security holder who wishes to communicate with stockholders. When the security holder demands a list of other stockholders from the corporation, the corporation may elect not to disclose the list, but to handle the mailing for him.

DERIVATIVE SUITS

A shareholder derivative suit is an effort to enforce a corporate right against insiders or outsiders, when those in control of the corporation refuse to enforce such corporate right. The derivative suit may provide protection for the whole community of corporate interests—creditors and shareholders. While the derivative suit serves a useful social purpose, it is susceptible to abuse by what are called "strike suits." These suits involve shareholders with small holdings of stock and their attorneys seeking a private settlement of the claim and their own self-enrichment. Abuses of the derivative remedy have led many jurisdictions to place restrictions by statute or judicial interpretations on shareholders seeking to sue derivatively.

One of the restrictions imposed on shareholders in derivative suits is the requirement that the shareholder must own shares contemporaneously with the wrong that occurred to the corporation. This requirement prevents individuals from "shopping around" for alleged corporate injuries and then buyig stock in such corporations to support a derivative suit. Numberous states have also required that dismissal or compromise of any derivative suit must first be approved by the court. Additional states have creative provisions that permit the corporation to require the plaintiff-shareholder to post some bond or security for corporate expenses should the litigation be decided against the plaintiff. Such provisions normally apply to shareholders with small holdings in the corporation.

Many states require the shareholder to exhaust all efforts to achieve an intracorporate remedy before proceeding in court. Exhaustion of an intracorporate remedy usually involves a demand on the board of directors and/or shareholders that they rectify the wrong against the corporation. The following case involves a derivative suit in which the plaintiff was charged with not fully exhausting intracorporate remedies which thereby precluded any further proceedings in the derivative suit.

MAYER v. ADAMS
141 A. 2d 458, (1958)
Supreme Court of Delaware

■ ■ ■

The case concerns Rule 23 (b) of the Rules of Court...relating to stockholders' derivative suits. The second sentence of paragraph (b) provides:

> The complaint shall also set forth with particularity the efforts of the plaintiff to secure from the managing directors or trustees and, if necessary, from the shareholders such action as he desires, and the reasons for his failure to obtain such action or the reasons for not making such effort.

The question is:

Under what circumstances is a preliminary demand on shareholders necessary?

Plaintiff is a stockholder of the defendant Phillips Petroleum Company. She brought an action to redress alleged frauds and wrongs committed by the defendant directors upon the corporation. They concern dealings between Phillips and defendant Ada Oil Company, in which one of the defendant directors is alleged to have a majority stock interest.

The amended complaint set forth reasons why demand on the directors for action would be futile and the sufficiency of these reasons was not challenged. It also set forth reasons seeking to excuse failure to demand stockholder action. The principal reasons were 1) that fraud was charged, which no majority of stockholders could ratify; and 2) that to require a minority stockholder to circularize more than 100,000 stockholders — in effect, to engage a proxy fight with the management — would be an intolerably oppressive and unreasonable rule, and in any event would be a futile proceeding. All defendants moved to dismiss on the ground that the reasons set forth were insufficient in law to excuse such failure.

The...(trial court) was of opinion that, notwithstanding these allegations, demand on stockholders would not necessarily have been futile. He accordingly dismissed the complaint. Plaintiff appeals.

In the view we take of the case, the issue between the ligitants narrows itself to this:

If the ground of the derivative suit is fraud, is demand for stockholder action necessary under the rule?

When it is said that a demand on stockholders is necessary in a case involving fraud, the inquiry naturally arises: demand to do what?

Let us suppose that the objecting stockholder submits to a stockholders' meeting a proposal that a suit be brought to redress alleged wrongs. He may do so either by attending the meeting, or, if the regulations of the Securities and Exchange Commission are applicable, by requiring the management to mail copies of the proposal to the other stockholders. (He is limited to 100 words of explanation. Rule X-14A-Sb.) Let us further suppose — a result quite unlikely— that the stockholder is about to file his suit. What additional force is given to the suit by the approval?

Let us suppose again that the proposal is disapproved by the majority stockholders — as common knowledge tells us it will ordinarily be. What of it? They cannot ratify the alleged fraud. . . .

If the foregoing is a correct analysis of the matter, it follows that the whole process of stockholder demand in a case of alleged fraud is futile and avails nothing.

The defendants vigorously assail this view of the matter. They say that the rule requires demand for action to be made upon the stockholders in all cases in which the board of directors is disqualified (as here) to pass upon the matter of bringing suit, because in such a case the power to determine the question of policy passes to the body of the stockholders. The stockholders may determine, when the matter is presented to them, upon any one of a number of courses. Thus, defendants say, they may authorize plaintiff's suit; they may determine to file the suit collectively — "take it over," so to speak; they may take other remedial action; they may remove the directors; and, finally, they may decide that the suit has no merit, or, as a matter of corporate policy, that is should not in any event be brought.

These answers do not impress us. As we have said, why is it "necessary" to have stockholders' approval of plaintiff's suit? Defendants say: to comply with the rule. This is arguing in a circle. The question is, does the rule make it necessary?

Finally it is suggested that the stockholders may 1) determine that the suit has no merit, or 2) that it is not good policy to press it.

As to the first suggestion, we think it clear that in the ordinary case the stockholders in meeting could not satisfactorily determine the probable merits of a minority stockholder's suit without a reasonably complete presentation and consideration of evidentiary facts. Perhaps some very simple cases might be handled in another manner, but they must be few. A stockholders' meeting is not an appropriate forum for such a proceeding.

The second suggestion, that the stockholders may, as a matter of policy, determine that the claim shall not be enforced and bind the minority not to sue, is really the cruz of this case. If the majority stockholders have this power, there would be much to be said for defendants' argument that in case of a disqualified or non-functioning board, the stockholders should decide the matter. . . .

But a decision not to press a claim for alleged fraud committed by the directors means, in effect, that the wrong cannot be remedied. It is conceded that the wrong cannot be ratified by the majority stockholders. . . To construe Rule 23 (b) as making necessary a submission of the matter to stockholders, because the stockholders have the power to prevent the enforcement of the claim, is to import into our law a procedure that would inevitably have the effect of seriously impairing the minority stockholder's now existing right to seek redress for frauds committed by directors of the corporation. This right he has always had under the Delaware law and practice. The policy of the General Corporation law for many years has been to grant to the directors, and to the majority stockholders in certain matters, very broad powers to detemine corporate management and policy. But, correlatively, the policy of our courts has always been to hold the directors and the majority stockholders to strict accountability for any breach of good faith in the exercise of these powers, and to permit any minority stockholder to seek redress in equity on behalf of the corporation for wrongs committed by the directors or by the majority stockholders. We cannot believe that Rule 23 (b) was intended to import into our law and procedures a radical change of this judicial policy.

We hold that if a minoirty stockholders' complaint is based upon an alleged wrong committed by the directors against the corporation, of such a nature as to be beyond ratification by a majority of the stockholders, it is not necessary to allege or prove an effort to obtain action by the stockholders to redress the wrong.

The question may be asked: In what circumstances is such demand necessary? Obviously the rule contemplates that in some cases a demand is necessary; otherwise, it would have not been adopted.

We are not called upon in this case to attempt to enumerate the various circumstances in which demand on stockholders is excused; and likewise we do not undertake to enumerate all the cases in which demand is necessary. It seems clear that one instance of necessary demand is a case involving only an irregularity or lack of authority in directorate action. . . .

■ ■ ■

Questions

1. What is the purpose in requiring a stockholder who desires a derivative suit to first submit the claim to the stockholders themselves?
2. Why was the derivatively suing stockholder in this instance excused from making a demand upon stockholders?
3. Does the decision in *Mayer* unnecessarily expose the corporation to "strikes suits" or aid the shareholders in protection against fraud against the corporation?

ASSET DISTRIBUTION

IN RE OLYMPIC NATIONAL AGENCIES, INC.
442 P. 2d 246 (1968)
Supreme Court of Washington

■ ■ ■

This is an appeal from a decree instructing the liquidating trustee to distribute the assets of Olympic National Agencies, Inc., after the preference of the preferred stock is satisfied, to the common and preferred stockholders on a pro rata basis.

. . .(The) decree. . .provided that the liquidating trustee should first pay $5 to each share of preferred stock, then $5 to each share of common stock and should then distribute any surplus pro rata to both classes of stock. The court based its conclusion on article V of Agencies' articles of incorporation, which reads:

> The preferred stock shall be entitled to a preferred non-cumulative dividend of seven percent (7%) per annum before any dividend shall be declared or paid on common stock. Dividends shall be out of the net earnings or surplus of the company, and shall be in such amount and payable at such times as shall be declared by the Board of Directors. The preferred stock shall further be preferred as to the assets of the corporation up to par value. . .

The articles of incorporation are a contract, and govern, save as statute may otherwise provide, the rights of the parties.

The articles should be read in the context of the usages and practices of businessmen. . .

The. . . question before us is whether a preference precludes the preferred stock from participating in the distribution of assets beyond the stated preference upon liquidation. In Squires v. Balbach Co., 177 Neb. 465, at 478, (1964), the court said:

> We conclude that provisions in corporate articles and memoranda that holders of preferred stock shall be paid the par value of their stock before any liquidation dividends are paid to the holders of common stock is exhaustive and mean that the preferred stock shall have its par preference on liquidation and nothing more. . . .

The articles of incorporation of Agencies resemble the charters involved in the *Mohawk Carpet Mills* case and the case of Re Isle of Thanet Electric Co., in that they expressly afford the preferred stock the right to participate in dividends beyond a stated preference. Thus, the absence of such a provision in regard to assets is significant. The concurring opinion in Williams v. Renshaw, explains why the New York court attached importance to such an omission:

> The trial court very aptly refers in this connection to the preference as to dividends, where it is provided that the preferred stock shall have first 8 per cent, then the common stock shall have 8 per cent; and, if there be further dividend distribution of earnings, the two stocks shall share equally. If it had been intended that there should be a like preference right in the distribution of assets, it would have been expressed. Had the contract been simply that the preferred stock should have an eight per cent dividend before the common stock could have any dividend, the preferred stock could have claimed no part in the distribution of earnings beyond 8 per cent. yet, if the net earnings had justified it, a 20 per cent dividend could have been paid on the common stock and a preferred stockholder could not have successfully contested. It seems to me very significant that, in drafting this certificate of incorporation as to the distribution of assets, nothing was stipulated with reference to the right of a preferred stockholder after he had once been paid "in full at par"; also that nothing is said as to the right of the common stockholder in the assets after the preferred holders are paid in full. The fair inference is that the remainder goes to the common stock... The right of the preferred stock having been specifically named, all further rights are excluded.

We hold that, under facts such as in the instant case, where one class of stock is afforded a stated preference as to assets on liquidation, and the articles of incorporation are silent as to any further participation, the clear implication is that the rights of the preferred stock are exhausted once the preference has been satisfied.

■ ■ ■

Questions

1. Preferred stock is to have a preference in liquidation. Explain your understanding of the extent of the preference in distribution of the assets.
2. How could the trial court have made such an error in the interpretation of the rights of preferred stock? What rules of interpretation did the Supreme Court of Washington follow in arriving at its decision?
3. When are stockholders entitled to dividends?

> It is a well-recognized principle of law that the directors of a corporation, and they alone, have the power to declare a dividend of the earnings of the corporation and to determine its amount...Courts...will not interfere in the management of the directors unless it is clearly made to appear that they are guilty of fraud or misappropriation of the corporate funds, or refuse to declare a dividend when the corporation has a surplus of net profits which it can, without detriment to its business, divide among its stockholders, and when a refusal to do so would amount to such an abuse of discretion as would constitute a fraud, or breach of that good faith which they are bound to exercise towards the stockholders. *Hunter v. Robers, Throp & Co.,* 47 N.W. 131, 134, (1890).

4. It is well-settled law that a shareholder of a corporation who sells his or her stock to the corporation while it is insolvent is liable to an injured creditor of the corporation for the amount paid to the shareholder for the stock. This liability is based on the adverse effect of the transaction on creditors, and not on the guilt or innocence of the shareholder, who is held liable even though there is no evidence of fraud. Why should the shareholder be liable? Is the shareholder ever permitted to sell his or her shares back to the corporation without incurring liability?

5. Should the directors be liable for repurchasing shares when the corporation is insolvent?

CORPORATE MANAGEMENT

Corporate management involves the functions of three groups within the corporation: shareholders, directors, and officers. Their roles are defined and limited by the corporation's charter, its bylaws, and the state's incorporation statutes. General management of the corporate business—making and implementing policy decisions—is delegated almost exclusively to the board of directors. However, the power to amend the corporate charter, sell all corporate assets, change the makeup of the corporation, and terminate corporate power remains with the shareholders. Making by-laws is also a shareholder function, unless this power is modified by statute.

The shareholders' principal control over the actions of the directors is through their voting power. The state incorporation statutes give the shareholders their voting power. The state incorporation statutes give the shareholders the right to remove a director with or without cause, and to elect a new director or board of directors. In large corporations, exercise of this right is hampered by the large number of shareholders and by management's control over proxy solicitation.

Because of the complexities of the modern corporation, the board of directors does not handle the daily activities of corporate business, delegating instead much of its authority to the officers of the company. The board retains a measure of control through its power of removal; it may remove an officer whenever it feels inclined to make a change.

While corporations are organized under an applicable state incorporation statute, most of the rules of management duties imposed on directors are, nevertheless, the product of court decision rather than statutory implementation. The various duties of directors are owed directly to the corporation as an entity. Generally speaking, the duties of management are threefold in nature: (a) obedience, (b) diligence, and (c) loyalty.

The duty of obedience requires the directors to act "intra vires" (within authority) as related to both the corporate charter and the by-laws, as well as statutory constraints. Willful or negligent disobedience will result in director liability to the corporation.

The duty of diligence contemplates the exercise of due care by directors in the conduct of their office. While the standard of care varies in different jurisdictions, the general scheme is described as the care which ordinarily prudent men would exercise under similar circumstances in like positions. When this duty of diligence is breached, the director is liable to the corporation for damages caused by his or her negligence.

The duty of loyalty contemplates the fiduciary principles of good faith and fair dealing. The director must refrain from any personal activities that injure or take advantage of the corporation. Any such disloyalty by a director to his or her profit will result in a disgorging of that profit to be returned to the corporation.

Under the "business judgment" rule, a court will not interfere with the internal management of a corporation and substitute its judgment for that of the directors as long as the directors exercise their judgment consistent with their duties of obedience, diligence, and loyalty. Having arrived at a decision, within the corporate powers and their authority, for which there is a reasonable basis, and acting in good faith, the "business judgment" rule will protect or immunize the directors from liability for a poor business judgment.

NEGLIGENCE IN OFFICE

BARNES v. ANDREWS
298 F. 614 (1924)
District Court of United States (SDNY)

■ ■ ■

The corporation was organized. . . to manufacture starters for Ford motors and aeroplanes. On October 9, 1919, about a year after its organization, the defendant took office as a director, and served until he resigned on June 21, 1920. During that period over $500,000 was raised by the sales of stock of the company, made through an agent working on commission. A force of officers and employees was hired at substantial salaries, and the factory, already erected when the defendant took office, was equipped with machinery. Starter parts were made in quantity, but delays were experienced in the production of starters as a whole, and the funds of the company were steadily depleted by the running charges.

After the defendant resigned, the company continued business until the spring of 1921, when the plaintiff was appointed receiver, found the company without funds, and realized only a small amount on the sale of its assets. During the incumbency of the defendant there had been only two meetings of directors, one of which. . .he attended; the other happening at a day when he was forced to be absent because of his mother's death. He was a friend of the president, who had induced him as the largest stockholder to become a director, and his only attention to the affairs of the company consisted of talks with the president as they met from time to time.

The theory of the bill was that the defendant had failed to give adequate attention to the affairs of the company, which had been conducted incompetently and without regard to the waste in salaries during the period before production was possible. This period was unduly prolonged by the incompetence of the factory manager, and disagreements between him and the engineer, upon whose patents the company depended. The officers were unable to induce these men to compose their differences, and the work languished from incompetence and extravagance. . .

The. . . liability must rest upon the defendant's general inattention to his duties as a director. He cannot be charged with neglect in attending director's meetings, because there were only two during his incumbency, and of these he was present at one and had an adequate excuse for his absence from the other. His liability must therefore depend upon his failure in general to keep advised of the conduct of the corporate affairs. The measure of a director's duties in this regard is uncertain; the courts contenting themselves with vague declarations, such as that a director must give reasonable attention to the corporate business. While directors are collectively the managers of the company, they are not expected to interfere individually in the actual conduct of its affairs. To do so would disturb the authority of the officers and destroy their individual responsibility, without which no proper discipline is possible. To them must be left the initiative and the immediate direction of the business; the directors can act individually only by counsel and advice to them. Yet they have an individual duty to keep themselves informed in some detail, and it is this duty which the defendant in my judgment failed adequately to perform.

All he did was to talk with Maynard as they met, while commuting from Flushing, or at their homes. That, indeed, might be enough, because Andrews had no reason to suspect Maynard's candor, nor has any reason to question it been yet disclosed. But it is plain that he did not press him for details, as he should. It is not enough to content oneself with general answers that the business looks promising and that all seems prosperous. Andrews was bound, certainly as the months wore on, to inform himself of what was going on with some particularity, and, if he had done so, he would have learned that there were delays in getting into production which were putting the enterprise in most serious peril. It is entirely clear from his letters of April 14, 1920, and June 12, 1920, that he had made no effort to keep advised of the actual conduct of the corporate affairs, but allowed himself to be carried along as a figurehead, in complete reliance upon Maynard. In spite of his own substantial investment in the company, which I must assume was as dear to him as it would be to other men, his position required of him more than this. Having accepted a post of confidence, he was charge with an active duty to learn whether the company was moving to production, and why it was not, and to consider, as best he might, what could be done to avoid the conflicts among the personnel, or their incompetence, which was slowly bleeding it to death.

Therefore I cannot acquit Andrews of misprision of his office, though his integrity is unquestioned. The plaintiff must, however, go further than to show that he should have been more active in his duties. . . The plaintiff must accept the burden of showing that the performance of the defendant's duties would have avoided loss, and what loss it would have avoided. . .

When the corporate funds have been illegally lent, it is a fair inference that a protest would have stopped the loan, and the director's neglect caused the loss. But when a business fails from general mismanagement, business incapacity, or bad judgment, how is it possible to say that a single director could have made the company successful, or how much in dollars he could have saved? . . .[T]he plaintiff must show that, had Andrews done his full duty, he could have made the company prosper, or at least could have broken its fall. He must show what sum he could have saved the company. Neither of these has he made any effort to do.

The defendant is not subject to the burden of proving that the loss would have happened, whether he had done his duty or not. If he were, it would come to this: that, if a director were once shown slack in his duties, he would stand charged prima facie with the difference between the corporate treasury as it was, and as it would be, judged by a hypothetical standard of success. How could such standard be determined? How could any one guess how far a director's skill and judgment would have prevailed upon his fellows, and what would have been the ultimate fate of the business, if they had? How is it possible to set any measure of liability, or to tell what he could have contributed to the event? Men's fortunes may not be subjected to such uncertain and seculative conjectures. It is hard to see how there can be any remedy, except one can put one's finger on a definite loss and say with reasonable asurance that protest would have deterred, or counsel persuaded, the managers who caused it. No men of sense would take the office, if the law imposed upon them a guaranty of the general success of their companies as a penalty for any negligence.

It is, indeed, hard to determine just what went wrong in the management of this company. Any conclusion is little better than a guess. Still some discussion of the facts is necessary, and I shall discuss them. The claim that there were too many general employees turned out to be true, but, so far as I can see, only because of the delay in turning out the finished product. Had the factory gone into production in the spring of 1920, I cannot say, and the plaintiff cannot prove, that the selling department would have been prematurely or extravagantly organized. The expense of the stock sales was apparently not undue, and in any event Andrews was helpless to prevent it, because he found the contract an existing obligation of the company. So far as I can judge, the company had a fair chance of life, if the factory could have begun to turn out starters at the time expected.

Suppose I charge Andrews with a complete knowledge of all that we have now learned. What action should he have taken, and how can I say that it would have stopped the losses? The plaintiff gives no definite answer to that question. Certainly he had no right to interject himself personally into the tangle; that was for Maynard to unravel. He would scarcely have helped to a solution by adding another cook to the broth. What suggestion could he have made to Maynard, or to his colleagues? The trouble arose either from an indifferent engineer, on whom the company was entirely dependent, or from an incompetent factory manager, who should have been dis-charged, or because the executives were themselves inefficient. Is Andrews to be charged for not insisting upon. . . or for not suggesting it? Suppose he did suggest it; have I the slightest reason for saying that the directors would have discharge him? Or, had they discharged him, is it certain that a substitute. . . would have speeded up production? Was there not as a fair chance that. . . (the two men) might be brought to an accomodation as there was in putting in a green man at that juncture? How can I, sitting here, lay it down that Andrews' intervention would have brought order out of this chaos, or how can I measure in dollars the losses he would have saved? Or am I to hold Andrews because he did not move to discharge Maynard? How can I know that a beter man was available? It is easy to say that he should have done something, but that will not serve to harnass upon him the whole loss, nor is it equivalent of saying that, had he acted, the company would now flourish.

True, he was not very well-suited by experience for the job he had undertaken, but I cannot hold him on that account. After all, it is the same corporation that chose him which now seeks to charge him...Directors are not specialists, like lawyers or doctors. They must have good sense, perhaps they must have acquaintance with affairs; but they need not — indeed, perhaps they should not — have any technical talent. They are the general advisers of the business, and if they faithfully give such ability as they have to their charge, it would not be lawful to hold them liable. Must a director guarantee that his judgment is good? Can shareholders call him to account for deficiencies which their votes assured him did not disqualify him for his office? While he may not have been the Cromwell for that Civil War, Andrews did not engage to play any such role.

I conclude, therefore...that there is no evidence that the defendant's neglect caused any losses to the company, and that, if there were, that loss cannot be ascertained...

■ ■ ■

Questions

1. Since the defendant was not acquitted of misprison of office or inattention to the company affairs, why did the court determine that the plaintiffs were not entitled to a recovery?
2. Is the burden too great on the plaintiff to prove that the director "caused" the loss? Would it be more equitable to require the director to show that the loss was not caused by his or her negligence?
3. Does the present allocation of burden of proof cause the director to be completely immune from liability for company failure?
4. Since the law gives the directors exclusive authority to manage the corporation, would it be appropriate to measure the performance of the directors against a "specialist" standard?

CORPORATE OFFICERS

The officers of a corporation are its agents. As such, their powers are controlled by the laws of agency, subject to limitations imposed by the charter and by-laws or by the instructions of the board of directors. Management positions usually carry broad authority to act on behalf of the corporation. Delegation to the officers involves two concepts: (1) basic policy implementation and (2) ordinary policy implementation. Basic policy involves those matters which require board approval, whereas ordinary policies may be acted upon by the chief executive officer alone.

Generally, the president is the presiding officer of the corporation. The treasurer, or controller, keeps corporate records and receives and disburses corporate funds. The secretary keeps the minutes of corporate meetings.

Where the officer performs solely an internal function, there are generally no incidental or inherent powers. The problems relating to the authority of the officers arises in transactions with persons outside the corporation. This usually involves the chief executive officer who is presumed to be able to do all things within the everyday business activity of the company. However, the third person must be aware of the usual limits of the authority of the officer with whom he or she is dealing and is responsible for his or her knowledge of the internal practices of the corporation and the customs of the trade.

The relation of the officers to the corporation, like that of the directors, is fiduciary. For this reason, the officers are liable for any secret profits made in connection with the business of the corporation. They are liable for willful or negligent acts resulting in damage to the corporation. On the other hand, they are not liable for mere errors in judgment committed while exercising their discretionary powers, provided they have acted with reasonable prudence and skill.

GOLDENBERG v. BARTELL BROADCASTING CORPORATION
262 N.Y.S. 2d 274 (1965)
Supreme Court, New York

■ ■ ■

The plaintiff seek(s) recovery of damages for an alleged breach of a written contract of employment. The...cause of action is against the defendant Bartell Broadcasting Corporation, an entity incorporated under the laws of the State of Delaware. It is alleged in substance that on or about March 16, 1961, the plaintiff and the defendant Bartell Broadcasting Corporation entered into a written contract wherein the plaintiff was engaged as an Assistant to Gerald A. Bartell, the president of the defendant Bartell Broadcasting Corporation. The plaintiff's primary duties were to engage in corporate development in the field of pay television. The contract which was for a period of three years, provided for (1) the payment to the plaintiff of $1,933.00 per month; and (2) for the delivery to plaintiff of 12,000 shares of "Free Registered" stock of defendant Bartell Broadcasting Corporation, which stock was payable in three installments of 4,000 shares in the months of January 1962, 1963 and 1964; and (3) the payment of plaintiff's traveling and living expenses in connection with his services to the employer; and (4) that defendant Bartell Broadcasting Corporation would provide the plaintiff with a private office and proper office facilities; and (5) that the agreement would be binding on any successor corporation or any corporation with which defendant Bartell Broadcasting Corporation would merge.

This written contract was signed by the plaintiff and by Gerald A. Bartell, in his capacity as the president of Bartell Broadcasting Corporation. It is further claimed that on or about May 1961, this contract was amended to increase plaintiff's monthly compensation from $1,933.00 to $2,400.00. It is further contended that the plaintiff was not paid his monthly compensation commencing with the month of November 1961; that the defendant Bartell Broadcasting Corporation failed to deliver the 4,000 shares of stock allegedly due in January 1962; and that in July 1962, the defendant Bartell Broadcasting Corporation denied the validity of plaintiff's employment contract...

A corporation can only act through its directors, officers and employees. They are the conduit by and through which the corporation is given being and from which its power to act and reason springs. Therefore in every action in which a person sues a corporation on a contract executed on behalf of the corporation by one of its officers, one of the issues to be determined is whether the officer had the express, implied or apparent authority to execute the contract in question....

The authority of an officer to act on behalf of a corporation may be express, implied or apparent. There has been no proof offered in this case indicating that Gerald A. Bartell, as president of the defendant Bartell Broadcasting Corporation, had express authority to enter into the agreement, dated March 16, 1961...

Did Gerald A. Bartell then have either *implied* or *apparent authority* to execute the contract?

Implied authority is a species of actual authority, which gives an officer the power to do the necessary acts within the scope of his usual duties. Generally, the president of the corporation has the implied authority to hire and fire corporate employees and to fix their compensation. However the president of a corporation does *not* have the implied power to execute "unusual or extraordinary" contracts of employment....

The agreement of March 16, 1961 not only provides for the payment of a substantial monthly compensation, but also requires the delivery of 12,000 shares of "free regis-tered" stock of the defendant Bartell Broadcasting Corporation. While the payment of the monthly compensation would not make the contract of March 16, 1961, "*unusual or extraordinary*," the Court is of the opinion that the inclusion in the contract of the provision requiring the delivery to plaintiff of 12,000 shares of "free registered stock," does bring the agreement within the category of being an "*unusual and extraordinary*" contract.

In *Gumpert v. Bon Ami Company*, 251 F. 2d 735, the plaintiff there sued on a one year employment contract under which he was to be paid $25,000 in cash and $25,000 in defendant's corporate stock. The contract was signed on behalf of the corporation's executive committee...The Federal court...wrote:

> *Even if Rosenberg was chief executive officer * * * it is doubtful that he would possess power to make such an arrangement as a normal incident of his position.____*

In *Noyes v. Irving Trust Company*, 294 N.Y.S. 2, the plaintiff there sued on an employment contract under which he was to be paid $400 per month together with a bonus based upon the net profits. The contract was signed on behalf of the defendant corporation by its sales manager. The court...wrote:

> It is well settled that a contract of this character is not the usual and ordinary contract which one authorized to employ agents and servants may make. *It would require express authority...*

The reason for the rule enunciated in the cases just cited, is easily discernible. Corporate stock is the sinew, muscle and bone upon which the financial structure of a corporation is constructed. Corporate stock is sold, traded or disposed of in exchange for money, labor, services or other property. Thus in this manner a corporation acquires the necessary assets needed for the fulfillment of the corporate purposes....

To permit the president of a corporation, without the express authority and approval of the corporation's Board of Directors, to barter or contract away the corporation's unissued (free)stock, would not only be an express violation of the statutes, but would also make possible the denudation of a corporation's assets, and the dilution of the value of the stock already issued to the detriment and disadvantage of the coprorate stockholders. It should be noted here that in the case at bar, the stock of both defendant corporations is publicly owned and traded.

Apparent authority is the authority which the principal permits the agent to represent that he possesses. Generally, persons dealing with officers of a corporation are bound to take notice that the powers of an officer are derived from statutes, by-laws and usages which more or less define the extent of the officer's authority. In a doubtful case one must at his peril acquaint himself with the exact extent of the officer's authority....The right of a third party to rely on the aparent authority of a corporate officer is subject to the condition that such third person has no notice or knowledge of a limitation in such authority....Although it is true that secret instructions or limitations upon the apparent general authority of an officer of a corporation will not affect one who deals with the officer in the general line of his authority, and knows nothing of such limitations; however, this rule is not applicable to any limitations which are provided for in statutes. Those who contract with a corporation do so with knowledge of the statutory conditions pertaining to a corporation....

The plaintiff is not a naive person, uninitiated in the business world, nor is he without knowledge of corporate financing or business practices. By his own testimony he is and was a stockholder, officer and director of several corporations. There is testimony that the plaintiff has engaged in the sale of securities to the general public....

With the varied and broad business experience acquired by the plaintiff in his wide business associations as evidenced by his own career resume furnished to the defendants...and by plaintiff's own testimony, it can be truly said that he not only presumed to have knowledge of the statutory provisions of the law pertaining to corporations, but that he apparently also had actual knowledge of such laws. It is reasonable to infer that the plaintiff was aware, or at the least, had reason to be aware, that the authority for the issuance of corporate stock rests solely within the powers of the Board of Directors of the corporation, and that in the absence of express authority, the president of a corporation does not have the implied or apparent authority to enter into an employment contract which provides for the issuance of corporate stock as compensation....

Questions

1. In what ways may a corporation be bound on a contract negotiated by its agent?

2. What documents would you want to look at to determine a corporate agent's express authority?

3. In *Employers Liability Assurance Corp. v. Hudson River Trust Co.*, 250 App. Div. 159. . . the court said: "In the case of an officer or agent of a private corporation dealing with its funds the authority of such officer or agent is not known to all but depends upon the authority conferred upon him by the corporation which he represents. In such class of cases a bank knowingly receiving corporate funds for deposit in the individual account of such officer or agent is held to be under the duty of making inquiry to ascertain the extent of his authority in the transaction." Explain.

4. "Are corporate officers and directors who take no steps to terminate their status as such, but simply abandon the corporation by ceasing to attend meetings and ceasing to perform the duties of their office, for whom no successors are elected, liable under the statute when the corporation subsequently is in default. . ."?
"The answer must be yes. A position of corporate trust, like a marriage, is not terminated merely by leaving the tent. Adequate protection of the myriad rights and interests involved in the sophisticated world of modern commerce requires something more than an Arabian directness and simplicity. It is to protect such interests that the statute exists. To ensure orderliness, as well as to locate corporate responsibility with certainty, a corporate officer or director retains his office until properly replaced by his successor (barring, perhaps, some particular by-law peculiarly bearing on the problem). Among the responsibilities of corporate offices, is the duty to see that the office is properly transferred into other hands." *Eberts Cadillac Co. v. Miller* 159 N.W. 2d 217 (1968).

ENDNOTE

1. "The History of Agency," 5 *Harv. L. Rev.* 1, 14.

PART III
GOVERNMENT REGULATION

The legal environment of the nineteenth century was devoted primarily to providing and, if necessary, creating the legal devices necessary for the economic expansion of the American continent. Fundamental public policy created a legal framework that encouraged individual initiative (private property) and guaranteed that the resonable expectations (contract rights) of this initiative could be realized. Business laws reflected society's notion of appropriate policy for a free enterprise system.

At the onset of the twentieth century, the United States had developed into an industrial nation of unparalleled power and wealth. This seemed to demonstrate conclusively the potential for economic growth in an environment relatively fee of legal restrictions and controls. However, certain events had placed too much of the power and wealth in the hands of individuals who recognized too few responsibilites to society.

Abuses of the privileges conferred by the free· enterprise system became more prevalent. For example, business utiliized the common law trust to create business combinations that enabled businessmen to control prices and restrict output of an entire industry. These anticompetitive arrangements caused the development of antitrust laws and regulations (Chapter 10 and 11) in an effort to perserve economic individualism, the opportunity to enter the marketplace, and the opportunity to fairly compete for the consumer's patronage. These efforts have evolved into direct consumer protection laws (Chapter 12). In additon, the law recognized the development of inequalities in bargaining power that came to exist between labor and management. As a result, new legal relationships and devices were created to provide the working-man with a larger share of the economic pie. Freedom of contract gave way to social welfare and a social concern for a fairer standard of work and living (Chapter 14). Federal regulation of the corporate security distribution process has emerged as one of the more pervasive controls on large business entities (Chapter 13). Finally, society's expression of concern over the natural environment has caused the enactment of recent legal constraints imposed by both state and federal environmental laws (Chapter 15). In short, the governmental policy of "promotionalism" of the nineteenth century has given way to the extensive regulations of the twentieth century.

10

GOVERNMENT REGULATION OF INDUSTRY STRUCTURE

From earliest U.S. history, the American businessman has place a firm faith in the workings of a free market economy. Protection against those who might exploit or abuse society in the production and distribution of the nations's goods and services was to be effectuated through the forces of competition. So strong was this faith in competition as an efficient regulator, the government, influenced by a *laissez faire* philosophy, offered little, if any, interference with the economy's operation. While this belief in competition as a virtue for society continues even today, the government has found it necessary to change its role from a passive observer of economic activity into a modern-day protector of "competition"; the theory being that by protecting and preserving competition, American will continue to reap the benefits of a free economy except for the historical role of a limited government.

Substantial government interference with trade activities is of fairly recent origin. Of course, the decisions concerning a change in the role of government and the variety of methods to be employed in trade regulation have not been accomplished without opposition. At the outset, debate centered on the nature of the "power" of the government to legislate and regulate economic activity. Additionally, the policy choices or alternative solutions selected to preserve "competition" have not received universal acceptance. The following materials deal with the power of the government to regulate economics matters and, secondly, the basic substantive regulations relating to the structure of industries; that is, government prohibitions of monopolies and illegal mergers and acquisitions that tend toward monopoly.

THE CONSTITUTIONAL BASIS OF REGULATION

In the past, the U.S. Supreme Court has reflected the ideological commitment to free competition in its acceptance of "laissez faire" as the rule for governmental policy. In fact, the Supreme Court utilized its power of judicial review to protect the American capitalistic system from the legislative or executive branches of government that attempted interferences with the fundamental basis of American capitalism; that is private property and the liberty to contract. The Supreme Court has utilized general clauses of the Constitution to restrict both state and federal legislative bodies to a *laissez faire* policy.

JUDICIAL RESTRICTIONS ON STATE LEGISLATURES

Efforts of the state legislatures to regulate their economic affairs is founded on the state's police power. To protect the health, safety, morals, or general welfare of the state citizenry, states may regulate economic affairs. However, the Supreme Court has utilized constitutional interpretation to limit state legislation over economic affairs. Since the Commerce Clause of the U.S. Constitution grants to the federal government the power to regulate interstate commerce, by implication the states were denied this power. The purposes of inserting the Commerce Clause in the Constitution was to prevent the states from imposing tariffs or duties on imports into their state or otherwise discriminating against interstate merchants transporting goods into the state. The Commerce Clause was intended to create a "free market" throughout the states of the Union. Consequently, the Supreme Court could utilize the clause to prohibit state governments from regulating certain aspects of commerce which the Court deemed to be interstate, and beyond the reach of state governments. The Supreme Court has stated that whenever the subject of economic regulation requires a national or uniform plan, Congress possesses *exclusive* power for legislative solution. And even if no uniformity of regulation is required, the Court has held that state regulations may not discriminate against interstate commerce or substantially and unduly burden interstate commerce. Only if the economic affair was not one requiring uniformity and the state law did not discriminate against or unduly burden interstate commerce, was the state free to regulate the economic activity.

A second judicial constraint was imposed on state governments in their efforts to regulate economic affairs. The Supreme Court extended the power of the "due process" clause of the Fourteenth Amendment from a "procedural" constraint to a "substantive" restraint on legislators. The Fourteenth Amendment provides that "life, liberty, or property" may not be deprived by the state without affording "due process of law." Initallly, process was a synonym for procedure and "due process of law" meant that appropriate procedure of law must be followed in depriving an individual of life, liberty, or property. Legislative due process would require that state congressional bodies follow their respective constitutional and statutory procedures before and during the enactment of laws. However, in contrast to procedural due process, "substantive" due process involves the Court's declaration of unconstitutionality of those state regulatory statutes which the Court determines to be *unreasonable* interferences with liberty or property. In this sense, the Due Process Clause was utilized to deprive state regulations whenever the court was convinced the statute was unreasonable or did not conform to the justices' concept of *laissez faire* philosophy. The Supreme Court, in effect, had the last word or a veto power over state legislatures by virtue of "substantive due process" interpretation.

Susbtantive due process restrictions on state legislatures began with Supreme Court review of the rates established by states over what may be termed public utilities. The Court determined that rates must allow a "fair return" on the invested value of property in such organizations. In these instances, the Court acted as a super-legislature and reviewed the reasonableness of the rates in any regulated industry. In other cases, as in *Allgeyer v. Louisiana* 165 U.S. 578 (1897) the court invalidated state statutes which prohibited their citizens from contracting with companies outside of the state. In the field of labor relations, numerous state statutes were held to be "unreasonable" interferences with liberty and consequently, in violationof the Due Process Clause. In *Lochner v. New York* 198 U.S. 45 (1905) the Court held a New York statute unconstitutional because it limited the hours of work by those employed in bakeries.

> In every case that comes before this court, therefore, where legislation of this character is concerned, and where the protection of the Federal Constitution is sought, the question necessarily arises: Is this a fair, reasonable, and appropriate exercise of the police power of the state, or is it an unreasonable, unnecessary, arbitrary interference with the right of the individual to his personal liberty, or to enter into those contracts in relation to labor which may seem to him appropriate or necessary for the support of himself and his family? . . .

We think the limit of the police power has been reached and passed in this case. There is, in our judgment, no reasonable foundation for holding this to be necessary and appropriate as a health law to safeguard the public health, or the health of individuals who are following the trade of baker.

Justice Holmes dissented from the *Lochner* decision and began an attack on substantive due process:

This case is decided upon an economic theory which a large part of the country does not entertain. If it were a question whether I agreed with that theory, I should desire to study it further and long before making up my mind. But I do not conceive that to be my duty, because I strongly believve that my agreement or disagreement has nothing to do with the right of a majority to embody their opinions in law. . . [A] Constitution is not intended to embody a particular legal theory, whether of paternalism and the organic relation of the citizen to the state or of *laissez faire*. It is made for people of fundamentally different views, and the accident of our finding certain opinions natural and familiar, or novel, and even shocking, ought not to conclude our judgment upon the question whether statutes emboding them conflict with the Constitution of the United States.

Nevertheless, the Supreme Court continued to use substantive due process to void state statutes. Thus, many statutory economic controls which the public desired were held to be unconstitutional during the era from 1890 to 1937.

JUDICIAL RESTRICTIONS ON THE FEDERAL LEGISLATURE

In the early history of the federal government there were only limited efforts in economic regulation. Federal economic regulation actually began with a Supreme Court decision involving state regulation of the railroads. The Court held that the interstate nature of the railroads required *uniform* regulations, which states could not supply. Therefore, the federal government found it necessary to pass the Interstate Commerce Act (ICC) of 1887 to deal with growing monopolistic abuses in the railroad industry. The Supreme Court upheld the ICC Act because railroads were involved in interstate commerce. The Supreme Court upheld other federal regulations under the Commerce Clause which involved questions of immorality. For example, the court allowed Congress to prohibit interstate lotteries, interstate shipment of adulterated food or drugs,, interstate transport of prostitutes, or interstate transportation of stolen motor vehicles. However, there were other Supreme Court interpretations of the Commerce Clause calculated to restrict the power of the federal government to regulate economic activities.

For example, the Court determined that "commerce among the several states" restricted the meaning of interstate commerce to *transportation* of goods from one state to another. The effect of this interpretation was to limit the Commerce Clause to transportation of goods between the states and to those activities surrounding transportation. Consequently, any federal legislation designed to deal with a particular subject area other than transporation were held to be beyond the powers of Congress. Insurance was held not be "commerce" and not subject to federal regulation. The Sherman Antitrust Act was initially held not to apply to local 'manufacturing" activities. One of the greatest impacts of the Supreme Court's narrow interpretation of the Commerce Clause was in labor relations. One of the most famous cases was *Hammer v. Dagenhart* 247 U.S. 251 (1918) which held that the Federal Child Labor Act was unconstitutional. The act attempted to prohibit the shipment in interstate commerce of articles manufactured from factories in which children under 14 years of age were employed in production. The Court concluded that this "manufacturing" was beyond the reach of the "interstate commerce" power.

During the economic depression of the 1930's, despite public demands for increased federal action, the Supreme Court struck down the National Industrial Recovery Act as unconstitutionally extending beyond the power conferred under the Commerce Clause. The Supreme Court also invalidated the Railroad Retirement Act of 1934 because the statute was said to deal with purely social ends without any "direct" relation to interstate commerce. The Bitumunous Coal Conservation Act of 1935, which set minimum wages and maximum hours for miners whose coal production was subsequently shipped in interstate commerce, was held unconstitutional. Mining was said to precede "commerce" and had only an "indirect" effect on interstate commerce and, consequently, was beyond the federal powers to control.

In total, the Supreme Court frustated both state and federal legislative attempts to deal with perceived economic problems. It was based on the Court's belief that its conception of economic theory and policy was best suited for Americans. It used its powers of judicial review in an effort to preserve *laissez faire* governmental policy.

NEW ERA OF LEGISLATIVE ECONOMIC POLICY

The decline of the use of substantive due process to veto state economic legislation began in the 1934 case of *Nebbia v. New York* 291 U.S. 502 (1934). The court ruled:

Neither property rights nor contract rights are absolute; for government cannot exist if the citizen may at will use his property to the detriment of his fellows, or exercise his freedom of contract to work them harm.

By 1941 the Supreme Court was writing:

We are not concerned, however, with the wisdom, need, nor appropriateness of the legislation. Differences of opinion on that score suggest a choice which "should be left where... it was left by the Constitution—to the states and to Congress."[1]

Later, the Court ruled:

This court... has consciously returned closer and closer to the earlier Constitutional principle that states have power to legislate against what are found to be injurious practices in their internal commercial and busines affairs, so long as their laws do not run afowl of some specific federal constitutional prohibition, or of some valid federal law. ...Under this doctrine the Due Process Clause is no longer to be so broadly construed that the Congress and the state legislatures are put in a strait-jacket when they attempt to suppress business and industrial conditions which they regard as offensive to the public welfare.[2]

By 1955, the Supreme Court was writing:

The day is gone when this Court uses the Due Process Clause of the Fourteenth Amendment to strike down state laws, regulatory of business and industrial conditions, because they may be unwise, inprovident, or out of harmony with a particular school of thought.[3]

In 1937, another series of Supreme Court decisions began which broadly interpreted the Commerce Clause, which thereby expanded the federal congressional power to deal with economic affirs. In the *National Labor Relations Board v. Jones & Laughlin Steel Corp.*, 301 U.S. 1 (1937), the Supreme Court upheld the National Labor Relations Act and its application in a *manufacturing* setting. In *U.S. v. Darby Lumber* 312 U.S. 100 (1941) the Supreme Court upheld the constitutionality of the Fair Labor Standards Act of 1938 and applied its provisions to an *intrastate* merchant who paid less than the federal minimum wage. The Supreme Court concluded that the commerce power may be utilized to exclude any article from interstate commerce whether the product itself is harmful or not. As an aftermath of *Darby Lumber*, Congress was empowered to eliminate from commerce items manufactured without payment of the minimum federal wage or, alternatively, impose a fine on those who violated the federal minimum wage law. Additional comprehensive federal regulation of a purely local commercial activity was proposed in the Agricultural Adjustment Act of 1938, which was challenged in the following case:

WICKARD v. FILBURN
317 U.S. 111 (1942)
Supreme Court of the United States

■ ■ ■

JACKSON, Mr. Justice:

It is urged that under the Commerce Clause of the Constitution, Congress does not possess the power it has in this instance sought to exercise. . . The sum of this is that the Federal Goverment fixes a quota including all that the farmer may harvest for sale or for his own farm needs, and declares that wheat produced on excess acreage may neither be disposed of nor used except upon payment of the penalty, or except it is stored as required by the Act or delivered to the Secretary of Agriculture.

Defandant says that this is a regulation of production and consumption of wheat. Such activities are, he urges, beyond the reach of Congressional power under the Commerce Clause, since they are local in character, and their effects upon interstate commerce are at most "indirect." In answer the Government argues it is sustainable as a "necessary and proper" implementation of the power of Congress over interstate commerce.

. . . Even today, when this power has been held to have great latitude, there is no decision of this Court that such activities may be regulated where no part of the product is intended for interstate commerce or intermingled with the subjects thereof. We believe that a review of the course of decision under the Commerce Clause will make plain, however, that questions of the power of Congress are not to be decided by reference to any formula which would give controlling force to nomenclature such as "production" and "indirect" and foreclose consideration of the actual effects of the activity in question upon interstate commerce. . .

It was not until 1887, with the enactment of the Interstate Commerce Act, that the interstate commerce power began to exert positive influence in American law and life. This first important federal resort to the commerce power was followed in 1890 by the Sherman Anti-Trust Act and, thereafter, mainly after 1903, by many others. These statutes ushered in new phases of adjudication, which required the Court to approach the interpretation of the Commerce Clause in the light of an actual exercise by Congress of its power thereunder.

When it first dealt with this new legislation, the Court adhered to its earlier pronouncements, and allowed but little scope to the power of Congress. . .

The Court's recognition of the relevance of the economic effects in the application of the Commerce Clause. . . has made the mechanical application of legal formulas no longer feasible. Once an economic measure of the reach of the power granted to Congress in the Commerce Clause is accepted, questions of federal power cannot be decided simply by finding the activity in question to be "production," nor can consideration of its economic effects be foreclosed by calling them "indirect." The present Chief Justice has said in summary of the present state of the law: "The commerce power is not confined in its exercise to the regulation of commerce among the states. It extends to those activities intrastate which so affect interstate commerce, or the exertion of the power of Congress over it, as to make regulation of them appropriate means to the attainment of a legitimate end, the effective execution of the granted power to regulate interstate commerce. . . The power of Congress over interstate commerce is plenary and complete in itself, may be exercised to its utmost extent, and acknowledges no limitations other than are prescribed in the Constitution. . . It follows that no form of state activity can constitutionally thwart the regulatory power granted by the commerce clause to Congress. Hence the reach of that power extends to those intrastate activities which in a substantial way interfere with or obstruct the exercise of the granted power." *United States v. Wrightwood Dairy Co.,* 315 U.S. 110, 119.

Whether the subject of the regulation in question was "production," "consumption," or "marketing" is, therefore, not material for purposes of deciding the question of federal power before us. That an activity is of local character may help in a doubtful case to determine whether Congress intended to reach it. The same consideration might help in determining whether in the absence of Congressional action it would be permissible for the state to exert its power on the subject matter, even though in so doing it to some degree affected interstate commerce. But even if (defendant's) activity be local and though it may not be regarded as commerce, it may still, whatever its nature, be reached by Congress if it exerts a substantial economic effect on interstate commerce, and this irrespective of whether such effect is what might at some earlier time have been defined as "direct" or "indirect."

The effect of consumption of home-grown wheat on interstate commerce is due to the fact that it constitutes the most variable factor in the disappearance of the wheat crop. Consumption on the farm where grown appears to vary in an amount greater than 20 per cent of average production. The total amount of wheat consumed as food varies but relatively little, and use as seed is relatively constant.

The maintenance by government regulation of a price for wheat undoubtedly can be accomplished as effectively by sustaining or increasing the demand as by limiting the supply. The effect of the statute before us is to restrict the amount which may be produced for market and the extent as well as to which one may forestall resort to the market by producing to meet his own needs. That defendant's own contribution to the demand for wheat may be trivial by itself is not enough to remove him from the scope of federal regulation where, as here, his contribution, taken together with that of many others similarly situated, is far from trivial.

It is well established by decisions of this Court that the power to regulate commerce includes the power to regulate the prices at which commodities in that commerce are dealt in and practices affecting such prices. One of the primary purposes of the Act in question was to increase the market price of wheat, and to that end to limit the volume thereof that could affect the market. It can hardly be denied that a factor of such volume and variability as home-consumed wheat would have a substantial influence on price and market conditions. This may arise because being in marketable condition such wheat overhangs the market and, if induced by rising prices, tends to flow into the market and check price increases. But if we assume that it is never marketed, it supplies a need of the man who grew it which would otherwise be reflected by purchases in the open market. Home-grown wheat in this sense competes with wheat in commerce. The stimulation of commerce is a use of the regulatory function quite as definitely as prohibitions or restrictions thereon. This record leaves us in no doubt that Congress may properly have considered that wheat consumed on the farm where grown, if wholly outside the scheme of regulation, would have a substantial effect in defeating and obstructing its purpose to stimulate trade therein at increased prices.

It is said, however, that this Act, forcing some farmers into the market to buy what they could provide for themselves, is an unfair promotion of the markets and prices of specializing wheat growers. It is of the essence of regulation that it lays a restraining hand on the self-interest of the regulated and that advantages from the regulation commonly fall to others. The conflicts of economic interest between the regulated and those who advantage by it are wisely left under out system to resolution by the Congress under its more flexible and responsible legislative process. Such conflicts rarely lend themselves to judicial determination. And with the wisdom, workability, or fairness, of the plan of regulation we have nothing to do.

■ ■ ■

Questions

1. Under the Interstate Commerce Clause, may the federal government regulate "marketing"? "Consumption"? "Production"? How far does the Interstate Commerce power extend into the states?

2. May the Court inquire into Congressional purposes for passing legislation in order to determine if Congress is regulating "economic affairs" and not some "social or moral" problem? In the *Heart of Atlanta Motel, Inc. v. U.S.*, 379 US 241 (1964) the Supreme Court ruled:

> ...In framing (the Civil Rights Act of 1964)...Congress was also dealing with what is considered a moral problem. But that fact does not detract from the overwhelming evidence of the disruptive effect that racial discrimination has had on commercial intercourse. It was this burden which empowered Congress to enact appropriate legislation, and, given this basis for the exercise of its power, Congress was not restricted by the fact that the particular obstruction to inter-state commerce with which it was dealing was also deemed a moral and social wrong. It is said that the operation of the motel here is of a purely local character. But, assuming this to be true, "(i)f it is interstate commerce that feels the pinch, it does not matter how local the operation which applies the squeeze." *United States v. Women's Sportswear Mfrs. Assn.,* 336 U.S. 460, 464 (1949)... Thus the power of Congress to promote interstate commerce also includes the power to regulate the local incidents thereof, including local activities in both the States of origin and destination, which might have a substantial and harmful effect upon that commerce. One need only examine the evidence which we have discussed above to see that Congress may —as it has—prohibit racial discrimination by motels serving travelers, however 'local' their operations may appear. Nor does the Act deprive appellant of liberty or property under the Fifth Amendment. The commerce power invoked here by the Congress is a specific and plenary one authorized by the Constitution itself. The only questions are (1) whether Congress had a rational basis for finding that racial discrimination by motels affected commerce, and (2) if it had such a basis, whether the means it selected to elimiate that evil are reasonable and appropriate. If they are, appellant has no "right" to select its guests as it sees fit, free from governmental regulation.

Society's commitment to a *laissez faire* philosophy of government has terminated. The Supreme Court's ideological commitment to *laissez faire* through a narrow interpretation of the Commerce Clause and through the use of substantive due process has likewise met its demise. Instead, the Supreme Court has abdicated its responsibilities to *laissez faire* philosphy and, in contrast, has expanded the reach of governmental power. The Court, through expansive definitions of interstate commerce, has created a federal legislative pre-eminence in the fashioning of national economic policy. Indeed, the new ideological commitment in the modern age appears to be one of governmental imperative in economic affairs. Individuals may differ as to the kinds and degree of governmental action, but, by far, the majority of individuals consider governmental action to be a necessity.

MONOPOLY POWER

The "trust" device is a judicial creation of the Chancery Court of England. American courts adopted it as a unique and flexible method for dispositions of property. It is a fiduciary relationship with respect to property, whereby the person who holds title to the property is subjected to equitable duties to deal with the property for the benefit of another person. A fiduciary relationship involves a duty on the part of the fiduciary (trustee) to act for the benefit of the second party called the beneficiary. In a trust, the trustee holds title to property and controls or manages the property for the beneficiary. The trustee has received the property from the party (setlor) setting up the trust who commands the trustee as to his duties in regard to the property and as to whom the property benefits are to be disbursed. The trustee is legally bound to follow the instructions as set forth in the instrument that created the trust.

The trust device has many very legitimate and socially desirable purposes. The will of parents who die at an early age can bequeath title to their property to a trustee for the benefit of the orphaned children. An individual could grant funds to a trustee to be invested for income which is to be used for charitable or scientific purposes. The variety of trust purposes is as wide as the imagination of man.

In the last part of the nineteenth century, the trust device was also used for the purpose of gaining monopolistic control of industries. The majority of the stock of competing companies would be transferred to a board of trustees and the previous stockholders would receive trust certificates naming them as beneficiaries entitled to dividends coming from the companies through the trust to them. The trustee board would be composed of various directors from the companies in the industry. The board would then make policy decisions for the supposedly competing companies and, in effect, run the legally separate companies in a monopolistic manner. It was this use of the trust device that brought in an era known as "trust busting" (that is, eliminating this type of trust purpose, not eliminating the trust device itself). The laws enacted to eliminate monopolistic practices in industry likewise became known as antitrust laws. The laws do not outlaw legitimate uses of trusts, rather the laws are designed to promote competition. In interpreting the first antitrust law, the Sherman Act, Justice Black said,

> The Sherman Act was designed to be a comprehensive charter of economic liberty aimed at preserving free and unfettered competition as a rule of trade. It rests on the premise that the unrestrained interaction of competitive forces will yield the best allocation of our economic resources, the lowest prices, the highest quality and the greatest material progress while at the same time providing an environment conducive to the preservation of our democratic political and social institutions. But even were that premise open to question, the policy unequivocally laid down by the Act is competition. *Northern Pac. R. Co. v. U.S.*, 356, U.S. 1, 4 (1958).

THE GOALS OF ANTITRUST

Justice Black predicated his understanding of the antitrust laws on the notion that competitive markets provide; (1) "the best allocation of our economic resources (and) the lowest prices," (economic efficiency) and (2) "the highest quality and the greatest material progress" (technological innovation and invention) and (3) "an environment conducive to the preservation of our democratic political and social institutions" (maintenance of political freedoms). Others have argued that competitive markets provide an equitable dispersion of income among society's participants (market valuation of worth and, hence, income levels) and that competitive markets, with flexible pricing and wage rates, make governmental policies of economic stabilization work better.

An ideological commitment to competition permeates society and is often supported by an almost religious fervor. It is not surprising, therefore, that statutory and common law reflect this ideological commitment to the competitive market system. However, while nearly everyone is in favor of competition, there is a great deal of debate concerning the degree or type of competition sufficient to bring about its benefits. In other words, what type of competition is to be accepted as a public policy *norm* with which to judge whether an industry is sufficently competitive. The determination of this policy norm is subject to considerable debate. There are basically three schools of thought (approaches) concerning the appropriate norm of "workable competition."

Conduct Approach. Advocates of the conduct approach argue that certain business practices which interfere with the efficient operation of the competitive marketplace should be reasonably identified and outlawed. They argue that standards of illegal "conduct" must be identified so that businessmen will have "fairly definite standards" to guide their behavior. They conclude that the criterion of intent to commit these illegal acts establishes a sensible test for determining antitrust enforcement. In effect, prohibition of illegal overt actions and behavior should be the only basis for judicial action in the field of antitrust. Since attorneys, who enforce antitrust law, are trained and conditioned to prosecution against behavior or conduct, instead of mere status, the conduct approach has had a definite impact upon the evolving antitrust laws.

Structuralist Approach. Structuralists believe that a norm of "workable competition" can be formulated from classical economic theory which can be modified for a realistic setting. They maintain that certain structural characteristics of an industry can be identified and that application of these characteristics to any specific industry can be used on a case-by-case basis to determine whether antitrust enforcement is needed. Such structural characteristics of a workably competitive market would include:

1. An appreciable number of traders (absence of concentration),
2. No firm powerful enough to be able to coerce a rival,
3. Responsiveness of the market participants to economic incentives rather than political purposes,
4. Minimization of product differentiation, and
5. Reasonable opportunity for entry by new traders.

These market structure tests place primary emphasis upon limitation of economic power in hands of private parties. Structuralists seek to employ antitrust laws to insure the continued existence of the competitive system with checks and balances against any private attempts to control the market. Structuralist also favor alternate governmental policies that encourage small businesses, the use of government procurement and surplus property programs to establish competing firms, and the imposition of taxes on increased advertising expenditures which can destroy the independence of consumers. Of course, more drastic remedies, such as divestiture of existing large firms, would also be an appropriate remedy to the structuralist.

Performance Approach. The pure economic performance test to determine appropriate antitrust policy includes criteria such as the following:

1. Is the industry economically efficient?
2. Is it technologically progressive?
3. Does it show a reasonable and socially useful profit pattern?
4. Does it have as much freedom of entry as the nature of the industry will permit?
5. Is it well suited to serve national defense needs?

Negative answers to these question suggest the need for antitrust action. Positive answers to these questions suggest an immunity from antitrust attack. However, it is extremely difficult to devise tests of performance which can be applied by the courts. The literature of performance economists summarize some of the tests as follows:

1. Progressiveness of the firm in product and process innovation
2. Whether cost reductions are passed on to consumers promptly
3. Whether investment is excessive in relation to output
4. Whether the profits are continuously and substantially higher than in industries exhibiting similar trends in sales and costs and innovations
5. Whether competitive effort is exhibited mainly by selling activities rather than improvements in services and products and price reductions.

To the extent that performance of the firm or industry as measured by these criteria is determined acceptable, antitrust attack against the industry is deemed inappropriate. Obviously, the pronouncements of large firms adopt the performance criteria and argue that their particular firm should not be subjected to antitrust action because their performance is acceptable.

Other viewpoints concerning the level of competition could be presented, but these three will suffice to indicate that the phrase "workable competition" means different things to different people. Most economists recognize that the classical economic model of "pure competition" does not provide a *norm* for enforcement of the antitrust laws. Instead a pragmatic approach in determination of appropriate "competitive markets" is utilized by each of the three approaches previously mentioned. However, the debate to determine an acceptable pragmatic norm of "workable competion" among these schools of though is continuous. For example, the structuralist of today argue for a policy which would prohibit the oil companies from also having interests in coal or atomic energy firms. Performance advocates maintain that such a structural limitation on oil companies would be inappropriate if adequate performance (that is, technological advancement and cross utilization of technology by oil and coal companies) could be obtained by the combination of alternate energy souce firms. More often than not, performance economists do not find a need for antitrust enforcement. Other aspects of the debate between these schools of thought will be discussed through the remainder of this chapter and the next.

REGULATION OF INDUSTRY STRUCTURE

Economists have prepared descriptions of competition, whether pure or imperfect, and its opposite extreme of monopoly. Based on certain assumptions, the competitive models suggest higher levels of production with lower prices will be achieved than with the monopolist, who seeks to restrain output to capture higher prices. As a result, few people advocate the creation of monopoly if a competitive market structure is a viable alternative. It was the belief that monopolies are undesirable that led to the enactment of Section 2 of the Sherman Act. Section 2 outlaws monopolization, attempts to monopolize, or conspiracies to monopolize. Congress outlawed monopoly and then, in effect, passed the buck to the courts to further articulate this law in specific situations. The courts have had a difficult time in applying this law. One reason is because economic theory, as illustrated by the differing views of the conduct, structuralist or performance schools of thought, has been little help. In addition, public consensus concerning specific cases has been lacking. As a result, the courts' decisions have been subjected to criticism and ridicule by one or more of the opposing economic viewpoints.

Section 2 of the Sherman Act uses the word "monopolize." The statutory language does not say that monopoly is prohibited, but rather "to monopolize" is to transgress the law. "Monopolize" was not defined by the statute, so such definition had to be determined by the courts. The Supreme Court has indicated that there is "monopolization" when two elements are present. First, the possession of monopoly power in the relevant market must be established, and secondly, the willful (intentional) acquisition or maintenance of that power must be shown. In *Standard Oil v. U.S.* 221 U.S. 1 (1911) the Supreme Court determined that Standard Oil's unification of power and control over petroleum and its products was the result of combinations, not the result of normal methods of industrial development. These large combinations afforded Standard Oil better than 90 percent control of the oil market. Coupled with these combinations were certain patterns of conduct which were essentially predatory in nature. These predatory actions were sufficient evidence to establish Standard Oil's intent and, consequently, violation of the Act. The use of predatory behavior as evidence of "intent" established a behavioral or conduct approach in determination of illegality.

In *U.S. v. U.S. Steel Corp.*, 251 U.S. 417 (1920) the Supreme Court found no violation of the Sherman Act and said:

> The corporation is undoubtedly of impressive size and it takes an effort of resolution not to be affected by it or to exaggerate its influence. But we must adhere to the law and the law does not make mere size an offense or the existence of unexerted power an offense. It, we repeat, requires overt acts. . .

This statement, when coupled with the previous case against Standard Oil, have been characterized as the "abuse theory" of monopoly. Under this theory the government must establish the monopolistic intent of the defendant with proof of overt acts and conduct which "abuse" the competitors. Without actions by the defendant indicating a wrongful intent, the government would be unable to prove the "abuse" of monopoly power.

The abuse theory of monopoly is consistent with the conduct approach for antitrust laws. Only the abusive practices and conduct of the defendant are outlawed. To the economists, a monopoly which restricts production and raises its price is contrary to the public interest, whether overt predatory conduct can be shown or not. It matters not how the monopolist obtained power or maintains its position. Consequently, the criticisms of economists and growing public concern over the inadequacy of antitrust laws (the conduct approach) caused the government to argue a different approach to the courts in the following case.

UNITED STATES v. ALUMINUM CO. OF AMERICA
148 F. 2d 416 (1945)
United States Court of Appeals, 2nd Cir.

■ ■ ■

L. Hand, Circuit Judge: The most important question in the case is whether the monopoly in "Alcoa's" production of "virgin" ingot, secured by the two patents until 1909...continued for the ensuing twenty-eight years; and whether, if it did, it was unlawful under §2 of the Sherman Act. It is undisputed that throughout this period "Alcoa" continued to be the single producer of "virgin" ingot in the United States; and the plaintiff argues that this without more was enough to make it an unlawful monopoly..."Alcoa's" position is that the fact that it alone continued to make "virgin" ingot in this country did not, and does not, give it a monopoly of the market; that it was always subject to the competition of imported "virgin" ingot, and of what is called "secondary" ingot; and that even if it had not been, its monopoly would not have been retained by unlawful means, but would have been the result of a growth which the Act does not forbid, even when it results in a monopoly...

There are various ways of computing "Alcoa's" control of the aluminum market—as distinct from its production—depending upon what one regards as competing in that market. The judge figured its share—during the years 1929-1938, inclusive—as only about thirty-three percent; to do so he included "secondary," and excluded that part of "Alcoa's" own production which it fabracted and did not therefore sell as ingot. If, on the other hand, "Alcoa's" total production, fabricated and sold, be included, and balanced against the sum of imported "virgin" and "secondary," its share of the market was in the neightborhood of sixty-four percent for that period. The percentage...over ninety—results only if we both include all "Alcoa's" production and exclude "secondary." That percentage is enough to constitute a monopoly; it is doubtful whether sixty or sixty-four percent would be enough; and certainly thirty-three percent is not. Hence it is necessary to settle what he shall treat as competing in the ingot market. That part of its production which "Alcoa" itself fabractes, does not of course ever reach the market as ingot;...(However)...the ingot fabricated by "Alcoa," necessarily had a direct effect upon the ingot market. All ingot—with trifling exceptions—is used to fabricate intermediate, or end products; and therefore all intermediate, or end, products which "Alcoa" fabricates and sells, pro tanto reduce the demand for ingot itself...We cannot therefore agree that the computation of the percentage of "Alcoa's" control over the ingot market should not include the whole of its ingot production...

In the case of a monopoly of any commodity which does not disappear in use and which can be salvaged, the supply seeking sale at any moment will be made up of two components: (1) the part which the putative monopolist can immediately produce and sell; and (2) the part which has been, or can be, reclaimed out of what he has produced and sold in the past. By hypothesis he presently controls the first of these components: the second he has controlled in the past, although he no longer does. During the period when he did control the second, if he was aware of his interest, he was guided, not alone by its effect at that time upon the market, but by his knowledge that some part of it was likely to be reclaimed and seek the future market. That consideration will to some extent always affect his production...The competition of "secondary" must therefore be disregarded, as soon as we consider the position of "Alcoa" over a period of years; it was as much within "Alcoa's" control as was the production of the "virgin" from which it had been derived. This can be well illustrated by the case of a lawful monopoly: e.g. a patent or a copyright. The monoplist cannot prevent those to whom he sells from reselling at whatever prices they please. Nor can he prevent their reconditioning articles worn by use, unless they in fact make a new article.... At any moment his control over the market will therefore be limited by that part of what he has formerly sold, which the price he now charges may bring upon the market, as second hand or reclaimed articles. Yet no one would think of saying that for this reason the patent or the copyright did not confer a monopoly. Again, consider the situation of the owner of the only supply of some raw material like iron ore. Scrap iron is a constant factor in the iron market; it is scavenged, remelted into pig, and sold in competition with newly smelted pig; an owner of the sole supply of ore must always face that competition and it will serve to put a "ceiling" upon his price, so far as there is enough of it. Nevertheless, no one would say that, even during the period while the pig which he has sold in the past can so return to the market, he does not have a natural monopoly.

We conclude therefore that "Alcoa's" control over the ingot market must be reckoned at over ninety percent; that being the proportion which its production bears to imported "virgin" ingot. . . The producer of so large a proportion of the supply has complete control within certin limits. It is true that, if by raising the price he reduces the amount which can be marketed—as always, or almost always, happens—he may invite the expansion of the small producers who will try to fill the place left open; not only is there an inevitable lag in this, but the large producer is in a strong position to check such competition; and, indeed, if he has retained his old plant and personnel, he can inevitably do so. There are indeed limits to his power; substitutes are available for almost all commodities, and to raise the price enough is to evoke them. . .

"Alcoa" was free to raise its prices as it chose, since it was free from domestic competition, save as it drew other metals into the market as substitues. Was this a monopoly within the meaning of §2? The judge found that, over the whole half century of its existence, "Alcoa's" profits upon capital invested, after payment of income taxes, had been only about ten percent, and, although the plaintiff puts this figure a little higher, the difference is negligible.

This assumed, it would be hard to say that "Alcoa" had made exorbitant profits on ingot,. . . But the whole issue is irrelevant anyway, for it is no excuse for "monopolizing" a market that the monopoly has not been used to extract from the consumer more than a "fair" profit. The Act has wider purposes. Indeed even though we disregarded all but economic considerations, it would by no means follow that such concentration of producing power is to be desired, when it has not been used extortionately. Many people believe that possession of unchallenged economic power deadens initiative, discourages thrift and depresses energy; that immunity from competition is a narcotic, and rivalry is a stimulant, to industrial progress; that the spur of constant stress is necessary to counteract an inevitable disposition to let well enough alone. Such people believe that competitors, versed in the craft as no consumer can be, will be quick to detect opportunities for saving and new shifts in production, and be eager to profit by them. In any event the mere fact that a producer, having command of the domestic market, has not been able to make more than a "fair" profit, is no evidence that a "fair" profit could not have been made at lower prices. . . . True, it might have been thought adequate to condemn only those monopolies which could not show that they had exercised the highest possible ingenuity, had adopted every possible economy, had anticipated every conceivable improvement, stimulated every possible demand. No doubt, that would be one way of dealing with the matter, although it would imply constant scrutiny and constant supervision, such as courts are unable to provide. Be that as it may, that was not the way that Congress chose; it did not condone "good trusts" and condemn "bad" ones; it forbad all. Moreover, in so doing it was not necessarily actuated by economic motives alone. It is possible, because of its indirect social or moral effect, to prefer a system of small producers, each dependent for his success upon his own skill and character, to one in which the great mass of those engaged must accept the direction of a few. These considerations, which we have suggested only as possible purposes of the Act, we think the decisions prove to have been in fact its purposes. . .

It does not follow because "Alcoa" had such a monopoly, that it "monopolized" the ingot market: it may not have achieved monopoly; monopoly may have been thrust upon it. If it had been a combination of existing smelters which united the whole industry and controlled the production of all aluminum ingot, it would certainly have "monopolized" the market. In several decisions the Supreme Court has decreed the dissolution of such combinations, although they had engaged in no unlawful trade practices...We may start therefore with the premise that to have combined ninety percent of the producers of ingot would have been to "monopolize" the ingot market; and, so far as concerns the public interest, it can make no difference whether an existing competition is put and end to, or whether prospective competition is prevented. ...Nevertheless, it is unquestionably true that from the very outset the courts have at least kept in reserve the possibility that the origin of a monopoly may be critical in determining its legality; and for this they had warrant in some of the congressional debates which accompanied the passage of the Act...This notion has usually been expressed by saying that size does not determine guilt; that there must be some "exclusion" of competitiors; that the growth must be something else than "natural" or "normal"; that there must be a "wrongful intent," or some other specific intent; or that some "unduly" coercive means must be used...

What engendered these compunctions is reasonably plain; persons may unwittingly find themselves in possession of a monopoly, automatically so to say: that is, without having intended either to put an end to existing competition, or to prevent competition from arising when none had existed; they may become monopolists by force of accident. Since the Act makes "monopolizing" a crime, as well as a civil wrong, it would be not only unfair, but presumably contrary to the intent of Congress, to include such instances. A market may, for example, be so limited that it is impossible to produce at all and meet the cost of production except by a plant large enough to supply the whole demand. Or there may be changes in taste or in cost which drive out all but one purveyor. A single producer may be the survivor out of a group of active competitors, merely by virtue of his superior skill, foresight and industry. In such cases a strong argument can be made that, although, the result may expose the public to the evils of monopoly, the Act does not mean to condemn the resultant of those very forces which it is its prime object to foster. The successful competitor, having been urged to complete, must not be turned upon when he wins...

It would completely misconstrue "Alcoa's" position in 1940 to hold that it was the passive beneficiary of a monopoly, following upon an involuntary elimination of competitors by automatically operative economic forces.

There were at least one or two abortive attempts to enter the industry, but "Alcoa" effectively anticipated and forestalled all competition, and succeeded in holding the field alone. True, it stimulated demand and opened new uses for the metal, but not without making sure that it could supply what it had evoked. There is no dispute as to this; "Alcoa" avows it as evidence of the skill, energy and initiative with which it has always conducted its business; as a reason why, having won its way by fair means, it should be commended, and not dismembered...

The only question is whether it falls within the exception established in favor of those who do not seek, but cannot avoid, the control of a market. It seems to us that that question scarcely survives its statement. it was not inevitable that it should always anticipate increases in the demand for ingot and be prepared to supply them. Nothing compelled it to keep doubling and redoubling its capacity before others entered the field. It insists that it never excluded competitors; but we can think of no more effective exclusion than progressively to embrace each new opportunity as it opened, and to face every newcomer with new capacity already geared into a great organization, having the advantage of experience, trade connections and the elite of personnel. Only in case we interpret "exclusion" as limited to manoeuvres not honestly industrial, but actuated solely by a desire to prevent competition, can such a course, indefatigably pursued, be deemed not "exclusionary." So to limit it would in our judgment emasculate the Act; would permit just such consolidations as it was designed to prevent...

We disregard any question of "intent." Although the primary evil was monopoly, the Act also covered preliminary steps, which, if continued, would lead to it. These may do no harm of themselves; but, if they are initial moves in a plan or scheme which, carried out, will result in monopoly, they are dangerous and the law will nip them in the bud. For this reason conduct falling short of monopoly, is not illegal unless it is part of a plan to monopolize, or to gain such other control of a market as is equally forbidden. To make it so, the plaintiff must prove what in the criminal kaw is known as a "specfic intent"; an intent which goes beyond the mere intent to do the act. By far the greatest part of the fabulous record piled up in the case at bar, was concerned with proving such an intent. The plaintiff was seeking to show that many transactions, neutral on their face, were not in fact necessary to the development of "Alcoa's" business, and had no motive except to exclude others and perpetuate its hold upon the ingot market. . . The plaintiff has so satisfied us, and the issue of intent ceases to have any importance; no intent is relevant except that which is relevant to any liability, criminal or civil: i.e. an intent to bring about the forbidden act.

In order to fall within § 2, the monopolist must have both the power to monopolize, and the intent to monopolize. To read the passage as demanding any "specific," intent, makes nonsense of it, for no monopolist monopolizes unconscious of what he is doing. So here, "Alcoa" meant to keep, and did keep, that complete and exclusive hold upon the ingot market with which it started. That was to "monopolize" that market, however innocently it otherwise proceeded. . .

■ ■ ■

Questions

1. Is the approach in *Alcoa* a conduct approach (abuse theory)?
2. In *Alcoa*, how did the court define the market in which Alcoa deals? What reasons for this definition did the court give? What percentages of this market did Alcoa control?
3. What was the court's response to Alcoa's assertion that it was only a "good" monopoly and charged only "fair" prices? Is this assertion relevant to a structuralist? To a performance economist?
4. What is a "thrust upon" defense? Can you give examples? Was the monopoly of Alcoa "thrust upon" it? What about a town with only one newspaper? Is the newspaper firm an illegal monopoly?
5. Did Alcoa "intend" to monopolize? What proof of intent did the court require? Considering the amount of evidence required by the court in *Alcoa*, is the court's approach that of a structuralist or of a performance economist?
6. Judge Wyzanski in *United States vs. United Shoe Machinery Corporation* summarized the existing law on Section 2 when he wrote:

> Since Judge Learned Hand's opinion in 1945 in United States v Aluminum Co of America. . ., and the 1948 opinion of the Supreme Court in United States v Griffith. . . that provision of § 2 of the Sherman Act. . . addressed to 'Every person who shall monopolize. . . any part of' interstate commerce has been so interpreted as to reach any enterprise that has exercised power to control a defined market, if that power is to any substantial extent the result of barriers erected by its own business methods (even though not predatory, immoral, or restraining trade in violation of § 1 of Sherman Act. . .) unless the enterprise shows that the barriers are *exclusively* the result of superior skill, superior products, natural advantages, technological or economic efficiency, scientific research, low margins of profit maintained permanently and without discrimination, legal licenses, or the like.

It appears as though one who has acquired an overwhelming share of the market may be held to have monopolized whenever he just carries on his business, "apparently even if there is no showing that his business involves any exclusionary practice." *U.S. v United Shoe Machinery Corp.* 391 U.S. 244 (1968). However, the corporation may avoid liability if it bears the burden of proving that "it owes its monopoly soley to superior skill, superior products, natural advantages, economic or technological efficiency, low margins of profit maintained permanently and without discrimination or licenses conferred by and used within the limits of law." Is this approach better in your mind than the "abuse theory" of monopoly? Is this a structural test or a performance test? Or a combination?

7. Wrongful intent may be predicated on wrongful contracts which prevent competitors from gaining raw materials or oppresive terms of sale upon buyers. *U.S. vs. Eastman Kodak Company,* 255 U.S. 578. In *Gamco, Inc. va. Providence Fruit & Produce Bldg., Inc.* 194 F.2d 484 (lst Cir. 1952) the defendants controlled a building specifically located and equipped for wholesale of produce. The defendants had the power to deny their competitors access. Abuse was deemed possible and this was sufficient to find a violation of Section 2. These cases indicate that once monopoly power exists, it is not difficult to find factors, which when coupled with the power, lead to finding a monopolization in violation of Section 2.

RELEVANT COMPETITIVE MARKET

UNITED STATES v. DuPONT & CO.
351 U.S. 377 (1956)
Supreme Court of the United States

■ ■ ■

REED, Mr. Justice.
The Government contends that, by so dominating cellophane production, duPont monopolized a "part of the trade or commerce" in violation of § 2. (Defendant) ...contends that the prohibition of § 2 against monopolization is not violated because it does not have the power to control the price of cellophane or to exclude competitors from the market in which cellophane is sold...

...Market delimitation is necessary under du Pont's theory to determine whether an alleged monopolist violates § 2. The ultimate consideration in such a determination is whether the defendants control the price and competition in the market for such part of trade or commerce as they are charged with monopolizing. Every manufacturer is the sole producer of the particular commodity it makes but its control in the above sense of the relevant market depends upon the availability of alternative commodities for buyers: i.e., whether there is a cross-elasticity of demand between cellophane and the other wrappings. This interchangeability is largely gauged by the purchase of competing products for similar uses considering the price, characteristics and adaptability of the competing commodities...

The burden of proof, of course, was upon the Government to establish monopoly ...Du Pont's power to set the price of cellophane has been limited only by the competition afforded by other flexible packaging materials. Moreover, it may be practically impossible for anyone to commence manufacturing cellophane without full access to du Pont's technique. However, du Pont has no power to prevent competition from other wrapping materials. The trial court consequently had to determine whether competition from the other wrappings prevented Du Pont from possessing monopoly power in violation of § 2. Price and competition are so intimately entwined that any discussion of theory must treat them as one. It is inconceivable that price could be controlled without power over competition or vice versa. This approach to the determination or monopoly power is strengthened by this Court's conclusion in prior cases that, when an alleged monopolist has power over price and competition, an intention to monopolize in a proper case may be assumed.

If a large number of buyers and sellers deal freely in a standardized product, such as salt or wheat, we have complete or pure competition. Patents, on the other hand, furnish the most familiar type of classic monopoly. As the producers of a standardized product bring about significant differentiations of quality, design, or packaging in the product that permit differences of use, competition becomes to a greater or less degree incomplete and the producer's power over price and competition greater over his article and its use, according to the differentiation he is able to create and maintain. A retail seller may have in one sense a monopoly on certain trade because of location, as an isolated country store or filling station, or because no one else makes a product of just the quality or attractiveness of his product, as for example in cigarettes. Thus one can theorize that we have monopolistic competition in every nonstandardized commodity with each manufacturer having power over the price and production of his own product. However, this power that, let us say, automobile or soft-drink manufacturers have over their trademarked products is not the power that makes an illegal monopoly. Illegal power must be appraised in terms of the competitive market for the product.

Determination of the competitive market for commodities depends on how different from one another are the offered commodities in character or use, how far buyers will go to substitute one commodity for another. For example, one can think of building materials as in commodity competition but one could hardly say that brick competed with steel or wood or cement or stone in the meaning of Sherman Act litigation; the products are too different. This is the interindustry competition emphasized by some economists.

On the other hand, there are certain differences in the formulae for soft drinks but one can hardly say that each one is an illegal monopoly. Whatever the market may be, we hold that control of price or competition establishes the existence of monopoly power under § 2. Section 2 requires the application of a reasonable approach in determining the existence of monopoly power. . . This of course does not mean that there can be a reasonable monopoly.

Our next step is to determine whether Du Pont has monopoly power over cellophane: that is, power over its price in relation to or competion with other commodities. . .

The Relevant Market. . . [W]here there are market alternatives that buyers may readily use for their purposes, illegal monopoly does not exist merely because the product said to be monopolized differs from others. It it were not so, only physically identical products would be a part of the market. To accept the Government's argument, we would have to conclude that the manufacturers of plain as well as moistureproof cellophane were monopolists, and so with films such as Pliofilm, foil, glassine, polyethylene, and Saran, for each of these wrapping materials is distinguishable. These were all exhibits in the case. New wrappings appear, generally similar to cellophane: is each a monopoly? What is called for is an appraisal of the "cross-elasticity" of demand in the trade. . . The varying circumstances of each case determine the result. In considering what is the relevant market for determining the control of price and competition, no more definite rule can be declared than that commodities reasonably interchangeable by consumers for the same purposes make up that "part of the trade or commerce," monopolization of which may be illegal. As respects flexible packaging materials, the market geographically is nationwide.

. . . In determining the market under the Sherman Act, it is the use or uses to which the commodity is put that control. The selling price between commodities with similar uses and different characteristics may vary, so that the cheaper product can drive out the more expensive. Or, the superior quality of higher priced articles may make dominant the more desirable. Cellophane costs more than many competing products and less than a few. But whatever the price, there are various flexible wrapping materials that are bought by manufacturers for packaging their goods in their own plant or sold to converters who shape and print them for use in the packaging of the commodities to be wrapped. . .

It may be admitted that cellphane combines the desirable elements of transparency, strength and cheapness more definitely than any of the others. . .

But, despite cellophane's advantages, it has to meet competition from other materials in every one of its uses... Thus, cellophane shares the packaging market with others. The overall result is that cellophane accounts for 17.9% of flexible wrapping materials, measured by the wrapping surface...

An element for consideration as to cross-elasticity of demand between products is the responsiveness of the sales of one product to price changes of the other. If a slight decrease in the price of cellophane causes a considerable number of customers of other flexible wrappings to switch to cellophane, it would be an indication that a high cross-elasticity of demand exists between them; that the products compete in the same market. The court below held that the "(g)reat sensitivity of customers in the flexible packaging markets to price or quality changes" prevented Du Pont from possessing monopoly control over price. The record sustains these findings.

We conclude that cellophane's interchangeability with the other materials mentioned suffices to make it a part of this flexible packaging material market.

The Government stresses the fact that the variation in price between cellophane and other materials demonstrates they are noncompetitive. As these products are all flexible wrapping materials, it seems reasonable to consider, as was done at the trial, their comparative cost to the consumer in terms of square area. Cellophane costs two or three times as much, surface measure, as its chief competitors for the flexible wrapping market, glassine and greaseproof papers. Other forms of cellulose wrappings and those from other chemical or mineral substances, with the exception of aluminum foil, are more expensive. The uses of these materials, ... are largely to wrap small packages for retail distribution. The wrapping is a relatively small proportion of the entire cost of the article. Different producers need different qualities in wrappings and their need may vary from time to time as their products undergo change. But the necessity for flexible wrappings is the central and unchanging demand. We cannot say that these differences in cost gave du Pont monopoly over prices in view of the findings of fact on that subject...

The facts above considered dispose also of any contention that competitors that have been excluded by du Pont from the packaging material market. That market has many producers and there is no proof du Pont ever has possessed power to exclude any of them from the rapidly expanding flexible packaging market... The record shows the multiplicity of competitors and the financial strength of some with individual assets running to the hundreds of millions.

The "market" which one must study to determine when a producer has monopoly power will vary with the part of commerce under consideration. The tests are constant. That market is composed of products that have reasonable interchangeability for the purposes for which they are produced—price, use and qualities considered. While the application of the tests remains uncertain, it seems to us that du Pont should not be found to monopolize cellophane when that product has the competition and inter-changeability with other wrappings that this record shows.

■ ■ ■

Questions

1. By a narrow definition of the market, the courts may find a monopoly (as in Alcoa) or the court may determine that no monopoly exists (as in *Du Pont)* when a broad definition of the market is accepted. In the determination of the relevant market, is "interindustry competition" relevant? What is the "test" to define the "product market?" Does the application of this test in any factual situation afford considerable leeway to the court?

2. What about Dr. Pepper soft drink? Does that company possess an illegal monopoly?

3. Besides relevant product markets, relevant geographical markets must also be established. While most monopolies involve national producers, the courts have not had to deal with the relevant geographical market often. Nevertheless, a defendant may possess a monopoly in a geographical market and be in violation of Section 2 of the Sherman Act.

4. From your understanding of the monopolization cases, if your firm controlled 60 percent of the relevant product market, would you take active competitive steps to try to increase your market share?
5. At the time of this writing the Justice Department is bringing suit against AT&T and IBM for monopolization. While it is impossible to predict the outcome of these cases, students and businessmen alike should pay close attention to these future decisions of the Court. They doubtlessly will drag on for many years before decision, unless settled.

ILLEGAL MERGERS AND ACQUISITIONS

Absent any attempt to monopolize, internal growth of assets is generally recognized as a legitimate method of corporate expansion. However, Congress was concerned about mergers and acquisitions as a means of growth and their effect of reducing competition or tending toward a monopoly. The original Section 7 of the Clayton Act established guidelines as to when mergers were to be held illegal. It differed from the Sherman Act in that "actual" restraints or monopolization did not have to be proved. The Clayton Act was designed to stop anticompetitive mergers before they resulted in creating the monopoly. This purpose was to be accomplished by the method of making illegal those mergers that "may" lessen competition. In this manner, anticompetitive activities were arrested in their early stages by lowering the government's burden of proof from an actual anticompetitve effect to a probable anticompetitive effect. This concept of attacking the evil practices in their incipiency is carried throughout the major sections of the Clayton Act.

The original language of Section 7 of the Clayton Act possessd several "loopholes" which had the effect of making Section 7 weak in terms of preventing mergers. The original text included language that for the merger to be illegal it must eliminate competition between the "acquiring" firm and the "acquired" firm. To eliminate competition *between* these two firms, they must themselves be in competition with each other. Consequently, the acquiring-acquired language indicated that the anti-merger law applied only to horizontal mergers (that is, those companies which compete with one another). Therefore, vertical or conglomerate mergers were free of antitrust attack under the original Section 7 language until the Justice Department decided to test this language in the late 1940s. In addition, the original language prohibited only the acquisition of *stock* in another company, where the probable effect was to substantially lessen competition. Therefore, any combination of companies, including horizontal, that wanted to avoid Section 7 would not acquire the *stock* of its competititor. Instead, acquisition of *assets* was used to avoid Section 7's prohibition of *stock* acquisitions. As a consequence, Section 7 of the Clayton Act had only minimal effect in prohibiting mergers. Indeed, antitrust enforcement officials reverted back to the use of the Sherman Act in an effort to prohibit mergers. However, the Sherman Act was found inadequate, also.

In 1950, the Celler-Kefauver Amendment modified Section 7 of the Clayton Act. This amendment omitted the acquiring-acquired language to indicate that horizontal, vertical, or conglomerate mergers were illegal if they had the probable effect of substantially lessening competition. In addition, the acquisition of stock or *assets* was deemed illegal if it had the prohibited effect. The first case interpreting the 1950 amendment to Section 7 was not decided until 1961.

Many reasons are given by the business community and the economic profession to justify mergers and combinations. They argue that mergers may provide opportunities for the firms to:

1. Gain economies of scale in production or distribution
2. Expand geographical markets
3. Enlarge the size to facilitate better use of financial markets

4. Insure sources of supply or marketing outlets
5. Reduce risks by diversification of product lines
6. Enter growing markets by acquiring experienced management

Congress recognized that mergers may bring about more economic efficiencies. Nevertheless, Congress sought to outlaw mergers which had the "probable efect" of substantially reducing competition in the relevant product or geographical markets. Consequently, the courts have not generally made substantial inquiries into the efficiencies alleged to have ben accrued by virtue of the proposed merger. Instead the court's analysis has concentrated on the anticompetitive impacts of the merger.

HORIZONTAL AND VERTICAL MERGERS

BROWN SHOE CO. v. UNITED STATES
370 U.S. 296 (1961)
Supreme Court of the United States

■ ■ ■

WARREN, Chief Justice.

This suit... (alleges) that a contemplated merger between the G.R. Kinney Company, Inc. (Kinney), and the Brown Shoe Company, Inc. (Brown)... would violate § 7 of the Clayton Act,... The compalint sought injunctive relief... to restrain consummation of the merger.

The industry

The District Court found that although domestic shoe production was scattered among a large number of manufacturers, a small number of large companies occupied a commanding position. Thus, while the 24 largest manufacturers produced about 35% of the Nation's shoes, the top 4... alone produced approximately 23% of the Nation's shoes or 65% of the production of the top 24...
The public buys these shoes through about 70,000 retail outlets...
The District Court found a "definite trend" among shoe manufacturers to acquire retail outlets...
And once the manufacturers acquired retail outlets, the District Court found there was a "definite trend" for the parent-manufacturers to supply an ever increasing percentage of the retail outlets' needs, thereby foreclosing other manufacturers from effectively competing for the retail accounts. Manufacturer-dominated stores were found to be "drying up" the available outlets for independent producers.
Another "definite trend" found to exist in the shoe industry was a decrease in the number of plants manufacturing shoes.

Brown Shoe.

Brown Shoe was found not only to have been a participant, but also a moving factor, in these industry trends... (I)n 1951, Brown... began to seek retail outlets by acquisitions...
The acquisition of these corporations was found to lead to increased sales by Brown to the acquired companies...
During the same period of time, Brown also acquired the stock or assets of seven companies engaged solely in shoe manufacturing. As a result, in 1955, Brown was the fourth largest shoe manufacturer in the country, producing about 4% of the Nation's total footwear production.

Kinney.

Kinney is principally engaged in operating the largest family-style shoe store chain in the United States. At the time of trial, Kinney was found to be operating over 400 such stores in more than 270 cities. These stores were found to make about 1.2% of all national retail shoe sales by dollar volume...

The Vertical Aspects of the Merger

Economic arrangements between companies standing in a supplier-customer relationship are characterized as "vertical." The primary vice of a vertical merger or other arrangement tying a customer to a supplier is that, by foreclosing the competitors of either party from a segment of the market otherwise open to them, the arrangement may act as a "clog on competition,"... which "deprive(s)... rivals of a fair opportunity to compete." Every extended vertical arrangement by its very nature, for at least a time, denies to competitors of the supplier the opportunity to compete for part of or all of the trade of the customer-party to the vertical arrangement. However, the Clayton Act does not render unlawful all such vertical arrangements, but forbids only those whose effect "may be substantially to lessen competition, or to tend to create a monopoly" "in any line of commerce in any section of the country."...

The "area of effective competition" must be determined by reference to a product market (the "line of commerce") and a geographic market (the "section of the country").

The Product Market

The outer boundaries of a product market are determined by the reasonable interchangeability of use or the cross-elasticity of demand between the product itself and substitutes for it. However, within this broad market, well-defined submarkets may exist which, in themselves, constitute product markets for antitrust purposes.

...The boundaries of such a submarket may be determined by examining such practical indicia as industry or public recognition of the submarket as a separate economic entity, the product's peculiar characteristics and uses, unique production facilities, distinct customers, distinct prices, sensitivity to price changes, and specialized vendors. Because §7 of the Clayton Act prohibits any merger which may substantially lessen competition "in *any* line of commerce", it is necessary to examine the effects of a meger in each such economically significant submarket to determine if there is a reasonable probability that the merger will substantially lessen competition. If such a probability is found to exist, the merger is proscribed.

Applying these considerations to the present case, we conclude that the record supports the District Court's finding that the relevant lines of commerce are men's, women's, and children's shoes. These product lines are recognized by the public; each line is manufactured in separate plants; each has characteristics peculiar to itself rendering it generally noncompetitive with the other; and each is, of course, directed toward a distinct class of customers.

The Geographic Market.

The relevant geographic market is the entire Nation...

The Probable Effect of the Merger

* * *

Since the diminution of the vigor of competition which may stem from a vertical arrangement results primarily from a foreclosure of a share of the market otherwise open to competitors, an important consideration in determining whether the effect of a vertical arrangement "may be substantially to lessen competition, or to tend to create a monopoly" is the size of the share of the market foreclosed... (Another)... important such factor to examine is the very nature and purpose of the arrangement...

...In 1955, the date of this merger, Brown was the fourth largest manufacturer in the shoe industry while Kinney... owned and operated the largest independent chain of family shoe stores in the Nation. Thus, in this industry, no merger between a manufacturer and an independent retailer could involve a larger potential market foreclosure. Moreover, it is apparent both from past behavior of Brown and from the testimony of Brown's President, that Brown would use its ownership of Kinney to force Brown shoes into Kinney stores...

Another important factor to consider is the trend toward concentration in the industry...

The existence of a trend toward vertical integration, which the District Court found, is well substantiated by the record. Moreover, the court found a tendency of the acquiring manufacturers to become increasingly important sources of supply for their acquired outlets. The necessary corollary of these trends is the foreclosure of independent manufacturers from markets otherwise open to them...

The District Court's findings, and the record facts... convince us that the shoe industry is being subjected to just such a cumulative series of vertical mergers which, if left unchecked, will be likely "substantially to lessen competition."

The Horizontal Aspects of the Merger

As economic arrangement between companies performing similar functions in the production or sale of comparable goods or services is characterized as "horizontal." The effect on competition of such an arrangement depends, of course, upon its character and scope... Where the arrangement effects a horizontal merger between companies occupying the same product and geographic market, whatever competition previously may have existed in that market between the parties to the merger is eliminated. Section 7 of the Clayton Act, prior to its amendment, focused upon this aspect of horizontal combinations by proscribing acquisitions which might result in a lessening of competition between the acquiring and the acquired companies. The 1950 amendments made plain Congress' intent that the validity of such combinations was to be gauged on a broader scale; their effect on competition generally in an economically significant market.

The Product Market.

...(W)e hold that the District Court correctly defined men's, women's, and children's shoes as the relevant lines of commerce... for considering the horizontal aspects of the merger.

The Geographic Market.

The criteria to be used in determining the appropriate geopraphic market are essentially similar to those used to determine the relevant product market... Moreover, just as a product sub-market may have §7 significance as the proper "line of commerce," so may a geographic submarket be considered the appropriate "section of the country." The geographic market selected must, therefore, both "correspond to the commercial realities" of the industry and be economically significant. Thus, although the geographic market is some instances may encompass the entire Nation, under other circumstances it may be as small as a single metropolitan area...

The District Court found that the effects of (the retail)... aspect of the merger must be analyzed in every city with a population exceeding 10,000 and its immediate contiguous surrounding territory in which Brown and Kinney sold shoes at retail through stores they either owned or controlled...

We therefore agree that the District Court properly defined the relevant geographic markets in which to analyze this merger as those cities with a population exceeding 10,000 and their environs in which both Brown and Kinney retailed shoes through their own outlets. Such markets are large enough to include the downtown shops and suburban shopping centers in areas contiguous to the city, which are the important competitive factors, and yet are small enough to exclude stores beyond the immediate environs of the city, which are of little competitive significance.

The Probable Effect of the Merger

The market share which companies may control by merging is one of the most important factors to be considered when determining the probable effects of the combination on effective competition in the relevant market. In an idustry as fragmented as shoe retailing, the control of substantial shares of the trade in a city may have important effects on competition. If a merger achieving 5% control were now approved, we might be required to approve future merger effort by Brown's competitors seeking similar market shares. The oligopoly Congress sought to avoid would then be furthered and it would be difficult to dissolve the combinations previously approved. Furthermore, in this fragmented industry, even if the combination controls but a small share of a particular market, the fact that this share is held by a large national chain can adversely affect competition. Testimony in the record from numerous independent retailers, based on their actual experience in the market, demonstrates that a strong, national chain of stores can insulate selected outlets from the vagaries of competition in particular locations and that the large chains can set and alter styles in footwear to an extent that renders the independents unable to maintain competitive inventories. . .

Other factors to be considered in evaluating the probable effects of a merger in the relevant market lend additional support to the District Court's conclusion that this merger may substantially lessen competition. One such factor is the history of tendency toward concentration in the industry. As we have previously pointed out, the shoe industry has, in recent years, been a prime example of such a trend. . .

We cannot avoid the mandate of Congress that tendencies toward concentration in industry are to be curbed in their incipiency, particularly when those tendencies are being accelerated through giant steps striding across a hundred cities at a time. In the light of the trends in this industry we agree with the Government and the court below that this is an appropriate place at which to call a halt.

■ ■ ■

Questions

1. Considering the vertical aspects of the merger, how did the court define the product market? Under what test? What is a product submarket? What criteria are to be used to determine a relevant submarket?
2. Considering the vertical aspects of the merger, how did the court determine the "probable effect" of the merger"
3. In considering the horizontal aspects of the merger, how did the court define the product and geographical markets? What tests were used by the court to define the markets?
4. In considering the horizontal aspects of the merger, how did the court determine the "probable effect" of the merger?

Decisions in the sixties continued to emphasize trends towards concentration as a determinative factor in deciding merger cases. During this era, dissenting justices criticized the Court's approach as amounting to an almost per se rule. If the aggregate numbers or relative percentages of the market foreclosed by the vertical or horizontal merger in relation to its industry were considered substantial by the court, the merger was outlawed. Of course, structuralist have favored this approach to halt the continuing trend toward concentration. Performance economists, on the other hand, argue that several pro-competitive mergers or mergers advancing the levels of economic efficiency are also prohibited and, consequently, society's interests are not being advanced by an almost per se illegality based on percentage of foreclosure alone. Nevertheless, the success of the Justice Department in gaining verdicts which outlawed mergers during the sixties led to the establishment of the Department of Justice Merger Guidelines. These Guidelines emphasize market structure as the basic determinant of whether mergers will be challenged by the Department of Justice. The Guidelines distinguish between concentrated industries and less concentrated industries. In the less concentrated industries, mergers may be allowed that would not be tolerated in oligopolistic industries. The Guidelines are not law, but are criteria for use by the Department of Justice in its determination of which mergers to challenge in the courts. However, because the Justice Department has been so successful in gaining favorable verdicts during the sixties, many merger proposals were forestalled when the parties determined that they would be challenged under the Guidelines. An example of the Horizontal Merger Guidelines is presented as follows:

Market Highly Concentrated. In a market in which the shares of the four largest firms amount to approximately 75% or more, the Department will ordinarily challenge mergers between firms accounting for, approximately, the following percentages of the market:

Acquiring Firm	Acquired Firm
4%	4% or more
10%	2% or more
15% or more	1% or more

(Percentages not shown in the above table should be interpolated proportionately to the percentages that are shown)

Market Less Highly Concentrated. In a market in which the shares of the four largest firms amount to less than approximately 75%, the Department will ordinarily challenge mergers between firms accounting for, approximately, the following percentages of the market:

Acquiring Firm	Acquired Firm
5%	5% or more
10%	4% or more
15%	3% or more
20%	2% or more
25% or more	1% or more

(Percentages not shown in the above table should be interpolated proportionately to the percentages that are shown.)

In 1974, the Supreme Court seemed to relax its almost *per se* orientation in determining the lawfulness of mergers. In the following case, the Supreme Court showed a willingness to consider competitive consequences of the merger through a specific economic investigation of the market involved. It did not utilize the mere "percentages" approach in determination of legality. Indeed, Justice Stewart, in writing the opinion of the Court, strongly criticized the major Supreme Court decisions in the sixties which followed the relative percentages approach.

However, the following case also involves peculiar facts. The facts lend themselves to be compared somewhat to the Failing Company Doctrine. Under this Doctrine, the Court ruled that a failing company could be merged with another successful company because the failing company was not a future competitor. It was about to be eliminated and, therefore, its merger did not eliminate any competition. In reviewing the decision of *General Dynamics,* the reader must evaluate the extent to which the peculiar facts limit the impact of this decision as establishing a new trend by the Court in eliminating its almost *per se* orientation.

NEW TREND

U.S. v. GENERAL DYNAMICS CORP.
415 U.S. 486 (1974)
Supreme Court of the United States

■ ■ ■

STEWART, Mr. Justice.

In prior decisions involving horizotal mergers between competitors, this Court has found prima facie violations of § 7 of the Clayton Act from aggregate statistics of the sort relied on by the United States in this case...

The effect of adopting this approach to a determination of a "substantial" lessening of competition is to allow the Government to rest its case on a showing of even small increases of market share or market concentration in those industries or markets where concentration is already great or has been recently increasing, since "if concentration is already great, the importance of preventing even slight increases in concentration and so preserving the possibility of eventual deconcentration is correspondingly great." *United States v. Aluminum Co. of America,* 377 U.S. 271, 279...

...[T]he statistical showing proffered by the Government in this case...would under this approach have sufficed to support a finding of "undue concentration" in the absence of other considerations...

In *Brown Shoe v. United States,* we cautioned that statistics concerning market share and concentration, while of great significance, were not conclusive indicators of anticompetitive effects...

In this case, the District Court assessed the evidence of the "structure, history and probable future" of the coal industry, and on the basis of this assessment found no substantial probability of anticompetitive effects from the merger.

...[T]he court discerned a number of clear and significant developments in the industry. First, it found that coal had become increasingly less able to compete with other sources of energy in many segments of the energy market...

Second, the court found that to a growing extent since 1954, the electric utility industry has become the mainstay of coal consumption...

Third, and most significantly, the court found that to an increasing degree, nearly all coal sold to utilities is transferred under long-term requirements contracts, under which coal producers promise to meet utilities' coal consumption requirements for a fixed period of time, and at predetermined prices...

...Because of these fundamental changes in the structure of the market for coal, the District Court was justified in viewing the statistics relied on by the Government as insufficient to sustain its case. Evidence of past production does not, as a matter of logic, necessarily give a proper picture of a company's future ability to compete. In most situations, of course, the unstated assumption is that a company that has maintained a certain share of a market in the recent past will be in a position to do so in the immediate future. Thus, companies that have controlled sufficiently large shares of a concentrated market are barred from merger by § 7 not because of their past acts, but because their past performances imply an ability to continue to dominate with at least equal vigor...

In the coal market, as analyzed by the District Court, however, statistical evidence of coal production was of considerably less significance. The bulk of the coal produced is delivered under long-term requirements contracts, and such sales thus do not represent the exercise of competitive power but rather the obligation to fulfill previously negotiated contracts at a previously fixed price. The focus of competition in a given time-frame is not on the disposition of coal already produced but on the procurement of new long-term supply contracts. In this situation, a company's past ability to produce is of limited significance, since it is in a position to offer for sale neither its past production nor the bulk of the coal it is presently capable of producing, which is typically already committed under a long-term supply contract. A more significant indicator of a company's power effectively to compete with other companies lies in the state of a company's uncommitted reserves of recoverable coal. A company with relatively large supplies of coal which are not already under contract to a consumer will have a more important influence upon competition in the contemporaneous negotiation of supply contracts than a firm with small reserves, even though the latter may presently produce a greater tonnage of coal. In a market where the availability and price for coal are set by long-term contracts rather than immediate or short-term purchases and sales, reserves rather than past production are the best measure of a company's ability to compete.

The testimony and exhibits in the District Court revealed that United Electric's coal reserve prospects were "unpromising." United's relative position of strength in reserves was considerably weaker than its past and current ability to produce...

United was found to be facing the future with relatively depleted resources at its disposal, and with the vast majority of those resources already committed under contracts allowing no further adjustment in price. In addition, the District Court found that "United Electric has neither the possibility of acquiring more reserves nor the ability to develop deep coal reserves," and thus was not in a position to increase its reserves to replace those already depleted or committed.

Viewed in terms of present and future reserve prospects—and thus in terms of probable future ability to compete—rather than in terms of past production, the District Court held that United Electric was a far less significant factor in the coal market than the Government contended or the production statistics seemed to indicate. While the company had been and remained a "highly profitable" and efficient producer of relatively large amounts of coal, its current and future power to compete for subsequent long-term contracts was severely limited by its scarce uncommitted resources. Irrespective of the company's size when viewed as a producer, its weakness as a competitor was properly analyzed by the District Court and fully substantiated that court's conclusion that its acquisition by Material Service (and General Dynamics) would not "substantially...lessen competition..."

■ ■ ■

CONGLOMERATE MERGERS

FTC v. PROCTOR & GAMBLE CO.
386 U.S. 568 (1966)
Supreme Court of the United States

■ ■ ■

DOUGLAS, Mr. Justice.

This is a proceeding by the Federal Trade Commission charging...that Procter's acquisition of Clorox might substantially lessen competition or tend to create a monopoly in the production and sale of household liquid bleaches.

At the time of the merger, in 1957, Clorox was the leading manufacturer in the heavily concentrated household liquid bleach industry. It is agreed that household liquid bleach is the relevant line of commerce. The product is used in the home as a germicide and disinfectant, and, more importantly, as a whitening agent in washing clothes and fabrics. It is a distinctive product with no close substitutes. Liquid bleach is a low-price, high-turnover consumer product sold mainly through grocery stores and supermarkets. The relevant geographical market is the Nation and a series of regional markets. Because of high shipping costs and low sales price, it is not feasible to ship the product more than 300 miles from its point of manufacture. Most manufacturers are limited to competition within a single region since they have but one plant. Clorox is the only firm selling nationally; it has 13 plants distributed throughout the Nation. Purex, Clorox's closest competitor in size, does not distribute its bleach in the northeast or mid-Atlantic States; in 1957, Purex's bleach was available in less than 50% of the national market.

At the time of the acquisition, Clorox was the leading manufacturer of household liquid bleach, with 48.8% of the national sales—annual sales of slightly less than $40,000,000. Its market share had been steadily increasing for the five years prior to the merger. Its nearest rival was Purex, which... accounted for 15.7% of the household liquid bleach market. The industry is highly concentrated; in 1957, Clorox and Purex accounted for almost 65% of the Nation's household liquid bleach sales, and, together with four other firms, for almost 80%. The remaining 20% was divided among over 200 small producers....

Since all liquid bleach is chemically identical, advertising and sales promotion are vital. In 1957 Clorox spent almost $3,700,000 on advertising, imprinting the value of its bleach in the mind of the consumer. In addition, it spent $1,700,000 for other promotional activities. The Commission found that these heavy expenditures went far to explain why Clorox maintained so high a market share despite the fact that its brand, though chemically indistinguishable from rival brands, retailed for a price equal to or, in many instances, higher than its competitors.

Procter is a large, diversified manufacturer of low-price, high-turnover household products sold through grocery, drug, and department stores. Prior to its acquisition of Clorox, it did not produce household liquid bleach... Procter has been marked by rapid growth and diversification. It has successfully developed and introduced a number of new products. Its primary activity is in the general area of soaps, detergents, and cleansers... Procter was the dominant factor in this area. It accounted for 54.4% of all packaged detergent sales. The industry is heavily concentrated—Procter and its nearest competitors, Colgate-Palmolive and Lever Brothers, account for 80% of the market.

In the marketing of soaps, detergents, and cleansers, as in the marketing of household liquid bleach, advertising and sales promotion are vital. In 1957, Procter was the Nation's largest advertiser, spending more than $80,000,000 on advertising and an additional $47,000,000 on sales promotion. Due to its tremendous volume, Procter receives substantial discounts from the media. As a multi-product producer Procter enjoys substantial advantages in advertising and sales promotion. Thus, it can and does feature several products in its promotions, reducing the printing, mailing, and other costs for each product. It also purchases network programs on behalf of several products, enabling it to give each product network exposure at a fraction of the cost per product that a firm with only one product to advertise would incur....

The decision to acquire Clorox was the result of a study conducted by Procter's promotion department designed to determine the advisability of entering the liquid bleach industry. The initial report noted the ascendancy of liquid bleach in the large and expanding household bleach market, and recommended that Procter purchase Clorox rather than enter independently. Since a large investment would be needed to obtain a satisfactory market share, acquisition of the industry's leading firm was attractive....

All mergers are within the reach of § 7, and all must be tested by the same standard, whether they are classified as horizontal, vertical, conglomerate or other. As noted by the Commission, this merger is neither horizontal, vertical, nor conglomerate. Since the products of the acquired company are complementary to those of the acquiring company and may be produced with similar facilities, marketed through the same channels and in the same manner, and advertised by the same media, the Commission aptly called this acquisition a "product-extension merger":

"By this acquisition... Procter has not diversified its interests in the sense of expanding into a substantially different, unfamiliar market or industry. Rather, it has entered a market which adjoins, as it were, those markets in which it is already established, and which is virtually indistinguishable from them insofar as the problems and techniques of marketing the product to the ultimate consumer are concerned. As a high offical of Procter put it, commenting on the acquisition of Clorox, 'While this is a completely new business for us, taking us for the first time into the marketing of a household bleach and disinfectant, we are thoroughly at home in the field of manufacturing and marketing low priced, rapid turn-over consumer products.' "...

The anticompetitive effects with which this product-extension merger is fraught can easily be seen: (1) the substitution of the powerful acquiring firm for the smaller, but already dominant, firm may substantially reduce the competitive structure of the industry by raising entry barriers and by dissuading the smaller firms from aggressively competing; (2) the acquisiton eliminates the potential competition of the acquiring firm.

The liquid bleach industry was already oligopolistic before the acquisition, and price competition was certainly not as vigorous as it would have been if the industry were competitive. Clorox enjoyed a dominant position nationally, and its position approached monopoly proportions in certain areas. The existence of some 200 fringe firms certainly does not belie that fact. Nor does the fact, relied upon by the court below, that, after the merger, producers other than Clorox "were selling more bleach for more money than ever before." In the same period, Clorox increased its share from 48.8% to 52%. The interjection of Procter into the market considerably changed the situation. There is every reason to assume that the smaller firms would become more cautious in competing due to their fear of retaliation by Procter. It is probable that Procter would become the price leader and that oligopoly would become more rigid.

The acquisition may also have the tendency of raising the barriers to new entry. The major competitive weapon in the successful marketing of bleach is advertising. Clorox was limited in this area by its relatively small budget and its inability to obtain substantial discounts. By contrast, Procter's budget was much larger; and, although it would not devote its entire budget to advertising Clorox, it could divert a large portion to meet the short-term threat of a new entrant. Procter would be able to use its volume discounts to advantage in advertising Clorox. Thus, a new entrant would be much more reluctant to face the giant Procter than it would have been to face the smaller Clorox.

Possible economies cannot be used as a defense to illegality. Congress was aware that some mergers which lessen competition may also result in economies but it struck the balance in favor of protecting competition.

The Commission also found that the acquisition of Clorox by Procter eliminated Procter as a potential competitor. The Court of Appeals declared that this finding was not supported by evidence because there was no evidence that Procter's management had ever intended to enter the industry independently and that Procter had never attempted to enter. The evidence, however, clearly shows that Procter was the most likely entrant. Procter had recently launched a new abrasive cleaner in an industry similar to the liquid bleach industry, and had wrested leadership from a brand that had enjoyed even a larger market share than had Clorox. Procter was engaged in a vigorous program of diversifying into product lines closely related to its basic products. Liquid bleach was a natural avenue of diversification since it is complementary to Procter's products, is sold to the same customers through the same channels, and is advertised and merchandised in the same manner. Procter had substantial advantages in advertising and sales promotion, which, as we have seen, are vital to the success of liquid bleach. No manufacturer had a patent on the product or its manufacture, necessary information relating to manufacturing methods and processes was really available, there was no shortage of raw material, and the machinery and equipment required for a plant of efficient capacity were available at reasonable cost. Procter's management was experienced in producing and marketing goods similar to liquid bleach. Procter had considered the possibility of independently entering but decided against it because the acquisition of Clorox would enable Procter to capture a more commanding share of the market.

It is clear that the existence of Procter at the edge of the industry exerted considerable influence on the market. First, the market behavior of the liquid bleach industry was influenced by each firm's predictions of the market behavior of its competitors, actual and potential. Second, the barriers to entry by a firm of Procter's size and with its advantages were not significant. There is no indication that the barriers were so high that the price Procter would have to charge would be above the price that would maximize the profits of the existing firms. Third, the number of potential entrants was not so large that the elimination of one would be insignificant. Few firms would have the temerity to challenge a firm as solidly entrenched as Clorox. Fourth, Procter was found by the Commission to be the most likely entrant. . .

■ ■ ■

Questions

1. What is a product-extension merger?
2. What is a potential competitor? What is the competitive effect of a potential entrant?
3. Besides eliminating a potential competitor, what other anticompetitive effects did the Court identify in *Proctor and Gamble?* Were these anticompetitive effects the results of the "deep-pockets" of Proctor and Gamble? In other words, what would be the competitive effect if Proctor and Gamble's financial resources were made available to Clorox who markets a product which involves extensive promotional expenditures to differentiate its otherwise competitively idential product?
4. Another possible anticompetitive effect of conglomerate mergers in some instances is reciprocity. In the *FTC v. Consolidated Foods,* 380 U.S. 592 (1965) Consolidated, a major retailer, acquired Gentry, Inc., a manufacturer of dehydrated onion and garlic. Since Consolidated made important purchases from several food processors, which needed substantial amounts of dehydraded onion and garlic, Consolidated was in a position to require or exert pressure on those seller-processors to buy their onion and garlic needs from Gentry. The Supreme Court found such attempts of reciprocity to create an unfair competitive advantage and outlawed the merger.

FUTURE REGULATION OF INDUSTRY STRUCTURE

Governmental regulation of industrial structure seems to favor the maintenance of the existing industry structure. Such conservation is based on the recognition that the U.S. economic system performs relatively well in comparison with other systems throughout the world. Instead of utilizing antitrust for structural reform, alternate governmental policies (as explored in subsequent chapters) are utilized to modify business behavior. Nevertheless, structuralists maintain that the rising tide of economic concentration threatens economic and political liberties and may also erode economic efficiencies. The continuing debate between structuralists and performance economists has been manifested in congressional halls and in the bills placed before Congress.

In the latter part of the seventies, structurally oriented senators have proposed another method for dealing with concentrated industry structure. They have proposed legislation to deal specifically with a single industry or firm. One bill was introduced which proposed breaking up AT&T. Another bill, the Petroleum Industry Competition Act, calls for the oil industry to eliminate its vertically integrated status among the eighteen largest U.S. oil firms. Another bill was proposed that the oil industry be prohibited from acquiring firms in other basic energy areas, such as coal or atomic energy. These proposals and others that are sure to be presented in the future deserve attention by business people. Increased research and more information are surely needed to formulate future public policies on these critical issues.

In addition, the Federal Trade Commission has decided to initiate attacks against the industrial structure of the ready-to-eat cereal producers and the oil industry. The amended FTC complaint against Kellogg, General Mills and General Foods alleges that the "big three" have a "shared monopoly" which hinders competition and increases the barriers to entry. The complaint suggests that the only appropriate remedy for this industry is compulsory divestiture of assets. Should the case be decided in favor of the FTC, it would have far-reaching legal implications. The FTC would thereby gain greater powers to deal with industrial structure perceived to be insufficiently competitive.

In the FTC suit against the oil industry, it has charged Exxon and seven other major vertically integrated oil producers with pursuing "a common course of action" in the production, refining, and marketing of crude and refined oil to the competitive disadvantage of nonvertically integrated competitors. The suit maintains that the larger oil companies share crude resources with one another and follow practices which "squeeze the profits" of the independent refineries. Such practices are alleged to be "unfair methods of competition." The FTC maintains that the only appropriate remedy for such behavior is the divestiture of the vertically integrated status of these eight oil companies. Again, should the FTC be successful in this litigation, it would thereby acquire new powers to regulate industrial structure. Whatever the decisions in these cases, they are not likely to be concluded for many years.

While the Supreme Court in *General Dynamics* may have relaxed the strict rules of illegality which it had fashioned for merger cases in the sixties, Congress has not similarily demonstrated any relaxation of its concern for outlawing mergers. In the 1976 Antitrust Improvements Act, Congress authorized the FTC and the Antitrust Division of the Department of Justice to prepare rules requiring firms desiring to merge to notify both the FTC and the Attorney General's Office. A mandatory waiting period of thirty days begins on the date the notice is received. The waiting period is intended to allow the government time to investigate the proposed merger and determine whether it would violate antitrust laws. During this period, either federal authority may request additonal information. If necessary, either of them can extend the period for a maximum of twenty days. At that point, the agencies must either permit the companies to proceed or go to court to block the proposal acquisition on antitrust grounds. Only companies meeting certain size tests are required to file. Generally, when a manufacturing company is acquired, notification must be filed if both parties have consolidated sales or assets of at least $10 million. For other acquisitions, notification is required when consolidated sales or assets of one party is at least $100 million and the other party is at least $10 million. Failure to comply with pre-merger rules can bring a civil penalty of $10,000 for each day of violation.

ENDNOTES

1. *Olsen v. Nebraska* 313 U.S. 236, 246-247, (1941).
2. *Lincoln Federal Labor Union v. Northwestern Iron & Metal Co.* 335 U.S. 325, 536-537, (1949).
3. *Williamson v. Lee Optical of Okla.* 348 U.S. 483, 487-488, (1955).

11

GOVERNMENT REGULATION OF MARKETING PRACTICES

Besides outlawing monopolies and attempting to arrest the "tide toward concentration" through antimerger laws, Congress felt that other anticompetitive practices must be prohibited also. Congress sought to prohibit firms from joining together to achieve results harmful to society in the same way that monopolies injure society. The initial reaction of Congress was passage of Section 1 of the Sherman Act which outlawed conspiracies and contracts in restraint of trade. However, it soon became apparent that the Sherman Act wasn't enough. Congress felt some large enterprises may utilize their size and power through marketing practices that, if continued, could result in greater concentration of monopolistic power. Therefore, Congress outlawed some specific anticompetitive marketing practices in the Clayton Act of 1914.

The Clayton Act was designed to stop anticompetitive practices before they resulted in creating *actual* restraints of trade outlawed under the Sherman Act. To deter anticompetitive practices before they became actual restraints of trade required a new approach. This was accomplished by making illegal those activities that "may" lessen competition. The Clayton Act reduces the government's burden of proof from actual anticompetitive effect to a *probable* anticompetitive effect.

This Chapter concentrates on anticompetitive marketing practices of competitors who join together or of an individual competitor which utilizes market power to lessen competitive conditions.

RULE OF REASON

Prior to the Sherman and Clayton Acts, the common law had established a body of law concerning restraints of trade. A contract was in restraint of trade when its performance would limit competition in any business or restrict some party in the exercise of an occupation. Such restraints on trade were illegal if the restraint was unreasonable. The rule of "reasonableness" had vague outlines which varied from state to state. The following decision illustrates the common law "rule of reason" in a modern case.

DUNN v. SHEPHERD
323 N.E. 2d 853 (1975)
Illinois Appellate Court

■ ■ ■

J. Glenn Dunn, plaintiff, commenced an action to declare a restrictive convenant in a contract between him and the defendant, Shepherd Insurance Agency, Inc., unenforceable, for an injunction against defendant's interference with his sale of insurance and for money damages. Defendant denied plaintiff's right to relief and in a counterclaim asked to have plaintiff enjoined from violating the restrictive covenant... The court... granted defendant's prayer for an injunction against the plaintiff...

Plaintiff entered into a series of three employment contracts with defendant, each of which contained a covenant not to compete in the event employment was terminated. In the last of these contracts the plaintiff agreed that in the event his employment terminated for any reason he would not solicit insurance orders from defendant's customers nor would he engage in the business of selling or serving any type of insurance in any capacity within the confines of Wabash, Edwards, Wayne, White and Lawrence (Counties), Illinois and Gibson and Knox Counties, Indiana, for a period of five years from the date of termination.

This is one of a large number of cases which have come before the courts of Illinois since before the turn of the century in which the validity of a covenant not to compete has been considered. The law is well established that such convenants can be enforced... Briefly, the conditions for supporting a covenant are:

1. That the time limitation be reasonable;
2. That the geographical limitation be reasonable:
3. That trade secrets or confidential information be in the possession of the promisor;
4. That the restriction not go beyond that necessary for the protection of a legitimate business interest;
5. That the covenant not be against public policy in denying to the public service of a kind which is needed.

In the instant case we find that the time and geographical limitations are reasonable in view of the nature of defendant's business; that a public policy question is not involved; that plaintiff obtained information about defendant's policy holders and the expiration dates of their policies; that such information has commercial value and when used by plaintiff would work to the detriment of defendant; and that the restriction does not go beyond the bounds necessary to protect legitimate business interest.

We find no error of law in this appeal.

■ ■ ■

When Congress passed the Sherman Act in 1890, Section 1 read:

> Every contract, combination... or conspiracy, in restraint of trade or commerce among the several states... is declared to be illegal...

This raised an obvious question: Are *reasonable* restraints of trade that are lawful under the common law made unlawful by the Sherman Act? In other words, did the word "every" in Section 1 mean "every"—including those reasonable common law restraints—and thereby outlaw all restraints on trade? Initially, the Supreme Court answered this question affirmatively by writing:

> ...[T]he plain and ordinary meaning of such language is not limited to that kind of contract alone which is in unreasonable restraint of trade, but all contracts are included in such language, and no exception or limitation can be added without placing in the act that which has been omitted by Congress... *U.S. v. Trans-Missouri Freight Association 166* U.S. 290 (1896).

This language by the Supreme Court indicated that the justices were following a "plain meaning" rule of statutory interpretation. They believed the plain meaning of the word as employed in the statute was the best evidence of the intention of Congress. They argued that if the legislators had meant something else, different words would have been used to indicate the alternate meaning. The dissenting justices favored a "purpose construction." They felt the statute should be interpreted in light of its "purpose" rather than according to the strictly literal language employed in the statute.

In 1911, the Court decided to adopt the "purpose" approach. The Court determined that the elimination of reasonable restraints of trade that were lawful under the common law was not within the "purpose" of the Sherman Act. Consequently, a "rule of reason" approach was accepted as the proper method to interpret the Sherman Act. So, while the Act itself may say "every" restraint of trade, the judicial interpretations of the Act have added the requirement of "unreasonableness" before the retraint of trade is to be ruled illegal. This rule of reason was first enunciated in the *Standard Oil Co. v. U.S.* 221 U.S. 1 (1911). One of the most frequently cited statements of the rule of reason is that of Justice Brandeis in *Chicago Board of Trade v. U.S.* 246 U.S. 231, 238 (1918):

> The true test of legality is whether the restraint imposed is such as merely regulates and perhaps thereby promotes competition or whether it is such as may suppress or even destroy competition. To determine that question the court must ordinarily consider the facts peculiar to the business to which the restraint is applied; its condition before and after the restraint was imposed; the nature of the restraint and its effect, actual or probable. The history of the restraint, the evil believed to exist, the reason for adopting the particular remedy, the purpose or end sought to be attained, are all relevant facts. This is not because a good intention will save an otherwise objectionable regulation or the reverse; but because knowledge of the intent may help the court to interpret facts and to predict consquences.

HORIZONTAL COMBINATIONS

Businessmen freely accept and publicly proclaim the advantages of competition and the free market. They maintain that the self-regulating aspects of competition promote the public welfare by assuring lower prices and greater productivity. However, businessmen also recognize that in planning for productive operations and in the development of marketing strategy cooperation among competitors may reduce the hazards associated with the competitive process. As Adam Smith wrote in *The Wealth of Nations*, "people of the same trade seldom meet together, even for merriment and diversion, but the conversation ends in a conspiracy against the public, or in some contrivance to raise prices." When such agreements are made between competitors at the same level of the distribution process, the agreements are considered horizontal combinations. Obvious examples include the agreements of manufacturers to fix prices they charge to the public, or wholeslers agreeing not to sell competing goods in each other's assigned territory. Such horizontal combinations eliminate competition between competing rivals. Society is then faced with higher prices and no alternative source of supplies. Because most of these practices present obvious harm to the competitive process, the courts have treated them as containing no redeeming social or economic value and, hence, unreasonable, *per se*. However, in many instances the conspiring merchants have attempted to convince the court that they only set or fix "reasonable" prices and achieve only "reasonable" profits as a result of the price-fixing agreement. In the following case, the conspirators also argued that their buying program to support prices merely eliminated "ruinous competition."

UNREASONABLE PER SE

U.S. v. SOCONY-VACUUM OIL CO.
310 U.S. 150 (1939)
Supreme Court of the United States

■ ■ ■

DOUGLAS, Mr. Justice.

The court charged the jury that it was a violation of the Sherman Act for a group of individuals or corporations to act together to raise the prices to be charged for the commodity which they manufactured where they controlled a substantial part of the interstate trade and commerce in that commodity. The court stated that where the members of a combination had the power to raise prices and acted together for that purpose, the combination was illegal; and that it was immaterial how reasonable or unreasonable those prices were or to what extent they had been affected by the combination...

In *United States v. Trenton Potteries Co.,* 273 U.S. 392, this Court sustained a conviction under the Sherman Act where the jury was charged that an agreement on the part of the members of a combination, controlling a substantial part of an industry, upon the prices which the members are to charge for their commodity is in itself an unreasonable restraint of trade without regard to the reasonableness of the prices or the good intentions of the combining units... This Court reviewed the various price-fixing cases under the Sherman Act... and said "...it has since often been decided and always assumed that uniform price-fixing by those controlling in any substantial manner a trade or business in interstate commerce is prohibited by the Sherman Law, despite the reasonableness of the particular prices agreed upon." This Court pointed out that the so-called "rule of reason" had not affected this view of the illegality of price-fixing agreements. And in holding that agreements "to fix or maintain prices" are not reasonable restraints of trade under the statute merely because the prices themselves are reasonable, it said...

> "The aim and result of every price-fixing agreement, if effective, is the elimination of one form of competition. The power to fix prices, whether reasonably exercised, or not, involves power to control the market and to fix arbitrary and unreasonable prices. The reasonable price fixed today may through economic and business changes become the unreasonable price of tomorrow. Once established, it may be maintained unchanged because of the absence of competition secured by the agreement for a price reasonable when fixed. Agreements which create such potential power may well be held to be in themselves unreasonable or unlawful restraints, without the necessity of minute inquiry whether a particular price is reasonable or unreasonable as fixed and without placing on the government in enforcing the Sherman Law and burden of ascertaining from day to day whether it has become unreasonable through the mere variation of economic conditions..."

Thus for over forty years this Court has consistently and without deviation adhered to the principle that price-fixing agreements are unlawful *per se* under the Sherman Act and that no showing of so-called competitive abuses or evils which those agreements were designed to eliminate or alleviate may be interposed as a defense.

Therefore the sole remaining question on this phase of the case is the applicability of the rule of the *Trenton Potteries* case to these facts.

In the first place, there was abundant evidence that the combination had the purpose to raise prices. And likewise, there was ample evidence that the buying programs at least contributed to the price rise and the stability of the spot markets, and to increases in the price of gasoline sold in the Mid-Western area during the indictment period. That other factors also may have contributed to that rise and stability of the markets is immaterial. For in any such market movement, forces other than the purchasing power of the buyers normally would contribute to the price rise and the market stability. So far as cause and effect are concerned it is sufficient in this type of case if the buying programs of the combination resulted in a price rise and market stability which but for them would not have happened... Proof that there was a conspiracy, that its purpose was to raise prices, and that it caused or contributed to a price rise is proof of the actual consummation or execution of a conspiracy under §1 of the Sherman Act.

Secondly, the fact that sales on the spot markets were still governed by some competition is of no consequence. For it is indisputable that the competition was restricted through the removal by defendants of a part of the supply which but for the buying programs would have been a factor in determing the going prices on those markets.

The elimination of so-called competitive evils is no legal justification for such buying programs. The elimination of such conditions was sought primarily for its effect on the price structure. Fairer competitive prices, it is claimed, resulted when distress gasoline was removed from the market. But such defense is typical of the protestations usually made in price-fixing cases. Ruinous competition, financial disaster, evils of price cutting and the like appear throughout our history as ostensible justifications for price-fixing. If the so-called competitive abuses were to be appraised here, the reasonableness of prices would necessarily become an issue in every price-fixing case. In that event the Sherman Act would soom be emasculated; its philosophy would be supplanted by one which is wholly alien to a system of free competition; it would not be the charter of freedom which its framers intended.

The resonableness of prices has no constancy due to the dynamic quality of business facts underlying price structures. Those who fixed reasonable prices today would perpetuate unreasonable prices tomorrow, since those prices would not be subject to continuous administrative supervision and readjustment in light of changed conditions. Those who controlled the prices would control or effectively dominate the market. And those who were in that strategic position would have it in their power to destroy or drastically impair the competitive system. But the trust of the rule is deeper and reaches more than monopoly power. Any combination which tampers with price structures is engaged in an unlawful activity. Even though the members of the price-fixing group were in no position to control the market, to the extent that they raised, lowered, or stabilized prices they would be directly interfering with the free play of marke forces. The Act places all such schemes beyond the pale and protects that vital part of our economy against any degree of interference...

Under the Sherma Act a combination formed for the purpose and with the effect of raising, depressing, fixing, pegging, or stabilizing the price of a commodity in interstate or foreign channels of trade, the power to fix prices exists if the combination has control of a substantial part of the commerce in that commodity... But there may be effective influence over the market though the group in question does not control it. Price-fixing agreements may have utility to members of the group though the power influence over the market thought the group in question does not control it. Price-fixing agreements may have utility to members of the group though the power possessed or exerted falls far short of domination and control. Monopoly power is not the only power which the Act strikes down, as we have said. Proof that a combination was formed for the purpose of fixing prices and that it caused them to be fixed or contributed to that result is proof of the completion of a price-fixing conspiracy under §1 of the Act. The indictment in this case charged that this combination had that purpose and effect. And there was abundant evidence to support it...

■ ■ ■

Questions

1. Did the Court accept the notion that reasonable prices and reasonable profits are justification for price-fixing?
2. Is the elimination of "ruinous competition" a justification for establishing a price-fixing scheme?
3. If the Supreme Court accepted reasonable prices and profits as justification for price-fixing and ruled that such pricing and profits were resonable, what would have to be done again if the parties changed their price structure? Would the Supreme Court become like a price control board? Do you think the Court wanted to get into such an activity?

4. When is an activity considered "unreasonable *per se*?" What reasons can be given for having such a rule? The Supreme Court said:

> ...[T]here are certain agreements or practices which because of their pernicious effect on competiton and lack of any redeeming virtue are conclusively presumed to be unreasonable and therefore illegal without elaborate inquiry as to the precise harm they have caused or the business excuse for their use. This principle of *per se* unreasonableness not only makes the type of restraints which are proscribed by the Sherman Act more certain to the benefit of everyone concerned, but it also avoids the necessity for an incredibly complicated and prolonged economic investigation into the entire history of the industry involved, as well as related industries, in an effort to determine at large whether a particular restraint has been unreasonable—an inquiry so often wholly fruitless when undertaken. *Northern Pac. R. Co. v. United States* 356 U.S. 1 (1957).

5. In *Socony-Vacuum Oil*, the activity challenged was price-fixing. Since Price-fixing is unreasonable *per se*, the only burden of proof to be met by the government is the agreement itself. Was that burden difficult in *Socony-Vacuum Oil?* Would it be more difficult today? Consider the following materials.

CONTRACT, COMBINATION...OR CONSPIRACY

Price-fixing has been ruled unreasonable *per se* since *Trenton Potteries*. Enforcement officials have consistently taken legal action against schemes to rig, control, or stabilize prices. No anticompetitive scheme is frowned on more than a price-fixing combination. Consequently, the Department of Justice believes that everyone, by now, should understand the illegality of price-fixing. Therefore, the Department of Justice often brings *criminal* charges against participants of price-fixing conspiracy. A criminal violation of the Sherman Act can be a felony and result in imprisonment for up to three years. The Act authorizes the imposition of fines of $100,000 per count for an idividual and a $1,000,000 fine per count for a corporation. These criminal penalties were upgraded in 1976 from more lenient provisions in the original Sherman Act. The increase in the level of penalties and the increased willingness of enforcement officials to proceed with criminal suits suggests that more prosecution and stiff sentencing of antitrust violators may well increase in the future. Business executives have been imprisoned for participation in price-rigging schemes.

Some businessmen attempt to circumvent the price-fixing prohibitions by concealing their conspiracy from the public. Historically, such conspiracies have been proven by presenting in evidence the actual documents or contracts of the price-fixing scheme. When such documents are not prepared or not discovered, circumstantial evidence is presented to establish the conspiracy. Meetings of competitors are often used as evidence of a conspiracy. In addition, business firms that sell their products at the same price are behaving "parallel" and such behavior may imply a conspiracy. "Conscious parallelism" of the competitors in following the same practices is often asserted as evidence of conspiracy. The following case deals with the questions of evidence of conspiracy and whether the "parallel behavior" of several competitors was the result of independent business judgment by each competitor or the result of a conspiratorial agreement.

ESCO CORPORATION v. UNITED STATES
340 F. 2d. 1000 (1965)
United States Court of Appeals, (9th Cir.)

■ ■ ■

This is an appeal from a jury verdict convicting appellant corporation of violating

Section 1 of the Sherman Act by means of its participation in an alleged price-fixing conspiracy, admittedly a *per se* violation of the Act...

The "central criminal design" charged herein was the restraint of trade by fixing prices on stainless steel pipe and tubing within the described market area. But, it is contended, Esco's "relationship" to the two... (Los Angeles) meetings and the Salt Lake City meeting of the competitors was "perfectly legal..." [A]ppellant's counsel (argues) "there is a compelled inference" that Tubesales, the biggest competitor called the meeting "not to ask for agreement, but simply to announce" its own pricing plans. Were we triers of fact, we might well ask if this were so, what purpose was to be served by a meeting of competitors?

Nor are we so naive as to believe that a formal signed-and-sealed contract or written resolution would conceivably be adopted at a meeting of price-fixing conspirators in this day and age. In fact, the typical price-fixing agreement is usually accomplished in a contrary manner.

While particularly true of price-fixing conspiracies, it is well recognized law that any conspiracy can ordinarily only be proved by inferences drawn from relevant and competent circumstantial evidence, including the conduct of the defendants charged... A knowing wink can mean more than words. Let us suppose five competitors meet on several occasions, discuss their problems, and one finally states—"I won't fix prices with any of you, but here is what I am going to do—put the price of my gidget at X dollars, now you all do what you want." He then leaves the meeting. Competitor number two says—"I don't care whether number one does what he says he's going to do nor not; nor do I care what the rest of you do, but I am going to price may gidget a X dollars." Number three makes a similar statement—"My price is X dollars." Number four says not a word. All leave and fix "their" prices at "X" dollars.

We do not say the foregoing illlustration compels an inference in this case that the competitors' conduct constituted a price-fixing conspiracy, including an agreement to so conspire, but neither can we say, as a matter of law, that an inference of no agreement is compelled. As in so many other instances, it remains a question for the trier of fact to consider and determine what inference appeals to it (the jury) as most logical and persuasive after it has heard all the evidence as to what these competitors had done before such meeting, and what actions they took thereafter, or what actions they did not take.

An accidental or incidental price uniformity, or even "pure" conscious parallelism of prices is, standing alone, not unlawful. Nor is an individual competitor's sole decision to follow a price leadership standing alone, a violation of law. But we do not find that factual situation here.

It is not necessary to find an express agreement, either oral or written, in order to find a conspiracy, but it is sufficient that a concert of action be contemplated and that defendants conform to the arrangement... Mutual consent need not be bottomed on express agreement, for any conformance to an agreed or contemplated pattern of conduct will warrant an inference of conspiracy... An exchange of words is not required... Thus not only action, but even a lack of action, may be enough from which to infer a combination or conspiracy...

Applying these rules to the facts at hand, the jury came to an opposite conclusion from that which appellant urges, and the fact that Esco's involvement was in but two of ten allegedly conspirational situations does not absolve Esco from participation in the entire conspiracy if its involvement in the two was unlawful and knowingly and purposely performed. We hold that sufficient evidence existed for the jury to find participation in a price-fixing conspiracy...

■ ■ ■

Questions

1. How many different types of evidence of a conspiracy or agreement are discussed in *Esco*?

2. Is pure "conscious parallalism "illegal? Is it evidence? Enough evidence to have a jury decide? What can the defendants do to rebut the evidence of their "parallel" behavior to avoid a jury verdict?

3. Is price leadership illegal?

4. Do you think it is wise to attend your competitor's announcement of new pricing plans? Is it ever wise to consult with your competitors?

GROUP BOYCOTTS

KLOR'S v. BROADWAY-HALE STORES
359 U.S. 207 (1959)
Supreme Court of the United States

■ ■ ■

BLACK, Mr. Justice.

Klor's, Inc., operates a retail store on Mission Street, San Francisco, California; Broadway-Hale Stores, Inc., a chain of department stores, operates one of its stores next door. The two stores compete in the sale of radios, television sets, refrigerators and other household appliances...

Klor's brought this action for treble damages and injunction in the United States District Court.

In support of its claim Klor's... (alleged): [M]anufacturers and distributors of such well-known brands as General Electric, RCA, Admiral, Zenith, Emerson and others have conspired among themselves and with Broadway-Hale either not to sell to Klor's or to sell to it only at discriminatory prices and highly unfavorable terms. Broadway-Hale had used its "monopolistic" buying power to bring about this situation... The concerted refusal to deal with Klor's has seriously handicapped its ability to compete and has already caused it a great loss of profits, goodwill, reputation and prestige.

The defendants did not dispute these allegations, but sought summary judgment and dismissal of the complaint for failure to state a cause of action. They submitted unchallenged affidavits which showed that there were hundreds of other household appliance retailers, some within a few blocks of Klor's who sold many competing brands of appliances, including those the defendants refused to sell to Klor's. From the allegations of the complaint, and from the affidavits supporting the motion for summary judgment, the District Court concluded that the controversy was a "purely private quarrel" between Klor's and Broadway-Hale, which did not amount to a "public wrong proscribed by the (Sherman) Act." On this ground the complaint was dismissed and summary judgment was entered for the defendants... [I]t held that here the required public injury was missing since "there was no charge or proof that by any act of defendants the price, quantity, or quality offered the public was affected, nor that there was any intent or purpose to effect a change in, or an influence on, prices, quantity, or quality..." The holding, if correct, means that unless the opportunities for customers to buy in a competitive market are reduced, a group of powerful businessmen may act in concert to deprive a single merchant, like Klor, of the goods he needs to compete effectively...

We think Klor's allegations clearly show one type of trade restraint and public harm the Sherman Act forbids, and that defendants' affidavits provide no defense to the charges. Section 1 of the Sherman Act makes illegal any contract, combination or conspiracy in restraint of trade, and §2 forbids any person or combination from monopolizing or attempting to monopolize any part of interstate commerce. In the landmark case of *Standard Oil Co. v. United States*, 221 U.S. 1, this Court read §1 to prohibit those classes of contracts or acts which the common law had deemed to be undue restraints of trade and those which new times and economic conditions would make unreasonable... The Court recognized that there were some agreements whose validity depended on the surrounding circumstances. It emphasized, however, that there were classes of restraints which from their "nature or character" were unduly restrictive, and hence forbidden by both the common law and the statute...

Group boycotts, or concerted refusals by traders to deal with other traders, have long been held to be in the forbidden category. They have not been saved by allegations that they were reasonable in the specific circumstances, nor by a failure to show that they "fixed or regulated prices, parcelled out or limited production, or brought about a deterioration in quality."

For, as this Court said in *Kiefer-Stewart Co. v. Seagram & Sons*, 340 U.S. 211, "such agreements, no less than those to fix minimum prices, cripple the freedom of traders and thereby restrain their ability to sell in accordance with their own judgment."

Plainly the allegations of this complaint disclose such a boycott. This is not a case of a single trader refusing to deal with another, nor even of a manufacturer and a dealer agreeing to an exclusive distributorship. Alleged in this complaint is a wide combination consisting of manufacturers, distributors and a retailer. This combination takes from Klor's its freedom to buy appliances in an open competitive market and drives it out of business as a dealer in the defendants' products. It deprives the manufacturers and distributors of their freedom to sell to Klor's at the same prices and conditions made available to Broadway-Hale, and in some instances forbids them from selling to it on any terms whatsoever. It interferes with the natural flow of interstate commerce. It clearly has, by its "nature" and "character" a monopolistic tendency." As such it is not to be tolerated merely because the victim is just one merchant whose business is so small that his destruction makes little difference to the economy. Monopoly can as surely thrive by the elimination of such small businessmen, one at a time, as it can by driving them out in large groups. In recognition of this fact the Sherman Act has consistently been read to forbid all contracts and combinations "which 'tend to create a monopoly,' " whether "the tendency is a creeping one" or "one that proceeds a full gallop."

■ ■ ■

Questions

1. The District Court ruled these facts merely demonstrated existence of a "private dispute" without any "public wrong." What did the court mean by no "public wrong proscribed by the Act"?
2. Why did the Supreme Court feel these facts revealed a "public wrong"?
3. Would there be illegal behavior if each distributor independently refused to deal with Klor's?

RELATIONS WITH COMPETITORS

Previous cases have revealed that Section 1 of the Sherman Act prohibits conspiracies and understandings that unreasonably restrain trade. Some kind of *joint or concerted* action between two or more persons or companies must exist for Section 1 of the Sherman Act to apply. But there need not be anything so formal as a written contract; "understandings" are enough, and these can be inferred by the court or jury from the way the parties have conducted themselves. Any kind of a mutual understanding which gives the parties a basis for expecting that a business practice or decision will be adopted by one and all, or at least not opposed, by the others is sufficient to establish a violation.

For Section 1 to be violated the joint action must have as its *purpose or effect* an unreasonable restraint of trade. If the *purpose* is unreasonable it does not matter whether the action taken by the parties is successful or fails. Such restraints of trade that are in their purpose considered unreasonable are identified as *"per se"* violations. Federal enforcement policy allows criminal prosecution of these *per se* offenses which include the following:

Price Fixing. This agreement need not be on a specific price. The law is violated by agreements on maximums or minimums; or on a common sales agent; or on terms or conditions of sale such as credit terms or discounts; or even on the mere exchange of price information if there is a stabilizing effect of prices. The agreement of price-fixing schemes can be inferred from a course of conduct, or from a history of telephone calls, meetings and the like between competitors followed by uniform price action. Price-fixing, in whatever form, is the antitrust violation most frequently prosecuted criminally.

Dividing Territory. Competitors may not agree as to geographical areas in which each will or will not sell. Any course of action whereby competitors avoid each other's territory may be a basis for a court finding of such an illegal agreement.

Dividing Customers. Competitiors may not agree that each will sell to a particular customer or class of customers and not to another. Neither may competitors agree on which of them will make any specific sales.

Dividing Products. Basically, competitors may not agree that one will not make or sell products made or sold by another.

Limiting Production. Competitors may not agree to restrict or limit production or production capacity. Violations of this form often involve a quota system.

Boycotting. Competing sellers must not agree among themselves not to sell to a particular customer or reseller, whatever the reason.

Suppression of quality competition. Competitors may not agree to restrict the development of improvements in the quality of their products. Nor may competitors agree to limit research for quality improvements. Most agreements of this type are, in effect, agreements not to compete and are contrary to the basic concepts of antitrust laws.

To avoid suspicion of a *per se* violation there should be no conversations or communications of any kind with competitors concerning the items above. If any comunications are made, a document should be prepared indicating the extent of the conversation and how the conversation was limited to avoid any violation of antitrust laws. If one of these subjects come up in conversation at a trade meeting attended by company employees, employees should terminate the conversation immediately or leave the gathering. Again, documentation of the incident should be recorded indicating the facts and the employee's noninvolvement. In all *per se* situations it makes no difference that an apparently sound business consideration may be involved also. There are no acceptable excuses nor such a thing as being just a "little bit" guilty.

Besides the *per se* offenses under the Sherman Act, the legality of other joint action by competitors turns on the reasonableness, under the circumstances, of any restraint on competition. Reasonableness of such restraints is measured in terms of both the purpose of the restraint and the effect of the restraint on competition. All these potential restraints must be tested on an individual basis. However, one should remember that a reasonable business purpose will not excuse joint action which has an unreasonable effect upon competition.

Joint activities of competitors to present views or make recommendations to governmental bodies are exempt from antitrust laws if they are limited to good faith efforts to influence governmental policy. However, the courts have ruled that such action must not be a mere sham to accomplish an otherwise illegal purpose. Therefore, before engaging with other companies in joint presentations before governmental bodies, each proposal should be reviewed to make certain that the project cannot be asserted to be a sham and thus lose its antitrust exemption status.

VERTICAL COMBINATIONS

Vertical combinations involve the relationships between manufacturers and distributors. It is often the desire of the manufacturer to impose contractual restrictions on the resale policies of the distributor. There are many reasons why the manufacturer may desire such vertical restraints. However, before discussing such reasons it should first be made clear that no manufacturer desires to allow his or her retailers to make above normal profits. Such a position would imply that the manufacturer is willing to pay more than necessary for retailing services. Above normal profits can be achieved by retailers only if they restrict sales to gain higher prices. Such restrictions would reduct the manufacturer's sales and, in effect, take money out of the manufacturer's own pocket. Consequently, when manufacturers attempt to impose vertical restraints (such as resale price maintenance or territorial divisions), it is because they believe such policies will induce dealer behavior that will make the distribution process more efficient. Additional profits from the restrictions are gained at the retail level in exchange for distribution efficiencies or expanded sales efforts which also accrue to the advantage of the manufacturer and consumers alike.

The most common justification raised for vertical restraints is the optimization or dealer-sales effort by the elimination of "free riding." Selling involves the provision of information and persuasion. It is in the nature of some products that dealers may need to invest money and time in carrying a full line of models for display, instructing sales personnel in the product's features and comparative advantages, and explaining the product and its uses to potential consumers. The dealer, of course, will do these things only if the cost can be recaptured in the price at which the product is sold. Some dealers will perceive the opportunity to avoid these costs and capture the consumer by offering a lower price.

Such dealers take a "free ride" on the other dealers' sale efforts. If free riding becomes common, no dealer will find it worthwhile to provide the sales effort that the manufacturer believes is optimal in the distribution of the products.

For the manufacturer to insure optimal dealer-sales effort and avoid "free riding," the manufacturer may divide dealer territories or fix minimum resale prices. When the product is of such a nature that it can be effectively sold through one or a few outlets in a given area, the manufacturer may employ the use of market divisions. However, where many outlets in an area is a preferable marketing strategy, the manufacturer may choose resale price maintenance provisions. Such restrictions eliminate competition between the dealers who sell the manufacturer's brand. Alternate brands of other manufacturers continue to compete in the marketplace for the consumers' dollars. Consequently, vertical restraints eliminate *intrabrand* competition, but may enhance *interbrand* competition.

The manufacturer will employ some type of vetical restraint only if consumers respond to the additional information provided through the dealer services. While some consumers may prefer lower prices without information, the technology of the distribution process may not allow such consumer preferences to be met. This is not uncommon in economic activity. Manufacturers often dictate a single model of a particular product even when a minority of consumers would prefer a lower priced model. The majority of consumers dictate the price and model of particular products available in the marketplace because the minority do not represent a significant enough "market" for separate recognition and service.

While pure economic analysis would suggest that the degree to which vertical restraints are exercised should be left to the free determination of the marketplace, several constraining influences have prevented this result. First, the courts and some economists have asserted that the elimination of intrabrand competition by use of vertical restraints may be part of a method or means to achieve conspiratorial horizontal restraints by the manufacturers. If manufacturers agree to fix prices, they would have the ability, if vertical restraints were lawful, to impose their price-fixing scheme, not only at the manufacturing level, but also at the retail level. Consequently, they argue that it is preferable to disallow intrabrand restrictions at the retail level to frustrate manufacturer efforts to extent their conspiratorial price-fixing scheme all that way through the distribution channels. However, the obvious answer to this contention is that conspiracies should be detected at their source and that efficient operations created by vertical restraints should not be outlawed to frustrate alleged conspiratorial conduct on a horizontal level. Nevertheless, the courts have developed judicial pronouncements against vertical restraints.

Secondly, many have argued that in some industries the intrabrand competition eliminated by vertical restraints is significant competiton that should not be lost. The elimination of any intrabrand competition in industries where only a few brands exist would have adverse effects upon consumer welfare. For example, it is often asserted that intrabrand competition in the auto industry is significant. A vertical price-fixing scheme for auto brands would eliminate significant price competition between dealerships selling the same brands. It is argued that such vertical restraints by manufacturers should be outlawed.

Beside these economic arguments, it is often advanced that the independent judgment of small retailers is destroyed by vertical constraints and U.S. "free" economy is thereby eroded. Also, resale price maintenance is believed to contain an inflationary bias. These arguments gain some constituency and force in the fashioning of antitrust rules and, therefore, the rules of antitrust in relation to vertical restraints have been inconsistent.

VERTICAL PRICE-FIXING

Resale price maintenance is an agreement or arrangement between a manufacturer and distributors to maintain a resale price, (vetical price-fixing). We have seen that any horizontal arrangement among manufacturers or among retailers involving price-fixing are illegal *per se*. The law on resale price maintenance, however, is less consistent. As early as 1911 the Supreme Court held that contractual agreements designed to maintain retail prices after the manufacturer has parted with title to the goods are injurious to the public interest and illegal, *Dr Miles Medical Co. v. John D. Park & Sons Co.* 220 U.S. 373 (1911). However, in 1919 the Supreme Court allowed resale price maintenance in *U.S. v. Colgate & Co.*, 250 U.S. 300 (1919). Colgate did not have "contractual agreements" with its dealers to maintain the resale price. Instead, it announced that it would "refuse to deal" with those distributors who did not cooperate with the announced resale price expected by Colgate. Therefore, the Supreme Court held that Colgate could not be charged with an "agreement" to vertically fix prices. The Colgate decision was distinguished from previous cases which were based on contracts between the manufacturer and the dealer. Thus, while the results (resale price maintenance) were the same in *Dr. Miles* and *Colgate*, the techniques used to achieve that result were different. Consquently, vertical price-fixing was both legal and illegal, depending upon the technique employed.

The Colgate Doctrine was later restricted by the Supreme Court in *FTC v. Beechnut Packing Co.*, 257 U.S. 441 decided in 1922. The Supreme Court held that Beechnut's methods of enforcement of its resale price maintenance program went beyond a simple refusal to sell goods to persons not maintaining the resale prices. Products were numbered by Beechnut to check whether the dealers were maintaining the resale price. Card files were maintained which listed undesirable price cutters. Beechnut refused to sell its products to continued violators. Beechnut would reinstate those previously cut-off on retailer assurances of intent to sell at the suggested price. The Supreme Court held that this plan in practice suppressed competition because of the reporting system, the card list, and the refusals to sell to nonconformists. Together, the techniques constituted an "unfair method of competition" which the Federal Trade Commission was empowered to suppress. The authority of the FTC to eliminate unfair methods of competition could not be frustrated by Beechnut's mere assertion that there was an absence of a contract or agreement to fix prices.

The following case represents another effort by the Supreme Court to cut back the utilization of the Colgate Doctrine to achieve resale price maintenance.

UNITED STATES v. PARKE, DAVIS & CO.
362 U.S. 29 (1960)
Supreme Court of the United States

■ ■ ■

BRENNAN, Mr. Justice.

The Government... (alleged) that Parke Davis conspired and combined, in violation of §1 of the (Sherman) Act., with retail and wholesale druggists... to maintain the wholesale and retail prices of Parke Davis pharmaceutical products...

Parke Davis makes some 600 pharmaceutical products which it markets nationally through drug wholesalers and drug retailers. The retailers buy these products from the drug wholesalers or make large quantity purchases directly from Parke Davis. Sometime before 1956 Parke Davis announced a resale price maintenance policy in its wholesalers' and retailers' catalogues...

There are some 260 drugstores in Washington, D.C., and some 100 in Richmond, Virginia... There are five drug wholesalers handling Parke Davis products in the locality who do business with the drug retailers. The wholesalers observed the resale prices suggested by Parke Davis. However, during the spring and early summer of 1956 drug retailers in the two cities advertised and sold several Parke Davis vitamin products at prices substantially below the suggested minimum retail prices... The Baltimore office manager of Parke Davis in charge of the sales district which included the two cities sought advice from his head office on how to handle this situation. The Parke Davis attorney advised that the company could legally "enforce an adopted policy arrived at unilaterally" to sell only to customers who observed the suggested minimum resale prices. He further advised that this meant that "we can lawfully say 'we will sell you only so long as you observe such minimum retail prices' but canot say 'we will sell you only if you agree to observe such minimum retail prices,' since... agreements as to resale price maintenance are invalid. "Thereafter in July the branch manager put into effect a program for promoting observance of the suggested minimum retail prices by the retailers involved. The program contemplated the participation of the five drug wholesalers. In order to insure that retailers who did not comply would be cut off from sources of supply, representatives of Parke Davis visited the wholesalers and told them, in effect, that not only would Parke Davis refuse to sell to wholesalers who did not adhere to the policy announced in its catalogue, but also that it would refuse to sell to wholesalers who sold Parke Davis products who did not observe the suggested minimum retail prices. Each wholesaler was interviewed indivudually but each was informed that his competitors were also being apprised of this. The wholesalers without exception indicated a willingness to go along.

Representatives called contemporaneously upon the retailers involved, individually, and told each, that if he did not observe the suggested minimum retail prices, Parke Davis would refuse to deal with him, and that furthermore he would be unable to purchase any Parke Davis products from the wholesalers. Each of the retailers was also told that his competitors were being similarly informed.

Several retailers refused to give any assurances of compliance and continued after these July interviews to advertise and sell Parke Davis products at prices below the suggested minimum retail prices. Their names were furnished by Parke Davis to the wholesalers. Thereafter Parke Davis refused to fill direct orders from such retailers and the wholesalers likewise refused to fill their orders. This ban was not limited to the Parke Davis products being sold below the suggested minimum prices but included all the company's products, even those necessary to fill prescriptions....

The *Colgate* case came to this Court... from a District Court judgment dismissing an indictment for violation of the Sherman Act. The Court said:

"The purpose of the Sherman Act is to prohibit monopolies, contracts and combinations which probably would unduly interfere with the free exercise of their rights by those engaged, or who wish to engage, in trade and commerce—in a word to preserve the right of freedom to trade. In the absence of any purpose to create or maintain a monopoly, the act does not restrict the long recognized right of trader or manufacturer engaged in an entirely private business, freely to exercise his own independent discretion as to parties with whom he will deal.

And, of course, he may announce in advance the circumstances under which he will refuse to sell."

The Government concedes for the purposes of this case that under the *Colgate* doctrine a manufacturer, having announced a price maintenance policy, may bring about adherence to it by refusing to deal with customers who do not observe that policy. The Government contends, however, that subsequent decisions of this Court compel the holding that what Parke Davis did here by entwining the wholesalers and retailers in a program to promote general compliance with its price maintenance policy went beyond mere customer selection and created combinations or conspiracies to enforce resale price maintenance in violation of § 1 of the Sherman Act....

The program upon which Parke Davis embarked to promote general compliance with its suggested resale prices plainly exceeded the limitations of the *Colgate* doctrine and...effected arrangements which violated the Sherman Act. Parke Davis did not content itself with announcing its policy regarding retail prices and following this with a simple refusal to have business relations with any retailers who disregarded that policy. Instead Parke Davis used the refusal to deal with the wholesalers in order to elicit their willingness to deny Parke Davis products to retailers and thereby help gain the retailers' adherence to its suggested minimum retail prices. The retailers who disregarded the price policy were promptly cut off when Parke Davis supplied the wholesalers with their names... In thus involving the wholesalers to stop the flow of Parke Davis products to the retailers, thereby inducing retailers' adherence to its suggested retail prices, Parke Davis created a combination with the retailers and the wholesalers to maintain retail prices and violated the Sherman Act. Although Parke Davis' originally announced wholesalers' policy would not under Colgate have violated the Sherman Act if its action thereunder was the simple refusal without more to deal with wholesalers who did not observe the wholesalers' Net Price Selling Schedule, that entire policy was tainted with the "vice of...illegality," when Parke Davis used it as the vehicle to gain the wholesalers' participation in the program to effectuate the retailers' adherence to the suggested retail prices...

■ ■ ■

Questions

1. What was the advice of the Parke-Davis attorney? Was it correct in light of Colgate Doctrine?
2. What did Parke-Davis do that "went beyond" a mere refusal to deal and transformed their unilateral behavior into bilateral or group practice?
3. Considering the *Parke-Davis* decision, is it possible to utilize the Colgate Doctrine to achieve resale price maintenance when the manufacturer sells through wholesalers?
4. A manufacturer may send goods to a dealer for sale to the public with the understanding that the manufacturer is to remain the owner of the goods and the dealer is to act as the manufacturer's agent in making the sale. The device of entrusting another person with the possession of property for the purpose of sale is commonly referred to as *selling on consignment*. Since the goods are still the property of the manufacturer, may he set the resale price of the items? In other words, may selling on consignment provide an alternative means of achieving resale price maintenance? The Supreme Court said the use of a consignment device in connection with a lease to coerce administered resale prices is illegal under the antitrust laws. Hence, the use of a "consignment device" will not protect the consignor from the charge of violation of Section 1 when the

maintenance of resell prices has an adverse effect on competition.

5. In 1937, Congress passed the Miller-Tydings Act which amended Section 1 of the Sherman Act. The purpose of the amendment was to permit manufacturers to set and maintain the retail price of their branded goods and to exempt such pricefixing from the federal antitrust laws if the particular state in which the goods were to be sold had enacted legislation permitting this resale price maintenance. The state legislation was usually called "fair trade" laws since the pretext for passing the state enactment was to create "fair" trade practices by stopping the discounter (free-rider) from selling goods at a lower price. Around twenty-two states had enacted such fair trade laws. However, in 1976 Congress repealled the Miller-Tydings Act and its companion statutes which had authorized fair trade laws.

CUSTOMER AND TERRITORIAL RESALE RESTRICTIONS

In resale price maintenance, antitrust law has advanced the basic premise that someone who has purchased a product should have the freedom to use it without restriction by the person by whom it was sold. Thus, any contractual agreement by the seller and the customer with respect to the resale price of the purchased product violates the law. Except for the very limited use of the Colgate Doctrine (and the repealed state "fair trade" laws), resale price maintenance has been considered illegal.

Other restrictions on the buyer's resale policies have been treated differently by the courts. Sellers sometimes attempt to restrict their customers as to whom they may resell or in what territorial area. On the permissive side, the courts have ruled that it is lawful to contractually make a buyer primarily responsible for adequately serving a given territorial area. This is true despite the fact that the buyer thereby may not have the time and resources to trade outside the assigned area. The courts also allow the seller to insist on delivery to a designated location only. Such "location" clauses usually prohibit "branching" by the dealer and thereby provide a form of territorial division of the market at the retail level. Together, the "primary responsibility for a designated area" clause and "location" clause provide sellers with a semblance of territorial division that is lawful. No actual contractual restraints are imposed upon the buyers from dealing in other territorial areas, but practical restraints of time and money brought about by "primary responsibility" and "location" clauses nearly accomplish the same results.

Some manufacturers, however, attempt to impose contractual territorial and customer resale restraints on their buyers. In *U.S. v. Schwinn* 388 U.S. 365 (1967), the Supreme Court ruled that contractual customer and territorial restrictions on buyers' resale policies were *per se* unreasonable. Strangely, the same Court ruled that "consignment" sales which imposed the same customer and territorial restraints were to be tested by the "rule of reason." On application of the reasonableness test in the bicycle market, the Court determined that Schwinn's use of customer and territorial restrictions in consignment sales were lawful because interbrand competition was sufficiently strong and the intrabrand restriction imposed by Schwinn was insignificant in the bicycle market. Though the customer and territorial restrictions imposed on the outright sales were the same as those imposed in the consignment sales in terms of market effect, the Court ruled the outright sales to be unreasonable *per se* without any analysis of the market effect. This dichotomy in approach which determines legality by the technique of sales was highly criticized in the legal and economic literature. Lower courts increasingly displayed ingenuity in finding interpretive ways around the *Schwinn per se* rule. Finally, the Supreme Court decided to reconsider *Schwinn's* strict rule of illegality which ignored market realities.

CONTINENTAL T.V., INC. v. GTE SYLVANIA, INC.
433 U.S. 36 (1977)
Supreme Court of the United States

[In an attempt to improve its market position by attracting more aggressive and competent retailers, Sylvania limited the number of retail franchises granted for any given area and required each franchisee to sell its products only from the location at which it was franchised. Petitioner, one of Sylvania's franchised retailers, claimed that Sylvania had violated § 1 of the Sherman Act by entering into and enforcing franchise agreements that prohibited the sale of Sylvania's products other than from specified locations.]

■ ■ ■

POWELL, Mr. Justice.

Both Schwinn and Sylvania sought to reduce but not to eliminate competition among their respective retailers through the adoption of a franchise system. [T]he Schwinn franchise plan included a location restriction similar to the one challenged here. These restrictions allowed Schwinn and Sylvania to regulate the amount of competition among their retailers by preventing a franchise from selling franchised products from outlets other than the one covered by the franchise agreement. To exactly the same end, the Schwinn franchise plan included a companion restriction, apparently not found in the Sylvania plan, that prohibited franchised retailers from selling Schwinn products to nonfranchised retailers. In *Schwinn* the Court expressly held that this restriction was impermissible under the broad principle started there. In intent and competitive impact, the retail customer restriction in *Schwinn* is indistinguishable from the location restriction in the present case. In both cases the restrictions limited the freedom of the retailer to dispose of the franchised products as he desired. The fact that one restriction was addressed to territory and the other to customers is irrelevant to functional anti-trust analysis, and indeed, to the language and broad thrust of the opinion in *Schwinn*.

The traditional framework of analysis under § 1 of the Sherman Act is familiar and does not require extended discussion. Section 1 prohobits "[e]very contract, combination. . . or conspiracy, in restraint of trade or commerce." Since the early years of this century a judicial gloss on this statutory language has established the "rule of reason" as the prevailing standard of analysis. Under this rule, the factfinder weighs all of the circumstances of a case in deciding whether a restrictive practive should be prohibited as imposing an unreasonable restraint on competition. *Per se* rules of illegality are appropriate only when they relate to conduct that is manifestly anti-competitive. . .

In essence, the issue before us is whether *Schwinn's per se* rule can be justified. . .

The market impact of vertical restrictions is complex because of their potential for a simultaneous reduction of intrabrand competition and stimulation of interbrand competition. . . .

Vertical restrictions reduce intrabrand competition by limiting the number of sellers of a particular product competing for the business of a given group of buyers. Location restrictions have this effect because of practical constraints on the effective marketing area of retail outlets. Although intrabrand competition may be reduced, the ability of retailers to exploit the resulting market may be limited both by the ability of consumers to travel to other franchised locations and, perhaps more importantly, to purchase the competing products of other manufacturers. . .

Vertical restrictions promote interbrand competition by allowing the manufacturer to achieve certain efficiencies in the distribution of his products. These "redeeming virtues" are implicit in every decision sustaining vertical restrictions under the rule of reason. Economists have identified a number of ways in which manufacturers can use such restrictions to compete more effectively against other manufacturers. For example, new manufacturers and manufacturers entering new markets can use the restrictions in order to induce competent and aggressive retailers to make the kind of investment of capital and labor that is often required in the distribution of products unknown to the consumer. Established manufacturers can use them to induce retailers to engage in promotional activities or to provide service and repair facilities necessary to the efficient marketing of their products. Service and repair are vital for many products, such as automobiles and major household appliances. The availability and quality of such services affect a manufacturer's good will and the competitiveness of his product. Because of market imperfections such as the so-called "free rider" effect, these services might not be provided by retailers in a purely competitive situation, despite the fact that each retailer's benefit would be greater if all provided the services than if none did....

...The question remains whether the *per se* rule stated in *Schwinn* should be... abandoned in favor of a return to the rule of reason...

...Such restrictions, in varying forms, are widely used in our free market economy. As indicated above, there is substantial scholarly and judicial authority supporting their economic utility. There is relatively little authority to the contrary. Certainly, there has been no showing in this case, either generally or with respect to Sylvania's agreements, that vertical restrictions have a "pernicious effect on competition" or that they "lack...any redeeming virtue." Accordingly, we conclude that the *per se* rule stated in *Schwinn* must be overruled...

In sum, we conclude that the appropriate decision is to return to the rule of reason that governed vertical restrictions prior to *Schwinn*.

■ ■ ■

Questions

1. When is a *per se* unreasonable rule appropriate?
2. Why was Schwinn's *per se* rule against resale constraint considered inappropriate?
3. What business reasons or pro-competitive effects did the court identify that may result from vertical resale restrictions?
4. The Court in a footnote in *Continental T.V.* provided this analysis:

> Interbrand competition is the competition among the manufacturers of the same generic product—television sets in this case—and is the primary concern of antitrust law. The extreme example of a deficiency of interbrand competition is monopoly, where there is only one manufacturer. In contrast, intrabrand competition is the competition between the distributors—wholesale or retail—of the product of a particular manufacturer.
> The degree of intrabrand competition is wholly independent of the level of interbrand competition confronting the manufacturer. Thus, there may be fierce intrabrand competition among the distributors of a product produced by a monopolist and no intrabrand competition among the distributors of a product produced by a firm in a highly competitive industry. But when interbrand competition exists, as it does among television manufacturers, it provides a significant check on the exploitation of intrabrand market power because of the ability of consumers to substitute a different brand of the same product.

Does this suggest when the Court would prohibit an intrabrand restraint?

5. Marketing efficiency is not the only legitimate reason for a manufacturer's desire to exert control over the manner in which products are sold and serviced. As a result of statutory and common law developments, society increasingly demands that manufacturers assume direct responsibility for the safety and quality of their products. For example, at the federal level, apart from more specialized requirements, manufacturers of consumer products have safety responsibilities under the Consumer Product Safety Act and obligations are imposed by state law. The legitimacy of these concerns has been recognized in cases involving vertical restrictions, as in *Tripoli Co. v. Wella Corp.,* 425 F.2d 932 (1970. 3rd Cir.) in which the Court of Appeals upheld a resale customer restriction to professional beauticians only. Sales to "consumers" were considered unsafe, and would subject the seller to "product liability" claims.

EXCLUSIVE DEALINGS

Section 3 of the Clayton Act clearly applies to a seller (or lessor) of goods (not services) who gains a commitment from his buyer (or lessee) not to buy from a competitor of the seller. The commitment may be embodied in a clause of exclusive dealing (promise not to buy elsewhere) or the commitment may be implied, as in a requirements contract. The requirements contract requires a buyer to purchase all (or substantially all) requirements of a product from the seller and, therefore, the buyer by implication is promising not to buy elsewhere. Whether these particular agreements are prohibited by law depends in each case on the determination of the *probable effect* of the agreement in substantially lessening competition in the relevant market. In determination of the substantiality of the probable effect, the early Supreme Court cases have been characterized as follows:

> Where the alleged violator dominated or was a leader in the industry, proof of such fact was...determined to be a sufficient predicate from which to conclude that the use of exclusive-dealing contracts was violative of Section 3 and other factors appeared to have been largely ignored.
> (Later)...the Supreme Court extended the rule to business organizations enjoying a powerful, though clearly not dominant, position in the trade and doing a substantial share of the industry's business by means of these contractual provisions and (the court) tacitly approved the trial court's refusal to consider other economic effects or merits of the system employed... *Dictograph Products v. FTC* 217 F. 2d 812 (1954).

The Supreme Court's utilization of such tests as "dominance of the seller" or a "powerful position" which included a "substantial share of the industry's business" without inquiry into the economic effects or merits of the exclusive dealing system amounts to an almost *per se* test of illegality by an firm that has a substantial share of the market. This test of substantiality was so strict that almost all exclusive dealings were illegal. This test became known as the "quantitive substantiality" because the Court emphasized the dollar volume of commerce tied-up in the exclusive-dealing contracts. The Court said that if a "not insubstantial amount of commerce was affected," then the exclusive-dealing contracts were illegal. The Court made no further inquiry concerning economic effects and made no market analysis of the impact of the exclusive-dealing arrangements. This quantitive substantiality test and its almost *per se* determination of illegality has received substantial criticism in the legal and economic literature. The Supreme Court retreated from this strict test and approved a more lenient test, which is generally referred to as "qualitative substantiality," in the following case.

TAMPA ELECTRIC CO. v. NASHVILLE CO.
365 U.S. 320 (1960)
Supreme Court of the United States

[Tampa Electric Co., a public utility in Florida, contracted with Nashville Coal Company for its expected coal requirements for two new units to be constructed. The agreement required Tampa Electric to purchase all its requirements of coal for a period of twenty years. Before the first shipment of coal was to be delivered, Nashville Coal Company advised Tampa Electric that the contract was illegal under the anti-trust laws and that no coal would be delivered. Tampa Electric purchased its coal requirements elsewhere and sued the defendants for breach of contract.]

■ ■ ■

CLARK, Mr. Justice...(The District Court and the Court of Appeals)...admitted that the contract "does not expressly contain the 'condition' " that Tampa Electric would not use or deal in the coal of (defendant's) competitors. Nonetheless, they reasoned, the "total requirements" provision had the same practical effect, for it prevented Tampa Electric for a period of 20 years from buying coal from any other source...[B]oth courts found, that the "line of commerce" on which th^ restraint was to be tested was coal... Both courts compared the estimated coal tonnage as to which the contract pre-empted competition for 20 years, namely, 1,000,000 tons a year by 1961, with the previous annual consumption of peninsular Florida, 700,000 tons. Emphasizing that fact as well as the contract value of the coal covered by the 20-year term, i.e., $128,000,000, they held that such volume was not "insignificant or insubstantial" and that the effect of the contract would "be to substantially lessen competition," in violation of the Act. Both courts were of the opinion that in view of the executory nature of the contract, judicial enforcement of any portion of it could not be granted without directing a violation of the Act itself, and enforcement was, therefore, denied.

Application of §3 of the Clayton Act.

* * *

In practical application, even though a contract is found to be an exclusive-dealing arrangement, it does not viloate the section unless the court believes it probable that performance of the contract will foreclose competition in a substantial share of the line of commerce affected. Following the guidelines of earlier decisions, certain considerations must be taken. *First*, the line of commerce, i.e., the type of goods, wares, or merchandise, etc., involved must be determined, where it is in controversy, on the basis of the facts peculiar to the case. *Second*, the area of effective competition in the known line of commerce must be charted by careful selection of the market area in which the seller operates, and to which the purchaser can practicably turn for supplies. In short, the threatened foreclosure of competition must be in relation to the market affected...

Third, and last, the competition foreclosed by the contract must be found to constitute a substantial share of the relevant market. That is to say, the opportunities for other traders to enter into or remain in that market must be significantly limited...

To determine substantiality in a given case, it is necessary to weigh the probable effect of the contract on the relevant area of effective competition, taking into account the relevant strength of the parties, the proportionate volume of commerce involved in relation to the total volume of commerce in the relevant market area, and the probable immediate and future effects which pre-emption of that share of the market might have on effective competition therein. It follows tht a mere showing that the contract itself involves a substantial number of dollars is ordinarily of little consequence.

The application of §3 Here.

In applying these considerations to the facts of the case before us, it appears that both the Court of Appeals and the District Court have not given the required effect to a controlling factor in the case—the relevant competitive market area. This omission, by itself, requires reversal, for, as we have pointed out, the relevant market is the prime factor in relation to which the ultimate question, whether the contract forecloses competition in a substantial share of the line of commerce involved, must be decided...

Relevant Market of Effective Competition.

* * *

We are persuaded that on the record in this case, neither peninsular Florida, nor the entire State of Florida, nor Florida and Georgia combined constituted the relevant market of effective competition. We do not believe that the pie will slice so thinly. By far the bulk of the overwhelming tonnage marketed from the same producing area as serves Tampa is sold outside of Georgia and Florida, and the producers were "eager" to sell more coal in those States. While the relevant competitive market is not ordinarily susceptible to a "metes and bounds" definition,.... it is of course the area in which (defendant) and the other 700 producers effectively compete.

The record shows that, like the (defendant), they sold bituminois coal "suitable for (Tampa's) requirements," mined in parts of Pennsylvania, Virginia, West Virginia, Kentucky, Tennessee, Alabama, Ohio and Illinois. We take notice of the fact that the approximate total bituminous coal (and lignite) product in the year 1954 from the districts in which these 700 producers are located was 359,289,000 tons, of which some 290,567,000 tons were sold on the open market. Of the latter amount some 78,716,000 tons were sold to electric utilities... From these statistics it clearly appears that the proportionate volume of the total relevant coal product as to which the challenged contract pre-empted competition, less than 1%, is, conservatively speaking, quite insubstantial. A more acurate figure, even assuming pre-emption to the extent of the maximum anticipated total requirements, 2,250,000 tons a year, would be .77%.

Effect on Competition in the Relevant Market.

It may well be that in the context of antitrust legislation protracted requirements contracts are suspect, but they have not been declared illegal *per se*... It is urged that the pesent contract pre-empts competition to the extent of purchases worth perhaps $128,000,000, and that this "is, of course, not insignificant or insubstantial." While $128,000,000 is a considerable sum of money, even in these days, the dollar volume, by itself, is not the test, as we have already pointed out.

The remaining determination, therefore, is whether the pre-emption of competition to the extent of the tonnage involved tends to substantially foreclose competition in the relevant coal market. We think not. That market sees an annual trade in excess of 250,000,000 tons of coal and over a billion dollars—multiplied by 20 years it runs into astronomical figures. There is here neither a seller with a dominant position in the market as in *Standard Fashions;* nor myriad outlets with substantial sales volume, coupled with an industrywide practice of relying upon exclusive contracts, as in *Standard Oil;*...

On the contrary, we seem to have only that type of contract which "may well be of economic advantage to buyers as well as to sellers." *Standard Oil Co. v. United States.* In the case of the buyer it "may assure supply," while on the part of the seller it "may make possible the substantial reduction of selling expenses, give protection against price fluctuations, and... offer the possibility of a predictable market." The 20-year period of the contract is singled out as the principal vice, but at least in the case of public utilities the assurance of a steady and ample supply of fuel is necessary in the public interest. In weighing the various factors, we have decided that in the competitive bituminous coal marketing area involved here, the contract sued upon does not tend to foreclose a substantial volume of competition...

■ ■ ■

Questions

1. How did the lower courts define the competitive geographical market? Did the Supreme Court agree?
2. How did the lower courts determine the "substantiality" of the probable anticompetitive effect? What is the proper test to determine "substantiality" of the probable anticompetitive effect?

FRANCHISES

The typical franchise contract involves the franchisor granting the franchisee the right to operate a business in a certain manner at a designated area and to use the franchisor's trademark or trade name in the operation. Because the franchisor normally has substantially more bargaining power than the franchisee, the franchise agreements contain provisions that restrict the franchisee's freedoms. Franchisees often agree not to compete with the franchisor or other franchised dealers in another territory. Franchisees also often agree not to sell competitors' brands from the franchised outlet. Franchise agreements sometimes require the franchisee to purchase supplies and services from the franchisor. Many of the restrictions imposed in franchise contracts would violate the antitrust laws except for the federal trademark statute, the Lanham Act. This Act requires the franchisors to exercise control over the use of their trademark so not to misrepresent the source of trademarked goods. Consequently, franchisors must exercise stringent quality control to maintain consistency in all franchised outlets to protect the product represented by the mark. Quality variance would negatively affect the public's attitude toward the mark in an economic sense and conflict with the policies of the Lanham Act. The following cases represent the efforts of the courts to recognize business realities and harmonize the apparently conflicting statutory requirements.

SUSSER v. CARVEL CORPORATION
332 F. 2d 505 (1964)
United States Court of Appeals, 2nd Cir.

■ ■ ■

The (plaintiffs) maintain that the franchise agreements embody violations of the Sherman and Clayton acts insofar as they require the dealer to refrain from selling any non-Carvel product...

Lacking economic data sufficient to meet the standard thus established in Tampa Electric, the (plaintiffs) here urge that the Supreme Court's decision in *Standard Oil Co. v. United States,* is controlling and that they need prove only that "competition has been foreclosed in a substantial share of the line of commerce affected."...(However) it seems indisputable that in *Tampa Electric* the Court deviated from the more rigorous and inflexible rule it had established in *Standard Oil* and erected criteria which demand close scrutiny of the economic ramifications of an exclusive dealing arrangement in order to determine the probable anti-competitive effects of such a device... We find it plain that the (plaintiffs) have failed to bear this burden. Instead of introducing evidence to establish the economic effects of the Carvel franchise structure, they merely protest that anti-competitive effects may be inferred solely from the existence of such a network of exclusive dealerships. But the whole tenor of *Tampa Electric* does not permit adherence to such a stringent standard of legality.

In any event, we need not rely solely upon the (plaintiff's) failure to adduce concrete evidence concerning the relevant line of commerce and geographical market and the probable anticompetitive effects of the Carvel arrangement. For in terms of at least one factor which the Supreme Court deemed significant in Tampa Electric—that of economic justification—the Carvel exclusive dealership arrangement withstands any attack on its legality.

As Judge Dawson found, "the cornerstone of a franchise system must be the trademark or trade name of a product." The fundamental device in the Carvel franchise agreement itself is the licensing to the individual dealer of the right to employ the Carvel name in his advertising displays, on the products he sells, and on the store itself. The stores are uniform in design, as well as in the public display of the ice cream machinery employed, the placement of advertising displays, and the products offered for sale. The requirement that only Carvel products be sold at Carvel outlets derives from the desirability that the public identify each Carvel outlet as one of a chain which offers identical products at a uniform standard of quality. The antitrust laws certainly do not require that the licensor of a trademark permit his licensees to associate with that trademark other products unrelated to those customarily sold under the mark. It is in the public interest that products sold under one particular trademark should be subject to the control of the trademark owner. . . Carvel was not required to accede to the requests of one or another of the dealers that they be permitted to sell Christmas trees or hamburgers, for example, which would have thrust upon Carvel the obligation to acquaint itself with the production and sale of these items so as to establish reasonable quality controls. Nor do the antitrust laws proscribe a trademark owner from establishing a chain of outlets uniform in appearance and operation. Trademark licensing agreements requiring the sole use of the trademarked item have withstood attack under the antitrust laws where deemed reasonably necessary to protect the goodwill interest of the trademark owner. . . and such agreements certainly are not unlawful *per se* under the antitrust laws.

. . . Judge Dawson was fully warranted in concluding that in the context of the entire Carvel franchise system the requirement that no non-Carvel products be sold at the retail level is reasonably necessary for the protection of Carvel's goodwill.

■ ■ ■

Questions

1. What test did the Court choose to use in determination of the legality of this exclusive dealing contract?
2. How is it "in the public interest that products sold under one particular trademark should be subject to the control of the trademark owner"?
3. Is exclusive dealing "reasonably necessary to protect the goodwill interest of the trademark owner"?

TY-IN ARRANGEMENTS

A ty-in agreement is a refusal to sell or lease one product or serice unless a different product or service is also bought or leased. In effect, the distributor forces its buyers to take a product or service of less desirability (the tied product) in order to obtain a more wanted item (the tying product). The courts have said that ordinarily there can be hardly any reason for tying two goods together except to use one's power over the tying product or service to gain a market for the tied product. Ty-in agreements limit competition in the market for the tied product in that rival sellers in the tied product market must overcome their competitor's economic power over the tying product to gain access to the available buyers of tied products. Because of this anticompetitive effect, ty-in arrangements receive close scrutiny by the courts which find the ty-in illegal if the firm has sufficient economic power in the tying product to restrict competition in the tied product market. For example, it is normally unreasonable to require that a buyer finance his purchase through the seller or to require that lessees of equipment use the lessor's supplies in the equipment. The courts generally give ty-ins an almost *per se* status of illegality unless the seller can produce an exceptional justification. The ty-in may be justified if the seller can prove that the new technology involved in a sensitive piece of equipment functions properly only if the seller's repair parts and service are used. If this is true, and only as long as this is true, the ty-in for repair parts and service would not be unreasonable. Besides this new business or new technology justification, ty-ins have received a rather inhospitable reception by the courts.

SIEGEL v. CHICKEN DELIGHT, INC.
448 F. 2d 43 (1971)
U.S. Court of Appeals (9th Cir.)

■ ■ ■

This antitrust suit is a class action in which certain franchisees of Chicken Delight seek treble damages for injuries allegedly resulting from illegal restraints imposed by Chicken Delight's standard form franchise agreements. The restraints in question are Chicken Delight's contractual requirements that franchisees purchase certain essential cooking equipment , dry-mix food items, and trade-mark bearing packaging exclusively from Chicken Delight as a condition of obtaining a Chicken Delight trade-mark license. These requirements are asserted to constitute a tying arrangement, unlawful per se under § of the Sherman Act...

In order to establish that there exists an unlawful tying arrangement plaintiffs must demonstrate *first*, that the scheme in question involves two distinct items and provides that one (the tying product) may not be obtained unless the other (the tied product) is also purchased. *Second,* that the tying product possesses sufficient economic power appreciably to restrain competition in the tied product market. *Third*, that a "not insubstantial" amount of commerce is affected by the arrangement. Chicken Delight concedes that the third requirement has been satisfied. It disputes the existence of the first two. Further it asserts that, even if plaintiffs should prevail with respect to the first two requirements, there is a *fourth* issue: whether there exists a special justification for the particular tying arrangement in question.

A. Two Products

Chicken Delight urges us to hold that its trade-mark and franchise licenses are not items separate and distinct from the packaging, mixes, and equipment, which it says are essential components of the franchise system. To treat the combined sale of all these items as a tie-in for antitrust purposes, Chicken Delight maintains, would be like applying the antitrust rules to the sale of a car with its tires or a left shoe with the right...

The historical conception of a trademark as a strict emblem of source of the product to which it ataches has largely been abandoned. The burgeoning business of franchising has made trade-mark licensing a widespread commercial practice and has resulted in the development of a new rationale for trade-marks as representations of product quality. this is particularly true in the case of a franchise system set up not to distribute the trade-marked goods of the franchisor, but, as here, to conduct a certain business under a common trade-mark or trade name. Under such a type of franchise, the trade-mark simply reflects the goodwill and quality standards of the enterprise which it identifies. As long as the system of operation of the franchisees lives up to those quality standards and remains as represented by the mark so that the public is not misled, neither the protection afforded the trade-mark by law nor the value of the trade-mark to the licensee depends upon the source of the components.

This being so, it is apparent that the goodwill of the Chicken Delight trade-mark does not attach to the multitude of separate articles used in the operation of the licensed system or in the production of its end product. It is not what is used, but how it is used and what results that have given the system and its end product their entitlement to trade-mark protection. It is to the system and the end product that the public looks with the confidence that established goodwill has created.

Thus, sale of a franchise license, with the attendant rights to operate a business in the prescribed manner and to benefit from the goodwill of the trade name, in no way requires the forced sale by the franchisor of some or all of the component articles...

B. Economic Power

Under the *per se* theory of illegality, plaintiffs are required to establish not only the existence of a tying arrangement but also that the tying product possesses sufficient economic power to appreciably restrain free competition in the tied product markets.

Chicken Delight points out that while it was an early pioneer in the fast food franchising field, the record establishes that there has recently been a dramatic expansion in this area, with the advent of numerous firms, including many chicken franchising systems, all competing vigorously with each other. Under the circumstances, it contends that the existence of the requisite market dominance remained a jury question...

The District Court ruled, however, that Chicken Delight's unique registered trade-mark, in combination with its demonstrated power to impose a tie-in, established as matter of law the existence of sufficient market power to bring the case within the Sherman Act...

Just as the patent or copyright forecloses competitors from offering the distinctive product on the market, so the registered trade-mark presents a legal barrier against competition... Accordingly we see no reason why the presumption that exists in the case of the patent and copyright does not equally apply to the trade-mark.

C. Justification

...Chicken Delight advances as justification the fact that when it first entered the fast food field in 1952 it was a new business and was then entitled to the protection afforded by United States v. Jerrold Electronics Corp. 365 U.S. 567 (1961).

We find no merit in this contention... To accept Chicken Delight's argument would convert the new business justification into a perpetual license to operate in restraint of trade.

(Another)... justification Chicken Delight offers is the "marketing identity" purpose, the franchisor's preservation of the distinctiveness, uniformity and quality of its product.

In the case of a trade-mark this purpose cannot be lightly dismissed. Not only protection of the franchisor's goodwill is involved. The licensor owes an affirmative duty to the public to assure that in the hands of his licensee the trade-mark continues to represent that which it purports to represent. For a licensor, through relaxation of quality control, to permit inferior products to be presented to the public under his licensed mark might well constitute a misuse of the mark.

However, to recognize that such a duty exists is not to say that every means of meeting it is justified. Restraint of trade can be justified only in the absence of less restrictive alternatives. In cases such as this, where the alternative of specification is available, the language used in Standard Oil Co. v. United States, 337 U.S. at 306, in our view states the proper test, applicable in the case of trade-marks as well as in other cases:

"* * * the protection of the goodwill of the manufacturer of the tying device—fails in the usual situation because specification of the type and quality of the product to be used in connection with the tying device is protection enough. * * * The only situation, indeed, in which the protection of goodwill may necessitate the use of tying clauses is where specifications for a substitute would be so detailed that they could not practicably be supplied."

The District Court found factual issues to exist as to whether effective quality control could be achieved by specification in the case of the cooking machinery and the dip and spice mixes. These questions were given to the jury under instructions: and the jury, in response to special interrogatories, found against Chicken Delight...

■ ■ ■

Questions

1. To establish a prima facie illegal ty-in, what three-prong test is utlized?
2. How do you determine if two products are involved?
3. What factors did the court identify as relevant in determination of "two products"?
4. What reasoning did the court use to determine whether Chicken Delight

possessed "sufficient economic power" to appreciably restrain competition?
5. Can a ty-in be justified? What two potential justifications are discussed in *Chicken Delight?* Why are these justifications normally not available to the defendant?
6. Can you distinguish between a trademarked good and a business under a trademark? What if the good itself was always trademarked. Could a buyer insist on buying it without the trademark tied thereto?

PRICE DISCRIMINATION

Section 2 of the Clayton Act as originally enacted prohibited price discrimination that had the probable anticompetitive effect of lessening competition. However, as drafted, Section 2 was not successful in eliminating price discrimination practices. Consequently, Congress enacted the Robinson-Patman Act in 1936 as an amendment to Section 2 of the Clayton Act. The Robinson-Patman Act had two main purposes which include:

1. The prevention of a seller from using its profits on higher priced interstate sales to unfairly subsidize its lower price in a regional market in competition with a regional seller.
2. The prevention of buyers from using their large purchasing power to exact discriminatory prices from suppliers to the unfair disavantage of smaller buyers.

To outlaw these practices, the Robinson-Patman Act makes it illegal to charge different prices to different buyers for goods of like grade and quality when the effect of the differences in prices may substantially lessen competition. To determine whether a Robinson-Patman problem is present under Section 2(a) of the Act, one should ask whether the company has made:

1. Sales at different prices within a reasonably contemporaneous time period (this time period may vary depending upon the competitive market, but six months is a good rule of thumb);
2. One of the two sales involving the different prices must have occurred in inter-state commerce (price-discrimination occurring totally intra-state is not covered by the Act);
3. The products sold must be of like grade and quality (i.e., substantial physical and chemical identity without any significant difference from the commercial standpoint);
4. Injury to competition at the seller, buyer or sub-buyer level will probably result.

If any of these is absent, no Robinson-Patman violation has occurred. Even if the above criteria of a Section 2(a) violation are present, the defendant may nvertheless avoid the violation of the law if he is able to prove a "justification" for the price discrimination. The Act authorizes three justifications.

One justification for price discrimination under the law is "difference in cost of manufacturer, sale, or delivery resulting from the differing methods or quantities in which such commodities are . . . sold or delivered." However, this defense is largely an illusion. Because of the difficulty in proving that the accounting standards utilized in the cost defense are the only or most appropriate standards, the defendant cannot establish a defense with acceptable evidence. Debates concerning allocation of over-head costs or other cost allocation techniques often cause the seller to fail to carry the burden of proof that the lower price was cost justified.

A second justification provided under the law is the privilege of charging different prices because of "changing conditions affecting the market for or the marketability of the goods concerned." This defense can be easily demonstrated by actual or eminent deterioration of perishable goods or obsolescence of seasonal goods. It also includes distress sales under court order or discontinuance of business.

The last justification under the Act is embodied in Section 2(b) of the Act. Section 2(b) grants the seller the privilege to lower a price in good faith to meet (but not beat) a price offered by a competitor. This defense has received considerable use in litigated cases.

Section 2(c) of the Robinson-Patman Act outlaws "phoney brokerage." Brokerage payments may not be paid by a seller to a buyer or an agent of the buyer except for services rendered to the seller. Often buyers attempt to by-pass brokers of the seller and then seek the commission the broker normally earns from the seller. However, the buyer has not rendered services to the seller and is not entitled to such brokerage commission. The buyer has rendered service to himself in bypassing the broker. These "phoney brokerage" allowances are illegal *per se*.

Section 2(d) and 2(e) of the Robinson-Patman Act seek to afford equitable treatment to competing customers of the seller. These sections require that promotional payments, services, or facilities (such as an advertising allowances or display materials) must be extended by the seller on proportionately equal terms to all the seller's customers who compete with each other. The law does not require the probable adverse competitive effect to be shown for violation of this section to occur. Equitable promotional services to all customers should be the general rule of the seller, unless he or she can justify failure to provide equitable treatment of promotional services on the ground that he or she was meeting in good faith a competing offer of assistance by a competitor.

COMPETITIVE INJURY

Price discrimination of goods of like grade and quality is illegal only if the (1) effect on such discrimination in any line of commerce may substantially lessen competition, or (2) its effect is to injure or prevent competition with any person who either (a) grants, or (b) knowingly receives the benefit of such discrimination, or (c) to customers of either of them. This language appears to indicate and the effect of court decisions seem to support the concept that under (1) above, the injury is to competition whereas under (2) above, the injury is to a competitor. However the courts have never officially recognized the concept of injury to a competitior unless such injury is a substantial injury to competition also. Rather than merely protecting a competitor, the FTC has chosen to use the injury to competition test. Of course, private litigants favor the use of the more easily proven injury to a competitor (namely, themselves) test. Some courts tend to find that competitive injury whenever there exists an injury to a competitor and hence cause some confusion as to which legal standard is to be applied.

From the language of the Act, it is possible to have competitive injury on various levels of business operations. For example, if seller A's price discrimination causes his competitive seller B to suffer injury, this would be primary line or seller's level injury. Seller A could sell in one market at a high price to subsidize his lower price in another market where he is competing with Seller B.

Figure 11-1
SELLER'S LEVEL INJURY (PRIMARY LINE INJURY)

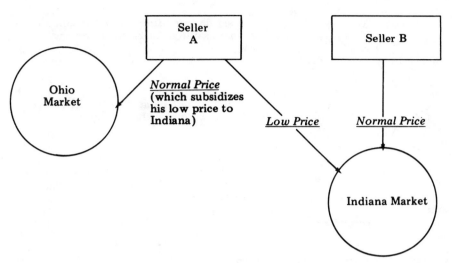

If the manufacturer sells his products at different prices to different buyers who compete with each other, the price discrimination will cause competitive injury at the buyer's level. This is called secondary line injury.

Figure 11-2
BUYERS LEVEL INJURY (SECONDARY LINE INJURY)

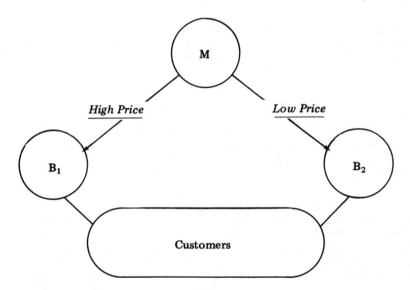

A third line injury occurs when the customers of the supplier's buyer are discriminated against in prices. This level is a more controversial means of showing competitive injury. While lawsuits alleging third-line injury rarely occur, it is possible for no primary line injury to be present and the secondary level buyers might not compete with each other so that secondary level injury is absent also. But nevertheless, if a lower price to a secondary level buyer allows the buyer to pass on a lower price to customers who compete with customers of another secondary level supplier, the competitive injury has occurred on the third line.

Figure 11-3

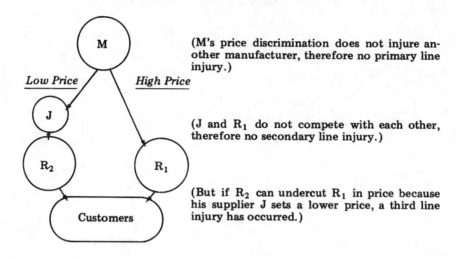

(M's price discrimination does not injure another manufacturer, therefore no primary line injury.)

Low Price   High Price

(J and R_1 do not compete with each other, therefore no secondary line injury.)

(But if R_2 can undercut R_1 in price because his supplier J sets a lower price, a third line injury has occurred.)

PROOF OF COMPETITIVE INJURY

UTAH PIE CO. v. CONTINENTAL BAKING CO.
386 U.S. 685 (1967)
Supreme Court of the United States

■ ■ ■

WHITE, Mr. Justice.

This suit for treble damages. . . was brought by petitioner, Utah Pie Company, against (defendants), Continental Baking Company, Carnation Company and Pet Milk Company. The complaint charged. . . violations by each (defendant) of § 2 (a) of the Clayton Act as amended by the Robinson-Patman Act. . . The jury found for petitioner on the price discrimination charge. . .

The product involved is frozen dessert pies. . . The period covered by the suit comprised the years 1958, 1959, and 1960 and the first eight months of 1961. Petitioner is a Utah corporation which for 30 years has been baking pies in its plant in Salt Lake City and selling them in Utah and surrounding States. It entered the frozen pie business in late 1957. . . Utah Pie's share of this market in those years was 66.5%, 34.3%, 45.5%, and 45.3% respectively, its sales volume steadily increasing over the four years. Its financial position also improved. Petitioner is not, however, a large company. . .

Each of the (defendants) is a large company and each of them is a major factor in the frozen pie market in one or more regions of the country. Each entered the Salt Lake City frozen pie market before petitioner began freezing dessert pies. None of them had a plant in Utah. . . They sold primarily on a delivered price basis.

The major competitive weapon in the Utah market was price. The location of petitioner's plant gave it natural advantages in the Salt Lake City marketing area and it entered the market at a price below the then going prices for (defendant's) comparable pies. For most of the period involved here its prices were the lowest in the Salt Lake City market. It was, however, challenged by each of the (defendants) at one time or another and for varying periods. There was ample evidence to show that each of the (defendants) contributed to what proved to be a deteriorating price structure over the period covered by this suit, and each of the (defendants) in the course of the ongoing price competition sold frozen pies in the Salt Lake market at prices lower than it sold pies of like grade and quality in other markets considerably closer to its plants. . .

Petitioner's case against Continental is not complicated. . . . Effective for the last two weeks of June it offered its 22-ounce frozen applie pies in the Utah area at $2.85 per dozen. It was then selling the same pies at substantially higher prices in other markets. The Salt Lake City price was less than its direct cost plus an allocation for overhead....

The Court of Appeals concluded that Continental's conduct had had only minimal effect, that it had not injured or weakened Utah Pie as a competitor, that it had not substantially lessened competition and that there was no reasonable possibility that it would do so in the future.

We again differ with the Court of Appeals. Its opinion that Utah was not damaged as a competitive force apparently rested on the fact that Utah's sales volume continued to climb in 1961...But this retrospective assessment fails to note that Continental's discriminatory below-cost price caused Utah Pie to reduce its price to $2.75. The jury was entitled to consider the potential impact of Continental's price reduction absent any responsive price cut by Utah Pie...The jury could rationally have concluded that had Utah not lowered its price, Continental, which repeated its offer once, would have continued it...It could also have reasonably concluded that a competitor who is forced to reduce his price to a new all-time low in a market of declining prices will in time feel the financial pinch and will be a less effective competitive force....

Section 2 (a) does not forbid price competition which will probably injure or lessen competition by eliminating competitors, discouraging entry into the market or enhancing the market shares of the dominant sellers. But Congress has established some ground rules for the game. Sellers may not sell like goods to different purchasers at different prices if the result may be to injure competition in either the sellers' or the buyers' market unless such discriminations are justified as permitted by the Act. This case concerns the sellers' market. In this context, the Court of Appeals placed heavy emphasis on the fact that Utah Pie constantly increased its sales volume and continued to make a profit. But we disagree with its apparent view that there is no reasonably possible injury to competition as long as the volume of sales in a particular market is expanding and at least some of the competitors in the market continue to operate at a profit. Nor do we think that the Act only comes into play to regulate the conduct of price discriminators when their discriminatory prices consistently undercut other competitors. It is true that many of the primary line cases that have rached the courts have involved blatant predatory price discriminations employed with the hope of immediate destruction of a particular competitor. On the question of injury to competition such cases present courts with no difficulty, for such pricing is clearly within the heart of the proscription of the Act. Courts and commentators alike have noted that the existence of predatory intent might bear on the likelihood of injury to competition. In this case there was some evidence of predatory intent with respect to each of these (defendants). There was also other evidence upon which the jury could rationally find the requisite injury to competition... We believe that the Act reaches price discrimination that erodes competition as much as it does price discrimination that is intended to have immediate destructive impact. In this case, the evidence shows a drastically declining price structure which the jury could rationally attribute to continued or sporadic price discrimination. The jury was entitled to conclude that "the effect of such discrimination," by each of these (defendants), "may be substantially to lessen competition...or to injure, destroy, or prevent competition with any person who either grants or knowingly receives the benefit of such discrimination..." The statutory test is one that necessarily looks forward on the basis of proved conduct in the past...

■ ■ ■

Questions

1. What evidence did the Court of Appeals rely on to determine that there was no "probable injury to competition"?
2. Must a predatory price discrimination be employed with the hope of immediate destruction of a particular competitor?
3. What evidence existed as to Continental's "predatory intent"? What motive could Continental have in selling its pies below cost?

GOOD FAITH MEETING OF COMPETITION

CADIGAN v. TEXACO, INC.
492 F. 2d 383 (1974)
U.S. Court of Appeals (9th Cir.)

[A former operator and lessee of a Texaco service station brought suit against Texaco alleging that Texaco's sale of gasoline to Wickland Oil at prices lower than the prices paid to Texaco by the plaintiff was a violation of the Robinson-Patman Act. Defendant's motion for summary judgement was granted because the price discrimination was made in good faith to meet equally low prices of a competitor. Plaintiff appeals.]

■ ■ ■

Plaintiff alleges that the price discrimination allowed Wickland's... stations to sell "Texaco" brand gas at a price lower than that at which he could sell the identical gas at his station across the street, and that as a result, he was driven out of business. Nevertheless, the district court's grant of summary judgment was entirely appropriate. Section 2(b) provides a complete defense to a prima facie case of price discrimination, despite any adverse effect on competition created by the price differential. The sole permissible inference which may be drawn from the uncontroverted facts is that Texaco offered the discriminatory discounts in a good faith effort to secure Wickland's business by matching prices offered by Texaco's competitors, Humble and American. Plaintiff having failed to introduce any evidence to support a contrary finding, a summary judgment motion was appropriate to establish the § 2(b) defense to plaintiff's claim....

Plaintiff also contends that summary judgment was improperly rendered because defendants, not having shown that the prices of Texaco's competitors were lawful, failed to bring themselves within the § 2(b) proviso. We reject this contention. A defendant need not prove the actual lawfulness of his competitor's price in order to secure the protection of the proviso. The well established rule is that § 2(b) is satisfied unless it appears that the defendant either knows the price being met is unlawful or that it is inherently unlawful.

Plaintiff has offered no proof to suggest that the competitor's prices were unlawful, much less that Texaco knew them to be such.

Finally, (plaintiff) argues that the § 2(b) defense can be asserted only when the price discrimination is made to retain old customers, and not, as in this case, when a seller meets competitive prices in order to obtain a new customer. The distinction is unsound and has been rejected by the courts, Sunshine Biscuits, Inc. v. FTC, 306 F.2d 48 (7th Cir. 1962); and is not applied by the Federal Trade Commission, *see* Beatrice Foods Co. [1967-70 Transfer Binder] Trade Reg. Rep. 19,045 (FTC 1970).

We agree with the Seventh Circuit that:

"If, in situations where the Section 2(b) proviso is applicable, sellers could grant good faith competitive price reductions only to old customers in order to retain them, competition for new customers would be stifled and monopoly be fostered. In such situations an established seller would have a monopoly of his customers and a seller entering the market would not be permitted to reduce his price to compete with his established rivals unless he could do so on a basis such as cost justification. Moreover, the distinction would create a forced price discrimination between a seller's existing customers to whom he had lawfully lowered his price under Section 2(b) and a prospective new customer. These results, we believe, are incompatible with the purpose for which the Robinson-Patman Act was enacted."

■ ■ ■

Questions

1. Is the "good faith meeting of competition" defense a complete defense to a prima facie case of price discrimination?
2. To take advantage of the 2(b) defense, must the seller prove the lawfulness of the competitor's price which he is meeting?
3. May the 2(b) defense be utilized "aggressively" to obtain new customers? Or is the 2(b) defense limited to the retention of old customers (defensive use)?

U.S. v. U.S. GYPSUM CO.
438 U.S. 422 (1978)
The Supreme Court of the United States

[Several officials of manufacturers of gypsum board were indicted for a price-fixing conspiracy in violation of the Section 1 of the Sherman Act. One of the actions allegedly taken in effectuating the conspiracy was interseller price verification, i.e., the practice of telephoning a competing manufacturer to determine the price being currently offered on gypsum board to a specific customer. The defendant's argued that the price information exchanges were necessary for them to prove their good faith in meeting-competition defense contained in Section 2(b) of the Robinson-Patman Act. The court of appeals held that verification of price concessions with competitors for the sole purpose of taking advantage of the meeting-competition defense precluded liability under Section 1 of the Sherman Act.]

■ ■ ■

BURGER, Chief Justice.

In *FTC v. A E Staley Manufacturing Co.,* 324 U.S. 746, (1945), the Court provided the first and still the most complete explanation of the kind of showing which a seller must make in order to satisfy the good-faith requirement of the § 2(b) defense:

> "Section 2(b) does not require the seller to justify price discriminations by showing that in fact they met a competitor's price. But it does place on the seller the burden of showing that the price was made in good faith to meet a competitor's.... We agree with the Commission that the statute at least requires the seller, who has knowingly discriminated in price, to show the existence of facts which would lead a reasonable and prudent person to believe that the granting of a lower price would in fact meet the equally low price of a competitor."

Appliaction of these standards to the facts in *Staley* led to the conclusion that the § 2(b) defense had not been made out. The record revealed that the lower price had been based simply on reports of salesmen, brokers, or purchasers with no efforts having been made by the seller "to investigate or verify" the reports or the character and reliability of the informants. Similarly, in *Corn Products v. FTC,* 324 U.S. 726, (1945), decided the same day, the § 2(b) defense was not allowed because "the only evidence said to rebut the *prima facie* case... of the price discriminations was given by witnesses who had no personal knowledge of the transactions, and was limited to statements of each witness's assumption or conclusion that the price discriminations were justified by competition."

Staley's "investigate or verify" language coupled with the *Corn Products'* focus on "personal knowledge of the transactions" have apparently suggested to a number of courts that, at least in certain circumstances, direct verification of discounts between competitors may be necessary to meet the burden of proof requirements of the § 2(b) defense...

A good-faith belief, rather than absolute certainty, that a price concession is being offered to meet an equally low price offered by a competitor is sufficient to satisfy the Robinson-Patman's § 2(b) defense. While casual reliance on uncorroborated reports of buyers or sales representatives without further investigation may not, as we noted earlier, be sufficient to make the requisite showing of good faith, nothing in the language of § 2(b) or the gloss on that language in *Staley* and *Corn Products* indicates that direct discussions of price between competitors are required. Nor has any court, so far as we are aware, ever imposed such a requirement. On the contrary, the § 2(b) defense has been successfully invoked in the absence of interseller verification on numerous occasions...

The so-called problem of the untruthful buyer...does not in our view call for a different approach to the § 2(b) defense. The good-faith standard remains the benchmark against which the seller's conduct is to be evaluated, and we agree with the government and the FTC that this standard can be satisfied by efforts falling short of interseller verification in most circumstances where the seller has only vague, generalized doubts about the reliability of its commercial adversary—the buyer. Given the fact specific nature of the inquiry, it is difficult to predict all the factors the FTC or a court would consider in appraising a seller's good faith in matching a competing offer in these circumstances. Certainly, evidence that a seller had received reports of similar discounts from other customers, or was threatened with a termination of purchases if the discount were not met, would be relevant in this regard. Efforts to corroborate the reported discount by seeking documentary evidence or by appraising its reasonableness in terms of available market data would also be probative as would the seller's past experience with the particular buyer in question.

There remains the possibility that in a limited number of situations a seller may have substantial reasons to doubt the accuracy of reports of a competing offer and may be unable to corroborate such reports in any of the generally accepted ways. Thus the defense may be rendered unavailable since unanswered questions about the reliability of a buyer's representations may well be inconsistent with a good-faith belief that a competing offer had in fact been made. As an abstract proposition, resort to interseller verification as a means of checking the buyer's reliability seems a possible solution to the seller's plight, but careful examination reveals serious problems with the practice.

Both economic theory and common human experience suggest that interseller verification—if undertaken on an isolated and infrequent basis with no provision for reciprocity or cooperation—will not serve its putative function of corroborating the representations of unreliable buyers regarding the existence of competing offers. Price concessions by oligopolists generally yield competitive advantages only if secrecy can be maintained; when the terms of the concession are made publicly known, other competitors are likely to follow and any advantage to the initiator is lost in the process.

Thus, if one seller offers a price concession for the purpose of winning over one of his competitor's customers, it is unlikely that the same seller will freely inform its competitor of the details of the concession so that it can be promptly matched and diffused. Instead, such a seller would appear to have at least as great an incentive to misrepresent the existence or size of the discount as would the buyer who received it. Thus verification, if undertaken on a one shot basis for the sole purpose of complying with the § 2(b) defense, does not hold out much promise as a means of shoring up buyers' representations.

The other variety of interseller verification is, like the conduct charged in the instant case, undertaken pursuant to an agreement, either tacit or express, providing for reciprocity among competitors in the exchange of price information. Such an agreement would make little economic sense, in our view, if its sole purpose were to guarantee all participants the opportunity to match the secret price concessions of other participants under § 2(b) of the Robinson-Patman Act. For in such circumstances, each seller would know that his price concession could not be kept from his competitors and no seller participating in the information exchange arrangement would, therefore, have any incentive for deviating from the prevailing price level in the industry. Regardless of its putative purpose, the most likely consequence of any such agreement to exchange price information would be the stablization of industry prices. Instead of facilitating use of the § 2(b) defense, such an agreement would have the effect of eliminating the very price concessions which provide the main element of competition in oligopolistic industries and the primary occasion for resort to the meeting competition defense.

Especially in oligopolistic industries such as the gypsum board industry, the exchange of price information among competitors carries with it the added potential for the development of concerted price-fixing arrangements which lie at the core of the Sherman Act's prohibitions...

We are left, therefore, on the one hand, with doubts about both the need for and the efficacy of interseller verification as a means of facilitating compliance with §2 (b) of the Robinson-Patman Act, and, on the other, with recognition of the tendancy for price discussions between competitors to contribute to the stability of oligopolistic prices and open the way for the growth of prohibited anticompetitive activity. To recognize even a limited...exception for interseller verification in such circumstances would be to remove from scrutiny under the Sherman Act conduct falling near its core with no assurance, and indeed with serious doubts, that competing antitrust policies would be served thereby. In *Automatic Canteen v. FTC*, 346 U.S. 61, (1953), the Court suggested that as a general rule the Robinson-Patman Act should be construed so as to insure its coherence with "the broader antitrust policies that have been laid down by Congress;" that observation buttresses our conclusion that exchanges of price information—even when putatively for purposes of Robinson-Patman Act compliance—must remain subject to close scrutiny under the Sherma Act. [Therefore, the Court of Appeals erred in treating interseller price verification as an exception which precludes Sherman Act liability.]

■ ■ ■

Questions

1. In *Staley* and *Corn Products*, the Court indicated a seller must "investigate or verify" the competing seller's lower price. How does the Court suggest such verification should procede?
2. Is a competing seller likely to inform the inquiring competitor of the details of a price concession? If all competitors freely exchange information of price consessions, is there any incentive to make such concessions?
3. Are exchanges of price information among competitors for purposes of verifying price concessions protected from Sherman Act attack by 2(b) of the Robinson-Patman Act?

BUYER LIABILITY

Knowingly inducing or receiving discriminatory price

§2 (f) It shall be unlawful for any person engaged in commerce, in the course of such commerce, knowingly to induce or receive a discrimination in price which is prohibited by this section.

From the foregoing language, it is easy to determine that the *buyer* may be in violation of this Act also. The buyer has committed a violation if he (1) receives an unlawful price discrimination and (2) the buyer has knowledge of its illegality. From the landmark *Automatic Canteen* case (346 U.S. 61, 1953), the court ruled that the FTC has the burden of "coming foreward with evidence" on the buyer's knowledge of illegality and that this burden extends to establishing that the buyer lacked knowledge of cost justification of the price discrimination. However, the FTC may establish its burden by "trade experience" evidence. In a FTC decision, the FTC established that it need only show that the buyer "should have known" of lack of cost justification. One Circuit Court has maintained that this is the same standard to be used in the meeting competition defense. The FTC must show that the buyer "should have known" that the price discrimination received was not justified and, therefore, the buyer had a "duty to inquire." (*Fred Meyer*, 9th Cir.).

Even if the buyer and seller are willing to violate the law and grant and receive special price concessions, the possiblity looms on the horizon that some competitor of the seller or of the buyer will discover the special price reduction and possibly bring a triple damage suit against either the buyer or the seller for violation of the Robinson-Patman Act.

KROGER CO.v. F.T.C.
438 F. 2d 1372 (1971)
U.S. Court of Apeals (6th Cir.)

■ ■ ■

The Korger Company brings this petition for review in which it complains of a cease and desist order of the Federal Trade Commission holding Kroger in violation of section 2(f) of the Clayton Act for having knowingly induced and received from Beatrice Food Company discriminatory prices on fluid milk and cottage cheese as prohibited by section 2(a) of the Act. In the same order the Commission absolved Beatrice from responsibility under section 2(a) of the Act on the ground that its lower price was offered in good faith to meet an equally low price of a competitor, a defense authorized under section 2(b) of the Act. Kroger seizes upon this circumstance contending that as a matter of law the discharge of Beatrice requires the acquittal of Kroger because there cannot be a violation of section 2(f) without there being one under section 2(a)...

defense absolving its seller under section 2(b) operated *ipso facto* for its own acquittal. However, even granting the validity of such a deduction, *arguendo*, it would not be available here. *Automatic Canteen*, 346 U.S. 61 (1953), holds only that buyers may avail themselves of discriminatory prices that a seller may lawfully grant or those that are "not known by him [the buyer] not to be within one of these defenses." The Commission found that Beatrice made a bona fide attempt to meet the Broughton bid which it was told by Kroger was the lower one. In so doing Beatrice was in good faith acting within a defense offered by section 2(b). On the other hand, Kroger knew that the Broughton bid was not lower and that the one of Beatrice was, therefore, not in fact responsive to an actual lower bid. In such a factual situation the seller's successful defense under §2(b) cannot exculpate the buyer since Kroger knew that the prices offered by Beatrice and received by Kroger were not in fact within the defense of section 2(b). To hold otherwise in this case would put a premium on the buyer's artifice and cunning in inducing discriminatory prices. In order for the buyer to be sheltered through the exoneration of the seller under section 2(b) the prices induced must come within the defenses of that section not only from the seller's point of view but also from that of the buyer. To hold otherwise would violate the purposes of the Act, and frustrate the intent of the Congress.

The findings of the Commission with regard to the misrepresentation of the Broughton bid are fully supported by substantial evidence throughout the record... Hutchinson, one of the Beatrice negotiators, testified that (Kroger's) Casserly told him "I have already got one at 20." And Stollings (another Beatrice negotiator) testified that Casserly said that "he had 20 per cent off from Broughton on this business." The bid actually averaged 10.9 per cent discount off the wholesale list price. We find no denial of this fact in the (Kroger's) briefs...

Finally, Kroger argues that the Commission failed to meet the burden of proving Kroger knew or should have known that Beatrice's prices were not cost justified, and there was no substantial evidence that the differentials on Kroger's private label product injured competition...

As to cost justification... Kroger was specifically warned by two dairy suppliers of Robinson-Patman Act problems that might result from the lower prices it sought. Still its expert in the purchasing and selling of dairy products, Mr. Casserly, pursued his course. He was a man of extremely wide experience in every line of the diary industry, including the production, processing and retailing of such products. He knew trade discounts, market conditions and cost accounting. Indeed, Casserly himself built up the cost formula which resulted in discriminations aggregating 39 per cent in some markets and as high as 41 per cent on cottage cheese. In these lights—coupled with the other circumstances surrounding the transaction—it is beyond question that Kroger knew—or should have known—that Beatrice's prices were not cost justified.

Likewise the differentials that Kroger received impaired competition...[A]s the Fifth Circuit said in *Foremost*: "It is unnecessary that there be evidence that the favored customer actually undersold his rivals."

The Commission properly inferred that there was a reasonable probability of substantial injury to competition since the discriminations were as high as 41 per cent (in cottage cheese); averaged in one market more than 28 percent, for other markets 17 per cent, and in Charleston, the most important area, more than 12 per cent. The discrimination here is among the highest in a litigated case under the Clayton Act. . The record shows that in the retail food business "competition is keen and profit margins are low."

In addition it is uncontested that dairy products are often used as "leaders" to attract customers. It follows that the injury found to be present involving a secondary-line here permits wide inferences of adverse competitive effects based on the existence of substantial price differentials.

Indeed, in wholesale fluid milk sales discounts from 5 percent to 12 percent have been held to have the required competitive effect on the secondary-line level...

■ ■ ■

Questions

1. Why was Beatrice not in violation of the Robinson-Patman Act?
2. How can Kroger be in violation of Section 2(f) if Beatrice is not in violation of Section 2(a)?
3. Did the Commission prove that Kroger knew or should have known that Beatrice's prices were not cost justified?
4. What evidence and reasoning did the Commission present to establish that there was probable anticompetitive effect resulting from Kroger's favored discount?
5. In buyer-level injury cases, the courts have developed two legal theories of injury. The "automatic inference" test is used when the industry is highly competitive, there is a substantial price difference, or very low profit margins exist in the industry. Under such conditions the court will infer a buyer-level injury. A second line of cases establishes the "ability to compete" test. This test requires more analysis of the effect on competitors resulting from the price discrimination before the court will rule on the probable effect on competition. Which theory is used in *Kroger*?
6. In a FTC decision of 1943 (Sherwin-Williams, 36 FTC 25), the Commission established the general rule that wholesale functional discounts are lawful. In effect, a manufacturer may give lower prices to wholesalers than to retailers because they do not compete and there is no competitive injury. However, if the wholesaler operates at retail also, the wholesaler is not entitled to the discount because competitive injury is present. In effect, the retailer (or a co-op of retailers) is performing self-functions (as wholesaler) and is seeking price concessions for his or her own labors. This type of activity is prohibited under the Act.

12

TRADE AND CONSUMER PROTECTION LAWS

Classical economists have advanced the theory of consumer sovereignty as an essential ingredient of free competitive markets. The informed consumer with equal bargaining power would interact with sellers in the marketplace to establish mutually satisfactory bargains. Government protection of either consumers or producers was considered unnecessary. Caveat emptor—let the buyer beware—was acceptable public policy because the seller and buyer generally had equal knowlege of the simple goods that revealed their quality through inspection. In effect, consumers could protect themselves. The consumer could avoid unsafe products because most goods did not contain hidden defects or dangerous tendencies. The nontechnical wares allowed consumers to protect themselves against fraud or deceit because they could inform themselves concerning the attributes of the product. In addition, the large number of sellers in the competitive market provided the consumer with the right to choose among producers and, thereby, forced producers to supply satisfactory quality and service at a fair price. And because the buyer and seller often dealt face to face, the consumers' complaints fell upon the sympathetic ears of producers who in their desire to make sales, responded to the consumers' voice.

During the final years of the nineteenth century, however, the marketplace began to change. New technology developed more sophisticated products, and producers began to organize into larger and fewer economic units. Initial outcries for consumer or public protection brought about congressional regulation of monopolistic practices of railroads and the passage of the antitrust laws. Subsequent legislation included the Federal Trade Commission Act in 1914 to prevent "unfair methods of competition" and to abort the trends toward monopoly and the erosion of consumer choice. In 1938, the Wheeler-Lea Amendment broadened the FTC's authority to prevent "unfair and deceptive practices in commerce" also. This provision empowered the FTC to prohibit practices deemed unfair or deceptive in relation to consumers.

Other laws of trade and consumer protection have been created in more recent times. While the development of these laws continues to be sporadic, President Kennedy's address concerning consumer protection in 1962 brought clarity and definition to the problems of consumers. The President asserted four basic *rights* of the consumer which included:

1. The right to choose (variety in products and services),
2. The right to be informed (avoid deceptions),

3. The right to safety (avoid hazardous goods),
4. The right to be heard (to assert consumer interests in the formulation of governmental policy).

These rights as enuciated by the President have given direction to the "consumer movement" throughout the sixties and seventies. They also provide some insights concerning future trends and legislation. For example, recent consumer advocates have advance the notion that consumers should also have the right to recover. The right of recovery is considered an esential consumer right, necessary to protect the other fundamental consumer rights. However, consumer rights, as advocated, have not been competely fulfilled in law. Consequently, the debate over the content and passage of consumer protection laws is continuous. This chapter attempts to provide a basic understanding of the present status and the principles of law that have been fashioned in the area of trade and consumer protection.

CONSUMER'S RIGHT TO CHOOSE

FEDERAL TRADE COMMISSION

The basic authority of the Federal Trade Commission (FTC) is enforcement of Section 5 which outlaws "unfair methods of competition" among competitors and "unfair or deceptive acts or practices" against consumers. The FTC is also empowered to enforce numerous other laws of trade and consumer protection (See Table 12-1). Investigations by the Commission to determine whether there are violations of Section 5, or of any law administered by the Commission, may be originated at the request of the President, Congress, governmental agencies, or on complaints by members of the public. Of course, the Commission may originate an investigation on its own initiative also. The Commission seeks voluntary cooperation in its investigations, but if the public interest requires, the Commission may invoke compulsory processes.

Whenever the Commission has reason to believe that any party is violating Section 5, it is authorized to issue a complaint against the party. However, when time and the nature of the proceeding permit, the Commission serves a notice on the party of the Commission's determination to institute a formal proceeding against the party. Within the prescribe time period, the party may file with the Secretary of the Commission a reply stating whether he or she is interested in having the proceedings disposed by the entry of a *consent order*. If the reply is in the negative, or if no reply is filed within the specified time, the complaint will be served. If on the other hand, the reply is in the affirmative, the party will be offered an opportunity to execute an appropriate settlement for consideration by the Commission.

The adjudicative proceedings of the Commission are commenced by the issuance and service of a complaint. The respondent named in the complaint has a specific number of days after service of the complaint to file an answer to the charges contained therein. Should the respondent elect not to contest the allegations of *fact* set forth in the complaint, he or she files, in effect, an admission answer which constitutes a waiver of hearing. If the answer is a denial of the allegations of fact contained in the complaint, the "case" then is heard by an Administrative Law Judge assigned to the Commission. During the hearings, counsel for the Commission has the burden of proving the allegations contained in the complaint. The Judge files an initial decision which includes (1) a statement of findings and conclusions, as well as the reasons or basis therefor, on all the material issues of fact, law, or discretion presented in the record, and (2) and appropriate order.

On appeal from, or review of, an initial decision of the Judge, the Commission will consider such parts of the record as necessary to resolve the issues presented. In rendering its decision, the Commission adopts, modifies, or sets aside the findings, conclusions, and order contained in the initial decision of the Judge and includes in its decision a statement of the reasons for its actions. Any party required by an order of the Commission to cease and desist, may obtain a review of such order by filing a written petition in a circuit court of appeals of the United States. On filing the petition, the Commission files with the court a record of the proceedings.

The appellate court has the power to enter a decree, affirming, modifying or setting aside the Commission's order. The statute provides that "findings of the Commission as to the facts, if supported by evidence, shall be conclusive." The judgment and decree of the appellate court is final, except that it shall be subject to review by the Supreme Court upon *certiorari*.

When an order of the Commission to cease and desist becomes final, either by failure to appeal or through affirmance by court action, and it is violated, the respondent is subjected to a fine of $10,000 per day for each violation. Furthermore, if an order of the commission is affirmed and adopted by an appellate court, so that the order of the commission becomes the order of the court, a violation thereof would constitute "contempt of court."

The Commission seeks, whenever possible, to avoid its formal procedures as a method to prevent the continuation of the practices which may violate any of the laws it administers. One method of "voluntary" enforcement is to permit any party to request advice from the Commission as to whether a proposed course of action violates any of its laws. The Commission informs the requesting party of the Commission's views, which will bind the Commission, so that if it changes these views, the inquiring party will be notified and given an opportunity to conform with the new views. However, a request is considered inappropriate (1) when the course of action is alredy being followed by the requesting party, (2) when the course of action is under investigation by the Commission or another governmental agency, or (3) when the proposed course of action is such that an informed decision could be made only after an extensive investigation. Another method of voluntary compliance is urged by the Commission through its issuance of "guides." These are administrative interpretations of law which aid the Commission's staff as well as businessmen in evaluating certain types of practices.

The rule-making powers of the FTC were confirmed and clarified in the FTC Improvement Act of 1975. The FTC is empowered to issue substantive rules with the force and effect of law which define and prohibit unfair and deceptive practices. Specific and detailed procedures for creating such rules are outlined in the Act. The FTC typically promulgates rules which relate to entire industries. While the FTC believes rule-making is a more efficient and a fairer process than the case-by-case procedure, both processes will continue to be utilized by the Commission to fashion laws for trade and consumer protection.

ANTITRUST ENFORCEMENT BY FTC

The Commission's initial goal was to enforce Section 5 of the FTC Act which prohibits "unfair methods of competition." This provision was conceived as a protection for honest businessmen from competitors utilizing unfair competitive practices. One question concerning enforcement of this section was: who is to decide what is an "unfair method of competition"—the Commission or the Court? A second question concerned whether a practice, not yet an antitrust violation under the Sherman or Clayton Acts, could nevertheless be an "unfair method of competition" and outlawed under Section 5? The following case provides answers.

FTC v. BROWN SHOE CO.
384 U.S. 316 (1965)
Supreme Court of the United States

■ ■ ■

BLACK, Mr. Justice.

...The Federal Trade Commission filed a complaint against the Brown Shoe Co.,

Inc., one of the world's largest manufacturers of shoes... The unfair practices charged against Brown revolve around the "Brown Franchise Stores' Program" through which Brown sells its shoes to some 650 retail stores. The complaint alleged that under this plan Brown... had "entered into contracts or franchises with a substantial number of its independent retail shoe store operator customers which require said customers to restrict their purchases of shoes for resale to the Brown lines and which prohibit them from purchasing, stocking or reselling shoes manufactured by competitors of Brown." Brown's customers who entered into these restrictive franchise agreements, so the complaint charged, were given in return special treatment and valuable benefits which were not granted to Brown's customers who did not enter into the agreements...

The... admissions of Brown as to the existence and operation of the franchise program were buttressed by many separate detailed fact findings of (the Administrative Law Judge), one of which findings was that the franchise program effectively foreclosed Brown's competitors from selling to a substantial number of retail shoe dealers. Based on these findings and on Brown's admissions the Commission concluded that the restrictive contract program was an unfair method of competition within the meaning of §5 and ordered Brown to cease and desist from its use.

Thus the question we have for decision is whether the Federal Trade Commission can declare it to be an unfair practice for Brown, the second largest manufacturer of shoes in the Nation, to pay a valuable consideration to hundreds of retail shoe purchasers in order to secure a contractual promise from them that they will deal primarily with Brown and will not purchase conflicting lines of shoes from Brown's competitors. We hold that the Commission has power to find, on the record here, such an anticompetitive practice unfair, subject of course to judicial review.

In holding that the Federal Trade Commission lacked the power to declare Brown's program to be unfair the Court of Appeals was much influenced by and quoted at length from this Court's opinion in *Federal Trade Comm'n v. Gratz*, 253 U.S. 421. That case, decided shortly after the Federal Trade Commission Act was passed, construed the Act... as giving the Commission very little power to declare any trade practice unfair. Later cases of this Court, however, have rejected the *Gratz* view and it is now recognized... that the Commission has broad powers to declare trade practices unfair. This broad power of the Commission is particularly well established with regard to trade practices which conflict with the basic policies of the Sherman and Clayton Acts even though such practices may not actually violate these laws. The record in this case shows beyond doubt that Brown, the country's second largest manufacturer of shoes, has a program, which requires shoe retailers, unless faithless to their contractual obligations with Brown, substantially to limit their trade with Brown's competitors. This program obviously conflicts with the central policy of both §1 of the Sherman Act and §3 of the Clayton Act against contracts which take away freedom of purchasers to buy in an open market. Brown nevertheless contends that the Commission had no power to declare the franchise program unfair without proof that its effect "may be to substantially lessen competition or tend to create a monopoly" which of course would have to be proved if the Government were proceeding against Brown under §3 of the Clayton Act rather than §5 of the Federal Trade Commission Act. We reject the argument that proof of this §3 element must be made for as we pointed out above our cases hold that the Commission has power under §5 to arrest trade restraints in their incipiency without proof that they amount to an outright violation of §3 of the Clayton Act or other provisions of the antitrust laws. This power of the Commission was emphatically stated in *F.T.C. v. Motion Picture Adv. Co.*, 344 U.S. 392, at pp. 394-395:

> "It is... clear that the Federal Trade Commission Act was designed to supplement and bolster the Sherman Act and the Clayton Act...to stop in their incipiency acts and practices which, when full blown, would violate those acts..."

We hold that the Commission acted well within its authority in declaring the Brown franchise program unfair whether it was completely full blown or not.

■ ■ ■

Questions

1. May the FTC rule a practice to be "unfair" (illegal) even if the practice is not an antitrust violation? What would the Commission have to show if it was trying to prove a Section 3 Clayton Act violation by Brown's exclusive dealing contracts? What must the FTC establish in order to prove an exclusive dealing is an "unfair method of competition"?
2. Why did the FTC rule this exclusive dealing program was "unfair" and other exclusive dealing franchise programs are not "unfair"? Does the answer have any connection with the outlawed Brown-Kinney merger in 1961?
3. How does this case relate to the consumer's right to choose?

ATLANTIC REFINING COMPANY v. F.T.C.
381 U.S. 357 (1965)
Supreme Court of the United States

■ ■ ■

CLARK, Mr. Justice.

The Federal Trade Commission has found that an agreement between the Atlantic Refining Company (Atlantic) and the Goodyear Tire & Rubber Company (Goodyear), under which the former "sponsors" the sale of the tires, batteries and accessory (TBA) products of the latter to its wholesale outlets and it retail service station dealers, is an unfair method of competition in violation of §5 of the Federal Trade Commission Act. Under the plan Atlantic sponsors the sale of Goodyear products to its wholesale and retail outlets on an overall commission basis. Goodyear is responsible for its sales and sells at its own price to Atlantic wholesalers and dealers for resale; it bears all of the cost of distribution through its warehouses, stores and other supply points and carries on a joint sales promotion program with Atlantic. The latter, however, is primarily responsible for promoting the sale of Goodyear products to its dealers and assisting them in their resale; for this it receives a commission on all sales made to its wholesalers and dealers...

Section 5 of the Federal Trade Commission Act...empowers the Commission, in the first instance, to determine whether a method of competition or the act or practice complained of is unfair. The Congress intentionally left development of the term "unfair" to the Commission rather than attempting to define "the many and variable unfair practices which prevail in commerce." Where the Congress has provided that an administrtive agency initially apply a broad statutory term to a particular situation, our function is limited to determining whether the Commission's decision "has 'warrant in the record' and a reasonable basis in law." While the final word is left to the courts, necessarily "we give great weight to the Commission's conclusion."

Certainly there is "warrant in the record" for the findings of the Commission here. Substantial evidence supports the conclusion that notwithstanding Atlantic's contention that it and its dealers are mutually dependent upon each other, they simply do not bargain as equals. Among the sources of leverage in Atlantic's hands are its lease and equipment loan contracts with their cancellation and short-term provisions... It must also be remembered that Atlantic controlled the supply of gasoline and oil to its wholesalers and dealers. This was an additional source of economic leverage, as was its extensive control of all advertising on the premises of its dealers

Furthermore, there was abundant evidence that Atlantic, in some instances with the aid of Goodyear, not only exerted the persuasion that is a natural incident of its economic power but coupled with it direct and overt threats of reprisal... In 1951, seven months after the sales-commission plan had gone into effect, Goodyear had enjoyed great success in signing contracts with Atlantic dealers despite the fact that a 1946-1949 servey had shown tht 67% of the dealers had preferred Lee tires and 76% Exide batteries.

With this background in mind, we consider whether there was a "reasonable basis in law" for the Commission's ultimate conclusion that the sales-commission plan constituted an unfair method of competition.

[N]either... the Commission (nor) the Court of Appeals held that the sales-commission arrangement was a tying scheme. What they did find was that the central competitive characteristic was the same—the utilization of economic power in one market to curtail competition in another. Here that lever was bolstered by actual threats and coercive practices. As our cases hold, all that is necessary in §5 proceedings to find a violation is to discover conduct that "runs counter to the public policy declared in the" Act.

...(The FTC's) use as a guideline of recognized violations of the antitrust laws was, we believe, entirely appropriate. It has long been recognized that there are many unfair methods of competition that do not assume the proportions of antitrust violations. When conduct does bear the characteristics of recognized antitrust violations it becomes suspect, and the commission may properly look to cases applying those laws for guidance...

Thus the Commission was warranted in finding that the effect of the plan was *as though* Atlantic had agreed with Goodyear to require its dealers to buy Goodyear products and had done so. It is beyond question that the effect on commerce was not insubstantial...

The short of it is that Atlantic with Goodyear's encouragement and assistance, has marshaled its full economic power in a continuing campaign to force its dealers and wholesalers to buy Goodyear products. The anticompetitive effects of this program are clear on the record and render unecessary extensive economic analysis of market percentages or business justifications in determining whether this was a method of competition which Congress has declared unfair and therefore unlawful.

■ ■ ■

Questions

1. What economic power did Atlantic possess over its dealers? Could Atlantic refuse the sale of its gasoline to any dealers who refused to purchase Goodyear TBA? Why not? Could it use its economic power to "urge" its dealers to buy Goodyear TBA? Why not?
2. How does this case relate to the consumer's right to choice?

NEW FTC INITIATIVES

Recently, the Federal Trade Commission has pursued some new policies in regard to antitrust enforcement. The FTC is attempting to enforce Section 5 in oligopoly and monopoly situations which are not provable violations of either Section 1 or 2 of the Sherman Act. If the FTC is successufl in this new approach and if it is upheld by the courts, the FTC may become the new umpire of industry structure, as well as trade behavior. An examination of some of the FTC's recent complaints reveals this new approach.

Oligopistic situations are normally attacked under Section 1 of the Sherman Act as a combination or conspiracy in restraint of trade. The government's burden of proof under Section 1 requires that it establish some sort of combination or agreement between the defendants. The defendants will contend that their activities are not conspired, but rather are the result of independent judgments and actions. If the government fails to prove the "agreement" by the defendants to act together, the government has failed to establish a Section 1 violation. However, the FTC maintains in recent complaints that despite its failure to prove concerted activity, the FTC may proceed to eliminate "common practices" which are "unfair methods of competition" without proof that the "common practices" are the result of an actual agreement.

In effect, if the "common behavior" of some members of an industry result in an adverse "effect" upon other industry competitors, the FTC maintains that it is empowered to eliminate the anticompetitive "effect" whether the "effect" arises from an agreement or not. Having established the anticompetitive "effect" and the need for a remedy, the FTC argues that it should establish an appropriate remedy, which may include divestiture of large oligopolists who follow "common practices." One complaint adopting this theory is the FTC action against eight major oil companies because of their "common practices" which the Commission feels are unfair to other competitors in the oil industry. The complaint indicates that the only appropriate remedy is divestiture of the refining activities from the production activities that are currently vertically integrated in major oil companies. In effect, the FTC is attempting to use its Section 5 powers to restructure the oil industry. Other industries where larger firms have "common practices" which have adverse (anticompetitive) effects on smaller competitors may be future targets of FTC complaints.

In another case, the FTC has initiated a complaint against the major manufacturers of cereals as a "shared monopoly" and requested divestiture of those firms. None of the firms alone could be charged with monopolization under Section 2 of the Sherman Act because no firm by itself controls a dominant share of the market.

One can determine from the new initiatives proposed in the FTC complaints that the Commission is directing itself more toward industry structure than toward particular competitor behavior. Should the Commission subsequently determine that "shared monopoly" or "common practices" are unfair under Section 5, the courts will have to decide whether the FTC's determination is within its statutory powers. These cases should take several years before a final decision is made. Nevertheless, they do indicate that the FTC is imaginatively attempting to enforce the spirit of the antitrust laws and to protect the consumers' right to choose between the products offered by "competitive" firms.

CONSUMER'S RIGHT TO BE INFORMED

COMMERCIAL ADVERTISING

In 1942 the Supreme Court in *Valentine v. Chrestensen,* 316 U.S. 52 held that "commercial advertising" was not protected by the First Amendment right of "free speech." In effect, the First Amendment imposed no restraints on governmental regulation of commercial advertising. The fact that advertising was a form of speech, a means of communicating ideas or information, and literally within the First Amendment's language was ignored by the Court. Consequently, the government and, in particular, the FTC had authority to regulate advertising without such governmental action being construed as an infringement on the advertiser's right to free speech. In so doing, the FTC had almost total authority to determine the meaning of the advertisement and to issue broad "fencing in" orders to avoid recurrence of the "illegal" ad.

However, in 1975 the Court began to critically examine its position concerning "commercial speech." Then, in *Virginia State Board v. Virginia Citizens Consumer Council,* 425 U.S. 748 (1976) the Court held that even if the advertiser's interest is "a purely economic one," it "hardly disqualifies him for protection under the First Amendment." The Court added:

> It is a matter of public interest that (private economic) decisions in the aggregate, be intelligent and well-informed. To this end, the free flow of commercial information is indispensable. . . . (E)ven if the First Amendment were thought to be primarily an instrument to enlighten public decision making in a democracy, we could not say that free flow of (commercial) information does not serve that goal.

However, the Court emphasized that its decision that "commercial speech, like other varieties, is protected" does not mean "it can never be regulated in any way." The Court acknowledged that reasonable "time, place, and manner" restrictions on speech are valid. The Court added:

[U]ntruthful speech, commercial or otherwise, has never been protected for its own sake... Obvisously, much commercial speech is not provably false, or even wholly false, but only deceptive or misleading. We foresee no obstacle to a state's dealing effectively with this problem.

The Court also recognized in a footnote, that because advertisements are calculated and supported by large financing, it is "less necessary to tolerate inaccurate statements for fear of silencing the speaker." These attributes "may also make it appropriate to require that a commercial message appear in such a form, or include such additional information, warnings, and disclaimers, as are necessary to prevent its being deceptive." Finally, the Court advised that the nature of commercial advertising "may also make inapplicable the prohibition against prior restraints."

The Court's language quickly aborts any foolish notion that the Court was attempting to repeal the Federal Trade Commission Act or any other laws prohibiting false and deceptive advertising. The Court wanted to make sure that its decision was not misconstrued as giving commercial speech the same degree of constitutional protection as political and literary speech. Advertising is to become coustitutionally protected speech, but advertisers do not need or deserve as much protection as politicans and editorial writers.

The law of advertising regulation will inevitably be affected by the introduction of the First Amendment as a relevant and important factor. While false and deceptive advertising will remain constitutionally unprotected, the Federal Trade Commission will not longer have complete autonomy in determing the "meaning" of the ad and its impact on the public. That issue now acquires a constitutional dimension on which the courts, not the FTC, will have the final say. In addition, regulators will find it necessary to more carefully articulate the necessity and justification for governmental control of particular advertising. The method of regulation or restriction imposed on the advertiser must be the least restrictive alternative available. For example, in *Chrysler Corporation v. the FTC,* 561 F.2d 357 (1977), the Court of Appeals struck down two provisions of an FTC order which the court felt were "potentially limitless" and "almost equally wide-ranging." Such decisions indicate that with First Amendment protection the courts will make a more searching examination of FTC and other governmental orders over advertising.

DECEPTIVE ADVERTISING

F.T.C. V. COLGATE-PALMOLIVE CO.
380 U.S. 374 (1964)
Supreme Court of the United States

■ ■ ■

WARREN, Mr. Chief Justice.

The basic question before us is whether it is a deceptive trade practice to represent falsely that a televised test, experiment, or demonstration provides a viewer with visual proof of a product claim, regardless of whether the product claim is itself true.

The case arises out of an attempt by respondent Colgate-Palmolive Company to prove to the television public that its shaving cream, "Rapid Shave,"... could soften even the toughness of sandpaper. Each of the commercials contained the same "sandpaper test." The announcer informed the audience that, "To prove RAPID SHAVE'S super-moisturizing power, we put it right from the can onto this tough, dry sandpaper. It was apply...soak...and off in a stroke." While the announcer was speaking, Rapid Shave was applied to a substance that appeared to be sandpaper, and immediately thereafter a razor was shown shaving the substance clean.

The Federal Trade Commission issued a complaint against respondent Colgate ...charging that the commercials were false and deceptive. The evidence before the... Administrative Law Judge (ALJ) disclosed that sandpaper of the type depicted in the commercials could not be shaved immediately following the application of Rapid Shave, but required a substantial soaking period of approximately 80 minutes. The evidence also showed that the substance resembling sandpaper was in fact a simulated prop, or "mock-up," made of plexiglass to which sand had been applied. However, the. . .(ALJ) found that Rapid Shave could shave sandpaper, even though not in the short time represented by the commercials, and that if real sandpaper had been used in the commercials the inadequacies of television transmission would have made it appear to viewers to be nothing more than plain, colored paper. . .

The Commission,. . .found that since Rapid Shave could not shave sandpaper within the time depicted in the commercials, (defendants) had misrepresented the product's moisturizing power. Moreover, the Commission found that the undisclosed use of a plexiglass substitue for sandpaper was an additional material misrepresentation that was a deceptive act separate and distinct from the misrepresentation concerning Rapid Shave's underlying qualities. Even if the sandpaper could be shaved just as depicted in the commercials, the Commission found that viewers had been misled into believing they had seen it done with their own eyes. As a result of these findings the Commission entered a cease-and-desist order against the (defendant). . . .

We accept the Commission's determination that the commercials involved in this case contained three representations to the public: (1) that sandpaper could be shaved by Rapid Shave; (2) that an experiment had been conducted which vertified this claim; and (3) that the viewer was seeing this experiment for himself. . . For the purposes of our review, we can assume that the first two representations were true; the focus of our consideration is on the third, which was clearly false. The parties agree that §5 prohibits the intentional misrepresentation of any fact which would constitute a material factor in a purchaser's decision whether to buy. They differ, however, in their conception of what "facts" constitute a "material factor" in a purchaser's decision to buy. (Defendant) submits, in effect, that the only material facts are those which deal with the substantive qualities of a product. The Commission, on the other hand, submits that the misrepresentation of *any* fact so long as it materially induces a purchaser's decision to buy is a deception prohibited by §5.

The Commission's interpretation of what is a deceptive practice seems more in line with the decided cases than that of (the defendant). . .

(Defendants) claim that all these cases are irrelevant to our decision because they involve misrepresentations related to the product itself and not merely to the manner in which an advertising message is communicated. This distinction misses the mark for two reasons. In the first place, the present case is not concerned with a mode of communication, but with a misrepresentation that viewers have objective proof of a seller's product claim over and above the seller's word. Secondly, all of the above cases, like the present case, deal with methods designed to get a consumer to purchase a product, not with whether the product, when purchased, will perform up to expectations. We find an especially strong similarity between the present case and those cases in which a seller induces the public to purchase an arguably good product by misrepresenting his line of business, by concealing the fact that the product is reprocessed, or by misappropriating another's trademark. In each the seller has used a misrepresentation to break down what he regards to be an annoying or irrational habit of the buying public—the preference for particular manufacturers or known brands regardless of a product's actual qualities, the prejudice against reprocessed goods, and the desire for verification of a product claim. In each case the seller reasons that when the habit is broken the buyer will be satisfied with the performance of the product he receives. . .It is generally accepted that it is a deceptive practice to state falsely that a product has received a testimonial from a respected source. In addition, the Commission has consistently acted to prevent sellers from falsely stating that their product claims have been "certified." We find these situations to be indistinguishable from the present case. We can assume that in each the underlying product claim is true and in each the seller actually conducted an experiment sufficient to prove to himself the truth of the claim. But in each the seller has told the public that it could rely on something other than his word concerning both the truth of the claim and the validity of his experiment. We find it an immaterial difference that in one case the viewer is told to rely on the word of a celebrity or authority he respects, in another on the word of a testing agency, and in the present case on his own perception of an undisclosed simulation....

We agree with the Commission, therefore, that the undisclosed use of plexiglass in the present commercials was a material deceptive practice, independent and separate from the other misrepresentation found. We find unpersuasive (defendant's) other objections to this conclusion. (Defendant) claims that it will be impractical to inform the viewing public that it is not seeing an actual test, experiment or demonstration, but we think it inconceivable that the ingenious advertising world will be unable, if it so desires, to conform to the Commission's insistence that the public be not misinformed. If, however, it becomes impossible or impractical to show simulated demonstrations on television in a truthful manner, this indicates that television is not a medium that lends itslef to this type of commercial, not that the commercial must survive at all costs...Nor was it necessary for the Commission to conduct a survey of the viewing public before it could determine that the commercials had a tendency to mislead, for when the Commission finds deception it is also authorized, within the bounds of reason, to infer that the deception will constitute a material factor in a purchaser's decision to buy...

We turn our attention now to the order issued by the Commission. It has been repeatedly held that the Commission has wide discretion in determining the type of order that is necessary to cope with the unfair practices found, and that Congress has placed the primary responsibility...for fashioning orders upon the Commission. For these reasons the courts should not "lightly modify" the Commission's orders. However, this Court has also warned that an order's prohibitions "should be clear and precise in order that they may be understood by those against whom they are directed"...

The Court of Appeals has criticized the reference in the Commission's order to "test, experiment or demonstration" as not capable of practical interpretation. It could find no difference between the Rapid Shave commercial and a commercial which extolled the goodness of ice cream while giving viewers a picture of a scoop of mashed potatoes appearing to be ice cream. We do not understand this difficulty. In the ice cream case the mashed potato prop is not being used for additional proof of the product claim, while the purpose of the Rapid Shave commercial is to give the viewer objective proof of the claims made. If in the ice cream hypothetical the focus of the commercial becomes the undisclosed potato prop and the viewer is invited, explicitly or by implication, to see for himself the truth of the claims about the ice cream's rich texture and full color, and perhaps compare it to a "rival product," then the commercial has become similar to the one now before us. Clearly, however, a commercial which depicts happy actors delightedly eating ice cream that is in fact mashed potatoes or drinking a product appearing to be coffee but which is in fact some other substance is not covered by the present order.

The crucial terms of the present order—"test, experiment or demonstration...represented...as actual proof of a claim"—are as specific as the circumstances will permit...

In commercials where the emphasis is on the seller's word, and not on the viewer's own perception, the defendants need not fear that an undisclosed use of props is prohibited by the present order. On the other hand, when the commercial not only makes a claim, but also invites the viewer to rely on his own perception for demonstrative proof of the claim, the defendants will be aware that the use of undisclosed props in strategic places might be a material deception. We believe that defendants will have no difficulty applying the Commission's order to the vast majority of their contemplated future commercials....

■ ■ ■

Questions

1. For an advertising misrepresentation to be illegal, must it relate false information about the substantive qualities of the product or misrepresent any fact that may induce a purchaser to buy the product?
2. Should misrepresenting mock-ups be allowed on television if the substantive facts behind the mock-up are true?
3. An advertisement showing a family enjoying ice cream uses mash potatoes for ice cream because of the hot lights in filming. Is this an illegal mock-up?
4. Must the Commission conduct a survey of the viewing public to determine if a commercial has a tendency to mislead? Must the Commission put some individual on the stand who will admit to being deceived?

CORRECTIVE ADVERTISING

Corrective advertising requires future advertising disclosures of wrong doing or of false impressions previously created by the advertiser. There have been consent orders in which companies have agreed to twelve months of advertising disclosures that correct previous false impressions created by advertising. However, the companies have not admitted to any wrongdoing or to the FTC's authority to order such corrective advertising. For example, ITT Continental Baking Corp., agreed to a twelve-month advertising disclosure that Profile Bread was not a dietary product. Ocean Spray Cranberries, Inc., likewise, admitted in corrective ads that cranberry juice had more "energy" only because it contained more calories. However, in the following case the FTC "ordered" the corrective advertising and the defendant, Warner-Lambert, challenged the authority of the Commission to issue such an order.

WARNER-LAMBERT CO. v. F.T.C.
562 F.2d 749 (1977)
U.S. Court of Appeals (D.C. Cir.)

■ ■ ■

The Warner-Lambert Company petitions for review of an order of the Federal Trade Commission requiring it to cease and desist from advertising that its product, Listerine Antiseptic mouthwash, prevents, cures, or alleviates the common cold. The FTC order further requires Warner-Lambert to disclose in future Listerine advertisements that: "Contrary to prior advertising, Listerine will not help prevent colds or sore throats or lessen their severity.". . .

Listerine has been on the market since 1879. Its formula has never changed. Ever since its introduction it has been represented as being beneficial in certain respects for colds, cold symptoms, and sore throats. Direct advertising to the consumer, including the cold claims as well as others, began in 1921. . . .

Petitioner contends that even if its advertising claims in the past were false, the portion of the Commission's order requiring "corrective advertising" exceeds the Commission's statutory power. The argument is based upon a literal reading of Section 5 of the Federal Trade Commission Act, which authorizes the Commission to issue "cease and desist" orders against violators and does not expressly mention any other remedies. The Commission's position, on the other hand, is that the affirmative disclosure that Listerine will not prevent colds or lessen their severity is absolutely necessary to give effect to the prospective cease and desist order; a hundred years of false cold claims have built up a large reservoir of erroneous consumer belief which would persist, unless corrected, long after petitioner ceased making the claims.

Petitioner's narrow reading of Section 5 was at one time shared by the Supreme Court. . .

But the modern view is very different. In 1963 the Court ruled that the Civil

Aeronautics Board has authority to order divestiture in addition to ordering cessation of unfair methods of competition by air carriers. *Pan American World Airways, Inc. v. United States,* 371 U.S. 296, (1963). The CAB statute, like Section 5, spoke only of the authority to issue cease and desist orders, but the Court said, "[W]here the problem lies within the purview of the Board,...Congress must have intended to give it authority that was ample to deal with the evil at hand...[The] power to order divestiture need not be explicitly included in the powers of an administrative agency to be part of its arsenal of authority..."

Later, in *FTC v. Dean Foods Co.,* the Court applied *Pan American* to the Federal Trade Commission. In upholding the Commission's power to seek a preliminary injunction against a proposed merger, the Court held that it was not necessary to find express statutory authority for the power. "Such ancillary powers have always been treated as essential to the effective discharge of the Commission's responsibilities."

Thus it is clear that the Commission has the power to shape remedies which go beyond the simple cease and desist order. Our next inquiry must be whether a corrective advertising order is for any reason outside the range of permissible remedies....

According to petitioner, "The first reference to corrective advertising in Commission decisions occurred in 1970, nearly fifty years and untold numbers of false advertising cases after passage of the Act." In petitioner's view, the late emergence of this "newly discovered" remedy is itself evidence that it is beyond the Commission's authority. This argument fails on two counts. First the fact that an agency has not asserted a power over a period of years is not proof that the agency lacks such power. Second, and more importantly, we are not convinced that the corrective advertising remedy is really such an innovation. The label may be newly coined, but the concept is well established. it is simply that under certain circumstances an advertiser may be required to make affirmative disclosure of unfavorable facts.

One such circumstance is when an advertisement that did not contain the disclosure would be misleading. For example, the Commission has ordered the sellers of treatments for baldness to disclose that the vast majority of cases of thinning hair and baldness are attributable to heredity, age, and endocrine balance (so-called "male pattern baldness") and that their treatment would have no effect whatever on this type of baldness. It has ordered the promoters of a device for stopping bedwetting to disclose that the device would not be of value in cases caused by organic defects or diseases. And it has ordered the makers of Geritol, an iron supplement, to disclose that Geritol will relieve symptoms of tiredness only in persons who suffer from iron deficiency anemia, and that the vast majority of people who experience such symptoms do not have such a deficiency.

Each of these orders was approved on appeal over objections that it exceeded the Commission's statutory authority...

Affirmative disclosure has also been required when an advertisement, although not misleading if taken alone, becomes misleading considered in light of past advertisements. For example, for 60 years Royal Baking Powder Company had stressed in its advertising that its product was superior because it was made with cream of tartar, not phosphate. But, faced with rising costs of cream of tartar, the time came when it changed its ingredients and became a phosphat aking powder. It carefully removed from all labels and advertisements any reference ◟◞ cream of tartar and corrected the list of ingredients. But the new labels used the familiar arrangement of lettering, coloration, and design, so that they looked exactly like the old ones. A new advertising campaign stressed the new low cost of the product and dropped all reference to cream of tartar. But the advertisements were also silent on the subject of phosphate and did not disclose the change in the product.

The Commission held, and the Second Circuit agreed, that the new advertisements were deceptive, since they did not advise consumers that their reasons for buying the powder in the past no longer applied. The court held that it was proper to require the company to take affirmative steps to advise the public. To continue to sell the new powder on the strength of the reputation attained through 60 years of its manufacture and sale and wide advertising of its superior powder, under an impression induced by its advertisements that the product purchased was the same in kind and as superior as that which had been so long manufactured by it, was unfair alike to the public and to the competitors in the baking powder business.

It appears to us that the order in *Royal...* (was) the same kind of remedy the Commission has ordered here. Like Royal...., Listerine has built up over a period of many years a widespread reputation. When it was ascertained that that reputation no longer applied to the product, it was necessary to take action to correct it. Here, as in *Royal,* it is the accumlated impact of *past* advertising that necessitates disclosure in *future* advertising. To allow consumers to continue to buy the product on the strength of the impression built up by prior advertising—an impression which is now known to be false—would be unfair and deceptive.

Having established that the Commission does have the power to order corrective advertising in appropriate cases, it remains to consider whether use of the remedy against Listerine is warranted and equitable...

The Commission has adopted the following standard for the imposition of corrective advertising:

> [I]f a deceptive advertisement has played a substantial role in creating or reinforcing in the public's mind a false and material belief which lives on after the false advertising ceases, there is clear and continuing injury to competition and to the consuming public as consumers continue to make purchasing decisions based on the false belief. Since this injury cannot be averted by merely requiring respondent to cease disseminating the advertisement, we may appropriately order respondent to take affirmative action designed to terminate the otherwise continuing ill effects of the advertisement.

We think this standard is entirely reasonable. It dictates two factual inquiries: (1) did Listerine's advertisements play a substantial role in creating or reinforcing in the public's mind a false belief about the product? and (2) would this belief linger on after the false advertising ceases? It strikes us that if the answer to both questions is not yes, companies everywhere may be wasting their massive advertising budgets. Indeed, it is more than a little peculiar to hear petitioner assert that its commercials really have no effect on consumer belief.

...(In any case) the Commission adduced survey evidence to support both propositions. We find that... survey data and the expert testimony interpreting them constitute substantial evidence in support of the need for corrective advertising in this case.

We turn next to the specific disclosure required: "Contrary to prior advertising, Listerine will not help prevent colds or sore throats or lessen their severity." Petitioner is ordered to include this statement in every future advertisement for Listerine for a defined period. In printed advertisements it must be displayed in type size at least as large as that in which the principal portion of the text of the advertisement appears and it must be separated from the text so that it can be readily noticed. In television commercials the disclosure must be presented simultaneously in both audio portions. During the audio portion of the disclosure in televsion and radio advertisements, no other sounds, including music, may occur.

These specifications are well calculated to assure that the disclosure will reach the public. It will necessarily attract the notice of readers, viewers, and listeners, and be plainly conveyed. Given these safeguards, we believe the preamble "Contrary to prior advertising" is not necessary. It can serve only two purposes: either to attract attention that a correction follows or to humiliate the advertiser. The Commission claims only the first purpose for it, and this we think is obviated by the other terms of the order. The second purpose, if it were intended, might be called for in an egregious case of deliberate deception, but this is not one. While we do not decide whether petitioner proffered its cold claims in good faith or bad, the record compiled could support a finding of good faith. On these facts, the confessional preamble to the disclosure is not warranted.

Finally, petitioner challenges the duration of the disclosure requirement. By its terms it continues until respondent has expended on Listerine advertising a sum equal to the average annual Listerine advertising budget for the period April 1962 to March

1972. That is approximately ten million dollars. Thus if petitioner continues to advertise normally the corrective advertising will be required for about one year. We cannot say that is an unreasonably long time in which to correct a hundred years of cold claims. But, to petitioner's distress, the requirement will not expire by mere passage of time. If petitioner cuts back its Listerine advertising, or ceases it altogether, it can only postpone the duty to disclose. The Commission concluded that correction was required and that a duration of a fixed period of time might not accomplish that task, since petitioner could evade the order by choosing not to advertise at all. The formula settled upon by the Commission is reasonably related to the violation it found.

■ ■ ■

Questions

1. The FTC Act authorizes the Commission to issue cease and desist orders. It does not expressly mention other remedies, such as "corrective advertising." Does this mean that the FTC does not possess the authority to order corrective advertising?
2. What two particular precedents did the Court of Appeals cite as containing essentially the same kind of remedy that the Commission ordered against Warner-Lambert?
3. When does the Commission feel corrective advertising is an appropriate remedy? What two factual inquires are necessary to impose corrective advertising?
4. Why did the court think that the preamble "contrary to prior advertising" was not necessary?

AD VISUALS

The FTC historically has been concerned with advertising which contained deceptive statements. Advertisers became increasingly wary of making deceptive claims in print. Therefore, the emphasis of advertisers shifted from verbal to visual. In response, the FTC's Bureau of Consumer Protection has indicated that the time has come for the FTC to start examining the nonverbal messages conveyed by the pictorial portion of the advertisements. They have argued that "healthy, happy" images should not be associated with such "unhealthy" products as alcohol and cigarettes. The FTC staff has asserted that if the message conveyed by the picture were put into words, it would be deceptive or misleading. Therefore, the FTC is considering different ways to get a consensus on the "implicit meaning" of visual images portrayed in advertising. Among the techniques being considered by the Commission are a panel of consumers, studies on consumer reactions, or opinions of media experts because "consumers may be unaware of subliminal effects." Then, once the picture's message has been determined, the FTC would rule on whether it constitutes false advertising.

LITTLE-FTC ACTS

In an effort to gain state aid to combat unfair trade practices, the Federal Trade Commission proposed a draft of an *Unfair Trade Practices and Consumer Protection Law* for states to enact. Forty-three states have enacted some version of this proposal, and six other states and the District of Columbia have adopted a variation of the *Uniform Consumer Sales Practices Act,* which was developed by the National Conference of Commissioners on Uniform State Laws. Consequently, fifty jurisdictions have enacted laws more or less like the Federal Trade Commission Act to prevent deceptive and unfair trade practices within their respective jurisdictions. In Alabama, which doesn't have such a law, the consumer complaint clearinghouse has been established to monitor action under existing laws and possibly recommend new legislation.

These "Little-FTC" Acts typically contain authorization for the administrating authority to conduct investigations through the use of subpoenas, to issue cease and desist orders, or to obtain court injunctions to halt the use of anticompetitive, deceptive, or unfair trade practices. Rules and regulations may be issued under the statutes in thirty-one states. The following cases illustrate the utilization of these state laws in the protection of the consumer's right to be correctly informed.

DECEPTIVE PRODUCTS

NEW YORK v. COLORADO STATE CHRISTIAN COLLEGE
346 N.Y.S.2d 482 (1973)
Supreme Court of New York

■ ■ ■

This action has been instituted pursuant to Section 349 of the General Business Law to enjoin, restrain and prohibit defendant from conferring or offering to confer upon any member of the public in the State of New York any academic or honorary degree; from directly or indirectly advertising, offering for sale or selling any academic or honorary degree to any member of the public in the State of New York; from representing itself as a "college" in any letter, advertisement, brochure, degree or other writing addressed to any member of the public in the State of New York; and from further engaging in deceptive acts and practices.

. . . The uncontroverted facts are that the Colorado State Christian College (of the Church of The Inner Power, Inc.) has been busily engaged in offering for sale and selling Ph.D. degrees in sundry and sorted areas of specialization. Its recipients, including New Yorkers, were selected and recruited from such publications as "Who's Who of American Women."

. . . The Colorado State Christian College . . . does not qualify as a college or institution of higher learning. It has no formal entrance requirements except a contribution of $100 or more accompanying the application for the honorary degree (which is claimed to be tax deductible). It has no faculty members who are trained and competent to teach accredited and recognized academic courses . . . In the words of the immortal bard of Avon, "its books are babbling brooks," it supports no other library or educationsl facilities. It has no resident students, no curriculum accredited by any official or recognized agency . . .

The legislative . . . (history) of Section 349 . . . (explains) . . . that where the act or practice complained of by the Attorney General is subject to and complies with the standards set by rules, regulations or statutes of the Federal Trade Commission, or the interpretation thereof by the Commission or the federal courts, the . . . defendant is exonerated. In so explaining, the (legislative) Report at p.8 states:

> "The Committee believes such a provision is necessary in order to protect businessmen from conflicting standards . . . and to make federal law and its interpretation of deceptive acts and practices applicable to state enforcement. The words 'rules and regulations' are intended to be broadly construed to cover all official policies of the Federal Trade Commission, including policy statements, advisory opinions and guides." . . .

It is thus clear that the legislative purpose in enacting § 349 . . . was to follow in the steps of the Federal Trade Commission with respect to the interpretation of deceptive acts and practices outlawed in Section 5 of the Federal Trade Commission Act . . .

The federal Courts have uniformly sustained Orders of the Federal Trade Commission prohibiting the use of trade name designations whch have a tendency to create an erroneous impression as to the nature of the business.

The Courts in New York have taken the same position . . .

Specifically, in regard to the use of the designation *college* numerous Federal Trade Commission administrative cease and desist orders have been issued and upheld by the Federal Courts prohibiting the use of the word "college" or "university" when the respondent as is the case here, is not in fact an institution of higher education; has no formal entrance requirements, nor resident students; nor library or other educational facilities; nor faculty members who are trained and competent to teach accredited and recognized college under-graduate or graduate courses of any kind.

In Branch v. F.T.C., 141 F. 2d 31 (7th Cir. 1941) the court upheld an F.T.C. cease and desist order prohibiting the use of the words "institute" or "university" in connection with the conduct of respondent's business which the Court described as a "diploma mill."

Most recently, the Federal Trade Commission has issued a cease and desist order against Ohio Christian College (of Calvary Grace Christian Churches of Faith, Inc.,...) The gravamen of the F.T.C. action is almost identical to that of the state herein (even the defendant's name is almost identical).

Defendant, by selling an honorary degree, (also) has clearly violated the provisions of Education Law § 224 (2). Furthermore, such conduct is violative of the declared public policy of this state to preserve and maintain the integrity of the education process.

By offering for sale and sale of honorary degrees in New York defendant places in the hands of individuals the means and instrumentalities by and through which they may deceive and mislead others as to the degrees and other academic qualifications said individuals possess and has aided and abetted such individuals in the violation of the Education Law § 224...

■ ■ ■

Questions

1. Is there danger of conflict between New York's Section 349 General Business Law and the Federal Trade Commission Rules?
2. How are the "Little-FTC" acts related to the consumer's right to be informed? What misinformation is supplied by the Colorado State Christian College?

Other examples of "unfair and deceptive trade practies" in relation to product claims are:

1. Misrepresentation of business or trade status—for example, misrepresentation of status as a "mill," "manufacturer," "wholesaler," or deceptive use of trademarks or trade names. For example, Carter Products Inc., was forced to excise it's "liver" from trademark when it was demonstrated that the drug had no effect on the liver.
2. False product claims—for example, false claims of composition, quality, quantity, characteristics, or effectiveness of the product. For example, Algoma Lumber Co. was precluded from the sale of yellow pine as "California white pine." Also, Winsted Hosiery Co. was prohibited from labeling some underwear manufactured from partly wool ingredients as "wool."
3. "Unfair" Product Claims—for example, unfair representations and claims not supported by substantiating tests or investigations. For example, it would be "unfair" to market a sunburn remedy containing well-known ingredients without "adequate and well-controlled tests" to support the claims made for the sunburn remedy. Many products that are marketed would require scientific testing to establish substantial data to support advertised claims. Another type of unfairness is improper "uniqueness" claims. For example, ITT Continental Baking Co. was not allowed to claim that its enriched breads contain some unique feature (nutritional) when it merely contained the ingredients that are in all manufacturers' bread.

DECEPTIVE SELLING INFORMATION

PEOPLE EX REL. DUNBAR v GYM OF AMERICA, INC.
493 P.2d 660 (1972)
Supreme Court of Colorado

■ ■ ■

The trial court held that the Colorado Consumer Protection Act is so vague and uncertain that it does not furnish a standard sufficiently definite to give notice of meaning to persons affected thereby and is thus in contravention of state and federal due process. In support of this conclusion, (defendant) claims that certain key words ...in the statute are either not defined at all or are so inadequately defined that one cannot determine which trade practices are allowed and which are prohibited...

We note that this statute is concerned with proscribing certain kinds of specific *future* conduct. As such, the statute provides sanctions of purely prospective effect, such as the restraining orders, injunctions, and assurances of discontinuance found in Section 7. This, of course, means that when the attorney general seeks an injunction he is not demanding that the defendant be punished with a penal sanction, but rather that the defendant be restrained from acting unlawfully in the future. It is unnecessary that such a statute provide absolutely precise warning before its equitable sanctions are applied. The adjudication itself provides notice to the defendant, and is prospective in its application. The result is that the defendant is provided with the explicit terms of the decree or order to tell him what practices are allowed without incurring penalties. Therfore, as will be seen below, a statute such as this whose sanctions are injunctions or assurances of discontinuance need not be as precise as a statute where the sanction is penal or criminal.

One should also take note... that the statute's subject matter... is the Colorado version of the Uniform Deceptive Trade Practices Act. It is clearly enacted to control various deceptive trade practices in dealing with the public and as such is obviously designed to both declare and enforce an important public policy. More significantly, the utility of general standards of actionability with respect to deceptive trade practices has been repeatedly recognized...

The question before the Court now is whether the... challenged phrases— "bait and switch," "disparagement," and "tie-in sales," as used in the Consumer Protection Act are so vague as to render their meaning intelligible to people affected by them. We believe that all... terms are not unconstitutionally vague...

The statute's "bait and switch" terminology is attacked on the ground that it has no commonly understood meaning and is therefore unconstitutionally vauge. This arugment must fall for several reasons. First, Section 2(1) (a) (o) (i) *specifically defines* "bait and switch" advertising as advertising which "consists of an attractive but insincere offer to sell a product or service which the seller in truth does not intend or desire to sell." Second, "bait and switch" advertising and selling techniques have long been recognized in the legal literature and have long been subject to equitable sanctions.

The use of the term "disparagement" in the statute is attacked on the basis that it has no widely understood meaning. It may be true that the Colorado Consumer Protection Act does not specifically define "disparagement" anywhere, but, in our view, the word "disparagement" has such a common meaning that to define it would be an exercise in redundancy. The legal literature contains many instances of the use of the word "disparagement" when dealing with forbidden trade practices.

In *Electrolux,* the New York Court of Appeals enjoined a sales promotion scheme whereby a business firm first advertised a product at a very attractive price in order to invite inquiry, then disparaged or "knocked" the product when members of the public made inquiry, and finally offered another item for sale which was more expensive than the first but which seemed like a "bargain" in comparison to the disparaged product that was originally advertised. This deceptive use of advertising as a lure to sell other nonadvertised products or services is exactly the kind of trade practice which the Colorado Consumer Protection Act and the Uniform Deceptive Trade Practices

Act... prohibit. This is also the "disparagement" that Gym of America is accused of engaging in when it allegedly told members of the public that club privileges on terms as advertised would not be available because the advertised terms were too short in duration to be of any benefit to their health, while an expensive membership of a longer period of time would be quite helpful.

(Defendant's) last contention concerning the statute's purported vagueness is that the Act's "tie-in-sales" language is too ambigious and uncertain to meet due process requirements. This argument must also fall for several reasons. The Colorado Consumer Protection Act specifically defines "tie-in-sales" to mean an "undisclosed condition to be met prior to selling the advertised product or service." Furthermore, the concept of a "tie-in-sale" is not new to the law as its practice has long been prohibited by the anti-trust laws. These guideposts, added to the fact that a "tie-in-sale," like "disparagement," and "bait and switch" tactics, is not a new or unfamiliar term to most business enterprises, leads us to conclude that its use in the Colorado Consumer Protection Act does establish a standard against which one's business and trade activities can be tested. There is a definite background of experience and precedent to illuminate the meaning of the words employed in the statute. No one would reasonably be misled thereby.

■ ■ ■

Questions

1. Why is it not necessary that a statute, such as the Colorado Consumer Protection Act, provide absolutely precise language in outlawing certain activity?
2. What is a "bait and switch" sales tactic?
3. What is the "disparagement" sale tactic?
4. What is a "tie-in sales" tactic?
5. How do these rules protect the consumer's right to be correctly informed?

FAIR LABELING

Closely related to the regulation of advertising and deceptive sales practices is the regulation of labeling and marking of products. Numerous federal statutes have been designed to give the consumer more accurate information about the product or precise warnings as to the dangers in the use of the product. Particular federal labeling statutes include the Fair Packaging and Labeling Act, the Fair Products Labeling Act, the Wool Products Labeling Act, the Cigarette Labeling and Advertising Act, and the Fedreal Hazardous Substances Labeling Act. Other statutes designed to protect the consumer from personal harm or economic loss also regulate labeling and disclosure of information.

The Fair Packaging and Labeling Act of 1966 directs the Secretary of Health, Education, and Welfare (in the case of food, drugs, devices, and cosmetics) and the Federal Trade Commission (in the case of all other commodities) to promulgate labeling requirements: (1) pertaining to the identification of the commodity's manufacturer, packer, or distributor; (2) pertaining to the location and legibility of a statement of net quantity of the contents; and (3) pertaining to any description in terms of weight, volume, or size. The Act authorizes the enforcement agencies to issue labeling regulations to prevent consumer deception and to determine what size packages may be represented by words such as "small," "medium," and "large." The Act grants additional authority to regulate the use of "cents-off" or "economy" sizes for packaging. It also requires a listing of the ingredients of commodities and authorizes regulations to prohibit "nonfunctional slack fill" or "packaged air."

The Federal Hazardous Substances Labeling Act of 1960 requires the manufacture to more precisely label a product to give a clear description of any danger inherent in the use of the products. The following case is illustrative.

MURRAY v. WILSON OAK FLOORING CO., INC.
475 F. 2d 129 (1973)
United States Court of Appeals (7th Cir.)

■ ■ ■

The plaintiff was the owner of a small brick residential property located in Chicago. On the evening of October 3, 1969, Murray was preparing to install a parquet-wood flooring on a portion of the second floor of this building, pursuant to a plan for overall remodeling. He planned to use Latex "45" Adhesive to hold the flooring in place...

Affixed to the fix-gallon can of Latex "45" Adhesive were two labels, one of which, bright red and diamond shaped, set forth its message in boldface black letters having the following content... "Keep Away From Fire, Heat and Open Flame Lights..." Another label was affixed to the opposite side of the can. White with red lettering, it set forth, in part, this message; "Caution: Inflammable Mixture, Do Not Use Near Fire or Flame... Use in Well Ventilated Area, Do Not Smoke—Extinguish flame—including pilot lights..." Prior to spreading any of the mastic, Murray thoroughly familiarized himself with the contents of these labels...

...While on his knees near the bathroom door, facing the front of the building and nearly finished with applying mastic, Murray heard an explosive noise, later described by him as a "whompf". This was accompanied by a bright orange flame... In an ensuing fire, Murray sustained burns which resulted in his permanent injury.

This suit for damages followed. Evidence produced at trial established that the warnings placed on the can of Latex "45" Adhesive were not in conformance with either the Federal Hazardous Substances Labeling Act or the Illinois Hazardous Substances Labeling Act. To comply with those Acts, a product having the combustibility of Latex "45"—equivalent to that of gasoline—would have required labeling which rad "danger" rather than "caution" and "extremely flammable" rather than "inflamable".

The evidence also established that the fire was caused when combustible vapors from the adhesive came in contact with one of the lit pilot lights, the most likely candidate being the pilot light of the water heater in the storage-utility room...

After hearing all of the evidence, the jury in the cause returned a verdict in favor of Murray, and assessed damages against Wilson in the sum of $20,429.00. Wilson then filed a motion for a judgment in its favor *non obstante veredicto* which was granted by the district judge. He based his decision on the following facts:

> [T]the plaintiff Frederick H. Murray admitted on the trial that at the time of the occurrence there were burners blazing and that he knew they were there. The product was plainly marked as inflamable. Said plaintiff's action was clearly a contributing cause of the explosion and fire that occurred, and he was therefore guilty of contributory negligence herein.

By "blazing burners" we take the judge to have meant the various pilot lights adjacent to the applied mastic.

We have carefully considered the evidence in this case, and conclude that the trial judge erred in entering a judgment *non obstante veredicto* for Wilson. Perhaps the most crucial fact relevant to our decision is the presence of the word "near" in the primary warning on Wilson's adhesive can, a term which we think must be taken to modify subordinate warnings on the same level. The most important of these is the recitation: "Do not smoke—Extinguish flame—*including pilot lights.*" (emphasis added). Reexamining the floor plan introduced as evidence in this case, and taking the evidence at its worst for Murray, it would appear that he spread mastic to within four or five feet of the water heater pilot light and within seven to eight horizontal feet of the stove pilot lights...

We cannot say as a matter of law that the term "near" was sufficient to inform Murray that his spreading of adhesive within four feet of a pilot light *located behind a closed door* and within eight feet of stove pilot lights three feet off the floor exposed him to the risk of an explosion and attendant fire damage. All of the evidence, when viewed in its aspect most favorable to Murray, fails to "so overwhelmingly [favor] movant [Wilson] that no contrary verdict based on that evidence could ever stand." Nearness is a matter of degree. To the president of Wilson, "near" included the entire house in which an application of Latex "45" was taking place. The reasonable man, we think, would disagree. Thus, whether "near" fairly encompassed the door and distances of this case was a question for the jury...

Lastly, we note... (the) evidence... establish(ed) (1) a case of *prima facie* negligence on the part of the defendant by failure to comply with industry-wide standards of warning, and (2) Murray was not an experienced carpenter with extensive practice in using the material causing the accident complained of.

■ ■ ■

Questions

1. How were the defendant's labels not in conformance with the Federal Hazardous Substance Labeling Act?
2. Why did the trial judge grant a judgment for the defendant *non obstante veredicto*?
3. Why did the Court of Appeals feel the judgment n.o.v. was inappropriate in this case?

LABELING STANDARDS

The implementation of labeling laws is not always easy. For example, in 1966 Congress recognized that there was great consumer confusion as to quality of tires offered for sale to the public and the meaning of the variety of trade terminology used in marketing new passenger car tires. This conclusion led to a provision in the National Traffic and Motor Vehicle Safety Act of 1966 that a system be established to assist the consumer in making an informed choice in purchasing new tires. The Department of Transportation (DOT) Act required the Secretary of Transportation to develop a "uniform quality grading system for motor vehicle tires." However, because of the failure of the tire industry to initially provide test and cost information requested by DOT and because of the technical difficulties in developing acceptable tire testing procedures, the tire-grading system was not implemented until 1979. Besides the difficulty in establishing product labeling standards, there is also the problem that consumers may not perceive the mandated labeling standard as in their best interest. Consider the dispute in the following case.

FEDERATION OF HOMEMAKERS v. HARDIN
328 F. Supp. 181 (1971)
U.S. District Court (D.C.)

■ ■ ■

[T]he Federation of Homemakers, a consumer organization dedicated to protecting the integrity of food products, challenges the use of "All Meat" labels on frankfurters when such products actually contain up to 15 percent of non-meat ingredients...

The underlying statute in this case is the Wholesome Meat Act, enacted to protect the health and welfare of consumers by ensuring that they have access to wholesome and properly marked meats...

The sections of the Wholesome Meat Act relating to misleading labeling, prohibit any meat product from being sold under a label which is misleading and provides a procedure whereby the Secretary (of Argriculture) may enfore the prohibition...

In reviewing the adoption of a regulation by an agency under its rule-making procedures, the Court is limited to considering whether the administrative action was "arbitrary, capricious, an abuse of discretion, or otherwise not in accordance with law." In this matter, the Secretary's determination that "All Meat" labels were authorized for frankfurters which contained up to 15 percent of non-meat ingredients represented a codification of a term in common use in the meat industry. However, there is nothing in the rcord to suggest that this "term of art" is understood by the general public..

The primary purpose of the Wholesome Meat Act is to benefit the consumer and to enable him to have a correct understanding of and confidence in meat products purchased. Prohibitions against mislabeling are an integral part of this purpose. Clearly, any rule-making procedure conducted under this Act which fails to primarily emphasize the understanding of the consumer is a procedure not conducted "in accordance with [the applicable] law" (the Act).

The leading case in this jurisdiction on the problem of mislabeling is *Armour and Company v. Freeman*... The Court stated:

> "To measure whether a label employing ordinary words of common usage is false or not, the words must be taken in their ordinary meaning."...

This Court finds the Armour case controlling. In applying the "ordinary meaning" test to the word "all", it is clear when that adjective is used on a label with the word "meat", the common understanding is that it describes a substance that is *totally and entirely* meat. The application of the "All Meat" label to frankfurters that are 15 percent nonmeat is a contradiction in terms and is misleading within the meaning of... (the Act). The use of the term "All Meat" or "All (*species*)" as applied to frankfurters is invalid, and the defendants should be enjoined from permitting any frankfurter product to be so labeled.

■ ■ ■

Questions

1. Why did the Secretary of Agriculture adopt a rule for labeling frankfurters "all meat" when they may contain up to 15 percent of nonmeat ingredients?
2. What was the reasoning of the Court to reject the Secretary's rule?

TRUTH-IN-LENDING

Title 1 of the consumer Credit Protection Act is more often referred to as the Truth-in-Lending Act. Section 102 (a) reveals the purposes of Congress:

> The Congress finds that economic stabilization would be enhanced and the competition among various financial institutions... would be strengthened by the informed use of credit. The informed use of credit results from an awareness of the cost thereof by consumers. It is the purpose of this title to assure a meaningful disclosure of credit terms so that the consumer will be able to compare more radily the various credit terms available to him and avoid the uninformed use of credit...

This Act was subsequently amended in 1974 to protect the consumer against inaccurate and unfair credit billing and credit card practices.

The Act authorizes the Federal Reserve Board to prescribe regulation Z to effectuate the purposes of the Act and prevent circumvention or evasion thereof. Regulation Z attempts to let consumers (borrowers) know the cost of credit so they can compare costs between various credit sources. Regulation Z also regulates the issuance of credit cards, sets maximum liability for the unauthorized use of credit cards and provides a procedure for resolving billing errors which occur in open-end credit accounts. It applies to credit card issuers and any individual or organization that extends or arranges consumer credit for which a finance charge is or may be payable or which is repayable by agreement in more than four installments. The law obviously applies to all financial institutions and may also apply to department stores, automotive, furniture and appliance dealers, craftsmen such as plumbers and electricians, and professional people.

Failure to make disclosures as required under the Truth-in-Lending Act subjects the violator to suit for actual damages by consumers plus twice the amount of the finance charge in the case of a credit transaction, as well as court costs and attorneys fees. Willfully or knowingly violating the Act or Regulation Z can result in criminal action and fines up to $5,000 or imprisonment for up to one year, or both. In addition, failure to comply with the fair credit billing provisions can result in a forfeiture penalty of up to $50.

GENERAL FINANCE CORP. v. GARNER
556 F. 2d 772 (1977)
U.S. Court of Appeals (5th Cir.)

■ ■ ■

In 1974, Ernest Garner purchased a car from Cantrell's Auto Sales in Columbus, Georgia. Garner signed a conditional sales contract granting the seller a security interest in the car. The contract required Garner to make 30 monthly payments of $86.19 each for a total of $2,585.70. In the same document, Cantrell's Auto Sales assigned the contract to General Finance Corp.

The record indicates that Garner made 11 monthly payments on the car. On February 11, 1975, after Ganer made the payment that was due for that month, he filed...a petition for relief under Chapter XIII of the Bankruptcy Act. Garner proposed to pay his creditors all that he owed them through the extension mechanism provided by Chapter XIII. Garner's plan called for a monthly payment to General Finance in the amount of $47.88.

General Finance rejected the plan. It filed a reclamation petition seeking possession of the car. Garner answered the petition alleging that the conditional sales contract violated the federal Truth-in-Lending Act. The bankruptcy judge agreed with Garner that the contract violated the Truth-in-Lending Act. The court concluded that Garner was entitled to a statutory penalty of $1,000.00 and to an attorney's fee of $150.00. The court, however, did not order General Finance to pay the penalty directly:

> The proof of claim filed by General Finance Corporation is in the amount of $1,637.61. We shall apply the $1,000.00 to this claim and allow the claim in the amount of $637.61. This would appear preferable to requiring General Finance Corporation to pay the sum of $1,000.00 to the debtor and increasing the payments under the plan to General Finance Corp. to $86.19 per month. The Chapter XIII Trustee should be instructed to pay to General Finance Corp. the sum of $47.88 per month as proposed in the original plan until General Finance Corporation has received the total of $637.61...

The district court approved the bankruptcy judge's conclusion that the conditional sales contract violated the disclosure provisions of the Truth-in-Lending Act and the Federal Reserve Board's regulations thereunder (Regulation Z), because the disclosure statement on the contract did not call attention to a provision in small type on the reverse side of the document dealing with a security interest in future indebtedness...

The Truth-in-Lending Act requires the creditor in the kind of transaction involved here to disclose

> [a] description of any security interest held or to be retained or acquired by the creditor in connection with the extension of credit, and a clear identification of the property to which the security interest relates.

The Federal Reserve Board's regulations require

> If after-acquired property will be subject to the security interest, or if other or future indebtedness is or may be secured by any such property, this fact shall be clearly set forth in conjunction with the description or identification of the type of security interest held, retained or acquired.

The future indebtedness term on the reverse side of the conditional sales contract here seems clearly to fall within the language both of the Act and of Regulation Z...

...General Finance contends that the spirit of the Truth-in-Lending Act will be served if disclosure is made at the time of any future advances, the theory being that Garner could then choose to go elsewhere for credit. This notion has been rejected by the Federal Reserve Board. Section 226.8(b)(5)... provides in part that

> [i]f after-acquired property will be subject to the security interest, or *if other or future indebtedness* is or may be secured by any such property, *this fact shall be clearly set forth* in conjunction with the description or identification of the type of security interest held, retained or acquired.

While this language is not without ambiguity... it is at least clear that the creditor may not wait until the future transaction to tell the debtor about the future indebtedness provision...

The implication of General Finance's argument is that it should be of no moment to the potential borrower that he is binding the collateral to cover any future debts owed to the creditor. We think, on the contrary, that Congress meant for the potential debtor to have such information when deciding whether he ought to deal with a particular lender...

■ ■ ■

Questions

1. What did General Finance Company fail to disclose in its credit terms with Garner which violated the Truth in Lending Act?
2. Do you agree that the consumer has the right to be informed of "credit terms" and of the various "security interests" retained by the creditor?

FEDERAL WARRANTY LEGISLATION

Consumers perceive warranties as added assurance of quantity and value. They assume that product performance is guaranteed if a written warranty accompanies its purchase. They view warranty provisions as a means of consumer redress for defective products. On the other hand,, marketers often regard warranties as promotional devices, rather than additional benefits for the consumer. They also view warranties as legal instruments which limit their obligations to consumers. The result of these opposing viewpoints is consumer confusion in comprehending warranty messages. The "legalese" language employed in warranties impedes the message to the consumers that the seller intends to limit his or her responsibilities in relation to the product sold. The resulting consumer dissatisfaction with warranties as an assurance of quality and consumer frustration with attempts to gain "satisfaction" through complex warranty provisions caused Congress to respond with the Magnuson-Moss Warranty Act which became law in 1975.

Even though the Warranty Act went into effect in 1975, its full impact has not yet been felt, because it provides only an outline of principles which must be further defined and implemented through rules promulgated by the Federal Trade Comission. While the Commission has prepared those rules that are mandatory under the Act, discretionary rule-making to further implement the Act are far from complete.

The Warranty Act has five primary purposes:

1. To improve the adequacy of warranty information available to consumers
2. To prevent deception with respect to warranties
3. To improve competition in warranties in the marketing of consumer products
4. To improve incentives for product reliability
5. To encourage warrantors to establish informal dispute settlement mechanisms

While the Act imposes no requirement that a consumer product be expressly warranted nor any requirement regarding the duration of expressed warranties, the Act does impose certain disclosure requirements and standards on warrantors who choose to give written warranties. Failure to comply with the Act's standards for warranties will subject the warrantor to action by the FTC or to action by a consumer class-action suit, if consumers have been damaged by the warrantor's failure to comply. The Act authorizes the court to award the consumer his legal expenses, including attorney's fees, as part of a judgment in favor of the consumer.

The Act applies when a written warranty is given in connection with the sale of consumer products—"any tangible personal property which is distributed in commerce and which is normally used for personal, family or household purposes." A warranty which is unambiguous and applying solely to services or workmanship is not covered by the Act. However, should the written warranty affirm both product performance and workmanship, such as basement waterproofing, it will be interpreted as a warranty subject to the terms of the Act. While a service contract may not be a warranty, the Act nevertheless stipulates that the terms of the service contract must be fully, clearly and conspicuously disclosed in simply and readily understood language.

Since products are capable of both personal and commercial uses, the "normal use" of the product is determinative in defining the scope of the Act. For example, the "normal use" of passenger autos is for personal or household purposes and, consequently, the auto warranty must comply with the Act as a consumer product. Finally, it should be noted that the Act does not apply to any warranty given in connection with the sale of real estate.

When a written warranty is given on a consumer product which costs the consumer more than ten dollas, the warranty must be clearly and conspicuously designated a "full warranty" or a "limited warranty." If a warranty is designated a full warranty, it must meet the Act's minimum standards for warranty:

1. There must be no charge for repairing the product if there is a defect within the warranty period.
2. There must be no limitation on the duration of implied warranty (such as merchantability).
3. Any exclusion or limitation of consequential damages for breach of express or implied warranty must appear clearly and conspicuously on the face of the warranty.
4. If the product cannot be repaired after a reasonable number of attempts, the consumer is permitted to elect either a replacement without charge or a refund.

This latter refund or replacement election of a consumer is often referred to as a "lemon-aid" provision because it aids a consumer who purchased a "lemon." Unfortunately, most consumers are not aware that "lemon-aid" is served only to those who purchase products under a "full warranty."

Two aditional requirements for full warranties under the Act include:

1. Warranty terms cannot be limited to the original purchaser only, but must extend to each purchaser who is a consumer of the product within the warranty period.
2. The warrantor may not impose any unreasonable duties on consumers as a condition of securing performance under the warranty.

While the Act did not establish any criteria for determing what is a "reasonable" duty to impose on a consumer, the FTC is authorized to develop rules to define such duties in detail in the future. Any warranty that does not meet the minimum standards for a full warranty must be designated as a "limited warranty."

Under the FTC Warranty Rule 702 sellers have the affirmative duty to make the text of the written warranties available for the buyer's review prior to sale. A variety of techniques are allowed by the FTC to accomplish this purpose. Rule 701 establishes the requirements for disclosure of warranty terms. It requires that the terms of the warranty clearly and conspiciously disclose the following:

1. The identity of the party to whom the warranty is extended
2. A clear identification of products, parts, or characteristics covered and excluded by the warranty
3. A statement of what the warrantor will do in the event of defect or failure of the product to perform
4. The point and time in which the warranty becomes effective if different from the purchase date
5. A step by step explanation of the procedure which the consumer should follow to obtain performance under the warranty
6. Information respecting any informal dispute settlement mechanism adopted by the warrantor
7. Certain mandatory statements if limitations are imposed on duration of implied warranties or consequential damages
8. A statement that the warranty confers specific legal rights

The Act allows warrantors an option to establish an informal dispute settlement procedure for resolving consumer complaints arising out of warranty obligations. Rule 703 defines the duties of the warrantor and the minimum requirements which must be met if the warrantor elects to implement such an informal procedure. The informal procedure must be disclosed in the written warranty and the warrantor must fund and operate the mechanism so that it is provided free of charge to consumers. If the warrantor provides such a mechanism, consumers may not bring civil suits under the Act until the dispute has been submitted to the informal proceedings. While the decision of the informal proceedings is not binding on the parties, it is admissable in evidence in subsequent civil suits relating to the matter decided.

Questions

1. How has the Warranty Act expanded the consumer's right to be informed?
2. What are the rights of the consumer under a "full warranty"?

CONSUMER'S RIGHT TO SAFETY

The consumer's right to safety involves protection against the marketing of goods which are hazardous to health, life, or economic well-being. Initially, the consumer's right to safety found expression in the common law doctrines that began the erosion of the concept of *caveat emptor*. Common law judges developed the implied warranties of merchantability and fitness for particular purpose which expressed the notion that consumers are entitled to some reasonable quality in goods to avoid personal harm. More recent trends include the judicial adoption of a strict tort liability on manufacturers who market defective goods which are hazardous to consumer health. However, the common law approach is one of compensating the consumer after he or she has become a victim of a defective product. The tort system is founded on the belief that the cost of the award to the injured consumer will motivate the manufacturer to improve production processes to avoid such costs arising from defective goods. However, society felt other *preventive* measures were necessary; consequently legislation attempting to prevent the marketing of unsafe products was created.

National product safey legislation consisted of a series of isolatd statutes designed to remedy specific hazards existing in a narrow range of product categories. For example, the Federal Food and Drug Administration was founded in 1931 to be responsible for the safety of drugs and medical devises and the purity of food. The Flammable Fabrics Act of 1953 was passed after serious injuries and deaths had resulted from the ignition of clothes made from synthetic fibers. The Federal Hazard Substances Labeling Act of 1960 mandated warnings on labels of potentially hazardous substances such as cleaning agents, and paint removers. The Child Protection Act of 1966 outlawed the marketing of potentially harmful toys and other articles intended for children.The Naional Traffic and Motor Vehicle Safety Act of 1966 was related specifically to automobiles. Among other things, tires must be labeled with the name of the manufacturer or retreader and with certain safety information, including the maximum permissible load for the tire. The Public Health Smoking Act and the Poison Prevention Packaging Act were both enacted in 1970 and in the following year the Lead-Based Paint Elimination Act was passed. The fragmentation of legislation and generally ineffective controls over product hazards prompted the Federal Government to introduce new product safety legislation to protect the consumer. The Consumer Product Safety Act of 1972 was the result.

CONSUMER PRODUCT SAFETY COMMISSION

The Consumer Product Safety Act created a five-member Consumer Products Safety Commission (CPSC) whose major function is to gather and disseminate information related to product injuries. The law require manufacturers to conduct testing programs to assure that their products conform to established safety standards. The law holds the manufacturer accountable for knowing all safety criteria applicable to the product, for testing the products, and for maintaining technical data relating to the performance and safety of the product. This information may have to be given to the consumer when purchasing the product. The Commission can require the use of specific labels that set forth the results of product testing. The manufacturer can be required to take corrective steps if he or she becomes aware of a defect that could created a substantial product hazard. The manufacturer may be required to publicize this information to consumers. The Commission can compel a manufacturer to refund the purchase price of the product, less a reasonable allowance for use, or to replace the product with a like or equivalent product that complies with the consumer product safety rules. The Commission can require manufacturers and distributors to establish and maintain books and records and make available information as the Commission deems necessary. The Commission also seeks to reduce product-related injury to consumers by mandating better designs and product instruction sheets. The commission is permitted to set product safety standards and to band those products which present "real" hazards to consumers which may not be made safe. Knowing violation of consumer product safety rules will subject the violator to a civil penalty of $2,000 for each offense or the maximum penalty of $500,000 for any related series of violations. Criminal penalties of $50,000, a year in jail, or both, can result when the Act is knowingly and wilfully violated after having received notice of noncompliance. In addition, the Commission may bring action to restrain the distribution of any consumer products that do not comply with its safety rules.

D. D. BEAN & SONS v. CONSUMER PRODUCTS SAFETY COM'N
574 F. 2d 643 (1978)
United States Court of Appeals (1st Cir.)

■ ■ ■

Petitioner D. D. Bean & Sons Co. (Bean), a manufacturer of paper book-matches..., seeks review of the Consumer Product Safety Commission's matchbook safety regulations... The Commission stated that the proposed regulation was "designed to reduce or eliminate...(e)ye injuries sustained by persons who use bookmatches that fragment and cause particles from such matches to lodge in a person's eye..."

The Commission's final rule contained the following design or "general" requirements...

"No matchhead in the matchbook shall be spilt, chipped, cracked, or crumbled."

The rule also listed the following "performance requirement" with which matchbooks must comply:

"A matchbook is defective... if it has, when tested...

"(b) A splint that separates into two or more pieces.
"(c)   A matchhead that produces fragments...

The commission will test for violations in accordance with detailed testing procedures that are set out at length in the Rule. The testing procedures call for a visual, post-manufacture inspection of matchbooks to insure compliance with the "general" requirements governing such matters as... splitting... of matchheads, etc. "Performance" defects are to be minimized by more elaborate testing. Samples from a lot are to be... tested under laboratory conditions for the incidence of fragmentation...

In ascertaining the sufficiency of the basis for the Commission's Rule we shall first inquire whether there is substantial evidence for its findings that... the listed hazard is in fact such. If it is, we shall next inquire whether the requirements addressed to... (the) hazard have been shown to be likely to reduce or eliminate it at a reasonable cost. Only after the existence of (the) hazard and the likelihood of its reduction at a reasonable cost have been established by the commission may it be said that the requirements are "reasonably necessary."

The commission's performance standards are fashioned to reduct the occurrene of matchhead fragmentation, and heads breaking off matches... The data from the Commission's survey of hospital emergency rooms and other studies indicate that roughly one-third of reported match-related injuries consist of fragments lodging in the eye. There are also some reported cases where a flaming fragment ignited a victim's clothing. One study indicated that entire matchheads occasionally fly off upon ignition, lodging in the eye or on clothing. We think therefore that there is sufficient evidence in the record to support the Commission's finding that a substantial hazard exists from matchhead fragmentation. We also think that the Commission was entitled to adopt the "general" requirements addressed to the fragmentation hazard. These call esentially for assurance that the matchbooks and matches do not contain obvious defects such as broken splints and matchheads and projecting staples which could lead to particles flying off when a match is struck. Compliance with these requirements may be insured by visual testing, a procedure which is presently the industry norm... And the design requirements themselves merely amount to insisting that the manufacturer produce matchbooks and matches that, on their face, do not contain obvious defects that seem logically to relate to a fragmentation risk. Since the cost of testing to ensure compliance with the general requirements geared to meeting the fragmentation hazard will therefore be slight, and the object of the requirements— ensuring a properly functioning product—seems only reasonable, we think that these requirements can be said to be "reasonably necessary" to reduce the risk from fragmentation.

However, we are not satisfied that the Commission has carried its burden of showing that the "performance" requirements geared to fragmentation are "reasonably necessary to eliminate or reduce" the risk to any significant degree. Performance requirements, unlike design requirements, cannot be tested for visually. The Commission itself conceds "that the principal cost effects on producers will arise from implementation of testing programs." Hence the effectiveness of these performance requirements in reducing risk is a matter of considerable importance.

There is a complete absence from the record of evidence tending to show the causes of fragmentation. The Commission has evidently proceeded on the assumption that fragmentation results from defective manufacturing procedures and will show up upon testing at the plant. However, manufacturers, in submissions to the commission, asserted that experience showed that post-manufacturer factors such as high humidity, perspiration, or misuse by consumers were principally responsible for fragmentation.

In view of the lack of evidence establishing the causes of fragmentation, and of the manufacturers' submissions claiming that post-manufacture handling causes most fragmentation, it is a large assumption that fragmentation is almost wholly attributable to the manufacturing process. Even then, the Commission's position on fragmentation establishes only that, at most "gross manufacturing errors" will be detected. But there is no evidence in the record from which the Commission could have determined that "gross errors," much less occasional defects occur with any frequency. It is just as possible to hypothesize that post-manufacture handling is the principal cause of fragmentation. We therefore think it speculative for the commission to find, on the present record, that the proposed fragmentation performance requirements will result in a significant decrease of the fragmentation risk. In view of this, the substantial, added cost of testing to insure compliance with the performance requirements cannot be justified...

■ ■ ■

Questions

1. What is the difference between a "design" requirement and a "performance" requirement?
2. What was the consumer "hazard" in *Bean*? What were the "requirements" to reduce the hazard? Were the requirements obtainable "at reasonable cost" to the manufacturer?

In late 1978, CPSC released its interpretative statement of the reporting requirements under the Consumer Product Safety Act. The CPSC allows five days for "reportable knowlege" to travel from "an official or employee who may reasonably be expected to be capable of appreciating the significance of the information" to the Chief Executive Office (CEO). Unless a written delegation of authority has been filed with CPSC, the CEO must notify the Commission within twenty-four hours of receiving reportable information. Reporting may be delayed an aditional ten days if the firm feels an investigation is needed to determine reportability. The commission will usually require a much more detailed "full report" at a later date. A "knowing" failure to report can result in a civil penalty (fine); and a "knowing and wilful" failure can result in a criminal penalty. It should be noted that the original equipment manufacturer and the component manufacturer are equally liable under the reporting requirements.

Under the new CPSC reporting policy, efficient internal procedures will be essential to insure that product safety information reaches the reporting officer. Internal controls will also be important to monitor the system to be sure that all the information is being transmitted quickly and accurately. People should be designated within the company (more than one if possible, to ensure cross checking) to bear responsibility for reporting to top officials even the slightest chance that a defect may be occurring. Employees should be notified in writing that they are exected to report possible product defect, and all parts suppliers should likewise be notified that the company expects immediate reporting of any posible defects that may cause a safety hazard. Once the reporting system is set up and a specific routine becomes mandatory, it should be regularily reviewed for effectiveness.

In 1978 Congress gave the CPSC a three-year life extension. The next three years will probably see CPSC action in the following areas: (1) enforcement of existing regulations, as with the product hazard reporting rules; (2) litigation, that is, proving "real risk" in the courts in order to uphold CPSC regulations; (3) research, such as dangers of asbestos, energy conservation devices, projectile toys, and smoke detectors; (4) policy development, such as with carcinogens and children's sleepwear; (5) voluntary standard development by outside groups; (6) establishing mandatory product safety standards; and (7) consumer education, as with the safe use of skateboards and bicycles.

As a result of the Supreme Court decision concerning OSHA's right to inspect without warrant, the CPSC has re-evaluated its own inspection procedures and determined that, henceforward, all employers will be given advance notice of CPSC inspections. the notice will include a statement that describes the purpose of the inspection and the nature of the information sought. Besides inspecting the premises, the CPSC inspector can obtain information from employees, examine all records, books, and documents, and obtain samples of any items and materials or substances necessary to an effective inspection. Should the employer refuse admittance to the CPSC official, the Commission may seek compulsory process by a search warrant, subpoena of witnesses, subpoena deposition, order a written interrogatory, issue orders seeking information, or oder an investigational hearing.

MANAGER'S RESPONSIBILITY

Governmental inspection of production, processing, and storage facilities of industry is an important means of preventing dangerous goods from reaching the consumer. However, for the government's inspection and warning system to work effectively, managers of business firms must instigate appropriate action to eliminate the discovered violations. The following case ilustrates the increasingly strict standards that the law is beginning to develop to help assure managerial action after governmental warnings.

U.S. v. PARK
421 U.S. 658 (1975)
Supreme Court of the United States

[Acme Markets, Inc. is a national retail food chain with over 800 retail outlets and 12 warehouses. Acme Markets, Inc. and its chief Executive Officer, Park, were charge with criminal violations of the Federal Food, Drug, and Cosmetic Act. It was alleged that Acme Markets, Inc. held food in a building accessible and exposed to contamination by rodents. In April, 1970 the FDA advised Park by letter of the unsanitary conditions in Acme's warehouse. A second inspection by the FDA in March, 1972 revealed continued evidence of rodent activity in the building. While Acme pleaded guilty, Park pleaded not guilty. Park moved for a judgment of acquittal on the grounds that the evidence did not show that he was personally concerned in this violation. He maintains that he directed a divisional vice president to investigate the situation and take corrective action. Park stated that he did not believe there was anything else he could have done more constructively than what he had done. Park was found guilty by a jury and sentenced to pay a fine of $50 on each of five counts. The Court of Appeals reversed.]

■ ■ ■

BURGER, Mr. Chief Justice.

The rule that corporate employees who have "a responsible share in the furtherance of the transaction which the statute outlaws" are subject to the criminal provision of the Act was not formulated in a vacuum. Cases under the Federal Food and Drugs Act of 1906 reflected the view both that knowledge or intent were not required to be proved in prosecutions under its criminal provision, and that responsible corporate agents could be subjected to the liability thereby imposed. Moreover, the principle had been recognized that a corporate agent, through whose act, default, or omission the corporation committed a crime, was himself guilty individually of that crime. The principle had been applied whether or not the crime required "consciousness of wrongdoing", and it has been applied not only to those corporate agents who themselves committed the criminal act, but also to those who by virtue of their managerial positions or other similar relations to the act could be deemed responsible for its commission.

In the latter class of cases, the liability of managerial officers did not depend on their knowledge of, or personal participation in, the act made criminal by the statute. Rather, where the statute under which they were prosecuted dispensed with "consciousness of wrongdoing", an omission or failure to act was deemed a sufficient basis for a responsible corporate agent's liability. It was enough in such cases that, by virtue of the relationship he bore to the corporation, the agent had the power to have prevented the act complained of...

...(T)he Court has reaffirmed the proposition that "the public interest in the purity of its food is so great as to warrant the imposition of the highest standard of care on distributors." In order to make "distributors of food the strictest censors of their merchandise," the Act punishes "neglect where the law requires care, or inaction where it imposes a duty." "The accused, if he does not will the violation, usually is in a position to prevent it with not more care than society might reasonably expect and no more exertion than it might reasonably exact from one who assumed his responsibilities." Similarly,... the court of appeals have recognized that those corporate agents vested with the responsibility, and power commensurate with that responsibility, to devise whatever measures are necessary to ensure compliance with the Act bear a "responsible relationship" to, or have a "responsible share" in, violations.

Thus... the cases which have followed reveal that in providing sanctions which reach and touch the individuals who execute the corporate mission—and this is by no means necessarily confined to a single corporate agent or employee — the Act imposes not only a positive duty to seek out and remedy violations when they occur but also and primarily a duty to implement measures that will insure that violations will not occur. The requirements of foresight and vigilance imposed on responsible corporate agents are beyond question demanding, and perhaps onerous, but they are no more stringent than the public has a right to expect of those who voluntarily assume positions of authority in business enterprises whose services and products affect the health and well-being of the public that supports them....

The Act does not... make criminal liability turn on "awareness of some wrongdoing" or "conscious fraud." The duty imposed by Congress on responsible corporate agents is, we emphasize, one that requires the highest standard of foresight and vigilance, but the Act, in its criminal aspect, does not require that which is objectively impossible. The theory upon which responsible corporate agents are held criminally accountable for "causing" violations of the Act permits a claim that a defendant was "powerless" to prevent or correct the violation to "be raised defensively at a trial on the merits." If such a claim is made, the defendant has the burden of coming forward with evidence, but this does not alter the Government's ultimate burden of proving beyond a reasonable doubt the defendant's guilt, including his power, in light of the duty imposed by the Act, to prevent or correct the prohibited condition. Congress has seen fit to enforce the acountability of responsible corporate agents dealing with products which may affect the health of consumers by penal sanctions cast in rigorous terms, and the obligation of the courts is to give them effect so long as they do not violate the Constitution....

■ ■ ■

Questions

1. Do managerial officers have to know of, or personally participate in the activity before they can be convicted of a crime?
2. Just what was the criminal behavior of Parks? Was he "powerless" to prevent the violation?

3. A previous court decision dealing with the same problem recognized that the Act dispenses with the need to prove "consciousness of wrong doing." As such, it may result in a hardship as applied to those who share "responsibility in the business process." But, the court added: "In such matters the good sense of prosecutors, the wise guidance of trial judges, and the ultimate judgment of juries must be trusted." Are these sufficient protections against a "hardship" prosecution?

FINANCIAL SAFETY

Recent legislation and FTC rule-making authority have been directed toward the protection of the consumer's "financial safety." Financial safety of the consumer involves protection against economic loss occurring by some method other than personal harm. For example, in previous discussion (Chapter 7) the FTC promulgated a rule to preserve consumers' defenses against a holder in due course of commercial paper. Another example is the Fair Credit Reporting Act of 1970. It was passed by Congress to protect consumers against the circulation of inaccurate or obsolete information, and insure that consumer reporting agencies exercise their responsibilities in a manner that is fair and equitable to consumers. Under the law the consumer has the right to be told the name of the consumer reporting agency that prepared the consumer report used to deny the consumer either credit, insurance, or employment. While the consumer does not have the right to request a copy or physically examine the file of the credit bureau, the consumer must be told the nature, substance, and sources of the information (except medical) collected. The consumer also has the right to have incomplete or incorrect information reinvestigated and inaccurate or unverifiable information removed from his or her files. Those individuals who previously received the incomplete information must be notified by the agency that such information has been deleted from the consumer's file. When a dispute between the consumer and the reporting agency exists over information in the consumer's file, the consumer has the right to have his or her version of the dispute placed in the file and included in future consumer reports.

To protect the privacy of the consumer, he or she must be notified by any business that is seeking information about him or her, which would constitute an "investigative consumer report." After notification, the consumer may request from that business more information about the nature and scope of the investigation and have such report withheld from anyone who under the law does not have a legitimate business need for the information. The consumer, of course, can discover the nature and substance (but not the sources) of the information that was collected for the report. Adverse information of the consumer which is over seven years old may be removed from the files, except for bankruptcy which must remain in the file for fourteen years. The consumer is empowered to sue the reporting agency for damages if it negligently violates the law. The consumer can collect attorney fees and court costs if succesful.

The Fair Credit Reporting Act also deals with credit cards in the following case:

NATIONAL COM'L BANK & TRUST CO. v. MALIK
339 N.Y.S. 2d 605 (1972)
Supreme Court, Albany County, N.Y.

■ ■ ■

...[T]he plaintiff seeks to recover the sum of $3,304.01 for unauthorized purchases made through the use of a Master Charge credit card which was issued by the plaintiff to Thomas S. Eldridge and his wife Ann R.Eldridge. While shopping at the defendant's gift store on April 13, 1971, Mrs. Eldridge used the credit card to make a purchase and inadvertently left the card at the defendants's store, and it was found by one of the defendant's employees. Mrs. Eldridge was notified by a telephone call from the defendant's employee that the credit card was there and she then requested that the credit card be held for her until she could pick it up on April 19, 1971. The defendant's employee agreed to hold it for her. Thereafter, the credit card disappeared from defendant's possession and was used to make unauthorized purchases of $3,304.01. The credit card was subsequently recovered by the authorities on April 23, 1971 at a store in Albany. On June 30, 1971, Thomas S. Eldridge and his wife Ann R. Eldridge assigned to the plaintiff all claims which they then had against the defendant resulting from the above-described events.

The complaint of the plaintiff assignee contains three causes of action. The first cause of action is predicated upon the fact that defendant wrongfully allowed the credit card to fall into the possession of unauthorized persons who used it to make unauthorized purchases... The second cause of action states that the loss of the credit card and the consequent damages were caused by the negligence of the defendant. The third cause of action is predicated on a breach of an alleged bailment of the credit card ...The Federal Truth in Lending Act, 15 U.S.C., Section 1643(a) states, in part, as follows:

> "A cardholder shall be liable for the unauthorized use of a credit card only if the card is an accepted credit card, the liability is not in excess of $50, the card issuer gives adequate notice to the cardholder of the potential liability, the card issuer has provided the cardholder with a self-addressed, prestamped notification to be mailed by the cardholder in the event of the loss or theft of the credit card, and the unauthorized use occurs before the cardholder has notified the card issuer that an unauthorized use of the credit card has occurred or may occur as the result of loss, theft, or otherwise...

Section 1643(c) makes this the greatest liability that can be imposed on a card holder regardless of all other applicable laws or agreements. Section 1643(d) states that the liability imposed by this section is the only liability to which a card holder can be subject for the unauthorized use of his credit card. Section 1643(b) places the burden of proof on the card issuer to show that the conditions of liability for the unauthorized use of a credit card as set forth in subsection (a) have been met.

The plaintiff does not contend that it complied with the Truth in Lending Act.

The assignors, the Eldridges, under the existing circumstances of this case and under the applicable statutes, cannot and were not subject to any liability for the misuse of their credit card and therefore suffer no damages through the loss of the card. The claims of the plaintiff assignee, herein, are therefore claims without damages.

The other two causes of action based on negligence and a bailment must also fail. the defendant herein was at most a gratuitous bailee, that is a depository without compensation for the benefit of the plaintiff's assignor, and therefore only liable for gross negligence. Liability for negligence depends on the existence of a duty or obligation recognized by law by one party to another; the breach of that duty; and a finding that the proximate cause of that breach resulted in damages, and actual loss or damage, and that the plaintiff be free of contributory negligence. The plaintiff herein fails to establish any of these elements.

■ ■ ■

Questions

1. There are a series of conditions that must exist before a card holder can be liable for unauthorized use of a credit card. What are those conditions?
2. If the Eldridges were not liable, why couldn't the defendant store be liable? Was the store liable for negligence or as a bailee?

FAIR DEBT COLLECTION PRACTICES

The Fair Debt Collection Practices Act became effective in 1978 and prohibits abusive, deceptive, and unfair debt collection practices by debt collectors. The law will not permit collectors to use unjust means when attempting to collect a debt.

Obviously, the law does not cancel genuine debts owed by the consumer. The law indicates that a debt collector may not contact the consumer in person at inconvenient or unusual times and places. The consumer can even stop a debt collector from contacting him by saying so in writing. The debt collector must not tell anyone else that the consumer owes money or utilize postcards or envelopes which identify the debt collector. The debt collector may not use threats or violence, repetitious phone calls, or advertise the consumer's debt. The debt collector may not use any false statements—such as implying that the collector represents the government, is an attorney, or that the consumer has committed a crime. Moreover, the debt collector may not say that any action will be taken against the consumer which cannot legally be taken.

The consumer has the right to sue the debt collector within one year from the date the law was violated for any damages suffered. The consumer is entitled to court costs and attorney fees if the violation is proven. Class action by consumers are authorized up to $500,000.

HOME SOLICITATION SALES

A number of statutes or administrative rules are aimed at the evils involved in home solicitation sales. To avoid the "slick talking" salesmen or high pressured sales tactics sometimes employed, the statute provides the consumer with a chance to think things over during a "cooling off period." If the consumer decides against the purchase, the law usually affords a right of cancellation. The following case involves the consumer's effort to utilize state law, federal law, and finally, an administrative rule to avoid a home solicitation sale.

DONNELLY v MUSTANG POOLS, INC.
374 N.Y.S. 2d 967 (1975)
Supreme Court of New York

■ ■ ■

On September 5, 1974, the plaintiffs and the defendant entered into an agreement for the construction of a 17 x 35 in-ground pool at the residence of plaintiffs. The contract provided for a cash price of $5500.00. By the terms of the contract, the plaintiffs were credited with a $50.00 down payment, leaving a balance of $5450.00 The contract also provided that a payment was due November 1st in the amount of $1800.00, leaving a balance of $3,650.00. The contract further provided that the sum of $3,000.00 would be paid upon delivery of the pool equipment; another $350.00 would be paid when the construction was half-completed and, finally, the balance of $300.00 was due on completion. The installment was to begin, as near as the Court is able to determine, in the Spring of 1975.

After the execution of the contract, the plaintiffs had second thoughts about the construction of this pool and sought to be relieved of whatever liability they might have under the contract. Sometime after the 23rd of April, 1975, the plaintiffs commenced this action against the defendant alleging in substance that the defendant failed and neglected to furnish plaintiffs with a statement of their right to cancel the contract within three days, allegedly as required by Article 10-A of the Personal Property Law and Regulation Z of the Federal Consumer Credit Code. Plaintiffs claim that because of the failure of the contract to provide for the right of cancellation, they have the right to rescind the contract absolutely. . .

Article 10-A of the Personal Property Law of the State of New York attempts to deal with the problems created by the so-called "door-to-door" sales. This Article of the Personal Property Law states as its purpose: ". . . to afford consumers, subjected to high pressure door-to-door sales tactics, a 'cooling-off' period." That Article defines a consumer transaction as a transaction wherein the money, property, or service which is the subject of the transaction is primarily for personal, family or household purposes.

There is no question that this agreement entered into between the parties for the construction of a pool at the residence of plaintiffs falls within the meaning of the definition as set forth in § 426.

Article 10-A, § 426, subd. 2 of the Personal Property Law defines a home solicitation sale as a consumer transaction in which payment of the purchase price *is deferred over time*, and the Seller or a person acting for him, is a person doing business who engages in a personal solicitation of the sale. The Buyer's agreement or purchase offer is made at a place other than the place of business of the Seller or a person acting for him.

The contract was executed at the residence of the plaintiffs and it meets one part of the definition of a home solicitation sale. However, the fact that the payments were not required to be made over a period of time, notwithstanding that payments were to be made at certain scheduled times prior to completion of the installation of the pool, does not bring the transaction within Article 10-A of the Personal Property Law. The contract, under a fair interpretation of all its terms, was a cash transaction upon completion and was not a "time payment plan" embracing the payment for the construction of the pool after its completion. Thus, the transaction, viewed as a whole, is a cash transaction, payable on completion and does not come within the definition of a home solicitation sale as set forth in Article 10-A of the Personal Property Law.

Plaintiffs contend, in the alternative, that the transction is governed by Regulation Z pursuant to the Federal Truth-in-Lending Act. The plaintiffs, relying on Regulation Z, claim that the fact that payments were required in more than four installments brings the transaction within the purview of Regulation Z, requiring a three day cooling off period which was, concededly, not contained in the contract in dispute. Subdivision (a) of § 1635 of Title 15 of U.S. Code provides, as it applies to this dispute:

"In the case of any consumer credit transaction in which a security interest is retained or acquired in any real property which is used or is expected to be used as the residence of the person to whom credit is extended, the obligor shall have the right to rescind the transaction until midnight the third business day following the consummation of the transaction or the delivery of the disclosures required under this part, whichever is later..."

Subdivision (k) of § 226.2 of Regulation Z provides:

" 'Consumer credit' means credit offered or extended to a natural person...for which either a finance charge is or may be imposed or which pursuant to an agreement,is or may be payable in more than four installments."

It appears therefore that the key to bringing this transaction within the purview of Regulation Z is the offering or extending of credit for which either a finance charge *is or may be imposed* or which pursuant to an agreement *is or may be payable in more than four installments...*

If you included the down payment, the contract in question would be clearly within the ambit of § 226.2(k) of Regulation Z, thus requiring the three day notice of cancellation in the contract in question.

The Court has examined the Truth-in-Lending Manual Supplement, Appendix E. submitted by the attorneys for the defendant. Advisory Letter No. 695, dated July 6, 1973, states that the staff's view is that in computing the number of installments, any down payment is not considered to be an installment for purposes of § 226.2(k) of Regulation Z.

In view of this, and since the contract calls for only four installment payments, exclusive of the down payment, the contract does not come within the notice of cancellation requirements of Regulation Z.

However, the plaintiffs are not without hope to extricate themselves from what they feel to be a difficult situation.

On October 18, 1972, the Federal Trade Commission promulgated a Trade Regulation Rule concerning a cooling-off period for door-to-door sales...The Rule provides that...it constitutes an unfair and deceptive act or practice for any seller to fail to furnish the buyer with a fully completed copy of the contract, and which contains a statement in substantially the following form:

"You, the buyer, may cancel this transaction at any time prior to midnight of the third business day after the date of this transaction. See the attached notice of cancellation form for an explanation of this right."

The Rule also defines a door-to-door sale as a sale, lease, or rental of consumer goods or services with a purchase price of $25.00 or more, whether under a single or multiple contracts, in which the Seller or his representative personally solicits the sale, including those in response to or following an invitation by the Buyer, and the Buyer's agreement or offer to purchase is made at a place other than the place of business of the Seller.

Clearly, the transaction with which we are concerned falls within the definition of the door-to-door sale as set forth in the Federal Trade Commission Regulation Rule effective June 7, 1974.

As pointed out earlier in this decision, the contract contained no notice of cancellation provision. The contract, although it did not fall within the purview of Article 10-A of the Personal Property Law of New York or Regulation Z, does fall within the purview of the Federal Trade Commission Rule.

Accordingly, since the contract failed to contain the required notice concerning the right to cancel the transaction, and in view of the fact that it did not contain the necessary notice of cancellation as required by the above referred to Trade Regulation Rule, the Court hereby declares that the contract entered into between the plaintiffs and the defendant is in violation of that Regulation and is therefore subject to cancellation by plaintiffs.

■ ■ ■

Questions

1. Why was the Personal Property Law in the State of New York ineffective as a means of cancellation for the consumer?
2. Why was the Truth-in-Lending Act's cancellation provision not available to the consumer?
3. What scheme of regulation is utilized by the Federal Trade Commission to provide "cooling off" periods in door-to-door sales?
4. How do these laws protect the consumer's "financial safety"?

CONSUMER'S RIGHT TO BE HEARD

The consumer's right to be heard includes the right to receive full consideration of the consumer's interests in the formulation of governmental policy. Incresingly, this right includes the right to fair and active participation by consumer advocates in hearings that formulate governmental policy.

In theory, regulatory agencies that oversee public utilities are charged to protect the public interest which also includes protection of the consumer. The law often grants monopolies over water, gas, electricity, telephone, public transportation, and others if the firms accept governmental restrictions imposed by administrative agencies. Since the services and goods produced by these regulated industries are paid for by the consumer, the agencies seek to balance a "fair price" to the consumer for these services and products with a "fair return" to the supplier. Regulation seeks, like competition, to provide satisfactory services at rates that make efficient use of natural resources. However, in practice, the performance of regulatory agencies has not always been satisfactory from the consumer's point of view. The regulatory agencies usually set price levels on a cost-plus basis and interfere little in the development of standards of quality for service or products. Many feel this performance results from the fact that the agencies are susceptible to great private pressures from the industries they regulate. In contrast, the appearance of consumer groups before agencies occurs less often and with less impact.

The imbalance of consumer advocacy in administrative hearings that determine policy has been increasingly recognized in judicial decisions and legislative debates and proposals. In *United Church of Christ v. FCC* 359 F. 2d 994 (D.C. Cir. 1966) an allegedly racist Mississippi radio station was applying for a renewal of its license before the Federal Communication Commission. The Church petitioned for a right to intervene and present evidence and arguments in opposition to the relicensing.The FCC refused to hear the Church on grounds that the listening public has not suffered an injury and that if the listeners had "standing to sue" in these cases, it would pose great administrative burdens on the agency. The court of appeals disagreed with the FCC and remanded the case back to the FCC with the provision that some "audience participation" be allowed in the new proceedings before the Commission. The court determined that unless consumers could be heard, there might be no one bringing program deficiencies or offensive commercialization to the attention of the Commission in an effective manner. As this case indicates,there is a growing body of case law in which the courts are requiring federal agencies to take in account the consumer groups that are being affected by the agency's decisions.

The concept of intervention before regulatory bodies by attorney generals is also growing. Since attorney generals are generally charged with the responsibility of representation before various bodies of state government, the attorney general may intervene to present various sides of an issue before a commission. It is not uncommon for two assistant attorney generals to appear on opposite sides on the same case before a commission.

There has also been a consumer movement to establish a federal consumer protection agency to represent the consumer interest in other federal agencies. In 1971, the House of Representatives passed a Consumer Protection Agency Bill by a vote of 344 to 44. However, the Senate did not pass a similar version and by 1975, the vote in the House on the proposed agency was only 208 to 199. In February of 1978 the House scuttled the Consumer Protection Agency Bill by a 227 to 198 vote. The consumer proponents of consumer advocacy have since proposed the Public Participation in Federal Agency Proceedings Act. The act would authorize federal agencies to pay the fees of lawyers and expert witnesses who participate in agency proceedings. When individuals and organizations that represent a consumer or public interest viewpoint would be forclosed from participation because the cost of representation would be prohibitive or the financial interest of the consumer groups would be too small in relation to the cost of representation, such participants would be eligible for payment under the act. The consumer proponents feel that the Participation Act does not have the same effect as the creation of an office of consumer representation. They feel the participation approach carries less of a "big government" connotation which was utilized to defeat the Consumer Protection Agency bill.

CONSUMER'S RIGHT TO RECOVER

At common law the consumer's remedy for deception and misrepresentation by the seller was an action for the tort of fraud. However, the elements to establish fraud are difficult barriers for the consumer to surmount. As a consequence, the consumer's right to recovery was and continues to be frustrated often. Therefore, alternate means to establish the consumer's right to recovery are slowly evolving

The FTC Improvement Act of 1975 provides that the FTC may seek "rescission or reformation of contracts, the refund of money or return of property, (or) the payment of damages" on behalf of consumers. This provision empowers the FTC to bring an action on behalf of consumers and seek recovery of monies for the consumers.

The Consumer Product Safety Commission has been empowered to compel a manufacturer to refund the purchase price of the product, less a reasonable allowance for use, or to replace the product with a like or equivalent product that complies with the consumer product safety rules. In like manner, the Department of Transportation's enforcement of the National Traffic and Motor Vehicle Safety Act against Firestone Tire and Rubber Company resulted in an agreement by Firestone to refund or replace a tire it sold which was alleged to be unsafe for consumers.

On the state level, "Little FTC" Acts authorize state officials to seek restitution for aggrieved consumers in forty-seven jurisdictions. Moreover, sixteen states allow for consumer class actions. Individual private actions by a consumer are authorized in forty-two states. While the consumer's right to recovery is being increasingly recognized in legislation, the right of recovery has been especially utilized as a scheme for consumer redress in the Uniform Consumer Credit Code (UCCC) which has been enacted in seven jurisdictions. The following case illustrates the UCCC approach to the consumer's right of recovery.

STRADER v. BENEFICIAL FINANCE COMPANY OF AURORA
551 P. 2d 720 (1976)
Supreme Court of Colorado

[Robert and Margaret Strader, petitioners, secured a loan from Beneficial Finance Company. The loan was closed on December 1, 1971, secured by a deed on Strader's residence and a security interest on their household furnishings. Beneficial failed to disclose the annual rate of interest as required by the UCCC making no entry in the blank provided for the disclosure on the statement furnished to the Straders. In June, 1972, the Colorado UCCC Administration made a routine audit of Beneficial and discovered that several disclosures, including those on the Straders' loan, had not been made. The Administration ordered corrections. In October, 1972, a follow-up audit revealed that the correction still had not been made. Beneficial informed the Straders of the correct percentage rate of 19.07 percent on or about November 17, 1972. The Straders, therefore, notified Beneficial by a letter dated November 20, 1972, of their intentions to rescind the loan. Beneficial took no action, and on December 7, 1972, the Straders filed the complaint with the Office of Consumer Affairs, requesting assistance in terminating the security interest held by Beneficial. The Straders also stopped making loan payments to Beneficial. This action was filed by the Straders in March, 1973.]

■ ■ ■

...The Straders argue that, under the facts of this case... section 5-5-204 of the UCCC relieves them from the remaining obligation on the note.

The trial court properly held that section 5-5-204(1) allows for a rescission of a consumer loan transaction in which a security interest is retained in land used as the debtor's residence. The right to rescind must be exercised, pursuant to the provisions in that section within three days of the "consummation of the transaction or the delivery of the disclosures required... whichever is later... " Recission is effected by the debtor's "notifying the creditor, in accordance with rules of the administrator, of his intention to do so." Section 5-5-204(1).

The Straders rely upon section 5-5-204(2) which states:

"(2) When a debtor exercises his right to rescind under subsection (1) of this section, he is not liable for any credit service charge, loan finance charge, or other charge, and any security interest given by the debtor becomes void upon the recission. Within ten days after receipt of notice of recission, the creditor shall return to the debtor the money or property given as earnest money, down payment, or otherwise, and shall take any action necessary or appropriate to reflect the termination of any security interest created under the transaction. If the creditor has delivered property to the debtor, the debtor may retain possession of it. Upon the performance of the creditor's obligations under this section, the debtor shall tender the property to the creditor, except that if return of the property in kind would be impracticable or inequitable, the debtor shall tender its reasonable value. Tender shall be made at the location of the property or at the residence of the debtor, at the option of the debtor. If the creditor does not take possession of the property within ten days after tender by the debtor, ownership of the property vests in the debtor without obligation on his part to pay for it.". . .

Section 5-5-204(2) states that upon recission, any security interest given by the debtor becomes void by law. The creditor is specifically obligated to take any action necessary or appropriate to reflect the termination of that security interest within ten days after receipt of the notice of recission. No duty is imposed upon the debtor until after the performance of the creditor's obligations. Until the obligations are performed, the debtor, as the court of appeals held, is entitled to retain possession of any property delivered from the creditor to the debtor.

Beneficial, in the present case, did not fulfill its obligations under the statute by releasing the security interests in the Straders' furniture and home. The Straders were forced to retain counsel and resort to litigation in order to compel Beneficial to meet its statutory obligations.

The creditor is required to remove cloud on the title of the debtor's residence within ten days. Then and only then is the debtor obligated to tender. After tender by the debtor, if the creditor fails to take possession of the property tendered "ownership of the property vests in the debtor without obligation to pay. . ." We hold that this statutory provision is intended as an impetus for the creditor to take immediate action to clear title and to fulfill its obligations. If not interpreted in this way, there is no stimulus for the creditor to comply with the statutory provisions requiring him to release the security interests within the ten day period. . .

We hold. . . that the requirement of tender arises only after the security interest is released. If it is not released within the ten days following notice of rescission, the debtor is relieved of the obligation to tender and the property vests in the debtor. As used, "property" is the unpaid principal balance of the loan, and the Straders have no obligation to pay that unpaid principal.

Beneficial argues that there is a distinction between "property", and the balance of a consumer loan. In other words, Beneficial would limit "property" to that purchased on credit. We do not agree. We think the consumer borrower and the consumer buyer are to be treated the same under the statute. Section 5-5-204, C.R.S. 1973 expressly applies to consumer credit sales and consumer loans.

We are not unmindful of. . . a split of authority in this regard, but think the holding here is the better view in light of the purposes and policies of the UCCC.

■ ■ ■

Questions

1. Which party is required by the UCCC to act first, the creditor releasing the security interest or the debtor returning the property?
2. What is the statutory scheme that "encourages" the creditor to release the security interest in the property?

13

SECURITIES LAW

Although securities and the trading of securities have deep historical roots, laws regulating the securities trading process are of most recent origin. The speculative pricing of securities in unchartered stock companies of England caused Parliament to pass the South Sea Bubble Act of 1720, which substantially prohibited the formation of unchartered corporations and outlawed the securities of unchartered companies. In the United States, however, the laws dealing with transactions in securities were not passed until states authorized general incorporation statutes during the industrialization process following the Civil War. In addition, to avoid fraudulent sales of securities, states passed "blue-sky" laws, so named because a judge once referred to a fraudulent security as having no more value "than so many fee of blue sky." Federal regulation of securities transactions began after the crash of the securities market in the late twenties.

BLUE-SKY LAWS

Nearly every state in the country has laws regulating the issuance of securities to its residents. The purpose of such laws is to prevent abuses by promoters of speculative ventures. The blue-sky laws differ from state to state. Most states have a fraud-type law with fraud-penalty provisions. A securities violation can result in criminal prosecution and injunctions barring future utilization of such practices. Other states require registration of brokers and dealers who sell securities. Such laws were enacted in an effort to regulate the person who sells securities in those states. Some states utilize a registration-type of securities law which requires the filing of information about the issuer with some state official. The laws of these states empower state officials to determine whether the securities themselves are "fair"deals in relation to the buying public. For example, in California, a security offering must meet a "fair, just, and equitable" standard before the security can be registered for distribution.

FEDERAL SCHEME OF REGULATION

When Congress determined to regulate securities, it had the advantage of surveying the various state efforts at security regulation before determing the federal approach to this problem. Congress rejected the notion that a federal bureaucracy should make a judgment concerning the worth or fairness of securities offered to the public. Instead, Congress utilized concepts embodied in blue-sky laws which include the designation of fraudulent activities, the registration of dealers in securities and the registration of information about the issuers of securities to be offered to the public. The essence of the federal approach is disclosure. The draftsmen of the federal laws viewed the responsibility of the federal government a being one primarily to assure investors access to enough information to enable them to arrive at rational decisions. The fundamental purpose of securities law is to substitute the philosophy of full disclosure for the philosophy of *caveat emptor* and thus achieve a higher standard of business ethics in the securities industry.

SECURITIES AND EXCHANGE COMMISSION

The financial community that deals in securities may be divided into two activities: the *distribution* (issuance) of securities and the *trading* of securities. The *distribution* involves the raising of capital for corporations and government entities through the new issuance of securities. The distribution function is often called "underwriting" and this activity is principally regulated by the Securities Act of 1933. On the other hand, *trading* of securities involves transactions whereby outstanding securities are traded or bought and sold among members of the public. Transactions are often executed through professional financial houses, through the exchanges or through the over-the-counter market. These secondary transactions are regulated primarily by The Securities Exchange Act of 1934

The Securities and Exchange Commission (SEC) was created by the Securities Exchange Act of 1934. As an independent, bipartisan agency, it administers laws which seek to protect investors and the general public in securities transactions. Laws administered by the SEC are briefly explained in Table 13-1. The Commission also advises federal courts in corporate reorganization proceedings under Chapter 10 of the National Bankruptcy Act. It studies any proposed reorganization plan and issues a report on whether the proposal is fair, feasible, and equitable.

THE ISSUANCE OF SECURITIES

THE WORK OF THE SECURITIES AND EXCHANGE COMMISSION
(Published by the SEC, March, 1973)

SECURITIES ACT OF 1933

■ ■ ■

This "truth in securities" law has two basic objectives: (a) to provide investors with material financial and other information concerning securities offered for public sale; and (b) to prohibit misrepresentation, deceit and other fraudulent acts and practices in the sale of securities generally (whether or not required to be registered).

REGISTRATION OF SECURITIES

The first objective applies to securities offered for public sale by an issuing company or any person in a control relationship to such company. Before the public offering of such securities, a registration statement must be filed with the commission by the issuer, setting forth the required information. When the statement has become effective, the securities may be sold. The purpose of registration is to provide disclosure of financial and other information on the basis of which investors may appraise the merits of the securities. To that end, investors must be furnished with a prospectus (selling circular) containing the salient data set forth in the registration statement to enable them to evaluate the securities and make informed and discriminating investment decisions...

Table 13-1

LAWS ADMINISTERED BY THE SEC

Securities Act of 1933	Previously administered by the Federal Trade Commission, this law is now under the jurisdiction of the SEC. It provides that securities which are offered to the public must be registered with the SEC unless there is a specific exemption for the transaction. Assuming no exemption, the registration statement containing a prospectus must be filed giving specified information and the SEC will judge the completeness and accuracy of the filing. The prospectus then must be delivered to potential buyers as means of disclosing critical information about the company. There are specific penalties for material mis-statement in registration.
Securities Exchange Act of 1934	This Act created the SEC and is concerned with the trading of securities. The companies listed on stock exchanges or having more than 500 shareholders must file certain regular reports with the SEC, including a Form 10-K annually, and Form 10-Q quarterly, annual proxy statements, and a Form 8-K for special events. The '34 Act also contains a general fraud provision applicable to all securities sold in interstate commerce, even though they are exempt from registration.
Public Utility Holding Company Act of 1935	This Act was enacted to correct abuses in the financing and operation of electric and gas public-utilities holding-company systems. Such systems had been complicated by the formation of large holding companies on top of the operating companies and a substantial amount of pyramiding.
Trust Indenture Act of 1939	This Act requires that publicly held debt be issued pursuant to contract, an indenture, which must contain specific provisions to protect the public. For each debt issued, there must be a trustee who is obligated in the event of default to protect the public debt holder as if the trustee were a "prudent man" acting on his own behalf.
Investment Company Act of 1940	This Act subjects investment holding companies (mutual funds) to certain statutory prohibitions and to Commission regulation deemed necessary to protect the interest of investors and the public. The Commission does not supervise the investment activities of these companies, but the law requires disclosure of their financial condition and investment policies to afford investors full and complete information about their activities.
Investment Advisors Act of 1940	This Act establishes a pattern of regulation of investment avisors. It requires that persons or firms who engage for compensation in the business of advising others about their securities transactions must register with the Commission and conform their activities to statutory standards designed to protect the interests of investors.

PURPOSE OF REGISTRATION

Registration of securities does not insure investors against loss in their purchase, nor does the Commission have the power to disapprove securities for lack of merit—and it is unlawful to represent otherwise in the sale of securities. The only standard which must be met in the registration of securities is an adequate and accurate disclosure of the material facts concerning the company and the securities it proposes to sell. The fairness of the terms of securities. . . have no bearing on the question whether securities may be registered. . .

THE REGISTRATION PROCESS

To facilitate the registration of securities by different types of issuing companies, the Commission has prepared special registration forms which vary in their disclosure requirements to provide disclosure of the essential facts pertinent in a given type of offering while at the same time minimizing the burden and expense of compliance with the law. In general, the registration forms call for disclosure of information such as (1) a description of the registrant's properties and business, (2) a description of the significant provisions of the security to be offered for sale and its relationship to the registrant's other capital securities, (3) information about the management of the registrant, and (4) financial statements certified by independent public accountants.

The registration statement and prospectus become public immediately on filing with the Commission; but it is unlawful to sell the securities until the effective date. After the filing of the registration statement, the securities may be offered orally or by certain sumaries of the information in the registration statement as permitted by rules of the Commission. The Act provides that registration statements shall become effective on the 20th day after filing (or on the 20th day after the filing of the last amendment thereto); but the Commission, in its discretion, may advance the effective date if. . . such action is deemed appropriate.

Registration statements are examined by the Division of Corporation Finance for compliance with the disclosure requirements. If a statement appears to be materially incomplete or inaccurate, the registrant usually is informed by letter and given an opportunity to file correcting or clarifying amendments. The Commission, however, has authority to refuse or suspend the effectiveness of any registration statement if it finds, after hearing, that material representations are misleading, inaccurate, or incomplete. Accordingly, if material deficiencies in a registration statement appear to stem from a deliberate attempt to conceal and mislead, or if the deficiencies otherwise are of such nature as not to lend themselves readily to correction through the informal letter process, the Commission may conclude that it is the public interest to resort to a hearing to develop the facts by evidence and to determine on the evidence whether a stop order should issue refusing or suspending effectiveness of the statement.

A stop order is not a permanent bar to the effectiveness of the registration statement or sale of the securities, for the order must be lifted and the statement declared effective if amendments are filed correcting the statement in accordance with the stop order decision. The Commission may issue stop orders after the sale of securities has been commenced or completed. Although losses which may have been suffered in the purchase of securities are not restored to investors by the stop order, the Commission's decision and the evidence on which it is based may serve to put investors on notice of their rights and aid in their own recovery suits.

This examination process naturally contributes to the general reliability of the registration disclosures—but it does not give positive assurance of the accuracy of the facts reported. Even if such a verification of the facts were possible, the task, if not actually prohibitive, would involve such a tremendous undertaking (both in time and money) as to seriously impede the financing of business ventures throught the public sale of securities. . .

■ ■ ■

THE BASIC PROHIBITION

Section 5 of the 1933 Act contains a double prohibition. First, it is unlawful for any person *to offer to sell* a security unless a registration statement has been *filed* with the SEC. Second, it is unlawful to *sell* a security unless a registration statement is *effective*. These prohibitions, in effect, mean that only when a preliminary prospectus has been filed is it permissible for the securities to be offered to the public, but no sales can take place until the prospectus has become effective. The preliminary prospectus contains wording in red ink which declares that the instrument is subject to amendment and that the securities described in the prospectus may not be sold prior to the time the registration statement becomes effective. Because of the red ink utilized in the preliminary prospectus, it is often referrred to as a "red herring."

The period of time between the preliminary filing and the effective date is known as the waiting period in which the public may become familiar with the new proposed offering. The management of the offering company must be careful during this period to avoid publicity which "puffs" the value of the company securities. The SEC's Release 5180 urges companies to respond factually to unsolicited inquiries from securities analysts during this period, but companies often limit communication while "in registration." Companies desire to avoid an inadvertent violation of the 1933 Act by releasing some statement that may be perceived by the SEC as initiating publicity which may subject the company's new offer to an SEC stop order. A stop order can have disastrous consequences because the timing of the offering of securities is critical in ever changing financial markets.

SECTION 2: A "SECURITY"

Section 2 of the 1933 Act defines a "security." The section includes any note, stock, treasury stock, investment contract, guarantee, warrants, and any interest or instrument commonly known as a security. However, there are many cases in which various obscure financial instruments are determined to be securities, as the following case illustrates.

SEC v. GLENN W. TURNER ENTERPRISES, INC.
474 F. 2d 476 (1973)
United States Court of Appeals (9th Cir.)

■ ■ ■

This is an appeal from an order granting the SEC a preliminary injuction. The injunction prohibits offering and selling by defendants of certain of their "Adventures" and "Plans"... Dare To Be Great, Inc. (Dare), a Florida corporation is a wholly owned subsidiary of Glenn W. Turner Enterprises, Inc. The individual defendants are, or were, officers, directors, or employees of the defendant corporations.

The trial court's findings, which are fully supported by the record, demonstrate that defendants' scheme is a gigantic successful fraud. The question presented is whether the "Adventure" or "Plan" enjoined are "securities" within the meaning of the federal securities laws...

The five courses offered by Dare ostensibly involve two elements. In return for his money, the purchaser is privileged to attend seminar sessions and receives tapes, records, and other material, all aimed at improving self-motivation and sales ability. He also receives, if he purchases either Adventure III or IV or the $1,000 Plan, the opportunity to help to sell the courses to others; if successful he receives part of the purchase price as his commission. There is no doubt that this latter aspect of the purchase is in all respects the significant one...

It is apparent from the record that what is sold is not of the usual "business motivation" type of courses. Rather, the purchaser is really buying the possibility of deriving money from the sale of the plans by Dare to individuals whom the purchaser has brought to Dare. The promotional aspects of the plan, such as seminars, films, and records, are aimed at interesting others in the Plans. Their value for any other purpose, is, to put it mildly, minimal.

Once an individual has purchased a Plan, he turns his efforts toward bringing others into the organization, for which he will receive a part of what they pay. His task is to bring prospective purchasers to "Adventure Meetings."

These meetings are like an old time revival meeting, but directed toward the joys of making easy money rather than salvation. Their purpose is to convince prospective purchasers, or "prospects," that Dare is a sure route to great riches....

Once he has bought a plan that empowers him to help sell the plans to others, the task of the purchaser is to find prospects and induce them to attend Adventure Meetings. He is not to tell them that Dare To Be Great, Inc. is involved. Rather, he catches their interest by intimating that the result of attendance will be significant wealth for the prospect. It is at the meetings that the sales effort takes place. The "salesman" is told that to maximize his chances of success he should impart an aura of affluence, whether spurious or not—to pretend that through his association with Dare he has obtained wealth of no small proportions. The training that he has received at Dare is educating him on this point. He is told to "fake it 'til you make it," or to give the impression of wealth even if it has not been attained. He is urged to go into debt if necessary to purchase a new and expensive automobile and flashy clothes, and to carry with him large sums of money, borrowing if necessary, so that it can be ostentatiously displayed. The purpose of all this is to put the prospect in a more receptive state of mind with respect to the inducements that he will be subject to at the meetings....

The 1933 and 1934 Acts are remedial legislation, among the central purposes of which is full and fair disclosure relative to the issuance of securities. It is a familiar canon of legislative construction that remedial legislation should be construed broadly. The Acts were designed to protect the American public from speculative or fraudulent schemes of promoters. For that reason Congress defined the term "security" broadly, and the Supreme Court in turn has construed the definition liberally...In *SEC v. W.J. Howey Co.* the Court stated that the definition of a security "embodies a flexible rather than a static principle, one that is capable of adaptation to meet the countless and variable schemes devised by those who seek the use of the money of others on the promise of profits."...

In *SEC v. W.J. Howey Co.* the Supreme Court set out its by now familiar definition of an investment contract:

> "The test is whether the scheme involves an investment of money in a common enterprise with profits to come solely from the efforts of others."

In *Howey* the Court held that a land sales contract for units of a citrus grove, together with a service contract for cultivating and marketing the crops, was an investment contract and hence a security. The Court held that what was in essence being offered was "an opportunity to contribute money and to share in the profits of a large citrus fruit enterprise managed and partly owned by respondents." The purchasers had no intention themselves of either occupying the land or developing it; they were attracted only "by the prospects of a return on their investment." It was clear that the profits were to come "solely" from the efforts of others.

For purposes of the present case, the sticking point in the *Howey* definition is the word "solely," a qualification which of course exactly fitted the circumstances in *Howey*. All the other elements of the *Howey* test have been met here. There is an investment of money, a common enterprise, and the expectation of profits to come from the efforts of others. Here, however, the investor, or purchaser, must himself exert some efforts if he is to realize a return on his initial cash outlay. He must find prospects and persuade them to attend Dare Adventure Meetings, and at least some of them must then purchase a plan if he is to realize that return. Thus it can be said that the returns or profits are not coming "solely" from the efforts of others.

We hold, however, that in light of the remedial nature of the legislation, the statutory policy of affording broad protection to the public and the Supreme Court's admonitions that the definition of securities should be a flexible one, the word "solely" should not be read as a strict or literal limitation on the definition of an investment contract, but rather must be construed realistically, so as to include within the definition those schemes which involve in substance, if not form, securities...

Strict interpretation of the requirement that profits to be earned must come "solely" from the efforts of others has been subject to criticism. Adherence to such an interpretation could result in a mechanical, unduly restrictive view of what is and what is not an investment contract. It would be easy to evade by adding a requirement that the buyer contribute a modicum of effort. Thus the fact that the investors here were required to exert some efforts if a return were to be achieved should not automatically preclude a finding that the Plan or Adventure is an investment contract. To do so would not serve the purpose of the legislation. Rather we adopt a more realistic test, whether the efforts made by those other than the investor are the undeniably significant ones, those essential managerial efforts which affect the failure or success of the enterprise.

In this case, Dare's source of income is from selling the Adventures and the Plan. The purchaser is sold the idea that he will get a fixed part of the proceeds of the sales. In essence, to get that share, he invests three things: his money, his efforts to find prospects and bring them to the meetings and whatever it costs him to create an illusion of his own affluence. He invests them in Dare's get-righ-scheme. What he buys is a share of the proceeds of the selling efforts of Dare. Those efforts are the . . . (basis) of the scheme; those efforts are what keeps it going; those efforts are what produces the money which is to make him rich. In essence, it is the right that he buys. In our view, the scheme is no less an investment contract merely because he contributes some effort as well as money to get into it.

Let us assume that in *Howey* the sales and service agreements had provided that the buyer was to buy and plant the citrus trees. Unless he did so, there would be no crop to cultivate, harvest and sell, no moneys in which he could share. The essential nature of the scheme, however, would be the same. He would still be buying, in exchange for money, trees and planting, a share in what he hoped would be the company's success in cultivating the trees and harvesting and marketing the crop. We cannot believe that the Court would not have held such a scheme to be an investment contract. So here. Regardless of the fact that the purchaser here must contribute something besides his money, the essential managerial efforts which affect the failure or success of the enterprise are those of Dare, not his own...

■ ■ ■

Questions

1. What is the definition of a security? What are the elements of the *Howey* Test?
2. To create a "security," must the profit to be realized from the investment of money be gained "solely" from the efforts and management of others?

EXEMPTIONS

Because the definition of security under Section 2 is so broad and all encompassing, Section 5 appears to prohibit the sale of any security without an effective registration statement. However, Section 3 of the 1933 Act exempts certain securities and Section 4 exempts certain transactions from the registration requirements. Section 3 exempts commercial paper, securities of government, banks, charitable organizations, savings and loans associations, common carriers, insurance policies, annuity contracts, and securities issued in bankruptcy reorganizations. In addition, "intrastate offerings" are exempt. However, to qualify under this exemption certain elements must be established. The following case illustrates the difficulties of complying with the "intrastate offering" exemption.

INTRASTATE OFFERING

SEC v. McDONALD INVESTMENT CO.
343 F. Supp. 343 (1972)
U.S. District Court, Minnesota

■ ■ ■

The question presented to the court is whether the sale exclusively to Minnesota residents of securities, consisting of unsecured installment promissory notes of the defendants, a Minnesota corporation, whose only business office is situate in Minnesota, is exempt from the filing of a registration statement under § 3(a)(11) of the 1933 Securities Act, when the proceeds from the sale of such notes are to be used principally, if not entirely, to make loans to land developers outside of Minnesota...

Plaintiff, the Securities and Exchange Commission, instituted this lawsuit...The defendants are McDonald Investment Company, a Minnesota corporation, and H.J. McDonald, the company's president, treasurer, and owner of all the company's outstanding common stock. Plaintiff requests that the defendants be permanently enjoined from offering for sale and selling securities without having complied with the registration requirements of Section 5 of the Act....

Section 3(a)(11) of the Act, however, sometimes called the intrastate exemption, exempts from registration:

> "(11) Any security which is a part of an issue offered and sold only to persons resident within a single State or Territory, where the issuer of such security is a person resident and doing business within or, if a corporation, incorporated by and doing business within, such State or Territory."...

The plaintiff predicates its claim for a permanent injunction on the ground that the defendants will be engaged in a business where the income producing operations are located outside the state in which the securities are to be offered and sold and therefore not availabe for the 3(a)(11) exemption...

In *Truckee v. Showboat* the exemption was not allowed because the proceeds of the offering were to be used primarily for the purpose of a new unrelated business in another state, i.e., a California corporation acquiring and refurbishing a hotel in Las Vegas, Nevada. Likewise, in *Chapman v. Dunn* the 3(a)(11) exemption was unavailable to an offering by a company in one state, Michigan, of undivided fractional oil and gas interests located in another state, Ohio. The *Dunn* court specifically stated at page 159:

> "...in order to qualify for the exemption of § 3(a)(11), the issuer must offer and sell his securities only to persons resident within a single State and the issuer must be a resident of that same State. *In addition to this, the issuer must conduct a predominant amount of his business within this same State.* This business which the issuer must conduct within the same State refers to the income producing operations of the business in which the issuer is selling the securities..." [Emphasis added]

This language would seem to fit the instant case where the income producing operations of the defendant, after completion of the offering, are to consist entirely of earning interest on its loans and receivables invested outside the state of Minnesota. While the defendant will not participate in any of the land developer's operations, nor will it own or control any of the operations, the fact is that the strength of the installment notes depends perhaps not legally, but practically, to a large degree on the success or failure of land developments located outside Minnesota, such land not being subject to the jurisdiction of the Minnesota court. The investor obtains no direct interest in any business activity outside of Minnesota, but legally holds only an interest as a creditor of a Minnesota corporation, which of course would be a prior claim on the defendant's assets over the shareholder's equity...

This case does not evidence the deliberate attempt to evade the Act as in the example posed by plaintiff of a national organization or syndicate which incorporates in several or many states, opens an office in each and sells securities only to residents of the particular state, intending nevertheless to use all the proceeds whenever realized in a venture beyond the boundaries of all, or at best all but one of the states. Defendant corporation on the contrary has been in business in Minnesota for some period of time, is not a "Johnny come lately" and is not part of any syndicate or similar enterprise; yet to relieve it of the federal registration requirements where none or very little of the money realized is to be invested in Minnesota, would seem to violate the spirit if not the letter of the Act...

Exemptions under the Act are strictly contrued, with the burden of proof on the one seeking to establish the same.

Defendant notes that agreements with land developers under Minnesota law; that the income producing activities will be the earnings of interest which occurs in Minnesota; that the Minnesota registration provides at close proximity all the information and protection that any investor might desire; that whether or not registered with the Securities and Exchange Commission, a securities purchaser has the protection of 15 U.S.C. § 77e which attaches liability to the issuer whether or not registration of the securities are exempted for fraudulent or untrue statements in a prospectus or made by oral communications; that plaintiff blurs the distinction between sale of securities across state lines and the operation of an intrastate business; and that if injunction issues in this case it could issue in any case where a local corporation owns an investment out of the particular state in which it has its principal offices and does business such as accounts receivable from its customers out of state. While these arguments are worthy... on balance and in carrying out the spirit and intent of the Securities Act of 1933, plaintiff's request for a permanent injunction should be granted.

■ ■ ■

Questions

1. Must the revenue from the security sales be applied or invested in the state itself to come within the "intrastate offering" exemption?
2. Should the intrastate offering exemption be narrowly or broadly interpreted?
3. Does the reasoning in the *MacDonald Investment Co.* decision make it difficult to comply with the intrastate offering exemption?

RULE 147

To avoid confusion concerning the scope of the intrastate offering exemption, the SEC has adopted Rule 147 which outlines a series of guidlines to determine the applicability of Section 3. Under Rule 147, a firm incorporated and doing 80 percent of its business within a state may sell its securities without registering them if at least 80 percent of the proceeds of the offering are used within the state and all offerees are residents of that state. In addition, resales of the stock for nine months must be limited to state residents and the stock certificates must bear a legend indicating these restrictions. As one can imagine, the limitations of Rule 147 are too severe for its wide utilization. Therefore, businesses with a substantial volume of interstate sales or interstate purchasers of the stock would be denied a intrastate offering exemption.

In an effort to aid small businesses in their efforts to raise risk capital, the SEC has authority to exempt issues smaller than $500,000. The Commission has promulgated Regulation A to cover these situations. Under a "Reg. A" procedure, the offeror prepares a short form of registration to be filed with the SEC.

PRIVATE PLACEMENTS

Section 4 provides that the registration requirements shall be inapplicable to "transactions by an issuer not involving any public offering." The courts have struggled to come up with a useful definition of a "nonpublic offer," which is often referred to as a private placement. The following case illustrates some of the appropriate criteria used by the courts to determine whether or not the offering is nonpublic.

HILL YORK CORP. v. AMERICAN INTERNAT'L FRANCHISES, INC.
488 F. 2d 680 (1971)
U.S. Court of Appeals (5th. Cir.)

■ ■ ■

It is conceded that no registration statement had been filed with the S.E.C. in connection with this offering of securities. The defendants contend, however, that the transactions come within the exemptions to registration found in...Section 4(2). Specifically, they contend that the offering of securities was not a public offering...

The S.E.C. has stated that the question of public offering is one of fact and must depend upon the circumstances of each case. We agree with this approach...

The following specific factors are relevant:

1. The number of offerees and their relationship to each other and to the issuer.

    In the past the S.E.C. has utilized the arbitrary figure of twenty-five offerees as a litmus test of whether an offering was public. A leading commentator in the field has noted, however, that in recent years the S.E.C. has increasingly disavowed any safe numerical test...Obviously, however, the more offerees, the more likelihood that the offering is public. The relationship between the offerees and the issuer is most significant. If the offerees know the issuer and have special knowledge as to its business affairs, such as high executive officers of the issuer would possess, then the offering is apt to be private. The Supreme Court laid special stress on this consideration in *Ralston Purina* by stating that "[t]he focus of the inquiry should be on the need of the offerees for the protections afforded by registration. The employees here were not shown to have access to the kind of information which registration would disclose." Also to be considered is the relationship between the offerees and their knowledge of each other. For example, if the offering is being made to a diverse and unrelated group, i.e. lawyers, grocers, plumbers, etc., then the offering would have the appearance of being public; but an offering to a select group of high executive officers of the issuer who know each other and of course have similar interests and knowledge of the offering would more likely be characterized as a private offering.

2. The number of units offered.

    Here again there is no fixed magic number. Of course, the smaller the number of units offered, the greater the likelihood the offering will be considered private.

3. The size of the offering.

    The smaller the size of the offering, the more probability it is private.

4. The manner of offering.

    A private offering is more likely to arise when the offer is made directly to the offerees rather than through the facilities of public distribution such as investment bankers or the securities exchanges. In addition, public advertising is incompatible with the claim of private offering.

Even an objective testing of these factors without determining whether a more comprehensive and generalized prerequisite has been met, is insufficient..."The design of the statute is to protect investors by promoting full disclosure of information thought necessary to informed investment decisions."Thus the ultimate test is whether " 'the particular class of persons affected need the protection of the Act.' ". . .The evidence indicates that this offering was limited to sophisticated businessmen and attorneys who planned to do business with the new firm. . .

The defendants rely most strongly on the fact that the offering was made only to sophisticated businessmen and lawyers and not the average man in the street. Although this evidence is certainly favorable to the defendants, the level of sophistication will not carry the point. In this context, the relationship between the promoters and the purchasers and the "access to the kind of information which registration would disclose" becomes highly relevant factors. . .Obviously if the plaintiffs did not possess the information requisite for a registration statement, they could not bring their sophisticated knowledge of business affairs to bear in deciding whether or not to invest in this franchise sales center. There is abundant evidence to support the conclusion that the plaintiffs did not in fact possess the requisite information. The plaintiffs were given: 1. a brochure representing that the defendants had just left the very successful firm of Nationwide, but without disclosing the fact that Nationwide was then under investigation by the S.E.C.; 2. a brochure representing Browne as an expert in capitalization consulting, when in fact he had no expertise in such consulting; 3. a brochure stating that the franchise fee would be 25,000 dollars, when in fact the franchise fee turned out to be 25,000 dollars plus a 1,000 dollar per month royalty; 4. a brochure representing that the existing sales centers were successfully operating, without disclosure of the fact that most of them were under investigation by various state securities commissions. No reasonable mind could conclude that the plaintiffs had access to accurate information on the foregoing points since the only persons who reasonably could have relieved their ignorance were the ones that told them the untruths in the first instance. This proof. . . inexorably leads to the conclusion that even the most sanguine of the purchasers would have entertained serious, if not fatal, doubts about investing in this scheme if completely accurate information had been furnished.

While defendants allude to other evidence in this case, the paucity of evidence pertaining to the relative considerations remains stark. The record contains no evidence as to the number of offerees. The fact that there were only thirteen actual purchasers is of course irrelevant. We do know that the purchasers were a diverse and unrelated group, or at least this was so at the time the offering occurred. Furthermore, the defendants admit that the plaintiffs had never met or in any way communicated with them prior to purchasing their stock. . .

This Court reviews cases, it neither tries nor retries fact issues. . . Faced with the state of evidentiary development when the parties rested, the court below could properly reach the same conclusion as the court in Repass v. Rees, 174 F. Supp. 898, 904 (D. Colo. 1959):

> * * * there is no evidence as to the experience of the buyers other than the plaintiffs. And there is no evidence as to how many offers were made to other persons, or the experience of those persons. The defendants did not testify that they had made no other offers. Without such evidence in the record the Court cannot determine whether the class needed protection. It was incumbent on the defendants to submit this evidence. Since they did not, they must suffer the consequences.

■ ■ ■

Questions

1. What are the relevant factors identified by the court to be considered in determining whether the offer is "public"?
2. If the securities are offered to "sophisticated businessmen and lawyers," will this entitle the offering to be designated as private?
3. On what other issues did the court say that evidence was lacking which would be necessary to establish the nature of a private offering?

RULE 146

In 1974 the SEC adopted Rule 146, which defines criteria to establish the clearly legal "private placement." However, if one is not able to fully comply with all the criteria of Rule 146, the offering may be held nevertheless to be a private offering under case law. Consequently, lawyers in the securities field try to comply with Rule 146 as much as possible in an effort to satisfy the court of the private nature of the offering. The provisions of Rule 146 require that there be a limitation of offerees to around thirty-five persons, that no solicitation or general advertising be undertaken, that the offerees or their representative be sophisticated investors with access to or disclosure of company information (by employment or economic bargaining power), and that the purchasers buy the securities for their own account without intent to resale.

After having acquired securities in a private placement, the investor is prohibited from reselling the securities unless he or she complies with provisions of Rule 144. Rule 144 is the only way for persons who have purchase securities under a private placement to resell their securities without being designated a "underwriter" who is selling securities without registration. Rule 144 requires a holding of the securities for two years from the date of the purchase and the amount of distribution must be limited to less than 1 percent of the average market trading volume within a four-week period. In addition, information must be delivered to the public prior to such distributions. This requirement means the company must have "gone public"(through registration) so that the general public will have information on which to evaluate whether to purchase the stock. To be absolutely safe in selling a security obtained in a private offering, the seller should follow Rule 237 which requires a holding period of five years and a sale of no more than $50,000 worth of securities within a one year period. In this fashion, the seller can avoid being charged as an underwriter.

ANTIFRAUD PROVISION

The 1933 Act also contains a general antifraud provision in Section 17(a). It prohibits fraudulent transactions in securities whether or not the security is entitled to an exemption from registration. The following case illustrates the utilization of this antifraud provision.

SEC v. MANOR NURSING CENTERS, INC.
458 F. 2d. 1082 (1972)
U.S. Court of Appeals (2d. Cir.)

■ ■ ■

The conduct of appellants in conection with the public offering of Manor shares, upon analysis, demonstrates beyond a peradventure of a doubt that they violated the antifraud provisions of the federal securities laws—§ 17(a) of the 1933 Act and § 10(b) of the 1934 Act.

The gravamen of this case is that each of the appellants participated in a continuing course of conduct whereby public investors were fraudulently induced to part with their money in the expectation that Manor and the selling stockholders would return the money if all Manor shares were not sold and all the proceeds from the sale were not received by March 8, 1970. It is undisputed that, as of March 8, Manor and the selling stockholders had not sold all the 450,000 shares and that all the proceeds expected from the sale had not been received. Moreover, it is clear that all appellants knew, or should have known, the the preconditions for their retaining the proceeds of the offering had not been satisfied. Nevertheless, rather than complying with the terms of the offering by returning the funds of public investors, appellants retained these funds for their own financial benefit. This misappropriation of the proceeds of the Manor offering constituted a fraud on public investors and violated the antifraud provisions of the federal securities laws...

It also is clear that appellants violated the antifraud provisions of the federal securities laws by offering Manor shares when they knew, or should have known, that the Manor prospectus was misleading in several material respects. After the registration statement became effective on December 8, 1969, at least four developments occurred which made the prospectus misleading: the public's funds were not returned even though the issue was not fully subscribed: and escrow account for the proceeds of the offering was not established; shares were issued for consideration other than cash; and certain individuals received extra compensation for agreeing to participate in the offering. These developments were not disclosed to the public investors. That these developments occurred after the effective date of the registration statement did not provide a liscense to appellants to ignore them. Post-effective developments which materially alter the picture presented in the registration statement must be brought to the attention of public investors. "The effect of the antifraud provisions of the Securities Act (§ 17(a)) and of the Exchange Act (§ 10(b) and Rule 10b-5) is to require the prospectus to reflect any post-effective changes necessary to keep the prospectus from being misleading in any material respect."

While appellants admit that public investors were defrauded, they seek to exculpate themselves from liability for their acts by arguing that they acted in good faith.

We hold, however, that the evidence established that appellants. . . did not act in good faith. Feinberg, as the district court properly found, has had considerable experience in complex financing arrangements. Thus, it would strain credulity to suggest that Feinberg did no know that the closing. . . was invalid. . .

Ezrine's claim that he acted in good faith likewise is belied by the evidence adduced at trial. As an experienced securities lawyer, he was well aware that failure to correct a misleading prospectus and retention of the proceeds even though the issue had not been fully subscribed constituted violations of the antifraud provisions of the securities laws. Indeed, Ezrine's knowledge that the federal securities laws required public disclosure of developments which occurred subsequent to the effective date of the registration statement is indicated by his supplementing the Manor prospectus on Februry 24 to reflect (a new participate) in the offering as an underwriter. . .

Having concluded that appellants had violated the federal securities laws, the district court permanently enjoined all appellants. . . from further violations of the antifraud provisions of the 1933 and 1934 Acts. . .

In addition to granting the SEC's request for injunctive relief, the district court ordered appellants to disgorge all the proceeds. . . received in connection with the public offering of Manor stock; appointed a trustee to receive such funds, to distribute them to defrauded public investors and to report to the court on the true state of affairs; and, to prevent a wasting of assets, ordered a temporary freeze on appellants' assets pending transfer of the funds to the trustee. . .

■ ■ ■

Questions

1. Identify the fraudulent activities of the defendants in *Manor Nursing Center?*
2. Must a registration statement be "up-dated" by subsequent developments which would be materially important to public investors?
3. Why were the defendants unable to convince the court that they acted in good faith?
4. What actions did the court take to protect public investors?

LIABILITIES FOR ILLEGAL SALES AND REGISTRATION

The SEC can enjoin the illegal distribution of securities without a registration statement and obtain a $5,000 fine or up to five years imprisonment for violation of the 1933 Act. Private parties also have the right to litigate securities violations under the 1933 Act.

Under Section 12(1) purchasers of securities may directly sue for rescission or damages any person who violated Section 5 be selling the securities to them without the required registration. Section 12(2) imposes liability for material misstatement or omissions in the distribution of securities. Since Section 12 contains a requirement of "privity," purchasers may sue only their immediate sellers and not the issuer. Consequently, Section 12 is drafted to impose potential liability upon broker-dealers who violate the Act in merchandising of securities.

Section 11 of the 1933 Act contains potential liability for the issuer of a security should a registration statement be filed which contains material misstatements or omissions. Section 11 entitles any person acquiring a security not knowing of the misstatement or omission to sue every person who has signed the registration statement, including the issuer. All directors who have signed the registration statement and the underwriters who have also signed are subject to suit. Even a director who has not signed the registration statement may not be relieved of potential liability. However, Section 11 also provides that no person, other than the isuer, shall be liable if the person can establish his "due diligence" defense. The following case illustrates the efforts of the defendants to establish their due diligence defense.

ESCOTT v. BARCHRIS CONSTRUCTION CORP.
283 F. Supp. 643 (1968)
U.S. District Court, (S.D.N.Y.)

■ ■ ■

The action is brought under Section 11 of the Securities Act of 1933. Plaintiffs allege that the registration statement with respect to these debentures filed with the Securities and Exchange Commission, which became effective on May 16, 1961, contained false statements and material omissions.

Defendants fall into three categories: (1) the persons who signed the registration statement; (2) the underwriters, consisting of eight investment banking firms, led by Drexel & Co. (Drexel); and (3) BarChris's auditors, Peat, Marwick, Mitchell & Co. (Peat, Marwick)...

It is a prerequisite to liability under Section 11 of the Act that the fact which is falsely stated in a registration statement, or the fact that is omitted when it should have been stated to avoid misleading, be "material."...

Early in the history of the Act, a definition of materiality was given in Matter of Charles A. Howad, 1 S.E.C. 6.8 (1934), which is still valid today. A material fact was there defined as:

"* * * a fact which if it had been correctly stated or disclosed would have deterred or tended to deter the average prudent investor from purchasing the securities in question."...

Judged by this test, there is no doubt that many of the misstatements and omissions in this prospectus were material. This is true of all of them which relate to the state of affairs in 1961, i.e., the overstatement of sales and gross profit for the first quarter, the understatement of contingent liabilities as of April 30, the overstatement of orders on hand and the failure to disclose the true facts with respect to officers' loans, customers' delinquencies, application of proceeds and the prospective operation of several alleys...

The "Due Diligence" Defenses

Every defendant... has pleaded these affirmative defenses. Each claims that (1) as to the part of the registration statement purporting to be made on the authority of an expert (which for convenience, I shall refer to as the "expertised portion"), he had no reasonable ground to believe and did not believe that there were any untrue statements or material omissions, and (2) as to the other parts of the registration statement, he made a reasonable investigation, as a result of which he had reasonable ground to believe and did believe that the registration statement was true and that no material face was omitted....

The only expert, in the statutory sense, was Peat, Marwick, and the only parts of the registration statement which purported to be made upon the authority of an expert were the portions which purported to be made on Peat, Marwicks's authority...

I turn now to the question of whether defendants have proved their due diligence defenses.

Russo

Russo was, to all intents and purposes, the chief executive officer of BarChris. He was a member of the executive committee. He was familiar with all aspects of the business. He was personally in charge of dealings with the factors. He talked with customers about their delinquencies...

In short, Russo knew all the relevant facts. He could not have believed that there were no untrue statements or material omissions in the prospectus. Russo has no due diligence defenses.

Vitolo and Pugliese

They were the founders of the business... Vitolo was president and Pugliese was vice president...

Vitolo and Pugliese are each men of limited education. It is not hard to believe that for them the prospectus was difficult reading, if indeed they read it at all...

The liability of a director who signs a registration statement does not depend upon whether or not he read it or, if he did, whether or not he understood what he was reading.

And in any case, Vitolo and Pugliese were not as naive as they claim to be. They were members of BarChris's executive committee. At meetings of that committee BarChris's affairs were discussed at length. They must have known what was going on. Certainly they knew of the inadequacy of cash in 1961. They knew of their own large advances to the company which remained unpaid...

All in all, the position of Vitolo and Pugliese is not significantly different, for present purposes, from Russo's. They could not have believed that the registration statement was wholly true and that no material facts had been omitted. And in any case, there is nothing to show that they made any investigation of anything which they may not have known about or understood. They have not proved their due diligence defenses.

Kircher

Kircher was treasurer of BarChris and its chief financial officer. He is a certified public accountant and an intelligent man. He was thoroughly familiar with BarChris's financial affairs... He knew of the customers' deliquency problem...

Moreover, as a member of the executive committee, Kircher was kept informed as to those branches of the business of which he did not have direct charge...

Kircher worked on the preparation of the registration statement... He supplied information... about the company's business. He read the prospectus and understood it. He knew what it said and what it did not say.

Kircher's contention is that he had never before dealt with a registration statement, that he did not know what it should contain, and that he relied wholly on (the attorneys) and Peat, Marwick to guide him...

There is an issue of credibility here. In fact, Kircher was not frank in dealing with (the attorneys). He withheld information from them. But even if he had told them all the facts, this would not have constituted the due diligence contemplated by the statute. Knowing the facts, Kircher had reason to believe that the expertised portion of the prospectus, i.e., the 1960 figures, was in part incorrect. He could not shut his eyes to the facts and rely on Peat, Marwick for that portion.

As to the rest of the propsectus, knowing the facts, he did not have a reasonable ground to believe it to be true. On the contrary, he must have known that in part it was untrue. Under these circumstances, he was not entitled to sit back and place the blame on the lawyers for not advising him about it.

Kircher has not proved his due diligence defenses...

Birnbaum

Birnbaum was a young lawyer, admitted to the bar in 1957, who, after brief periods of employment by two different law firms and an equally brief period of practicing in his own firm, was employed by BarChris as house counsel and assistant secretary in October 1960. Unfortunately for him, he became secretary and a director of BarChris on April 17, 1961, after the first version of the registration statement had been filed with the Securities and Exchange Commission. He signed the later amendments, thereby becoming responsible for the accuracy of the prospectus in its final form...

One of Birnbaum's more important duties, first as assistant secretary and later as full-fledged secretary, was to keep the corporate minutes of BarChris and its subsidiaries. This necessarily informed him to a considerable extent about the company's affairs. Birnbaum was not initially a member of the executive committee, however, and did not keep its minutes at the outset...

It seems probable that Birnbaum did not know of many of the inaccuracies in the prospectus. He must, however, have appreciated some of them. In any case, he made no investigation and relied on the others to get it right... [H]e was entitled to rely upon Peat, Marwick for the 1960 figures, for as far as appears, he had no personal knowledge of the company's books of account or financial transactions. But he was not entitled to rely upon Kircher, and (attorneys) for the other portions of the prospectus. As a lawyer, he should have known his obligations under the statute. He should have known that he was required to make a reasonable investigation of the truth of all the statements in the unexpertised portion of the document which he signed. Having failed to make such an investigation, he did not have reasonable ground to believe that all these statements were true. Birnbaum has not established his due diligence defenses except as to the audited 1960 figures.

Auslander

Auslander was an "outside" director, i.e., one who was not an officer of BarChris. He was chairman of the boad of Valley Stream National Bank in Valley Stream, Long Island. In February 1961 Vitolo asked him to become a director ofBarChris. Vitolo gave him an enthusiastic account of BarChris's progress and prospects. As an inducement, Vitolo said that when BarChris received the proceeds of a forthcoming issue of securities, it would deposit $1,000,000 in Auslander's bank...

Auslander was elected a director on April 17, 1961. The registration statement in its original form had already been filed, of course without his signature. On May 10, 1961, he signed a signature page for the first amendment to the registration statement which was filed on May 11, 1961. This was a separate sheet without any document attached. Auslander did not know that it was a signature page for a registrtion statement. He vaguely understood that it was something "for the SEC."

Auslander attended a meeting of BarChris's directors on May 15, 1961. At that meeting he, along with the other directors, signed the signature sheet for the second amendment which constituted the registration statement in its final form. Again, this was only a separate sheet without any document attached. Auslander never saw a copy of the registration statement in its final form.

At the May 15 directors' meeting, however, Auslander did realize that what he was signing was a signature sheet to a registration statement. This was the first time that he had appreciated that fact. A copy of the registration statement in its earlier form as amended on May 11, 1961 was passed around at the meeting. Auslander glanced at it briefly. He did not read it thoroughly.

At the May 15 meeting, Russo and Vitolo stated that everything was in order and that the prospectus was correct. Auslander believed this statement.

In considering Auslander's due diligence defenses, a distinction is to be drawn between the expertised and nonexpertised portions of the prospectus. As to the former, Auslander knew that Peat, Marwick had audited the 1960 figures. He believed them to be correct because he had confidence in Peat, Marwick. He had no reasonable ground to believe otherwise.

As to the non-expertised portions, however, Auslander is in a different position...

It is true that Auslander became a director on the eve of the financing. He had little opportunity to familiarize himself with the company's affairs. The question is whether, under such circumstances, Auslander did enough to establish his due diligence defense with respect to the non-expertised portions of the prospectus...

Section II imposes liability in the first instance upon a director, no matter how new he is. He is presumed to know his responsibility when he becomes a director. He can escape liability only by using that reasonable care to investigate the facts which a prudent man would employ in the management of his own property. In my opinion, a prudent man would not act in an important matter without any knoledge of the relevant facts, in sole reliance upon representations of persons who are comparative strangers and upon general information which does not purport to cover the particular case.

To say that such minimal conduct measures up to the statutory standard would, to all intents and purposes absolve new directors from responsibility merely because they are new. This is not a sensible construction of Section II, when one bears in mind its fundamental purpose of requiring full and truthful disclosure for the protection of investors.

I find and conclude that Auslander has not established his due diligence defense...

Grant

Grant became a director of BarChris in October 1960. His law firm was counsel to BarChris in matters pertaining to the registration of securities...

Grant is sued as a director and as a signer of the registration statement. This is not an action against him for malpractice in his capacity as a lawyer. Nevertheless, in considering Grant's due diligence defenses, the unique position which he occupied cannot be disregarded. As the director most directly concerned with writing the registration statement and assuring its accuracy, more was required of him in the way of reasonable investigation than could fairly be expected of a director who had no connection with this work...

I find that Grant honestly believed that the registration statement was true and that no material facts had been omitted from it.

In this belief he was mistaken, and the fact is that for all his work, he never discovered any of the errors or omissions...

Grant contends that a finding that he did not make a reasonable investigation would be equivalent to a holding that a lawyer for an issuing company, in order to show due diligence, must make an independent audit of the figures supplied to him by his client. I do not consider this to be a realistic statement of the issue. There were errors and omissions here which could have been detected without an audit. The question is whether, despite his failure to detect them, Grant made a reasonable effort to that end...

It is claimed that a lawyer is entitled to rely on the statements of his client and that to require him to verify their accuracy would set an unreasonably high standard. This is too broad a generalization. It is all a matter of degree. To require an audit would obviously be unreasonable. On the other hand, to require a check of matters easily verifiable is not unreasonable. Even honest clients can make mistakes. The statute imposes libility for untrue statements regardless of whether they are intentionally untrue. The way to prevent mistakes is to test oral information by examining the orignal written record...

Grant was entitled to rely on Peat, Marwick for the 1960 figures. He had no reasonable gound to believe them to be inaccurate. But the matters which were not within the expertised protion of the prospectus... Grant was obliged to make a reasonable investigation. I am forced to find that he did not make one... In my opinion, this finding on the evidence in this case does not establish an unreasonably high standard in other cases for company counsel who are also directors. Each case must rest on its own facts. I conclude that Grant has not established his due diligence defenses except as to the audited 1960 figures.

The Underwriters and Coleman

The underwriters other than Drexel made no investigation of the accuracy of the prospectus. They all relied upon Drexel as the "lead" underwriter.

Drexel did make an investigation. The work was in charge of Coleman, a partner of the firm... Drexel's attorneys acted as attorneys for the entire group of underwriters. Ballard did the work, assisted by Stanton.

On April 17, 1961 Coleman became a director of BarChris. He signed the first amendment to the registration statement filed on May 11 and the second amendment, constituting the registration statement in its final form, filed on May 16. He thereby assumed a responsibility as an underwriter...

After Coleman was elected a director on April 17, 1961, he made no further independent investigation of the accuracy of the prospectus. He assumed that Ballard was taking care of this on his behalf as well as on behalf of the underwriters.

In April 1961 Ballard instructed Stanton to examine BarChris's minutes for the past five years and also to look at "the major contracts of the company." Stanton went to BarChris's officer for that purpose on April 24... He read the minutes of the board of directors and discovered interleaved in them a few minutes of executive committee meetings in 1960. He asked Kircher if there were any others. Kircher said that there had been other executive committee meetings but that the minutes had not been written up...

As to the "major contracts," all that Stanton could remember seeing was an insurance policy. Birnbaum told him that there was no file of major contracts... His visit, which lasted one day, was devoted primarily to reading the director's minutes...

Ballard did not insist that the executive committee minutes be written up so that he could inspect them, although he testified that he knew from experience that executive committee minutes may be extremely important. If he had insisted, he would have found the minutes highly informative... Ballard did not ask to see BarChris's schedule of delinquencies...

I have already held that this procedure is not sufficient in Grant's case...

The underwriters say that the prospectus is the company's prospectus, not theirs. Doubtless this is the way they customarily regard it. But the Securities Act makes no such distinction. The underwriters are just as responsible as the company if the prospectus is false. And prospective investors rely upon the reputation of the underwriters in deciding whether to purchase the securities...

The purpose of Section 11 is to protect investors. To that end the underwriters are made responsible for the truth of the prospectus. In order to make the underwriters' participation in this enterprise of any value to the investors, the underwriters must make some reasonable attempt to verify the data submitted to them. They may not rely solely on the company's officers or on the company's counsel. A prudent man in the management of his own property would not rely on them.

It is impossible to lay down a rigid rule suitable for every case defining the extent to which such verification must go. It is a question of degree, a matter of judgment in each case. In the present case, the underwriters' counsel made almost no attempt to verify management's representations. I hold that that was insufficient.

On the evidence in this case, I find that the underwriters' counsel did not make a reasonable investigation of the truth of those portions of the prospectus which were not made on the authority of Peat, Marwick as an expert. Drexel is bound by their failure. It is not a matter of relying upon counsel for legal advice. Here the attorneys were dealing with matters of fact. Drexel delegated to them, as its agent, the business of examining the corporate minutes and contracts. It must bear the consequences of their failure to make an adequate examination.

The other underwriters, who did nothing and relied solely on Drexel and the lawyers, are also bound by it. It follows that although Drexel and the other underwriters believed that those portions of the prospectus were true, they had no reasonable ground for that belief, within the meaning of the statute. Hence, they have not established their due diligence defense, except as to the 1960 audited figures.

The same conclusions must apply to Coleman. He made no investigation after he became a director. When it came to verification, he relied upon his counsel to do it for him. Since counsel failed to do it, Coleman is bound by that failure. Consequently, in his case also, he has not established his due diligence defense except as to the audited 1960 figures.

Peat, Marwick

Section 11(b)... defines the due diligence defense for an expert. Peat, Marwick has pleaded it.

The part of the registration statement purporting to be made upon the authority of Peat, Marwick as an expert was the 1960 figures... (The) question is whether at that time Peat, Marwick, after reasonable investigation, had reasonable ground to believe and did believe that the 1960 figures were true and that no material fact had been omitted from the registration statement which should have been included in order to make the 1960 figures not misleading. In deciding this issue, the court must consider not only what Peat, Marwick did in its 1960 audit, but also what it did in its subsequent "S-1 review." The proper scope of that review must also be determined...

Most of the actual work was performed by a senior accountant, Berardi...

It is unnecessary to recount everything that Berardi did in the course of the audit. We are concerned only with the evidence relating to what Berardi did or did not do with respect to those items which I have found to have been incorrectly reported in the 1960 figures in the prospectus...

First and foremost is Berardi's failure to discover that (a subsidiry)... had not been sold. This error affected both the sales figure and the liability side of the balance sheet.

As to factors' reserves, it is hard to understand how Berardi could have treated this item as entirely a current asset when it was obvious that most of the reserves would not be released within one year. If Berardi was unaware of that fact, he should have been aware of it.

Berardi erred in computing the contingent liability on Type B leasebeack transactions at 25 percent. Berardi did not examine the documents which are in evidence which established that BarChris's contingent liability on this type of transaction was in fact 100 percent. Berardi did not make a reasonable investigation in this instance.

The S-1 Review

The purpose of reviewing events subsequent to the date of a certified balance sheet (referred to as an S-1 review when made with reference to a registration statement) is to ascertain whether any material change has occured in the company's financial position which should be disclosed in order to prevent the balance sheet figures from being misleading. The scope of such a review, under generally accepted auditing standards, is limited. It does not amount to a complete audit.

Peat, Marwich prepared a written program for such a review. I find that this program conformed to generally accepted auditing standards...

Berardi made the S-1 review in May 1961. He devoted a little over two days to it, a total of 20½ hours. He did not discover any of the errors or omissions pertaining to the state of affairs in 1961 which I have previously discussed at length, all of which were material. The question is whether, despite his failure to find out anything, his investigation was reasonable within the meaning of the stature.

What Berardi did was to look at a consolidating trial balance as of March 31, 1961 which had been prepared by BarChris, compare it with the audited December 31, 1960 figures, discuss... certain unfavorable developments which the comparison disclosed, and read certain minutes. He did not examine any "important financial records" other than the trial balance...

In substance, what Berardi did is similar to what Grant and Ballard did. He asked questions,, he got answers which he considered satisfactory, and he did nothing to verify them...

Since he never read the prospectus, he was not even aware that there had ever been any problem about loans from officers.

There had been a material change for the worse in BarChris's financial position. That change was sufficiently serious so that the failure to disclose it made the 1960 figures misleading. Berardi did not discover it. As far as results were concerned, his S-1 review was useless.

Accountants should not be held to a standard higher than that recognized in their profession. I do not do so here. Berardi's review did not come up to that standard. He did not take some of the steps which Peat, Marwick's written program prescribed. He did not spend an adequate amount of time on a task of this magnitude. Most important of all, he was too easily satisfied with glib answers to his inquiries.

This is not to say that he should have made a complete audit. But there were enough danger signals in the materials which he did examine to require some further investigation on his part. Generally accepted accounting standards required such further investigation under these circumstances. It is not always sufficient merely to ask questions.

Here again, the burden of proof is on Peat, Marwick, I find that that burden has not been satisfied, I conclude that Peat, Marwick has not established its due diligence defense.

■ ■ ■

Questions

1. As to the nonexpert protion of the registration statement, what must a director do to establish his "due diligence" defense?
2. Identify some of the things that the "insiders" failed to do to establish their reasonable investigations and reasonable belief in the accuracy of the registration statement?
3. What did the underwriters fail to do to establish their due diligence defense?
4. What did the expert accountants have to do to establish their due diligence defense? What did they fail to do to establish the defense?

THE TRADING OF SECURITIES

THE WORK OF THE SECURITIES AND EXCHANGE COMMISSION
(Published by the SEC, March, 1973)
SECURITIES EXCHANGE ACT OF 1934

■ ■ ■

By this Act, congress extended the "disclosure" doctrine of investor protection to securities listed and registered for public trading on our national securities exchanges; and... the Securities Acts Amendments of 1964 applied the disclosure and reporting provisions to equity securities of hundreds of companies traded over-the-counter...

CORPORATE REPORTING

Companies which seek to have their securites listed and registered for public trading on such an exchange must file a registration application with the exchange and the Commission. A similar registration form must be filed by companies whose equity securities are traded over-the-counter if they (are of a certain) size... The Commissions's rules prescribe the nature and content of these registration statements, including certified financial statements. These data are generally comparable to, but less extensive than, the disclosures required in Securities Act registration statements. Following the registration of their securities, such companies must file annual and other periodic reports to keep current the information contained in the original filing.

Since trading by and between public investors, whether involving listed or over-the-counter securites, involves transactions between holders of outstanding securities (not an offer of securities for sale by the issuing company), there is no provision for dissemination of the reported data to investors through use of a prospectus or similar medium. However, the reported information is available for public inspection, both at the offices of the comission and the exchanges. It is also used extensively by publishers of securities manuals, securities advisory services, investment advisers, trust departments, brokers and dealers in securities, and similar agencies, and thus obtains widespread dissemination. In addition... copies of any of the reported data may be obtained from the commission at nominal cost.

The law prescribes penalties for filing false statements and reports with the Commission, as well as provision for recovery by investors who suffer losses in the purchase or sale of registered securites in reliance thereon...

MARKET SURVEILLANCE

The Securities Exchange Act also provides a system for regulating securities trading practices in both the exchange and the over-the-counter markets. In general, transactions in securities which are effected otherwise than on national securities exchanges are said to take place "over the counter." Designed to protect the interests of investors and the public, these provisions seek to curb misrepresentations and deceit, market manipulation and other fraudulent acts and practices and to establish and maintain just and equitable principles of trade conducive to the maintenance of open, fair and orderly markets.

While these provisions of the law establish the general regulatory pattern, the Commission is responsible for promulgating rules and regulations for their implementation. Thus, the Commission, has adopted regulations which, among other things, (1) define acts or practices which constitute a "manipulative or decetive devise or contrivance" prohibited by the statute, (2) regulate short selling, stabilizing transactions and similar matters, (3) regulate the hypothecation of customers' securities and (4) provide safeguards with respect to the financial responsibility of brokers and dealers.

REGISTRATION OF EXCHANGES AND SECURITIES ASSOCIATIONS

In addition, the law requires registration with the Commission of (1) "national scurities exchanges" (those having substantial securities trading volume); and (2) brokers and dealers who conduct an over-the-counter securities business in interstate commerce.

To obtain registration exchanges must show that they are so organized as to be able to comply with the provisions of the statute and the rules and regulations of the Commission and that their rules contain provisions which are just and adequate to insure fair dealing and to protect investors. Among other things, exchange rules must provide for the expulsion, suspension or other disciplining of members for conduct inconsistent with just and equitable principles of trade. While the law contemplates that exchanges shall have full opportunity to establish self-regulatory measures insuring fair dealing and the protection of investors, it empowers the Commission by order, rule or regulation to "alter or supplement" the rules of exchanges with respect to various phases of their activities and trading practices if necessary to effectuate the statutory objective. For the most part, exchange rules and revisions thereof, suggested by exchanges or by the Commission, reach their final form after discussions between representatives of the exchange and the Commission without resort to formal proceedings..

By an amendment to the law enacted in 1938, Congress also provided for creation of a self-policing body among over-the-counter brokers and dealers... (only one such association, the National Association of Securities Dealers, Inc., [NASD] is registered with the Commission under this provision of the law.)

Not all broker-dealer firms are members of the NASD; thus, some are not subject to supervison and control by that agency. To equalize the regulatory pattern, Congress provided in the 1964 Amendments that the Commission should undertake to establish investor safeguards applicable to non-NASD firms comparable to those applicable to NASD members. Among the controls adopted by the Commission is a requirement that persons associated with non-NASD firms meet certain qualification standards similar to those applied by the NASD to its members.

BROKER-DEALER REGISTRATION

Applications for registration as broker-dealers and amendments thereto are examined by the Office of Registrations and Reports with the assistance of the Division of Market Regulation The registration of brokers and dealers engaged in an interstate over-the-counter securities business also is an important phase of the regulatory plan of the Act. They must conform their business practices to the standards prescribe in the law and the Commission's regulations for the protection of investors (as well as to the fair trade practice rules of their association); in additon...they may violate these regulations only at the risk of possible loss of registration with the Commission and the right to continue to conduct an interstate securities business, or of suspension or explusion from the association and of the benefits of such membership...

INVESTIGATION AND ENFORCEMENT

It is the duty of the commission under the laws it administers to investigate complaints or other indications of possible law violations in securities transactions, most of which arise under the Securities Act of 1933 and the Securities Exchange Act of 1934. Investigation and enforcement work is the primary responsibility of the Commission's Regional Offices, subject to review and direction by the Division of Enforcement.

The more general types of investigations concern the sale without registration of securities subject to the registration requirement of the Securities Act, and misrepresentation or omission of material facts concerning securities offered for sale (whether or not registration is required). The anti-fraud provisions of the law also apply equally to the purchase of securities, whether involving outright misrepresentations or the withholding or omissionof pertinent facts to which the seller was entitled. For example, it is unlawful in certain situations to purchase securities from another person while withholding material information which would indicate that the securities have a value substantially greater than that at which they are being acquired. Such provisions of the law apply not only to transactions between brokers and dealers and their customers but also to the reacquisition of securities by an issuing company or its "insiders."...

...(One) common... type of violation involves the broker-dealer who, on gaining the trust and confidence of a customer and thereby establishing an agency relationship demanding the highest degree of fiduciary duty and care, takes secret profits in his securities transactions with or for the customer over and above the agreed brokerage (agency) commission. For example the broker-dealer may have purchased securities from customers at prices far below, or sold securities to customers at prices far above, their current market prices. In most such cases, the broker-dealer subjects himself to no risk of loss, since his purchases from customers are made only if he can make simultaneous sales of the securities at prices substantially in excess of those paid to the customers, and his sales to customers are made only if he can make simultaneous purchases of the securities at prices substantially lower than those charged the customer. Or the firm may engage in large-scale in-and-out transactions for the customer's account ("churning") to generate increased commissions, usually without regard to any resulting benefit to the customer...

STATUTORY SANCTIONS

It should be understood that Commission investigations (which for the most part are conducted in private) are essentially fact finding inquiries. The facts so developed by the staff are considered by the Commission only in determining whether there is *prima facie* evidence of a law violation and whether an action should be commenced to determine whether, in fact, a violation actually ocurred and, if so, whether some sanction should be imposed.

Assuming that the facts show possible fraud or other law violation, the laws provide serveral courses of action or remedies which the Commission may pursue:

1. Civil injunction. The Commission may apply to an appropriate United States District Court for an order enjoining those acts or practices alleged to violate the law or Commission rules.
2. Criminal prosecution. If fraud or other willful law violation is indicated, the Commission may refer the facts to the Department of Justice with a recommendation for criminal prosecution of the offending persons. That Department through its local United States Attorneys (who frequently are assisted by Commission attorneys), may present the evidence to a Federal grand jury and seek an indictment.
3. Administrative remedy. The Commission may, after hearing, issue orders suspending or expelling members from exchanges or the over-the-counter dealers association; denying, suspending or revoking the registrations of broker-dealers; or censuring individuals for misconduct or barring them (temporarily or permanently) from employment with a registered firm...

■ ■ ■

INSIDER TRADING

SEC v. TEXAS GULF SULPHUR COMPANY
401 F. 2d 833 (1968)
United States Court of Appeals, (2nd Cir.)

■ ■ ■

This action was commenced by the Securities and Exchange commission (the SEC) against Texas Gulf Sulphur Company (TGS) and several of its officers, directors and employees, to enjoin certain conduct by TGS and the individual defendants said to violate Section 10(b) of the Act, and Rule 10 b-5 (the Rule), promulgated thereunder, and to compel the rescission by the individual defendants of securities transactions assertedly conducted contrary to law...

This action derives from the exploratory activities of TGS begun in 1957 on the Canadian Shield in eastern Canada... These operations resulted in the detection of numerous anomalies, i.e., extraordinary variations in the conductivity of rocks, one of which was on the Kidd 55 segment of land located near Timmins, Ontario.

...Drilling of the inital hole, K-55-1, at the strongest part of the anomaly was commenced on November 8 and terminated on November 12 at a depth of 655 feet.

Visual estimates... of the core of K-55-1 indicated an average copper content of 1.15% and an average zinc content of 8.64% over a length of 599 feet. This visual estimate convinced TGS that it was desirable to acquire the remainder of the Kidd 55 segment, and in order to facilitate this acquisition TGS President Stephens instructed the exploration group to keep the results of K-55-1 confidential and undisclosed even as to other officers, directors, and employees of TGS. The hole was concealed and a barren core was intentionally drilled off the anomaly. Meanwhile, the core of K-55-1 had been shipped to Utah for chemical assay which, when received in early December, revealed an average mineral content of 1.18% copper, 8.26% zinc, and 3.94% ounces of silver per ton over a length of 602 feet. These results were so remarkable that neither Clayton, an experienced geophysicist, nor four other TGS expert witnesses, had ever seen or heard of a comparable initial exploratory drill hole in a base metal deposit. So, the trial curt concluded. "There is no doubt that the drill core of K-55-1 was unusually good and that it excited the interest and speculation of those who knew about it." By March 27, 1964, TGS decided that the land acquisition program had advanced to such a point that the company might well resume drilling, and drilling was resumed on March 31.

During this period, from November 12, 1963 when K-55-1 was completed, to March 31, 1964 when drilling was resumed, certain of the individual defendants... purchased TGS stock or calls thereon. Prior to these transactions these persons had owned 1135 shares of TGS stock and possessed no calls; thereafter they owned a total of 8235 shares and possessed 12,300 calls...

When drilling was resumed on March 31, hole K-55-3 was commenced 510 feet west of K-55-1 and was drilled easterly at 45° angle so as to cross K-55-1 in a vertical plane. Daily progress reports of the drilling of this hole K-55-3 and of all subsequently drilled holes were sent to defendants... On the basis of these findings relative to the foregoing drilling results, the trial court concluded... that "There was real evidence that a body of commercially mineable ore might exist."...

Rule 10b-5, on which this action is predicated, provides:

> It shall be unlawful for any person, directly or indirectly, by the use of any means or instrumentality of interstate commerce, or of the mails, or of any facility of any national securities exchange,
>
> (1) to employ any device, scheme, or artifice to defraud,
> (2) to make any untrue statement of a material fact or to omit to state a material fact necessary in order to make the statements made, in the light of the circumstances under which they were made, not misleading, or
> (3) to engage in any act, practice, or course of business which operates or would operate as a fraud or deceit upon any person,
> in connection with the purchase or sale of any security.

Rule 10b-5 was promulgated pursuant to the grant of authority given the SEC by congress in Section 10(b) of the Securities Exchange Act of 1934. By that Act Congress purposed to prevent inequitable and unfair practices and to insure fairness in securities transactions generally, whether conducted face-to-face, over the counter or on exchanges. The Act and the Rule apply to the transactions here, all of which were consummated on exchanges... [T]he Rule is based in policy on the justifiable expectation of the securities market place that all investors trading on impersonal exchanges have relatively equal access to material information. The essence of the Rule is that anyone who, trading for his own account in the securities of a corporation has "access, directly or indirectly, to information intended to be available only for corporate purpose and not for the personal benefit of anyone" may not take "advantage of such information knowing it is unavailable to those with whom he is dealing," i.e., the investing public. Insiders, as directors or management officers are, of course, by this Rule, precluded from so unfairly dealing, but the Rule is also applicable to one possessing the information who may not be strictly termed an "insider" within the meaning of Sec. 16(b) of the Act. Thus, anyone in possession of material inside information must either disclose it to the investing public, or, if he is disabled from disclosing it in order to protect a corporate confidence, or he chooses not to do so, must abstain from trading in or recommending the securities concerned while such inside information remains undisclosed. So, it is here no justification for insider activity that disclosure was forbidden by the legitimate corporate objective of acquiring options to purchase the land surrounding the exploration site; if the information, was, as the SEC contends, material, its possessors should have kept out of the market until disclosure was accomplished.

Material Inside Information

An insider is not, of course, always foreclosed from investing in his own company merely because he may be more familiar with company operations than are outside investors. An insider's duty to disclose information or his duty to abstain from dealing in his company's securities arises only in "those situations which are essentially extraordinary in nature and which are reasonably certain to have a substantial effect on the market price of the security if (the extraordinary situation is) disclosed."

Nor is an insider obligated to confer upon outside investors the benefit of his superior financial or other expert analysis by disclosing his educated guesses or predictions. The only regulatory objective is that access to material information be enjoyed equally, but this objective requires nothing more than the disclosure of basic facts so that outsiders may draw upon their own evaluative expertise in reaching their own investment decisions with knowledge equal to that of the insiders...

...[M]aterial facts include not only information disclosing the earnings and distributions of a company but also those facts which affect the probable future of the company and those which may affect the desire of investors to buy, sell, or hold the company's securities...

The core of Rule 10b-5 is the implementation of the congressional purpose that all investors should have equal access to the rewards of participation in securities transactions. It was the intent of congress that all members of the investing public should be subject to identical market risks,—which market risks include, of course the risk that one's evaluative capacity or one's capital available to put at risk may exceed another's capacity or capital. The insiders here were not trading on an equal footing with the outside investors. They alone were in a position to evaluate the probability and magnitude of what seemed from the outset to be a major ore strike; they alone could invest safely, secure in the expectation that the price of TGS stock would rise substantially in the event such a major strike should materialize, but would decline little, if at all, in the event of failure, for the public, ignorant at the outset of the favorable probabilities would likewise be unaware of the unproductive exploration, and the additional exploration costs would not significantly affect TGS market prices. Such inequities based upon unequal access to knowledge should not be shrugged off as inevitable in our way of life, or in view of the congressional concern in the area, remain uncorrected.

We hold, therefore, that all transactions in TGS stock or calls by individuals apprised of the drilling results of K-55-1 were made in violation of Rule 10b-5. Inasmuch as the visual evaluation of that drill core (a generally reliable estimate though less accurate than a chemical assay) constituted material information, those advised of the results of the visual evaluation as well as those informed of the chemical assay traded in violation of law...

■ ■ ■

Questions

1. What is the purpose of Rule 10b-5? How did the defendants violate this rule?
2. When are "insiders" precluded from trading in securities of the company they represent?
3. Must a corporation immediately disclose all material information?

Case Note

The insiders of Texaco Gulf Sulphur who are found to be in violation of Rule 10b-5 were ordered to pay money into an escrow account with the company which was to be used to pay parties injured by their illegal trading on inside information. The amount each had to pay into the fund was determined by comparing the price of Texas Gulf Sulphur stock after the disclosure of the extradorinary information with the purchase price paid by the insider prior to disclosue. The difference plus interest was to be disgorged from the insiders.

In addition, some of the individual defendants were enjoined from violating this aspect of the securities law again. Any future violation by these defendants would subject them to a "contempt of court" charge and the possibility of a prison sentence.

MISLEADING PRESS RELEASE

REYNOLDS v. TEXAS GULF SULPHUR COMPANY
309 F. Supp. 548 (1970)
United States District Court, Utah

■ ■ ■

Neither the ('34) statute nor the (10b-5) Rule provides for private civil remedies for fraud or misrepresentation in connection with a purchase or sale of any security, manipulative or deceptive practices, or for failing to disclose material information not otherwise available to the other party to a transaction. Judicial decisions, however, have firmly established such civil remedies as being implicit in the provisions.

Plaintiffs here contend that they have been damaged by violations of the statute and the rule by... the corporation... in issuing an inacurate, misleading and deceptive press release, which was published April 13, 1964...

Plaintiff Reynolds made two purchases of TGS stock, 300 shares o January 7, 1960, at $18-5/8 a share and 200 shares on May 18, 1962, at $15 per share. He sold his 500 shares early on the morning of April 16, 1964, after hearing about a "rumor" and a "flurry" in the stock, but before he learned that there had been an announcement of a "major strike" or "discovery." He testified that he sold on the strength of the April 12, 1964 press release, a summary of which came over the wires on the morning of April 13th.

From the record the court concludes that the press release dated April 12, 1964, was inaccurate, misleading and deceptive with respect to material matters disclosed by the company's drilling near Timmins... (T)he court finds the release dated April 12 was deceptive, misleading and inaccurate and violated both the statutory section 10(b) and the Rule provision 10b-5, and finds that plaintiff Reynolds was misled and deceived to his detriment and is entitled to recover damages...

The aim of courts in cases of this type is to put the plaintiffs in the position they would have been in if they had not been motivated by defendant's fraudulent press release to sell their stock...

The variety of situations in which a 10(b) or 10b-5 violation may be found makes it difficult to formulate a comprehensive rule of damages...

It seems to this court that the true and just measure of damages in these cases should be...the highest intermediate value reached by the stock between the time of the wrongful act complained of and a reasonable time after the injured party received, or should have received notice of it, a time within which he has a reasonable opportunity to replace the stock.

The obligation of the plaintiff shareholder is to exercise ordinary and reasonable care and diligence to look out for himself. The notice required is that which he received, or should have received, in the exercise of reasonable care and diligence.

We must draw the line somewhere, and this is an attempt to give a twenty trading day period within which the average of the highest daily prices is the measure of damages, and a period within which the shareholders received, or should have received, notice of the Texas Gulf Sulphur announcement of April 16...

The court deems it fair and just therefore, to take the average of all of the highest market prices on the 20 trading days, rather than the single highest market price during the period.

The average of the high market prices during such 20-day period is $50.75, which the court adopts as the measure of damages in these cases.

Damages to be awarded to Plaintiff Reynolds are computed by deducting from $50.75 the price he received for each share, $33.625, and multiplying the resulting figure of $17.125 by 500, the number of shares he sold, to arrive at damages at $8,562.25. Interest on that amount at the rate of 6% per annum from the date he sold his stock to the date of judgment is allowed...

■ ■ ■

Questions

1. How did Texas Gulf Sulphur violate Rule 10b-5?
2. How did the court compute the amount of damages to be awarded to the plaintiff?

Case Note

On December 30, 1971 the majority of cases brought by stockholders against Texas Gulf Sulphur were settled. Texas Gulf Sulphur paid $2.7 million in settlement to stockholder plaintiffs.

TIPPEE LIABILITY

SHAPIRO v. MERRILL LYNCH, PIERCE, FENNER & SMITH, INC.
495 F. 2d 228 (1974)
United States Court of Appeals, (2nd. Cir.)

■ ■ ■

...This case involves the liability of non-trading "tippers" and trading "tippees" under Section 10(b) and Rule 10b-5...

On August 21, 1970, plaintiffs commenced the instant action... They sued on behalf of themselves and all others similarly situated (a "class action") who purchased Douglas common during the period June 21 through June 24, 1966...

Plaintiffs do not claim to have purchased specific shares of Douglas stock sold by any of the selling defendants. The complaint demands damages sustained by plaintiffs and an accounting of profits realized by defendants...

Here, upon the question of whether Section 10(b) and Rule 10b-5 were violated, the critical facts—admitted for purposes of this appeal—are that Merrill Lynch, a prospective managing underwriter of a Douglas debenture issue, and some of the officers, directors and employees of Merrill Lynch, divulged to certain of its customers, the selling defendants, material adverse inside information regarding Douglas' earnings; the selling defendants, without disclosing to the investing public this inside information, sold Douglas' common stock on a national securities exchange; and as a result of such trading Merrill Lynch and the individual defendants received commissions and other compensation, the selling defendants minimized their losses, but the investing public comprised of uninformed outsiders, including plaintiffs, who purchased Douglas stock during the same period sustained substantial losses.

Our holding that such conduct on the part of all defendants violated Section 10(b) and Rule 10b-5 is based chiefly on our decision in SEC v. Texas Gulf Sulphur Co.

Defendants argue, however, that Texas Gulf is inapplicable here because... Rule

10b-5 does not impose upon these defendants a duty to disclose material inside information in question to these plaintiffs who did not purchase the actual stock sold by defendants.

...We hold that defendants owed a duty—for the breach of which they may be held liable in this private action of damages—not only to the purchasers of the actual shares sold by defendants (in the unlikely event they can be indentified) but to all persons who during the same period purchased Douglas stock in the open market without knowledge of the material inside information which was in the possession of defendants...

We are not persuaded by the selling defendants' argument that as tippees they were not able to make effective public disclosure of information about a company with which they were not associated; for the duty imposed is not a naked one to disclose, but a duty to abstain from trading unless they do disclose. Since upon the admitted facts befoe us the selling defendants knew or should have known of the confidential corporate source of the revised earnings information and they knew of its non-public nature, they were under a duty not to trade in Douglas stock without publicly disclosing such information.

...While the concepts of reliance and causation have been used interchangeably in the context of a Rule 10b-5 claim, the proper test to determine whether causation in fact has been established in a non-disclosure case is "whether the plaintiff would have been influenced to act differently than he did act if the defendant had disclosed to him the undisclosed fact.". ...

Our holding that causation in fact has been established despite the fact that all transactions took place on a national securities exchange is consistent with the underlying purpose of Section 10(b) and Rule 10b-5 "to prevent inequitable and unfair practices and to insure fairness in securities transactions generally, whether conducted face-to-face, over the counter, or on the exchanges... The Act and the Rule apply to the transactions here, all of which were consummated on exchanges."

For the reasons set forth above, we hold that defendants are liable in this private action for damages to plaintiffs who, during the same period that defendants traded in or recommended trading in Douglas common stock, purchased Douglas stock in the open market without knowledge of the material inside information which was in the possession of defendants.

■ ■ ■

Questions

1. How did Merrill Lynch gain access to the inside information of Douglas?
2. Are the "tippees" of Merrill Lynch liable under Rule 10(b)-5?

Note

While all the legal issues involving "insider" trading have not been resolved, hardly anyone is complaining. The SEC and shareholder suits involving the misuse of the inside information no longer appear to be significant threats to business. Instead, the SEC has been able to impose "self-regulation" on business, by encouraging corporations to adopt internal guidelines for the proper handling of inside information. However, government suits based on insider trading and tipping are still possible. The SEC in early 1978 brought the first *criminal* case based on misuse of inside information.

ACCOUNTANTS AND RULES 10b-5

If accountants (or attorneys and underwriters) were to intentionally participate in a fraudulent or misleading scheme with their clients, it would be clear that they have violated Rule 10b-5. However, it is a more difficult question to determine if the accountant should be liable for negligent failure to expose a client's fraud. The following case examines this specific question.

ERNST & ERNST v. HOCHFELDER
425 U.S. 185 (1976)
Supreme Court of the United States

■ ■ ■

POWELL, Mr. Justice.

Petitioner, Ernst & Ernst, is an accounting firm. From 1946 through 1967 it was retained by First Securities Company of Chicago (First Securities), a small brokerage firm and member of the Midwest Stock Exchange and of the National Asociation of Securities Dealers, to perform periodic audits of the firm's books and records. In connection with these audits Ernst & Ernst prepared for filing with the Securities and Exchange Commission (the Commission) the annual reports required of First Securities under § 17(a) of the 1934 Act...

Respondents were customers of First Securities who invested in a fraudulent securities scheme perpetrated by Leston B. Nay, president of the firm and owner of 92 percent of its stock. Nay induced the respondents to invest funds in "escrow" accounts that he represented would yield a high rate of return. Respondents did so from 1942 through 1966, with the majority of the transactions occurring in the 1950's. In fact, there were no escrow accounts as Nay converted respondents' funds to his own use immediately upon receipt. These transactions were not in the customary form of dealings between First Securities and its customers. The respondents drew their personal checks payable to Nay or a designated bank for his acount. No such escrow accounts were reflected on the books and records of First Securities, and none was shown on its periodic accounting to respondents in connection with their own investments. Nor were they included in First Securities' filings with the Commission...

This fraud came to light in 1968 when Nay committed suicide, leaving a note that describe First Securities as bankrupt and the escrow accounts as "spurious." Respondents subsequently filed this action for damages against Ernst & Ernst... The complaint charge that Nay's excrow scheme violated § 10(b) and Commission Rule 10b-5, and that Ernst & Ernst had "aided and abetted" Nay's violations by its "failure" to conduct proper audits of First Securities. As revealed through discovery, respondents' cause of action rested on a theory of negligent nonfeasance. The premise was that Ernst & Ernst had failed to utilize "appropriate auditing procedures" in its audits of First Securities, thereby failing to discover internal practices of the firm said to prevent an effective audit. The practice principally relied on was Nay's rule that only he could open mail addressed to him at First Securities or addressed to First Securities to his attention, even if it arrived in his absence. Respondents contended that if Ernst & Ernst had conducted a proper audit, it would have discovered this "mail rule." The existence of the rule then would have been disclosed in reports to the Exchange and to the Commission by Ernst & Ernst as an irregular procedure that prevented an effective audit. This would have revealed the fraudulent scheme. Respondents specifically disclaimed the existence of fraud or intentional misconduct on the part of Ernst & Ernst....

We granted Certiorari to resolve the question whether a private cause of action for damages will lie under § 10(b) and Rule 10b-5 in the absence of any allegation of "scienter" — intent to deceive, manipulate, or defraud....

Section 10(b) makes unlawful the use or employment of "any manipulative or deceptive device or contrivance" in contravention of Commission rules. The words "manipulative or deceptive" used in conjunction with "device or contrivance" strongly suggest that § 10(b) was intended to proscribe knowing or intentional misconduct....

In its *amicus curiae* brief, however, the Commission contends that nothing in the language "manipulative or deceptive device or contrivance" limits its operation to knowing or intentional practices. In support of its view, the Commission cites the overall congressional purpose in the 1933 and 1934 Acts to protect investors against false and deceptive practices that might injure them.... The Commission then reasons that since the "effect" upon investors of given conduct is the same regardless of whether the conduct is negligent or intentional, Congress must have intended to bar all such practices and not just those done knowingly or intentionally. The logic of this effect-oriented approach would impose liability for wholly faultless conduct where such conduct results in harm to investors, a result the commission would be unlikely to support... The arugment simple ignores the use of the words "manipulative," "device," and "contrivance." terms that make unmistakable a congressional intent to proscribe a type of conduct quite different from negligence. Use of the word "manipulative" is especially significant. It is and was virtually a term of art when used in connection with securities markets. It connotes intentional or wilful conduct designed to deceive or defraud investors by controlling or artifically affecting the price of securities....

...The commission contends, however, that subsections (2) and (3) of Rule 10b-5 are cast in language which — if standing alone — could encompass both intentional and negligent behavior. These subsections respectively provide that it is unlawful "[t]o make any untrue statement of a material fact or to omit to state a material fact necessary in order to make the statements made, in light of the circumstances under which they were made, not misleading..." and "to engage in any act, practice, or course of business which operates or would operate as a fraud or deceit upon any person...." Viewed in isolation the language of subsection (2), and arguably that of subsection (3), could be read as proscribing, respectively, any type of material misstatement or omission, and any course of conduct, that has the effect of defrauding investors, whether the wrongdoing was intentional or not.

We note first that such a reading cannot be harmonized with the administrative history of the rule, a history making clear that when the Commission adopted the rule it was intended to apply only to activities that involved scienter. More importantly, Rule 10b-5 was adopted pursuant to authority granted the Commission under § 10(b). The rulemaking power granted to an administrative agency charged with the administration of a federal statute is not the power to make law. Rather, it is " 'the power to adopt regulations to carry into effect the will of congress as expressed by the statute.' "

...Thus, despite the broad view of the Rule advanced by the Commission in this case, its scope cannot exceed the power granted the Comission by Congress under § 10(b). For the reasons stated above, we think the Commission's orginal interpretation of Rule 10b-5 was compelled by the language and history of § 10(b) and related section of the Acts.... When a statute speaks so specifically in terms of manipulation and deception, and of implementing devices and contrivances — the commonly understood terminology of international wrongdoing — and when its history reflects no more expansive intent, we are quite unwilling to extend the scope of the statute to negligent conduct....

■ ■ ■

Questions

1. What do the respondents contend was the "error" of Ernst & Ernst in auditing First Securities? Was the error intentional or fraudulent? Was the error negligence? Did the Court decide whether E&F was negligent?
2. Should the language "manipulative or deceptive device for contrivance" limit the use of Rule 10b-5 to "intentional" practices?
3. What impact did the administrative history of the Rule have on the Court's interpretation?

SHORT-SWING PROFITS

Section 16 of the 1934 Act attempts to prohibit the use of inside information by insiders to reap profits on short-swing transactions in securities markets. Section 16(a) requires that all directors, officers, and beneficial owners of at least 10 percent of the stock file a form with the SEC disclosing the amount of securities of the issuer which they hold. Subsequently, a report must be filed whenever a change in beneficial ownership occurs during any calendar month. These reports are public information and scrutinized by individuals who may be interested in instituting lawsuits against the insiders. Section 16(b) allows recovery of "short-swing" profits realized by a director, officer, or 10 percent beneficial stockowner resulting from any sale or purchase, or purchase and sale, of any equity security of the company within a period of less than six months. The suit may be instituted by the company or by any owner of stock of the company, if the company refuses to bring suit within sixty days after request by the complaining stockholder. It is possible for an indiviudal to purchase one share of the company stock and bring suit in the name of the company to recover short-swing profits. The person's motivation for bringing the suit is often explained by the right of the person's attorney to claim an attorney's fee out of the short-swing profits recovered by the suit. In this manner, private litigants serve as "enforcers" of Section 16.

A person may be held to be a "beneficial" owner of securities which are legally owned by a spouse, minor children, or any relative who resides in his or her home. Moreover, securities owned by a trustee who is under the direction of an insider also are considered to be beneficially owned by the insider.

In determination of whether a short-swing profit has been secured, the courts arbitrarily match purchases and sales during any 6 month period. For example, consider the following transactions:

Day 1, a purchase of 100 shares @ $10 per share.
Day 2, a sale of 100 shares @ $8 per share.
Day 3, a purchase of 100 shares @ $5 per share.
Day 4, a sale of 100 shares @ $3 per share.

It would appear that in this declining price market the insider has suffered losses. However, the court would compare the purchase at $5/share with the sale at $8/share and determine a short-swing profit has been obtained. In addition, the courts have held that any losses incurred during the 6 month period (the purchase at $10/share and the sale at $3/share) could not be used as a set-off against the profits obtained during the same period. Consequently, the insider would be obligated to pay the "short-swing profit to the corporation.

The following case involves a U.S. Supreme Court interpretation of Section 16(b). While the director did not keep his short-swing profit, his partners did retain short-swing profits. The question before the court is whether the partners' share was a violation of 16(b).

BLAU v. LEHMAN
368 U.S. 403 (1962)
Supreme Court of the United States

■ ■ ■

BLACK, Mr. Justice.

. . . Blau, a stockholder in Tide Water Associated Oil Company, brought this action in a United States District Court on behalf of the company under § 16(b) of the Securities Exchange Act of 1934 to recover with interest "short swing" profits. . . alleged to have been "realized" by respondents in Tide Water securities dealings. Respondents are Lehman Brothers, a partnership engaged in investment banking, securities brokerage and in securities trading for its own account, and Joseph A. Thomas, a member of Lehman Brothers and a director of TideWater. The complaint alleged that Lehman Brothers. . . (deputized) ". . . Thomas, to represent its interests as a director on the Tide Water Board of Directors," and that within a period of six months in 1954 and 1955 Thomas, while representing the interests of Lehman Brothers as a director of Tide Water and "by reason of his special and inside knowledge of the affairs of Tide Water, advised and caused the defendants, Lehman Brothers, to purchase and sell 50,000 shares of. . . stock of Tide Water, realizing profits thereon which did not insure to and [were] not recovered by Tide Water."

The case was tried before a district judge without a jury. The evidence showed that

Lehman Brothers had in fact earned profits out of short-swing transactions in Tide Water securities while Thomas was a director of that company...

From the... testimony the District Court found that "there was no evidence that the firm of Lehman Brothers deputed Thomas to represent its interests as director on the board of Tide Water" and that there had been no actual use of inside information, Lehman Brothers having bought its Tide Water stock "solely on the basis of Tide Water's public announcements and without consulting Thomas."

On the basis of these findings the District Court refused to render a judgment, either against the partnership or against Thomas individually, for the $98,686.77 profits which it determined that Lehman Brothers had realized... Despite its recongition that Thomas had specifically waived his share of the Tide Water transaction profits, the trial court nevertheless held that within the meaning of § 16(b) Thomas had "realized" $3,893.41, his proportionate share of the profits of Lehman Brothers. The court consequently entered judgment against Thomas for that amount... the questions presented by the petition are whether the courts below erred: (1) in refusing to render a judgment against the Lehman partnership for the $98,686.77 profits they were found to have "realized" from their "short-swing" transactions in Tide Water stock, (and) (2) in refusing to render judgment against Thomas for the full $98,686.77 profits. ...

Both the petitioner and the Commission contend on policy grounds that the Lehman partnership should be held liable even though it is neither a director, officer, nor a 10 percent stockholder, Conceding that such an interpretation is not justified by the literal language of § 16(b) which plainly limits liability to directors, officers, and 10 percent stockholders, it is argued that we should expand § 16(b) to cover partnerships of which a director is a member in order to carry out the congressionally declared purpose "of preventing the unfair use of information which may have been obtained by such beneficial owner, director, or officer by reason of his relationship to the issuer..." Failure to do so, it is argued, will leave a large and unintended loophole in the statute — one "substantially eliminating the great Wall Street trading firms from the statutes operation." These firms it is claimed will be abled to evade the Act and take advantage of the "inside" information available to their members as insiders of countless corporations merely by trading "inside" information among the various partners.

The argument of petitioner and the commission seems to go so far as to suggest that § 16(b)'s forfeiture of profits should be extended to include all persons realizing "short swing" profits who either act on the basis of "inside" information or have the possibility of "inside" information. One may agree that petitioner and the Commission present persuasive policy arguments that the Act should be broadened in this way to prevent "the unfair use of information" more effectively than can be acomplished by leaving the Act so as to require forfeiture of profits only by those specifically designated by Congress to suffer those losses. But this very broadening of the categories of persons on whom these liabilities are imposed by the language of § 16(b) was considered and rejected by Congress when it passed the Act. Drafts of provisions that eventually became § 16(b) not only would have made it unlawful for any director, officer or 10 percent stockholder to disclose any confidential information regarding registered securities, but also would have made all profits received by anyone, "insider" or not, "to whom such unlawful disclosure" had been made recoverable by the company.

Not only did Congress refuse to give § 16(b) the content we are now urged to put into it by interpretation, but with knowledge that in 1952 the Second Circuit Court of Appeals refused, in the Rattner case, to apply § 16(b) to Lehman Brothers in circumstances substantially like those here, Congress has left the Act as it was...

Second. The petitioner and the Commission contend that Thomas should be required individually to pay to Tide Water the entire $98,686.77 profit Lehman Brothers realized on the ground that under partnership law he is co-owner of the entire undivided amount and has therefore "realized" it all. "[O]nly by holding the partner-director liable for the entire short-swing profits realized by this firm," it is urged, can "an effective prophylactic to the stated statutory policy... be fully enforced." But liability under § 16(b) is to be determined neither by general partnership law nor by adding to the "prophylactic" effect Congress itself clearly prescribed in § 16(b). That section leaves no room for judicial doubt that a director is to pay to his company only "any profit realized by him" from short-swing transactions. (Emphasis added.) It would be nothing but a fiction to say that Thomas "realized" all the profits earned by the partnership of which he was a member. It was not error to refuse to hold Thomas liable for profits he did not make...

■ ■ ■

Questions

1. Did the court determine that Thomas was a "deputy" of Lehman Brothers?
2. What reason did the Court give for not extending the reach of Section 16(b) to include the partnerships of a director?

FRAUD BY INVESTMENT ADVISORS

The Investment Advisor's Act of 1940 requires that persons who advise others on a compensatory basis about their transactions in securities must register with the Commission and conform their activities to statutory standards which protect investors. The Act contains provisions governing investment advisors much like the Securities Exchange Act provisions which govern the activities of brokers and dealers who merchandise securities. The registration of investment advisors can be denied, suspended, or revoked if the Commission determines such action is in the public interest. The Act also contains antifraud provisions which empower the Commission to adopt rules which define fraudulent and manipulative acts and practices. The following case is illustrative of the SEC's determination of fraudulent activities by investment advisors.

S.E.C. v. CAPITAL GAINS RESEARCH BUREAU
375 U.S. 180 (1963)
Supreme Court of the United States

■ ■ ■

GOLDBERG, Mr. Justice.

We are called upon in this case to decide whether under the Investment Advisers Act of 1940 the Securities and Exchange Commission may obtain an injunction compelling a registered investment adviser to disclose to his clients a practice of purchasing shares of a security for his own account shortly before recommending that security for long-term investment and then immediately selling the shares at a profit upon the rise in the market price following the recommendation. The answer to this question turns on whether the practice — known in the trade as "scalping" — "operates as a fraud or deceit upon any client or prospective client" within the meaning of the Act. We hold that it does and that the Commission may "enforce compliance" with the Act by obtaining an injunction requiring the adviser to make full disclosure of the practice to his clients...

An adviser who, like respondents, secretly trades on the market effect of his own recommendation may be motivated — consciously or unconsciously — to recommend a given security not because of its potential for long-run price increase (which would profit the client), but because of its potential for short-run price increase in response to anticipated activity from the recommendation (which would profit the adviser). An investor seeking the advice of a registered investment adviser must, if the legislative purpose is to be served, be permitted to evaluate such overlapping motivations, through appropriate disclosure, in deciding whether an adviser is serving "two masters" or only one, "especially... if one of the masters happens to be economic self-interest." Accordingly, we hold that the Investment Advisers Act of 1940 empowers the courts, upon a showing such as that made here, to require an adviser to make full and frank disclosure of his practice of trading on the effect of his recommendations....

■ ■ ■

FOREIGN CORRUPT PRACTICES ACT

The scandal of illegal corporate payments in the seventies was largely uncovered by the SEC. The staff of the SEC heard testimony in the Senate Watergate Hearings that the Republican Party regularly received secret donations from corporations in violation of the maximum amount that corporations are legally permitted to contribute to political parties. Thereafter, the SEC brought suits against a few corporations, alleging such secret payments were improperly withheld from the disclosure documents that the corporations were required to file with the Commission. However, since corporate disclosure regulation pursuant to the Securities Acts is limited to *material* information, corporate officials often asserted that the SEC cannot require the disclosure of most secret corporate payments for political or foreign bribes, because the amounts were usually small compared to sales or earnings of the company. The SEC argued, nevertheless, that information that affects the integrity of management, or the integrity of the company's books and records, is material even if the dollar amount is very small. Since secret corporate payments often involve mislabeling of accounts in the books and records, the SEC contended that the transactions are generally material and required disclosure.

The SEC argued further that books and records must be accurately maintained for the company's financial statements to be relied upon by stockholders. Congressional agreement with the SEC's position was subsequently evidenced in the Foreign Corrupt Practices Act (FCPA) of 1977, which amended the 1934 Securities Act in prohibiting the making of false entries in books and records of publicly traded companies. The Act requires that the company's books, records and accounts accurately and fairly reflect, in reasonable detail, the transactions and dispositions of the company's assets. Since the reliability of the company's books and records is dependant upon the effectiveness of the company's system of internal accounting controls, the Act also requires that each company devise and maintain a system of internal accounting controls sufficient to provide reasonable assurances that accurate records are being kept. Companies found to have willfully violated the accounting standards provisions of the FCPA are subject to fines of not more than $10,000 or imprisonment of not more than five years or both. The possibility also exists that a violating company may be subjected to civil litigation brought by third parties. The SEC has also indicated its intention to require management to report publicly on its internal accounting controls.

The sections of the Act that deal with "foreign corrupt practices" are quite limited in scope, but can involve a fine of up to one million dollars for a violation. There are five separate parts that make up a violation: (1) the use of an instrumentality of interstate commerce (such as the telephone or mails) in furtherance of, (2) a payment, or even an offer to pay, "anything of value," directly or indirectly, (3) to any foreign official with discretionary authority or to any foreign political party or foreign political candidate, (4) if the purpose of the payment is the "corrupt" one of getting the recipient to act (or refrain from acting), (5) in such a way as to assist the company in obtaining or retaining business for or with or directing business to any person.

The Act provides that a foreign official does not include any government employee whose duties are "essentially ministerial or clerical." Consequently, there is no prohibition against paying substantial sums to minor officials, so long as their duties are ministerial or clerical. Such payments are frequently called "grease" or "facilitating" payments to minor foreign officials to get them to perform customary services that they might refuse to perform, or only slowly perform, in the absence of such payments.

For the payments to be illegal under the Act, the word "corruptly" is used to make clear that the offer, payment, promise, or gift must be intended to induce the recipient to misuse his or her official position to wrongfully direct business to the payor or the client, or to obtain preferential legislation or regulation. The word "corruptly" connotes an evil motive or purpose, but there is no requirement that the payment violate the law of the host country for it to be labeled "corrupt."

While not in the Act itself, Congress made clear in its hearings that it did not attempt to outlaw an extortion payment. However, no precise guidance is provided in this area except that Congress expects the U.S. diplomatic service to render aid to American businesses abroad who are threatened by extortion.

CORPORATE GOVERANCE

The SEC has often settled suits of alleged wrongdoing by corporate officials by requiring the defending companies to appoint " independant" persons to investigate the full extent of wrongdoing. In-house investigators were either outside directors of the company or especially hired lawyers and accountants who were to report to a committee of the board of directors, such as an audit committee. This technique became the basis of the SEC's handling of the "Corporate Payment Scandal." The SEC requested companies to participate in a "voluntary disclosure program." Almost 400 companies agreed to conduct independant internal investigations and make the findings available to the SEC. A summary of the internal investigation was reported to investors. The SEC also required the participating companies to develop corporate codes of conduct which prohibit illegal payments, require proper recordkeeping, and prohibit other types of unethical conduct. The codes also established compliance and monitoring procedures so that, in effect, the codes became in-house extensions of the securities laws.

As the "voluntary disclosure program" indicates, corporate disclosure regulation appears to be expanding from merely providing information to investors. Instead, disclosure rules are becoming instruments for social regulation. Critics of the "corporate system" have asserted that companies are "undemocratic" because management controls the nomination procedures for the board of directors. Opposing shareholders must bear an expensive proxy fight to nominate any other person for a directorship. As a response to these criticisms Congress and the SEC held public hearings on corporate governance in 1977. Most reform proposals have involved the corporate disclosure machinery as a means for shareholders to gain greater control over boards of directors. Such reforms attempt to make companies more responsible, accountable, and democratic.

While the SEC already requires many shareholder social accountability proposals to be included in management's proxy materials, the SEC appears to believe that an increase in federal intervention into corporate control is unjustified by past corporate transgressions. The SEC is satisfied with the disclosure program and hopes to convince Congress not to set precedence in government regulation of corporate decision making.

In an attempt to stave off tougher Congressional legislation (federal chartering, public directors, or business-in-the-sunshine board meetings), the SEC is developing new disclosure rules for directors. Future proxy statements may include materials concerning the composition anf responsibilities of the board's audit, nominating, conflicts of interest, and compensation committees. Increased disclosure concerning the business and personal relationship between directors and management may be required in proxy materials. Information concerning the directors attendance at meetings, other directorships held, reasons for director resignations, and director compensation may become required disclosure items, also. Finally, rules relating to increased shareholder participation in director elections will probably follow soon.

CRITICISMS AND REFORMS

New academic theories and congressional criticism have raised fundamental questions about the federal disclosure system of security regulation. These questions will undoubtedly affect the future course of innovation in this field. One fundamental issue is whether disclosure is an effective remedy to deal with the ills which affect the securities markets. For example, the federal securities laws were passed in part as a reaction to the 1929 stockmarket crash. However, the federal securities laws have not prevented continuing gyration in securities markets. The goal of stability in the financial markets has not been achieved. Yet, in theory, full information revealed by the disclosure system should result in prices which are more stable. However, conclusions on this matter are difficult to determine since the instability of markets may result more from uncertainty and imperfectability of financial and economic predictions and forecasts, rather than from the failure of securities laws to make adequate disclosures of historical facts.

Connected with this criticism is the debate about historical cost financial statements. Such statements do not reflect current market values or provide information of future projection, which are more valuable to the professional or average investor. In addition, the overly permissible treatment of accounting standards tends to destroy the comparability of financial information published through the registration process. Historically, the SEC has essentially delegated the regulation of accounting principles to the accounting profession. In January of 1977, however, a Senate Subcommittee led by Senator Lee Metcalf lambasted the SEC and the accounting profession. Senator Metcalf reported:

> Corporations presently have substantial discretion in choosing among alternative accounting standards to report similar business transactions. As a result, the amounts of earnings or losses reported to the public can vary drastically depending on which accounting alternatives are chosen...In particular, I am disturbed by two...findings. The first is the extraordinary manner in which the SEC has insisted upon delegating its public authority and responsibilities on accounting matters to private groups with obvious self-interests in the resolution of such matters. The second is the alarming lack of independance and the lack of dedication to public protection shown by the large accounting firms.

As a consequence of the Metcalf report, the SEC is likely to place increasing pressure on the accountants' Financial Accounting Standards Board to set more specific accounting standards to allow for comparability of financial statements. The flexibility of accounting standards will probably be reduced and the relationship of the SEC to the accounting profession will continue to be a source of controversy for years to come.

One example of the continuing efforts of the SEC in prodding the accounting profession to make the financial statements more accurately reflect reality is the SEC accounting release which requires the disclosure of replacement costs in addition to historical costs. This involves the SEC's efforts to make financial statements reflect current value.

Another example of SEC reform is its new rule which allows companies to make projections (forecasts) in financial information. Because of the value of such data to security analysts, the SEC is likely to continue these efforts. The SEC was previously concerned that companies would use overly optimistic forecasts. The SEC is now considering ways to encourage projections by absolving a company from liability if its forecast is competently prepared but is later shown to have been inaccurate. The SEC has issued a voluntary program of guidelines to encourage the publishing of financial projections in reports, proxy, and registration statements. Nearly all the details of the forecast, including the items to be projected, assumptions underlying the projections, projection periods and frequency, and third party review are left to the discretion of management. As a further inducement to disclose, the SEC is likely to adopt a so-called "safe-harbor" rule. Two versions are currently under consideration, but both would shelter the company and its management from liability for projections which fail the test of time if forecasts were: (1) "reasonably prepared" and (2) "disclosed in good faith." The safe-harbor rule will cover stockholder reports and commission filings. One version would place the burden of proving good faith and reasonableness on the company. The other version would require investors to prove lack of good faith. Most observers believe that after two or three years of voluntary forecasting, the program will be made mandatory.

Another criticism of the present disclosure system is that the disclosed data is beyond the skills and background of the average investor to understand. The system attempts to protect relatively unsophisticated individuals who are presently inundated with overly complex material. It will be a continuing problem of the SEC to develop simpler documents and otherwise provide a more meaningful disclosure to the average investor.

Companies and critics have complained also of the extensive paperwork that must be filed with the Commission. The Advisory Committee on Corporate Disclosure has recommended that the SEC create one "continuous disclosure report" which could be used for all 1933 and 1934 Act filings. Furthermore, the SEC is anticipating recommendations of the American Law Institute which will soon propose a bill to Congress which combines the 1933 and 1934 Acts. The new Act would deemphasize the public company's offerings of securities and make the company's annual report become the "key-disclosure document."

Finally, some have argued that the disclosures mandated by the securities laws have not been effective in preventing fraud. They maintain that scandals such as Bar Chris, Manor Nursing Centers, and Equity Funding were not prevented by the securities law. However, it is impossible to know what frauds would have been perpetuated had the securities laws not been enacted. The incident of fraud and manipulation may well have been reduced by virtue of disclosure requirements. The fact that some frauds exist does not preclude the possible conclusion that some frauds have been prevented by the securities laws. Moreover, many have argued that the requirement of full disclosure results not only in the prevention of fraud, but also reduces shareholder-management conflicts of interest and deters other questionable practices.

All the efforts of the SEC are designed to promote investor confidence in American capital markets, which are the soundest in the world. While no one doubts that these disclosure practices involve a great deal of cost, the confidence of investors in American capitalistic markets is essential to the preservation of the vigor of the capital raising system of the United States. Only a few can doubt the economic and social benefits accruing from the efficient U.S. capital-raising system are less than the costs associated with the securities laws.

14

LAWS OF EMPLOYMENT

The years after the Civil War were the time of building industrial empires. The technological developments of the Industrial Revolution created a need for large-scale industrial establishments. The increasing concentration of economic power was not greatly reduced by the passage of the Sherman Act. However, the growth of the large corporations had significant consequences for the workers. It ended the personal relationship that had existed between the employer and employee and put the employee at a considerable bargaining disadvantage. Unionism appeared to be essential to give laborers an opportunity to deal with their employers on an equal basis.

As a consequence of the changing economic conditions, modern labor laws regulate nearly all aspects of the relation between employer and employee. Employers must concern themselves not only with the National Labor Relations Act but also with fair employment practices, fair labor standards, minimum wage, workmen's compensation, unemployment compensation, safety rules, and numerous other legislative prohibitions and regulations. Nevertheless, collective bargaining is the heart of labor law. Despite the detailed regulations provided by law, it is the negotiation and administration of the collectively bargained labor contracts that primarily guarantee the social and economic security that American workers enjoy. As a result, modern unions and collective bargaining have emerged as significant institutions in U.S. society. Moreover, the evolving legal doctrines concerning labor disputes focus attention on the limitations of law. It is largely through the private arena, grievance, and arbitration procedures, that detailed regulations most vitally affecting workers in their daily lives are made.

Within the context of this understanding the question arises, "What role should the court play?" The following cases elaborate some of the history involved in the legislation of labor laws, some of the basic legislative pronouncements themselves, and the appropriate role for the courts. Within the context of particular labor disputes, the reader may gain a more significant understanding of the tremendous social issues involved.

ANTITRUST AND ANTI-INJUNCTION

NORRIS-LAGUARDIA ACT

In 1932 Congress passed the Federal Anti-injunction Act (Norris-LaGuardia Act).

The Act protects legitimate union activity from federal court injunctions attempting to prohibit such activity. The Act was passed as a congressional disapproval of the courts' utilization of injunctions in spite of the Clayton Act which had, without clarity, exempted labor activities from the antitrust laws. As a consequence, the provisions of the Norris-LaGuardia Act divest federal courts of injunctive power in cases growing out of a "labor dispute," unless the private complaintant can prove in court, under cross-examination, the following elements:

1. Unlawful acts have been threatened or committed.
2. Injury to property will result.
3. Injury to complaintant will be greater than injury to defendant unless the unlawful acts are enjoined.
4. Complaintant has no adequate "damages" remedy.
5. Public officials (police) are unable or unwilling to provide protection to the complaintant's property.
6. Complaintant must petition the court with "clean hands" by having made reasonable efforts to negotiate a settlement.

Since all these elements will be difficult to establish, private parties (employers) will most likely be unable to obtain a federal court injunction against labor activities. Even if an injunction is issued, it can enjoin only the specific acts complained of in the petition.

A "labor dispute" is broadly defined in the Act to include a list of events in which the federal courts are restricted in the issuance of injunctions against labor activities. Consequently, federal courts are denied the power to issue an injunction to prohibit such "labor disputes" as ceasing or refusing to perform work, joining a labor organization, assembling peacefully, advising others, or giving publicity to any labor dispute. Nor can the federal courts issue injunctions to prohibit the paying of strike or unemployment benefits that may be available to participants in a labor dispute.

The anti-injunction provisions of the Norris-LaGuardia Act establish a policy which is in opposition to the policy of the antitrust laws. Yet, the anti-injunction law does not repeal antitrust laws. Therefore, the courts must "accomodate" or reconcile the two Acts, just as the Court attempted in *Allen Bradley*.

ALLEN BRADLEY CO. v. LOCAL UNION NO. 3
325 U.S. 797, (1945)
Supreme Court of the United States

■ ■ ■

BLACK, Mr. Justice.

Our problem in this case is...(whether) labor unions violate the Sherman Act when, in order to further their own interests as wage earners, they aid and abet businessmen to do the precise things which that Act prohibits?

The Sherman Act as originally passed contained no language expressly exempting any labor union activities. Sharp controversy soon arose as to whether the Act applied to unions...

Federal courts...applied the law to unions in a number of cases. At the same time, employers invoked injunctions to restrain labor union activities even where no violation of the Sherman Act was charged.

Vigorous protests arose from employee groups. The unions urged congressional relief from what they considered to be two separate, but partially overlapping evils— application of the Sherman Act to unions, and issuance of injunctions against strikes, boycotts and other labor union weapons...All of this is a part of the well-known history of the era between 1890 and 1914.

To amend, supplement, and strengthen the Sherman Act against monopolistic business practices, and in response to the complaints of the unions against injunctions and application of the Act to them, Congress in 1914 passed the Clayton Act...

...Section 6 declared that labor was neither a commodity nor an article of commerce, and that the Sherman Act should not be "construed to forbid the existence and operation of labor, agricultural, or horticultural organizations, instituted for the purposes of mutual help..." Section 20 limited the power of the courts to issue injunctions in a case "involving or growing out of a labor dispute over terms or conditions of employment..." It declared that no restraining order or injunction should prohibit certain specified acts, and further declared that no one of these specified acts should be "held to be violations of any law of the United States." This Act was broadly proclaimed by many as labor's "Magna Carta," wholly exempting labor from any possible inclusion in the antitrust legislation; others, however, strongly denied this.

This Court later declined to interpret the Clayton Act as manifesting a congressional purpose wholly to exempt labor unions from the Sherman Act...

Again the unions went to Congress. They protested against this Court's interpretation, repeating the arguments they had made against application of the Sherman Act to them. Congress adopted their viewpoint, at least in large part, and...passed the Norris-LaGuardia Act. That Act greatly broadened the meaning this Court had attributed to the words, "labor dispute," further restricted the use of injunctions in such a dispute, and emphasized the public importance under modern economic conditions of protecting the rights of concerted activities for the purpose of collective bargaining or other mutual aid and protection."...

The result of all this is that we have two declared congressional policies which it is our responsibility to try to reconcile. The one seeks to preserve a competitive business economy; the other to preserve the rights of labor to organize to better its conditions through the agency of collective bargaining. We must determine here how far Congress intended activities under one of these policies to neutralize the results envisioned by the other.

Aside from the fact that the labor union here acted in combination with the contractors and manufacturers, the means it adopted to contribute to the combination's purpose fall squarely within the "specified acts" declared by Sec. 20 not to be violations of federal law...Consequently, had there been no union-contractor-manufacturer combination, the union's actions here, coming as they did within the exemptions of the Clayton and Morris-LaGuardia Acts, would not have been violations of the Sherman Act. We pass to the question of whether unions can with impunity aid and abet business men who are violating the Act...

It must be remembered that the exemptions granted the unions were special exceptions to a general legislative plan. The primary objective of all the antitrust legislation has been to preserve business competition and to proscribe business monopoly. It would be a surprising thing if Congress, in order to prevent a misapplication of that legislation to labor unions, had bestowed upon such unions complete and unreviewable authority to aid business groups to frustrate its primary objective. For if business groups, by combining with labor unions, can fix prices and divide up markets, it was little more than a futile gesture for Congress to prohibit price fixing by business groups themselves. Seldom, if ever, has it been claimed before, that by permitting labor unions to carry on their own activities, Congress intended completely to abdicate its constitutional power to regulate interstate commmerce and to empower interested business groups to shift our society from a competitive to a monopolistic economy. Finding no purpose of Congress to immunize labor unions who aid and abet manufacturers and traders in violating the Sherman Act, we hold that the district court correctly concluded that the respondents had violated the Act.

Our holding means that the same labor union activities may or may not be in violation of the Sherman Act, dependent upon whether the union acts alone or in combination with business groups. This, it is argued, brings about a wholly undesirable result—one which leaves labor unions free to engage in conduct which restrains trade. But the desirability of such an exemption of labor unions is a question for the determination of Congress. It is true that many labor union activities do substantially interrupt the course of trade and that these activities, lifted out of the prohibitions of the Sherman Act, include substantially all, if not all, of the normal peaceful activities of labor unions...

Thus, these congressionally permitted union activities may restrain trade in and of themselves. There is no denying the fact that many of them do so, both directly and indirectly. Congress evidently concluded, however, that the chief objective of antitrust legislation, preservation of business competition, could be accomplished by applying the legislation primarily only to those business groups which are directly interested in destroying competition...

■ ■ ■

Questions

1. In its early history, was the Sherman Act applied to union activities?
2. Does the Clayton Act "wholly exempt" labor unions from the Sherman Act? When might a labor union violate the Sherman Act?
3. Are agricultural associations exempt from antitrust laws?
4. What is the purpose of the Norris-LaGuardia Act? Does it prohibit a federal court injunction against unilateral labor activities which may violate the Sherman Act?
5. Is it congressional intention that the Sherman Act apply only against employer combinations and not labor combinations?

The Court in *Allen Bradley* stated that the union could have achieved its purpose by acting alone. Such results would be "the natural consequence of labor union activities exempted by the Clayton Act from the coverage of the Sherman Act." However, any *agreement* between the union and the employer whereby the union imposes certain restrictions on other employers would not be exempt from an antitrust charge. For example, in the *United Mine Workers v. Pennington*, 381 U.S. 657, (1965), the Court ruled:

> a union forfeits its exemption from the antitrust laws when it is clearly shown it has agreed with one set of employers to impose a certain wage scale on other bargaining units. One group of employers may not conspire to eliminate competitors from the industry and the union is liable with the employers if it becomes a party to the conspiracy. This is true even though the union's part in the scheme is an undertaking to secure the same wages, hours, or other conditions of employment from the remaining employers in the industry.

While the union may not agree with the employer, the Court said:

> the union may make wage agreements with the multi-employer bargaining unit and may in pursuance of its own union interests seek to obtain the same terms from other employers. No case under the antitrust laws could be made out on evidence limited to such union behavior.

The Court has subsequently said:

> Union success in standardizing wages ultimately will affect price competition among employers, but the goals of federal labor law never could be achieved if this effect on business competition were held a violation of the antitrust laws. The Court therefore has acknowledged that labor policy requires tolerance for the lessenting of business competition... *Connell Co. v. Plumbers and Steamfitters* 421 U.S. 616 (1975).

NATIONAL LABOR RELATIONS ACT

Congress determined that the denial by some employers of the right of employees to organize and collectively bargain led to strikes and other forms of industrial strife which had the effect of obstructing commerce. They felt the inequality of bargaining power between employees who did not possess full freedom of association and employers who were organized in the corporate form substantially burdened the free flow of commerce. Consequently, Congress declared the policy of the United States, through the National Labor Relations Act of 1932, was to eliminate these obstructions by encouraging the practice and procedure of collective bargaining. This involved the protection of the exercise by workers of the full freedom to self-organize and designate representatives of their own choosing to negotiate terms and conditions of their employment with their employers.

The National Labor Relations Board was created by Section 3 of the Act and consists of five members, appointed by the President with the advice and consent of the Senate. The Board shall have the authority to make, amend, and rescind such rules and regulations as may be necessary to carry out the provisions of the Act.

The two most important portions of the National Labor Relations Act are Section 7 and 8. Section 7 as originally enacted reads as follows:

> Employees shall have the right to self-organization, form, join or assist labor organizations to bargain collectively through representatives of their own choosing, and to engage in other concerted activities for the purpose of collective bargaining or other mutual aid or protection.

There are three parts to the right guaranteed by Section 7. First, employees are secured the freedom to form, join, or assist labor organizations. Secondly, they are guaranteed the right to engage in concerted activities, such as strikes and picketing. Without the right to engage in strikes and picketing, the other rights may have been nothing more than empty slogans.

The rights granted to employees in Section 7 are protected against employer interference by Section 8, which details five prohibited practices by employers deemed unfair to labor.

Section 8 (1) declares it to be an unfair labor practice for an employer to "interfere with, restrain, or coerce employees in the exercise of rights guaranteed in Section 7." This provision outlaws such anti-union tactics as beating of labor organizers, company lock-outs of employees to destroy efforts to organize a union and other use of the employer's economic power to prevent unionization. This section also prohibits some subtle anti-union tactics, such as wage increases carefully timed to demonstrate to employees that nothing would be gained by joining a union.

Section 8(2) outlaws "company unions" which are dominated and controlled by the company. Such "company unions" granted the employees the *form* of an organization, but denied then any substantive rights in control. Section 8(3) prohibits discrimination in the hiring or firing of employees to influence affiliation. Subsection (4) provides protection for employees against reprisals from the company becuase of the employee's filing of charges or giving testimony with the National Labor Relations Board. Section 8(5) declares that it is unfair labor practice for the company to refuse to bargain collectively with the duly designated representative of the employees.

The National Labor Relations Board has exclusive jurisdiction over both unfair labor practices and questions of which union organization is to represent the employees. The Board has the authority to designate or separate the employees into appropriate "bargaining units." The employees of each bargaining unit by majority vote determine if they desire a union and which union will represent the unit. Such elections are controlled by the labor laws. The following cases illustrate situations in which alleged Section 8 violations occured.

INTERFERENCE WITH UNIONIZING

NLRB v. GISSEL PACKING CO., INC.
395 U.S. 575 (1969)
Supreme Court of the United States

■ ■ ■

WARREN, Mr. Chief Justice.

When petitioner's president first learned of the Union's drive in July, he talked with all of his employees in an effort to dissuade them from joining a union. He particularly emphasized the results of the long 1952 strike, which he claimed "almost put our company out of business," and expressed worry that the employees were forgetting the "lessons of the past." He emphasized, secondly, that the Company was still on "thin ice" financially, that the Union's "only weapon is to strike," and that a strike "could lead to the closing of the plant," since the parent company had ample manufacturing facilities elsewhere. He noted, thirdly, that because of their age and the limited usefulness of their skills outside their craft, the employees might not be able to find re-employment if they lost their jobs as a result of a strike. Finally, he warned those who did not believe that the plant could go out of business to "look around Holyoke and see a lot of them out of business." The president sent letters to the same effect to the employees in early November, emphasizing that the parent company had no reason to stay in Massachusetts if profits went down.

During the two or three weeks immediately prior to the election.... the president sent the employees a pamphlet captioned "Do you want another 13-week strike?" stating that "We have no doubt that the Teamsters Union can again close the Wire Weaving Department and the entire plant by a strike. We have no hopes that the Teamsters Union Bosses will not call a stike...The Teamsters Union is a strike happy outfit." Similar communications followed...including one stressing the Teamsters' "hoodlum control."... He repeated that the Company's financial condition was precarious; that a possible strike would jeopardize the continued operation of the plant; and that age and lack of education would make re-employment difficult. The Union lost the election 7-6, and then filed both objections to the election and unfair labor practice charges which were consolidated for hearing before the trial examiner.

The Board agreed with the trial examiner that the president's communications with his employees, when considered as a whole, "reasonably tended to convey to the employees the belief or impression that selection of the Union in the forthcoming election could lead [the Company] to close its plant, or to the transfer of the weaving production with the resultant loss of jobs to the wire weavers." Thus, the Board found that under the "totality of the circumstances" petitioner's activities constituted a violation of §8(a)(1) of the Act. The Board further agreed with the trial examiner that petitioner's activities, because they "also interfered with the exercise of a free and untrammeled choice in the election," and "tended to forclose the possibility" of holding a fair election required that the election be set aside...Consequently, the Board set the election aside, entered a cease-and-desist order, and ordered the Company to bargain on request...

We consider petitioner['s]...First Amendment challenge to the holding of the Board...At the outset we note that the question raised here most often arises in the context of a nascent union organizational drive, where employers must be careful in waging their anti-union campaign...But we do note than employer's free speech right to communicate his views to his employees is firmly established and cannot be infringed by a union or the Board. Thus, §8(c) merely implements the First Amendment by requiring that the expression of "any views, argument or opinion" shall not be "evidence of an unfair labor practice," so long as such expression contains "no threat of reprisal or force or promise of benefit" in violation of §8(a)(1). Section 8(a)(1), in turn, prohibits interference, restraint or coercion of employees in the exercise of their right to self-organization.

Any assessment of the precise scope of employer expression, of course, must be made in the context of its labor relations setting. Thus, an employer's rights cannot outweight the equal rights of the employees to associate freely, as those rights are embodied in §7 and proctectd by §8(a)(1) and the proviso to §8(c). And any balancing of those rights must take into account the economic dependence of the employees on their employers, and the necessary tendency of the former, because of that relationship, to pick up intended implications of the latter that might be more readily dismissed by a more disinterested ear. Stating these obvious principles is but another way of recognizing that what is basically at stake is the establishment of a nonpermanent, limited relationship between the employer, his economically dependent employee and his union agent, not the election of legislators or the enactment of legislation whereby that relationship is ultimately defined and where the independent voter may be freer to listen more objectively and employers as a class freer to talk.

Within this framework, we must reject the Company's challenge to the decision below and the findings of the Board on which it was based. The standards used below for evaluating the impact of an employer's statements are not seriously questioned by petitioner and we see no need to tamper with them here. Thus, an employer is free to communicate to his employees any of his general views about unionism or any of his specific views about a particular union, so long as the communications do not contain a "threat of reprisal or force or promise of benefit." He may even make a prediction as to the precise effects he believes unionization will have on his company. In such a case, however, the prediction must be carefully phrased on the basis of objective fact to convey an employer's belief as to demonstrably probable consequences beyond his control or to convey a management decision already arrived at to close the plant in case of unionization. If there is any implication than an employer may or may not take action solely on his own initiative for reasons unrelated to economic necessities and known only to him, the statement is no longer a reasonable prediction based on available facts but a threat of retaliation based on misrepresentation and coercion, and as such without the protection of the First Amendment. We therefore agree with the court below that "conveyance of the employer's belief, even though sincere, that unionization will or may result in the closing of the plant is not a statement of fact unless, which is most improbable, the eventuality of closing is capable of proof." As state elsewhere, any employer is free only to tell "what he reasonably believes will be the likely economic consequences of unionization that are outside his control," and not "threats of economic reprisal to be taken solely on his own volition."

Equally valid was the finding by the court and the Board that petitioner's statements and communications were not cast as a prediction of "demonstrable economic consequences," but rather as a threat of retaliatory action. The Board found that petitioner's speeches, pamphlets, leaflets, and letters conveyed the following message: that the company was in precarious financial condition: that the "strike-happy" union would in all likelihood have to obtain its potentially unreasonable demands by striking, the probable result of which would be a plant shutdown, as the past history of labor relations in the area indicatd; and that the emloyees in such a case would have great dificulty finding employment elsewhere. In carrying out its duty to focus on the question "What did the speaker intend and the listener understand," the Board could reasonably conclude that the intended and understood import of that messge was not to predict that unionization would inevitably cause the plant to close but to threaten to throw employees out of work regardless of the economic realities. In this connection, we need go no further than to point out (1) that petitioner had no support for its basic assumption that the union, which had not yet even presented any demands, would have to strike to be heard, and that it admitted at the hearing that it had no basis for attributing other plant closings in the area to unionism; and (2) that the Board has often found that employees, who are particularly sensitive to rumors of plant closings, take such hints as coercive threats rather than honest forecasts.

Questions

1. Under Section 8(c) the employer may express "any views, arguments, or

opinions." However, Section 8(c) contains a proviso which limits the employer's free speech. What are the limitations on the employer's speech?

2. How did the Court justify this limitation upon the free speech of the employer?

3. What words of the employer were held not to be protected by Section 8(c)?

COMPANY UNION

N.L.R.B. v. POST PUBLISHING COMPANY
311 F. 2d 565 (1962)
United States Court of Appeals, 7th Cir.

■ ■ ■

This case is before us on the petition of National Labor Relations Board for enforcement of its order issued against respondent, ...The Post Publishing Company, on March 15, 1962...

The Board found, in agreement with the Trial Examiner, that respondent violated §8(a)(2) and (1) of the Act by offering contributing financial and other assistance and support of the Appleton Post-Crescent Craftsmen's Union, herein called PCCU.

At the time of the dispute in question, PCCU was an independent union and since 1921 had been the lawfully recognized bargaining agent and representative of respondent's mechanical employees.

The charging party in this case is Appleton, International Typographical Union, AFL-CIO, herein called ITU. It was seeking to replace PCCU as the bargaining representative of respondent's mechanical employees.Thus, it appears at the outset that respondent found itself in the middle of a representation dispute between the two unions....

On April 4, 1961, ITU held an organizational meeting for employees in Appleton which was attended by some mechanical employees of respondent.

Subsequently, following an exchange of correspondence between respondent and ITU, the latter demanded recognition as the representative of a majority of the mechanical employees. Respondent refused such recognition because of its current contract with PCCU.

This was followed by an interunion struggle between ITU and PCCU for control, and PCCU apparently won out. In any event, ITU has never petitioned for a Board-conducted election.

Subsequently, ITU filed the charges resulting in this action. It charged respondent with the following alleged violations: (1)... (2) giving PCCU illegal support by allowing it to use respondent's cafeteria for union meetings; (3) giving PCCU illegal support by permitting it to print its union notices on respondent's machines; and (4) furnishing PCCU illegal support by permitting it to retain the profits from the operation of the cafeteria and coffee vending machine.

The trial examiner... found that the conduct complained of in the second and third charges, standing alone, would not constitute a type of "support" that amounted to a violation of the Act.

However, on the fourth charge, he ruled that the receipt of profits from the operation of the cafeteria and coffee vending machine was violative of the Act. He then considered the conduct alleged in charges 2 and 3 as contributing to such violation as a part of an overall pattern of continued and substantial support of PCCU "which was well calculated to coerce and restrain employees in the exercise of their right freely to choose or change their bargaining representative."

The Board approved and adopted the trial examiner's report without change and entered an appropriate order thereon.

The trial examiner agreed there was no evidence showing that respondent had made use of this "support" to gain concessions from PCCU in bargaining and that respondent had not threatened to discontinue such "support" if the employees left PCCU and joind ITU.

The narrow issued before us is whether the granting of annual financial benefits of its 38-year history of amicable relationship with this independent union, constituted illegal financial support by respondent in violation of the Act.

At the outset the resolution of this issue must be made in the light of the Board's concession that *there is no claim that respondent was the motivating factor in the organization of PCCU* and that *no claim is made that respondent dominated this independent union.*

We conclude that the Board erred in failing to properly distinguish between "support" and "cooperation." The findings of proscribed support under the Act are unsupported by substantial evidence in the record considered as a whole and are contrary to law.

The course of conduct engaged in by respondent in its relationship with PCCU follows that pattern of friendly and courteous cooperation, or even generous action, of the sort we feel brings about the end result in labor-management relations sought by the underlying philosophy motivating the National Labor Relations Act.

This course of conduct flows directly from union request. Absent any showing of employer domination, we fail to find in the record that showing of proscribed motivation warranting an inference drawn by the Board that it was calculated to unlawfully coerce or restrain the employees in their right to freely choose or change their bargaining representative.

The fact that the union members chose to eliminate dues and forego the provision for many fringe benefits to its members was a decision it made. Respondent did not participate in any way in the decision of the union as to how it would derive its income, or in what manner it would incur expenses in the conduct of its business. All that respondent did was to assist the employees in carrying out their independent activities. No one ever complained until a representation dispute was precipitated. That complaint was made by the dominant international organization in its effort to oust the small independent group. . . .

We have carefully reviewed the many cases cited by the Board. In practically all of them, the facts clearly demonstrate antiunion bias by the employer, financial support combined with union domination by the employer, discriminatory discharges, threats or other unfair labor practices interwoven with acts of alleged illegal financial support. Such is not the case here.

We hold, absent any showing of employer motivation in the original organization of the independent union or any showing of subsequent employer domination thereof, that a course of conduct over a period of years by an employer in its amicable relationship for 38 years with an independent union acting as a bargaining agent for employees (1) in permitting the union to hold meetings in its cafeteria (after working hours), (2) in permitting the union to print notices on the employer's duplicating machines, (3) and in permitting the union to retain annual profits of about $600 from the operation of the union of employer's cafeteria for employees and about $120 annually from the operation of a coffee vending machine for employees on its premises by the Union, all at the instance and request of the union and under the circustances as herein earlier set out, is a permissible form of friendly cooperation designed to foster and resulting in uninterrupted harmonious labor-management relations, and is not the form of "support" designed to interfere with, restrain or coerce employees in the free exercise of their right to choose or change their bargaining representative.

For the foregoing reasons, we deny the Board's petition for enforcement of its order against respondent.

■ ■ ■

SECTION 8(a) 3

This section prevents an employer from discharging or refusing to hire an employee as a technique to encourage or discourage membership in a labor orgainization. However, it does not restrict the employer in a normal exercise of his or her judgment in selecting or discharging employees for proper cause. Nevertheless, the question arises as to whether the employer may close his or her shop and open another business elsewhere to avoid unionization of the plant? Or whether the employer can choose to go out of business altogether in order to avoid unionization? The following excerpt provides some answers.

TEXTILE WORKERS UNION v. DARLINGTON MANUFACTURING CO.
380 U. S. 263 (1965)
Supreme Court of the United States

■ ■ ■

HARLAN, Mr. Justice.

We are not presented here with the case of a "runaway shop," whereby Darlington would transfer its work to another plant or open a new plant in another locality to replace its closed plant. Nor are we concerned with a shutdown where the employees, by renouncing the union, could cause the plant to reopen. Such cases would involve discriminatory employer action for the purpose of obtaining some benefit in the future from the new employees. We hold here only that when an employer closes his entire business, even if the liquidation is motivated by vindictiveness towards the union, such action is not an unfair labor practice...

The closing of an entire business, even though discriminatory, ends the employer-employee relationship; the force of such a closing is entirely spent as to that business when termination of the enterprise takes place. On the other hand, a discriminatory partial closing may have repercussions on what remains of the business, affording employer leverage for discouraging the free exercise of §7 rights among remaining employees of much the same kind as that found to exist in the "runaway shop" and "temporary closing" cases. Moreover, a possible remedy open to the Board in such a case, like the remedies available in the "runaway shop" and "temporary closing" cases, is to order reinstatement of the discharged employees in the other parts of the business. No such remedy is available when an entire business has been terminated. By analogy to those cases involving a continuing enterprise we are constrained to hold, in disagreement with the Court of Appeals, that a partial closing is an unfair labor practice under §8(a)(3) if motivated by a purpose to chill unionism in any of the remaining plants of the single employer and if the employer may reasonably have foreseen that such closing will likely have that effect.

■ ■ ■

BARGAIN IN GOOD FAITH

N.L.R.B. v. KATZ
369 U.S. 736 (1961)
Supreme Court of the United States

■ ■ ■

BRENNAN, Mr. Justice.

Is it a violation of the duty " to bargain collectively" imposed by §8(a)(5) of the National Labor Relations Act for an employer, without first consulting a union with which it is carrying on bona fide contract negotiations, to institute changes regarding matters which are subjects of mandatory bargaining under §8(d) and which are in fact under discussion? The National Labor Relations Board answered the question affirmatively in this case, in a decision which expressly disclaimed any finding that the totality of the respondents' conduct manifested bad faith in the pending negotiations...

The first meeting between the company and the union took place on August 30, 1956. On this occasion, as at the ten other conferences held between October 2, 1956, and May 13, 1957, all six companies were in attendance and represented by the same counsel. It is undisputed that the subject of merit increases were raised at the August 30, 1956, meeting although there is an unresolved conflict as to whether an agreement was reached on joint participation by the company and the union in merit reviews, or whether the subject was simply mentioned and put off for discussion at a later date. It is also clear that proposals concerning sick leave were made. Several meetings were held during October and one in November, at which merit raises and sick leave were each discussed on at least two occasions. It appears, however, that little progress was made.

Meanwhile, on April 16, 1957, the union had filed the charge upon which the General Counsel's complaint later issued. As amended and amplified at the hearing and construed by the Board, the complaint's charge of unfair labor practices particularly referred to three acts by the company: unilaterally granting numerous merit increases in October 1956 and January 1957; unilaterally announcing a change in sick-leave policy in March 1957; and unilaterally instituting a new system of automatic wage increases during April 1957. As the ensuing litigation has developed, the company has defended against the charges along two fronts: First, it asserts that the unilateral changes occurred after a bargaining impasse had developed through the union's fault in adopting obstructive tactics. According to the Board, however, "the evidence is clear that the Respondent undertook its unilateral actions before negotiations were discontinued in May 1957, or before, as we find on the record, the existence of any possible impasse." 126 N.L.R.B., at 289-290. There is ample support in the record considered as a whole for this finding of fact...

The second line of defense was that the Board could not hinge a conclusion that §8(a)(5) though the employer has every desire to reach agreement with the union upon employer's subjective bad faith at the bargaining table; and that the unilateral actions were merely evidence relevant to the issue of subjective good faith.

The duty "to bargain collectively" enjoined by §8(a)(5) is defined by §8(d) as the duty to "meet...and confer in good faith with respect to wages, hours, and other terms and conditions of employment." Clearly, the duty thus defined may be violated without a general failure of subjective good faith: for there is no occasion to consider the issue of good faith if a party has refused even to negotiate *in fact*—"to meet... and confer"—about any of the mandatory subjects. A refusal to negotiate *in fact* as to any subject which is within §8(d), and about which the union seeks to negotiate, violates §8(a)(5) though the employer has every desire to reach agreement with the union upon an over-all collective agreement and earnestly and in all good faith bargains to that end. We hold that an employer's unilateral change in conditions of employment under negotiation is similarly a violation of §8(a)(5), for it is a circumvention of the duty to negotiate which frustrates the objectives of §8(a)(5) as much as does a flat refusal.

The unilateral actions of the respondent illustrate the policy and practical considerations which support our conclusion... At the April 4, 1957, meeting the employers offered, and the union rejected, a three-year contract with an immediate across-the-board increase of $7.50 per week, to be followed at the end of the first year and again at the end of the second by further increases of $5 for employees earning less than $90 at those times. Shortly thereafter, without having advised or consulted with the union, the company announced a new system of automatic wage increases whereby there would be an increase of $5 every three months up to$74.99 per week; an increase of $5 every six months between $75 and $90 per week; and a merit review every six months for employees earning over $90 per week. It is clear at a glance that the automatic wage increase system which was instituted unilaterally was considerably more generaous than that which had shortly theretofore been offered to and rejected by the union. Such action conclusively manifested bad faith in the negotiations, *Labor-Board v. Crompton-Highland Mills,*337 U.S. 217, and so would have violated §8(a)(5) even on the Court of Appeals' interpretation, though no additional evidence of bad faith appeared. An employer is not required to lead with his best offer; he is free to bargain. But even after an impasse is reached he has no license to grant wage increases greater than any he has ever offered the union at the bargaining table, for such action is necessarily inconsistent with a sincere desire to conclude an agreement with the union. . . .

. . . But the Board *is* authorized to order the cessation of behavior which is in effect a refusal to negotiate, or which directly obstructs or inhibits the actual process of discussion, or which reflects a cast of mind against reaching agreement. Unilateral action by an employer without prior discussion with the union does amount to a refusal to negotiate about the affected conditions of employment under negotition, and must of necessity obstruct bargaining, contrary to the congressional policy. It will often disclose an unwillingness to agree with the union. It will rarely be justified by any reason of substance. it follows that the Board may hold such unilateral action to be an unfair labor practice in violation of §8(a)(5), without also finding the employer guilty of over-all subjective bad faith. While we do not foreclose the possiblity that there might be circumstances which the Board could or should accept as excusing or justifying unilateral action, no such case is presented here.

■ ■ ■

Questions

1. What was the "bad faith" bargaining in *Katz*?
2. The duty to bargain collectively is defined in Section 8(d). This duty relates only to certain mandatory subjects. What are they?
3. Is the refusal to "meet. . . and confer" about a mandatory subject a violation of 8(a)5?

LABOR - MANAGEMENT RELATIONS ACT

The Labor-Management Relations Act of 1947 (Taft-Hartley Act) was the product of diverse forces. Many business firms continued to attack "unionism" and gladly joined in the effort to develop an anti-union law. Others criticized the unions for abuse of power. John L. Lewis and the United Mine Workers had carried on two long strikes during World War II in defiance of the government. There were news reports that many so-called "labor unions" were really rackets and controlled by unsavory individuals. Often violence was promoted by union leaders when peaceful measures failed to achieve union objectives. In a few unions the membership rolls were closed to outsiders and jobs passed from father to son. Others criticized the use of secondary boycotts by unions to achieve their purposes. The Taft-Hartley Act attempted to deal with these perceived problems by amending the National Labor Relations Act and in formulating other policies for labor law.

Severl changes in labor law were created by the Taft-Hartley Act. First, the labor injunction was revived in a modified and restrictive form. As one example, an injunction could be secured by the National Labor Relations Board to eliminate statutorily defined unfair union practices. Secondly, Section 7 of the National Labor Relations Act was amended to allow individuals the freedom to refrain from union activities as a right equal to Section 7's previously announced right to join a union. Moreover, Section 8 of the National Labor Relations Act was amended [8(b)(1)] to prohibit union restraint or coercion of workers who attempted to exercise the right not to join the union.

Prior to 1947 the union could secure a "union security" provision in the contract negotiated with the employer whereby the employer would refuse to hire those who were not members of the union. In effect, the union determined who would be hired.

This system was called a closed shop and was outlawed by the Taft-Hartley Act. Instead, the Taft-Hartley amendments to the NLRA established that the employer could legally agree to a union membership provision only if it allowed the employer to select employees without regard to pre-hire union membership. Membership in the union could only be required after thirty days of employment. If the employee thereafter refused to pay union initiation fees and dues, the membership provision of the collectively bargained contract would require the employer to discharge the employee. This type of union security agreement is referred to as a union shop.

While the rules of federal law apply to all employers whose operations affect interstate commerce, Congress has chosen to explicitly exclude employers from the permissible union shop provisions of federal law in those states that have enacted the so-called "right-to-work laws." Section 14(b) of the NLRA excludes state employers when state law refuses to enforce any contractual commitments of employers and unions which attempt to mandate membership in labor organizations. Twenty states have enacted such laws which, in effect, outlaw union shops in their jurisdictions.

Besides the amendment of Section 8 to protect the right of the individual worker to refrain from union membership, subsection (2) through (6) of Section 8(b) also outlawed the following concerted union activities:

(2) attempt to cause an employer to discriminate against an employee, except where the employee fails to pay dues,
(3) refusal to bargain in good faith with the employer,
(4) strikes to compel an employer to commit some unfair labor practice or secondary boycotts: i.e. the refusal to work for employer A, unless he ceases to do business with employer B, with whom the union has its real dispute,
(5) requirements of excessive or discriminatory initiation fees,
(6) "feather-bedding" practices of pay without work performed.

The following cases discuss portions of the Section 8(b) and relate in more detail some of the particular union practices held to be illegal.

FAIR REPRESENTATION

LOCAL UNION, NO. 12, UNITED RUBBER WORKERS v. NLRB
368 F. 2d 12 (1966)
United State Court of Appeals, 5th Cir.

■ ■ ■

At the outset it must be reiterated that every union decision which may in some way result in overriding the wishes... of..., even an appreciable number of employees, does not in and of itself constitute a breach of the fiduciary duty of fair representation. Even in the administration stage of the bargaining contract..., the union must necessarily retain a broad degree of discretion in processing individual grievances. Thus, where the union after a good faith investigation of the merits of a grievance, concludes that the claim is insubstantial and refuses to encumber fruther its grievance channels by continuing to process the unmeritorious claim, its duty of fair representation may well be satisfied. Such good-faith effort to reprsent fairly the interests of individual employees, however, is not evidenced in this controversy. To the contrary, Local 12 in open disregard of the recommendations of its International has continued to refuse to represent the vital interests of a segment of its membership.... Undoubtedly, the duty of fair representation can be breached by discriminatory inaction in refusing to process a grievance as well as by active conduct on the part of the union...

We thus conclude that where the record demonstrates that a grievance would have been processed to arbitration but for arbitrary and discriminatory reasons, the refusal to so process it constitutes a violation of the union's duty to represent its members "without hostile discrimination, fairly, impartially, and in good faith."

Similarly, with respect to the grievances concerning the segregated nature of plant facilities, the union not only refused to process such claims but actively opposed desegregation of shower and toilet facilities. It is impossible for us to look upon such conduct as anything other than an effort to discriminate against Negro employees with respect to conditions of employment. . . As the Board properly concluded, "whatever may be the bases on which a statutory representative may properly decline to process grievances, the bases must bear a reasonable relation to the Union's role as bargaining representative or its functioning as a labor organization; manifestly racial discrimination bears no such relationship."

. . .Local 12, in refusing to represent the complainants in a fair and impartial manner, thereby violated section 8(b)(1)(A) by restraining them in the exercise of their secion 7 right to bargain collectively through their chosen representatives.

■ ■ ■

Questions

1. May the union refuse to further prosecute a grievance of an individual union member? What valid justification might be advanced by the union for refusing to prosecute a union member's claim?
2. Why was the refusal to prosecute grievances of union members by Local Union No 12 in violation of federal law?

SECONDARY BOYCOTTS

N.L.R.B. v. LOCAL 825, INTERNAT'L U. OF OPERATING ENG.
400 U.S. 297 (1971)
Supreme Court of the United States

■ ■ ■

MARSHALL, Mr. Justice.

In this cause we are asked to determine whether strikes by Operating Engineers at the site of the construction of a nuclear power generator plant at Oyster Creek, New Jersey, violated §8(b)(4)(B) of the National Labor Relations Act. Although the National Labor Relations Board found the strikes to be in violation of this section, the Court of Appeals refused to enforce the Board's order. . .

The general contractor for the project, Burns & Roe,Inc., subcontracted all of the construction work to three companies—White Construction Co., Chicago Bridge & Iron co., and Poirier and McLane Corp. All three employed operating engineers who were members of Local 825, International Union of Operating Engineers. But White, unlike Chicago Bridge and Poirier, did not have a collective-bargaining agreement with Local 825.

In the latter part of September 1965, White installed an electric welding machine and assigned the job of pushing the buttons that operated the machine to members of the Ironworkers Union, who were to perform the actual welding. Upon learning of this work assignment, Local 825's job steward and its lead engineer threatened White with a strike if operating engineers were not given the work. White, however, refused to meet the demand. On September 29, 1965, the job steward and lead engineer met with the construction manager for Burns, the general contractor. They informed him that the members of Local 825 working at the jobsite had voted to strike unless Burns signed a contract, which would be binding on all three subcontractors as well as Burns, giving Local 825 jurisdiction over all power equipment, including electric welding machines, operated on the jobsite. On October 1, after White and Burns refused to accede to the demands, the operating engineers employed by Chicago Bridge and Poirer as well as those employed by White walked off the job. . .

Congressional concern over the involvement of third parties in labor disputes not their own prompted §8(b)(4)(B). This concern was focused on the "secondary boycott," which was conceived of as pressure brought to bear, not "upon the employer who alone is a party [to a dispute], but upon some third party who has no concern in it" with the objective of forcing the third party to bring pressure on the employer to agree to the union's demands.

Section 8(b)(4)(B) is, however, the product of legislative compromise and also reflects a concern with protecting labor organizations' right to exert legitimate pressure aimed at the employer with whom there is a primary dispute. this primary activity is protected even though it may seriously affect neutral third parties.

Thus there are two threads to §8(b)(4)(B) that require disputed conduct to be clasified as either "primary" or "secondary." And the tapestry that has been woven in classifying such conduct is among the labor law's most intricate. But here the normally difficult task of classifying union conduct is easy. As the Court of Appeals said, the "record amply justifies the conclusion that [Burns and the neutral subcontractors] were subjected to coercion in the form of threats or walkouts, or both." And, as the Board said, it is clear that this coercion was designed "to achieve the assignment of [the]disputed work" to operating engineers.

Local 825's coercive activity was aimed directly at Burns and the subcontractors that were not involved in the dispute. The union engaged in a strike against these neutral employers for the specific, overt purpose of forcing them to put pressure on White to assign the job of operating the welding machine to operating engineers... It was...using a sort of pressure that was unmistakably and flagrantly secondary.

The more difficult task is to determine whether one of Local 825's objectives was to force Burns and the other neutrals to "cease doing business" with White as §8(b)(4)(B) requires. The Court of Appeals concluded that the union's objective was to force Burns "to use its influence with the subcontractor to change the subcontractor's conduct, not to terminate their relationship" and that this was not enough. That court read the statute as requiring that the union demand nothing short of a complete termination of the business relationship between the neutral and the primary employer Such a reading is too narrow.

Some disruption of business relationships is the necessary consequence of the purest form of primary activity. These foreseeable disruptions are, however, clearly protected. Likewise, secondary activity could have such a limited goal and the foreseeable result of the conduct could be, while disruptive, so slight that the "cease doing business" requirement is not met.

Local 825's goal was not so limited nor were the foreseeable consequences of its secondary pressure slight The operating engineers sought to force Burns to bind all the subcontractors on the project to a particular from of job asignments. The clear implication of the demands was that burns would be required either to force a change in White's policy or to terminate White's contract. The strikes shut down the whole project. If Burns was unable to obtain White's consent, Local 825 was apparently willing to continue disruptive conduct that would bring all the employers to their knees.

Certainly, the union would have perferred to have the employers capitulate to its demands; it wanted to take the job of operating the welding machines away from the Ironworkers. It was willing, however, to try to obtain this capitulation by forcing neutrals to compel White to meet union demands. To hold that this flagrant secondary conduct with these most serious disruptive effects was not prohibited by §8(b)(4)(B) would be largely to ignore the original congressional concern...

Since the Court of Appeals did not believe that §8(b)(4)(B) was applicable, it did not consider the propriety of the portion of the Board's order relating to that section... [S]o we must remand these cases for the Court of Appeals to consider whether the order is necessary to further the goals of the Act.

■ ■ ■

Questions

1. What is a "secondary boycott"? Are all secondary boycotts illegal?
2. How did the court interpret the requirement that the secondary boycott must cause the neutral employer to "cease doing business" with the primary employer?

INFORMATIONAL PICKETING

N.L.R.B. v. FRUIT PACKERS
377 U.S. 58 (1963)
Supreme Court of the United States

■ ■ ■

BRENNAN, Mr. Justice.

Under... the National Labor Relations Act, as amended, it is an unfair labor practice for a union "to threaten, coerce, or restrain any person," with the object of "forcing or requiring any person to cease using, selling, handling, transporting, or otherwise dealing in products of any other producer... or to cease doing business with any other person... " A proviso excepts, however, "publicity, *other than picketing,* for the purpose of truthfully advising the public... that a product or products are produced by an employer with whom the labor organization has a primary dispute and are distributed by another employer, as long as such publicity does not have an effect of inducing any individual employed by any person other than the primary employer in the course of his employment to refuse to pick up, deliver, or transport any goods, or not to perform any services, at the establishment of the employer engaged in such distribution." The question in this case is whether the respondent unions violated this section when they limited their secondary picketing of retail stores to an appeal to the customers of the stores not to buy the products of certain firms against which one of the respondents was on strike.

Respondent Local 760 called a strike against fruit packers and warehousemen doing business in Yakima, Washington. The struck firms sold Washington State apples to the Safeway chain of retail stores in and about Seattle, Washington. Local 760... instituted a consumer boycott against the apples in support of the strike. They placed pickets who walked back and forth before the customers' entrances of 46 Safeway stores in Seattle. The pickets—two at each of 45 stores and three at the 46th store—wore placards and distributed handbills which appealed to Safeway customers, and to the public generally, to refrain from buying Washington State apples, which were only one of numerous food products sold in the stores. Before the pickets appeared at any store, a letter was delivered to the store manager informing him that the picketing was only an appeal to his customers not to buy Washington State apples, and that pickets were being expressly instructed "to patrol peacefully in front of the consumer entrances of the store, to stay away from the delivery entrances and not to interfere with the work of your employees, or with deliveries to or pickups from your store." A copy of written instructions to the pickets—which included the explicit statement that "you are also forbidden to request that the customers not patronize the store"—was enclosed with the letter. Since it was desired to assure Safeway employees that they were not to cease work, and to avoid any interference with pickups or deliveries, the pickets appeared after the stores opened for business and departed before the stores closed. At all times during the picketing, the store employees continued to work, and no deliveries or pickups were obstructed. Washington State apples were handled in normal course by both Safeway employees and the employees of other employers involved. Ingress and egress by customers and others was not interfered with in any manner.

A complaint issued on charges that this conduct violated §8(b)(4) as amended...

that "by literal wording of the proviso (to Section 8(b)(4)) as well as through the interpretive gloss placed theron by its drafters, consumer picketing in front of a secondary establishment is prohibited."

The Board's reading of the statute—that the legislative history and the phrase "other than picketing" in the proviso reveal a congressional purpose to outlaw all picketing directed at customers at a secondary site—necessarily rested on the finding that Congress determined that such picketing always threatens, coerces or restrains the secondary employer... We therefore have a special responsibility... to examine the legislative history for confirmation that Congress made that determination. Throughout the history of federal regulation of labor relations, Congress has consistently refused to prohibit peaceful picketing except where it is used as a means to achieve specific ends which experience has shown are undesirable. "In the sensitive area of peaceful picketing congress has dealt explicitly with isolated evils which exprience has established flow from such picketing." *Labor Board v. Drivers Local Union*, 362 U.S. 274, 284. We have recognized this congressional practice and have not ascribed to Congress a purpose to outlaw peaceful picketing unless "there is the clearest indication in the legislative history," that Congress intended to do so as regards the particular ends of the picketing under review. Both the congressional policy and our adherence to this principle of interpretation reflect concern that a broad ban against peaceful picketing might collide with the guarantees of the First Amendment.

We have examined the legislative history of the amendments to §8(b)(4), and conclude that it does not reflect with the requisite clarity a congressional plan to proscribe all peaceful consumer picketing at secondary sites, and, particularly, any concern with peaceful picketing when it is limited, as here, to persuading Safeway customers not to buy Washington State apples when they traded in the Safeway stores. All that the legislative history shows in the way of an "isolated evil" believed to require proscription of peaceful consumer picketing at secondary sites, was its use to persuade the customers of the secondary employer to cease trading with him in order to force him to cease dealing with, or to put pressure upon, the primary employer. This narrow focus reflects the difference between such conduct and peaceful picketing at the secondary site directed only at the struck product. In the latter case, the union's appeal to the public is confined to its dispute with the primary employer, since the public is not asked to withhold its patronage from the secondary employer, but only to boycott the primary employer's goods. On the other hand, a union appeal to the public at the secondary site not to trade at all with the secondary employer goes beyond the goods of the primary employer, and seeks the public's assistance in forcing the secondary employer to cooperate with the union in its primary dispute. This is not to say that this distinction was expressly alluded to in the debates. It is to say, however, that the consumer picketing carried on in this case is not attended by the abuses at which the statute was directed....

Peaceful consumer picketing to shut off all trade with the secondary employer unless he aids the union in its dispute with the primary employer, is poles apart from such picketing which only persuades his customers not to buy the struck product. The proviso indicates no more than that the Senate conferees' constitutional doubts led Congress to authorize publicity other than picketing which persuades the customers of a secondary employer to stop all trading with him, but not such publicity which has the effect of cutting off his deliveries or inducing his employees to cease work. On the other hand, picketing which persuades the customers of a secondary employer to stop all trading with him was also to be barred.

In sum, the legislative history does not support the Board's finding that Congress meant to prohibit all consumer picketing at a secondary site, having determined that such picketing necessarily threatened, coerced, or restrained the secondary employer. Rather, the history shows that Congress was following its usual practice of legislating against peaceful picketing only to curb "isolated evils."

This distinction is opposed as "unrealistic" because, it is urged, all picketing automatically provokes the public to stay away from the picketed establishment. The public will, it is said, neither read the signs and handbills, nor note the explicit injunction that "This is not a strike against the store or market." Be that as it may, our holding today simply takes note of the fact that Congress has never adopted a broad condemnation of peaceful picketing, such as that urged upon us by petitioners and an intention to do so is not revealed with the "clearest indication in the legislative history," which we require.

We come then to the question whether the picketing in this case, confined as it was to persuading customers to cease buying the product of the primary employer, falls within the area of secondary consumer picketing which Congress did clearly indicate its intention to prohibit under §8(b)(4)(ii). We hold that it did not fall within that area, and therefore did not "threaten, coerce, or restrain" Safeway. While any diminution in Safeway's purchase of apples due to a drop in consumer demand might be said to be a result which causes respondents' picketing to fall literally within the statutory prohibitions, "it is a familiar rule, that a thing may be within the letter of the statute and yet not within the statute, because not within its spirit, nor within the intention of its makers.". . . When consumer picketing is employed only to persuade customers not to buy the struck product, the union's appeal is closely confined to the primary dispute. the site of the appeal is expanded to include the premises of the secondary employer, but if the appeal succeeds, the secondary employer's purchases from the struck firms are decreased only because the public has diminished its purchases of the struck product. On the other hand, when consumer picketing is employed to persuade customers not to trade at all with the secondary employer, the latter stops buying the struck product, not because of a falling demand, but in response to pressure designed to inflict injury on his business generally. In such case, the union does more than merely follow the struck product; it creates a separate dispute with the secondary employer.

We disagree therefore with the Court of Appeals that the test of "to threaten, coerce, or restrain" for the purposes of this case is whether Safeway suffered or was likely to suffer economic loss. A violation of §8(b)(4)(ii)(B) would not be established, merely because respondents' picketing was effective to reduce Safeway's sales of Wahsington State apples, even if this led or might lead Safeway to drop the item as a poor seller.

The judgment of the Court of Appeals is vacated and the case is remanded with direction to enter judgment setting aside the Board's order.

■ ■ ■

Questions

1. What "evil" was Congress legislating against in Section 8(b)4?
2. Why did Congress feel the "proviso" was necessary in this legislation?
3. As a result of the decision in *Fruit Packers,* under what conditions is "secondary picketing" permitted?
4. Could a publicity campaign *without secondary picketing* be directed to consumers requesting their *total* boycott of retailers selling goods of the primary employer?
5. Could publicity be directed to employees or deliverymen of a secondary employer?

FEATHERBEDDING OF MAKE-WORK?

N.L.R.B. v. GAMBLE ENTERPRISES
345 U.S. 117 (1952)
Supreme Court of the United States

■ ■ ■

BURTON, Mr. Justice

The question here is whether a labor organization engages in an unfair labor practice, within the meaning of §8(b)(6) of the National labor Relations Act, as amended by the Labor Management Relations Act, 1947, when it insists that the management of one of an interstate chain of theaters shall employ a local orchestra to play in connection with certain programs, although that management does not need or want to employ that orchestra...

For generations professional musicians have faced a shortage in the local employment needed to yield them a livelihood. They have been confronted with the competition of military bands, traveling bands, foreign musicians on tour, local amateur organizations and, more recently, technological developments in reproduction and broadcasting. To help them conserve local sources of employment, they developed local protective societies. Since 1896, they also have organized and maintained on a national scale the American Federation of Musicians, affiliated with the American Federation of Labor. By 1943, practically all professional instrumental performers and conductors in the United States had joined the Federation, establishing a membership of over 200,000, with 10,000 more in Canada.

The Federation uses its nationwide control of professional talent to help individual members and local unions. It insists that traveling band contracts be subject to its rules, laws and regulations. Article 18 §4, of its By-Laws provides: "Traveling members cannot, without the consent of a Local, play any presentation performances in its jurisdiction unless a local house orchestra is also employed."

From this background we turn to the instant case. For more than 12 years the Palace Theater in Akron, Ohio, has been one of an interstate chain of theaters managed by respondent, Gamble Enterprises, Inc., which is a Washington corporation with its principal office in New York. Before the decline of vaudeville and until about 1940, respondent employed a local orchestra of nine union musicians to play for stage acts at that Theater. When a traveling band occupied the stage, the local orchestra played from the pit for the vaudeville acts and, at times, augmented the performance of the traveling band.

Since 1940, respondent has used the Palace for showing motion pictures with occasional appearance of traveling bands. Between 1940 and 1947, the local musicians, no longer employed on a regular basis, held periodic rehearsals at the theater and were available when required. When a traveling band appeared there, respondent paid the members of the local orchestra a sum equal to the minimum union wages for a similar engagement but they played no music.

The Taft-Hartley Act, containing §8(b)(6), was passed, over the President's veto, June 23, 1947, and took effect August 22. Between July 2 and November 12, seven performances of traveling bands were presented on the Palace stage. Local musicians were neither used nor paid on those occasions. They raised no objections and made no demands for "stand-by" payments. However, in October, 1947, the American Federation of Musicians, Local No 24 of Akron, Ohio, here called the union, opened negotiations with respondent... for the latter's employment of a pit orchestra of local musicians whenever a traveling band performed on the stage The pit orchestra was to play overtures, "intermissions" and "chasers" (the latter while patrons were leaving the theater). The union required acceptance of this proposal as a condition of its consent to local appearances of traveling bands. Respondent declined the offer and a traveling band scheduled to appear November 20 canceled its engagement on learning that the union had withheld its consent.

May 8, 1949, the union made a new proposal. It sought a guaranty that a local orchestra would be employed by respondent on some number of occasions having a relation to the number of traveling band appearances. This and similar proposals were declined on the ground that the local orchestra was neither necessary nor desired. Accordingly, in July, 1949, the union again declined to consent to the appearance of a traveling band desired by respondent and the band did not appear...

In 1949, respondent filed charges with the National labor Relations Board asserting that the union was engaging in the unfair labor practice defined in §8(b)(6)....

We accept the finding of the Board, made upon the entire record, that the union was seeking actual employment for its members and not mere "stand-by" pay. The Board recognized that, formerly, before §8(b)(6) had taken effect, the union had received "stand-by" payments in connection with traveling band appearances. Since then, the union has requested no such payments and has received none. It has, however, requested and consistently negotiated for actual employment in connection with traveling band and vaudeville appearances. It has suggested various ways in which a local orchestra could earn pay for performing competent work and, upon those terms, it has offered to consent to the appearance of traveling bands which are Federation-controlled. Respondent, with equal consistency, has declined these offers as it had a right to do.

Since we and the Board treat the union's proposals as in good faith contemplating the performance of actual services, we agree that the union has not, on this record, engaged in a practice proscribe by §8(b)(6). It has remained for respondent to accept or reject the union's offers on their merits in the light of all material circumstances. We do not find it necessary to determine also whether such offers were "in the nature of an exaction." We are not dealing here with offers of mere "token" or nominal services. The proposals before us were appropriately treated by the Board as offers in good faith of substantial performances by competent musicians. There is no reason to think that sham can be substituted for substance under §8(b)(6) any more than under any other statute. Payments for "standing-by," or for the substantial equivalent of "standing-by," are not payments for services performed, but when an employer receives a bona fide offer of competent performance of relevant services, it remains for the employer, through free and fair negotiation, to determine whether such offer shall be accepted and what compensation shall be paid for the work done.

■ ■ ■

Questions

1. What is "feather-bedding"? Had the local musicians in *Gamble Enterprises* ever engaged in feather-bedding?
2. What is "make-work"? Is it illegal?

FEDERAL PREEMPTION

Through constitutional decisions the Supreme Court has allocated to Congress the power (1) to enact national labor legislation and (2) to forbid the application of State laws in labor relations. The Congress may choose not to exercise this power or to use only part. However, the actual enactment of federal legislation does not necessarily exclude the jurisdiction of State tribunals nor the application of State law. But the expansion of national power over industrial relations raised significant questions concerning the portion of government power shared between the states and the nation.

First, how far does actual federal regulation of labor relations extend? The National Labor Relations Act is the most significant labor legislation in the United States. In upholding the constitutionality of the NLRA, the Supreme Court assumed without so holding that the Act asserted federal power to the outermost limits of the commerce power. But in fact, the National Labor Relations Board exercises more narrow jurisidction. Congress has never appropriated sufficient funds to the Board to fully cover the scope of the Act. Therefore, through self-restraint imposed by limited funds and administrative descretion, several million employees and employers are left outside the Board's jurisdiction. In the 1957 decision of *Guss v. Utah Labor Relations Board*, 353 U.S. 1, the Supreme Court held that State agencies could not take jurisdiction in areas over which the NLRB declined to exercise its statutory jurisdiction. The result was a "no man's land" in which the federal agency declined to act and the States were excluded by federal legislation. Finally in 1959, the Congress allowed the State law to operate in the area over which the NLRB had declined to exercise jurisdiction. The same legislation prohibits the NLRB from any further contractions of its jurisdiction.

Second, how far does federal regulation of labor relations exclude the application of supplementary State law? The Court has determined that, with limited exceptions, the states have no authority over the aspects of labor relations under NLRB jurisdiction. A State may not decide questions of union representation, remedy employer unfair labor practices, or regulate the concerted activities (picketing and strikes) of employees when such activities are arguably within the juridiction of the NLRB. These activities lie within the protection of Section 7 or the prohibition of Section 8 of the NLRA. As such, they are areas that are exclusive to the NLRB and excluded from State courts. The principal judge-made exception is the power of State courts to enjoin or award damages resulting from conduct marked by violence or imminent threats to public order. Previously in *San Diego Building Trades Council v. Garman,* 359 U.S. 236 (1959), the court had concluded that the states need not yield jurisdiction "where the activity regulated was a merely peripheral concern of the Labor Management Reltions Act.... Or where the regulated conduct touched interests so deeply rooted in local feeling and responsibility that, in the absence of compelling congressional direction, we could not infer that Congress had deprived the States of the power to act." Consequently, States may legislate to supplement the federal law if such legislation does not concern an area of labor relations arguably within the area covered by federal legislation. The "peripheral" aspects of labor relations are within the reach of State legislation.

COURT ENFORCEMENT OF LABOR CONTRACTS

As previously indicated, the Norris-LaGuardia Act generally prohibits federal court injunctions in labor disputes. However, Section 301 of the Taft-Hartley Act provides that unions may sue and be sued as an entity. Suits for violation of labor contracts may be brought in any district court and money judgments against labor unions or the employer may be obtained. However, the language of the Taft-Hartley Act did not expressly overrule the Norris-LaGuardia anti-injunction provisions. Thereafter, the question naturally arose as to whether the courts could use an injunction against either party to a labor contract who refused to artibrate when the collective bargaining agreement made such a provision.

TEXTILE WORKERS UNION v. LINCOLN MILLS
353 U.S. 448 (1957)
Supreme Court of the United States

■ ■ ■

DOUGLAS, Mr. Justice.

Petitioner-union entered into a collective bargaining agreement in 1953 with respondent-employer... The agreement provided that there would be no strikes or work stoppages and that grievances would be handled pursuant to a specified procedure. The last step in the grievance procedure—a step that could be taken by either party—was arbitration.

This controversy involves several grievances that concern work loads and work assignments. The grievances were processed through the various steps in the grievance procedure and were finally denied by the employer. The union requested arbitration, and the employer refused. Thereupon the union brought this suit in the District Court to compel arbitration.

The District Court concluded that it had jurisdiction and ordered the employer to comply with the grievance arbitration provisions of the collective bargaining agreement. The Court of Appeals reversed by a divided vote...

The starting point of our inquiry is § 301 of the Labor Management Relations Act of 1947...

There has been considerable litigation involving § 301 and courts have construed it differently... (Most Courts)... hold that § 301 (a) is more than jurisdictional—that it authorizes federal courts to fashion a body of federal law for the enforcement of these collective bargaining agreements and includes within that federal law specific performance of promises to arbitrate grievances under collective bargaining agreements. That is our constructionof § 301 (a), which means that the agreement to arbitrate grievance disputes, contained in this collective bargaining agreement, should be specifically enforced...

Congress was interested in promoting collective bargaining that ended with agreements not to strike... Thus collective bargaining contracts were made "equally binding and enforceable on both parties." As stated in the House Report, the new provision makes labor organizations equally responsible with employers for contract violation and provides for suit by either against the other in the United States district courts." To repeat, the Senate Report summed up the philosphy of §301 as follows: "Statutory recognition of the collective agreement as a valid, binding, and enforceable contract is a logical and necessary step. It will promote a higher degree of responsibility upon the parties to such agreements, and will thereby promote industrial peace."

Plainly the agreement to arbitrate grievance disputes is the *quid pro quo* for an agreement not to strike. Viewed in this light, the legislation does more than confer jurisdiction in the federal court over labor organizations. It expresses a federal policy that federal courts should enforce these agreements on behalf of or against labor organizations and that industrial peace can be best obtained only in that way...

The question remains whether jurisdiction to compel arbitration of grievance disputes is withdrawn by the Norris-LaGuadia Act. Section 7 of that Act prescribes stiff procedural requirements for issuing an injunction in a labor dispute. The kinds of acts which had given rise to abuse of the power to enjoin are listed in §4. The failure to arbitrate was not a part and parcel of the abuses against which the Act was aimed. Section 8 of the Norris-LaGuarida Act does, indeed, indicate a congressional policy toward settlement of labor disputes by arbitration, for it denies injuctive relief to any person who has failed to make "every reasonable effort" to settle the dispute by negotiation, mediation, or "voluntary arbitration." Though a literal reading might bring the dispute within the terms of the Act, we see no justification in policy for restricting § 301 (a) to damage suits, leaving specific performance of a contract to arbitrate grievance disputes to the inapposite procedural requirements of that Act... The congressional policy in favor of the enforcement of agreements to arbitrate grievance disputes being clear, there is no reason to submit them to the requirements of § 7 of the Norris-LaGuardia Act.

■ ■ ■

Questions

1. Why did Congress feel that collectively bargained labor contracts should be legally forceable?
2. Does the Norris-LaGuardia Act prohibit a court injunction which orders an employer to arbitrate as agreed in the labor contract?

BOYS MARKETS, INC. v. RETAIL CLERKS LOCAL 770
398 U.S. 235, (1970)
Supreme Court of the United States

■ ■ ■

BRENNAN, Mr. Justice.

In this case we re-examine the holding of Sinclair Refining Co. v. Atkinson, 370 U.S. 195 (1962), that the anti-injunction provisions of the Norris-LaGuardia Act preclude a federal district court from enjoining a strike in breach of a no-strike obligation under a collective bargaining agreement, even though that agreement contains provisions, enforceable under § 301(a) of the Labor-Management Relations Act for binding arbitration of the grievance dispute concerning which the strike was called. The Court of Appeals for the Ninth Circuit, considering itself bound by *Sinclair*, reversed the grant by the District Court... of petitioner's prayer for injunctive relief...

In February 1969, at the time of the incidents that produced this litigation, petitioner and respondent were parties to a collective bargaining agreement which provided that all controversies concerning its interpretation or application should be resolved by adjustment and arbitration procedures set forth therein and that during the life of the contract, there should be "no cessation or stoppage of work, lock-out, picketing or boycotts...." The dispute arose when petitioner's frozen foods supervisor and certain members of his crew who were not members of the bargaining unit began to rearrange merchandise in the frozen food cases of one of petitioner's supermarkets. A union representative insisted that the food cases be stripped of all merchandise and be restocked by union personnel. When petitioner did not accede to the union's demand, a strike was called and the union began to picket petitioner's establishment. Thereupon petitioner demanded that the union cease work stoppage and picketing and sought to invoke the grievance and arbitration procedures specified in the contract....

The literal terms of § 4 of the Norris-LaGuardia Act must be accommodated to the subsequently enacted provisions of § 301(a) of the Labor-Management Relations Act and the purposes of arbitration. Statutory interpretation requires more than concentration upon isolated words; rather, consideration must be given to the total corpus of pertinent law and the policies which inspired ostensibly inconsistent provisions.

The Norris-LaGuardia Act was responsive to a situation totally different from that which exists today. In the early part of this century, the federal courts generally were regarded as allies of management in its attempt to prevent the organization and strengthening of labor unions; and in this industrial struggle the injunction became a potent weapon which was wielded against the activities of labor groups. The result was a large number of sweeping decrees, often issued *ex parte,* drawn on an *ad hoc* basis without regard to any systematic elaboration of national labor policy.

In 1932 Congress attempted to bring some order out of the industrial chaos that had developed and to correct the abuses which had resulted from the interjection of the federal judiciary into union-management disputes on the behalf of management. Congress, therefore, determined initially to limit severely the power of the federal courts to issue injunctions "in any case involving or growing out of any labor dispute...." Even as initally enacted, however, the prohibition against federal injunctions was by no means absolute. Shortly thereafter Congress passed the Wagner Act, designed to curb various management activities which tended to discourage employee participation in collective action.

As labor organizations grew in strength and developed toward maturity, congressional emphasis shifted from protection of the nascent labor movement to the encouragement of collective bargaining and to administrative techniques for the peaceful resolution of industrial disputes. This shift in emphasis was acomplished, however, without extensive revision of many of the older enactments, including the anti-injunction section of the Norris-LaGuardia Act. Thus it became the task of the courts to accommodate, to reconcile the older statutes with the more recent ones.

A leading example of this acommodation process is Brotherhood of R.R. Trainmen v. Chicago River & Ind. R.R., 353 U.S. 30 (1957). There we were confronted with a peaceful strike which violated the statutory duty to arbitrate imposed by the Railway Labor Act. The Court concluded that a strike in violation of a statutory arbitration duty was not the type of situation to which the Norris-LaGuardia Act was responsive, that an important federal policy was involved in the peaceful settlement of disputes through the statutorily-mandated arbitration procedure, that this important policy was imperiled if equitable remedies were not available to implement it, and hence that Norris-LaGuardia's policy of nonintervention by the federal courts should yield to the overriding interest in the successful implementation of the arbitration process.

The principles elaborated in *Chicago River* are equally applicable to the present case. To be sure, *Chicago River* involved arbitration procedures established by statute. However, we have frequently noted, in such cases as *Lincoln Mills,* the *Steelworkers Trilogy,* and *Lucas Flour,* the importance which Congress has attached generally to the voluntary settlement of labor disputes without resort to self-help and more particularly to arbitration as a means to this end. Indeed, it has been stated that *Lincoln Mills,* in its exposition of § 301(a), "went a long way towards making arbitration the central institution in the administration of collective bargaining contracts."

The *Sinclair* decision, however, seriously undermined the effectiveness of the arbitration technique as a method peacefully to resolve industrial disputes without resort to strikes, lockouts, and similar devices. Clearly employers will be wary of assuming obligations to arbitrate specifically enforceable against them when no similarly efficacious remedy is available to enforce the concomitant undertaking of the union to refrain from striking. On the other hand, the central purpose of the Norris-LaGuardia Act to foster the growth and viability of labor organizations is hardly retarded—if anything, this goal is advanced—by a remedial device which merely enforces the obligation that the union freely undertook under a specifically enforceable agreement to submit disputes to arbitration. We conclude, therefore, that the unavailability of equitable relief in the arbitration context presents a serious impediment to the congressional polciy favoring the voluntary establishment of a mechanism for the peaceful resolution of labor disputes, that the core purpose of the Norris-LaGuardia Act is not sacrificed by the limited use of equitable remedies to further this important policy, and consequently that the Norris-LaGuardia Act does not bar the granting of injunctive relief in the circumstances of the instant case.

■ ■ ■

ARBITRATION

Labor arbitration is the process in which a neutral third party, selected jointly by labor and management, decides a dispute which the parties have been unable to resolve. The arbitrator's decision is final and binding and enforceable through the courts. The Supreme Court has approved of labor arbitration in a series of cases in 1960. These cases establish arbitration as the preeminent process in deciding contract disputes. In one case, the company refused to arbitrate what the lower court called a frivolous and patently baseless claim by the union. Consequently, the lower court held the employer was not subject to arbitration under the labor contract. The Supreme

Court reversed the lower court's determination and ordered arbitration. The Court identified the proper role of the lower courts in the following language:

> The collective agreement calls for the submission of grievances in the categories which it describes, irrespective of whether a court may deem them to be meritorious. In our role of developing a meaningful body of law to govern the interpretation and enforcement of collective bargaining agreements, we think special heed should be given to the context in which collective bargaining agreements are negotiated and the purpose which they are intended to serve.... The function of the court is very limited when the parties have agreed to submit all questions of contract interpretation to the arbitrator. It is confined to ascertaining whether the party seeking arbitration is making a claim which on its face is governed by the contract. Whether the moving party is right or wrong is a question of contract interpretation for the arbitrator. In these circumstances the moving party should not be deprived of the arbitrator's judgment, when it was his judgment and all that it connotes that was bargained for.

> The courts, therefore, have no business weighing the merits of the grievance, considering whether there is equity in a particular claim, or deteriming whether there is particular language in the written instrument which will support the claim. The agreement is to submit all grievances to arbitration, not merely those which the court will deem meritorious. The processing of even frivolous claims may have therapeutic values of which those who are not a part of the plant environment may be quite unaware.

> The union claimed in this case that the company had violated a specific provision of the contract. The company took the position that it had not violated that clause. There was, therefore, a dispute between the parties as to "the meaning, interpretation and application" of the collective bargaining agreement. Arbitration should have been ordered. When the judiciary undertakes to determine the merits of a grievance under the guise of interpreting the grievance procedure of collective bargaining agreements, it usurps a function which under that regime is entrusted to the arbitration tribunal. *United Steelworkers of Am. v. American Mfg. Co.*, 363 U.S. 564 (1960).

Questions

1. Is the Court to separate frivolous and meritorious claims before ordering arbitration?
2. What therapeutic value could result from processing even frivolous claims?

NATIONAL EMERGENCIES

The Taft-Hartley Act sets forth detailed procedures to govern strikes which are deemed to create a national emergency. The Act provides that if the President believes a strike will imperil the national health or safety, he may impanel a board of inquiry. This board is directed to investigate the causes and circumstances of the labor controversy and report to the President. After reviewing the report, the President may direct the Attorney General to petition a federal district court for an injunction. If the district court finds the continuation of the strike will imperil the national health and safety, the court has jurisdiction to enjoin the strike. Thereafter, bargaining between the parties is to continue under the aid of the Federal Mediation and Conciliation Service. After sixty days, the board of inquiry must submit another report detailing the current status of the dispute and the employer's last offer of settlement. Within the next fifteen days, a vote is to be taken among the employees to determine whether they will agree to accept the last offer of the employer. If no settlement is reached, the injunction is dissolved at the end of eighty days.

The hope of the "eighty-days cooling-off period" is that the parties will be able to reach an agreement. If no agreement is reached, the employees may strike again and no further injunctions are provided by law. Accordingly, Congress must deal with the "national emergency" in some fashion. In 1963, the railroad unions threatened a strike because the railroad companies had proposed modifications of certain work rules. In an effort to avoid the strike, Congress enacted a law requiring compulsory arbtration over the two most controversial work rule changes (the retention of fireman on diesels and the size and compliment of train crews). The arbitration panel satisfactorily settled the controversy and avoided the strike. While most elements in American industry and labor would reject the compulsory arbitration alternative as a solution to major labor disputes, nevertheless compulsory arbitration has been utilized on one occasion and the possibility of its subsequent employment, now that it has been used once, cannot be ruled out. The fear by both labor and management of congressional action often helps formulate an agreement.

LABOR MANAGEMENT REPORTING AND DISCLOSURE ACT

The Labor Management Reporting and Disclosure Act of 1959 (Landrum-Griffin Act) regulates the internal affairs of unions. During the 1950s, congressional hearings produced evidence of misconduct by the officials of some unions. To cope with the abuses, such as embezzlement and "sweetheart" contracts with employers, Congress enacted a wide variety of provisions. Certain provisions, often referred to as a union member's "bill of rights," require elections to be held periodically for union officers and that union members be assured the right to vote, nominate candidates, run for office, or comment upon qualifications of candidates for office. Moreover, union members were given the right to attend membership meetings and participate in the voting and deliberations of such meetings. Other provisions of the Act require filing of extensive information concerning the financial affairs of the union and its officials. The Act outlaws embezzlement of union funds and restricts the making of loans by the union to its officials in excess of a stipulated amount.

In *Hall v. Cole* 83 LRRN 1390 (1973) a union member introduced a set of resolutions alleging undemocratic actions and misguided policies on the part of union officers in the Seafarers Union. When the resolutions were defeated by the union membership, the member was expelled from the union on the gounds that the resolutions violated a union rule prohibiting "deliberate and malicious vilification with regard to execution of the duties of any office." Finding no success with efforts to secure an intra-union remedy, the expelled member filed suit under the Labor-Management Reporting and Disclosure Act, claiming that his expulsion violated the union member's right of free speech. The courts regained union membership for the petitioner and awarded $5,500 in legal fees. The petitioner's vindication of free speech rights was conceived by the courts to have worked to the benefit of all member of the union and,, hence, justified the union's bearing the expense of the petitioner's litigation.

When members of the unions feel their rights under the Labor-Management Reporting and Disclosure Act have been violated and internal union procedures are exhausted, the union member may complain to the Secretary of Labor who, after investigation, may bring an action in court for the vindification of the union member's rights.

TRBOVICH v. UNITED MINE WORKERS OF AMERICA
404 U.S. 528 (1972)
Supreme Court of the United States

■ ■ ■

MARSHALL, Mr. Justice.

The Secretary of Labor instituted this action under §402(b) of the Labor-Management Reporting and Disclosure Act of 1959 (LMRDA), to set aside an election of officers of the United Mine Workers of America (UMWA), held on December 9, 1969. He alleged that the election was held in a manner that violated the

LMRDA in numerous respects, and he sought an order requiring a new election to be held under his supervision.

Petitioner, a member of the UMWA, filed the initial complaint with the Secretary that eventually led him to file this suit. Petitioner now seeks to intervene in the litigation pursuant to Fed. Rule Civ. Proc. 24(a), in order (1) to urge two additional grounds for setting aside the election, (2) to seek certain specific safeguards with respect to any new election that may be ordered, and (3) to present evidence and argument in support of the Secretary's challenge to the election. The District Court denied his motion for leave to intervene, on the ground that the LMRDA expressly stripped union members of any right to challenge a union election in the courts, and gave that right exclusively to the Secretary.

The LMRDA was the first major attempt of Congress to regulate the internal affairs of labor unions. Having conferred substantial power on labor organizations, Congress began to be concerned about the danger that union leaders abuse that power, to the detriment of the rank-and-file members. Congress saw the principle of union democracy as one of the most important safeguards against such abuse, and accordingly included in the LMRDA a comprehensive scheme for the regulation of union elections.

Title IV of the statute establishes a set of substantive rules governing union elections, and it provides a comprehensive procedure for enforcing those rules. Any union member who alleges a violation may initiate the enforcement procedure. He must first exhaust any internal remedies available under the constitution and bylaws of his union. Then he may file a complaint with the Secretary of Labor, who "shall investigate" the complaint. Finally, if the Secretary finds probable cause to believe a violation has occurred, he "shall... bring a civil action against the labor organization" in federal district court to set aside the election if it has already been held, and to direct and supervise a new election. With respect to elections not yet conducted, the statute provides that existing rights and remedies apart from the statute are not affected. But with respect to an election already conducted, "[T]he remedy provided by this subchapter... shall be exclusive."

The critical statutory provision for present purposes is § 403, making suit by the Secretary the "exclusive" post-election remedy for a violation of Title IV. This Court has held that § 403 prohibits union members from initiating a private suit to set aside an election. But in this case, petitioner seeks only to participate in a pending suit that is plainly authorized by the statute; it cannot be said that his claim is defeated by the bare language of the Act. The Secretary, relying on legislative history, argues that § 403 should be construed to bar intervention as well as initiation of a suit by the members. In his view the legislative history shows that Congress deliberately chose to exclude union members entirely from any direct participation in judicial enforcement proceedings under Title IV. The Secretary's argument rests largely on the fact that two alternative proposals figured significantly in the legislative history of Title IV, and each of these rejected bills would have authorized individual union members to bring suit. In the words of the District Court:

> "We think the fact that congress considered two alternatives—suit by union members and suit by the Secretary—and then chose the latter alternative and labelled it 'exclusive' deprives this Court of jurisdiction to permit the former alternative via the route of intervention.."

That argument misconceives the legislative history and misconstrues the statute. A review of the legislative history shows that Congress made suit by the Secretary the exclusive post-election remedy for two principal reasons: (1) to protect unions from frivolous litigation and unnecessary judicial interference with their elections, and (2) to centralize in a single proceeding such litigations as might be warranted with respect to a single election. Title IV as enacted serves these purposes by referring all complaints to the Secretary so that he can screen out frivolous ones, and by consolidating all meritorious complaints in a single proceeding, the Secretary's suit in federal district court. The alternative proposals were rejected simply because they failed to accomplish these objectives. These is no evidence whatever that Congress was opposed to participation by union members in the litigation, so long as that participation did not interfere with the screening and centralizing functions of the Secretary. . . .

Invervention by union members in a pending enforcement suit, unlike initiation of a separate suit, subjects the union to relatively little additional burden. The principal intrusion on internal union affairs has already been acomplished in that the union has already been summoned into court to defend the legality of its election. Intervention in the suit by union members will not subject the union to burdensome multiple litigation, nor will it compel the union to respond to a new and potentially goundless suit. Thus, at least insofar as petitioner seeks only to present evidence and argument in support of the Secretary's complaint, there is nothing in the languace or the history of the LMRDA to prevent such intervention.

The question is closer with respect to petitioner's attempt to add to the Secretary's complaint two additional grounds for setting aside the union election. These claims that the Secretary has preseumably determined to be without merit. Hence, to require the union to respond to these claims would be to circumvent the screening function assigned by statute to the Secretary. We recognize that it is less burdensome for the union to respond to new claims in the context of the pending suit than it would be respond to a new and independent complaint. Nevertheless, we think Congress intended to insulate the union from any complaint that did not appear meritorious to both a complaining member and the Secretary. Acordingly, we hold that in a post-election enforcement suit, Title IV imposes no bar to intervention by a union member, so long as that intervention is limited to the claims of illegality presented by the Secretary's complaint. . . .

The statute plainly imposes on the Secretary the duty to serve two distinct interests, which are related, but not identical. First, the statute gives the individual union members certain rights against their union and "the Secretary of Labor in effect becomes the union member's lawyer" for purposes of enforcing those rights. And second, the Secretary has an obligation to protect the "vital public interest in assuring free and democratic union elections that transcends the narrower interest of the complaining union member." Both functions are important, and they may not always dictate precisely the same approach to the conduct of the litigations. Even if the Secretary is performing his duties, broadly conceived, as well as can be expected, the union member may have a valid complaint about the performance of "his lawyer." Such a complaint, filed by the member who initiated the entire enforcement proceeding, should be regarded as sufficient to warrant relief in the form of intervention. . .

■ ■ ■

FAIR EMPLOYMENT PRACTICES

There are four major federal laws which regulate fair and equal rights in employment. Title VII of the Civil Rights Act of 1964, as amended by the Equal Employment Opportunities Act of 1972, forbids unions and employer discrimination based on race, color, religion, sex, or national origin. The Equal Pay Act of 1963 requires equal pay for men and women doing equal work. The Age Discrimination Employment Act of 1967 prohibits discriminatory hiring practices against job applicants between the ages of 40 and 65. The Fair Labor Standards Act of 1938 has three broad objectives: (a) the establishment of minimum wages, reflecting concepts of a "rudimentary minimum standard of living;" (b) the encouragement of a ceiling on hours of labor which was to result in an increase in the scope of employment by increasing the cost of overtime work, defined as work in excess of forty hours perweek; and (c) the discouragement of "oppressive child labor." Several amendments have been made to the 1938 Act increasing the minimum hourly wage rate and enlarging the scope of the Act by expanding its coverage.

EQUAL EMPLOYMENT OPPORTUNITY

One of the major purposes of Title VII of the Civil Rights Act of 1964 is to eliminate job discrimination based on race, color, religion, sex, or national origin. The Act prevents employer or union discrimination for any of these reasons in regard to discharge, refusal to hire, compensation, or conditions of employment. The Act is generally applicable to employers or labor unions with fifteen or more employees and employment agencies of any size.

The Civil Rights Act of 1964 created the Equal Employment Opportunities Commission (EEOC) which is granted the authority to investigate and conciliate grievances under the Act. The Commission investigates complaints after giving a similar state agency an opportunity to handle the problem. If the Commission is unable to satisfactorily resolve the dispute through conciliation, the EEOC may litigate the issues in federal court. If a "pattern and practice" of discrimination exists, the Commission may bring a class action suit. The Agency through the issuance of standards has put employers on notice about personnel policies which could lead to a charge of "pattern and practice" discrimination. The outlined six standards include:

1. Employers who follow policies and practices that result in "low utilization" of available minorities and women despite the law's requirement that they recruit, hire and promote such persons.
2. Employers who pay minorities and women less than other employers who use such workers for comparable work.
3. Companies that pay minorities and women less than other workers in comparable job categories.
4. Employers who follow personnel policies that have an "adverse impact" on those protected by federal antidiscrimination laws when such policies can't be justified by "business necessity."
5. Employers whose discriminatory practices are likely to be emulated by other employers because of the company's size, influence in the community, or competitive position in the industry.
6. Employers who have an opportunity to hire and promote more minorities and women because of expansion or high turnover rates but neglect such workers in filling those positions.

Certain exemptions are provided in the Act. It is not an unlawful employment practice for an emloyer to hire employees on the basis of his or her religion, sex, or national origin where these items have a bona fide occupational qualification reasonably necessary to the normal operation of the particular enterprise. However, it should be noted that there is no bona fide occupational qualification exemption for either race or color.

To prevent the Civil Rights Act of 1964 from violating the constitutional protection of free exercise of religion, a provision was inserted that states it is not unlawful for religious organizations to hire employees of a particular religion to perform work connected with carrying on its activities. Consequently,, the Catholic Church could legally refuse to hire anyone other than members of the Catholic faith in carrying out is religious activities. However, secular employers have a statutory obligation to make reasonable accommodations for the religious observance or practice of its employees, if such accommodations are not an undue hardship on the employer. Consider the person whose religion regarded Saturday as the Sabbath and forbade work on the Sabbath. The union refused to allow any violations in the seniority system and the person had insufficient seniority to bid for a shift with Saturdays off. The Company refused to permit the employee to work a four-day week or to replace the employee with another worker on the fifth day. Nevertheless, the employee's discharge did not violate the law because "accommodations" to the employee's beliefs would have caused an "undue hardship" on the employer.

RACIAL DISCRIMINATION

GRIGGS v. DUKE POWER CO.
401 U.S. 424 (1971)
Supreme Court of the United States

■ ■ ■

BURGER, Chief Justice.

We granted the writ in this case to resolve the question whether an employer is prohibited by the Civil Rights Act of 1964, Title VII, from requiring a high school education or passing of a standardized general intelligence test as a condition of employment in or transfer of jobs when (a) neither standard is shown to be significantly related to sucessful job performance, (b) both requirements operate to disqualify Negroes at a substantially higher rate than white applicants, and (c) the jobs in question formerly had been filled only by white employees as part of a long-standing practice of giving preference to whites.

...All the petitioners arc employed at the Company's Dan River Steam Station, a power generating facility located in Draper, North Carolina. At the time this action was instituted, the Company had 95 employees at the Dan River Station, 14 of whom were Negroes; 13 of these are petitioners here....

The objective of Congress in the enactment of Title VII is plain from the language of the statute. It was to achieve equality in employment opportunities and remove barriers that have operated in the past to favor an identifiable group of white employees over other employees. Under this Act, practices, procedures, or tests neutral on their face, and even neutral in terms of intent, canot be maintained if they operate to "freeze" the status quo of prior discriminatory employment practices.

The Court of Appeals' opinion, and the partial dissent, agreed that, on the record in the present case, "whites fare far better on the Company's alternative requirements" than Negroes. This consequence would appear to be directly traceable to race. Basic intelligence must have the means of articulation to manifest itself fairly in a testing process. Because they are Negroes, petitioners have long received inferior education in segregated schools.... Congress did not intend by Title VII, however, to guarantee a job to every person regardless of qualifications. In short, the Act does not command that any person be hired simply because he was formerly the subject of discrimination, or because he is a member of a minority group. Discrimination perference for any group, minority or majority, is precisely and only what Congress has proscribed. What is required by Congress is the removal of artificial, arbitrary, and unnecessary barriers to employment when the barriers operate invidiously to discriminate on the basis of racial or other impermissible classifications.

...The Act proscribes not only overt discrimination but also practices that are fair in form, but discriminatory in operation. The touchstone is business necessity. If an employment practice which operates to exclude Negroes cannot be shown to be related to job performance, the practice is prohibited.

On the record before us, neither the high school completion requirement nor the general intelligence test is shown to bear a demonstrable relationship to successful performance of the jobs for which is was used. Both were adopted, as the Court of Appeals noted, without meaningful study of their relationship to job-performance ability. Rather, a vice president of the Company testified, the requirements were instituted on the Company's judgment that they generally would improve the overall quality of the work force.

The evidence, however, shows that employees who have not completed high school or taken the tests have continued to perform satisfactorily and make progress in departments for which the high school and test criteria are now used. The promotion record of present employees who would not be able to meet the new criteria thus suggests the possiblity that the requirements may not be needed even for the limited purpose of preserving the avowed policy of advancement within the Company...

The Court of Appeals held that the Company had adopted the diploma and test requirements without any "intention to discriminate against Negro employees." We do not suggest that either the District Court or the Court of Appeals erred in examining the employer's intent; but good intent or absence of discriminatory intent does not redeem employment procedures or testing mechanisms that operate as "built-in headwinds" for minority groups and are unrelated to measuring job capability....

The facts of this case demonstrate the inadequacy of broad and general testing devices as well as the infirmity of using diplomas or degrees as fixed measures of capability. History is filled with examples of men and women who rendered highly effective performance without the conventional badges of accomplishment in terms of certificates, diplomas, or degrees. Diplomas and tests are useful servants, but Congress has mandated the common-sense proposition that they are not to become masters of reality.

The Company contends that its general intelligence tests are specifically permitted by §703(h) of the Act. That section authorizes the use of "any professionally developed ability test" that is not "designed, intended, *or used* to discriminate because of race...."(Emphasis added.)

The Equal Employment Opportunity Commission, having enforcement responsibility, has issued guidelines interpreting §703(h) to permit only the use of job-related tests. The adminstrative interpretation of the Act by the enforcing agency is entitled to great deference. Since the Act and its legislative history support the Commission's construction, this affords good reason to treat the Guidelines as expressing the will of Congress....

Nothing in the Act precludes the use of testing or measuring procedures; obviously they are useful. What Congress has forbidden is giving these devices and mechanisms controlling force unless they are demonstrably a reasonable measure of job performance. Congress has not comanded that the less qualified be preferred over the better qualified simply because of minority origins. Far from disparaging job qualifications as such, Congress has made such qualifications the controlling factor, so that race, religion, nationality, and sex become irrelevant. What Congress has commanded is that any tests used must measure the person for the job and not the person in the abstract.

■ ■ ■

Questions

1. Must the employer "intend" to discriminate before his employment practice is unlawful?
2. Why did the intelligence test used by the Duke Power Company fail to be an acceptable exception to the Act of 1964?

Once it is shown that an employment practice (testing mechanisms) has a discriminatory impact, the Court in *Griggs* said the burden is on the employer to prove that any given requirement has a "manifest relationship" to the jobs in question and respesents a "business necessity." The Justices also said that "Congress directed the thrust of the Act to the *consequences* of employment practices, not simply motivation." For an employer to safely use a testing mechanism and satisfy the "job-relatedness" test of *Griggs*, the employer must fully comply with the 1978 Uniform Guidelines on Employee Selection Procedures prepared by federal enforcement agencies. One district court ruled that an alledgedly discriminatory promotion examination cannot be saved by a "job relatedness" study that fails to address alternative selection procedures. Such a study alone is unimpressive for providing the "business necessity" element to rebut a prima facie case of racial discrimination in violation of Title VII. Alternative selection procedures might be capable of being developed which would not have had the same racially discriminatory impact.

In the *Griggs* dicision the seniority rights of the discrimination victims were "to be considered on a plant-wide, rather than a departmental, basis." The Court added, "to apply a strict departmental seniority would result in the continuation of present effects of past discrimination." Since the *Griggs* decision, most courts and employers had operated on the principle that any seniority system locking-in minorities or women in positions of previous discrimination was illegal. Addressing the question in *U.S. vs Teamsters* 431 U.S. 324 (1977) the Supreme Court said that a seniority system that perpetuated the effects of discrimination that took place before Title VII became law (July, 1965) was legal. The Court refused to bar a departmental seniority system that was part of a bona fide labor contract when it was neutral and equally applied. The Company seniority system can perpetuate past discrimination, but only if it is part of a bona fide labor contract and the original discrimination took place before July, 1965 and has not happened since (a combination of circumstances time is rapidly erasing).

REVERSE DISCRIMINATION

UNITED STEELWORKERS v. WEBER
443 U.S. — (1979)
Supreme Court of the United States

■ ■ ■

BRENNAN, Mr. Justice.

In 1974 petitioner United Steelworkers of America (USWA) and petitioner Kaiser Aluminum & Chemical Corporation (Kaiser) entered into a master collective-bargaining agreement covering terms and conditions of employment at 15 Kaiser plants. The agreement contained an affirmative action plan designed to eliminate conspicious racial imbalances in Kaiser's then almost exclusively white craft work forces. Black craft hiring goals were set for each Kaiser plant equal to the percentage of blacks in the respective local labor forces. To enable plants to meet these goals, on-the-job training programs were established to teach unskilled production workers—black and white—the skills necessary to become craft workers. The plan reserved for black employees 50% of the openings in these newly created in-plant training programs.

This case arose from the operation of the plan at Kaiser's plant in Gramercy, La. Until 1974 Kaiser hired as craft workers for that plant only persons who had had prior craft experience. Because blacks had long been excluded from craft unions, few were able to present such credentials. As a consequence, prior to 1974 only 1.83% (five out of 273) of the skilled craft workers at the Gramercy plant were black, even though the work force in the Gramercy area was approximately 39% black.

Pursuant to the national agreement Kaiser altered its craft hiring practice in the Gramercy plant. Rather than hiring already trained outsiders, Kaiser established a training program to train its production workers to fill craft openings. Selection of craft trainees was made on the basis of seniority, with the proviso that at least 50% of the new trainees were to be black until the percentage of black skilled craft workers in the Gramercy plant approximated the percentage of blacks in the local labor force.

During 1974, the first year of the operation of the Kaiser-USWA affirmative action plan, 13 craft trainees were selected from Gramercy's production work force. Of these, 7 were black and 6 white. The most junior black selected into the program had less seniority than several white production workers whose bids for admission were rejected. Thereafter one of those white production workers, respondent Brian Weber, instituted this class action in the United States District Court for the Eastern District of Louisiana.

The complaint alleged that the filling of craft trainee positions at the Gramercy plant pursuant to the affirmative action program had resulted in junior black employees receiving training in preference to more senior white employees, thus discriminating against respondent and other similarly situated white employees in violation of §§703 (a) and (d) of Title VII...

We emphasize at the outset the narrowness of our inquiry. Since the Kaiser-USWA plan does not involve state action, this case does not present an alleged violation of the Equal Protection Clause of the Constitution. Further, since the Kaiser-USWA plan was adopted voluntarily, we are not concerned with what Title VII requires or with what a court might order to remedy a past proven violation of the Act. The only question before us is the narrow statutory issue of whether Title VII *forbids* private plans that accord racial preferences in the manner and for the purpose provided in the Kaiser-USWA plan...

Respondent argues that Congress intended in Title VII to prohibit all race-conscious affirmative action plans. Respondent's agrument rests upon a literal inter-pretation of §§703 (a) and (d) of the Act. Those sections make it unlawful to "discriminate...because of...race" in hiring and in the selection of apprentices for training programs. Since, the argument runs,...the Kaiser-USWA affirmative action plan operates to discriminate against white employees solely because they are white, it follows that the Kaiser-USWA plan violates Title VII.

Respondent's argument is not without force. But it overlooks the significance of the fact that the Kaiser-USWA plan is an affirmative action plan voluntarily adopted by private parties to eliminate traditional patterns of racial segregation. In this context respondent's reliance upon a literal construction of §703 (a) and (d)...is misplaced. It is a "familiar rule, that a thing may be within the letter of the statute and yet not within the statute, because not within its spirit, nor within the intention of its makers." The prohibition against racial discrimination in §§703 (a) and (d) of Title VII must therefore be read against the background of the legislative history of Title VII and the historical context from which the Act arose...

Congress' primary concern in enacting the prohibition against racial discrimination in Title VII of the Civil Rights Act of 1964 was with "the plight of the Negro in our economy." Before 1964, blacks were largely relegated to "unskilled and semi-skilled jobs." As a consequence "the relative position of the Negro worker [was] steadily worsening...

Congress feared that the goals of the Civil Rights Act—the integration of blacks into the mainstream of American society—could not be achieved unless this trend were reversed. And Congress recognized that that would not be possible unless blacks were able to secure jobs "which have a future."... Accordingly, it was clear to Congress that "the crux of the problem [was] to open employment opportunities for Negroes in occupations which have been traditionally closed to them," and it was to this problem that Title VII's prohibition against racial discrimination in employment was primarily addressed.

It plainly appears from the House Report accompanying the Civil Rights Act that Congress did not intend wholly to prohibit private and voluntary affirmative action efforts as one method of solving this problem. The Report provides:

> "No bill can or should lay claim to eliminating all the causes and consequences of racial and other types of discrimination against minorities. There is reason to believe, however, that national leadership provided by the enactment of Federal legislation dealing with the most troublesome problems *will create an atmosphere conducive to voluntary or local resolution of other forms of discrimination."* H. R. Rep. No. 914, 88th Cong., 1st Sess. (1963), at 18. (Emphasis supplied.)

Given this legislative history, we cannot agree with respondent that Congress intended to prohibit the private sector from taking effective steps to accomplish the goal that Congress designed Title VII to achieve. The very statutory words intended as a spur or catalyst to cause "employers and unions to self-examine and to self-evaluate their employment practices and to endeavor to eliminate, so far as possible, the last vestiges of an unfortunate and ignominious page in this country's history," cannot be interpreted as an absoulte prohibition against all private, voluntary, race-conscious affirmative action efforts to hasten the elimination of such vestiges. It would be ironic indeed if a law triggered by a Nation's concern over centuries of racial injustice and intended to improve the lot of those who had "been excluded from the American dream for so long." constituted the first legislative prohibition of all voluntary, private, race-conscious efforts to abolish traditional patterns of racial segregation and hierarchy.

Our conclusion is further reinforced by examination of the language and legislative history of §703 (j) of Title VII. Opponets of Title VII raised two related arguments against the bill. First, they argued that the Act would be interpreted to *require* employers with racially imbalanced work forces to grant preferental treatment to racial minorities in order to integrate. Second, they argued that employers with racially imbalanced work forces would grant preferental treatment to racial minorities, even if not required to do so by the Act. Had Congress meant to prohibit all race-conscious affirmative action, as respondent urges, it easily could have answered both objections by providing that Title VII would not require or *permit* racially preferential integration efforts. But Congress did not choose such a course. Rather Congress added §703 (j) which addresses only the first objection. The section provides that nothing contained in Title VII "shall be interpreted to *require* any employer . . . to grant preferental treatment . . . to any group because of the race . . . of such . . . group on account of" a defacto racial imbalance in the employer's work force. The section does *not* state that "nothing in Title VII shall be interpreted to *permit*" voluntary affirmative efforts to correct racial imbalances. The natural inference is that Congress chose not to forbid all voluntary race-conscious affirmative action.

The reasons for this choice are evident from the legislative record. Title VII could not have been enacted into law without substantial support from legislators in both Houses who traditionally resisted federal regulations of private business. Those legislators demanded as a price for their support that "management prerogatives and union freedoms . . . be left undisturbed to the greatest extent possible." . . . Clearly, a prohibition against all voluntary, race conscious, affirmative action efforts would disserve these ends. Such a prohibition would augment the powers of the Federal Government and diminish traditional management preogatives while at the same time impeding attainment of the ultimate statutory goals. In view of this legislative history and in view of Congress' desire to avoid undue federal regulation of private businesses, use of the word "require" rather than the phrase "require or permit" in §703 (j) fortifies the conclusion that Congress did not intend to limit traditional business freedom to such a degree as to prohibit all voluntary, race-conscious affirmative action.

We therefore hold that Title VII's probitition is §§703 (a) and (d) against racial discrimination does not condemn all private, voluntary, race-conscious affirmative action plans . . .

We conclude, therefore, that the adoption of the Kaiser-USWA plan for the Gramercy plant falls within the area of discretion left by Title VII to the private sector voluntarily to adopt affirmative action plans designed to eliminate conspicuous racial imbalance in traditionally segregated job categories. . . .

Questions

1. Why was the charge of "reverse discrimination" not within the purpose of Title VII?
2. Did Congress intend to prohibit all race-conscious affirmative action? What language could Congress have used if it intended to accomplish that goal?

EQUAL PAY FOR EQUAL WORK

WIRTZ, SECRETARY OF LABOR, v. BASIC INC.
256 F. Supp 786 (1966)
United States Distric Court of Nevada

■ ■ ■

...The case for the plaintiff was presented by a feminine attorney of the Departmet of labor, resisted by a masculine attorney of the Nevada Bar, and considered by a Judge who, for the purposes of this case at least, must be sexless, a possibility not apparent when the oath of office was taken and one which may bespeak the appointment of older judges....

The employees involved in the instant dispute are laboratory analysts Jo Ann Barredo, Ann Jones, and Byron O'Dell. Barredo was hired by Thompson, the then Chief Chemist, on September 1, 1959, and was trained under his supervision to perform the analytical tests required to determine the metallurgy of the various ores and compounds required to be analyzed. She had had no previous experience. Jones was hired by Thompson in 1953 and was trained by him. She had had no previous experience. O'Dell was hired by Thompson in March, 1962. He was trained by Thompson, with the assistance of Barredo and Jones, in the particular analytical procedures used at Basic. In his early life, he had been employed as a miner and mill superintendent and from 1949 until 1962, was employed by Standard Slag Co. at Gabbs, Nevada, as a laboratory analyst, using similar analytical procedures to those at Basic to determine the metallurgy of similar ores and products....

The primary work of all three laboratory analysts is the running of relatively simple, standardized chemical tests on various materials performed strictly in accordance with the company's testing manual and directives....

After the passage of the Equal Pay Act of 1963, the then Chief Chemist, Thompson, discussed with his superiors the necessity of either equalizing the pay of the laboratory analysts or setting up legal job classifications of jobs requiring different skill, effort, or responsibility or which were to be performed under different working conditions, but no final action was taken. Thompson resigned before September 1, 1964, and the present Chief Chemist, Lawson, succeeded him...

The defendant's answer to the Complaint, after denying any discrimination among employees on the basis of sex, affirmatively alleges:

> "Any lesser pay received by Jo Ann Barredo and Ann Jones results from the fact that their work requires less skill, effort, and/or responsibility than the work of higher paid employees who work under similar conditions."...

The burden of proof in this case is upon the Secretary to show that the jobs under consideration require equal work, equal skill, equal effort, and equal responsibility and are performed under similar working conditions. The defendant has invoked none of the statutory exceptions permitting payment differentials made pursuant to a seniority system, a merit system, a system which measures earnings by quantity or quality of production or a differential based on any other factor other than sex, which are affirmative defenses the burden of proof of which would be borne by the employer.

The Secretary has promulgated comprehensive regulations interpreting the equal pay provisions. Such regulations are generally valid and binding... and our perusal of them persuades us that the Secretary has produced a helpful and reasonable aid to a correct interpretation of the law.

Fundamental in the application of the law is the premise that it establishe an objective standard requiring that a judgement with respect to alleged discrimination between sexes be based upon the requirements of the particlar jobs being compared, rather than a comparison of the skill of individual employees, the effort of individual employees, or their previous training and experience. "Application of the equal pay standard is not dependent on job clasifications or titles but depend rather on actual job requirements and performance." Equal does not mean identical and insubstantial differences in the skill, effort, and responsibility requirements of particular jobs should be ignored. The job requirements should be viewed as a whole.

The preponderance of the evidence clearly shows that the work performed by O'Dell, Barredo, and Jones is substantially equal and that their jobs as laboratory analysts require substantially equal skill, effort, and responsibility. The only require-ment, as we see it, as to which there is room for a reasonable difference of opinion concerns the existence of similar working conditions.

We have no doubt that this defendant may, as it apparently has attempted to do, establish a poistion for a male analyst designated "Shift Analysts," if you will, where the working conditions are different from other analysts' jobs, provided the classifica-tion is made in good faith and there is no unreasonable discrimintion on the basis of sex. The Secretary agrees. "However, in situations where some employees performing work... have working conditions substantially different from those required for the performance of other jobs the equal pay principle would not apply." The evidence shows that O'Dell's swing shift work every two weeks is performed under substantially different working conditions; the supervising chemists are absent after 5 p.m., the other analysts are absent after 5 p.m., and part of the work is at night.

The difficulty here is that what the defendant company has done belies any announced intention to differentiate between a day shift and a swing shift analyst on the basis of dissimilar working conditions. The facts are: Between June 11, 1964, the effective date of the Equal Pay Act, and September 1, 1964, O'Dell, Barredo, and Jones all worked the day shift, performed the same work, and received different wages; since September 1, 1964, O'Dell has worked a swing shift every alternate two-week period and has received an additional five cents per hour for such work; during the alternate two-week periods that O'Dell works the day shift, his job requires substan-tially the same skill, effort, and responsibility as those performed by Barredo and Jones, yet he receives a higher hourly rate of compensation. We think these facts compel the consclusion that the job classification "Swing Analyst" is a paper classifi-cation unrelated to the true working conditions, and that the five-cent pay differential for swing shift work is intended to compensate for the different working conditions.

Section 800.145 of the Regulations states:

> "When applied without distinction to employees of both sexes, shift differentials, incen-tive payments, production bonuses, performance and longevity raises, and the like will not result in equal pay violations. For example, in an establishment where men and women are employed on a job, but only men work on the night shift for which a night shift differential is paid, such a differential would not be prohibited. However, the payment of a higher hourly rate to all men on that job for all hours worked because some of the men may occasionally work nights would result in a prohibited wage differential."

These provisions seem reasonable on their face and as applied to our situation. There could be no effective enforcement of the equal pay provisions if differentials between sexes were permitted for all hours worked because of the substantially different working conditions and responsibilities entailed in a specific part of the work performed at identifiable times and places. As a "Shift Analyst," O'Dell is entitled to a different rate of pay while he is working as a shift analyst, but not while working on the day shift. He and the company apparently have agreed that five cents per hour is a reasonable differential.

The Equal Pay Act of 1963, which, like other Congressional enactments concerning employment practices, was induced by social conditions and working conditions pertaining in metropolitan and industrial areas, presents unique headaches in applica-tion to an agrarian-mining-tourist economy such as Nevada's where employers of large numbers of employees are few and far between. Nevertheless, just as the interpretive opinions of the Act by industrially oriented courts in Michigan, New York, Ohio, California, and elsewhere will be persuasive authority for us in future cases, so should we interpret the law with deference to the expressed intention of Congress in the light of its nationwide application. Provincial differences in business practices and customs are not excepted by the law.

Anomalously, the compensation of two females, Barredo and Jones, will also be equalized by our decree. We see no escape from this result. The last proviso of 29 U.S.C. 206(d)(1) states:

"That an employer who is paying a wage rate differential in violation of this subsection shall not, in order to comply with the provisions of this subsection, reduce the wage rate of any employee."

We cannot adjust O'Dell's wage rate downward, and inasmuch as Barredo and Jones are doing equal work, must increase the wage rate of both their jobs to equal O'Dell's.

■ ■ ■

Questions

1. Must jobs be identical in all respects to require equal pay?
2. What justifications are allowed for differences in wage rates?

AGE DISCRIMINATION

COATES v. NATIONAL CASH REGISTER CO.
433 F. Supp. 655 (1977)
U.S. District Court (WD. Va)

■ ■ ■

Section 623(a)(1) of the Age Discrimination in Employment Act... states that it is unlawful for an employer to discharge or to discriminate against any individual "because of such individual's age." The phrase "because of such individual's age" is used several times throughout the prohibitory sections of ADEA and constitutes the standard by which to judge employment decisions. The problem with this standard for courts has been to interpret how much weight age must be given in the employment decision before the Act is violated....

The court in *Laugesen v. Anaconda Co.*, 510 F. 2d 307 (6th Cir. 1975) adopted a "determining factor" test and explained how the jury should judge the legality of the employment decision:

[W]e believe that it was esential for the jury to understand from the instructions that there could be more than one factor in the decision to discharge him and that he was nevertheless entitled to recover if one such factor was his age and if in fact it made a difference in determining whether he was retained or discharged. This is so even though the need to reduce the employee force generally was also a strong, and perhaps even more compelling reason....

NCR had several reasons for its reduction of the Danville field engineers staff, including deteriorating economic conditions in mid-1975. While the company can discharge its employees, it cannot base the decision about which employee to discharge on age or on factors created by age discrimination.

NCR's decision to discharge plaintiff was not directly based on age, but it was based on the training of plaintiffs. The evidence clearly established that the relative training levels of NCR employees was directly related to the age of the employees. So by using the training level as the basis of the discharge decision, NCR indirectly discharged plaintiffs because of their age. Therefore this court holds that the training or lack of traning, which ostensibly is an objective and valid criterion for employment decisions cannot form the basis of an employment decision when that lack of training is created by age discrimination. The age discrimination which invalidates an employment decision need not be direct or intentional. This court further holds that both plaintiffs were discharged "because of" their "age".

Damages

Besides asking for reinstatement, plaintiffs requested back wages from May 2, 1975 until reinstatement, liquidated damages and atorney's fees and costs....

To summarize the measure of back pay, it is still the difference between the salary an employee would have received but for the violation of the Act and the salary actually received from other employment. The period of back pay is measured from the time of the loss of employment as a result of the violation to the time when the employee accepts or declines reinstatement at his former position or at a position of comparable status, salary, benefits, and potential for advancement. The back pay amount computed in this way must be reduced by severance pay received, unemployment compensation collected, and any amounts earnable with reasonable diligence. Finally, the back pay amount should be increased by the value of any pension benefits, health insurance, seniority, leave-time, or other fringe benefits which the employee would have accrued during the back pay period but for the violation of the Act.

Another aspect of damages involves damages for pain and suffering....

...[I]t is the holding of this court that damages for pain and suffering are allowable under ADEA. The bases of this holding are... (1) the ADEA...creates a new statutory tort, and the existence of such a statutory right implies the existence of necessary and appropriate remedies: (2) the emotional and psychological losses occasioned by age discrimination were clearly recognized by the Congress in its deliberations on the Act; (3) compensatory awards for pain and suffering have been found appropriate in other discrimination contexts, including employment and housing; (4) the cases denying damage awards for pain and suffering in Title VII actions have been premised on that statute's express limitation of relief to equitable remedies, whereas the ADEA contains a specific allowance of legal relief.

Based on the evidence adduced at the trial, this court is in accord with the jury's determination that both plaintiffs suffered damages for pain and suffering. Their discharges disrupted their lives and caused them considerable embarrassment.

Both plaintiffs also prayed for liquidated damages and attorney's fees and costs. Liquidated damages are only available for "willful violations" of ADEA.

In this case, the advisory jury was instructed that they should find that the discharges were wilful violations of ADEA only if the acts were "done voluntarily and intentionally, and with the specific intent to do something which is forbidden by law." This court finds that neither discharge was a willful violation of the law; therefore, no liquidated damages are available to plaintiffs.

Finally, it is well settled that plaintiffs who are victims of age dicrimination are entitled to reasonable attorney's fees and costs.

■ ■ ■

Questions

1. In what fashion did NCR discriminate on the basis of age?
2. Besides gaining reinstatement, what damages were ordered to be paid to the plaintiffs?
3. Should "pain and suffering" damages be allowed in an age discrimination case? In *Dean v. American Security Insurance Co.* the Supreme Court left standing a fifth Circuit Court of Appeals ruling that ADEA does not permit awards for pain and suffering. Were such awards possible, the lower court said, they would undermine attempts to conciliate disputes before they escalate into court cases.
4. When the Supreme Court ruled in *McMann v. United Airlines* that retirement could be forced when an employeee reached an age prescribed in a bona fide retirement pension plan, it suggested that if Congress wanted to change that rule, it should pass a law. As a result, Congress passed a law in 1978 which forbids the involuntary retirement of an employee at any age up to 70. The new rule was to be phased in with differing dates for differing types of employees, but generally applicable to all by the beginning of 1980. Can one expect that Congress will eventually eliminate all compulsory retirement ages?

UNEMPLOYMENT AND INJURY PROTECTION

Considerable state and federal legislation has been enacted to protect the employee from physical injury and loss of job. The principal statutes covering these risks are unemployment compensation laws, workman's compensation laws, and the Occupational Safety & Health Act of 1970.

UNEMPLOYMENT COMPENSATION

Unemployment compensation is usually administered jointly by the states and the federal government. It provides compensation to the unemployed. While qualifications vary from state to state, the employee generally must be off the job for at least a week, remain ready for work in other jobs requiring similar training and experience, and must not have quit his previous employment without cause or been fired for misconduct. Generally, if the unemployment is the result of a labor dispute in which the employee is actively participating, the employee is disqualified. The following case involves an administrative officer's determination of whether the employee was qualified for unemployment compensation when unemployment resulted from a labor dispute.

ARMSTRONG v. PROPHET FOODS CO.
287 N.E. 2d 286 (1972)
Common Pleas Court of Richland County

■ ■ ■

Denver Armstrong and some 19 other claimants have appealed from a decision of the Board of Review, Ohio Bureau of Employment Services dated June 30, 1971... which in effect disallowed claimants' claims for benefits on the basis that their unemployment was due to a labor dispute.

General Motors Corporation owned and operated one of its Fisher Body Plants new Mansfield and the production workers were members of a local union of United Auto Workers. A labor dispute developed between the union members and General Motors and this culminated in a strike by said local union...[P]icket lines were set up around the entrance to the plant.

Now there existed... at said plant, some two cafeterias and one dining room... (which) were provided for and used by the production workers and other workers for the General Motors Corporation. Prophet Foods Company handled the cafeterias (and) dining room... under an agreement with General Motors...

When the picket lines were set up the Prophet Foods Company employees were thrown out of work...

Now, Prophet Foods is a totally separate corporation from General Motors, and no one at General Motors either controls or has the right to control the activity of any employee of Prophet Foods. Prophet Foods had its own collective bargaining agreement with Prophet Foods employees, and this was in full force during all times involved herein. At none of the times involved herein was there any labor dispute between Prophet Foods and any of its employees. At no time was there any labor dispute between employees of Prophet Foods and General Motors or any other employer.

It was after the labor dispute started at General Motors that appellants were laid off by Prophet Foods, since there was no work available—no customers to serve.

...[T]he referee denied said claimed rights to receive unemployment compensation benefits because their unemployment was due to what he termed the dispute between the General Motors corporation and the United Auto Workers...

R.C. 4141.29 (d)(1)(a), provides: ...[N]o individual may serve a waiting period or be paid benefits under the following conditions: (1) For any week with respect to which the administrator finds that: (a) His unemployment was *due to a labor dispute* other than a lockout *at* any *factory*, estalishment, or other *premises* located in this or any other state *owned or operated by the employer by which he is or was last employed;* and for so long as his unemploymment is due to such labor dispute. * * * "(Emphasis by the court.)

The court notes that before an amendment to the law in 1963 the statutory disqualification in effect then provided:

"Lost his employment or has left his employment by reasons of a labor dispute * * * *at* the factory, establishment, or other premises *at* which he was employed."(Emphasis by the court.)

It appears a dispute "at the factory, establishment or other premises" under the old law would have involved all employees or any employer. But the law was changed. This change was effective October 20, 1963. It will be noted that a word was stricken and the phrase now reads "owned or operated by the employer by which" he was employed. Under the present law, status of the employee takes on a new significance. If an employer in a labor dispute thus shuts down or reduces oerations at another location it owns or operates, then its employees at such other location would be disqualified. If the employer is in a labor dispute resulting in a supplier receiving no orders and thus has to lay off people then those people are not disqualified. Their employer, the supplier, is not in the labor dispute. He is a separate employer. From the evidence in the instant case, the referee initially adopted the two-unit theory with relationship between Prophet Foods and General Motors. The plant was not viewed as a single unit. According to the theory adopted there are two distinct premises within the gates at General Motors, their manufacturing facility and the second which is the cafeteria operations by Prophet Foods.

It naturally follows under the theory adopted, it must be accepted that a labor dispute at the establishment or premises that is operated by General Motors is not a labor dispute at the establishment or premises that is operated by Prophet Foods. Under the statute appellant would be entitled to receive unemployment compensation unless their unemployment was due to a labor dispute at the premises operated by Prophet Foods. The referee expressly found that General Motors did not operate the premises used by Prophet and that the unemployment of apellants herein was due solely to the labor dispute at General Motors. There was no labor dispute at the food operation business of Prophet Foods. Further, the Unemployment Compensation Act must be liberally construed. A referee cannot broadly construe a proviso or exception which restricts the general scope of the Act. Such must be strictly construed.

The courts in other states have not disqualified claims where somebody else's employer has a labor dispute with his employees...

Ordinarily an employee can't receive unemployment compensation if unemployment results from a labor dispute of the employer and the employees of the same company. If employees under such circumstances could rely on unemployment compensation, it would place the employers at a disadvantage. But in our case at hand these workers are mere victims of the circumstances, the type of situation prompting the adoption of unemployment compensation laws for relief.

The decision of the Board of Review denying appellants compensation as prayed for is unlawful, unreasonable and contrary to the manifest weight of the evidence and is hereby reversed.

■ ■ ■

WORKMEN'S COMPENSATION

In common law, if an employee was injured as the result of the negligence of the employer, the employee was entitled to recover money damages. However, the common law also provide the employer with three defenses known as (1) assumption of risk, (2) contributory negligence, and (3) the fellow servant rule. These defenses normally provided the employer with an escape from liability to the employee. For example, if an employer knowingly supplied a hazardous working tool for employees an employee injured in handling the equipment would be entitled to recover damages. However, if the employee had understood the hazards of the defective equipment and knowingly assumed the risk of this injury, the employee would be barred from recovery. In addition, the employee could not recover it he or she was in some way contributorially negligent in the manner in which the machine was handled. Finally, if a fellow servant was negligent and caused the injury to the employee, the employee was denied recovery under the fellow servant rule. Hence, at common law it was only in rare instances that an employee was able to gain a recovery against an employer because of an injury sustained in the working environment.

State workman's compensation statutes were enacted to provide a system to pay workers or their families if a worker was accidentally killed or injured while employed. In addition, occupational diseases which arise out of and in the course of employment are likewise covered. Under these Acts, the negligence or fault of the employer in causing the employee injury is not an issue. Instead, the law affords the employee an assured recovery and in turn, limits the dollar amount of damages that the employer must pay to the injured employee. Normally, the employers pay monies into a state fund and an industrial commisison decides which employees are entitled to a recovery. Some states allow an emloyer to be covered or to purchase insurance for the protection of the employees.

The following case illustrates a typical workman's compensation situation.

BUNKLEY v. REPUBLIC STEEL
30 Ohio Misc. 39 (1972)
Common Pleas Court of Cuyahoga County

■ ■ ■

. . . The Republic Steel company, is a self insurer under the Workmen's Compensation Act of Ohio. It is the claim of the plaintiff that he ruptured himself when he, and two other workmen, were lifting, by hand, a heavy article called a "twyer" or "twill" which weighed approximately 175 to 200 pounds and inserting it into an opening in a Republic furnace at an elevation about five feet above the floor level of the defendant's mill. . .

It is the contention of Republic that claimant is not entitled to have a judgment entered which would have the effect of requiring Republic to pay his surgical and hospital expenses incidental to the repairing of his hernia, compensation for temporary, total disability for the period when he was hospitalized for the surgery and subsequent convalescence and for such other allowances as he is entitled to receive as a result of his injury, including an award for attorney fees payable by Republic because of the necessity for bringing this lawsuit

The bases for Republic's contention as to why plaintiff should not be entitled to the benefits of the Workmen's Compensation Act with reference to his rupture may be summarized as follows:

1. The incident in which claimant contends he was ruptured did not occur. The jury found, upon the basis of adequate testimony, that the incident did in fact occur.
2. The words used by the claimant in his description of the incident were not such as to describe the sustaining of an injury as required by R.C. 4123.01. . .

There is no validity to any of these contentions of Republic.

R.C. 4123.01 provides as follows:

"(C) 'Injury' includes any injury, whether caused by external accidental means or accidental in character and result, received in the course of, and arising out of the injured employee's employment."

"Accident" is defined as follows:

> "An event which takes place without one's foresight or expectation; or an unusual effect of a known cause and, therefore, not expected; an event which under the circumstances, is unusual and not expected to the person to whom it happens."

Counsel for the defendant wasted considerable trial time in this action in attempting to elicit statements from the plaintiff to the effect that there was no unexpected, unusual, or fortuitous happening in connection with plaintiff's injury, other than the occurrence of the injury.

Testimony of such a happening was unnecessary in order to establish plaintiff's right to recovery even though his testimony did include such evidence.

Plaintiff testified that on the day of the injury, the twill in the furnace had burned out and that it became necessary for himself and two other workmen to replace it; that a twill is inserted into the furnace by lifting it up by hand to a point where there is an opening in the furnace at about his shoulder height—above five feet; that:

'You can't put it in straight. You have to put it in sideways in order to get it in and sometimes that quill [sic] will get stuck and you jerk on it and that is when I felt this pain (indicating in the groin area);" "I went over and sat down for awhile and the pain left;" "I went back to work. It wasn't long before it was time to quit anyway;" "Well, that pain kept coming but it never stayed. It come and go till I notice it begin to swell. I had swelled up. It would swell up and go back down and it starts having pains and that is when I went to this Dr. Oppenheim;" He testified he was having the swelling in the same spot where he felt the pain; that he was operated on there; that he had never previously had any swelling over there...

It was the contention of Republic that before a workman can participate in the Workmen's Compensation Fund as a result of an injury sustained while at work and engaged in the advancement of the work of the employer, that an unusual occurrence such as a slip, fall, jerk, jar, external force, unusual strain, pressure, etc., must be described as having brought about the injury, even though it was sustained when a workman was extending himself beyond his physical capabilities in order to further this business of his employer.

Beyond question, the plaintiff's description of the occurrence, even though in less than artful words, if believed by the jury, sufficiently complied with the...statutory requirements that are brought into question herein by Republic.

OSHA

The Occupational Safety and Health Act of 1970 (OSHA) was the result of testimony and documentary evidence presented before Congress which pointed out that the American work site was a place of peril. More than 14,500 workers were killed annually in connection with their job, a mortality rate two and one-half times greater than experienced by U.S. troops in Vietnam. More than 2,200,000 workers were disabled in America each year, and this represents a loss of about 250 million man-days of work which is in excess of lost work time due to strikes. Of course, these statistics do not measure the social and emotional cost to the individuals injured.

The Act requires businessmen to maintain their organizations free from recognized hazards. The duty placed on the employer is no more than the common law concept that a person must refrain from actions which will cause harm to others. Three federal agencies were created to develop and enforce occupational safety and health standards. The Occupational Safety and Health Administration is a component part of the Department of Labor with authority to promulgate standards, make inspections, and enforce the Act. The Nationa Institute for Occupational Safety and Health (NIOSH) is a component part of the Department of Health, Education, and Welfare. Its primary function is to conduct research on various safety and health problems and recommend standards for OSHA to adopt. The Occupational Safety and Health Review Commission is an independent agency whose primary functions are to handle all appeals from actions taken by OSHA and to assess penalties recommended by OSHA. The enforcement machinery of OSHA is more streamlined than traditional administrative procedure. As a consequence, the enforcement structure of OSHA has been challenged as unconstitutional in many instances, such as in the following case.

ENFORCEMENT STRUCTURE

ATLAS ROOFING CO. v. OCCUPATIONAL S. & H. REV. COM'N
518 F.2d 990 (1975)
U.S. Court of Appeals (5th Cir.)

■ ■ ■

Atlas Roofing Company petitions this Court to review an order of the Occupational Safety and Health Review Commission (OSHRECOM) affirming a $600.00 penalty assessed by the Secretary of Labor under the Occupational Safety and Health Act of 1970 (OSHA)...Petitioner challenges the order...on the grounds that the basic structure of OSHA is constitutionally defective because (1) the civil penalties under OSHA are really penal in nature and call for the constitutional protections of the Sixth Amendment....

This issue has importance even beyond the case at hand because the streamlined enforcement procedure embodied in OSHA, although presently prescribed in only a few instances, has been recommended as a blueprint for a major revision of the enforcement systems of *all* federal agencies....

The Enforcement Structure of OSHA

Designed with the ambitious but socially laudable goal "to assure so far as possible every working man and woman in the Nation safe and healthful working conditions and to preserve our human resources," OSHA applies to all workers employed in businesses that affect interstate commerce.

To accomplish this vast objective, Congress passed a labor safety standards form of administrative program. Under OSHA, the Secretary of Labor (Secretary) is vested with the power to both promulgate and enforce compliance with the safety standards set for individual industries throughout the country. As enforcement measures, OSHA provides for both civil and criminal penalties. The Justice Department prosecutes employers in federal district court when job conditions are deemed to warrant criminal prosecution, but the Secretary enforces the civil penalties before the autonomous forum of the OSHRECOM...

The enforcement procedures of OSHA have three stages—citation, administrative hearing, and court review. Each stage is distinct because unless the employer initiates the next level of review, the penalty becomes final and unreviewable.

The citation procedure begins when an inspector, acting in response to a complaint or on his own investigation, determines that the employer has violated either a specific safety standard or the general duty provision requiring the employer to provide a safe working environment. The citation given by the inspector lists the nature of the violation as well as the time set for abatement.

Within a reasonable time thereafter, the Secretary shall assess and notify the employer of the penalty, if any, that will itself be based on the nature of the violation. For initial violations of OSHA an employer may be subject to a $10,000 penalty for either (1) willful violations or for violations that are determined to be serious, i.e., "* * * [have] a substantial probability that death or serious harm could result from a condition that exists * * * unless the employer did not, and could not with the exercise of due diligence know of the presence of the violation."

Alternatively, criminal proceedings may be triggered by conditions that the Secretary considers both willful and serious and the employer shall upon conviction be subject to a fine of up to $10,000 and six months in jail.

On receipt of the Secretary's citation, an employer has 15 days to notify the Secretary that he intends to challenge the penalty or the penalty becomes final and unreviewable. Once such a challenge is made, the Secretary is required to initiate the administrative hearing by notifying OSHRECOM. The ALJ conducts a full hearing and thereafter makes a report that will itself become the final decision of OSHRECOM unless the parties seek and the Commission grants discretionary review.

Thereafter the final stage is review in the Court of Appeals and thereafter the discretionary review by the Supreme Court. The Court of Appeals review is on the APA substantial-evidence-on-the-record-considered-as-a-whole-standard. The Courts, however, may direct the Commission to consider additional evidence if it is found that the evidence is both material and reasonable grounds existed for the failure to admit it in the hearing before the Commission....

The Government argues that OSHA successfully survives the Atlas Sixth Amendment attack because the provisions for civil and criminal enforcement specified in the statute are precise and distinct and, additionally, because the legislative history clearly demonstrates that Congress purposefully chose remedial rather than punitive consequences to accompany the civil provisions. The Government naturally stresses the long accepted maxim that Congress may use either civil or criminal measures to control similar conduct....

...[T]aken as a whole, we think that Atlas has failed to demonstrate that Congress meant the statute to reprimand rather than regulate. The focus of the statute—the control of job site safety practices and health conditions—has a demonstrable and legitimate government concern. The fact that the civil enforcement sanctions are inherently disabilities does not alter the nature of the Congressional purpose. And finally the Congressional purpose carefully to establish both civil and criminal sanctions and distinguishable procedures for imposing and reviewing them eliminate any question of Congressional intent...

■ ■ ■

Questions

1. What are the three stages of enforcement procedures of OSHA?
2. For a violation of OSHA, what potential monetary penalty may be assessed against the employer?
3. Taken as a whole, does OSHA regulate or reprimand in a fashion similar to the criminal law?

EMPLOYER'S DUTIES

To aid in the enforcement of the Act, employers are required to make reports of work-related injuries and diseases to OSHA. The administrators of OSHA summarize the data and make periodic reports to the President and Congress on the progress of their administration. Moreover, OSHA utilizes the data received from industry to promulgate rules of safety which must be followed by employers. In *Ace Sheeting & Repair Co.* the employer was charged with having violated a standard promulgated by the Secretary of Labor.

ACE SHEETING & REPAIR v. OCCUP. S. & H. REVIEW COM'N
555 F.2d 439 (1977)
U.S. Court of Appeals (5th Cir.)

■ ■ ■

The facts are undisputed. Petitioner Ace Sheeting and Repair Company is a roof repair company. In September 1973 J. C. Ledger, the owner of Ace, and employee Stroud were replacing corrugated metal panels on the roof of a warehouse in Houston. The roof was pitched rather steeply and contained 60 skylight openings arranged in two rows running the length of the building. The skylights were covered with a translucent plastic material called coralux. There was no guard rail or cover around or over any of these skylights. While walking to another section of the roof to obtain additional materials Stroud stepped in the middle of one of the coralux sheets. The sheet gave way beneath his 175-pound weight, and Stroud fell 25 feet to his death.

A few days after this fatality the Secretary of Labor inspected the job site. On the basis of this inspection, Ace was served with a citation for violation of § 1926.500(b)(4). That section provides:

> Wherever there is danger of falling through a skylight opening, it shall be guarded by a fixed standard railing on all exposed sides or a cover capable of sustaining the weight of a 200-pound person.

This regulation was promulgated by the Secretary under the Act. Title 29 U.S.C.A. § 654 (a)(2) imposes on all employers covered by the Act the duty to comply with such regulations. The proposed penalty in the citation served on Ace was a $30 fine.

Ace challenged the citation, and a hearing was held before an administrative law judge... The administrative law judge vacated the citation on the ground that the Secretary had failed to prove that compliance with the regulation was feasible under the circumstances. The Commission reversed by a two-to-one vote. Ace petitioned this Court for review of that decision...

The outcome of this case turns on who has the burden of proof. Must the Secretary prove that compliance with the regulation is feasible, as thought by the administrative law judge; or is feasibility of compliance assumed unless the employer proves otherwise?

Title 29 U.S.C.A. § 654(a) creates two kinds of obligations requiring employers to take steps for the occupational safety and health of their employees:

> Each employer—
> (1) shall furnish to each of his employees employment and a place of employment which are free from recognized hazards that are causing or are likely to cause death or serious physical harm to his employees;
> (2) shall comply with occupational safety and health standards promulgated under this chapter.

Paragraph (1) has come to be called the "general duty clause," while paragraph (2) is referred to as the "specific duty clause." This case involves a safety standard promulgated under the specific duty clause. The Act itself gives no guidance as to who must bear the burden of proving the feasibility of eliminating a particular hazard under either clause.

Ace relies on *National Realty & Construction Co., Inc. v OSHRC,* 489 F.2d 1257 (1973), to show that this burden is properly place on the Secretary. But *National Realty* dealt with the general duty clause. No regulation or standard guided the employer as to the way to eliminate the hazard there involved. The D.C. Circuit for that reason placed the burden on the Secretary of demonstrating in what manner the Company's conduct fell short of the statutory mandate. The court reasoned that "the Secretary must be constrained to specify the particular steps a cited employer should have taken to avoid citation, and to demonstrate the feasibility and likely utility of those measures."

Two circuits have extended the *National Realty* principle to "specific duty clause" situations...

In both (of those cases)... however, there was no specific direction as to what the employer should do. The regulations involved did nothing more than create, in effect, a general duty of the employer to meet a safety standard, without stating what specific employer conduct was required for compliance.

Here, the regulation stated specific ways for the employer to eliminate the hazard. If the employer put up guard rails or covered the skylights, the safety standard would have been met. If for any reason guard rails or covers are not feasible, the employer knows this better than anyone else, and it is reasonable to require him to come forward with the evidence to prove it.

Regulations are promulgated only after industry-wide comment during which time general feasibility considerations can be voiced. If a regulation contains a proposed method of abating a safety hazard which employers consider to be infeasible in the ordinary case, they can directly challenge the regulation as factually unsupported. Futhermore a particular employer who finds that he cannot comply with the safety measures required by the regulations can request a variance... When the citation stage is reached, it is eminently reasonable for courts to cast upon the employer the burden of proving impossibility of compliance.

The standard prescribed the precise conduct required of the employer. It may be easily complied with in many shops. Others may have difficulty, but where compliance with either of two specific alternatives, a guard rail or a cover, would eliminate the hazard with which the deceased employee in this case was confronted, the employer should prove why he cannot meet either of those alternatives. We therefore hold that where a specific duty standard contains the method by which the work hazard is to be abated, the burden of proof is on the employer to demonstrate that the remedy contained in the regulation is infeasible under the particular circumstances.

To state this rule is to decide the present case. The factual decisions of the Commission are to be sustained if supported by substantial evidence on the record as a whole. Ace argues that even if it did have the burden of showing infeasibility, that burden was carried by the testimony of the Secretary's witnesses. Ace itself presented no evidence as to why it could not use skylight covers on this particular roof. Although the Secretary's witnesses did express some concern that skylight covers might slide off the pitched roof, the possibility of using "some type of abrasive surface on the bottom of a covering to...prevent the covering from sliding off the roof" was also discussed. In any event, on the state of the record, it was not the Secretary's job to describe precisely how covers or guard rails could be placed on Ace's premises. There is therefore sufficient evidence in the record to support the Commission's finding that "[i]impossibility has not been established in this case." That being so, the citation for violation of 29 C.F.R. § 1926.500(b)(4) was proper, and the Commission's decision enforcing the $30 penalty is affirmed.

■ ■ ■

Questions

1. What is the employer's "general duty" under the Act?
2. What is the employer's responsibility under the "specific duty clause"?
3. Does OSHA empower the employee to determine his working conditions are "unsafe" and protect his job when he refuses to work? The Fifth Circuit Court of Appeals answered "no." The court said:

> While Congress envisioned that workers play an integral role in achieving the salutary purpose of assuring safe and healthful working conditions, in relation to preventing imminent dangers, OSHA expressly provides the contours of the part that workers play: (1) They may notify the Secretary of those conditions and practices that they *believe* present an imminent danger and request an immediate inspection, and (2) they may provide the inspector with information during the investigation. Before an imminent danger is enjoined, however, four independent judgments must be integrated in the decision-making calculus: (1) The Secretary must conclude that the worker's notice provides reasonable grounds to believe that an imminent danger exists. (2) An OSHA inspector must conclude upon inspecting the workplace that the danger cannot be prevented through normal enforcement procedures but requires immediate injunctive relief and recommend to the Secretary that he seek relief. (3) The Secretary must conclude that the inspector is correct and proceed to federal court. (4) A federal district court must find that an imminent danger exists at the worksite such that requires immediate injunctive relief. At no point does the Act permit workers to make a determination that a dangerouse condition exists *in fact* and that their employment or their employer's business operations may be halted by their refusal to work. Indeed the Secretary... has acknowledged this with the following language: "[R]eview of the Act and examination of the legislative history discloses that, as a general matter, there is no right afforded by the Act which would entitle employees to walk off the

job because of potential unsafe conditions at the workplace." Marshall v. Daniel Const., Co., Inc. 563 F.2d 707 (1977).

The Sixth Circuit Court of Appeals has upheld an OSHA regulation allowing workers to walk off jobs they consider hazardous. This court agreed with the dissent in *Daniel* which noted that "the same Congress which wanted employees to work in safe and healthful surroundings could not have meant for them to die at their posts." Which of these conflicting decisions seems correct?

15

A QUALITY NATURAL ENVIRONMENT

Most societies at some time in their development have expressed concern over the pollution of their natural environment. The task of defining what constitutes pollution is dependent upon society's choice in the use of its environment and resources. It is society's concept of "public interest," therefore, that becomes the controlling factor in defining pollution. Once defined, however, there are legal maxims dating back to ancient Roman Law which establish the notion of a citizen's fundamental right to a quality environment.

The earliest form of "pollution control" in this country involved the protection of individual property rights. The rights developed under the tort system included the right to be free of neighboring nuisances and to be compensated for any harm caused to one's property which resulted from the intentional or negligent conduct of another. If a plaintiff could show that polluted air was injuring his or her house or crops, he could secure judicial aid to prevent the injury and obtain compensation from the pollutor. However, if the plaintiff could not establish that he or she sustained specific harm which was distinct from the harm which all members of the public at large sustained, the plaintiff would be denied standing to object to the pollutor's behavior. Moreover, the crowding conditions of urban and industrial society made it more difficult for the plaintiff to establish which pollutor was the single cause of the harm. Without proof of causation, plaintiff was not entitled to injunctive relief nor to compensatory damages. As a result, the tort system was not effective in the elimination of the growing levels of pollution in the industrial and urban society.

The growing crisis of environmental pollution necessitated governmental efforts to protect society's health and welfare. The imposition of governmental controls, however, oftens comes in conflict with the concern of society for individual rights, the concept of private property, and the total economic growth of society. Road construction, for example, will provide jobs and serve society's transportation needs. However, it also creates the problems of soil erosion, stream pollution, engine exhaust, and people displacement. It becomes evident that the job of establishing and enforcing the standards of control must weigh the cost of controlling pollution against the cost of other goals of society. The legislatures establish guidelines and priorities in identifying society's right to a quality environment. The implementation and enforcement of environmental improvement lies with the decisional process of administrative agencies and the courts.

STATE ACTION

In the early days of public outcry for pollution abatement, state and local governments were the first to respond with laws of environmental protection. The power of the states to promulgate controls over environmental deterioration arises from the inherent police power of society which allows the governing body to take such steps as are reasonably necessary for the protection of the health, safety, morals or well-being of society and its individual members. The steps taken by local governments to improve the environment almost always involved increasing economic costs for private or public enterprises. To minimize pollution abatement costs, the polluters have tried many arguments to avoid the local laws. One argument often advanced is the notion that the Commerce Clause of U.S. Constitution requires uniformity of regulation which is not achieved by state and local ordinances of pollution control and, consequently, the local ordinances are said to be in violation of the U.S. Constitution. The court in the following case had to deal with this argument in relation to Oregon's new "bottle law."

BOTTLE LAW

AMERICAN CAN CO. v. OREGON LIQUOR CONTROL COM'N
517 P.2d 691 (1974)
Court of Appeals of Oregon

■ ■ ■

This is an appeal from a circuit court decree declaring that Oregon's so-called bottle bill, is valid and denying plaintiffs'...application for injunctive relief against the enforcement of the law. Plaintiffs are (a) manufacturers of cans...(b) brewers in California and Arizona...(c) out-of-state soft drink canners...(d) soft drink companies...and(e) the Oregon Soft Drink Association....

The primary legislative purpose of the bottle bill is to cause bottlers of carbonated soft drinks and brewers to package their products for distribution in Oregon in returnable, multiple-use deposit bottles toward the goals of reducing litter and solid waste in Oregon and reducing the injuries to people and animals due to discarded "pull tops."...

Plaintiffs' most substantial challenge to the bottle bill is under the Commerce Clause of the United States Constitution.

The development of the one-way container provided a great technological opportunity for the beverage industry to turn logistical advantages into economic advantages. By obviating the expensive necessity of reshipping empty bottles back to the plant for refilling, the new containers enabled manufacturers to produce in a few centralized plants to serve more distant markets. The industry organized its manufacturing and distribution systems to capitalize maximally on the new technology.

The Oregon legislature was persuaded that the economic benefit to the beverage industry brought with it deleterious consequences to the environment and additional cost to the public. The aggravation of the problems of litter in public places and solid waste disposal and the attendant economic and esthetic burden to the public outweighed the narrower economic benefit to the industry. Thus the legislature enacted the bottle bill over the articulate opposition of the industries represented by plaintiffs.

As with every change of circumstance in the market place, there are gainers and there are losers. Just as there were gainers and losers, with plaintiffs apparently among the gainers, when the industry adapted to the development of non-returnable containers, there will be new gainers and losers as they adapt to the ban. The economic losses complained of by plaintiffs in this case are essentially the consequences of readjustment of the beverage manufacturing and distribution systems to the older technology in order to compete in the Oregon market.

The purpose of the Commerce Clause...was to assure to the commercial enterprises in every state substantial equality of access to a free national market. It was not meant to usurp the police power of the states which was reserved under the Tenth Amendment. Therefore, although most exercises of the police power affect interstate commerce to some degree, not every such exercise is invalid under the Commerce Clause.

Plaintiffs acknowledge the authority of the state to act, but assert that the state exercise of its police power must yield to federal authority over interstate commerce because, they claim, the impact on interstate commerce in this case outweighs the putative benefit to the state and because alternative methods exist to achieve the state goal with a less deleterious impact on interstate commerce...

Specifically upholding the authority of the states to enact environmental legislation affecting interstate commerce, the court held in Huron Cement Co. v. Detroit, 362 U.S. 440, (1960):

> "* * * Legislation designed to free from pollution the very air that people breathe clearly falls within the exercise of even the most traditional concept of what is compendiously known as the police power. In the exercise of that power, the states and their instrumentalities may act, in many areas of interstate commerce and maritime activities, concurrently with the federal government."

The United States Supreme Court has also made clear that it will not only recognize the authority of the state to exercise the police power, but also its right to do so in such manner as it deems most appropriate to local conditions, free from the homogenizing constraints of federal dictation...

The Oregon legislature is thus constitutionally authorized to enact laws which address the economic, esthetic and environmental consequences of the problems of litter in public places and solid waste disposal which suit the particular conditions of Oregon even though it may, in doing so, affect interstate commerce.

The enactment of the bottle bill is clearly a legislative act in harmony with federal law. Congress has directed that the states take primary responsibility for action in this field. By enacting the Federal Solid Waste Disposal Act, (1970), Congress specifically recognized that the proliferation of new packages for consumer products has severely taxed our disposal resources and blighted our landscapes. It disclaimed federal preemption and assigned to local government the task of coping with the problem with limited federal fiscal assistance... Congress has recently reaffirmed that allocation of state and federal responsibility by enactment of the Environmental Quality Improvement Act, (1970), which provides:

> "(b) (1) The Congress declares that there is a national policy for the environment which provides for the enhancement of environmental quality. This policy is evidenced by statutes heretofore enacted relating to the prevention, abatement, and control of environmental pollution, water and land resources, transportation, and economic and regional development.
> (2) The primary responsibility for implementing this policy rests with State and local governments.
> "* * *"

While it is clear that the Oregon legislature was authorized to act in this area, plaintiffs assert that the means incorporated in the bottle bill are not effective to accomplish its intended purpose and that alternative means are available which will have a lesser impact upon interstate commerce. Particularly, they offered evidence to show: (1) that the deposit system is inadequate to motivate the consuming public to return containers, (2) that mechanical means are being developed for improved collection of highway litter; and (3) that public education, such as the "Pitch In To Clean Up America" campaign, is a desirable means of dealing with container litter.

Selection of a reasonable means to accomplish a state purpose is clearly a legislative, not a judicial, function... In particular, the courts may not invalidate legislation upon the speculation that machines may be developed or because addtional and complementary means of accomplishing the same goal may also exist. The legislature may look to its imagination rather than to traditional methods such as those which plaintiffs suggest, to develop suitable means of dealing with state problems, even though their methods may be unique. Each state is a laboratory for innovation and experimentation in a healthy federal system. What fails may be abandoned and what succeeds may be emulated by other states. The bottle bill is now unique; it may later be regarded as seminal.

We conclude, therefore, that the bottle bill was properly enacted within the police power of the state of Oregon and that it is imaginatively, but reasonably, calculated to cope with problems of legitimate state concern....

■ ■ ■

Questions

1. What scheme of regulation was developed by Oregon to reduce litter and solid waste?
2. Does the Commerce Clause of the U.S. Constitution usurp the police power of the state?
3. Does the state's police power include aesthetic values which may be protected by government?
4. Have federal laws indicated the proper role for states to take in dealing with environmental pollution?

ADOPTION OF STANDARDS

The "bottle bill" in Oregon represents the more modern efforts of pollution control by states. However, the states also have been involved in efforts to control the traditional areas of pollution. In dealing with air and water pollution, many states developed systems of administrative boards to prepare statewide plans and adopt standards that could be used in measuring and controlling the level of pollution abatement required. The following case discusses some of the difficulties in setting standards and assigning those standards to particular localities.

TOWN OF WATERFORD v. WATER POLLUTION CONTROL BD.
156 N.E. 2d 427 (1959)
Court of Appeals of New York

■ ■ ■

In this...proceeding, instituted pursuant to...the Public Health Law...the Town and the Village of Waterford, hereinafter called appellants, are challenging the right of the Water Pollution Control Board of this State, hereinafter called the Board, to classify the waters of that section of the Mohawk River Drainage Basin extending from its mouth to the first dam above Cohoes Falls as Class C waters.

...The system provides seven classes for fresh surface waters according, in essence, to the highest and best use to which the water may be put, and may be briefly summarized as follows:

AA and A: Drinking water (the only difference between the two being the type of treatment required to render the water fit to drink)
B: Bathing
C: Fishing
D: Agricultural or industrial water supply
E: Sewage or waste disposal and transportation
F: Sewage or waste disposal only, under such conditions as will not cause a public nuisance.

Classes AA to D require sewage treatment; classes E and F do not...

As already noted, the Board established a system of classification in 1950, and in implementing this system sections 1208 and 1209 envisaged a four-step procedure...(1) a survey of all the waters throughout the State; (2) the classification and assignment of appropriate quality standards to all such waters or segments thereof; (3) the development of comprehensive programs for the abatement of pollution which contravenes the standards established for such waters, and (4) the execution of these programs through co-operative endeavors so far as possible, or if necessary, through the issuance and enforcement of orders requiring abatement of pollution.

In the instant case we are concerned with step 2 of this procedure, whereby a section of the Mohawk River—not a "mountain rill"—bordering on the Town and the Village of Waterford was classified as C water. As a result of such classification, appellants, who for a long period had been discharging sewage into the river without any kind of treatment, may be required to cease such practice and eventually to construct sewage treatment facilities. They contend on this appeal that the C classification should be set aside.

Their first contention is that in assigning the C classification to the waters involved, the Board failed to comply with...the Public Health Law in that it failed to give any consideration to the fiscal and economic aspects of its classification. Section 1209, which recognizes that "no single standard of quality and purity of the waters is applicable to all waters of the state or to different segments of the same waters," provides that the classification of waters made by the Board "shall be made in accordance with considerations of *best usage* in the interest of the public and with regard to the considerations mentioned in subdivisions three hereof." Subdivision 3 reads as follows:

"In adopting the classification of waters and the standards of purity and quality above mentioned, consideration shall be given to:
"(a) the size, depth, surface area covered, volume, direction and rate of flow, stream gradient and temperature of the water;
"(b) the character of the district bordering said waters and its peculiar suitability for the particular uses, and with a view of conserving the value of the same and encouraging the most appropriate use of lands bordering said waters, for residential, agricultural, industrial or recreational purposes;
"(c) the uses which have been made, are being made or may be made, of said waters for transportation, domestic and industrial consumption, bathing, fishing and fish culture, fire prevention, the disposal of sewage, industrial waste and other wastes, or other uses within this state, and, at the discretion of the board, any such uses in another state on interstate waters flowing through or originating in this state;
"(d) the extent of present defilement or fouling of said waters which has already occurred or resulted from past discharges therein."

Appellants insist that in deciding whether a particular classification is in the "public interest" and encourages "the most appropriate use of lands bordering the waters for 'residential' and 'industrial' purposes" the Board, in order to comply with the statute, must take into account the "economic and fiscal" impact of the classification upon the municipalities affected... In other words, they maintain,...that in classifying the waters of this State "to prevent and control the pollution" thereof...the Board's determination as to "reasonable standards of purity" or impurity should depend not on the actual facts, but rather in some measure on how much it will cost to abate or prevent pollution. It is another way of saying that a physician may not diagnose a serious disease as such if the patient cannot afford the cost of cure.

...There is nothing in the statute that requires the Board to consider probable costs or relative priorities as between municipal public works projects, *at the time it adopts a classification* for particular waters. Nowhere in the statute, which sets out the criteria to govern a particular classification, is there any mention of financial costs, fiscal conditions or public works priorities. The statute does recognize...that financial disability might impede the construction of the facilities needed to *comply with* adopted classifications; the relief provided for, however, is not the annulment of the classification previously assigned but an extension of time in which to effect the needed improvements.

...At this stage, the Board is merely applying its over-all system of water classifications and quality standards to a particular body of water, in accordance with the "best usage" of that water and in the light of hydrologic factors, the character of the surronding district, the past, present and foreseeable uses of such waters and the extent of present pollution. The proper time to consider the financial ability of affected municipalities to comply with established standards is when the Board, in accordance with its previously assigned classifications, evolves a comprehensive program to abate pollution in the classified waters. If at that time a municipality demonstrates that it is financially unable to provide the treatment works necessary to cure existing pollution, the Board is empowered to grant extensions of time.

The...Legislature well knew that a comprehensive water purification program would impose a financial burden upon the municipalities of the State, but determined, by enacting the Pollution Control Act, that the pressing need for water purification outweighed any financial hardships incident thereto....

Although the only relief appellants seek... is a remission to the Board to re-evaluate the classification in the light of probable costs, it is quite clear from their petition... that the proper classification of the waters in question would, in their opinion, have been Class E, entitling them to continue to discharge sewage into the Mohawk River without treatment. The appellants seem to ignore completely the severe menace to public health posed by polluted waters, as well as the deleterious effects of pollution on neighboring waters and on the natural resources of the State, which were among the prime considerations that motivated the enactment of the Act... Furthermore, no section of the Mohawk River proper has been classified lower than C and, in fact, much of it has been classified as A and B. Of a total of 618 classifications of the waters of the Mohawk Drainage Basin, only three *creeks* were classified lower than D....

■ ■ ■

Questions

1. What was the four-step procedure envisioned by the Water Pollution Control Act to establish and implement a system of classification of waters in New York?
2. Must the classification of waters give consideration to the fiscal and economic aspects of cleaning the water to meet such classification?
3. Were the plaintiffs bringing their suit at the proper time?

SUFFICIENCY OF EVIDENCE

PEOPLE v. INTERNATIONAL STEEL CORP.
226 P. 2d 587 (1951)
Supreme Court, Appellate Div., L.A., California

■ ■ ■

The defendants,...were convicted on charges of violating the Health and Safety Code, which is a part of the law for the formation of air pollution control districts, enacted...for the purpose of reducing air contamination, popularly known as "smog." Defendants...contend...that the evidence does not support the findings of guilt, and that the court erred in rulings on evidence. The general purpose of the law

...is to reduce air contamination... [It] provides that: "A person shall not discharge into the atmosphere from any single source of emission whatoever any air contaminant for a period or periods aggregating more than three minutes in any one hour which is: (a) As dark or darker in shade as that designated as No. 2 on the Ringelmann Chart, as published by the United States Bureau of Mines, or (b) Of such opacity as to obscure an observer's view to a degree equal to or greater than does smoke described in subsection (a) of this section."

This provision is attacked on the ground that it sets forth no ascertainable standard of guilt and is fatally uncertain, by reason of its reference to the Ringelmann Chart for the description of the forbidden air contaminant. The complaint here specified smoke as the air contaminant discharged, so we limit our further discussion to smoke.

The term "air contaminant" is defined... to include smoke and a variety of other specified emanations. All that is needed further for certainty, as it aplies here, is some means of determining the density or opacity of smoke that is forbidden. "That is certain which can be made certain." This rule is as applicable to statutes as to other expressions of ideas. A statute may refer to and adopt, for an expression of the legislative intent, a statute, or rules or regulations of another state or of the United States.

We think it is equally permissible for a statute to refer to and adopt, for description of a prohibited act, an official publication of any United States board or bureau established by law, such as the United States Bureau of Mines. The publications of that bureau are as readily available for examination by those seeking information on the effect of the statute as were the statutes and regulations, references to which were approved in the cases just cited. It is no more necessary here than it was in those cases that provision be made for free or other public distribution of the matter referred to. The courts take judical notice of the official acts of the Bureau of Mines Code of Civil Procedure, and private citizens who are concerned with them are also charged with notice of them.

While, as already stated, the courts take notice of the Ringelmann Chart, our notice in this case is fortified by a copy which was introduced in evidence and is in the record. It is a plain white piece of paper divided into four sections, numbered from 1 to 4 and each about 5-¾ x 8-¾ inches in size. On each of these sections is printed a series of intersecting heavy black lines of uniform width for each section, with the lines growing progressively wider from section 1 to section 4, until on section 4 the black covers much more than half of the surface. This chart refers to Bureau of Mines Information Circular No. 6888, a copy of which is also in the record. From the chart and this circular, it appears that the chart is to be posted at a distance of 50 feet from the observer. When so posted the black lines and the white spaces merge into each other, by a process of optical illusion, so as to present the appearance of a series of gray rectangles of different color densities, No. 4 being the densest. Estimates of the density of smoke may be made by glancing from this chart so displayed to smoke, and picking out the section on the chart which most nearly resembles the smoke. This mode of measuring the density of smoke has been in use, it appears, for over fifty years. This affords a reasonably certain mode of determining and stating the density and opacity of smoke, and we think that the statute adopting it is not lacking in certainty....

Three witnesses testified regarding the smoke discharged from the defendants' place of busniness on the occasions specified in the complaint, and its degree of density and opacity as compared with the Ringelmann Chart. Defendants complain that these witnesses showed no qualifications sufficient to enable them to give expert testimony on this subject, and that their observations were not sufficient because they had no Ringelmann Charts with them when those observations were made. Assuming that the comparative density and opacity of the smoke is a matter for expert testimony only, we see no error in the rulings of the court admitting in evidence and refusing to strike the testimony of these witnesses. The air pollution control district established under the statute in Los Angeles County maintained a school where its inspectors were trained to "read smoke," as they called it, by the aid of the Ringelmann Chart, and after they became experienced they no longer needed to look at the Chart. The witnesses just mentioned attended this school before making the observations to which they testified, and by that and other experience acquired the ability to estimate the opacity and color of smoke such as they testified to with reference to the Ringelmann Chart without actually using the chart. Their testimony was sufficient in these respects to justify the ruling of the court that they were competent to testify as experts...

■ ◿ ■

Questions

1. What technique was utilized by Los Angeles County to determine that the smoke was too dark? Was the technique operative with sufficient certainty?
2. Were the witnesses against the defendant sufficiently qualified?

The efforts of local government to regulate air pollution have ranged across a broad spectrum of techniques. Basic ordinances, such as in *People v. International Steel Corp.*, are aimed at the prevention of certain conduct which is determined to be excessive or unreasonable. While these primitive techniques are still utilized in many municipalities, most local authorities now have enacted comprehensive emission control ordinances to regulate all emissions. Still other authorities have enacted ambient air quality ordinances which seek to control air pollution by achieving a given atmospheric quality. The increase in air quality control has been made possible by better measuring instruments to determine the quality of the air and the types of pollutants therein.

NATIONAL ENVIRONMENTAL POLICY

Public Law 91-190
91st Congress, S. 1075
January 1, 1970

Be it enacted by the Senate and House of Representatives of the United States of America in Congress assembled, That this Act may be cited as the "National Environmental Policy Act of 1969."

PURPOSE

Sec. 2. The Purpose of this Act are: To declare a national policy which will encourage productive and enjoyable harmony between man and his environment; to promote efforts which will prevent or eliminate damage to the environment and biosphere and stimulate the health and welfare of man; to enrich the understanding of the ecological systems and natural resources important to the Nation; and to establish a Council on Environmental Quality.

TITLE I

DECLARATION OF NATIONAL ENVIRONMENTAL POLICY

Sec. 101. (a) The Congress, recognizing the profound impact of man's activity on the interrelations of all components of the natural environment, particularly the profound influences of population growth, high-density urbanization, industrial expansion, resource exploitation, and new and expanding technological advances and recognizing further the critical importance of restoring and maintaining environmental quality to the overall welfare and development of man, declares that it is the continuing policy of the Federal Government, in cooperation with State and local governments, and other concerned public and private organizations, to use all practicable means and measures, including financial and technical assistance, in a manner calculated to foster and promote the general welfare, to create and maintain conditions under which man and nature can exist in productive harmony, and fulfill the social, economic, and other requirements of present and future generations of Americans.

(b) In order to carry out the policy set forth in this Act, it is the continuing responsibility of the Federal Government to use all practicable means, consistent with other essential considerations of national policy, to improve and coordinate Federal plans, functions, programs, and resources to the end that the Nation may—

(1) fulfill the responsibilities of each generation as trustee of the environment for succeeding generations;

(2) assure for all Americans safe, healthful, productive, and esthetically and culturally pleasing surroundings;

(3) attain the widest range of beneficial uses of the environment without degradation, risk to health or safety, or other undesirable and unintended consequences;

(4) preserve important historic, cultural, and natural aspects or our national heritage, and maintain, wherever possible, an environment which supports diversity and variety of individual choice;

(5) achieve a balance between population and resouce use which will permit high standards of living and a wide sharing of life's amenities; and

(6) enhance the quality of renewable resources and approach the maximum attainable recycling of depletable resources.

(c) The Congress recognizes that each person should enjoy a healthful environment and that each person has a responsibility to contribute to that preservation and enhancement of the environment.

Administration. Sec. 102. The Congress authorizes and directs that, to the fullest extent possible: (1) the policies, regulations, and public laws of the United States shall be interpreted and administered in accordance with the policies set forth in this Act, and (2) all agencies of the Federal Government shall—

(A) utilize a systematic, interdisciplinary approach which will insure the integrated use of the natural and social sciences and the environmental design arts in planning and in decision-making which may have an impact on man's environment;

(B) identify and develop methods and procedures, in consultation with the Council on Environmental Quality established by title II of this Act, which will insure that presently unquantified environmental amenities and values may be given appropriate consideration in decision making along with economic and technical considerations;

(C) include in every recommendation or report on proposals for legislation and other major Federal actions significantly affecting the quality of human environment, a detailed statement by the responsible official on—

(i) the environmental impact of the proposed action,

(ii) any adverse environmental effects which cannot be avoided should the proposal be implemented,

(iii) alternatives to the proposed action,

(iv) the relationship between local short-term uses of man's environment and the maintenance and enhancement of long-term productivity, and

(v) any irreversible and irretrievable commitments of resources which would be involved in the proposed action should it be implemented. . . .

(D) study, develop, and describe appropriate alternatives to recommended courses of action in any proposal which involves unresolved conflicts concerning alternative uses of available resources;

* * *

Questions

1. What are the advantages for articulating a national environmental policy?
2. What duties are imposed on "all agencies of the federal government" by this Act?

3. In Section 102(C) a detailed statement must be prepared by a responsible official. What elements must be contained in this report?

ENVIRONMENTAL IMPACT STATEMENT

NATURAL RESOURCES DEFENSE COUNCIL, INC. v. MORTON
458 F.2d 827 (1972)
U.S. Court of Appeals (D.C. Cir.)

■ ■ ■

This appeal raises a question as to the scope of the requirement of the National Environmental Policy Act (NEPA) that environmental impact statements contain a discussion of alternatives. Before us is the Environmental Impact Statement filed October 28, 1971, by the Department of Interior with respect to its proposal, under §8 of the Outer Continental Shelf Lands Act, for the oil and gas general lease sale, of leases to some 80 tracts of submerged lands, primarily off eastern Louisiana... Opening of bids for the leases was scheduled for December 21, 1971, and three conservation groups brought this action on November 1, to enjoin the proposed sale. On December 16, the District Court held a hearing and granted a preliminary injunction enjoining the sale of these leases pending compliance with NEPA. The Government appealed, and filed a motion in this court for summary reversal....

Statement—Adverse Environmental Impact Disclosed

While the Statement presents questions, subsequently delineated, this document—67 pages in length, exclusive of appendices—is not challenged on the ground of failure to disclose the problems of environmental impact of the proposed sale. On the contrary, these problems are set forth in considerable range and detail. Indeed, the complaint voiced by the Audubon Society's witness in testimony was that the draft Statement gives a green light for the sale while its contents seem to cry out for the opposite conclusion. Without purporting to summarize, we identify some of the Statement's highlights:

Adjacent to the proposed lease area is the greatest estuarine coastal marsh complex in the United States, some 7.9 million acres, providing food, nursery habitat and spawning ground vital to fish, shellfish and wildlife, as well as food and shelter for migratory waterfowl, wading birds and fur-bearing animals. This complex provides rich nutrient systems which make the Gulf of Mexico, blessed also with warm waters and shallow depths, the most productive fishing region of the country. It yielded $71 million of fish and shellfish to Louisiana and Mississippi commercial fishermen in 1970, and some 9 million man-days of sport fishing.

The coastal regions of Louisiana and Mississippi contain millions of acres suitable for outdoor recreation, with a number of state and federal recreation areas, and extensive beach shorelines...

As to probable impact of issuance of leases on the environment the Statement did not anticipate continuation of debris from drilling operations, in view of recent regulations prohibiting dumping of debris on the OCS. The Statement acknowledged some impact from construction of platforms, pipelines and other structures. A concluding section (III D) on "Unavoidable Adverse Environmental Effects" particularly noted the destruction of marsh and of marine species and plants from dredging incident to pipeline installation, and the effect of pipeline canals in *e.g.*, increasing ratio of water to wetlands and increasing salt water intrusion.

Oil pollution is the problem most extensively discussed in the Statement and its exposition of unavoidable adverse environmental effects. The Statement acknowledges that both short and long term effects on the environment can be expected from spillage, including in that term major spills (like that in the Santa Barbara Channel in 1969); minor spills from operations and unidentified sources; and discharge of waste water contaminated with oil.

These adverse effects relate both to the damage to the coastal region—beaches, water areas and historic sites; and the forecast that oil pollution "may seriously damage the marine biological community"—both direct damage to the larger organisms, visible more easily and sooner, and to smaller like stages which would lead one step removed to damage later in the food chain.

The Statement noted the diverse conclusions and comments in existing reports on oil spills, some minimizing damage done, others stressing that oil spillage has effects beyond the period of visible evidence; that oil may mix with water, expecially in a turbulent sea, and disperse downward into the sea; that emulsifiers used to remove surface oil may have toxic consequences, etc.

The Statement asserted that while past major spills in the Gulf resulted in minimal damage, this was due to the fortunate combination of offshore winds and surface currents...

Need to discuss environmental consequences of alternatives

...A sound construction of NEPA, which takes into account both the legislative history and contemporaneous executive construction, requires a presentation of the environmental risks incident to reasonable alternative courses of action. The agency may limit its discussion of environmental impact to a brief statement, when that is the case, that the alternative course involves no effect on the environment, or that their effect, briefly described, is simply not significant. A rule of reason is implicit in this aspect of the law as it is in the requirement that the agency provide a statement concerning those opposing views that are responsible.

Alternative as to oil import quotas

We think the Secretary's Statement erred in stating that the alternative of elimination of oil import quotas was entirely outside its cognizance. Assuming, as the Statement puts it, that this alternative "involves complex factors and concepts, including national security, which are beyond the scope of this statement," it does not follow that the Statement should not present the environmental effects of that alternative. While the consideration of pertinent alternatives requires a weighing of numerous matters, such as economics, foreign relations, national security, the fact remains that, as to the ingredient of possible adverse environmental impact, it is the essence and thrust of NEPA that the pertinent Statement serve to gather in one place a discussion of the relative environmental impact of alternatives.

The Government also contends that the only "alternatives" required for discussion under NEPA are those which can be adopted and put into effect by the official or agency issuing the statement. The Government seeks to distinguish the kind of impact statement required for a major Federal action from that required with a legislative proposal...

While we agree with so much of the Government's presentation as rests on the assumption that the alternatives required for discussion are those reasonably available, we do not agree that this requires a limitation to measures the agency or official can adopt. This approach would be particularly inapposite for the lease sale of offshore oil lands. The scope of this project is far broader than that of other proposed Federal actions discussed in impact statements, such as a single canal or dam. The Executive's proposed solution to a national problem, or a set of inter-related problems, may call for each of several departments or agencies to take a specific action; this cannot mean that the only discussion of alternatives required in the ensuing environmental impact statements would be the discussion by each department of the particular actions it could take as an alternative to the proposal underlying its impact statement.

When the proposed action is an integral part of a coordinated plan to deal with a broad problem, the range of alternatives that must be evaluated is broadened. While the Department of the Interior does not have the authority to eliminate or reduce oil import quotas, such action is within the purview of both Congress and the President, to whom the impact statement goes. The impact statement is not only for the exposition of the thinking of the agency, but also for the guidance of these ultimate decision-makers, and must provide them with the environmental effects of both the proposal and the alternatives, for their consideration along with the various other elements of the public interest....

In defense of the Statement as written Government counsel suggest that nothing else was required because it was apparently assumed that there would be no adverse environmental impact from increased imports. This was not stated—and, for all we know, a contrary implication may have been intended by the Statement (at p. 37) when it referred to the problem of spillage from drilling as not even approaching the pollution from routine discharges of tankers and other vessels. As to this contention—like another statement of counsel, unsupported in the record, that offshore drilling has less adverse environmental impact than onshore drilling becasue the oil produced has lower sulfur content—our comment is simply this: The subject of environmental impact is too important to relegate either to implication or to subsequent justification by counsel. The Statement must set forth the material contemplated by Congress in form suitable for the enlightenment of the others concerned....

What NEPA infused into the decision-making process in 1969 was a directive as to environmental impact statements that was meant to implement the Congressional objectives of Government coordination, a comprehensive approach to environmental management, and a determination to face problems of pollution "while they are still of manageable proportions and while alternative solutions are still available" rather than persist in environmental decision-making wherein "policy is established by default and inaction" and environmental decisions "continue to be made in small but steady increments" that perpetuate the mistakes of the past without being dealt with until "they reach crisis proportions."

We reiterate that the discussion of environmental effects of alternatives need not be exhaustive. What is required is information sufficient to permit a reasoned choice of alternatives so far as environmental aspects are concerned. As to alternatives not within the scope of authority of the responsible official, reference may of course be made to studies of other agencies—including other impact statements. Nor is it appropriate, as Government counsel argues, to disregard alternatives merely because they do not offer a complete solution to the problem. If an alternative would result in supplying only part of the energy that the lease sale would yield, then its use might possibly reduce the scope of the lease sale program and thus alleviate a significant portion of the environmental harm attendant on offshore drilling....

We think there is merit to the Government's position insofar as it contends that no additional discussion was requisite for such "alternatives" as the development of oil shale, desulfurization of coal, coal liquefaction and gasification, tar sands and geothermal resources.

The Statement sets forth that while these possibilites hold great promise for the future, their impact on the energy supply will not likely be felt until after 1980, and will be dependent on environmental safeguards and technilogical developments. Since the Statement also sets forth that the agency's porposal was put forward to meet a near-term requirement, imposed by an energy shortfall projected for the mid-1970's, the possibility of the environmental impact of long-term solutions requires no additional discussion at this juncture...

Still different considerations are presented by the "alternatives" of increasing nuclear energy development, listed in the Statement, and the possibilites, identified by the District Court as a critical omission, of federal legislation or administrative action freeing current offshore and state-controlled offshore production from state market demand prorationing, or changing the Federal Power Commission's natural gas pricing policies.

The mere fact that an alternative requires legislative implementation does not automatically establish it as beyond the domain of what is required for discussion, particularly since NEPA was intended to provide a basis for consideration and choice by the decision-makers in the legislative as well as the executive branch. But the need for an overhaul of basic legislation certainly bears on the requirements of the Act. We do not suppose Congress intended an agency to devote itself to extended discussion of the environmental impact of alternatives so remote from reality as to depend on, say, the repeal of the antitrust laws.

In the last analysis, the requirement as to alternatives is subject to a construction of reasonableness, and we say this with full awareness that this approach necessarily has both strengths and weaknesses.

A final word. In this as in other areas, the functions of courts and agencies, rightly understood, are not in opposition but in collaboration, toward achievement of the end prescribed by Congress. So long as the officials and agencies have taken the "hard look" at environmental consequence mandated by Congress, the court does not seek to impose unreasonable extremes or to interject itself within the area of discretion of the executive as to the choice of the action to be taken.

Informed by our judgment that discussion of alternatives may be required even though the action required lies outside the Interior Department, the Secretary will, we have no doubt, be able without undue delay to provide the kind of reasonable discussion of alternatives and their environmental consequences that Congress contemplated.

■ ■ ■

Questions

1. What adverse environmental impact may result from oil production on the outer continental shelf lands?
2. Does the Act require discussion of the environmental consequences of *suggested* alternatives?
3. Must the Secretary of the Interior in the environmental impact statement discuss alternatives which may be outside his or her authority?
4. For whom is the environmental impact statement prepared?
5. What is the purpose of the environmental impact statement? Must the federal agencies consider and discuss every conceivable alternative?

PRIVATE ENFORCEMENT

SIERRA CLUB v. MORTON
405 U.S. 727 (1972)
Supreme Court of the United States

■ ■ ■

STEWART, Mr. Justice.

The Mineral King Valley is an area of great natural beauty nestled in the Sierra Nevada Mountains in Tulare County, California, adjacent to Sequoia National Park. It has been part of the Sequoia National Forest since 1926, and is designated as a national game refuge by special Act of Congress. Though once the site of extensive mining activity, Mineral King is now used almost exclusively for recreational purposes. Its relative inaccessibility and lack of development have limited the number of visitors each year, and at the same time have preserved the valley's quality as a quasi-wilderness area largely uncluttered by the products of civilization.

The United States Forest Service which is entrusted with the maintenance and administration of national forests...(invited) bids from private developers for the construction and operation of a ski resort that would also serve as a summer recreation area. The proposal of Walt Disney Enterprises, Inc., was chosen... To provide access to the resort, the State of California proposes to construct a highway 20 miles in length. A section of this road would traverse Sequoia National Park, as would a proposed highvoltage power line needed to provide electricity for the resort. Both the highway and the power line require the approval of the Department of the Interior, which is entrusted with the preservation and maintenance of the national parks.

Representatives of the Sierra Club, who favor maintaining Mineral King largely in its present state... filed the present suit in the United States District Court... seeking a declaratory judgment that various aspects of the proposed development contravene federal laws and regulations governing the preservation of national parks, forests, and game refuges, and also seeking preliminary and permanent injuctions restraining the federal officals involved from granting their approval or issuing permits in connection with the Mineral King project. The petitioner Sierra Club sued as a membership corporation with "a special interest in the conservation and the sound maintenance of the national parks, game refuges and forests of the country," and invoked the judicial-review provisions of the Administrative Procedure Act....

The first question presented is whether the Sierra Club has alleged facts that entitle it to obtain judicial review of the challenged action. Whether a party has a sufficient stake in an otherwise justiciable controversy to obtain judicial resolution of that controversy is what has traditionally been referred to as the question of standing to sue... Where... Congress has authorized public officials to perform certain functions according to law, and has provided by statute for judicial review of those actions under certain circumstances, the inquiry as to standing must begin with a determination of whether the statute in question authorizes review at the behest of the plaintiff.

The Sierra Club relies upon § 10 of the Administrative Procedure Act (APA), § 702, which provides:

> "A person suffering legal wrong because of agency action, or adversely affected or aggrieved by agency action within the meaning of a relevant statute, is entitled to judicial review thereof."

Early decisions under this statute interpreted the language as adopting the various formulations of "legal interest" and "legal wrong" then prevailing as constitutional requirements of standing. But, in... (later decisions) we held more broadly that persons had standing to obtain judicial review of federal agency action under § 10 of the APA where they had alleged that the challenged action had caused them "injury in fact," and where the alleged injury was to an interest "arguably within the zone of interests to be protected or regulated" by the statutes that the agencies were claimed to have violated....

The injury alleged by the Sierra Club will be incurred entirely by reason of the change in the uses to which Mineral King will be put, and the attendant change in the aesthetics and ecology of the area. Thus, in referring to the road to be built though Sequoia National Park, the complaint alleged that the development "would destroy or otherwise adversely affect the scenery, natural and historic objects and wildlife of the park and would impair the enjoyment of the park for future generations." We do not question that this type of harm may amount to an "injury in fact" sufficient to lay the basis for standing under § 10 of the APA. Aesthetic and environmental well-being, like economic well-being, are important ingredients of the quality of life in our society, and the fact that particular enviornmental interests are shared by the many rather than the few does not make them less deserving of legal protection through the judicial process. But the "injury in fact" test requires more than an injury to a cognizable interest. It requires that the party seeking review be himself among the injured.

The impact of the proposed changes in the environment of Mineral King will not fall indiscriminately upon every citizen. The alleged injury will be felt directly only by those who use Mineral King and Sequoia National Park, and for whom the aesthetic and recreational values of the area will be lessened by the highway and ski resort. The

Sierra Club failed to allege that it or its members would be affected in any of their activities or pastimes by the Disney development. Nowhere in the pleadings or affidavits did the Club state that its members use Mineral King for any purpose, much less that they use it in any way that would be significantly affected by the proposed actions of the respondents. The Club apparently regarded any allegations of individualized injury as superfluous, on the theory that this was a "public" action involving questions as to the use of natural resources, and that the Club's longstanding concern with and expertise in such matters were sufficient to give it standing as a "representative of the public." this theory reflects a misunderstanding of our cases involving so-called "public actions" in the area of administrative law....

The trend of cases arising under the APA and other statutes authorizing judicial review of federal agency action has been toward recognizing that injuries other than economic harm are sufficient to bring a person within the meaning of the statutory language, and toward discarding the notion that an injury that is widely shared is *ipso facto* not an injury sufficient to provide the basis for judicial review. We noted this development with approval in *Data Processing,* 397 U.S., at 154, in saying that the interest alleged to have been injured "may reflect 'aesthetic, conservational, and recreational' as well as economic values." But broadening the categories of injury that may be alleged in support of standing is a different matter from abandoning the requirement that the party seeking review must himself have suffered an injury.

Some courts have indicated a willingness to take this latter step by conferring standing upon organizations that have demonstrated "an organizational interest in the problem" of environmental or consumer protection. It is clear that an organization whose members are injured may represent those members in a proceeding for judicial review. But a mere "interest in a problem," no matter how longstanding the interest and no matter how qualified the organization is in evaluating the problem, is not sufficient by itself to render the organization "adversely affected" or "aggrieved" within the meaning of the APA. The Sierra Club is a large and long-established organization, with a historic commitment to the cause of protecting our Nation's natural heritage from man's depredations. But if a "special interest" in this subject were enough to entitle the Sierra Club to commence this litigation, there would appear to be no objective basis upon which to disallow a suit by any other bona fide "special interest" organization however small or short-lived. And if any group with a bona fide "special interest" could initiate such litigation, it is difficult to preceive why any individual citizen with the same bona fide special interest would not also be entitled to do so.

The requirement that a party seeking review must allege facts showing that he is himself adversely affected does not insulate executive action from judicial review, nor does it prevent any public interests from being protected through the judicial process. It does serve as at least a rough attempt to put the decision as to whether review will be sought in the hands of those who have a direct stake in the outcome. That goal would be undermined were we to construe the APS to authorize judicial review at the behest of organizations or individuals who seek to do no more than vindicate their own value preferences through the judicial process. The principle that the Sierra Club would have us establish in this case would do just that.

...[T]he Court of Appeals was correct in its holding that the Sierra Club lacked standing to maintain this action...

DOUGLAS, Mr. Justice, dissenting.

The critical question of "standing" would be simplified and also put neatly in focus if we fashioned a federal rule that allowed environmental issues to be litigated before federal agencies or federal courts in the name of the inanimate object about to be despoiled, defaced, or invaded by roads and bulldozers and where injury is the subject of public outrage. Contemporary public concern for protecting nature's ecological equilibrium should lead to the conferral of standing upon environmental objects to sue for their own preservation...

■ ■ ■

Questions

1. What are the elements that must be established to possess standing to sue under the Administrative Procedure Act? What is an "injury in fact?" What is "adversely affected" or "aggrieved?" What did the Sierra Club fail to establish?
2. The Supreme Court recognized that other courts have taken a different approach in the determination of standing to sue. What is that alternate approach? Could this explain why three conservation groups in *Natural Resources Defense Council v. Morton* were able to bring an action against the Secretary of the Interior while the Sierra Club was denied standing to sue in this case?
3. How would the dissenting justice settle the question of standing?
4. Which rule for standing do you prefer?

ENVIRONMENTAL PROTECTION AGENCY

The Environmental Protection Agency (EPA) was created on December 2, 1970, to coordinate and administer major federal legislation over the environmental problems of air and water pollution, solid waste control, dangerous pesticides, radiation, and noise. The EPA is a regulatory agency which must set standards, timetables, and limitations that are to be utilized in the administration and enforcement of laws to improve the environment. The EPA also conducts studies of pollution sources and supports universities and other research institutions with grants and contracts to discover and develop techniques for pollution control. The EPA also expends considerable energies dispersing information to the public through workshops, seminars, bulletins, and manuals which describe methods to improve environmental quality.

SPECIFIC AREAS OF POLLUTION

AIR POLLUTION

Air pollution represents a serious danger to the health of citizens of any industrial society. Air quality is affected by such natural conditions as wind speed, geographic features, stationary high-pressure areas, and other natural phenomena. However, major contributions to air pollution result from industrial operations and automobile exhaust. Consequently, combating air pollution is not strictly a local affair. If it is to be effectively controlled, action must be taken at all levels of government. The following two cases represent efforts by the city of New York to improve its air quality. Thereafter, a case involving "interstate pollution" requires federal authorities to enforce federal laws.

FUEL AND REFUSE BURNERS

ORIENTAL BOULEVARD COMPANY v. HELLER
316 N.Y.S. 2d 226 (1970)
Court of Appeals of New York

■ ■ ■

...(Two) principal contentions are (that) the local ordinance is impossible of compliance within the time schedule provided (and) the upgrading of equipment is disproportionately costly... Plaintiffs (also) particularly urge that the effect of the ordinance in reducing air pollution would be either non-existent or so minimal as not to justify the extraordinary expense imposed on property owners.

The amended ordinance is a detailed statute aimed at multiple dwelling uses of fuel and refuse burners... It requires the commissioner of air pollution control to issue operating certificates for fuel burners and incinerators...Owners must conduct such tests as the commissioner deems necessary to determine the compliance of equipment with the new standards...

The law sets new standards for lower sulphur content of fuel. It requires the owners to install suplhur emission monitoring and recording devices, and to forward the records to the commissioner...Installation of apparatus in the fuel burners, entailing substantial outlays, was required within two years...Varying with the number of apartments dependent upon an incinerator, owners are required to install additional apparatus within staggered periods up to two years...After compliance dates have passed, the commissioner is empowered to seal any equipment for which permits have not been obtained as explicitly required by the ordinance, and, in addition, but only after notice and hearing, to seal any other equipment which is emitting harmful substances. A fine from $25 to $200 a day and imprisonment up to 60 days may be imposed for each day of improper operation of an incinerator.

The ponderous argument made that pollution caused by incinerators and oil burning equipment is of trivial effect in the overall solution of a massive problem is fallacious. Accepting the contention that there is only a 2% daily contribution of pollutants by private apartment housees, this contribution still aggregrates over 186 tons per day. Moreover, government is and must be entitled to attack massive problems piecemeal, and to select those most susceptible areas which permit of the least destructive effect on the economy. Thus, while, by common belief, the automobile is the grossest offender in air pollution, the only immediate corrective, evidently, would be its banishment, a socially and economically intolerable solution worse than the condition to be cured.

This is not to say that there are not serious questions raised as to the wisdom and the practicality of the undoubtedly rigorous measures required by the ordinance. But the ultimate conclusion must be that these are questions within the domain of legislative and executive discretion becasue they involve choices among alternative reasonable courses of action based on the presently limited knowledge of the extent of the pollution evil and methods of cure. So long as there is reasonable basis in available information, and rationality in chosen courses of conduct to alleviate an accepted evil, there is no constitutional infirmity...

On another somewhat simliar issue plaintiffs urge that the regional shortage of pollution control engineers and related service firms would have prevented many multiple dwelling owners from complying with the ordinance had all sought at one time to comply with the ordinance within its time limits. Because plaintiffs do not contend that they, rather than all owners, found timely performance impossible, they fail to show that they are aggrieved. Statutes will not be struck down unless the plaintiffs are actually aggrieved.

It is not without practical significance, if not theoretical relevance, that more than two and four years have passed since the respective local laws were enacted, in which time much, if not all, of the change-overs required could have been accomplished. In the meantime, plaintiffs have made no effort to comply. Hence, it is not persuasive, on the limited issue affecting the compliance time schedule, that, as plaintiffs argue, performance is not possible because all could not have performed within the original time schedules in the amended ordinance. Plaintiffs may have been reasonable in resisting enforcement of the ordinance for other reasons, but not because all members of the class could not have complied.

While it is true that compliance in particular buildings will involve the outlay of varying substantial sums in the range of $3,500 to $14,000, or even $19,000, to upgrade fuel burners and incinerators, the amounts only seem enormous when totaled as a whole for the city. Related to the particular properties, considering the serious health hazard represented by aerial pollution, there is no showing that the amounts are disproportionate to the capital investment or the benefits to be obtained. Equally significant outlays have been required in the past from owners of multiple dwellings and sustained as constitutional...At a time when weather agencies in the city report almost daily that the air is unsatisfactory or unhealthy, it is hardly permissible to allow aerial pollution to continue untrammeled because the necessary outlays to avoid the condition would cut into profit margins or require "hardship" adjustments in controlled rents. In any event, there is no patent unconstitutionality involved and the balance to be struck is a legislative and not a judicial obligation.

■ ■ ■

Questions

1. Is an ordinance unconstitutional because its reduction of air pollution is miniminal in relation to the extraordinary expense imposed upon property owners to comply? Is this question for the court to decide?
2. Did the defendants have enough time to comply with the law?

AUTO EXHAUST

ALLWAY TAXI, INC. v. CITY OF NEW YORK
340 F. Supp. 1120 (1972)
U.S. District Court (S.D.N.Y.)

■ ■ ■

Plaintiffs, fifteen corporations owning and operating licensed taxicabs in New York City, move...for a preliminary injunction against enforcement of a New York City ordinance requiring exhaust emission controls for licensed taxicabs....

The ordinance requires licensed taxicabs to use gasoline containing no more than specified low levels of lead and to use only non-leaded gasoline after January 1, 1974. The ordinance also requires pre-1970 federal standards and later models to be equipped with such emission control devices which comply with 1970 federal standards and later models to be equipped with such emission control devices as may be specified by the New York City Taxi and Linousine Commission....

Plaintiff's claim...depends on the validity of their contention that the ordinance is null and void because the field of motor vehicle emission control has been preempted by the federal Clean Air Act.

A local ordinance will be upheld against a claim of preemption unless there is such an actual conflict between the local and federal regulatory schemes that both cannot stand in the same area or unless there is clear evidence of congressional intent to preempt the field.

Plaintiffs rely upon two sections of the Clean Air Act, which, they claim, show a clear congressional intent to preempt the regulation of automobile exhaust emissions.

The first preemption section...prohibits states of their subdivisions from regulating fuel and fuel additives if the federal administrator has found that no control is necessary or has already prescribed standards. Since plaintiffs neither show nor contend that either condition has been full-filled here, we see no conflict at present between the City's regulation of the lead content of gasoline and this preemption section.

The second preemption section...prohibits states...from creating standards for exhaust emission control devices for new motor vehicle engines. It also prohibits states from setting standards of approval as conditions precedent to the initial sale or registration of new motor vehicles.

Where exercise of the local police power serves the purpose of a federal Act, the preemptive effect of that Act should be narrowly construed. We think the purpose of the federal Act is served by the challenged ordinance. Surely, New York City has the power at least to try to clean the very air that people breathe. Plainly, that is the purpose of the ordinance, and it is clearly compatible with the goal of the federal Clean Air Act. Moreover, both the history and text of the Act show that the second preemption section was made not to hamstring localities in their fight against air pollution but to prevent the burden on interstate commerce which would result if, instead of uniform standards, every state and locality were left free to impose different standards for exhaust emission control devices for the manufacture and sale of new cars.

Thus, the second preemption section restricts states and localities from setting their own standards for new motor vehicles, which are defined as motor vehicles, "the equitable or legal title to which...[have] never been transferred to an ultimate purchaser." The statutory definition reveals a clear congressional intent to preclude states and localities from setting their own exhaust emission control standards only with respect to the manufacture and distribution of new automobiles. That narrow purpose is further suggested by the remainder of the section, which prohibits states and localities from setting standards governing emission control devices before the initial sale or registration of an automobile. Finally, congress specifically refused to interfere with local regulation of the use or movement of motor vehicles after they have reached their ultimate purchasers.

We do not say that a state or locality is free to impose its own emission control standards the moment after a new car is bought and registered. That would be an obvious circumvention of the Clean Air Act and would defeat the congressional purpose of preventing obstruction to interstate commerce. The preemption sections, however, do not preclude a state or locality from imposing its own exhaust emission control standards upon resale or reregistration of the automobile. Nor do they preclude a locality from setting its own standards for the licensing of vehicles for commercial use within that locality. Such regulations would cause only minimal interference with interstate commerce, since they would be directed primarily to intrastate activities and the burden of compliance would be on individual owners and not on manufacturers and distributors.

The challenged ordinance would, at most, require taxicab owners, seeking a license to operate in the City, to meet at their own expense emmission control standards established by the Taxi and Limousine Commission. Such a requirement is fully supported by the congressional call for local cooperation toward the prevention and control of air pollution. We conclude that the ordinance is neither in conflict with, nor precluded by, the second preemption section of the Clean Air Act....

Plaintiffs' third agreement is that the emission control devices required by the ordinance will be significantly expensive. The requirement of such devices for pre-1970 taxicabs is virtually moot, since taxicabs are traded every 16 to 18 months. As for vehicles manufactured in 1971 and thereafter, the present New York City standards are no stricter than federal standards. Although the ordinance gives the Taxi and Limousine Commission authority to set stricter standards, the commission has not yet done so and, thus, taxicab owners face no present threat of increased cost.

■ ■ ■

Questions

1. Which government has the authority to impose auto exhaust emission control devices on new automobiles?
2. Under what circumstances would New York's ordinance which requires a nonleaded gasoline become preempted by the federal law?
3. Did the court believe the plaintiff's arguments of excessive expense to comply?

INTERSTATE AIR POLLUTION

UNITED STATES v. BISHOP PROCESSING COMPANY
423 F.2d 469 (1970)
U.S. Court of Appeals (4th Cir.)

■ ■ ■

This appeal is the most recent chapter in a long series of proceedings, in and out of court, stretching over more than a decade. The states of Delaware and Maryland, later joined by the federal government, have been endeavoring to bring relief to affected communities from alleged air pollution stemming from the appellant's rendering plant.

From approximately 1959 to 1965 the two states engaged in futile efforts to induce Bishop Processing Company, operator of the rendering and animal reduction plant located near Bishop, Maryland, to abate the malodorous air pollution which allegedly moves across the state line to pollute the air of nearby Selbyville, Delaware. Finally in 1965, the United States Secretary of Health, Education and Welfare received a request from the Delaware authorities to "take necessary action under...the Clean Air Act to secure the abatement of the air pollution problem." In response to this request the Secretary initiated hearing procedures provided in the Act.

...[T]he initial step was a conference held in Selbyville on November 9 and 10, 1965. The parties attending the conference represented, as specified in the Act, the air pollution control agencies of the states and municipalities concerned. The Secretary forwarded to the participants a summary of the conference discussions and recommendations, which called upon Maryland to require Bishop to take certain remedial action by September 1, 1966.

Since the recommended remedial action was not taken, the Secretary instituted the next step envisioned in the Act, by calling a public hearing which was held on May 17 and 18, 1967. At this hearing Bishop was represented by counsel who extensively cross-examined witnesses and otherwise fully participated. The hearing board forwarded its findings and recommendations to the Secretary, who in turn transmittd them to Bishop with the instruction to abate the pollution not later than December 1, 1967 by installing adequate and effective pollution control systems.

This step also proving fruitless, the Secretary...filed a complaint on March 7, 1968 in the United States District Court for Maryland seeking to enjoin Bishop from discharging malodorous air pollutants. There followed discussions between the parties and on October 4, 1968 the appellant proposed settlement of the case, specifying the terms he would accept. On November 1, 1968, the action then pending was disposed of by settlement. A consent decree was entered in which Bishop agreed, in the precise terms it had suggested, to "cease all manufacturing and processing" upon the "filing of an affidavit by the Director, Air Pollution Control Division, State of Delaware Water and Air Resources Commission, stating that the defendent is discharging malodorous air pollution reaching the State of Delaware * * *"

The Director accordingly instituted a surveillance program to determine to what extent, if any, the obnoxious odors persisted and reached Delaware. Odor logs were kept at the instance of the Director and he made personal observations. On this basis the Director found that Bishop had been recurringly discharging malodorous air polluants which reached the State of Delaware since November 1, 1978. These findings and conclusions the Director embodied in an affidavit.

Based upon this affidavit and pursuant to the consent decree, the United States moved for an order directing the defendant to cease operations. A hearing on this motion was held on March 3 and 4, 1968, in which the District Judge declared that the "Court would prefer to have more evidence" that Bishop is engaging in air pollution, and announced his interpretation of the consent decree "for the guidance of * * * members of the staff who may be participating in any further investigations." In this way the judge indicated to the parties the type of evidence he would consider requisite for a showing of air pollution upon which an order could be based.

On September 12, 1969, the United States filed a second motion accompanied by affidavits in compliance with the consent decree and the court prescribed evidentiary requirements. After a further hearing, the court found the evidence substantial and entered the order to cease operations. The appeal is from this order.

The appellant presses the contention that the District Court erred in ruling that the

Director performed his duties in accordance with the consent decree. Bishop argues that the decree was entered into with various "understandings" which contemplated certain procedures to be followed by the Director in his investigation. Specifically, Bishop asserts its "understandings" that (1) the Director was not to rely on citizen complaints or on testimony of representatives of the federal government in determining whether it committed air pollution and, (2) that the Director's finding was to be based upon "generally accepted sampling techniques."

Whatever merit this arguement might have in other circumstances, it must fail here. The consent decree is plain in its terms. Nowhere and at no time was it intimated that any finding of air pollution was to be based upon unexpressed "understandings" with respect to the investigative procedures. Neither before the entry of the consent decree, nor when the judge held a hearing and announced his interpretation of the decree for the guidance of the parties did Bishop disclose the existence of any "understandings" or reservations on its part.

Bishop had ample opportunity to propose incorporation in the decree of any protection it may have felt necessary, and to object to procedures it deemed contrary to its understanding of the decree's terms. It cannot now ask the court to revise the decree by inserting language or to interpret it to embrace matters which, if present at all, were lurking in the recesses of Bishop's corporate mind....

Bishop's further contentions, variously repeated, are in substance an attack on the sufficiency of the evidence upon which the finding of air pollution was based. As above stated, at the first hearing the District Judge explained, with no caveat whatever from Bishop, the type and quantum of evidence he felt was necessary. After a second hearing he found that the Government had complied with his directions and adduced sufficient evidence to show that Bishop continues to pollute the air. Certainly the factual finding, so carefully arrived at, cannot be deemed clearly erroneous.

Pollution is a severe and increasing problem of which the courts and other branches of government have become acutely conscious. The residents of the area in the neighborhood of Bishop's plant have the right to demand that the air they breathe shall not be defiled by what witnesses described as a "horrible" and "nauseating" stench. The afflicted neighbors have striven long and in vain to vindicate that right. Relief is due them now....

This court is not unmindful of the serious consequences to appellant's business from the District Court's order. It is, however, precisely the remedy which Bishop suggested and agreed to in order to avoid a trial, and seems inescapable since it has over a long period failed to take effective measures to solve the problem.

■ ■ ■

Questions

1. What procedural steps did the Secretary of HEW go through before bringing action to cease all manufacturing by the defendant?
2. Was the District Judge careful in his determination of whether Bishop had violated the consent decree?
3. Was the defendant successful in arguing that the director could not take action unless he could support his contention of air pollution by "generally accepted sampling techniques"?

The Clean Air Act Amendments of 1970 were the culmination of previous legislation which included the 1955 Air Pollution Control Act, 1963 Clean Air Act, the major amendments of 1965 and 1967, and the Air Quality Act of 1967. The 1970 Amendments provide primary legislation for the air quality management in the United States today. The enforcement of these acts is under the administration of the Environmental Protection Agency. The Act provides for a system of national air quality standards based on geographic regions and establishes maximum levels for auto pollution. They require the EPA to give guidance and to set "standards" for air quality which must be met by industrial firms and governmental units to curb hazardous pollutants from being emitted into the atmosphere.

State and local governments are important instruments in the prevention of air pollution under the federal law. Each state has developed a plan for air quality improvement in its geographic area and such plans have been approved by the EPA. State agencies investigate the quality of air and aid in the enforcement of regulations that upgrade air quality.

The EPA may notify a polluter that he or she is in violation of the law and issue a stop order. If these efforts fail, the EPA may seek a court injunction. The Clean Air Amendments Act of 1972 authorizes a private suit by "any person" in a federal district court to stop a violation of EPA pollution standards.

The initial efforts of the federal laws were concentrated on cleaning up the dirty regions of the country with little thought to preventing significant deterioration in clean regions. As a result of the 1970 Amendments, the EPA promulgated the National Ambient Air Quality Standards (NAAQS). The 1970 legislation outlined how the NAAQS were to be achieved and maintained. The 1970 legislation also asserted the goal "to protect and enhance the quality of the nation's air resources," which implied that deterioration of air quality in clean areas was to be avoided. However, the intent of Congress never specified enforcement procedures. Consequently, industry moved into clean areas and fouled the air there up to the level of the national standards. Consequently, numerous suits by environmental groups were brought against the EPA demanding stricter interpretations to avoid significant deterioration of air quality in clean air regions. To avoid continued litigation of these issues, Congress established provisions in the Clean Air Act Amendments of 1977 to prevent the significant deterioration of air quality in clean areas.

WATER POLLUTION

The Rivers and Harbors Act of 1899 empowered the Army Corps of Engineers to prevent discharges into navigable waterways. While the Act was obviously designed to protect the navigability of rivers and harbors, its language has been interpreted by the courts to prohibit pollution discharges into the waterways also. However, in 1956 Congress began programs specifically designed to deal with water pollution by enacting the Federal Water Pollution Control Act. The Water Quality Act of 1965 created the Federal Water Pollution and Control Administration to aid the states in preparation of stream quality standards and to prepare plans to meet the standards. The Clean Water Restoration Act of 1966 imposed statewide water quality standards and provided substantial federal monies to aid in the development of water pollution control. Subsequently, the Federal Water Pollution Control Administration was merged into the Environmental Protection Agency. The Water Quality Improvement Act of 1970 and the Federal Water Pollution Control Act Amendments of 1972 strengthened the federal powers and established the goal to eliminate all pollution in navigable waters by 1985. According to the 1972 amendments, industrial firms must apply the "best practical control technology currently available" (best conventional technology) to achieve a cleaner water environment. By 1984 the firms must be using the "best available technology economically achievable" (best available technology) to remove foreign matter from water discharged from their premises.

While enforcement of the various pollution laws remains the primary responsibility of the state water pollution control agencies, the EPA may enforce state and federal regulations if state authorities are not accomplishing the task.

The Safe Drinking Water Act of 1974 was passed to provide for the safety of drinking water supplies throughout the United States by setting and enforcing national drinking water standards for public water systems. A public water system is defined as one that provides piped water for human consumption and has at least fifteen service connections or regularly serves at least twenty-five people. The EPA has the primary responsibility of establishing national standards while the states are responsible for enforcing the standards and supervising the public drinking water supply systems.

UNITED STATES v. HOLLAND
373 F.Supp. 665 (1974)
U.S. District Court (Fa.)

■ ■ ■

This is an action brought by the United States to enjoin allegedly unlawful landfilling operations in an area known as Harbor Isle, adjoining Papy's Bayou, St. Petersburg, Florida. The government contends that the defendants have begun filling the waters of the bayou with sand, dirt, dredged spoil and biological materials without the permits required by 33 U.S.C. §§ 403, 407 and 1311 (a). For relief the government requests a stoppage of further filling and a restoration of some mangrove wetland....

The government charged the defendants with past and continuing violations of Section 301 (a) of the Federal Water Pollution Control Act Amendments of 1972 (FWPCA). To sustain this allegation two showings had to be made. First it had to be established that the defendants' acts were such as to be prohibited if done in waters within federal jurisdiction, and second, that the waters receiving the impact of the prohibited conduct were indeed within that jurisdictional ambit.

The FWPCA is an admirably comprehensive piece of legislation. It was designed to deal with all facets of recapturing and preserving the biological integrity of the nation's water by creating a web of complex interrelated regulatory programs. Section 301 (a), the enforcement hub of the statute, however, is stated very simply. It provides that except as otherwise permitted within the Act "the discharge of any pollutant by any person shall be unlawful." The plainness of the prohibition is matched by the breadth given the definition of a "discharge of a pollutant":

(A) Any addition of any pollutant to navigable waters from any point source,
(B) Any addition of any pollutant to the waters of the contiguous zone or the ocean from any point source...other than a vessel or other floating craft.

"Pollutant" is in turn defined as

...*Dredged spoil*, solid waste, incinerator residue, sewage, garbage, sewer sludge, munitions, chemical vastes, *biological materials,* radioactive materials, heat, wrecked or discarded equipment, rock, *sand*, cellar dirt and *industrial,* municipal, and agricultural waste discharged into water....

And "point source" is

...any discernible, confined and discrete conveyance, *including* but not limited to any *pipe, ditch,* channel, tunnel, conduit, well, discrete fissure, container, *rolling stock,* concentrated animal feeding operation, or vessel or other floating craft, from which pollutants are or may be discharged.

The evidence substantiates the defendants" admission that without a permit they have discharged and would continue to discharge from point sources, including dump trucks, drag lines, and bulldozers, materials defined as pollutants. Whether these pollutants were discharged into waters within federal jurisdiction was the key issue....

For years the mainstays of the federal water pollution effort were Sections 10 and 13 of Ribers and Harbors Act of 1899. Section 10 makes it illegal to fill, excavate, alter or modify the course, condition or capacity of waters within the boundaries of a navigable waterway without authorization from the Corps of Engineers. Section 13 prohibits the deposit of refuse in, or on the bank of, a navigable waterway without a Corps of Engineers' permit. Both of these laws are by their terms limited to waters that are deemed navigable. Because of this limitation past discussion of federal jurisdiction over water pollution was largely a question of the navigability of the waterway being affected.

Why the Congress limited the Rivers and Harbors Act to navigable waters is no insoluble mystery. Although the Constitution does not mention navigable waters, it vests in Congress the power to "regulate commerce with foreign nations and among the several states."[4] Since much of the interstate commerce of the 19th century was water borne, it was early held that the commerce power necessarily included the power to regulate navigation....

On October 18, 1972, the Congress exercised its power under the commerce clause by enacting the FWPCA, establishing regulatory programs to combat pollution of the nation's waters. Even though it seems certain that Congress sought to broaden federal jurisdiction under the Act, it did so in a manner that appears calculated to force courts to engage in verbal acrobatics. Although using the term "navigable waters" in the prohibitory phase of the statute, the definition of "navigable waters" is stated to be "waters of the United States, including the territorial seas." The definition stands with no limiting language.

If indeed the Congress saw fit to define away the navigability restriction, the sole limitation on the reach of federal power remaining would be the commerce clause. Thus two questions emerge. Did Congress intend to define away the old "navigability" restriction? And does the Congress have such power?

The answer to the first question is in the affirmative. The Court is of the opinion that the clear meaning of the statutory definition may be ascertained on its face without having to rely on the well established judicial philosophy that "forbids a narrow, cramped reading" of water pollution legislation....

It is beyond question that water pollution has a serious effect on interstate commerce and that the Congress has the power to regulate activities such as dredging and filling which cause such pollution....

Congress and the courts have become aware of the lethal effect pollution has on all organisims. Weakening any of the life support systems bodes disaster for the rest of the interrelated life forms. To recognize this and yet hold that pollution does not affect interstate commerce unless committed in navigable waters below the mean high water line would be contrary to reason. Congress is not limited by the "navigable waters" test in its authority to control pollution under the Commerce Clause.

Having thus ascertained that Congress had the power to go beyond the "navigability" limitation in its control over water pollution and that it intended to do so in the FWPCA, the question remains whether the Congress intended to reach the type of activities involved in the instant case—the pollution of non-navigable mosquito canals and mangrove wetland areas....

The conclusion that Congress intended to reach water-bodies such as these canals with the FWPCA is inescapable. The legislative history quoted manifests a clear intent to break from the limitations of the Rivers and Harbors Act to get at the sources of pollution. Polluting canals that empty into a bayou arm of Tampa Bay is clearly an activity Congress sought to regulate. The fact that these canals were man-made makes no difference. They were constructed long before the development scheme was conceived. That the defendants used them to convey the pollutants without a permit is the matter of importance.

The Court is of the opinion that the waters of the mosquito canals were within definition of "waters of the United States" and that the filling of them without a permit was a violation of the FWPCA....

One of the sources of pollution in the instant case was the discharge of sand, dirt and dredged spoil on land which, although above the mean high water line, was periodically innundated with the waters of Papy's Bayou. Defendants argue that such activities are beyond the reach of the FWPCA. This Court does not agree. Even the occasional lapping of the bayou waters has conveyed these pollutants into the waters of the United States. That the pollutants are not so conveyed every day is of no consequence. Pollutants have been introduced into the waters of the United States without a permit and the mean high water mark cannot be used to create a barrier behind which such activities can be excused. The environment cannot afford such safety zones.

The Court is of the opinion that the mean high water line is no limit to federal authority under the FWPCA. While the line remains a valid demarcation for other purposes, it has no rational connection to the aquatic ecosystems which the FWPCA is intended to protect. Congress has wisely determined that federal authority over water pollution properly rests on the Commerce Clause and not on past interpretations of an act designed to protect navigation. And the Commerce Clause gives Congress ample authority to reach activities above the mean high water line that pollute the waters of the United States.

The defendants' filling activities on land periodically innundated by tidal waters constituted discharges entering "waters of the United States" and, since done without a permit, were thus in violation of 33 U.S.C. § 1311 (a).

■ ■ ■

Questions

1. The court in *Holland* determined that "two showings" had to be made by the government. What were these two items of proof?
2. What is the purpose of the federal Water Pollution Control Act? What is a "pollutant?"
3. Why had Congress in 1899 limited the effect of the Rivers and Harbors Act to navigable waters? Does this suggest a limitation on the power of Congress to reach waters that are not navigable for purposes of pollution control?

In July of 1978 the first person was sent to prison for violating the federal Clean Water Act. The defendant had pleaded guilty and was sentenced to six months in prison, a $20,000 fine, and four-and-a-half years on probation. He had been cited for more than a hundred state pollution violations over the past thirteen years. His most recent conviction, which resulted in the six months sentence, was for pouring thousands of gallons of hazardous industrial wastes into the Delaware River, close to its city drinking-water plant. The 1972 Clean Water Act makes it a crime to willfully dump such waste into a river without a permit. The defendant had poured the waste materials into the river through a manhole in his warehouse.

In addition, jail terms are possible for water polluters who do not disclose their discharge of harmful quantities into the water. The EPA has designated 271 substances as hazardous to public health when discharged into the waters. Anyone "in charge of" a facility that does not notify the U.S. government immediately of water polluting by these substances at levels determined by the EPA to be "harmful" is subject to a $10,000 fine, imprisonment for not more than one year, or both. The "owner or operator" of the offending facility stands to lose up to $500,000 to the EPA, depending on such factors as the size of the discharge, the culpability of the owner, and any mitigating efforts undertaken by the owner. In addition, the owner may be liable to the government for all costs incurred in the removal of the pollutant. There are only four defenses against liability. The discharge must be shown to have been caused by one or more of the following:

1. An act of God
2. An act of war
3. Negligence on the part of U.S. government
4. An act or omission of a third party without regard to whether the omission was or was not negligent

SOLID WASTE POLLUTION

The Solid Waste Disposal Act of 1968 was subsequently placed under the jurisdiction of the Environmental Protection Agency. Primarily, the Act encourages the development of improved techniques and planning for solid waste disposal. The EPA is required to develop guidelines and establish a national materials policy to guide the conservation and wise use of U.S. national resources. The federal law assists and provides information to state and local authorities in the development of solid waste disposal systems. Moreover, the state law often defers responsibility to the local authorities to handle waste disposal.

NOISE POLLUTION

While previous federal legislation has dealt with noise control in specific situations, the Noise Control Act of 1970 and 1972 declare a federal policy to protect the health and welfare of all Americans from ill effects of environment noise. The administrator of the EPA is given authority to establish noise emission standards for a variety of areas. Aircraft, railroads, and motor carriers are subjected to noise abatement regulations. And in factories, tolerable occupation noise levels are determined for enforcement by the Occupational Safety and Health Administration

AIR TRANSPORT ASSOCIATION OF AMERICA v. CROTTI
389 F. Supp. 58 (1975)
U.S. District Court (N. Calif.)

■ ■ ■

The federal statutes intending to regulate the intensity of noise generated by aircraft in flight and incident thereto are the Noise Control Act of 1972, as it amends the Federal Aviation Act of 1958, and the regulations now and to be promulgated thereunder. Of particular note is Section 2(a)(3) of the Noise Control Act, which reads:

"The Congress finds...

"(3) that, while primary responsibility for control of noise rests with State and local governments, Federal action is essential to deal with major noise sources in commerce control of which require national uniformity of treatment."

...[T]he California Public Utilities Code, required the California Department of Aeronautics to adopt noise regulations governing the operations of airports and of aircraft at all airports in California operating mandatorily under a permit issued by the Department of Aeronautics... [T]he county in which the airport is situated is given responsibility to enforce the noise regulations adopted by the Department. The airport's non-compliance subject their permit to suspension or cancellation

Some of the means available in order to meet California's airport noise standards are set out in the Administrative Code, which is entitled "Methodology for Controlling and Reducing Noise Problems," and which reads as follows:

"The methods whereby the impact of airport noise shall be controlled and reduced include but are not limited to the following:

"(a) Encouraging use of the airport by aircraft classes with lower noise level characteristics and discouraging use by higher noise level aircraft classes;

"(b) Encouraging approach and departure flight paths and procedures to minimize the noise in residential areas;

"(c) Planning runway utilization schedules to take into account adjacent residential areas, noise characteristics of aircraft and noise sensitive time periods;

"(d) Reduction of the flight frequency, particularly in the most noise sensitive time periods and by the noisier aircraft;

"(e) Employing shielding for advantage, using natural terrain, buildings, ...and

"(f) Development of a compatible land use within the noise impact boundary.

"Preference shall be given to actions which reduce the impact of airport noise on existing communities. Land use conversion involving existing residential communities shall normally be considered the least desirable action for achieving compliance with these regulations."

Hence, the Code recommends certain procedures which can be employed in order to attain the established noise reduction standards, but no particular procedure is mandatory. Airport authorities are left to choose among the suggested means at their own discretion, tailoring their own programs to their peculiar needs and inclinations. Furthermore, airport authorities are left free to devise and employ other noise control measures beyond those suggested in the Code.

Specifically, the regulations fall into two categories: (a) CNEL (Community Noise Equivalent Level) standards prescribed for continued operation of airports with monitoring requirements, which focus upon the arrival of a prescribed ultimate maximum noise level and limiting the land uses subjected thereto around airport facilities; and (b) SENEL (Single Event Noise Exposure Levels) prohibitions applied to the inseparable feature of noise generated by an aircraft directly engaged in flight...

The Airlines' position narrows to the simple contention that any control and the federal goverment; accordingly, each of the CNEL standards and related monitoring requirements and SENEL prohibitions are per se void and unenforeceable under the holdings of *Burbank v. Lockheed Air Terminal* 411 U.S. 624 (1973),

> The "Act [the Noise Control Act of 1972, EPA, amending the Federal Aviation Act of 1958, FAA, and regulations thereunder] reaffirms and reinforces the conclusion that FAA, now in conjunction with EPA, has full control over aircraft noise, pre-empting state and local control."

The Airports counter (that an)...exemption (for)...a *proprietor of an airport* from the pre-emption by the federal government...flows from the following footnote 14 to *Burbank:*

> "The letter from the Secretary of Transportation also expressed the view that 'the proposed legislation will not affect the rights of a State or local public agency, *as the proprietor of an airport,* from issuing regulations or establishing requirements as to the permissible level of noise which can be created by aircraft using the airport. Airport owners *acting as proprietors* can presently deny the use of their airports to aircraft on the basis of noise considerations so long as such exclusion is nondiscriminatory'..."

We believe that the Airlines' total reliance upon *Burbank* is misplaced. The factual picture supporting *Burbank* is of narrow focus, a single police power ordinance of a municipality—not an airport proprietor—intending to abate aircraft noise by *forbidding* aircraft flight at certain night hours. The holding in *Burbank* is limited to that proscription as constituting an unlawful exercise of police power in a field pre-empted by the federal government, and we take as gospel the words in footnote 14 in *Burbank:* "[A]uthority that a municipality may have as a landlord is not necessarily congruent with its police power. *We do not consider here what limits, if any, apply to a municipality as a proprietor."*

It is now firmly established that the airport proprietor is responsible for the consequences which attend his operation of a public airport... Manifestly, such proprietary control necessarily includes the basic right to determine the type of air service a given airport proprietor wants its facilities to provide, as well as the type of aircraft to utilize those facilities. The intent of Congress not to interfere with such basic airport control is made clear in the legislative history the Federal Aviation Act of 1958...

The monitoring provisions in the California airport noise abatement scheme are innocuous to aircraft traffic. The monitoring of noise levels at and near airports is a passive function involving ground noise measuring machines and recording sound volume data which in no wise intrude upon or affect flight operations and air space management in commerce.

The State dictated employment of shielding and ground level facility configurations, as well as development of compatible land uses under the provisons of CNEL, is so patently within local police power control and beyond the intent of Congress in the federal legislation that further discussion would be wasteful...

We conclude that the CNEL provisions and regulations are not per se invalid as delving into and regulating a field of aircraft operation engaged in direct flight, which is pre-empted unto the federal government under the Constitution and the laws of the United States.

Whether or not the CNEL requirements and regulations are *in fact*... an unreasonable burden upon interstate and foreign commerce as utilized by aircraft, is not before us upon undisputed facts and must await a future day of judgment.

The SENEL provisions and regulations are not so favored. We are satisfied and conclude that the SENEL provisions and regulations of noise levels which occur when an aircraft is in direct flight and for the levying of criminal fines for violations, are a per se unlawful exercise of police power into the exclusive federal domain of control over aircraft flights and operations, and air space management and utilizations in interstate and foreign commerce. The thrust of the Single Event Noise Exposure Levels is clear and direct and collides head-on with the federal regulatory scheme for aircraft flights delineated by and central to the *Burbank* decision.

According we conclude as a matter of law that the airlines are entitled to a partial summary judgment declaring each of the SENEL regulations, and particularly those levying criminal fines, void and unenforceable as in contravention of the Constitution and laws of the United States, and enjoining the implementation and enforcement thereof by any official or officer of the... State of California...

■ ■ ■

Questions

1. Under the Federal Noise Control Act of 1972, which government has primary responsibility for the control of noise?
2. When should federal action preempt efforts of local authorities to control noise? What scheme of regulation was utilized by the California Law?
3. What is the major holdings of the *Burbank v. Lockheed Air Terminal?* Why did the court determine that SENEL regulations were unenforceable and the CNEL regulations were within the power of California?

TOXIC SUBSTANCES

The purpose of the Toxic Substances Control Act (TOSCA) of 1976 is to eliminate unreasonable threats to human health or the environment arising from chemical substances or mixtures and the products containing such elements. The new law requires chemical manufacturers to test new chemical substances or mixtures according to rules issued by the EPA, so that their affect on health environment may be evaluated. Such data must be submitted to the EPA at least ninety days before the chemicals are to go into commercial production. The data must include the proposed product's molecular structure, its intended use, production estimates, the number of employees exposed to the chemical during manufacture and any known health or environmental effects of its components. If the EPA decides that such data provides grounds for prohibiting the new chemical, it must notify the company within forty-five days. The company can submit counter arguments to the EPA and is afforded some "due process" by forcing the agency to seek a court injunction to prohibit the distribution of the chemical.

The EPA is also authorized to seek a court order banning or restricting an *existing* chemical if it believes the chemical to be "imminently hazardous." The law establishes an interagency task force that will draw up a list of marketed products for the EPA to check for potential hazards. The EPA is authorized to spend $10 million on toxic substances control in 1977, $12.6 million in 1978 and $16.2 million in 1979. These figures contrast sharply with the annual operating budget of $100 million for water pollution and $39.8 million for pesticide control. The inadequate funding and uncertainty involved with any new law preclude determination of the full impact of this law on the chemical and manufacturing industry and on the reduction of risk to human health and the environment occasioned by chemical elements.

ENDANGERED SPECIES

TENNESSEE VALLEY AUTHORITY v. HILL, et. al.
98 S. Ct. 2279 (1978)
Supreme Court of the United States

[The Tennessee Valley Authority, a public corporation of the United States, began constructing the Tellico Dam on the Little Tennessee River in 1967. When fully operational, the dam would impound water covering some 16,500 acres and thereby convert the river's shallow, fast-flowing waters into a deep reservoir over 30 miles in length. In 1973, an unknown species of perch, the snail darter, was discovered in the waters of the Little Tennessee. Some four months after its discovery, Congress passed the Endangered Species Act of 1973 which protects the "critical habitat" of these creatures.]

■ ■ ■

BURGER, Mr. Chief Justice.

We begin with the premise that operation of the Tellico Dam will either eradicate the known population of snail darters or destroy their critical habitat. In any event, under §4(a)(1) of the Act, the Secretary of the Interior is vested with exclusive authority to determine whether a species such as the snail darter is "endangered" or "threatened" and to ascertain the factors which have led to such a precarious existence. By §4(d) Congress has authorized—indeed commanded—the Secretary to "issue such regulations as he deems necessary and advisable to provide for the conservation of such species." As we have seen, the Secretary promulgated regulations which declared the snail darter an endangered species whose critical habitat would be destroyed by creation of the Tellico Reservoir.

Starting from the above premise, two questions are presented: (a) would TVA be in violation of the Act if it completed and operated the Tellico Dam as planned?; (b) if TVA's actions would offend the Act, is an injunction the appropriate remedy for the violation? For the reasons stated hereinafter, we hold that both questions must be answered in the affirmative.

It may seem curious to some that the survival of a relatively small number of three-inch fish among all the countless millions of species extant would require the permanent halting of a virtually completed dam for which Congress has expended more than $100 million. The paradox is not minimized by the fact that Congress continued to appropriate large sums of public money for the project, even after congressional appropriations committees were appraised of its apparent impact upon the survival of the snail darter. We conclude however, that the explicit provisions of the Endangered Species Act require precisely that result.

One would be hard prssed to find a statutory provision whose terms were any plainer than those in §7 of the Endangered Species Act. Its very words affirmatively command all federal agencies "to *insure* that actions *authorized, funded,* or *carried out* by them do not *jeopardize* the continued existence" of an endangered species or "*result* in the destruction or modification of habitat of such species...." This language admits of no exception. Nonetheless, petitioner urges, as do the dissenters that the Act cannot reasonably be interpreted as applying to a federal project which was well under way when Congress passed the Endangered Species Act of 1973. To sustain that position, however, we would be forced to ignore the ordinary meaning of plain language. It has not been shown, for example, how TVA can close the gates of the Tellico Dam without "carrying out" an action that has been "authorized" and "funded" by a federal agency. Nor can we understand how such action will *"insure"* that the snail darter's habitat is not disrupted. Accepting the Secretary's determinations, as we must, it is clear that TVA's proposed operation of the dam will have precisely the opposite effect, namely the *eradication* of an endangered species.

Concededly, this view of the Act will produce results requiring the sacrifice of the anticipated benefits of the project and of many millions of dollars in public funds. But examination of the language, history and structure of the legislation under review here indicates beyond doubt that Congress intended endangered species to be afforded the highest of priorities.

When Congress passed the Act in 1973, it was not legislating on a clean slate. The first major congressional concern for the preservation of the endangered species had come with passage of the Endangered Species Act of 1966...

In 1969 Congress enacted the Endangered Species Conservation Act, which continued the provisions of the 1966 Act while at the same time broadening federal involvement in the preservation of endangered species...

Despite the fact that the 1966 and 1969 legislation represented "the most comprehensive of its type to be enacted by any nation" up to that time, Congress was soon persuaded that a more expansive approach was needed if the newly declared national policy of preserving endangered species was to be realized. By 1973, when Congress held hearings on what would later become of the Endangered Species Act of 1973, it was informed that species were still being lost at the rate of about one per year, and "the pace of disappearance of species" appeared to be "accelerating."...

The legislative proceedings in 1973 are, in fact, replete with expressions of concern over the risk that might lie in the loss of *any* endangered species. Typifying these sentiments is the report of the House Committee on Merchant Marine and Fisheries ...which stated:

"As we homogenize the habitats in which these plants and animals evolved, and as we increase the pressure for products that they are in a position to supply (usually unwillingly) we threaten their—and our own—genetic heritage.
"The value of this genetic heritage is, quite literally, incalculable.

"From the most narrow possible point of view, *it is in the best interests of mankind to minimize the losses of genetic variations.* The reason is simple: they are potential resources. They are keys to puzzles which we cannot solve, and may provide answers to questions which we have not yet learned to ask.
"To take a homely, but apt, example: one of the critical chemicals in the regulation of ovulations in humans was found in a common plant. Once discovered, and analyzed, humans could duplicate it synthetically, but had it never existed—or had it been driven out of existence before we knew its potentialities—we would never have tried to synthesize it in the first place.
"Who knows, or can say, what potential cures for cancer or other scourges, present or future, may lie locked up in the structures of plants which may yet be undiscovered, much less analyzed?...Sheer self-interest impels us to be cautious.
  "The institutionalization of that caution lies at the heart of H.R. 37...."

As the examples cited here demonstrate, Congress was concerned about the *unknown* uses that endangered species might have and about the *unforeseeable* place such creatures may have in the chain of life on this planet.

In shaping legislation to deal with the problem thus presented, Congress started from the finding that "[t]he two major causes of extinction are hunting and destruction of natural habitat." Of these twin threats, Congress was informed that the greatest was destruction of natural habitats...

Witnesses recommended, among other things, that Congress require all land-managing agencies "to avoid damaging critical habitat for endangered species and to take positive steps to improve such habitat." Virtually every bill introduced in Congress during the 1973 session responded to this concern by incorporating language similar, if not identical, to that found in the present §7 of the Act....

It is against this legislative background that we must measure TVA's claim that the Act was not intended to stop operation of a project which, like Tellico Dam, was near completion when an endangered species was discovered in its path. While there is no discussion in the legislative history of precisely this problem, the totality of congressional action makes it abundantly clear that the result we reach today is wholly in accord with both the words of the statute and the intent of Congress. The plain intent of Congress in enacting this statute was to halt and reverse the trend toward species extinction, whatever the cost. This is reflected not only in the stated policies of the Act, but in literally every section of the statute. All persons, including federal agencies, are specifically instructed not to "take" endangered species, meaning that no one is "to harass, harm, pursue, hunt, shoot, wound, kill, trap, capture, or collect" such life forms. Agencies in particular are directed by §§2 (c) and 3 (2) of the Act to "use *all methods* and procedures which are necessary" to preserve endangered species. In addition, the legislative history undergirding § 7 releals an explicit congressional decision to require agencies to afford first priority to the declared national policy of saving endangered species...

Furthermore, it is clear Congress foresaw that § 7 would, on occasion, require agencies to alter ongoing projects in order to fulfill the goals of the Act....

Notwithstanding Congress' expression of intent in 1973, we are urged to find that the continuing appropriations for Tellico Dam constitute an implied repeal of the 1973 Act, at least insofar as it applies to the Tellico Project. In support of this view, TVA points to the statements found in various House and Senate appropriations committees' reports...

There is nothing in the appropriations measures, as passed, which state that the Tellico Project was to be completed irrespective of the requirements of the Endangered Species Act. These appropriations, in fact, represented relatively minor components of the lump sum amounts for the *entire* TVA budget. To find a repeal of the Endangered Species Act under these circumstances would surely do violence to the "cardinal rule...that repeals by implication are not favored."...

Here we are urged to view the Endangered Species Act "reasonably," and hence shape a remedy "that accords with some modicum of commonsense..." But is that our function? We have no expert knowledge on the subject of endangered species, much less do we have a mandate from the people to strike a balance of equities on the side of the Tellico Dam. Congress has spoken in the plainst of words, making it abundantly clear that the balance has been struck in favor of affording endangered species the highest of priorities, thereby adopting a policy which is described as "institutionalized caution."

Our individual appraisal of the wisdom or unwisdom of a particular course consciously selected by the Congress is to be put aside in the process of interpreting a statute. Once the meaning of an enactment is descerned and its constitutionality determined, the judicial process comes to an end. We do not sit as a committee of review, nor are we vested with the power of veto...

We agree with the Court of Appeals that in our constitutional system the commitment to the separation of powers is too fundamental for us to pre-empt congressional action by judicially decreeing what accords with "commonsense..." Our Constitution vests such responsibilities in the political Branches.

■ ■ ■

Questions

1. What social purposes are advanced by protecting "endangered species"?
2. Did Congress impliedly repeal the Endangered Species Act in relation to the Tellico project by appropriating money for the dam?
3. Should the Endangered Species Act be amended by the "commonsense" of the judiciary?

Case Note

Later in 1978, proponents of the Tellico Dam persuaded Congress to amend The Endangered Species Act and empower the President to establish an Endangered Species Committee to resolve disputes over public projects that threatened the existence of rare animals and plants. The Committee established by President Carter voted unanimously to protect the snail darter from the Tennessee Valley Authority dam and reservoir project. The Committee declared that there was a "reasonable and prudent alternative" to completing the dam. The Committee said virtually equal benefits could be realized by developing the scenic river rather than flooding it. The Committee noted that the valley had numerous Indian and early white settlers historic and archaeological sites. It also contains some of the richest farmland in east Tennessee. These values, along with the saving of the snail darter, provided sufficient incentive to opt for a workable alternative to the dam project. Nevertheless, in 1979 Congress, by providing an exception to the Endangered Species Act, voted to complete the Tellico dam. The dam will provide electrical power while saving consumption of oil. Also over 700 snail darters have been transplanted from the Little Tennessee to the Hiwassee River and seem to be thriving.

LANDMARK PRESERVATION LAWS

In *Penn Central Transportation Co. v. City of New York,* 98 S. Ct. 2646 (1978), the Supreme Court upheld New York City's Landmark Preservation Law. It had been challenged by the owner of Grand Central Terminal as an improper exercise of the police power. The famous station in New York had been designated a "landmark" by the city's Landmark Preservation Commission in 1967. Thereafter, any future developments involving Grand Central Terminal was to be approved by the Commission. The Supreme Court ruled that New York's law did not constitute a "taking" of property without "just compensation" in violation of the fifth and the fourteenth amendments. The law, according to the Court, permitted continued use of the terminal by the owner and permitted the owner a reasonable return on his or her investment. In addition, the Court said the law did not completely restrict the potential use of the terminal's airspace in spite of the fact that the owner could not erect a fifteen-story office building on the site which had not been approved by the Landmark Preservation Commission. All fifty states and over 500 municipalities have landmark preservation laws. While any property designated a "landmark" will gain in prestige, the owner's option to change that property will be lawfully restricted.

Glossary

Abandoned property. Property the title to which has been surrendered by owner.

Abate. To reduce or put a stop to a nuisance; to reduce or decrease a legacy because the estate is insufficient.

Ab initio. From the begining. An agreement is said to be "void ab initio" if it at no time had any legal validity.

Abrogate. To annul, repeat.

Acceleration clause. A provision in a contract or another legal instrument that upon occurrence of a stated event, the time for performance shall be advanced.

Acceptance. The act by which a person obligates himself, or the inference that a person intends to obligate himself, to the terms of a contract offered him. Also, the act by which the person on whom a draft is drawn assents to the request of the drawer to pay it or makes himself liable to pay it when it falls due.

Accessory after the fact. One who, after a felony has been committed, knowingly assists the felon.

Accessory before the fact. One who was not present at the commission of a crime but nevertheless had some part in its commission.

Accommodation paper. A negotiable instrument to which the acceptor, drawer, or indorser has put his name, without consideration, for the purpose of benefiting or accommodating some other party who desires to raise money on it and who is to pay the instrument when it becomes due.

Accord and satisfaction. The substitution of a second agreement between contracting parties in satisfaction of a former one, and the execution of the latter agreement. Accord is the agreement to substitute; satisfaction is the performance of the accord.

Acknowledgment. The act by which a party who has executed an instrument goes before a competent officer or court and affirms that its execution was a genuine and voluntary act on his part; certification by an authorized person on the face of an instrument that it has been acknowledged.

Action. A suit brought to enforce a right.

Act of God. Any injury or damage that happens by the direct and exclusive operation of natural forces, without human intervention, and that could not have been prevented or escaped from by any reasonable degree of care or diligence.

Adjudication. The giving or pronouncing of a judgment in a case; also the judgment given.

Ad litem. While an action is pending.

Administrator. A person appointed by the court to administer the estate of a deceased person.

Advisory opinion. An opinion rendered by the court when there is no actual controversy before it upon a matter submitted to obtain the court's opinion.

Affidavit. A written declaration made voluntarily and confirmed by the oath of the party making it, taken before a person having authority to adminster such an oath.

Affiant. One who makes or attests to an affidavit.

A fortiori. By a stronger reason.

Agency. A relationship created by an express or implied contract or by law whereby one party (the principal) delegates the transaction of some business to another person (the agent), who undertakes a commercial transaction for him.

Agent. One who represents and acts for another under an agency relationship.

Alienability. Transferability.

Alienation. The transfer of property from one person to another.

Allegation. The statement of a party to an action, made in a pleading, set forth the charges he expects to prove.

Allege. To state or charge, to make an allegation.

Alteration. Any material change of the terms of a written instrument.

Ambulatory. Not effective.

Amicus curiae. A friend of the court, a person appointed by the court to assist in litigation by offering his opinion on some important matter of law.

Amortize. To provide for the paying of a debt in installments.

Ancillary. Auxiliary.

Annexation. The attachment of personalty to real property in such a manner as to make it part of the realty.

Answer. In a pleading, the written statement made by the defendant setting forth his defense.

Antenuptial contract. A contract made prior to marriage between a prospective wife and her prospective husband.

Appeal. The removal of an adjudicated case from a trial court to a court of appellate jurisdiction for the purpose of obtaining a review or retrial.

Appearance. A coming into court as plaintiff or as defendant.

Appellant. A party who takes an appeal from one court to another.

Appellate jurisdiction. The power of a court to hear cases on appeal from another court or an administrative agency.

Appellee. The party in a legal action against whom an appeal is taken.

Appurtenance. An incidental adjunct to some thing that is considered the principal thing.

Arrest of judgment. The act of staying a judgment or refusing to render judgment in an action at law after the verdict has been given, for some matter appearing on the face of the record that would render the judgment, if given, reversible.

Assault. A threat of an "offensive or injurious touch" to a person made by another person who is able to carry out the threat.

Assumpsit. A form of action brought to recover damages for the non-performance of a contract.

Attachment. Seizure of the property of a debtor of the service of process upon a third person who is in possession of the property.

Attest. To act as a witness to.

Attestation clause. A clause at the end of an instrument stating that the document has been properly executed.

"Attractive nuisance." The courts hold a landowner liable for injuries sustained by small children while they were playing on his land if they were reasonably attracted there by something on the property.

Averment. A positive statement of fact.

Bad faith. The intent to mislead, deceive, or take unfair advantage of another.

Bailment. The giving up of the possession of personal property to another for some purpose, upon the accomplishment of which the goods are to be redelivered to the owners.

Battery. An unlawful beating, wrongful physical violence, or "offensive touch" inflicted on another without his consent.

Bearer. The holder of a commercial paper.

Beneficiary. A person for whose benefit property is held by a trustee, administrator, or executor.

Bequeath. To give personal property to another by a will.

Bequest. A gift of personal property by will.

Bill. A formal, written declaration, complaint, or statement of fact.

Bill in equity. The complaint in an action in equity.

Bill of Attainder. A legislative act which inflicts punishment without a judicial trial.

Bill of particulars. A written statement giving the details of the demand for which an action is brought, or of a defendant's counterclaim against such a demand, furnished by one of the parties to the other, either voluntarily or in compliance with a court order.

Bill of sale. Written evidence of the completion of a sale.

Blank indorsement. The signing of one's name to a commercial paper.

Blue-Sky Laws. State laws regulating the sale of stocks and bonds to the general public.

Bona fide. In good faith.

Brief. A written statement of a party's case.

Burden of proof. The necessity of proving the facts at issue in court.

Case. A dispute to be resolved in a court of law or equity.

Case law. Legal principles evolved from case decisions.

Cause of Action. Perhaps best defined as the fact or facts which give rise to a right of action, in other words, give to a person a right to judicial relief.

Caveat emptor. Let the buyer beware.

Caveat venditor. Let the seller beware.

Certificate of deposit. A writing that acknowledges that the person named has deposited in the issuing bank a specified sum of money and that the bank will repay the money to the named individual, or to his order, or to some other person named in the instrument as payee.

Cestui que trust. A person who is the beneficial owner, or beneficiary, of property held in trust.

Charter. A grant of authority to exist as a corporation, issued by a state.

Chattel. An article of personal property.

Chattel mortgage. An instrument of sale of personalty that conveys the title of the property to the mortgagee and specifies the terms of defeasance.

Check. A draft drawn upon a deposit of funds in a bank directing the unconditional payment on demand of a sum certain in money to the person named on the instrument, or to his order, or to bearer.

Chose in action. A right to personal property that is not in the owner's possession, but to which he has a right of action for its possession.

Chose in possession. Personal property that is in the owner's possession and to which he has a right of possession.

Circumstantial evidence. Evidence relating to the circumstances of a case from which the jury may deduce what actually happened.

Civil rights. Private rights, protected by law, or members of society.

Closed shop. Such shop exists where the worker must be a member of the union as condition precedent to employment.

Cloud on title. Evidence that a third person has a claim to property.

Class action. A legal action brought by a limited number of persons on behalf of a larger number of persons similarly situated.

Codicil. An addition to a will, executed in the same manner as the will itself.

Cognovit. Admission by the defendant of the legitimacy of the plaintiff's claim.

Cognovit Note. A promissory note which contains a provision authorizing any attorney, agent or other representative to confess judgment on the instrument and direct entry of such judgment.

Collusion. An agreement between two or more persons to defraud, or a conspiracy for some other illegal purpose.

Color of title. Apparent title; the misleading appearance that someone owns something, when in fact legitimate title may lie elsewhere.

Common law. A body of unwritten law based on the customs, habits, and usages of society.

Complainant. The plaintiff in a legal or an equitable pleading.

Complaint. The first pleading on the part of the plaintiff in a civil action(corresponding to a declaration in common law). Also, a charge, preferred before a court in order to begin prosecution, that the person named (or a certain person whose name is unknown) has committed a certain offense, together with an offer to prove the facts alleged.

Composition. An agreement between an insolvent debtor and his creditors whereby the latter agree to accept an amount less than the whole of their claims, to be distributed pro rata, in discharge and satisfaction of the entire debt.

Compos mentis. Of sound mind.

Compounding a felony. The offense committed by a person who, after having been directly injured by a felony, makes an agreement with the felon that he will not prosecute him, on the condition that the latter will make reparation or will tender him a bribe.

Concealment. The failure to volunteer relevant facts not apparent to the other party.

Conditional sale. A sale under the terms of which the passage of title depends on the performance of a stated act.

Confession of judgment. The act by which a debtor permits a judgment to be entered against him by his creditor without any legal proceedings having taken place.

Connivance. Secret or indirect consent to, or permission for, the commission of an unlawful act.

Conservator. The court-appointed guardian of someone's property.

Consideration. The inducement to a contract; the thing of value which induces a contracting party to enter into a contract.

Consignee. One to whom a consignment is made; the person to whom goods are shipped for sale.

Consignor. One who sends or makes a consignment; a shipper of goods.

Conspiracy. An agreement between two or more persons to work together to commit a criminal act.

Constructive. Inferred, legally interpreted to be so; construed by the courts to have a particular character or meaning other than or beyond what is actually expressed.

Contempt. Conduct that is disruptive of a legislative or judicial proceeding or disobedience of a lawful order of a legislative or judicial body.

Contract. An agreement enforceable in a court of law.

Contribution. The sharing of a loss or a payment among several individuals; also reimbursement of a surety who has paid the entire debt by his co-sureties.

Contributory negligence. Negligence on the part of the plaintiff that contributes to his injury. At common law a person guilty of such negligence cannot recover damages.

Conversion. The unauthorized assumption of ownership of goods belonging to another.

Copyright. A grant to an author or publisher of an exclusive right to publish and sell literary work for a period of years, renewable for a second period.

Corporation. An aritifical legal person, created by the state, which for some purposes may act as a natural person and be treated as such.

Corporeal property. Property that is discernible by the senses and may be seen and handled (as opposed to incorporeal property, which cannot be seen or handled and exists only in contemplation).

Corpus delicti. Evidence that a crime has been committed.

Count. A division of a complaint, declaration, bill of petition wherein a separate cause of action is stated.

Counterclaim. A claim made by the defendant against the plaintiff; a cross-complaint.

"Court above"—"Court below." The "court above" is the court to which a case is removed for review; the "court below" is the court from which the case is removed.

Court of record. A court in which a permanent record is kept of proceedings.

Covenant. An agreement or promise of two or more parties, given in a written, signed delivered deed, by which one party promises the other than something either is done or shall be done, or by which one party stipulates the truth of certain facts. Also, a promise contained in such an agreement.

Covenants of title. Covenants made by the grantor of real property that guarantee such matters as his right to make the conveyance, his ownership of the property, and the freedom of the property from encumbrances.

Crime. A violation of the law punishable as an offense against the state.

Cross-complaint. A counterclaim made by the defendant against the plaintiff.

Cross-examination. The examination of a party's witness by the attorney for the other party.

Culpable. Evil or criminal.

Damage. Loss or injury to one's person or property caused by the negligence or intentional actions of another.

Damages. Compensation claimed or awarded in a suit for damage suffered.

Deceit. A fraudulent misrepresentation made by one or more persons who is ignorant of the true facts, to his injury.

Deed. An instrument purporting to convey an interest in real property, delivered by the party who is to be bound thereby and accepted by the party to whom the contract is given.

De facto. In fact; actually.

Defalcation. Embezzlement.

Default. Failure to perform.

Defeasance clause. A term of a mortgage that enables the mortgagor to defeat a foreclosure claim of the mortgagee by paying off the amount of his obligation.

Defendant. The person against whom a declaration or complaint is filed and who is named therein.

Deficiency judgment. A judgment against a debtor for the amount that still remains due after a mortgage foreclosure that did not discharge the full amount of the debt.

De jure. Of right; legitimate, lawful.

Delictum. A tort.

Delivery. The physical or constructive transfer of an instrument or of goods from one person to another.

De minimus. Smallest, being of the smallest size.

Demise. (1) A conveyance of an estate to another for life, for a term of years, or at will; a lease. (2) Death of decease.

Demonstrative evidence. Evidence that consists of physical objects.

Demurrer. A plea by the defendant that concedes the truth of the facts in the case but alleges that the plaintiff does not have a cause of action.

De novo. Anew, over again.

Deponent. One who takes an oath in writing that certain facts are true.

Deposition. The testimony of a witness in response to questioning not given in court, but taken for use in court.

Derivative action. Action brought by shareholders to enforce a corporate cause of action.

Dictum. A statement of law by a judge in an opinion that is not essential to the determination of that controversy.

Directed verdict. An instruction by the trial judge to the jury to return a verdict in favor of one of the parties to an action. The party requests the instruction.

Domestic corporation. A corporation chartered by the state in which it is doing business.

Domicile. The home of a person; the state in which a corporation was incorporated.

Dower. An estate for life, to which a widow is entitled in that portion of her husband's estate to which she has not given up her right during the marriage.

Drawee. The person to who a draft is addressed and who is requested to pay the sum of money therein named.

Drawer. The person drawing a draft and addressing it to the drawee.

Due care. The degree of care that a reasonable man can be expected to exercise in order to prevent harm that, under given circumstances, is reasonably foreseeable should such care not be taken.

Duress. A use of force or threat of force that deprives the victim of free will.

Earnest. A payment of a part of the price of goods sold, or a delivery of part of such goods, in order to make a contract binding.

Easement. A right to use the land of another for a special purpose.

Ejectment. An action to determine the title to certain land.

Emancipation. The act by which all rights and obligations in regard to a child are given up by his parents.

Embezzlement. The fraudulent appropriation to one's own use or benefit of property or money entrusted to the appropriator by another.

Eminent domain. The right of the government to take private property for public use in the name of the people.

Encumbrance. A claim or lien that affects title to real property.

Entirety. The whole (as opposed to a part). When land is conveyed to a husband and wife jointly, both own the entirety.

Equitable. Just, fair, or right; existing in equity.

Equity. A field of jurisdiction different in its orgin, theory, and methodology from the common law.

Error. A mistaken judgment or incorrect belief of a trial court as to the existence or effect of matters of fact, or a false or mistaken conception or application of the law. (1) *Assignment of errors.* A statement of the errors upon which an appellant will reply, submitted to assist an appellate court in its examination of the transcript of a case under appeal. (2) *Harmless error.* An error committed during the progress of a trial that was not prejudicial to the rights of the party assigning it and for which therefore, an appellate court will not reverse a judgment. (3) *Reversible error.* An error in original proceedings for which an appellate court will reverse the judgment under review.

Escheat. The reversion of the property of a decedent to the government when there is no legal heir.

Escrow. A deed that is held by a third person until a specified condition is fulfilled.

Estate. An interest in land or in any other subject of property.

Estoppel. A rule of law designed to prevent a person from denying a fact that his conduct influenced others to believe was true.

Et ux. And his wife.

Eviction. The act of depriving a person of the possession of lands held by him, pursuant to a court order.

Evidence. Any type of proof legally presented at a trial through witnesses, records, documents, or physical objects, for the purpose of inducing belief in the mind of the court or the jury as to the truth or falsity of the facts at issue.

Exception. A formal objection to the action of the court raised during a trial, implying that the objecting party does not agree with the decision of the court and that he will seek a reversal of the judgment handed down.

Ex contractu. From or out of a contract. The term is usually used to refer to a cause of action arising from a contract.

Eculpatory. Tending or serving to exculpate or clear from alleged fault or guilt.

Ex delicto. From a tort or crime.

Executed. Completed; fully carried into effect.

Executor. A person appointed by a testator to carry out the directions and requests in his will and to dispose of his property according to the testamentary provisions of the will.

Executory. Something that is yet to be executed or performed; that which is incomplete or dependent upon a future performance or event.

Exemplary damages. Damages in excess of the amount needed to compensate the plaintiff for his injury, awarded to punish the defendant for malicious or willful conduct.

Exemption. A privilege allowed by law to a debtor by which he may hold a certain amount of property or certain classes of property free from all liability—free from seizure and sale by court order or from attachment by his creditors.

Ex parte. On one side only; by one party; done for, or on behalf of, one party only.

Ex post facto law. A law which, in its operation, makes that criminal which was not so at the time of the act, or which increases the punishment, or, in short, which, in relation to the offense or its consequences, alters the situation of a party to his disadvantage.

Express. Set forth in direct and appropriate language (as opposed to that which is implied from conduct).

Fee simple. The most complete form of ownership of real property.

Felony. An offense punishable by confinement in prison or by death, or an offense that statute has expressly deemed a felony.

Fiction. An assumption of the law.

Finis opus coronat. A finish, a fine, the end work, labor, benefit.

Fisc. Fiscal, belonging to the public treasury or revenue.

Fixture. Personal property attached to real property in such a manner that it is considered part of the realty.

F.O.B. Free on board. A shipping term designating a seller's intention to deliver goods on board a car of ship at a designated place without charge to the buyer.

Forcible detainer. The offense of keeping possession of lands by force and without legal authority.

Forcible entry. The offense or a private wrong committed by taking possession of lands by force and without legal authority.

Foreclosure. A proceeding by which the rights of the mortgagee of real property are enforced against the mortgagor.

Foreign corporation. A corporation created by, or organized under, the laws of another state government.

Forgery. The fraudulent making of an instrument that, if genuine, would appear to create contractual liability in another.

Franchise. Any special privilege conferred by a governmental body upon an individual or a corporation.

Fraud. A knowing and intentional misinterpretation of a material fact made in order to deprive another of his rights or to induce him to enter into a contract.

Fungible goods. Goods of a class in which any unit is the equivalent of any other unit.

Future estate. An estate that will not take effect until the termination of the present estate.

Garnishment. See *Attachment.*

General creditor. A creditor who has an unsecured claim against a debtor.

General verdict. The ordinary form of verdict, either for the plaintiff or for the defendant.

Gift causa mortis. A gift made by the donor in contemplation of his supposedly imminent death.

Good faith. Honest intentions.

Grant. To convey real property.

Gravamen. The material part or gist of a charge.

Guaranty. A promise to be responsible for the performance of another.

Habeus corpus. A writ obtained to test whether a prisoner is being lawfully held.

Habendum clause. The clause in a deed describing the estate granted.

Hearsay. Evidence attested by a witness that is derived not from his personal knowledge but from what others have told him.

Heirs. Persons entitled to receive an estate or a portion of an estate that a decedent has not effectively disposed of by will.

Hereditaments. Things capable of being inherited.

Holder. The person in possession of a negotiable instrument.

Hung jury. A jury that are unable to agree upon a verdict.

Hypothecation. Deposit of stocks, bonds, or negotiable instruments with another to secure the repayment of a loan, and with the power to sell the same in case the debt is not paid to reimburse himself of the proceeds.

Illusory. Appears to be, but is not.

Immunity. Freedom from legal duties and obligations.

Impanel. To make a list of those who have been selected for a jury.

Implied. Found from the circumstances of the case.

In camera. In chambers; secretly.

Inchoate. Not perfect, nor perfected.

Inculpatory. Free from guilt or blameless.

Indemnify. To make good another's loss caused by a specified act or ommission.

Indemnity. That which is given or granted to a person to prevent his suffering damage.

Indicia. A sign or indication.

Indictment. The formal written accusation of a crime, presented by a grant jury.

Indorsee. The person to whom draft, promissory note, or other commercial paper is assigned by indorsement and who therefore has a cause of action if payment is not made.

Indorsement. The signature of a payee, a drawee, or accomodation indorser, or a holder of a negotiable instrument, written on the back of the instrument, in order to transfer it to another.

Indorser. One who makes an indorsement.

Infant. A person under lawful age; a minor.

Information. In criminal law, an accusation by a public officer (as distinguished from a finding by a grand jury) that is made the basis of a prosecution of a crime.

Injunction. An order issued by a court of equity directing a person or a group to do, or to refrain from doing, a specified act.

Injury. Any wrong or damage to the person, rights, reputation, or property of another.

In pari delicto. In equal fault; equally guilty.

In personam. Against a specific person (as opposed to *In rem).*

In re. In the matter.

In rem. Against a thing; directed at specific property or at a specific right or status.

Insolvency. A state in which debts and liabilities exceed assets.

Interlocutory appeal. Incidence to a suit still pending; as an order or decree, made during the progress of a case, which does not amount to a final decision.

Interpleader. A form of action by which a third person who holds property or monies to which he has no claim and against whom conflicting claims are made may bring the complaining parties into court to settle their claims.

Inter alia. Among other things or matters.

Inter se. Between or among themselves.

Inter vivos. Any transaction that takes place among living persons.

Intestate. Without a will.

Intestate succession. A distribution, directed by statute, of property owned by a decedent and not effectively disposed of by will.

Ipso facto. By the fact itself.

Jointly. Acting together. When persons are jointly liable, they all must be sued or none can be sued.

Jointly and severally. Acting together and separately. Anyone so liable can sue (or be sued) with or without the others joining (or being joined) in the action.

Joint tenancy. An estate in entirety held by two or more persons with the right of survivorship.

Judgment. The final order of a court, entered upon the completion of an action.

Judgment note. A note authorizing a judgment to be entered against a debtor if the note is not paid when it falls due.

Judgment on the pleadings. A judgment entered upon the request of either party to an action after the pleadings have been filed, when it is apparent from the content of the pleadings that one party is entitled to a decision in his favor without proceeding further.

Judicial sale. A sale made under a court order by an officer appointed to make the sale.

Jurisdiction. The power and authority conferred upon a court, either constitutionally or by statute.

Justiciable. Liable to trial in a court of justice.

"Last clear chance." In accident cases, the courts hold that if the defendant had the last clear chance to avoid an accident, he is liable even though the plaintiff may been guilty of contributory negligence.

Leading question. A question that suggests to the witness what his response should be.

Lease. A conveyance of lands or tenements to a person for life, for a term of years, or at will, in consideration of a return of rent or some other form of compensation.

Leasehold. An estate held under a lease; an estate for a fixed term of years.

Legal tender. A medium of exchange that the law compels a creditor to accept in payment of a debt when it is legally offered to him by the debtor.

Lessee. One to whom a lease is made.

Lessor. One who grants a lease.

Let. To demise, to lease.

Levy. To exact, collect, gather, seize.

Lex loci. The law of the place where an accident occurred.

Lex loci contractus. The law of the place where a contract was made

Lex loci fori. The law of the place where an action was brought.

License. A personal privilege on authority to do something which would otherwise be inoperative.

Lien. A claim against, or a right to, property.

Life estate. An estate the duration of which is limited to the life of the person named in the grant; a freehold estate that cannot be pased on to one's heirs.

Life tenant. One who holds an estate in lands for the period of his own life or that of another person named.

Limitation. Anything that defines or limits, either by words or by implication, the time during which an estate granted may be enjoyed.

Lineal heirs. Those directly descended from an ancestor; children or grandchildren, for example.

Liquidated. Determined, clarified, fixed.

Liquidated damages. A sum stipulated and agreed upon by the parties, at the time of entering into a contract, as being payable as compensation for loss suffered in the event of a breach.

Lis pendens. A suit pending; the filing of legal notice that there is a dispute about the title to property.

Maker. One who executes a legal instrument or promissory note.

Malfeasance. The performance of an unlawful act.

Malum in se. An act that is wrong in itself.

Malum prohibitum. An act that is prohibited by law.

Mandamus. A court order compelling an individual to fulfill an official duty.

Maturity. The due date of an instrument.

Mechanic's lein. A claim created by statute for the benefit of person supplying materials for the construction of a building, giving them a lien on the building.

Mens rea. The state of mind of the actor.

Merchantable. Of good quality; salable in the regular course of business or intended purpose.

Merger. A joining of two corporations whereby one company retains its original identity.

Mesne. Intermediate, intervening.

Minor. A person who is under the age of legal competence specified by statute; usually, a person under twenty-one years of age.

Misdemeanor. A crime that is neither a felony nor treason.

Misfeasance. The performing of a lawful act in an improper manner.

Misprison. Maladministration, concealing, embezzlement.

Misrepresentation. An intentionally false statement of fact.

Mitigation of damages. The duty of the plaintiff to avoid increasing his damages and to limit them where possible.

Moiety. One-half.

Motion to dismiss. To dismiss the defendant from the suit for lack of good cause shown to retain.

Motion to quash. See *motion to dismiss;* usually only consider questions of law as apparent on the face of the record.

Moot case. A hypothetical or nonexisting controversy.

Mutuality. Reciprocation of understanding. Both parties to a contract must have a clear understanding of the legal obligations of their agreement.

Necessaries. That which is reasonably needed to maintain one's accustomed standard of living.

Negative covenant. An agreement in a deed to refrain from doing something.

Negligence. The failure to do something that a reasonable man would do or the commission of an act that a reasonable man would not commit, that results, in an ordinary and natural sequence, in damage to another.

Negotiable instrument. An instrument containing an obligation for the payment of a sum certain in money, the legal title to which may be transferred from one person to another by indorsement and delivery by the holder or by delivery only.

Nisi prius. A trial court (as distinguished from an appellate court).

Nolo contendere. Not contesting the charge, it has the effect of a guilty plea in a criminal action.

Nominal damages. A token sum awarded to the plaintiff when he has suffered no actual damage.

Non compos mentis. Not sound of mind; insane.

Non est factum. A plea that a note sued on was never made or executed.

Nonfeasance. The neglect or failure to do something that one ought to do.

Non obstante veredicto. A judgment given that is contrary to the verdict of the jury.

Nonsuit. An abandonment of suit by the plaintiff.

Novation. Release by agreement from a contractual obligation by substitution of a third party for the original obligor.

Nudum pactum. An agreement or promise made without consideration and thus not legally enforceable under normal circumstances.

Nuisance. Improper personal conduct, or the unresonable use by a person of his own property, that obstructs the rights of others or of the public and produces material inconvenience or hardship.

Obliteration. An erasure or crossing out that makes all or portions of a will impossible to read. Sections so altered and considered to be revoked when the changes were made by the testator for the purpose of revocation.

Operation of law. The automatic attaching of certain legal consequences to certain facts.

Opinion evidence. The conclusions that a witness draws from what he has observed (as opposed to the observation itself).

Option. A contract to hold an offer open for a fixed period of time.

Ordinance. A statutory enactment of the legislative branch of a municipal government.

Ostensible agency. An implied agency that exists when a supposed principal by his conduct induces another to believe that a third person is his agent, although the principal never actually employed him.

Ostensible partner. A partner whose name is publicly made known (as opposed to a silent partner).

Parens patriae. The father of the country constituted in law by the state; in the capacity of legal guardian of persons not sui juris.

Parol. Oral, spoken.

Parol evidence rule. The construction that parol evidence is not considered by the courts to alter a written contract that is complete on its face.

Partition. A divison of real property between co-owners.

Patent. The giving of a privilege or property by a government to one or more individuals. (1) The conveyance by which a government grants lands in the public domain to an individual. (2) The privilege given to an inventor allowing him the exclusive right to make and sell his invention for a definite period of time.

Pawn. A bailment of goods to a creditor as security for a debt; a pledge.

Payee. One to whom a negotiable instrument is made payable.

Per curiam opinion. An opinion written with the concurrence of all the members of the court.

Perform. To do any action, other than making payment, in discharge of a contract.

Performance. The fulfillment of a contractual obligation according to the terms of the agreement.

Per se. By itself; standing alone; not related to other matters.

Petition. The first pleading by the plaintiff in a civil case, also called the complaint.

Petty jury, petit jury. The jury in a trial court.

Plaintiff. One who brings an action.

Plaintiff in error. A party who bases his appeal on an error in a judgment rendered by a trial court.

Plead. To make, deliver,or file a pleading.

Pleadings. The papers filed by the parties in an action.

Pledge. A bailment of goods as security for a debt.

Pledgee. One to whom the goods are pledged.

Pledgor. The party delivering the goods in a pledge.

Police power. The power of the state to enact laws for the protection of the public health, safety, welfare, and morals.

Polling the jury. Asking each member of the jury in open court how he voted on the verdict.

Possessory lien. The right to retain property as security for a debt.

Postdate. To record a date later than the date of execution of an instrument.

Precatory. Indicate a desire or wish; opposite of command.

Preference. The payment of money or the transfer of property to one creditor in priority to other creditors.

Presentment. The exhibition of a draft to the drawee for his acceptance or to the acceptor for payment; also, the exhibition of a promissory note to the maker, with a demand for payment.

Personal jurisdiction. Court power to deal with the person by reason of proper service of process (summons).

Presumption. An inference of the truth or falsehood of a proposition or a fact, in the absence of actual certainty as to its truth or falsehood, by a process of probable reasoning.

Prima facie. At first sight; on first appearance; presumably.

Privileged communication. A communication concerning which a witness may refuse to testify in open court because of his relationship with the person from whom he received the information; a communication between a lawyer and his client, for example.

Privity. An immediate relationship. A party to a contract is said to have "privity" with regard to the making of the contract.

Process. A court order informing the defendant that he is required to appear in court.

Promissory note. A promise in writing to pay a specified sum within a certain time, on demand, or at sight. to a named person, to his order, or to bearer.

Promoters. The organizers of a corporation.

Prosecute. To bring suit and carry on an action against a person in court.

Pro tanto. For so much; as far as it goes.

Protest. A formal, written statement, made by a notary at the request of the holder of a commercial paper, that the draft or note was presented for payment (or acceptance) and that payment (or acceptance) was refused. The protest also states the reasons if any, given, for the dishonor.

Proximate cause. That act which is the effective cause of an injury; an act from which the injury could reasonably be expected to result.

Proximate damage. Damage that is a reasonably foreseeable result of an action.

Prurient interest. To itch or crave wantonly and restlessly or to be lascivious (lewd, lustful), in thought or desire.

Punitive damages. Damages over and above the amount necessary to compensate an injured party. They are imposed to punish a wrongdoer.

Qualified acceptance. A conditional or modified acceptance of a draft that in some way changes the terms of the instrument.

Qualified indorsement. An indorsement containing the words "without recourse," or words of similar import, evidencing the indorser's intent not to be bound should the primary party fail to pay.

Quantum meruit. As much as he deserved.

Quasi. As if it were; having the characteristics of.

Quasi contract. A contract implied in law.

Quid pro quo. Something for something.

Quiet title. An action brought to settle claims against the title to a piece of property.

Quit-claim deed. A deed purporting to transfer whatever interest, if any, the grantor has in the property concerned.

Quo warranto. An action compelling someone (usually a corporation) to show by whose authority he is transacting business.

Ratification. The acceptance of responsibility for, and the undertaking of the obligations incurred by, a previous act committed either by oneself or by one's agent.

Real property. A general term for land and everything attached to it.

Receipt. Acceptance of something delivered.

Receiver. A person appointed by the court to collect the rents and profits of land, or the growth of personal estates, or to transact other business that the court thinks not reasonable that either party should transact or that a party is incompetent to transact.

Recognizance. An obligation entered into before a court or magistrate to do a particular act—for example, to appear in court or to pay a debt.

Recovery. The collection of a debt through an action at law. (See also *Right of Recovery.*)

Redemption. A buying back of property. A mortgage conveys the title to property to the mortgagee, subject to a right of redemption of the mortgagor. The mortgagor has a right to defeat the conveyance of the title by paying the amount of the debt secured by the mortgage.

Release. The giving up of a right or privilege by the person in whom it existed to the person against whom it might have been demanded or enforced.

Remainder. An estate that takes effect and may be enjoyed only after another estate is determined.

Remand. To send a case back to a trial court for a new trial in accordance with the decision of an appellate court.

Remedial. Pertaining to a legal remedy, or to the form or procedural details of such a remedy, that is to be taken after a legal or an equitable wrong has been committed.

Remedy. The means by which the violation of a right is prevented or compensated for.

Replevin. A personal action brought to recover possession of goods taken from one unlawfully.

Recission. Cancellation of a contract by one or both parties.

Residuary. Constituting the residue; entitled to the residue.

Residuary estate. The part of a testator's estate and effects that remains after all particular devises and bequests have been made.

Respondeat superior. A legal maxim that a master is liable in certain cases for the wrongful acts of his servant, and a principal for those of his agent.

Respondent. One who makes an answer to or argues against an appeal.

Reversal. The decision of an appellate court to annul or vacate a judgment or decree of a trial court.

Revocation. The recall of some power, authority, or thing granted; also, the destruction or voiding of a legal document.

Right of entry The right of taking or resuming possession of land by entering peaceably on it.

Right of recovery. A right of action deriving from a legal wrong committed in a given case.

Right to redeem. The right of a debtor whose property has been mortgaged; then sold to another to pay a debt, to repurchase the property.

"Right to work." Section 14(b) of the National Labor Relations Act leaves to the various states the power to enact laws limiting or prohibiting labor agreements which make union membership a condition of employment. Such state laws simply declare unlawful any agreement which conflicts with the policy that individuals have the right to work without abridgement on account of non-membership in any labor organization.

Riparian. Relates to the bank of a river.

"Run with the land." Certain convenants in a deed to land are deemed to "run" or pass with the land in order that whoever owns the land is bound by or entitled to the benefit of the covenants, even though the agreements are not in the public record.

Sale or return. A sale in which, although title passes to the buyer at the time of the agreement, he has the option of returning title to the seller.

Satisfaction. The act of discharging an obligation owed to a party by paying what is due him or what is awarded to him by the judgment of a court.

Scienter. Knowingly.

Scintilla. A spark, a remaining particle; hence, the lease evidence.

Set-off. A counterclaim, a cross-demand.

Severable contract. A contract one part of which may be separated from the other parts and performed or enforced alone.

Severalty. The sole ownership of real property.

Short sale. A sale of stock which the seller does not possess at the time, but which he expects to acquire subsequently for delivery under his contract.

Silent partner. A partner whose name or connection with a firm is not known to the public (as opposed to an ostensible or acknowledge partner).

Slander. Oral defamation of character.

Slander per se. Words slanderous in themselves whether or not damage can be proven to result from them. To have a case, it is necessary merely to allege that they have been published.

Special agent. An agent authorized to conduct a specific transaction.

Special appearance. A person's appearance in court for a specific purpose, without his submitting to the jurisdiction of the court.

Special Damages. Damages that are the actual and natural, although not the necessary, result of the proximate cause of an injury. They must be proven according to the special circumstances of a particular case.

Specific performance. An equitable remedy by which a contracting party is compelled to perform his obligations under the terms of the contract.

State of the forum. The state in which the court sits or has its hearing or forum.

Stare decisis. To stand by that which has been decided. A case decision serves as a legal precedent in the deciding of subsequent similar cases.

(SIC). So, thus, simply, in this manner. (Confirms a word that might be questioned.)

Stipulation. An agreement between opposing counsel that they will accept certain things in evidence without the necessity of proof.

Statute of frauds. A statute that requires certain contracts to be in writing before they will be accepted as valid, enforceable contracts. It is designed to prevent contracts based upon perjured testimony.

Statute of limitations. A statute that limits the period of time in which an enforceable cause of action may be brought.

Subrogation. The substitution of one thing for another, or of one person in place of another, with respect to rights, claims, or securities.

Subscribe. To write one's name at the bottom or end of a writing.

Sua sponte. Upon its own responsibility or motion, as an order "sua sponte" made by a court without prior motion be either party.

Substantive law. That part of the law that creates, defines, and regulates rights (as opposed to procedural law, which prescribes methods enforcing rights or obtaining remedies for this invasion).

Sui generis. Of its own kind of class.

Sui juris. Of his own right; having legal capacity to manage his own affairs.

Summary. Immediate; rendering without a hearing.

Summary judgment. A judgment entered by a court when no substantial dispute of fact exists; consequently, there is no need for a trial.

Summary proceeding. A brief proceeding, usually conducted with less formality than a normal court proceeding.

Summons. A writ served upon a defendant to secure his appearance in court.

Supra. Noted above or previously.

Surety. A person who makes himself liable for the obligations of another.

Survivorship. The right of a surviving tenant (or tenants) to take the share (or shares) of a tenant who dies.

Tangible. Having physical qualities.

Tenancy at sufferance. An illegal staying on by a tenant after a lease has expired.

Tenancy at will. The possession of land for an indefinite period of time that may be terminated at any time by either party without notice being given.

Tenancy for years. A tenancy for any fixed period of time. (The period may be less than year.)

Tenancy from year to year. A tenancy that continues indefinitely from year to year (or any other period of time) until terminated.

Tenancy in common. The ownership of property by two or more persons.

Tenancy in partnership. The form of ownership of partnership property that was created by the Uniform Partnership Act.

Tender. An unconditional offer by a party who is able to complete an obligation.

Tenor. The true meaning or effect of an instrument.

Terminable Fee. An estate that may be terminated upon the occurrence of some event.

Testamentary. To take effect at death.

Testamentary capacity. The capacity to make a will.

Testate. Having left a will.

Testate succession. The distribution of a testator's estate according to the terms of his will.

Third-party beneficiary. A third person who is directly benefited by the making of a contract to which he is not a party.

Toll the statute. To stop the operation of the time period specified by the statute of limitations.

Tort. A wrong committed upon the person or property of another; an invasion of a private right.

Tort feasor. One who commits a tort.

Tortious. Wrongful.

Transcript. A copy of a writing; a court record.

Trespass. (1) An injury to the person, property, or rights of another. (2) A common-law action for money damages for injury to one's person, property, or rights.

Trier of fact. Usually a jury.

Trust. An equitable right to land or other property, held for a beneficiary by another person, in whom the legal title rests.

Trustee. One appointed to execute a trust; a person in whom an estate interest, or power is vested under an agreement that he shall administer or exercise if for the benefit or use of another.

Ultra vires. Beyond the powers conferred upon a corporation by its charter.

Undisclosed principal. A principal whose existence and identity are unknown to third parties.

Undue influence. Dominance of one person in a fiduciary relationship over another, sufficient to inhibit or destroy the weaker party's free will.

Unilateral contract. A contract consisting of a promise made by one party in return for an act to be done by the other.

Unincorporated association. A combination of two or more persons to achieve a common end.

Union shop. Such shop exists where the employer is permitted to employ a non-union worker but such worker is required to join the union as a requisite to his continuing employment.

Usque ad coelum. As far as heaven—referring to a rule in law that the owner of land owns the air space above it indefinitely upward.

Usury. The charging of an illegally high interest rate.

Vacation of judgment. The setting aside of a judgment by a court.

Valid. Legally sufficient.

Vendee. A purchaser, a buyer.

Vendor. A seller.

Venire. To appear in court. A writ of venire is used to summon a jury.

Verdict. The decision of a jury.

Vested. Accrued, settled, absolute; not contingent upon anything; having an immediate right to the enjoyment of property.

Void. Having no legal effect; not binding.

Voidable. Subject to being declared ineffectual. A contract is voidable when one party has grounds for refusing to perform his obligations.

Voidable preference. A preference given by a bankrupt person or firm to one creditor over others. It may be set aside by the trustee in bankruptcy.

Voir dire examination. An examination to determine the qualifications of a juror or witness.

Volenti non fit injuria. He who consents cannot be injured.

Voluntary nonsuit. A means available to the plaintiff for stopping a trial in a civil suit without prejudice to bring the suit again.

Waiver. The giving up of a legal right.

Ward. A person under the care of court.

Warrant. A guaranty that certain facts are true as represented.

Warranty of authority. An implied warranty that an agent possesses the authority that he represents himself as possessing.

Waste. A reduction in value to property caused by the person in possession.

Watered stock. Stock recorded in the books of a corporation as being fully paid when in fact it is not because the property received by the corporation is valued less than the value of the stock issued.

Will. The legal expression of a person's wishes regarding the disposition of his property after his death.

Witness. An individual who testifies under oath in a legal action.

Writ of certiorari. An order from an appellate court to a lower court requesting the record of a case that is to be reviewed by the appellate court.

Writ of error. The order of an appellate court authorizing a lower court to remit to it the official record of the proceedings in a case where an error sufficient to invalidate the verdict is claimed.

Index